Contributions to Economics

The series *Contributions to Economics* provides an outlet for innovative research in all areas of economics. Books published in the series are primarily monographs and multiple author works that present new research results on a clearly defined topic, but contributed volumes and conference proceedings are also considered. All books are published in print and ebook and disseminated and promoted globally. The series and the volumes published in it are indexed by Scopus and ISI (selected volumes).

Zhenying Wang

Trading Economics

New Theory for Trading System Evolution

Springer

Zhenying Wang
Shanghai Gold Exchange
Shanghai, China

ISSN 1431-1933 ISSN 2197-7178 (electronic)
Contributions to Economics
ISBN 978-981-99-9874-6 ISBN 978-981-99-9875-3 (eBook)
https://doi.org/10.1007/978-981-99-9875-3

The translation was done with the help of an artificial intelligence machine translation tool. A subsequent human revision was done primarily in terms of content.

This Springer imprint is published by the registered company Springer Nature Singapore Pte Ltd.
The registered company address is: 152 Beach Road, #21-01/04 Gateway East, Singapore 189721, Singapore

Preface

In the preface of *The Price of Inequality*, renowned American economist Joseph E. Stiglitz poses the question: Why is the American economic system a failure for most Americans? Why has inequality escalated to this extent today?[1] As the world's most developed economy, a country known as the "city upon a hill," and once hailed as the "beacon of freedom" for humanity, why has America experienced a failure in its economic system? If the American economic system, once considered by American political scientist Fukuyama as nearly the ultimate system for human society, has failed, which country's economic system is successful?

In today's world, although the increasingly severe problem of polarization has long become a chronic disease hindering the healthy development of human society, it is difficult to find a systematic argument about inequality and polarization in the exquisite models of equilibrium theory in mainstream economic theory. In fact, the puzzling economic issues are far more than these. What is the ultimate outcome of the evolution of the trading system? Can human society maintain growth forever? These are the ultimate questions facing economists.

The predicament faced by economic theory shows that mainstream economic theory is not a complete theoretical system, and it cannot even respond to important economic issues that people generally care about. This indicates that the perspective of mainstream economics is not the only possible choice. Outside of mainstream economics, there should be other different perspectives. By choosing a new perspective, we can gain more valuable economic knowledge. More than a century ago, Max Weber warned people not to let liberal political economics blind their eyes, and that a single perspective is dangerous. In his view, when a way of looking at problems is so confidently advancing, there is already the danger of falling into illusion, that is, overestimating the importance of one's own perspective, especially treating a fairly

[1] Joseph E. Stiglitz (2022) The Price of Inequity (trans: Ziyuan ZHANG), China Machine Press, Beijing.

limited perspective as the only perspective.[2] Today, Max Weber's warning has very important implications for economists.

Trading economics, with the trading system as its research object, integrates all economic activities of human society into the trading system through the expansion of the concept of trading. It assumes that the maximization of expected return is the basic assumption of the behavior of trading agents, and the limited rationality of trading agents under incomplete information is the premise. It reveals the instability characteristics of the trading system and the natural tendency of the trading potential to polarize. It reveals that under the free market system, the market's "invisible hand" cannot maintain effective allocation of resources in the long term. Free competition without government participation and institutional constraints will inevitably lead to polarization of wealth distribution, market monopoly, manipulation of law and justice, and other social chronic diseases.

Trading economics and mainstream economics have a complementary relationship. Mainstream economics focuses on the operating mechanism of the trading system, while trading economics focuses on the evolutionary laws. Both have their emphasis in the time dimension, thus forming a complete picture of the trading system. In terms of the entire human economic and social evolution process, mainstream economics focuses on a short-term analytic perspective. The theoretical analysis is carried out under the premise that the economic structure remains basically stable, and the research is focused on the interaction among economic variables. Trading economics focuses on the large-scale evolutionary process of the trading system from a long-term evolutionary perspective. As theories studying human economic society, trading economics and mainstream economics respectively study the trading system in different time dimensions; hence, their complementarity is obvious.

In terms of application, mainstream theory has outstanding advantages in analyzing and predicting the market. It can build accurate and clear economic models through the logical relationship of many economic variables, which is very convenient for understanding the causal relationship among economic variables. The advantage of trading economics lies in revealing the basic characteristics of the trading system and the internal driving forces and mechanisms that promote the evolution of the trading system, including the stability of the trading system, the evolutionary trend of polarization in the trading system, the internal causes of trading cascades, and how do trading states phase change, spread and diffuse in the trading system. These issues are crucial for our understanding of the operation of human economic society, and for how to achieve social stability, harmony, and efficient development through institutional arrangements and government control. However, these issues have not been emphasized in the research vision of mainstream economics.

---

[2] Qixuan HUANG (2018) General Political Economy - History, Classics, Reality, Orient Publishing Center, Beijing, p 16.

Trading economics does not merely provide a methodology for dealing with complex economic phenomena but constructs a complete economic evolution theory system. Trading economics studies five dimensions of the trading system. These five dimensions are: first, the compactness of the trading system. This is used to describe the intensity of the connection and interaction among the agents within the trading system. Compactness has strong evolutionary characteristics. With the continuous evolution of the trading system, the compactness of the trading system shows an increasing trend. The enhancement of the compactness of the trading system means that the nonlinear characteristics of the trading system are strengthened, and the difficulty of linear theory in describing and analyzing the trading system with strong compactness is more prominent.

Second, the network structure of the trading system. The multi-level complex internal structure is the basis for all complex systems, and the trading system, as a super complex system, is no exception. The internal structure of the trading system presents a network shape, which we call the trading network. The trading network has complex aggregation structures, link structures, and time limit structures. The trading network is the basic tool for trading economics to study the trading system. By studying the trading communities on the trading network, it reveals the mechanism by which the trading agents and the entire trading system are linked and interact with each other within the trading system; and the information exchange mechanism between individuals and the environment.

Third, the distribution structure of the trading potential in the trading system. The trading potential is a quantitative description of the importance of trading agents on the trading network. Trading economics accepts the ubiquitous reality of differences, takes the differentiation of trading agents as the logical starting point of analysis, and reveals that with the evolution of the trading system, the distribution of the trading potential develops in the direction of polarization, and there is a phenomenon of advantage accumulation among trading agents. On the large scale of the evolution of the trading system, increasing marginal returns play a dominant role.

Fourth, the distribution structure of the trading state in the trading system. The trading state is an important trading characteristic of the trading agent, playing a crucial role in trading decisions. The trading state distribution in the trading system will directly affect the circulation of the trading network, ultimately becoming a significant factor influencing the speed of economic growth. Trading agents in the trading network are influenced and constrained by trading flows and information flows from all directions. The trading state of the trading agent is both the result of the network environment and the driving force for changes in the network environment. The trading state propagates and spreads in the trading network, forming the rhythm of the evolution of the trading network's trading state distribution, presenting itself in the operation of the trading system as an economic cycle.

Fifth, the trading space structure in the trading system. Each trading agent in the trading system has its own trading space. The size of the trading space reflects the status of the trading agent in the trading system. The larger the trading space, the higher the status of the trading agent in the trading system. This spatial distribution structure defined by the trading space of the trading agent continuously adjusts and changes with the evolution of the trading system. Some trading agents' trading spaces are constantly expanding, while others are continuously shrinking. The different evolution trends of trading spaces constitute the vivid picture of the evolution of the trading system.

In terms of exploring the characteristics of the trading system, we have deeply discussed the inherent mechanism of equilibrium in the trading system and the causes that induce the trading system to deviate from equilibrium. The study found that the trading system has a spontaneous motive to deviate from equilibrium, and the balance sheet of the trading agent is constantly updated and reconstructed in trading activities. The trading constraints continue to change, which determines that the dominant strategy of the trading agent must change at each time step. The perfect match of dominant strategies among a large number of trading agents at the same time is just one of countless probabilistic events and belongs to a small probability event. Therefore, it can be seen that operating on the perfect curve is an abnormal state of the trading system, while deviating from equilibrium is the normal state of the trading system. The study also found that the ability of the trading system to spontaneously return to equilibrium is limited. When the effective matching degree of the trading system exceeds a certain threshold, the trading system loses its ability to self-regulate, resulting in pole residence. Therefore, it can be seen that the trading system is a weakly stable system, its stability is very fragile, and the equilibrium situation is extremely easy to be broken.

The trading system is not perfect and has inherent flaws. Due to the spontaneous polarization tendency of the trading system, the result of free competition cannot achieve Pareto optimality, let alone maximizing social welfare. This means that human society cannot rely solely on an unrestricted free market system to achieve its ultimate development goals.

Based on the multi-dimensional and broad perspective research on the trading system, trading economics adopts a theoretical paradigm different from mainstream economics and constructs economic cycle models, economic growth models, and trading pricing models. In these areas deeply cultivated by mainstream economics, trading economics provides a new perspective, broadening people's cognitive space for economic phenomena and deepening their understanding of these phenomena.

Trading economics provides us with such a picture of economic operation: the trading network connects a large number of trading agents to form a trading system, and the continuous profit-seeking behavior of countless trading agents drives the evolution of the trading system to enhance its resource allocation and trading efficiency; the evolution of the trading system in turn reshapes the trading agents, forcing them to adjust in behavior and internal organization in time to adapt to new changes in the trading system.

Trading economics, commencing from the principle of expected return maximization and using evolutionary game theory, comprehensively delineates the behavioral characteristics of trading agents in various complex scenarios, elucidates the evolutionary process of the trading system from simplistic trading communities to complex hierarchical phase structure and aggregation structure, and thoroughly manifests the logical progression of "simplicity engendering complexity," which is a significant academic contribution of trading economics.

Frankly speaking, trading economics has not discovered any surprising "economic truths", whether it is the weak stability of the trading system, or the divergence between equilibrium state and Pareto optimality, all of which are involved in mainstream economic theory or theories of different schools. From this perspective, trading economics can hardly be considered a new theory. What differs from mainstream economics is that trading economics conducts systematic research on the trading system from the perspective of trading, obtaining many existing conclusions through different logical paths. These conclusions were originally scattered in different academic schools and different branches of mainstream economics. Under the vision of trading economics, a cognitive picture with stronger logical consistency and more natural clarity appears.

The main theoretical contribution of trading economics is to examine the evolution process and ultimate results of the trading system from an evolutionary perspective. This global perspective provides us with the overall trend of human social evolution and development. Through meticulous logical argumentation, trading economics has proven the conclusion that a perfect economic system does not exist. This proves that any economic system needs to be continuously reformed and optimized in practice, and adjustments and corrections to the basic system need to be made. Only in this way can the healthy and stable operation of the trading system be maintained continuously. The impossibility theorem of trading economics fundamentally dispels people's illusions of finding a perfect economic system and dispels people's illusions of solving possible problems in social development by constructing a perfect system.

Trading Economics is a companion piece to *The Principle of Trading Economics*, with each book having its own emphasis. *The Principle of Trading Economics* focuses on the ideological concepts of trading economics, philosophical thinking of economic systems and phenomena, and the construction of conceptual systems with a broad coverage, and can be regarded as the origin of theory of trading economics. *Trading Economics* focuses on quantitative analysis and argumentation as well as the rigor of theoretical architecture and is the systematization of thought of trading economics. In terms of methods, *Trading Economics* widely adopts game theory methods, including argument analysis and model construction. The widespread use of game theory strengthens the micro-analytical foundation of trading economics making trading economics a more solid real-world foundation.

Trading Economics further refines some of the concepts proposed in *The Principle of Trading Economics*, striving to be more simplified in the use of concepts and more rigorous in the logical. It eliminates concepts that are not closely related to the main line of logic and lack later application scenarios; it adjusts the meaning of the trading potential and applies the concept of the trading potential to measure the trading status of trading agents and no longer applies to the measurement of trading strength.

After the publication of *The Principle of Trading Economics* in 2016, I received a lot of support from colleagues in the economics field, which greatly encouraged me. Professors Songcheng Sheng, Guoqiang Tian from Shanghai University of Finance and Economics, and Prof. Weisen Li from Fudan University, each wrote review articles or prefaces for *The Principle of Trading Economics*. While giving an objective evaluation of trading economics, they also put forward many criticisms and suggestions for improvement. Their help is invaluable, for which I express my heartfelt thanks.

I would like to thank Prof. Songzuo Xiang from Renmin University of China, who highly appreciated the ideas expressed in trading economics and provided valuable comments on the layout of this book.

I would also like to thank the postdocs at the Shanghai Gold Exchange Postdoctoral Workstation, namely Dr. Guanping Lu, Dr. Jiangping Li, Dr. Qinggong Zhao, Dr. Lin Zhu, Dr. Zhicheng Weng, Dr. Minghui Xin, and Dr. Kaiyang Chen. They have participated in the trading economics discussion many times. The young students are active in thinking and strong in accepting new knowledge. Each discussion brings me a lot of inspiration and enlightenment. In particular, Dr. Jiangping Li, Dr. Kaiyang Chen and Dr. Dapeng Dou spent a lot of time helping me find references and calibrate formulas, as well as proofread the manuscript. This has been of great help to me in successfully completing the writing of this book. Furthermore, the English edition of *Trading Economics* could not be published without the help of my five colleagues from Shanghai Gold Exchange: They are Dr. Tingting Huang, Mr. Ming Yang, Ms. Lingyin Zeng, Ms. Sha He and Mr. Jian Chen. I would like to express my deepest gratitude to them.

I would also like to express my special thanks to Ms. Yingying Zhang from the China headquarters of Springer Publishing. The successful publication of *Trading Economics* by Springer is due to her strong support. In addition, Ms. Yingying Zhang also provided very valuable help for the translation of *Trading Economics*. For this, I express my heartfelt gratitude to her.

When mentioning Springer Publishing, I could not forget Mr. Rajasekar Ganesan, the project coordinator, who offered great support and assistance in my preparation of the manuscripts. Only with his patient guidance and coordination, could the successful publication of *Trading Economics* (English edition) by Springer become a reality, Therefore, please allow me to express my sincere gratitude to him as well.

Finally, I would like to conclude with a quote from the master of neoclassical economics, Alfred Marshall, in the preface to the first edition of *Principles of Economics*, as a tribute to the master's profound wisdom. "Economic conditions are constantly changing, and each generation looks at its own problems in its own way. In England, as well as on the Continent and in America, Economic studies are being more vigorously pursued now than ever before; but all this activity has only shown the more clearly that Economic science is, and must be, one of slow and continuous growth. Some of the best work of the present generation has indeed appeared at first sight to be antagonistic to that of earlier writers; but when it has had time to settle down into its proper place, and its rough edges have been worn away, it has been found to involve no real breach of continuity in the development of the science. The new doctrines have supplemented the older, have extended, developed, and sometimes corrected them, and often have given them a different tone by a new distribution of emphasis; but very seldom have subverted them."[3]

West Bank of Huangpu River
Midsummer 2023

Zhenying Wang

[3] Alfred, Marshall (1890) Principles of Economics, London, Macmillan.

Praise for *Trading Economics*

"Trading economics comes at a time when people are yearning for a new economic theory. Starting with bounded rationality, it reconstructs economic theory and reveals the connections behind such phenomena as the 'animal instinct' of stock investors, stagflation, community poverty, and gambler behavior from a fresh perspective. In the context of COVID-19, trading economics shows that direct assistance to the 'fulcrum players' of a trading network works better than stimulating consumption, thus providing a theoretical framework for macroeconomic management. The book *Trading Economics* is the culmination of 20 years of research by Dr. Zhenying Wang and a major accomplishment on the subject. I am honored to recommend it."

—Songcheng Sheng, *President of the Institute of China Chief Economist Forum, Professor at China Europe International Business School, and former Director of the Statistics and Analysis Department of the People's Bank of China*

"The modern market economy is a complex and expansive system with currency as the medium of exchange and goods, services, transportation, catering, entertainment, finance, securities, futures, information, and AI as the carrier. Examining the foundation and mechanics of the market system from individual transactions, therefore, will yield a more insightful and realistic picture of how the world runs. Dr. Zhenying Wang is the author of the *Principles of Trading Economics*, which represents decades of theory building and is now in its second edition (plus an English edition). *Trading Economics* refines the theoretical framework of this earlier work and explains the principles and ideas behind trading economics in a clearer and more logical language. The advent of trading economics, itself a theoretical breakthrough, also made the dream of Friedrich von Hayek—the great 20th-century economist from Austria—to establish *catallactics* (roughly translated as 'science of exchanges in a free market') a reality."

—Weisen Li, *National First-Class Professor of Philosophy and Social Sciences, Professor of Economics, Fudan University*

"This is an interdisciplinary, insightful, and highly readable work, with a scope as broad as the content is rich. Its one major contribution is to reveal and systematize the threads that underpin the evolution of economics. On the whole, Dr. Zhenying Wang's research on the theories of trading economics can be seen as part of a broader development and innovation of modern economics in China. His penetrating views are valuable to creating an economic theory right for China."

—Guoqiang Tian, *Alfred F. Chalk Professor Department of Economics Texas A&M University*

"*Trading Economics* is an original work on economics. It examines the evolution of the economic system from a refreshing perspective—the birth and dynamics of the whole trading system—rather than the static supply-demand equilibrium that anchors current mainstream theories. Furthermore, it cuts deep into the internal laws that govern a trading system, while putting forward a wealth of new ideas such as the trading potential, trading space, and the trading equation, which merit further studies. Moreover, by reframing the most important topics in economics including general equilibrium, economic growth, economic cycle, and price changes from the angle of evolving trading systems and networks, it opens up a new way to bridge the gap between micro- and macroeconomics. For decades, Dr. Zhenying Wang has been dedicated to developing the basic theory of trading economics, with fruitful outcomes. His scholarly pursuits and inquiring mind are much admired."

—Songzuo Xiang, *Author of The New Capitalism and New Economics*

Book At a Glance

Part I—Fundamentals of Trading Economics

Chapter 1: Trading System

A brief review of the evolution of trading in human history leads to the conclusion that trading drives the progress of human civilization. Whether it is the institutional choice of human society, the construction of the rule of law, or technological innovation, the ultimate goal is to trade and allocate resources more efficiently. This chapter introduces the concept, basic structure, and evolution of trading system, and explains the law of efficiency, which is the basic law governing that evolution.

Chapter 2: Trading Agents

Trading economics is a study of the roles of families and enterprises, collectively referred to as trading agents. It does not arbitrarily presuppose families as consumers and enterprises as suppliers. Rather, families and enterprises are viewed as agents that jointly observe the principle of maximizing expected returns, and need to constantly switch between the different trading roles.

Chapter 3: Accounting Matrix

The accounting matrix is the basic analytical tool of trading economics and the foundation of its conceptual framework. It enables us to quantitatively describe the economic characteristics of families and enterprises as well as expanding the concept of trading, constructing the expected return function, and establishing the concept of accounting space.

Chapter 4: Expansion of Trading Concepts

Trading economics expands the concept of trading, and unifies all kinds of economic activities, such as consumption, investment, and production into the concept of trading. On this basis, we introduce the concepts of trading direction, trading time limit and valuation time domain, further enriching the concept of trading.

Chapter 5: Expected Return Function

In the logical framework of trading economics, the expected return function is the basis for the decision-making of trading agents. The expected return function satisfies the conditions of von Neumann's utility axioms and encompasses all kinds of trading scenarios of families and enterprises, providing the basis for a highly consistent analytical framework of trading economics.

Chapter 6: Principle of Maximizing of Expected Return

Trading economics classifies trading motives into three types, namely profit-seeking motives, asset diversification motives and liquidity motives, and concludes that trading under these different motives follows the principle of maximizing expected returns. Thus, the entire theory of trading economics is based on the principle of maximizing expected returns.

Part II—Birth and Structural Evolution of Trading Network

Chapter 7: Trading Community

Trading community is the seed of a trading network and an important part of the state synergy set of trading agents. It is the bridge between the local and the wider trading networks, and plays a vital role in the decision-making of trading agents.

Chapter 8: Generation of Trading Networks

Starting from the trading community, trading activities knit trading agents into an organic whole–trading network. Starting from the direct exchange and based on the principle of maximizing expected return, this chapter deduces the evolution of the trading network from small to large and from simple to complex, and gives the conditions for the emergence of important phenomena such as currency, specialization and economic globalization.

Chapter 9: Expression of Trading Network

This chapter gives quantitative indicators describing the characteristics of trading networks from eight dimensions, namely trading network capacity, node degree, degree distribution function, trading network density, trading network cycle rate, trading efficiency, trading network connectivity and trading network reconnection rate. These indicators are the basic parameters for constructing various models in trading economics.

Chapter 10: Layered Structure of Trading Network

This chapter discusses the layered structure of trading networks under supply, time, and synergistic constraints. At the end of this chapter, we analyze the impact of layered evolution of trading networks on the efficiency of resource allocation.

Chapter 11: Trading Network Phase Structure

This chapter focuses on market types such as polycentric markets, monocentric markets, and random trading markets. Starting from the phase structure, trading economics revisits topics that have been studied in depth in mainstream economics and obtains conclusions that go beyond mainstream economic models.

Chapter 12: Aggregation Structure of Trading Networks

The trading network shows non-uniform aggregation characteristics. It aggregates at five levels, namely community aggregation, city aggregation, economic beltaggregation, national aggregation, and international aggregation. This chapter discusses the evolutionary trend of trading network aggregation and constructs city aggregation model and migration models.

Chapter 13: Compactness of Trading Systems

Compactness is a quantitative measure of the nonlinearity of the trading system. In this chapter, we study the various factors that affect the compactness of the trading system in depth, reveal how that compactness evolves over time, and discuss the impact of the increasing compactness on the risk transmission, system robustness and the behaviors of trading agents.

Part III—Mechanism of Interaction Among Trading Agents and Polarization of Trading Potential

Chapter 14: Trading Equation

The trading equation is the primary analytical tool in trading economics; it captures how trading agents evaluate the various trading strategies. The trading equation connects the community to which a trading agent belongs with the whole trading network, and describes the interaction between individuals and between a part and the whole of a trading network, thereby solving the longstanding problem of detailing the microscopic mechanics of a nonlinear system.

Chapter 15: Interpretation of Trading Phenomena

This chapter uses the trading equation to explain the "peculiar phenomena"—the trading cascade, technological innovation, community poverty, gambler behaviors, and industrial agglomeration—that confound the mainstream economic theories. This showcases the interpretative power of the trading equation and the effectiveness of trading economics.

Chapter 16: Trading Loop

Trading loop is a unique concept of trading economics and the principal tool for macroeconomic analysis. The trading loop is the main contributor to large market volatility. It is the driving force behind both accelerated economic growth and economic crisis. By analyzing the equivalent equation of the trading loop, we reveal the close connection between economic chaos and trading loop.

Chapter 17: Distribution of Trading Potential

Trading potential is a quantitative measure of the competitiveness of trading agents. By studying how trading potential evolves, we draw the important conclusion that a trading system necessarily tends towards one of two extremes. A proof shows that when the trading system meets certain conditions, the distribution function of the trading potential follows the power law. From this we have simulated the distribution of the trading potential and the speed of polarization.

Chapter 18: Equation of the Trading System Evolution

The evolution equation of trading system describes the quantitative relationship between economic growth, degree of financialization, and magnitude of trading potential polarization. We draw three conclusions from this equation. First, the polarization of the trading potential is self-reinforcing. Second, economic growth and financialization are its main drivers. Third, agents with super trading potential will dictate the evolution of a trading system. The more successful these super-trading agents are, the more dynamic the society becomes.

Chapter 19: Evolution of Trading Space

The trading trajectory equation lays out the laws shaping an agent's trading trajectory. With this equation, we prove the weak reducibility of the trading space, the inevitability of social stratification, the existence of "black holes" (i.e., asymptotically closed sets) and "poverty trap." These characteristics of the trading space once again reveal the polarized nature of the trading system.

Part IV—Trading Economics Model

Chapter 20: Trade Phase Transition

Trading states are the types of strategy adopted by trading agents. We derive the phase transition equation of trading states from the trading equation, followed by a discussion of how trading states propagate in different types of communities, and reveal the expanding mechanism of the trading states in the trading network.

Chapter 21: Economic Cycle Model

Trading economics sees the economic cycle as the synchronization of trading states in a trading network. After introducing state entropy, we construct the cycle model of trading economics. This model shows that the effectiveness of monetary policies is closely related to the compactness of the trading system.

Chapter 22: Economic Growth Model

In mainstream theories, economic growth is the culmination of the economic activities of families and enterprises and the accumulated value they create. Trading economics believes it is the result of an expanding trading network, rather than a simple superposition of the behaviors of trading agents. This idea is fully reflected in the growth model of trading economics, which is constructed from the extension and connotation factors of the trading network.

Chapter 23: Trading Pricing Model

The trading pricing model is created based on the principle of maximizing expected return and the structural characteristics of a modern price system. This model allows us to explain the acceleration of inflation and the inner workings of stagflation, and shows how currency affects price changes in various scenarios.

Part V—Nature and Evolutionary Endpoint of Trading System

Chapter 24: Trading System Equilibrium

Equilibrium is a state of the trading system where all agents are trading at the optimal strategy. It is nearly impossible to achieve in the real world. From the bounded rationality hypothesis, we introduce the concepts of α-equilibrium and pole residence, and prove the weak stability of the trading system.

Chapter 25: Efficiency Decay of Trading System

With the social welfare function of trading economics, we prove that polarization is the main culprit behind the falling resource allocation efficiency of a trading system. The other common contributing factors are institutional suppression and population aging.

Chapter 26: The Imperfection of the Trading System

In trading economics, an institutional system is a set of rules. The perfect institutional system is a set of incentivizing rules that are both efficient and fair. This chapter shows that, against all our hopes for building a utopian world on top of a trading system, an institutional system is necessarily imperfect.

Contents

A Quick Guide to the Symbols

T	Trading system
a, b	Trading agent
A, B	The accounting matrix of trading agent, balance sheet
s	Trading strategy
S	Trading strategy set of trading agent, social system
Ω	Trading community, trading space
ω	Network density
φ	Trading system compactness
θ	Circulation rate of trading network
γ	Price squeeze coefficient
Γ	Price squeeze risk coefficient of the trading system
E	Expected return
Z	Value of commodity
μ	Trading efficiency coefficient, rational structure parameters
Gr	Economic growth
Fr	Financialization rate of asset
ψ	Trading potential
τ	The lag in the transmission of monetary policy
χ	Trading potential polarization index of the trading system
η	Distribution ratio of trading system
v	Value parameters of trading system
α, β	Parameters
i, j, l, k	Superscript of natural numbers
n, m, N, M	Natural numbers

Part I
Fundamentals of Trading Economics

This part consists of six chapters. It begins by introducing the concept of trading system and establishing the research direction of trading economics, followed by the definition of trading agents, the methods of describing them, and the expanded definition of trading. The subsequent chapters derive the expected return function on the basis of accounting matrix and discuss the motives of trading in various scenarios. These discussions come to the conclusion that one basic law governs all trading activities—the principle of maximizing expected return.

As the theoretical basis of trading economics, this part communicates an important idea throughout its chapters: As society evolves, the trading system continues to expand and grow in importance, and efficiency promotion is the basic direction of trading system evolution. The basic driving force behind the expansion and evolution of trading system is the pursuit of profits by trading agents.

Chapter 1
Trading System

Trading is the basic form of human economic activity and the source of the driving force for human progress. Trading system is the core of modern society. Once it stops operating, society will collapse, and the large and complex social organization will disintegrate. The national economy is essentially an open trading system. Human society develops, evolves, and accumulates under the support of trading system, ultimately creating a brilliant and splendid human civilization.

1.1 The Significance of Trading

The history of human civilization began with trading activities. Around 8000–6000 BC, human civilization first appeared in the Tigris and Euphrates river basins.[1] At this time, trading had begun to play an important role. The raw materials for the handicraft industry in the Mesopotamia region, including copper, silver, lead, and timber, had to be bought from other regions. To repay these imports, handicraft products had to be provided in exchange.[2]

Trading promotes the development of civilization and also creates a way for the spread of civilization. Through cross-regional trading activities, farming and irrigation techniques spread from Mesopotamia and western Iran to the east. By 3500 BC at the latest, these techniques had been widely disseminated in eastern Iran, Afghanistan, Baluchistan, and the Indus River basin.[3]

As early as the beginning of the Neolithic period, when agricultural civilization was just budding in China, trading activities had already begun in the Central Plains. The first dynasty recorded in Chinese characters—the Shang Dynasty—already had merchant groups whose basic means of livelihood was trading. The eight hundred years of history with "Shang" as its name,[4] is enough to show how powerful the influence of trading activities was.

Z. Wang, *Trading Economics*, Contributions to Economics,
https://doi.org/10.1007/978-981-99-9875-3_1

Trading has fundamentally changed the course of human society evolution in two ways. First, trading has shifted the goal of human pursuit from survival to wealth accumulation; second, trading has promoted social division of labor, driving the continuous evolution of human society towards increasingly complex organizational structures.

Once trading activities emerged, the concept of wealth entered people's consciousness. The more assets people have for trading, the wealthier they are considered. Thus, the goal of human survival shifted from the initial pursuing a full meal to pursuing wealth. This shift in goals has profound implications for human society evolution, representing a leap from material to number, from concrete to abstract goals. The pursuit of humans has never stopped from this point on, and human potential is maximally exploited in the pursuit of infinite wealth. The history of human society evolution has since entered a continuously accelerating trajectory.

There is an old Chinese saying, "People die for wealth, and birds die for food," which reveals the fundamental difference between humans and animals in terms of survival goals. In this sense, trading is not only a uniquely human behavior but also a key activity that guides humans to stand out from animal species and ultimately leave other species far behind.

In the diverse ecosystems, many species have relatively developed division of labor systems. For example, there is a strict division of labor within bee colonies, but these divisions belong to the category of physiological division of labor. Just like the division of labor between males and females exists in almost all species, this is due to the basic needs for species continuation. The division of labor caused by trading belongs to the category of social division of labor, which is not based on special physiological structures, but on individual skill differences and environmental endowment characteristics. The purpose of physiological division of labor is survival, while the purpose of social division of labor is efficiency.

After the emergence of social division of labor, human society evolved into increasingly complex organizational structures. The efficiency and function of complex systems invariably require the support of complex structures. The higher the efficiency and the stronger the function, the more complex the system structure.

Adam Smith believed that the key difference between rich and poor countries lies in whether the division of labor is sufficient. Trading is a key factor determining the level of division of labor; the more frequent the trading, the broader the market, the more detailed the division of labor.[5] The history of human society development is also the history of the evolution of trading. Even today, when various complex systems in human society have far exceeded people's imagination, complex social organizations, political systems, legal systems, education, healthcare, pensions, defense, arts, etc., are almost inexhaustible, but trading remains the basic activity that maintains social operation. When the economy begins to slump, supermarkets, department stores, and giant shopping centers are deserted, unemployment begins to rise, the national fiscal deficit begins to increase, the pressure brought by the economic depression is deeply felt by everyone from politicians to ordinary people, from banks to businesses, and the source of widespread social pain is the change in trading activities.

In Chinese history, there was once the famous "Needham's Question," named after the renowned British historian Joseph Needham. This is a question raised by Joseph Needham in his monumental work "Science and Civilization in China", a question that greatly puzzled Needham: given that ancient China made significant contributions to the development of human science and technology, why didn't the modern science and industrial revolution occur in modern China? Qian Xuesen, a renowned scientist in China, also raised a similar question, which is referred to as "Qian's Question" in academia. Whether it's "Needham's Puzzle" or "Qian's Question", a great deal of research has been conducted in the field of history, but no general consensus has been reached to date. From the perspective of trading economics, the idea of "emphasizing agriculture and suppressing commerce" that originated in the Warring States period is directly related. In China's feudal history spanning over two thousand years, agriculture has always been regarded as the foundation of governing the country and ensuring its stability, while commerce has always been strictly restricted and considered a "marginal occupation". Under the dominance of the idea of "emphasizing agriculture and suppressing commerce", not only were heavy taxes imposed on commerce, but it also had to bear unfair corvée. In order to restrict commercial activities, hotel services were abolished by government, which further limit long-distance travel of merchants.[6] Commercial activities were suppressed for a long time in Chinese history. Both modern science and the industrial revolution are built on the basis of refined social division of labor, and commercial activities are the most effective and fundamental way to promote social division of labor. The most important driving force for the evolution of human society from ancient times to modern civilization comes from social division of labor, and trading activities are at the bottom of the logic of division of labor. When trading activities are restricted, social division of labor cannot be fully realized, and social evolution will inevitably stumble. Under such a main line of historical evolution, "Needham's Puzzle" and "Qian's Question" naturally become self-evident issues.

Trading is fundamental to the healthy development of the trading system. Human society is a typical dissipative system. A dissipative system must maintain its existence through continuous energy exchange with the outside world, and a country or a city must also maintain its healthy operation through extensive trading activities with the outside world. Once the trading connection with the outside world is cut off, the isolated social system will inevitably collapse. In this regard, human history provides a lot of vivid evidence, the decline of the Athenian Empire and the Roman Empire are typical cases. In the early development of Athens, Athens gradually became powerful with the support of prosperous trading activities with neighboring city-states. During this period, the Athenian city-state traded city handicrafts for grain and food in rural areas. Later, the Athenians replaced voluntary trading exchange with a tribute system through conquer other city-states. The tribute system had to be maintained and consolidated through warfare, which inevitably caused a certain degree of destruction to the trading system. This is exactly the opposite of the effect produced by trading. The latter continuously nourishes the trading system and accumulates more and more wealth. The Athenian city-state abandoning the voluntary trading system eventually led to the gradual decline of the city-state. The situation of the Roman Empire was almost identical that of the Athenian city-state in its later period. The Roman Empire mainly relied on the tribute from the conquered areas to maintain the operation of the empire, and was a true "parasitic city". When the Germans became increasingly powerful and began to invade the territory of the Roman Empire, the tribute system of the Roman Empire was destroyed, and the once invincible Roman Empire eventually collapsed.[7]

Trading is the driver of wealth accumulation, the creator of wealth, and the measure of wealth. Without trading, humans lose the motivation and means to accumulate wealth, and without trading, it is impossible to achieve wealth growth and accumulation. The essence of wealth lies in that "Wealth" that cannot be traded is just an item, not real wealth.

Trading pursues profit, and profit drives innovation. Technological progress drives the development of human civilization. With the help of increasingly rapid technological progress, humans have achieved achievements they could not imagine before. Human footsteps have crossed the solar system and are advancing into the vast depths of space; on a microscopic level, humans have entered the nano era. Humans can carry out processes on a two-nanometer scale and can perform self-gene repair and modification. All of these are the results of trading activities aimed at profit.

Trading requires rules, and rules generate laws. Trading promotes the evolution of the rule of law in human society, and law is the greatest invention of mankind. The law provides order for human activities and guards the steady and far-reaching progress of human civilization.

1.2 Structure of the Trading System

The trading system is a subsystem evolved from the social system, and its core function is to achieve efficient resource allocation through trading. The trading system is an important part of human society and is in a continuous evolution process, which is the driving force for the evolution of human society.

The trading system is a system composed of four components: trading agents, trading bases, trading rules, and various government supervision and management mechanisms. In the long process of human society evolution, the trading system and the social system have the basic division of functions. The trading system undertakes the function of resource allocation, and its main value orientation is efficiency. In terms of resource allocation, the larger the input–output ratio, the higher the resource allocation efficiency; in terms of wealth distribution, the more intense the competition induced by the distribution system, the more effective this distribution system is. In general, the efficiency of resource allocation in the trading system refers to the system's ability to use various resources, including natural resources and human resources. To evaluate the efficiency of the trading system, we need to see whether all kinds of resources are fully and effectively used, and whether there is idle or waste of resources.

Corresponding to the functionality of the trading system, the social system mainly undertakes the function of consolidating the public and provides a stable and harmonious operating environment for the trading system. Its main value orientation is social justice. Social justice is manifested as the rationality of morality and social inclusiveness. The social system should provide potential development opportunities for every citizen, provide basic life guarantees for competition losers, avoid polarization of wealth distribution, avoid solidification of social hierarchy, and avoid restrictions on the potential for free development of citizens.

The social system is a typical ecosystem. The ecosystem is a cycle of material carriers and energy supported by a large number of interconnected components and complex structures. The trading system closely links a large number of trading agents through the trading network and realizes the circulation of goods and values through trading. Under the promotion of trading activities, an increasingly complex social organizational structure has evolved.

On the surface, there is a certain conflict in value orientation between the trading system and the social system. Fairness requires sacrificing efficiency, and efficiency may lead to a loss of fairness. However, on a deeper level, the two systems interact and restrain each other, forming a collaborative organic whole. In the social system, efficiency and fairness are closely related aspects of the same agent, and a significant decline in either will lead to the destruction of the social system, challenging its sustainability. When wealth distribution lacks fairness, a small portion of people gain a large amount of wealth with little effort, while the majority work hard but reap little wealth. If the incentive mechanism of the trading system has problems at the grassroots level, it will inevitably dampen the enthusiasm of the trading agents, leading to a decline in the efficiency of the trading system. The internal circulation mechanism of the trading system will stagnate, the trading network will not be able to achieve efficient circulation, and the social system will inevitably collapse.

However, if one blindly pursues absolute fairness, it will harm the competitiveness of the trading agents, leading to a decline in the efficiency of the trading system. A large amount of resources, including human resources, will fall into idle or semi-idle states, leading the trading system towards the same outcome—the operation of the social system becomes unsustainable, eventually leading to collapse.

Fairness and efficiency are two dimensions of the robustness of the social system. Like the relationship between the two poles of Yin and Yang in natural systems, they restrict and generate each other, and depend on each other. Only by maintaining a relatively balanced relationship can the social system operate healthily. The healthy relationship between society and economy should be that the economy provides means to support social justice, and social justice promotes economic development.

The operation of the trading system is governed by rules, while the operation of the social system is dominated by morals. Rules and morals complement each other, maintaining the delicate balance of the social system. A society lacking morals has high trading costs and unbearable trading risks. Conversely, a trading system lacking efficiency cannot support a society with a good moral standard.

From the evolution of human civilization to today, a basic trend is the rising status of the trading system in the social system, the continuous expansion of the functions of the trading system, and more and more social activities being included in the scope of trading. In traditional rural areas, neighbors helping each other was entirely a moral activity. With the evolution of society, people today are no longer ashamed to talk about money, but pay according to the price of labor per day. The family is an important place for social activities and a major manifestation of sociability. Housework is an important part of family functions, with most female members responsible for housework, including cooking, sewing, and caring for young children; male members work outside to support the family. Nowadays the division of labor among family members has already changed, with most of the housework already transferred or being transferred to the market, with resource allocation completed through the trading system. Family elder care, once one of the core functions of the family, is also moving towards socialization. Even medical care, which reflects the warmth among family members, is facing professional transformation, solving problems through the trading system. The externalization of family functions has become a major sign of the expansion of the trading system into society.

From the perspective of trading, morality can be seen as a fuzzy rule for intertemporal trading activities, regulating the intertemporal payment behavior between people and between individuals and society. The nurturing of children by parents and the reciprocation by children to their parents, as important content of moral norms, is essentially a form of intertemporal trading. Parents pay first, and children reciprocate later. This intertemporal payment behavior cannot be regulated by contracts. Contracts require arbitration and supervision, and for a large number of family groups, moral norms are the most economical. However, moral norms are not always effective, and the constraints of morality on people's behavior are very limited. As human society expands and the connections among people become increasingly close, the powerlessness and paleness of morality become increasingly prominent. The social costs caused by disputes and contradictions are rapidly rising, gradually becoming an unbearable social burden. Against this backdrop, a large number of social activities have shifted from the realm of morality to the trading system, with the former moral norms replaced by trading rules. This evolutionary trend in human society represents progress from extensive to refined, and from low efficiency to high efficiency.

Accompanying the expansion of the trading system within the social system, the efficiency of the social system is constantly improving. From the perspective of social evolution, the position of the trading system in the social system represents the level of social development. The higher the position occupied by the trading system, the more developed the social system, and the faster the pace of social progress; conversely, the more developed a society, the higher the degree of social civilization, the more important the position of the trading system in the social system.

Looking at the entire process of human social development and evolution, the expansion of the trading system in the social system is limited. We will prove later that the trading system has a natural tendency to polarize. If the polarization of the trading system is allowed to develop, the social system will eventually be torn apart in the polarization. As the matrix of the trading system, the social system needs to continuously reform and optimize the institutional system, effectively correct the polarization, and curb the increasingly intensified polarization of the trading system. Only in this way can the sustainable development of the entire social system be maintained and the continuous evolution of human civilization be realized.

Among the components that make up the trading system, trading rules include both micro trading rules, i.e., agreements reached by the parties to the trading, and various laws and regulations that support micro trading rules. Compared with micro rules, laws and regulations have a wider range of application scenarios and belong to macro rules. The supervision and management mechanism is composed of the corresponding execution agencies and various regulations. The execution agencies include various government departments, market supervision organizations, etc. Supervision and management belong to two different categories. Market access, market behavior supervision, financial supervision, etc. belong to the category of trading supervision; monetary policy, fiscal policy, tax policy, trading investment policy, foreign exchange management policy, etc. belong to the management category of trading. Supervision and management are part of the self-regulation of the trading system. By continuously strengthening supervision and management, the smooth and efficient operation of the trading system is achieved, avoiding the spontaneous collapse of the trading system. If trading is a great invention of mankind, trading supervision and management are a great wisdom of mankind.

The dynamic relationship between the trading system and the social system can be graphically represented as follows.

Figure 1.1 shows the position of the trading system in the social system, which continues to expand over time, absorbing more and more social functions into the trading process.

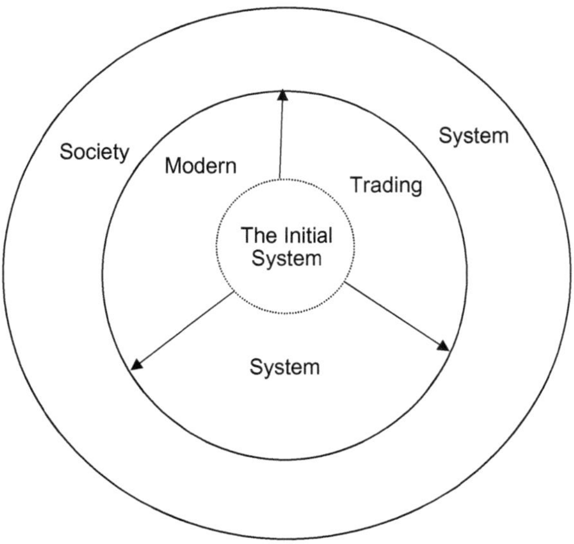

Fig. 1.1 The evolutionary trend of the trading system and social system

1.3 The Efficiency Law of Trading System Evolution

The second law of thermodynamics suggests that the universe we are born into, which encompasses everything, is not changing aimlessly, but has a clear evolutionary direction—that is, the direction of increasing entropy. In the vast universe, entropy is like a ubiquitous hand, breaking the original order and dragging the world into deeper chaos. However, the world we live in has chosen to deviate from the direction of increasing entropy and evolve towards increasing efficiency. The evolution of dissipative structures is inevitably efficiency-oriented. Efficiency is the basis of the "life" of dissipative systems. The trading system is a typical dissipative system. The higher the efficiency of the system, the less input is required to maintain a given output, the stronger the vitality of the system, and the more advantageous it is in competition.

Efficiency is a very broad philosophical concept, a description of the ability to achieve goals. Efficiency is an ancient concept, which began to be used as early as the eighth century BC in ancient Greece. Two ancient Greek philosophers, Hesiod and Xenophon, were very concerned about efficiency. As a farm owner, Hesiod naturally noticed the issue of efficiency. For ancient Greek philosophers, economics is closely related to efficiency. Xenophon was the first to use the term economics, and named his work "Economics", which originally meant effective management at the enterprise or household level, and believed that economics is the study of efficiency.[8]

In physics, the definition of efficiency refers to the percentage of useful work in total work when machinery and electrical appliances are working. The higher the proportion of useful work, the higher the efficiency of the equipment. In everyday language, efficiency is used to mark the amount of work done in a unit of time, the more work completed and the greater the workload, the higher the efficiency. In this case, efficiency is the speed of work. In economics, efficiency refers to the utilization rate of resources, that is, the less resources consumed and the shorter the time invested under a given goal, the higher the efficiency of the adopted approach or method; otherwise, the efficiency is lower. There are many indicators that can quantitatively describe the efficiency of the economy, including per capita GDP, productivity, the output value per unit of time; at the micro level, indicators such as per capita input, profit rate, etc. can be used.

It is very difficult to measure the efficiency of the entire trading system. At the intuitive level, efficiency is manifested as the pace of work and life that people feel. Whether comparing the pace of life and compactness of business management in developed and less developed countries, or comparing the pace of life in economically developed regions and underdeveloped regions within a country, or comparing urban life with rural life, or comparing the pace of life in ancient, modern and contemporary times, we will conclude that our pace of life is accelerating.

Generally speaking, the pace of life in less developed economies is slower, and businesses in these regions tend to be more lax in their management, with poorer rationality in the pace and process of work; whereas in developed countries and regions, the pace of life is much faster, the content of life is much richer than in less developed countries and regions, and time seems more precious. Regardless of whether it is in developed countries or developing countries, there is always a gap in the pace of life between cities and rural areas. Although rural areas are also changing and the pace is accelerating compared to the past, compared to cities of the same period, the pace of life will always be much slower. In traditional agricultural societies, people have been living and working strictly according to the rhythm of nature for thousands of years, living their daily lives according to the rule of working at sunrise and resting at sunset; in a year, they decide the arrangement of farming activities according to the rotation of spring, summer, autumn and winter seasons. China's twenty-four solar terms are actually a work schedule for farmers in the Yellow River basin. Throughout the agricultural economic era, neither Eastern nor Western societies had an accurate concept of time or unit of hours, let alone minutes and seconds. In Europe, there was no accurate concept of minutes until the eighteenth century. Traditional Chinese timekeeping methods used sundials, with units using the twelve equal scales of Zi, Chou, Yin, Mao, etc., and one time unit being two hours.

In the late Middle Ages, despite the heavy obstacles of guilds and churches, the pace of Europe gradually began to accelerate. In the late Middle Ages, Europe was the first to invent clocks, dividing time into equal lengths through mechanical movement. From then on, it broke away from the dependence on nature in time measurement. The trend of accelerating rhythm first appeared in some cities. In the fifteenth and sixteenth centuries in Europe, with the overall population growth, the population of some large cities also began to expand rapidly. In the 200 years of the fifteenth and sixteenth centuries, the European population doubled from 50 to 105 million. As the urban population increased, interactions became frequent, the division of labor within the city became increasingly refined, and trading drove changes in everything from accounting, information transmission, to transportation, and then to production organization methods. The urban network became denser, and the frequency of trading began to increase.

In the fifteenth century, it took 11–20 days in summer and 13–24 days in winter to send a letter from Lübeck to Bruges; in the process of accelerating progress, the mail in the seventeenth century shortened this postal route to 8 days in summer and 10 days in winter. In order to deliver goods to their destination faster and cheaper, sea transportation began to play an increasingly important role. The speed of land transportation in the Middle Ages was 5–7 km per day, while sea transportation reached 18–20 nautical miles per day, and even 24–32 nautical miles when sailing directly. The speed of sea transportation is several times that of land. In the sixteenth century, the Dutch developed the flute-shaped merchant ship, which was not only faster, but also had a larger load. Therefore, due to the speed, the Netherlands occupied the maritime advantage for as long as 200 years.

In the trading system evolution, once speed changes in a link or a certain part, this change will gradually spread, eventually elevating the operating speed of the entire trading network to a new level. Take the technological development of the textile industry as an example. In 1733, John Kay invented the flying shuttle technology, greatly increasing the speed of weaving; while spinning technology was still lagging behind, with the efficiency ratio of weaving to spinning reaching 12:1, i.e., 12 spinners were needed to meet the cotton yarn demand of one weaver. In 1769, the Spinning Jenny and the Water-Power Spinning Machine were introduced; in 1799, the mule spinning machine was introduced. Spinning efficiency increased by 200 times, and the problem of yarn supply was completely solved. Then, a new problem arose, the carding and cotton combing process before spinning became the bottleneck restricting the efficiency of the textile industry; the invention of the rocker carding machine solved this problem, increasing the speed of carding and cotton combing. With the resolution of these issues, the dyeing and printing process emerged as the new bottleneck. In 1783, a British dyeing factory invented the roller printing method, replacing the traditional single-block printing process. After the technology in each link of the textile industry was comprehensively improved, another problem that did not exist before began to emerge—the shortage of workers. Therefore, the issue of textile automation was put on the agenda, and after continuous experiments, the third generation of mechanical looms came out in the 1920s, increasing the weaving speed by 3 times.

Speed not only propagates through different production process links, but also spreads rapidly among countries through competitive pressure and demonstration effects. When the Industrial Revolution turned Britain into the world's number one power, countries on the European continent followed suit, hoping to quickly catch up with Britain's development level. Countries on the European continent sent delegation to Britain to study advanced technologies, then arranged to establish industrial association in their home countries. Also, they published the most advanced technologies that Britain had been using on magazines. European governments also sent the delegation of specialists to Britain to learn technologies, and purchased machines in government's own name. Machines on the purchasing list were all specially permitted by the prime minister of Britain, so that they would not have any problem when shipping aboard. These machines were exhibited in Gewebe-Institut in Berlin, in Polytechnischen Verein in Muenchen, in Conservatoire in Paris and in Polytechnischen Institut in Wien respectively, so that other countries were able to learn and copy the technology, and provided convenience for technicians and engineers in research. Technicians from Britain were hired by other countries on the continent as well. According to statistics, there were about 20,000 British technicians employed in different countries in Europe in 1825.[9]

As more and more mechanical equipment is introduced into production and life, and the pace of life and work continues to accelerate, people begin to pay attention to the optimization of their own behavior. Faced with increasingly fierce competition, companies must improve management efficiency to survive, and employees must improve their work skills and optimize operating procedures to get good remuneration and promotion. Starting from the 1920s, Taylorism began to rise. As a management scientist, Taylor suggested that companies evaluate each link of the production process, using time as the measure of the efficiency of a technology and process; eliminate some initially seemingly necessary, but actually inefficient links, processes, and technologies in the evaluation. Under the promotion of Taylorism, the efficiency of enterprises further improved, and according to Taylor's method, the efficiency of an ordinary blacksmith worker increased by 4 times. Following Taylor's thinking, a large number of management techniques to improve enterprise efficiency and speed up work emerged.

As production efficiency and the pace of life continue to increase, information technology is bringing the world closer together, allowing people all over the world to know almost instantly about events happening in every corner of the world. "In 1962, Telstar, the communication satellite, firstly transferred the television image between the US and Europe. In 1963, the first synchronous satellite was send into orbit. Distance between countries was greatly narrowed to the minimum that hardly existed. The popularity of TV camera also accelerated the development of fashion industry. Fashion trend in one place soon became a trend of the world through the media. In the twentieth century, the development of economics and technology has been unprecedentedly accelerating. The telecommunication speed has been increased by 10 million times; public transportation speed and disease control speed have been improved by 100 times; data processing speed has been increased by 10 million times."[10] The acceleration of production and life rhythm makes people's bodies tense, and the acceleration of information transmission makes people's eyes busier.

The speed upgrade of computers obeys Moore's Law.[11] In fact, the entire human society is also governed by Moore's Law. The operation speed of human society also has a Moore's Law, which also shows an exponential trend of acceleration. A history of human social development is actually a history of speed acceleration and efficiency promotion. Acceleration is not a choice of human nature, nor is it individual behavior, but the result of the interaction of social network mechanisms. Ultimately, the pursuit of efficiency drives society to accelerate its pace, and efficiency dominates the evolution of the trading system.

Notes

1. Rondo Cameron, Larry Neal (2009) A Concise Economic History World: From Paleolithic Times to the Present (trans: Ning PAN), 4th edn. Shanghai Translation Publishing House, Shanghai, p 20–26.
2. L. S. Stavrianos (2006) A Global History: From Prehistory to the 21 Century (trans: Xiangying WU, Chimin LIANG, Shuhui DONG), 7th edn. Peiking University Press, Beijing, p 49–53.
3. Rhoads Murphey (2004) A History of Asia (trans: Lin HUANG), Hainan Publishing House, p 3–6.
4. Wenlan FAN (1964) A Brief Compilation of Chinese General History, 4th edn. People's Press, Beijing, The first book: p 111–118.
5. Adam Smith (2009) The Wealth of the Nation (trans: Changming HU), Ch3. On the division of labour being limited by the scope of the market, People's Daily Press.
6. Kezhong ZHENG, A Study on the Origin of the Thought of Suppressing Business in Ancient China and the Theoretical Mistakes It Trapped in,1999.
7. Arthur O′Sullivan (2015) Urban Economics (trans: Jingkui ZHOU), Peiking University Press, p 19.
8. Harry Landreth, David C. Colander (2014) History of Economic Thoughts (trans: Wen ZHOU), 4th edn. Posts & Telecom Press, Beijing, p 33.

9. L. S. Stavrianos (2006) A Global History: From Prehistory to the 21 Century (trans: Xiangying WU, Chimin LIANG, Shuhui DONG), 7th edn. Peiking University Press, Beijing, p 44.
10. L. S. Stavrianos (2006) A Global History: From Prehistory to the 21 Century (trans: Xiangying WU, Chimin LIANG, Shuhui DONG), 7th edn. Peiking University Press, Beijing, p 175.
11. In the mid-1960s, Gordon Moore, one of the founders of Intel, predicted that the transistors in a silicon wafer would grow exponentially, doubling every 18–24 months. This is known as the Moore's Law.

Chapter 2
Trading Agents

Identifying trading agents is both the logical starting point of theoretical analysis and an important part of constructing the trading network to find nodes. The choice of trading agents must consider the convenience of description and the uniformity among different types of agents, which will have a significant impact on the simplicity of the theory.

2.1 Choice of Trading Agents

In the mainstream economic theory system, the treatment of trading agents or behavioral agents is relatively vague. Consumers can be natural persons or family organizations. But in fact, for a logically rigorous theory, it is very important to clarify the behavioral agent. The behavioral agent is the logical starting point of economics. Only on the basis of clearly defining the research object can we establish a characteristic description of the behavioral agent and study the relationship between the organizational structure of the agent and its behavior.

People are the agents of society and the basic components of the trading system. From the perspective of systems theory, only by forming organizational structures through multi-level aggregation iteration, assigning specific functions to different organizational structures, can we achieve efficient system operation through coordination among organizations.[1] Theoretically, any organizational unit at each level of the trading system can be the agent of study, becoming the agent of economics, including individuals, families and enterprises, industrial clusters, regions, countries, etc. The choice of the behavioral agent depends on the focus of the theory and the method used, as well as the perspective of system research. Different perspectives not only dictate the trajectory of theoretical logic evolution, but also induce different theoretical propositions. The challenges for economics lies in dealing with the causal relationships of numerous variables in multi-level systems. However, phenomena at

Z. Wang, *Trading Economics*, Contributions to Economics,
https://doi.org/10.1007/978-981-99-9875-3_2

different levels not only have different "agent" objects, but their laws of motion are also different, which inevitably leads to the super complexity of the theory. Faced with the ambition to find a bottom-up unified description of the operating laws of the trading system, economists often helplessly stop at the reality separately constructed at macro and micro levels. Trading economics takes a different approach, adopting a method to reduce the levels of theoretical construction, placing families and enterprises directly in the position of agents, and viewing the trading system as a space formed by the trading network among agents.

Families and enterprises, as two basic trading agents, have symmetry in function, and their organizational forms and their evolution process are based on a common principle—the principle of maximum expected return. Using families and enterprises as research objects, compared to mainstream economics, it seems to be just a difference in number. In fact, the derived theoretical effects are extremely wide, leading to fundamental mutations in the theoretical system.

In trading activities, complex interpersonal organization construction will inevitably have an impact on the actors that cannot be ignored. The essence of organizational construction is a definition of a relationship of rights and responsibilities. Different rights and responsibilities induce different behavioral patterns. The same individual, due to different rights and responsibilities, may have completely different behavioral patterns in state-owned enterprises than in private enterprises. The trading agent is a re-editing of human nature, showing more profit-seeking characteristics.

The simplicity of the theory depends on whether the unity behind the appearance of huge differences can be discovered. In trading economics, the role layout of producers and consumers is abandoned, and enterprises and families are simply regarded as trading agents of different organizational forms. During the trading, there are no absolute suppliers or demanders, and each agent is constantly switching roles between supply and demand. No matter how the role changes, the goal pursued by the trading agent shows a high degree of stability and consistency.

Based on the above analysis, trading economics defines the behavioral agent as follows: the trading agent refers to an organization that has independent decision-making ability and bears the consequences of actions, and has a clear boundary of full economic rights and responsibilities with other agents.

Whether it is a family or an enterprise, as a trading agent, it has a clear legal status, and the independence of property is recognized and protected by law and custom. From the perspective of accounting, as a natural person who is a member of a family, there is a lack of clear property boundaries with other family members, and it is impossible to establish a complete balance sheet. In a legal sense, family members share certain civil responsibilities and obligations with one another, including debts, claims, compensation, and inheritance and succession, etc. Cohabitation is an increasingly common family form in modern society. From the surface, cohabitants have almost the same life content as legal marriage, but they lack legal relationship recognition and do not have the right to share property and the obligation to share debt responsibilities, hence cannot be regarded as the sametrading agent.

The determination of the trading agent is not only related to the organizational structure, but also closely related to rules and regulations. For families, the age at which children can act as independent civil liability persons should be defined according to the laws and social customs of different countries. Customs are factors that cannot be ignored. Even though children have reached the legal age of adulthood, they still live in their parents' homes and share various rights and interests of their parents. In this case, adult children should still be regarded as members of their parents' family, not as an independent trading agents.

Altruistic strategies within the family require members to consider the interests of other members. Parents need to consider the needs of their children when consuming and investing, including arrangements for expenditures in education, medical care, etc.; and children's consumption usually requires the approval and supervision of their parents. The family is based on marriage and kinship, and appears as a community of interests in the entire economic decision-making process. Although family members can have their own expectations, they must be based on the interests of the entire family. Therefore, it is realistic and rational to regard the family as an independent unit participating in the trading.

Based on the legal provisions of the civil subject, we can establish a complete financial accounting system for families. Just like enterprises, they have balance sheets, income statements, and cash flow statements, etc. In addition, there is another important reason to regard families as trading agents, only on the basis of the balance sheet can we discover the essence of the trading, and accurately give the connotation and extension of the trading concept.

There is still an internal structure within the trading agent. At the level of the agent's internal hierarchy, the organization is structured by natural persons, just like cells achieve specific functions through aggregation, and the further aggregation of organs with different functions can form a vigorous and powerful life body. Enterprises and families are the cells of the trading system, and the trading network connects these cells to realize the macroeconomic operation.

2.2 Family

In the modern trading system, the family and the enterprise are like a binary star system, interacting and depending on each other, and the interaction between the family and the enterprise becomes the basic driving force of economic operation, and also constitutes the basic framework of the trading system. Although the family no longer plays the role of producer in the modern trading system, and has relatively independent division of labor with the enterprise, fundamentally speaking, the family is the same as the enterprise in terms of trading decision-making mechanisms, both trying to maximize expected return under their own constraints. The difference is only manifested in decision-making procedures and trading methods.

In the long history of human evolution, the family form has undergone various changes. In different historical periods, in different cultural groups, the organizational form of the family is not exactly the same. Before the modern family appeared, the family went through five forms. The earliest was the endogamous family, which was the most primitive form of human society. At that time, the number of humans was extremely limited, and the main survival pressure faced by humans was not competition among groups, but harsh natural conditions and fierce beasts. The number of groups was very small, and the probability of one group encountering another group was very low. Under these conditions, in order to maintain the reproduction of the group, it was necessary to adopt marriage within the group. Compared with today's families, primitive families had many more members, and there was no definite generational structure. The only certainty was that within the family, there was a certain blood relationship among all members. After experiencing the long history of human evolution, it is no longer possible to find direct evidence of the existence of this family form, and can only get indirect confirmation from historical and religious legends.

With the increase in family population, single family continues to split into more families. When the number of families in a region reaches a certain threshold, the survival pressure of the family needs to face includes not only the challenges of the harsh environment, but also the competition among groups. The result of survival of the fittest is that families that adopt exogamy have stronger physiques and higher IQs, and hence have greater advantages in competition.

Early exogamy lacked stability. The marital behavior between a person and the opposite sex from another group was completely random, giving rise to a problem: between the two sexes, to whom should the children belong? Answering such a simple question took humans two to three hundred thousand years. The right of children not only relates to the issue of family organization structure, but also to which gender has a higher status in the group. Obviously, this is not a case issue, but a systemic issue. When human footprints have not yet spread across the world, as long as the bloody wars among groups have not risen to the main challenge of group survival, the absolute authority of men in the group cannot appear. It is most natural for children to belong to their mother. Therefore, it is inevitable that the matrilineal clan becomes the second form of human family. At this time, the family is based on the clan, and a clan is a family. Every member of the family shares the family's wealth, including food, shelter, etc. Throughout the long years of the entire Paleolithic and early Neolithic, the matrilineal family was the basic form of family existence. The tribe, as a union of clan families with certain blood relations, has more military significance. Connect to defend against foreign enemies, carry out military attacks to expand territory and other activities. But the unit of economic activity is still the clan family.

With the increase of clan families, wars caused by territorial competition among clans are becoming more frequent. Males with aggressive characteristics gradually move to the center of the family, and the patrilineal clan family gradually becomes dominant. From matrilineal clans to patrilineal clans, although only the gender of inheritance has changed, it has caused structural changes in the family, and it has laid the groundwork for the emergence of individual families and the disintegration of clan families. Compared with matrilineal clans, the blood relationship among family members has become thinner. The evolution from clan family to modern monogamous family has gone through a transition from group marriage to couple, and then to monogamy. The establishment of the monogamous family form announced the disintegration of the clan family. The original public society also declared the end.

Behind the evolution of family forms is the change in the mode of production. In primitive society, the family existed in the form of a clan, and the clan members were tied together by blood relations, belonging to an organizational unit that combined human self-production, economy, and military. After entering the agricultural civilization, the state function was separated from the family, and the functions undertaken by the family focused on two aspects: one is the reproduction function; the other is the agricultural production function. In that era, the family as an economic organization unit had a strong constraint on each member, and each member's labor, consumption, and inheritance were strictly limited under the management rules of the family organization. The traditional moral system also requires adaptation to this economic organizational form.

After entering the industrial age, the constraints of the family on its members greatly weakened. The production function gradually separated from the family, and family members entered social activities at a very young age. From kindergarten, primary school, middle school, university, to employment, the function of the family finally purified to maintaining human reproduction, providing leisure for members, and a place to share consumption. Compared with the original family, the functions have been continuously simplified, and more and more functions are replaced by social division of labor.

Regardless of how the form of the family evolves, the essence of the family has always been the smallest population unit that shares property, and it is the foundation of social and economic activities. The edge of the family is determined by the property sharing relationship. The more fully the members share, the closer they are to the core of the family.

The economic decision-making power of the family also evolves with social development. In traditional Chinese society, the decision-making power of the family is not held by the creator of the family income, but is usually decided by the elders of the family. In the agricultural era, a family's decision was very simple, and there was not much change year after year. Only building houses or buying and selling land were the most significant decisions a family faced. With the advent of the industrial age, the decision-making situation and content faced by the family are becoming more and more complex, including family financial management, children's career choices, real estate investment, etc. Not only has the content become richer, but the dynamic characteristics are becoming prominent. These complex decisions can no longer be completed by an elderly person who is far away from social activities. Such a development result naturally leads to changes in the family structure. While the family becomes simpler, the decision-making power also shifts from the elderly to the creators of wealth—the young people.

Accompanied by the weakening of family functions, the family is constantly evolving towards miniaturization. Although the family organization is influenced by cultural traditions, the characteristics and development level of economic activities are the ultimate determinants. Generally speaking, the higher the level of economic development, the smaller the family size (Table 2.1).

The size of the composite family containing multiple generations receives influenced by the degree of partial engineering. The higher the degree of external division of labor, the greater the possibility of internal division of labor being replaced by external division of labor. There are two reasons: one is that external division of labor is in a larger range of competition, which is more efficient than the division of labor within the family. The second is that the larger the family size, the phenomenon of hitchhiking and escaping responsibility within the family will increase. The family size is the balance of the two advantages, i.e., the advantage of cooperation within the family and the advantage of external division of labor.

Of course, the family size cannot be infinitely reduced. The core family is the lowest mode with production functions, i.e., a couple plus a few underage children. The number of children is influenced by family functions and rearing costs. The simplification of family functions will inevitably reduce the demand for the number of children. With the development from traditional society to modern society, family functions have also been simplified from the production of life materials and goods and providing for the elderly, to the function of live together to reduce costs and increase the joy of life, and the demand for children is also greatly compressed.

Table 2.1 Comparison of family size among countries and regions in different times[2]

Region or country	Average family size	Family standard deviation
India (1970–1971)	6.64	3.61
USA (1970)	3.11	1.82
USA (1689)	5.85	2.88
Syria (1970)	5.91	3.00
Thailand (1970)	5.82	2.81
France (1778)	5.04	2.55
Japan (1713)	4.97	2.49
England (1599)	4.75	3.35
Florence (1427)	5.92	2.42

Unit: Person

2.3 Enterprises

Enterprises have separated from families, taking on the basic function of creating benefits. For the trading system, enterprises are as important as the heart, acting as the engine that drives the operation and development of the trading system. Enterprises play the role of the most important trading in any economy. The organizational management and technological innovation capabilities of an enterprise directly determine the vitality and efficiency of the trading system.

2.3.1 The Emergence of Enterprises

In modern society, enterprises have become organizations with independent functions, but historically speaking, for a considerable period, the functions of enterprises were undertaken by families. Enterprises originated from families. In the long history of human development, the time when families served as production units far exceeded that of enterprises with independent functions. The step into civilization was accompanied by the transition from gathering and hunting to production. After entering the civilized era, the first dominant economic form was agriculture, with fishing and animal husbandry only existing as supplements. Under the agricultural economic form, the family was the only place of production. A large amount of archaeology around the world proves that the revolutionary transition of humans from gatherers to producers began in the Neolithic Age. In stone tool making, Neolithic people used grinding methods, the stones used were harder, the tools made were more durable, sharper, and had a wider range of uses. The change in the way humans obtain food has profound significance in the evolution of civilization. The emergence of agriculture is not just a change in the way food is obtained, but more importantly, agricultural production and the resulting fixed residence make wealth accumulation possible, thereby opening the door to human pursuit of wealth. The subsequent evolution of human society is ultimately centered on the production, distribution, and possession of wealth.

After the agricultural revolution, the demands generated by settled communities were much more diverse than those of nomadic life, including the need for housing and furniture, various agricultural tools, etc., all of which were absent in the hunting era. This diversified demand quickly gave birth to social division of labor, and handicraft and commerce separated from agricultural production. Craftsmen and merchants became the main inhabitants of early towns. These craftsmen and merchants also operated on a family basis. They were the direct source of modern enterprises. After the industrial revolution, these family-based enterprises, with the help of new technologies and financial tools, turned into modern enterprises—companies, organizations with legal person status. From then on, enterprises formally separated from families. Without this transformation, people might even feel that there is no need to create a separate term for enterprises. Even today, family enterprises of various sizes and systems in the economy still play an important role that cannot be ignored. Among the numerous micro and individual enterprises in various countries, the organization combining family and enterprise is still mainstream.

Modern enterprises first appeared in Europe. In the early eighteenth century, some European villages saw the emergence of family workshop-style textile enterprises, with labor based on families, and both parents and children participated in the labor of the family workshops. These families also owned land, balancing labor in workshop and farming. The raw materials used and the products produced by these family workshops were mostly provided and sold by town merchants, and the products were sold to distant markets. These characteristics distinguish these concentrated rural workshops from the previous, long-standing family handicraft workshops. The large-scale rural factories of this period not only greatly expanded the market radius of the products, but also produced under the organization and coordination of merchants. Rural workshops were the predecessors of modern enterprises and their activities were the direct precursors of the industrial revolution.[3] Therefore, the industrial development of this period is called proto-industrialization by historians, to emphasize the inheritance between the industrial development of this period and the industrial revolution.[4]

Not all regions' industrialization has a transitional stage of proto-industrialization (such as Ireland), while the phenomenon of proto-industrialization is still very common. In the early 1980s at the beginning of China's reform and opening up, a large number of township enterprises emerged, most of which were of the nature of family workshops, with the characteristics of primitive enterprises, i.e., small in scale, using simple equipment, and almost all or at least mainly supported by family members or relatives. This type of production organization does not have clear institutional norms, quite a few have not even registered with the industrial and commercial administration department, and never borrow from formal financial institutions. In the early 1980s, the township enterprises spread all over China were once an important force driving the development of reform and opening up. Even today, after more than forty years of development, the traces of these early developments are still faintly visible in some areas, like the sock knitting industry in Zhuji City, Zhejiang Province, and the denim clothing processing industry in Xintang Town, Zengcheng, Guangdong Province, which are still important pillars of the local economy, and the main supporting force behind them is still family enterprises.

In the history of enterprise development, commercial enterprises were the first to separate from the family, acting as a catalyst for the development of productive enterprises. The history of commerce can be traced back to the origins of agricultural civilization, or even earlier, to the origins of human civilization. In the development process of any economy, capital accumulation always starts with commerce. Merchants accumulate capital far beyond that of small enterprise owners through trading, and by leveraging their understanding of the market, they connect scattered small enterprise owners, forming a proto-industrial market operation model. In this period, the trading network was centered around merchants. Superior trading positions gave merchants an absolute advantage in rapidly accumulating wealth.

The partnership form of organization was widely used in economic fields before the Industrial Revolution. From the perspective of system evolution, partnership enterprises can easily evolve into joint-stock enterprises. As the number of partners continues to increase, the difference between partnership enterprises and joint-stock enterprises becomes increasingly blurred. Once a partner sells their "rights", the nature of the partnership enterprise has actually transformed into a joint-stock enterprise. The specific situations stipulated by the partnership enterprise system vary from country to country. In England, enterprise partners generally bear unlimited liability; but in France, partnership enterprises can have three different system arrangements: unlimited liability companies, partially limited liability, and limited liability. Unlimited liability requires all partners to bear unlimited liability; partial limited liability requires some partners to bear limited liability, but the remaining partners bear unlimited liability; and limited liability means that partners only bear the responsibility for their investment, which is essentially no different from a limited liability company. Furthermore, as an important feature of modern enterprises, the mechanism of separating property rights and management rights has already appeared in large partnership enterprises. These enterprises are mostly concentrated in industries such as coal mining, smelting, and beer manufacturing. In fact, partnership enterprises prevalent in the proto-industrial era have fully prepared for the mainstream enterprise organization model of the industrial age—limited liability companies—in terms of property rights system and enterprise model.

The partnership enterprise system has far exceeded family enterprises in terms of resource integration and allocation capabilities. By increasing the number of partners, previously scattered small enterprises in the same industry are brought together, and this integration can even be carried out across regions. The integrated enterprise shows stronger advantages in market competition.[5] Before the widespread establishment of modern corporate systems around the world, partnerships were the mainstream organizational system for enterprises. However, in the absence of a comprehensive legal system, partnership enterprises were essentially just an extension of natural person's family business. The enterprise did not have an independent "personality" and was merely an item owned by all the enterprise owners. At this time, the enterprise had not truly separated from the family, so there was no distinction between enterprise responsibilities and family responsibilities. It was quite natural for enterprise investors to bear unlimited liability. This situation existed in the UK until the mid-nineteenth century. It should be noted that in the absence of a firmly established credit system based on the rule of law, the unlimited liability of enterprises was an efficient institutional choice. However, at the same time, facing market uncertainty, unlimited liability undoubtedly deterred many potential investors. In this respect, the unlimited liability system hindered economic expansion.

Although entities similar to joint-stock companies appeared as early as the fifteenth century (or even earlier, such as partnership groups raising funds for wars between city-states in the Middle Ages, or associations lending to city-states in exchange for privileges),[6] the first modern permanent joint-stock company was established in the Netherlands in the seventeenth century (the Dutch East India Company was established in 1602). However, the emergence of a large number of companies was accompanied by the Industrial Revolution. Initially, the joint-stock company was merely a temporary organization for a specific profit-making activity, not a legal entity that could exist indefinitely. The first agreement of the East India Company was only valid for one voyage, and the agreement ended after the profits were divided upon return. The company was essentially just a loose group of merchants. In 1613, the company raised £429,000 for four voyages; in 1617, it raised £1.7 million for seven voyages; it was not until 1657 that the East India Company obtained permission to operate continuously for a limited period. It was not until 1720 that it obtained the right to operate permanently. Not only in the UK, but also in France at that time, the licenses for joint-stock companies were time-limited.[7] From today's perspective, the initial joint-stock companies were more like a financial management activity for the wealthy at the time.

Modern enterprises are the natural result of the development of trading to a certain extent. New institutional economics believes that enterprises are a choice against trading costs. In fact, from the evolutionary history of enterprises, early enterprises were family-based, and large-scale enterprises, or enterprises with modern significance emerged only after the Industrial Revolution, which is obviously closely related to technological progress. The emergence of modern factories from family workshops was first the result of technological process innovation and the application of new technologies. Large-scale factories appeared in the early sixteenth century, when Englishman John Winchcombe established a textile factory in Newbury, he employed more than 2000 workers. He divided the woolen textile production into several separate processes and applied a strict division of labor among the workers: 200 women carders, 150 children pickers, 200 girl spinners, 200 weavers with 200 boys at the spools, 80 teasers, 50 shearers, 40 dyers and 20 fullers.[8] The key to the Industrial Revolution is production technology, therefore, the correct conclusion should be: the emergence of modern enterprises is due to technological reasons, and the development of the number and scale of enterprises in the economy depends on the reduction of trading costs.

As an organization that independently assumes civil liability, a company requires the support of a series of related laws. The introduction of the concept of corporate legal person is foundational to the development of enterprises and their important role in economic activities. However, the establishment and widespread application of the concept of a legal person has undergone a long evolutionary process. The concept of a legal person originated in the Roman Empire. Although the concept of a legal person did not explicitly appear in the "Roman Law", the spirit of a legal person was already implied in it. The "Roman Law" regarded the state, autonomous cities, religious groups, industry organizations, etc. as associations, as a conceptual unit. To this day, records of some association activities at that time can still be found on the inscriptions left by ancient Rome, such as the Shipowners Association, which is a typical association organization of this period, undertaking the task of grain transportation and benefiting from it. Although there was no clear concept of a legal person in Roman times, the concept of a "legal person" has already emerged in various legal provisions. In the Roman legal compilation "Digest" compiled between 530 and 534 AD, there are two clauses that show the spirit of modern corporate legal persons: (1) What the company owns is not owned by individuals; (2) What is owed to the company is not owed to individuals, and what the company owes is not owed by individuals. Obviously, these provisions already contain the affirmation of the independent personality of the company.

Entering the Middle Ages, the Roman Church further clarified the concept of a legal person. The Roman Catholic Church, in order to argue the status of the church and clarify the property rights of the church, further clarified the concept of a legal person in the "Roman Law". The church, as a legal person, is independent of any individual, has the characteristic of immortality, which coincides with the eternal life of God. From then on, the concept of "legal person" clearly entered the process of social development. In this regard, the positive role of Christianity in nurturing modern economic society is undeniable.

The modernization of the concept of a legal person was completed in the United States. Although legal persons have been involved in trading, finance and other fields in the UK for a long time, these legal persons were all established by the authorization of the parliament or the king. It can be imagined that it is very difficult for ordinary people to obtain a charter to establish a legal person. It was not until the early nineteenth century when the United States enacted the "General Corporation Act" that corporate legal persons entered a new era. The legal person completed the historic transition from charter to registration according to law. Not only the registration of corporate legal persons has a chapter to follow, but also obtaining a legal person license has become a very easy thing, unlike obtaining through special legislation or the grace of the king in the past. From then on, as a legal person with a personality status, the enterprise has a solid legal basis, and has officially entered the modern development stage. The legal person, as a legal technique to simplify legal relationships, has played an immeasurable role in promoting the establishment of modern corporate systems and even the process of human social development.

The major reform of the enterprise system began in the late nineteenth century, driven by modern transportation and communication technologies, including the emergence of railways, telegraphs, steamships, and submarine telegraphs. Before this, enterprises were managed and operated by the owners themselves; the profits of the enterprise were the income of the enterprise owner. The emergence of new technologies has unprecedentedly expanded the market, the scale of enterprises has expanded accordingly, the complexity and professionalism of enterprise management have increased, a salaried management level has appeared, and the separation of enterprise property rights and management rights has begun, and the modern enterprise system was born.[9] Today, the modern corporate system characterized by the separation of property rights and operational rights has become the basic governance model for enterprises, especially large ones. The economy dominated by this corporate system, where property rights and management rights are separated, is referred to as managerial capitalism by American scholar Alfred D. Chandler, Jr. Despite this, the organizational forms of enterprises are still diverse and varied.

2.3.2 Corporate Trading Objectives

What distinguishes humans from animals is the ability to transcend the present, set goals in the future, and make everything currently done a means to achieve distant goals, even if the appearance of the means often contradicts the goals. As a means, the choice of current behavior is always a discretion made under specific circumstances, which is variable compared to long-term goals, while goals are relatively stable. This ability to transcend time and space is key to distinguishing human intelligence from animal intelligence. Human activities driven by various goals constitute the ever-changing world, driving the never-ending development and evolution of human society.

However, the goal of an enterprise has become one of the most fiercely debated issues in the field of economics. The firm assumption of neoclassical economic theory, which dominates the mainstream—that enterprises pursue the goal of profit maximization, has been mostly questioned and various new assumptions have been proposed: maximizing sales; maximizing the number of employees and compensation utility; maximizing enterprise growth; maximizing shareholder wealth; maximizing cash flow; minimizing capital costs and manager satisfaction goals, etc. Some scholars suggest using a multi-goal model; some even question the maximization behavior model itself and suggest abandoning any assumptions about enterprise goals.[10]

As a living entity, an enterprise is always in a state of continuous development and evolution. From property structure, to organizational model; to enterprise goals and philosophy, everything is constantly changing. Historically, when enterprises first separated from families, they had a clear temporary nature. The operating rights of chartered companies were strictly time-limited, and enterprise activities were limited to a single trading. In this case, the goal pursued by the enterprise is very clear, which is to make as much money as possible in a single chartered trading, maximizing the return on investment. This is the template for the firm theory in classical economics regarding enterprise goal assumptions. Even the enterprises in the early stages of the Industrial Revolution—the model of merchants + rural family workshops—still did not escape the short-term nature of enterprise goals. Because this enterprise model is very loose, the cooperative relationship between merchants and family workshops is not based on a strict legal contract, in most cases it can only be a personalized agreement. At this time, there was no conscious marketing in the enterprise, and enterprise management was very simple: calculating profit and loss after each trading. With the evolution of the enterprise system, enterprises theoretically have an immortal life, and the emergence of joint-stock companies provides institutional and capital guarantees for long-term enterprise operations, which also encourages enterprises to pursue more long-term and comprehensive goals. In the historical process of enterprise development, the long-term trend of enterprise goals is becoming more and more prominent, and short-term profits can no longer explain the behavior of long-term enterprises well. Enterprise operations are shifting from a single goal to multiple goals and from a pure profit goal to a development in various aspects such as market share, industry influence, pricing power, and innovation ability.

Evolutionary economics denies the teleological model in enterprise operations and decision-making, arguing that people make decisions under the premise of bounded rationality. Therefore, it is "impossible to know what is profit maximization and optimal decision-making, so the development of socio-economics will not unfold in a teleological manner, nor will it necessarily tend towards a perfect equilibrium state."[11] Undeniably, enterprises are constrained by bounded rationality and incomplete information in the decision-making process, which cannot guarantee the scientific rationality of each decision, nor can it ensure that each action will achieve the expected goals. However, this cannot be used to deny the role of goals in decision-making, nor can it deny the basic behavioral patterns of humans. The purposefulness of human behavior and the multi-level nature of the goal system are key to distinguishing humans from animals. Society, as a macro system, cannot achieve the same purposefulness as a single individual. This is due to the goal differences and interactions of countless individuals, and also because society itself is not a decision-making agent, but a stage for many decision-making agents, and there is no issue of purposefulness of behavior. But this should not deny the goal-driven model of individual behavior.

Although theoretically, an enterprise as a legal entity can exist indefinitely, with an infinite lifespan, historical experience shows that the decline and bankruptcy of enterprises are often unavoidable. At each stage, enterprises will have different operating strategies and goals. In the early stages of an enterprise, rapid expansion and increasing market share are the strategies adopted by most new enterprises. Just like all young life forms, the main danger facing new enterprises is death, and only about 40% of new enterprises can survive to three years. Under the threat of death, new enterprises hope to quickly leap over the early death trap by expanding their scale and increasing their market share, which is the enterprise strategy adopted by most new enterprises. For these enterprises, the operating goal of growing enterprises has a clear scale expansion orientation, "growth" is the goal of the enterprise.

When an enterprise enters maturity, after scale expansion reaches a critical upper limit, the enterprise usually enters a period of diversified development. This period is mainly about range expansion, including expanding the operating range from the original section to the upstream, or downstream, or both, and some enterprises even expand into new industries.

The real-world situation is much more complex, changes in market cycles, differences in competitive environments, all affect the enterprise's operating goals. For example, for enterprises in the expansion phase, when the market enters a recession cycle, scale expansion could lead to huge losses, forcing enterprises to shift their focus to fully exploiting existing potential, making cost control the main task of current operations, and thus achieving profit maximization. It can be seen that the goals of enterprises are very complex and cannot be simply reduced to "profit maximization" or "scale maximization" or "maximizing market share", etc. Only by placing each decision of an enterprise in a longer valuation time domain can the diverse decisions of enterprises in various trading be concluded to a unified purpose.

2.4 Unification of Trading Motives

In neoclassical economics, enterprises act as the supply side of the market, while families act as the demand side. By analyzing the production of enterprises, we can predict market supply, and then by analyzing family income, we can predict market demand. The price trend is then determined through the relationship between supply and demand. This is the basic analytical framework of neoclassical economics. In reality, enterprises are not purely suppliers. In the economic cycle, before becoming suppliers, enterprises are first demanders, needing to purchase raw materials, labor, and various consumables. Continuous observation of the economic cycle reveals that we cannot strictly distinguish when an enterprise is a supplier and when it is a demander in terms of time. Enterprises are both suppliers and demanders at almost every point in time. The same is true for families. They not only demand various consumer goods but also provide labor and capital to the market. For families, the behaviors of demand and supply often occur simultaneously. The entire trading system operates with the continuous transformation of the trading roles. In an economy, the people who make up the two types of organizations, enterprises and families, are the same group of people. They are called enterprises when they organize production, and families when they gather together to live after work. But from the perspective of trading, both families and enterprises are constantly trading, with the only difference being the content of the trading and the structure of rights and responsibilities. The intrinsic unity of the trading agent is rooted in human nature. Human nature does not change because one works in an enterprise during the day and returns home after work. In terms of property rights, apart from a few state-owned enterprises, most enterprises belong to different families. Even for state-owned enterprises, in essence, their property rights ultimately belong to the resident families of the country. This ownership indicates that the motivation for enterprises to pursue profits still comes from families. Without the pursuit of wealth by families, enterprises could not have differentiated from families, let alone become organizations focused on profits. The pursuit of economic benefits by enterprises is actually a manifestation of the motivation of families. Enterprises are also composed of individuals who come from families. They work in enterprises in order to earn as much salary as possible. In this sense, there is no essential difference between families and enterprises. It can be seen that the goal setting in the trading process of these two basic agents, families and enterprises, can be unified, which provides a solid foundation for establishing a logically consistent theoretical system.

Notes

1. Harry Landreth, David C. Colander (2014) History of Economic Thoughts (trans: Wen ZHOU), 4th edn. Posts & Telecom Press, Beijing, p 236–237.
2. Gary S. Becker, A Treatise on the Family (1991) Harvard University Press, p 46–47.

3. The use of the term "industrial revolution" has been questioned by some economic historians (e.g., T.S. Ashton). Through quantitative analyses of economic data from the eighteenth and nineteenth centuries, it is found that there was no growth in the scale of economic activity or structural changes during this period that could be described as the outbreak of a revolution, the so-called industrial revolution was in fact a gradual process.
4. Rondo Cameron, Larry Neal (2009) A Concise Economic History World: From Paleolithic Times to the Present (trans: Ning PAN), 4th edn. Shanghai Translation Publishing House, Shanghai, p 162–163.
5. Postan, M. M., Coleman D.C., Peter Mathias (2004) The Cambridge Economic History, Vol. 5, Cambridge University Press, p 362–415.
6. Charles P. Kindleberger (2007) A Financial History of Western Europe (trans: Zijian XU), 1st edn. China Financial Publishing House, p 209.
7. Charles P. Kindleberger (2007) A Financial History of Western Europe (trans: Zijian XU), 1st edn. China Financial Publishing House, p 209.
8. Postan, M. M., Coleman D.C., Peter Mathias (1977) The Cambridge Economic History, Vol. 5, Cambridge University Press, p 470–471.
9. Alfred D. Chandler., Jr (1999) Economies of Scale and Scope of Enterprise - the driving force of industrial capitalism, China Social and Science Press, Beijing.
10. Daniel Houseman (2007) The Philosophy of Economics (trans: Jiangfeng DING), Ch16: Firms and Economists, Shanghai People's Publishing House, Shanghai.
11. Zhaohan SHENG, Depeng JIANG (2002) Evolutionary Economics, Shanghai Joint Publishing Press, Shanghai. A Treatise on the Family.

Chapter 3
Accounting Matrix

The accounting matrix provides a means of quantitatively describing trading agents and is the basis for establishing new trading concepts.

3.1 Accounting Statements

The trading system is actually a dynamic system composed of a large number of trading agent accounts and the interaction among accounts. As Wassily Leontief pointed out, the entire economic activity of a country can be imagined as a comprehensive huge be concluded to accounting system. Not only all industrial, agricultural and transportation sectors, but also all private budgets are included in this system. Each company or each family is treated as an independent accounting unit. A complete thin record system is composed of a large number of different accounts.[1] This is also under the dominance of the idea of interconnection within the trading system, Leontief established the analysis theory of national economic input and output.

Analyzing economic behavior and phenomena from the perspective of accounting has become a theoretical concept for some economists. In the history of economic theory, the first economist that explicitly proposed the building of economic theory on the balance sheet was Professor Kenneth E. Boulding from the University of Michigan. In his 1962 publication *A Reconstruction of Economics*, he placed economic behaviors such as investment, consumption, and savings on the balance sheet for overall examination. He used a core concept—the preferred asset ratio, to establish various economic behavior analysis frameworks on the balance sheet.

The earliest human accounting records appeared around 4000 BC. The double-entry bookkeeping method with modern characteristics was invented by Venetian priest Luca Pacioli in the late fifteenth century.[2] The accounting method provided Venetian merchants with a navigator that could sail in the commercial sea, allowing them to grasp their business performance in time to better manage their business.

Z. Wang, *Trading Economics*, Contributions to Economics,
https://doi.org/10.1007/978-981-99-9875-3_3

Accounting is so important to the modern economy that no institution can survive without accounting calculations. A large society needs to operate on the basis of orderly accounting calculations. Adjustments to the accounting system will have a major impact on all aspects of economic activity—from corporate profits to national taxes; from capital markets to investor confidence. The accounting system and its supporting regulations have become the institutional foundation of the modern economy.

The statement of assets and liabilities occupies a central position in accounting calculations. The statement of assets and liabilities reflects the composition of an institution's assets and liabilities and owner's equity, contains important information about the accounting entity's ability to pay, and reflects the final result of all economic activities of the accounting entity. The statement of assets and liabilities reflects the economic strength of the accounting entity and provides very important information for predicting the future development trend of the institution.

Another important component of the accounting statements is the income statement, which reflects the profitability of the accounting entity. The balance sheet depicts a static picture of the financial situation of the accounting entity, while the income statement provides the specific causes of changes in assets and liabilities within an accounting period, which is a dynamic picture. The main composition of the income statement is the remainder after deducting various expenses from various incomes. It includes various income items and expense items. Income items such as business income, investment income, other income, etc.; expenditure items include wage expenditure, raw material expenditure, interest expenditure, water and electricity expenditure, etc. Unlike the statement of assets and liabilities, the income statement is not a balance sheet, but an addition and subtraction sheet.

The cash flow statement is part of the statement of changes in financial position, reflecting the dynamic situation of the source and use of funds of the accounting entity. The importance of cash is self-evident, money is the basis of trading. No matter how large the scale of assets, if there is a lack of sufficient liquidity, it will face the risk of bankruptcy. The emphasis on cash flow is due to the deviation between corporate profits and cash income caused by the massive emergence of financial innovations, leading to the phenomenon of "profitable bankruptcy", which is particularly prominent when an economic crisis or financial crisis breaks out.

Through three accounting statements, we can obtain the basic trading information of the accounting entity, and have a clear understanding of the entity's solvency, profitability, and asset-liability structure. Among the three basic accounting statements, the statement of assets and liabilities plays a fundamental role. If we can obtain all the statements of assets and liabilities at all time points, and when the items on the statement of assets and liabilities are detailed enough, the changes in income and cash flow can be directly derived from the statement of assets and liabilities.

Although accounting is an effective means of business operation accounting and management, it cannot be directly used as a theoretical tool for economic analysis. This is because accounting calculations mainly describe the operation of enterprises, while as a tool for economic analysis, it must include families and their various activities; moreover, accounting calculations require objectivity, accuracy, and comparability, while economic analysis tools need to have the ability to explain the motives of trading agents.

3.2 Accounting Matrix

Drawing on the description method of accounting entities in accounting, we introduce the concept of an accounting matrix, corresponding each trading agent to an accounting matrix. All economic activities of the trading agent will be reflected in the accounting matrix.

3.2.1 *Concept of Accounting Matrix*

Similar to the statement of assets and liabilities, the accounting matrix is a matrix composed of asset vectors arranged by various assets and liability vectors arranged by various liabilities, mainly used to reflect the overall situation of the trading agent's assets and liabilities. The difference from the statement of assets and liabilities is that the accounting matrix no longer adheres to the principle of balance on both sides, and no longer sets up the owner's equity items.

In the trading system, the economic conditions of the trading agent are so diverse, and the corresponding accounting matrices are vastly different. It is actually impossible to stipulate an accounting matrix form that adapts to all situations. The number of items set up in the accounting matrix and the specific definition of each item need to be determined according to the specific research content.

The accounting matrix is represented by A and the general form can be expressed as follows:

$$A = \begin{bmatrix} a_1 & l_1 \\ a_2 & l_2 \\ \vdots & \vdots \\ a_i & l_i \\ \vdots & \vdots \\ a_n & l_n \end{bmatrix} \tag{3.2.1}$$

where, a_{i} and l_j represent the asset items and liability items respectively. For the convenience of calculation, we agree that all items of assets in the accounting matrix are positive; all items of liabilities are negative, that is $a_i \geq 0, l_i \leq 0, i = 1, 2, \ldots, n$. For an accounting matrix composed of n rows, it is called an n-level accounting matrix, or simply an n-level matrix. In practical applications, if the number of items in the asset vector and that in the liability vector is inconsistent, use 0 to fill the shorter vector to ensure the integrity of the matrix.

The more detailed the division of items in the asset and liability vectors, and the greater the amount of information reflected by the accounting matrix. However, the larger the accounting matrix, the more calculations are related, and the more complex the processing.

For families, people rarely use the concepts of assets and liabilities, and are more accustomed to using concepts such as wealth and consumption levels. This is because many family assets, such as home appliances and furniture, are difficult to find buyers after a period of use and have almost no market liquidity, hence it is difficult to determine their market value. In addition, the main purpose of family holding assets is for family members to use, not for appreciation or preservation of value. However, regardless of the purpose of holding, assets in the hands of families or enterprises indicate the rights of the holders in terms of the benefits, services, and disposal brought by the possession of assets.

For accounting, it has a certain time cycle. Once a year or a quarter, a financial statement is prepared after accounting for business activities, and this length of time is called the accounting cycle. Whether from a technical level or a management demand level, it is impossible to do accounting every day, let alone every moment. The accounting matrix, as a description of the economic status of the trading agent, is theoretically in a state of dynamic change at all times. Each trading and change in prices will cause corresponding changes in the accounting matrix. In this sense, the accounting matrix is a function of time, and at each point in time, there is an accounting matrix corresponding to the trading agent.

As an analytical tool of economic theory, the accounting matrix changes continuously with time t, and uninterruptedly tracks and reflects the characteristics of the economic status of the trading agent. The dynamic changes of the accounting matrix come from the income and expenditure of various trading of the trading agent. Therefore, the accounting matrix also contains the income information and cash flow information of the trading agent. It can comprehensively describe the economic status of the trading agent, thereby providing full information for trading decisions.

3.2.2 Trading Base

The essence of assets is rights, and the essence of liabilities is obligations. The asset vector and liability vector of the accounting matrix are also based on the same principle. The asset column and liability column reflect the relationship of value attribution. The factors that determine the order and structure of the accounting matrix come from two aspects: one is the scale of the trading base. The more types of goods available for trading in the trading system, the higher the order of the accounting matrix; the second is the diversity of commodity trading method. On a limited commodity base, innovative trading methods can also increase the order of the accounting matrix. For example, if an enterprise uses a commercial bill as a payment tool to purchase a commodity, the change caused in the seller's accounting matrix is a corresponding decrease in inventory and an equivalent increase in notes receivable; for the buyer, the corresponding asset item in the accounting matrix increases, and the corresponding amount of notes payable on the liability side increases. If the enterprise uses money to purchase, the buyer has less money, and the corresponding assets increase; the seller's money increases, and the inventory decreases. It can be seen that after introducing the commercial bill trading method, notes receivable and notes payable appear in the accounting matrix. Despite this, the trading base plays a more basic role in the trading system and is the key to determining the order of the accounting matrix.

The trading base is a collection of all goods available for trading in the trading system. The trading base has a certain elasticity and can determine the degree of refinement according to research needs. It can either divide the types of goods very finely, for example, in a category of home appliances, different models and grades of home appliances are divided into different types, or it can put home appliances with the same attribute together as a category to deal with, and this depends on the research needs.

Use g_i to represent a commodity, use G to represent the trading base, as shown below:

$$G = \{g_0, g_1, g_2, \ldots, g_n\} \tag{3.2.2}$$

Money is a special commodity in the trading system, occupying the core position of all commodity trading, represented by g_0; there are $n + 1$ goods in the trading base, including physical goods and service goods.

With the evolution of the trading system, the trading base is in a continuous expansion process. The more developed the economy, the wider the range of goods. The development of the economy inevitably accompanies the deepening of economic division of labor. With unchanged economic scale and technological level, the finer the division of labor, the more types of goods, and the larger the trading base. Goods are the carrier of trading, and division of labor inevitably promotes trading, and the two complement each other. In addition, technological innovation is an important driving force for the expansion of the trading base. Generally speaking, the higher the innovation level of the trading system, the larger the trading base.

In the modern economy, no trading system can be absolutely closed to the outside world. The goods circulating in the trading system cannot all be produced domestically, and a considerable part comes from abroad. Therefore, the trading base of the trading system is composed of two parts, namely the endogenous base and the exogenous base. The endogenous base is produced within the trading system; the exogenous base is produced abroad but circulates domestically. The trading base structure formed by the endogenous base and the exogenous base constitutes an important aspect of the trading system structure. Generally speaking, the higher the degree of openness of the trading system, the higher the proportion of the exogenous base in the trading base. It can be predicted that with the continuous deepening of globalization, the intensity of each country's participation in international division of labor is also constantly increasing, and the proportion of the exogenous base of each country's trading system will continue to increase.

Based on the above analysis, goods and their trading status are the two elements that constitute the items of the accounting matrix. The larger the trading base of the trading system, the more trading methods, the more items in the accounting matrix. Specifically, if there are n goods in the trading base, and each type of goods has an average of m trading methods, since each trading method generates different asset items or liability items on the accounting matrix of the trading parties, the maximum order of the accounting matrix is $2\,m \times n$.

3.2.3 Example of Accounting Matrix

Due to the differences in the types, business operations, scale, and asset structure of different trading agents, it is difficult to standardize the content of the accounting matrix. Even for the same type of trading agents, the differences in the accounting matrix can be significant.

Below is the accounting matrix of a transportation service company a, with the pricing unit in 10,000 yuan:

$$A_e = \begin{bmatrix} 50 & -60 \\ 30 & -100 \\ 500 & -20 \\ 50 & 0 \end{bmatrix} \tag{3.2.3}$$

In the accounting matrix A_e, the cash assets are 500,000 yuan, accounts receivable assets are 300,000 yuan, transportation equipment assets are 5 million yuan, office equipment is 500,000 yuan; on the liability side, accounts payable are 600,000 yuan, bank loans are 1 million yuan, and prepaid expenses are 200,000 yuan. According to the accounting matrix, the total assets of this transportation company are 6.3 million yuan, the total liabilities are 1.8 million yuan, the net assets are 4.5 million yuan, and the asset-liability ratio is 28.5%. It has a low level of liabilities and good payment ability.

Below is the accounting matrix of a manufacturing company b, with the pricing unit in 10,000 yuan:

$$B_e = \begin{bmatrix} 185 & -28 \\ 65 & -36 \\ 300 & -150 \\ 800 & -120 \end{bmatrix} \tag{3.2.4}$$

The accounting matrix B_e shows that the cash assets of this manufacturing company are 1.85 million yuan, accounts receivable are 650,000 yuan, inventory assets are 3 million yuan, fixed assets are 8 million yuan; on the liability side, accounts payable are 280,000 yuan, taxes payable are 360,000 yuan, bank loans are 1.5 million yuan, long-term bond liabilities are 1.2 million yuan. The total assets are 13.5 million yuan, the total liabilities are 3.34 million yuan, the net assets are 10.16 million yuan, and the asset-liability ratio is 24.7%.

Comparing the accounting matrices of company a and company b, it can be seen that company a is significantly smaller in scale than company b with b's total assets being 2.14 times that of a. In terms of asset structure, a's main assets are transportation equipment, which fall under the category of movable assets, while b's main assets are fixed assets. In terms of liabilities, a's main liabilities come from bank loans, while b's main debts come from long-term bonds. Compared to a, b has better asset liquidity, but b has a problem of high inventory, with inventory accounting for 22% of total assets, posing a significant market risk.

Looking at the situation of company c, the pricing unit in the accounting matrix is still 10,000 yuan:

$$C_e = \begin{bmatrix} 130 & -430 \\ 100 & -30 \\ 29 & -60 \\ 35 & -600 \\ 300 & -53 \\ 1200 & -58 \\ 500 & -23 \end{bmatrix} \tag{3.2.5}$$

In the accounting matrix C_e, cash assets are 1.3 million yuan, inventory assets are 1 million yuan, raw materials are 290,000 yuan, prepaid goods are 350,000 yuan, intangible assets are 3 million yuan, fixed assets and equipment are 12 million yuan, receivable dividends are 5 million yuan; on the liability side, bank loans are 4.3 million yuan, internal fundraising is 300,000 yuan, corporate bonds are 600,000 yuan, payable dividends are 6 million yuan, payable taxes are 530,000 yuan, payable wages are 580,000 yuan, payable pensions are 230,000 yuan. Accounting matrix C_e shows that this is a company with strong profitability. After distributing 6 million yuan in dividends, it can still retain a large scale of cash assets.

Compared to enterprises, the accounting matrix of families is relatively simple. Below is the accounting matrix of family a, in units of 10,000 yuan.

$$A_f = \begin{bmatrix} 2 & -80 \\ 15 & -20 \\ 260 & -0.05 \\ 500 & 0 \end{bmatrix} \tag{3.2.6}$$

In the accounting matrix A_f, cash assets are 20,000 yuan, financial assets are 150,000 yuan, real estate and durable goods assets are 2.6 million yuan, human capital is 5 million yuan; on the liability side, bank mortgage loans are 800,000 yuan, installment payment balances are 200,000 yuan, payable bills are 500 yuan. From the accounting matrix, family a's economic situation is not affluent, with little liquid funds, only 20,000 yuan, and financial assets such as insurance are only 150,000 yuan, and the scale of real estate is not large. The payable bills are only 500 yuan, indicating that a's consumption level is not high. The most prominent in the accounting matrix is human capital, valued at 5 million yuan, which is the biggest advantage of this family and the hope for the future.

Let's look at the accounting matrix of family b:

$$B_f = \begin{bmatrix} 5.5 & -100 \\ 32 & -1.2 \\ 60 & -0.3 \\ 35 & 0 \\ 52 & 0 \\ 380 & 0 \\ 1500 & 0 \end{bmatrix} \tag{3.2.7}$$

In the accounting matrix of family b, cash assets are 55,000 yuan, bank deposits are 320,000 yuan, investment funds are 600,000 yuan, pension insurance is 350,000 yuan, family durable goods are 520,000 yuan, housing assets are 3.8 million yuan, human capital is 15 million yuan; on the liability side, bank mortgage loans are 1 million yuan, credit card loans are 12,000 yuan, payable bills are 3000 yuan.

Comparing family a and family b, it is clear that family b is more affluent, with larger human capital, indicating that family b has greater potential for wealth creation.

The items in the matrix can be set according to the needs of the study. The accounting matrix comes from the statement of assets and liabilities and can be seen as a transformation of the statement of assets and liabilities to adapt to economic analysis.

3.3 Processing of Accounting Matrix

In order to apply the accounting matrix to complex and diverse real-world problems, we need to make some conventions for the accounting matrix. For the treatment of asset items in the accounting matrix, some can refer to the provisions of accounting calculation, while others need to be independently agreed upon based on the feasibility of theory and the requirements for logical consistency.

3.3.1 *Pricing Principle of Accounting Matrix*

In accounting, there are multiple choices for the calculation method of the statement of assets and liabilities, including cost method, current price method, fair value method, etc. For the sake of theoretical application, the accounting matrix uniformly adopts the "fair value method", that is, the value of an asset that is expected to be realized in the market based on the information available to the trading agent.

The accounting matrix has both subjective and objective properties. On the one hand, the accounting matrix reflects the real financial situation of the trading agent, and the various indicators in the accounting matrix have real existence; on the other hand, the accounting matrix also contains the subjective expectations of the trading agent in the trading process. Due to the constraints of limited information, "fair value" may vary among different trading agents. The agent will form an expectation of the "fair value" of the trading assets based on his own experience and the information he understands. When the actual price is lower than the "fair value", the buyer will think that they get more in this trading; similarly, if the trading price is higher than the "fair value", the seller will think they have made a bargain, forming a trading surplus. Due to the different information sets of the trading parties, the trading parties may form a "fair value" with a large gap between each other. In this case, the expected price difference benefit obtained by the seller is not necessarily the expected price difference loss of the buyer. This forms a phenomenon contrary to common sense, where it is possible for both parties in the trading to think they have made a lot.

The "fair value" of the trading agent is constantly being revised in reality. Although "fair value" has a certain subjectivity, it is still limited within the objective range. For assets with a clear market value, the "fair value" and "market value" will not systematically deviate. Only for assets that lack clear market value information and have strong individual characteristics, such as human capital, intangible assets, etc., will "fair value" have more subjective characteristics. These asset valuations that are greatly influenced by subjective factors will change when the state of the trading agent changes. When the trading agent is in an aggressive state, the valuation of human capital and intangible assets tends to be overestimated; on the contrary, when the trading agent is in a conservative state, the valuation of assets with strong subjectivity is easily to be underestimated. These changes in valuation play an important role in the dynamic evolution of the trading system.

3.3.2 *Accounting for Human Capital*

Human capital is an important part of enterprise and family assets, corresponding to physical capital. The concept of human capital can be traced back to the classical economist Adam Smith, who regarded the useful abilities acquired by all nationals as part of capital, and believed that the fundamental reason for determining a country's wealth is the labor skills and proficiency of the nationals and their thinking and judgment power.[3] Initially, Adam Smith's view was not widely accepted, the prevailing view at the time was that people were considered the masters of wealth and should not be regarded as wealth. The concept of human capital once again attracted widespread attention in academia after World War II. Economists originally thought that it would take a long time for the economy to recover from the huge destruction of the war. The actual situation later showed that this pessimistic estimate was wrong. The key to this misjudgment was the neglect of human capital.[4]

Human capital is key to determining competitiveness, whether for macroeconomics or micro entities. In past theories, human capital has not been given the attention it deserves for two reasons: first, the calculation of human capital is very difficult, lacking clear boundaries and relevant statistical data; second, human capital is a relatively stable variable, whether at the national level, or at the level of enterprises and families, changing the status of human capital requires a considerable amount of time. For neoclassical theory, which focuses on short-term economic analysis, human capital can naturally be omitted from the analysis.

Introducing human capital into the accounting matrix not only makes up for the deficiencies of existing economic theories, but also completes the accounting matrix of families. In trading economics, human capital, as a kind of asset of the family, can be seen as a potential reserve for the family to generate income. This is somewhat different from the concept of human capital investment proposed by Schultz. Schultz's human capital is a macro concept, an asset for a trading system. In trading economics, human capital, as a micro concept, is a measure of the wealth creation potential of family members.

Human capital is manifested in three dimensions: a healthy body, a normal mind, and certain labor skills. All kinds of family consumption, including food consumption, health care consumption, leisure consumption, and education consumption, should be regarded as inputs to maintain human capital. The size of family consumption is an important factor affecting human capital. Human capital is an expected value, adjusted with changes in the wages and salaries of family members. Of course, human capital will also be adjusted with the health status of members.

Human capital is a residual value. The older the age, the smaller the residual value of human capital. Human capital increases with the input of education and skills training. From this, human capital is not always a decreasing function of time.

For enterprises, human capital is also an important soft asset. Like families, enterprises will invest in human capital, including employee training and various welfare inputs beyond employee salaries, which are common means for enterprises to increase human capital. In this regard, different enterprises have different emphasis on human capital, different estimates of the value of human capital, and therefore different inputs into human capital.

3.3.3 Intangible Assets

For an enterprise, intangible assets, being an important part of the enterprise's strength, are non-monetary assets held by the enterprise for the purpose of producing goods, providing services, leasing to others, or for management purposes, without physical form. These include goodwill, patents, non-patented but proprietary technology, trademark rights, copyrights, franchises, and land use rights, etc.[5] In order to improve goodwill, enterprises will invest a lot of money in advertising; they will also invest a lot of money in technology research and development activities, the results of these trading are the source of the increase in the enterprise's intangible assets.

For an enterprise, intangible assets are relatively easy to understand, and a mature calculation method has been formed in accounting. For families, the concept of intangible assets is rarely used. When we regard the family as a trading agent, intangible assets become very important. The social status of a family, including its reputation, trustworthiness, and degree of trust among neighbors and friends, is a major component of the family's intangible assets. Like enterprises, families also invest in intangible assets. Some consumption that seems purely out of vanity is actually an investment in intangible assets by the family. For example, a family buys a car that is not very useful in practice. Looking only at the direct benefits brought by the car, buying a car may not be cost-effective, but it can make the family look good in the neighborhood, making the neighbors think they are relatively wealthy, thereby bringing an increase in the family's intangible assets.

The difference between intangible assets and other assets is that intangible assets are not directly used for trading to obtain profits, but indirectly promote trading. For enterprises, intangible assets play an important role in enhancing market competitiveness and obtaining preferential financing opportunities; for families, intangible assets provide support for family members to participate in many market competitions—including labor markets, marriage markets, etc.

3.4 Accounting Matrix Indicators

Based on the accounting matrix, several financial indicators based on the accounting matrix can be calculated to reflect the financial status of the trading agent and to describe the characteristics of the accounting matrix.

Through the accounting matrix, the corresponding net asset size can be calculated. Net assets equal the difference between total assets and total liabilities. The part of total assets that exceeds total liabilities is called net assets. Net assets measure the amount of equity owned by the trading agent and are the main goal of the trading agent. Since net assets are the ultimate goal of trading, the means to achieve the goal can be diversified. Both enterprises and families will choose what they think is the most appropriate means according to their own financial situation and expectations of market trends, in order to achieve the goal of maximizing wealth. Use $|A|$ to represent the net assets of the accounting matrix A.

Liquidity is an important indicator of the accounting matrix. The importance of liquidity to business operation is self-evident. For families, maintaining a certain scale of liquidity, that is, holding a certain amount of monetary assets is the basic condition for maintaining normal family expenses.

Accounting analysis provides many indicators for analyzing liquidity conditions, including liquidity ratio, cash ratio, etc. Among them, the liquidity ratio is the ratio of liquid assets to liquid liabilities; the cash ratio is the ratio of cash plus tradable securities to liquid liabilities.[6] Use $L(A)$ to represent the liquidity of the accounting matrix A.

Asset scale is another important indicator of the trading agent's accounting matrix. Under the same asset-liability structure, enterprises with larger asset scales often have higher credit levels in the market and are in a relatively advantageous position in market competition. The same is true for families. Families with larger asset scales are undoubtedly wealthier and have a higher quality of life.

3.5 Accounting Matrix Synergy Effect

Trading closely link the accounting matrices among agents, forming a closely related, nested relationship. The enterprise is composed of people from different families, from enterprise decision-makers and management to ordinary employees. There is a close interest synergy between each employee's accounting matrix and the accounting matrix of the enterprise they belong to. If a trading is beneficial to the enterprise, it can bring about the expansion or optimization of the enterprise's accounting matrix, it will also bring certain benefits to the employees, which is conducive to the improvement of the employee's accounting matrix. Obviously, the synergy of the accounting matrix will have a significant impact on the cooperation among trading agents, we call this impact the synergy effect of the accounting matrix.

According to the direction of synergy transmission, accounting matrix synergy can be divided into two basic types: one is unidirectional synergy, such as the synergy relationship between the enterprise's accounting matrix and the employee's accounting matrix. The main characteristic of unidirectional synergy is the asymmetry of the status of the two parties in the synergy relationship, which can be divided into the leading party and the following party. Taking the synergy relationship between the enterprise and the employees as an example, the enterprise is the leading party in the accounting synergy relationship, and the initiative of how much effort and in what way to synergize with the employee's accounting matrix is in the enterprise, and the employee can only accept. In terms of sharing relationships, employees can share the enterprise's profits, but the enterprise cannot share the profits of the employee's family.

Another type of synergy relationship is bidirectional synergy. In this type, the status of both parties in the synergy of the accounting matrix has certain symmetry, and they can share each other's benefits in some way. Among enterprises with equity investment relationships, the equity investors can share the benefits of the beneficiary enterprises according to the proportion of equity; conversely, when the accounting matrix of the equity enterprise is improved, the market recognition of the beneficiary enterprise may be correspondingly improved, realizing the appreciation of intangible assets. At the beginning of this century, during the shareholding reform of Chinese state-owned banks, many internationally renowned financial institutions such as Bank of America, Temasek Holdings of Singapore, Royal Bank of Scotland, UBS Group, Asian Development Bank, Goldman Sachs, etc., were introduced as strategic investors. The purpose was not entirely to introduce equity capital, but more importantly, to enhance the market recognition of state-owned banks. The two-way coordination of the accounting matrix between these strategic investors and banks is typical.

In addition, between the guaranteeing enterprise and the guaranteed enterprise, a bidirectional synergy of the accounting matrix will also be formed; between families with blood or marital relationships, a subtle bidirectional synergy relationship will also be formed. It can be seen that the synergy of the accounting matrix is very common in the trading system and plays a very important role in the operation and evolution of the trading system.

There can be various ways to achieve accounting matrix synergy, which can be cash flow benefits or some kind of intangible assets. For accounting matrix synergy achieved through different ways, the synergy magnitude will be quite different. Generally speaking, the accounting matrix synergy achieved through cash flow benefits has a higher synergy intensity; while the accounting matrix synergy formed through intangible asset relationships has a weaker intensity. As a trading agent pursuing benefits, it will inevitably choose its cooperation strategy according to the synergy intensity of the accounting matrix.

The degree of accounting matrix synergy between any trading agents is limited, and the benefit synergy can only be manifested in specific aspects. Beyond a certain range, the synergy relationship between trading agents will no longer exist. We call the specific aspects of accounting matrix synergy the accounting matrix synergy points of trading agents. Obviously, trading agents are always looking for cooperation strategies that are beneficial to maximize their own benefits on the synergy points of the accounting matrix. Within the enterprise, according to the design of incentive mechanism, the synergy intensity and synergy points between each employee's accounting matrix and the enterprise's accounting matrix are different. In this case, employees will focus on the synergy points with the highest degree of synergy, and invest as little energy as possible in other aspects of the enterprise, so as to obtain the maximum possible return. If the market value of the enterprise is the maximum synergy point between the decision-maker's accounting matrix and the enterprise accounting matrix, the decision-maker will try to increase the market value of the enterprise, even if such behavior is not necessarily conducive to the sustainable development of the enterprise. The situation of employees will also be the same. If performance is the maximum benefit synergy point between the employee and the enterprise, the employee will focus on his own performance and ignore other aspects of the enterprise. In order to maximize their own performance, colleagues can even sabotage one another.

Cooperation inevitably involves some degree of rent-seeking motivation. When decision-makers serve the interests of the enterprise, there is a motive to use their positions to seek more benefits for themselves; while enterprise employees hope to evade supervision and get something for nothing; these various cooperative rent-seeking behaviors are endless. Among collaborators, people always hope that the other party can take on more responsibilities and pay higher costs for cooperation; they always hope that they can get as much benefit as possible and take on as little responsibility as possible.

The attitude and effort of trading agents towards cooperation depend on the degree of accounting matrix synergy. The higher the degree of synergy, the higher the willingness of trading agents to cooperate, striving to tap to achieve a win–win situation. Conversely, the lower the degree of synergy, the weaker the willingness of the trading agents to cooperate, and the less energy they will invest. If the degree of accounting matrix synergy is zero, it is impossible for any willingness to cooperate to arise between the trading agents.

The accounting matrix synergy is the foundation of cooperation between trading agents and a prerequisite for incentive compatibility. Fully leveraging the positive role of the synergy effect of the accounting matrix is not only an effective means to stimulate enterprises' market competitiveness, but also an important way to build a vibrant trading system. Any goal lacking the support of the synergy effect of the accounting matrix will inevitably fail to achieve its desired outcome.

Notes

1. Wassily Leontief (1993) 1919–1939, Economic structure of the United States–Empirical Application of Equilibrium Analysis, The Commercial Press, Beijing, p 12.
2. There is a theory that he did not invent double-entry bookkeeping, but that he merely worked on a method that was then circulating among the teachers and students of the Venetian commercial schools. See also Roger H. Hermanson, James Don Edwards, L. Gayle Rayburn, Financial Accounting, 4th edn. BPI IRWIN.
3. Adam Smith (2009) The Wealth of the Nations (trans: Changming HU), 1st edn. People's Daily Press, p 27.
4. Theodore W. Schultz (1990) Investment in Human Capital, Beijing Institute of Economics Press, p 3–8.
5. Ministry of Finance, Account Department (2001) Explanation of Business Accounting System, Chinese financial & Economic Publishing House, Beijing, p 143.
6. Gerald I. White, Ashwinpaul C. Sondhi & Dov. Fried (2003) The Analysis and Use of Financial Statement (trans: Zhiqiang LI), 3rd edn. Citic Press, Beijing, p 124–130.

Chapter 4
Expansion of Trading Concepts

With the evolution and progress of human society, trading activities have evolved from the simple trading mode of traditional society to today's dazzling variety of commodities and trading methods. The naive concept of trading can no longer meet the requirements for in-depth study of trading phenomena, hence it is necessary to expand the original concept. The expanded concept of trading extends to the scope of all economic activities. On this basis, we can incorporate all economic activities of people into the trading system for research.

4.1 Simple Trading

In the primitive trade of bartering, there are at least two trading agents, each holding goods needed by the other, and exchanging their goods to the other at a certain ratio, while receiving the other's goods. After the emergence of money, trading was given a modern meaning—the exchange of money and goods. In modern times, the connotation and extension of the concept of goods have been greatly expanded. Goods are no longer limited to specific forms of value, they can be any value that meets people's needs, tangible or intangible. In the modern economy, money is at the center of exchange. Trading activities are liberated from the demand correspondence of bartering, releasing increasingly powerful energy.

When trading enters the field of economic theory, the concept of trading is much more complex than actual trading. Scholars have different emphases on understanding trading. The founder of transaction cost theory, Oliver E. Williamson gave the definition of trading: trading occurs when a certain good or service is transferred from one technological boundary to another. At this point, one stage of action ends and another stage of action is declared to begin. This definition emphasizes the transfer of trading between two forms of value, which can occur both in the market and within the enterprise. This definition distinguishes between two types of trading,

Z. Wang, *Trading Economics*, Contributions to Economics,
https://doi.org/10.1007/978-981-99-9875-3_4

namely, internally-connected trading—the transfer of value within the enterprise; and externally-connected trading—the transfer of value that occurs in the market.

American institutional economist John Rogers Commons proposed another definition of trading, viewing it as the division and acquisition of future ownership of tangible goods between individuals. The focus of this definition is the transfer of property rights, paying more attention to rights rather than the form of value.

By examining the changes in the accounting matrix before and after trading, we will find some key features of trading. Suppose a_1, a_2 two agents carry out trading, where a_1 is the buyer, a_2 is the seller; a_1 pays 3000 yuan to a_2 to buy a TV, this trading causes changes in the accounting matrix of the two trading agents a_1 and a_2 respectively: on the asset vector of a_1, the cash assets decrease by 3000 yuan, and at the same time, a TV worth 3000 yuan is added to the physical assets; on the accounting matrix of a_2, the inventory assets decrease by a TV worth 3000 yuan, and at the same time, 3000yuan in cash is added to the monetary assets. This trading caused the co-movement between the accounting matrices of the two related agents a_1 and a_2.

Before the trading, the accounting matrices of the trading agents a_1 and a_2 are respectively:

$$A_1 = \begin{bmatrix} a_{11} & l_{11} \\ a_{12} & l_{12} \\ \vdots & \vdots \\ a_{1n} & l_{1n} \end{bmatrix} \tag{4.1.1}$$

$$A_2 = \begin{bmatrix} a_{21} & l_{21} \\ a_{22} & l_{22} \\ \vdots & \vdots \\ a_{2n} & l_{2n} \end{bmatrix} \tag{4.1.2}$$

where, A_1 is the accounting matrix of the trading agent a_1, and A_2 is the accounting matrix of the trading agent a_2. After standardization, the accounting matrix of the trading agent is uniformly an $n \times 2$ order matrix.

After the trading, the accounting matrices of a_1 and a_2 are respectively transformed into A_1' and A_2', that is:

$$A_1' = \begin{bmatrix} a_{11} - 3000 & l_{11} \\ a_{12} + 3000 & l_{12} \\ \vdots & \vdots \\ a_{1n} & l_{1n} \end{bmatrix} \tag{4.1.3}$$

$$A_2' = \begin{bmatrix} a_{21} + 3000 & l_{21} \\ a_{22} - 3000 & l_{22} \\ \vdots & \vdots \\ a_{2n} & l_{2n} \end{bmatrix} \tag{4.1.4}$$

Observing the changes in the accounting matrices of the two trading agents a_1 and a_2 before and after the television trading, we can define the concept of trading as follows: trading is an economic activity that cause the co-movement between the accounting matrices of two agents. The so-called co-movement between the statements of assets and liabilities refers to the change in one party's statement of assets and liabilities constituting the cause of the corresponding change in the other party's statement of assets and liabilities. The above definition of trading summarizes the characteristics of ordinary commodity trading, which we call narrow-sense trading.

4.2 Expansion of the Concept of Trade

In order to broaden the connotation and extension of trading, it is necessary to find common rules in various trading activities. Williamson guided two different forms of trading with different connotations—internally-connected trading and externally-connected trading. Here, we use the tool of accounting matrices to expand the concept of trading, so as to unify various economic activities under the concept of trading.

In an economic society, commodity exchange (i.e., narrow-sense trading activity) is indeed important, but it is not the entirety of economic activity. In addition to narrow-sense trading, there is another very important economic activity—production. Production is the source of value, without the support of production, narrow-sense trading activities become water without a source, and a tree without roots.

Generally speaking, an enterprise needs to purchase production equipment, raw materials, energy and water etc., and hire labor to organize a production, all of which can be realized through narrow-sense trading. Taking the production of color televisions as an example, the simplified accounting matrix of the enterprise before the production of televisions is as follows (only relevant agents are written out, other irrelevant agents are omitted; the pricing unit is 10,000 yuan):

$$\begin{bmatrix} 80 & 0 \\ 10 & 0 \\ 0 & 0 \end{bmatrix} \tag{4.2.1}$$

In matrix (4.2.1), raw materials are 800,000 yuan, prepaid wages are 100,000 yuan, and color TV inventory is 0 yuan. The liability items are not listed. In order to maintain the integrity of the accounting matrix, the liability items are all taken as 0.

In order to produce televisions, the enterprise purchases raw materials and hires labor and pre-pays wages before the start of color TV production, which constitute part of the enterprise's assets. Now the enterprise is ready for production, and the color TV inventory is 0.

After a production cycle, the accounting matrix changes:

$$\begin{bmatrix} 0 & 0 \\ 0 & 0 \\ 120 & 0 \end{bmatrix} \tag{4.2.2}$$

In the new matrix (4.2.2), raw materials are 0, prepaid wages are 0, and color TV inventory is 1.2 million yuan. Comparing the two accounting matrices, the production activity leads to the co-movement between related asset items in the enterprise's accounting matrix, resulting in value transfer and value change. The value of raw materials and prepaid wages is transferred to the color TV inventory assets. Because the market price of televisions is higher than the production cost, the enterprise's color TV inventory assets reach 1.2 million yuan. After deducting the production cost of 900,000 yuan, the enterprise realizes a profit of 300,000 yuan in this production cycle, with a gross profit margin of 33%.

The above production process can be summarized as: production is the process of value conversion and appreciation between asset items in the accounting matrix. Specifically, in the above example, it is the value transfer among raw materials, labor and color TV inventory. This conversion, accompanied by the expected growth of value, is the source of the enterprise's production motivation.

Comparing the representation of narrow-sense trading and production activities on the accounting matrix, it is not difficult to find that whether it is narrow-sense trading or production process, their common manifestation is the co-movement between items in the accounting matrix. This can be the co-movement between asset items, or the co-movement between assets and liabilities (financial trading); it can occur between two or more trading agents in the accounting matrix, or it can only occur within a single trading agent's accounting matrix. Based on these characteristics, we further expand the concept of narrow-sense trading to obtain the concept of broad-sense trading: trading is an action and process that causes changes in the structure of items in the accounting matrix. Generally speaking, trading is the activity characterized by changing the form of value held by the agent, and is characterized by the co-movement between two or more items in the accounting matrix. Trading where the co-moving items are distributed in two accounting matrices are called externally-connected trading; while trading where the co-moving items are in the same accounting matrix are called internally-connected trading.

After the extension of the concept of trading, not only are ordinary commodity trading included, but all economic activities such as production processes, technological research and development, financial activities, etc., are included. All economic activities are covered under the concept of trading. Whether it is commodity exchange or commodity production, it can be discussed, under the concept of trading, how trading agents maximize expected return through trading, which provides a unified conceptual framework for economic analysis.

In the definition of trading, the change in value form refers to the change in the nature of asset value, and the depreciation of value from new to old does not belong to the change in value form, but to the change in the amount of commodity value. Holding an asset, if the value changes during the holding process, it is not considered as trading due to the lack of co-movement between items. Social activities such as charity and gifts are also excluded from the category of trading due to the lack of co-movement between items in the accounting matrix.

In the broad-sense concept of trading, trading does not necessarily occur between two trading agents. A trading agent can complete trading independently without any trading partners, which is internally-connected trading. According to the logic of broad-sense trading, farmers working on their own land also belong to trading activities. The evolution from an agricultural economic form to an industrial economic form actually involves a wide range of externalization of trading. A history of human society is also a history of the externalization of trading activities. The self-sufficiency of agriculture is a typical form of internally-connected trading. As the industrial economic form gradually dominates, the proportion of externally-connected trading in the economy is increasing.

With the improvement of the trading environment and the reduction of trading costs, more and more trading are transformed from internally-connected to externally-connected, from self-sufficiency to market trading. The deepening of social division of labor and the trend of globalization can all be seen as manifestations of the law of trading externalization. Trading externalization and trading system expansion constitute the two basic characteristics of the evolution of the trading system.

4.3 Trading Direction

According to the direction of cash flow at the time of trading, externally-connected trading are divided into forward trading and reverse trading. Forward trading refers to trading where the trading agent sells goods and receives cash; reverse trading is the opposite of forward trading, referring to trading where cash is spent to acquire goods. Internally-connected trading no longer divide in terms of trading direction.

Due to the flexibility and diversity of trading payment methods, determining the direction of trading based on cash flow may cause some problems. For example, futures trading, forward trading, options trading, installment payments, and trading using various types of bills, especially the numerous types of trading of financial derivatives, will have a great deal of uncertainty when dividing the trading direction based on cash flow. Taking stock index futures as an example, the underlying asset of stock index futures is a basket of stocks represented by the pre-agreed stock index, with the difference between the index price on the contract expiration date and the initial trading index price as the basis for cash settlement,[1] the rise and fall of the stock index determine whether the long or short side pays cash to the other party, and the uncertainty of the stock price also determines the uncertainty of the direction of stock index futures trading. For all the above types of trading, regardless of the payment agreement of trading, the cash flow direction of the payment target is still the only standard to determine the trading direction.

For financial trading, the principal has commodity attributes. Whether the party holding the funds transfers the right to use the funds commodity for a limited or unlimited period in the form of deposits, bonds, or stock purchases, they all receive interest or dividends as a return.

4.4 Trading Time Limit

Each trading has different time requirements, constituting an important attribute of trading, which we call the trading time limit. The trading time limit is a time constraint attached to the trading, which is a time interval determined by the intrinsic relationship of the trading, requiring the trading to be completed within this time interval. For example, various consumption activities in daily life, most of which have strong trading time limit requirements, have clear time points. Regular payments for water, electricity, gas, and communication by families have a fixed time point each month; visits to the hospital cannot be timed according to wishes; one cannot stop food consumption because of recent price increases; when the child's school starts, tuition fees need to be paid, and the child cannot wait at home due to a tight budget. Enterprises' trading activities also have time limits, water and electricity fees, employee wages, office rents, etc., all have a determined payment time. For productive enterprises, normal production has a stable pace of time, and raw materials need to be purchased regularly. Thermal power companies need to buy coal regularly, car manufacturers need to purchase spare parts regularly, and clothing manufacturers need to buy cloth regularly. The trading mentioned above all have a determined time point, and these trading are called point-in-time trading.

Trading that is somewhat similar to point-in-time trading is bilateral time limit trading. These trading only make sense when they occur in a specific time interval, and seasonal trading is a case in point. During the traditional Chinese festival, the Spring Festival, each family sets off firecrackers and fireworks to celebrate. The lunar December to the first month of the new year is the time to set off firecrackers and fireworks, and this period is also the peak season for firecracker and firework trading. Each family needs to buy firecrackers during this period, otherwise, they will not buy them again. Seasonal clothing is also the case, summer clothing is generally sold from late spring to the end of summer. After entering winter, few people buy summer clothes. Similar situations include air conditioners for cooling, cold drinks in summer, etc., these trading basically occur within a specific time interval.

Unilateral time-limited trading can be further divided into upper time-limited trading and lower time-limited trading. Upper time-limited trading refers to trading with a starting time limit. If the trading occurs earlier than the specified time limit, the trading is meaningless. Lower time-limited trading refers to trading with a termination time limit. If the trading occurs later than the termination time limit, the trading is also meaningless. These two types of trading are mostly closely related to certain special events, such as the need to purchase renovation materials for house renovations, but these trading must wait until the house is available; a small vacuum cleaner for car interior cleaning only makes sense after the car is purchased. All of these are examples of unilateral time-limited trading.

Among the three types of trading mentioned above, the time limit for point-in-time trading is the strictest, and traders have almost no choice in terms of time; bilateral time-limited trading have slightly more choices in terms of time, and the trading agent can choose a favorable time to implement the trading according to changes in the situation. Relatively, unilateral time-limited trading give the trading agent a relatively large space for timing choices.

For trading with time constraints, the purpose is not necessarily to maximize profits, but may be to meet a specific goal. The trading agent can only optimize his choices within a limited range. Only non-time-limited trading allows decision-makers to fully consider various factors in an unrestricted situation, choose the best time, and maximize profits. Based on these characteristics, we divide trading into two major types, namely time-limited trading and non-time-limited trading. Time-limited trading includes point-in-time trading, unilateral time-limited trading, and bilateral time-limited trading; trading without a clear time limit is non-time-limited trading.

The factors determining the trading time limit can come from objective requirements or subjective wishes. Objective factors are relatively easy to understand, such as children going to school, medical treatment, daily consumption, etc.. Subjective factors mainly come from the subjective preferences of the trading agent. In the car market, a new model has just been launched, and the supply of cars is scarce. It often takes a long time to get a car. Some customers are willing to pay extra fees to car dealers in order to drive their favorite new car as soon as possible. Obviously, this eager mood is not the result of objective factors, but to satisfy psychological needs. The psychology of comparison will also affect the trading time limit. In family consumption, some consumption may not be very urgent, but because neighbors and friends have bought it, they also buy it due to the unwillingness to lag behind, and they can't wait for a long time. Obviously, the timeliness of such trading is entirely an artificial result.

Note

1. Guangping Zhang (2012), The Innovation of Renminbi Products, 3rd edn. China Financial Publishing House, Beijing, p 95–108.

Chapter 5
Expected Return Function

A rigorous quantitative analysis system in economics needs to be established on the basis of the behavioral objectives. Neoclassical economics uses utility as the behavioral objective of consumers and return as the behavioral objective of firms. Trading economics unifies consumers and firms under the concept of trading agents and uses the expected return function to cover the behavioral objectives of the two basic types of trading agents.

5.1 Utility Theory

To elucidate the inheritance relationship between the expected return function and utility, expected utility, and prospect theory, we first review the origin of the concept of utility in economics.

5.1.1 The Origin of the Concept of Utility

Utility is a fundamental concept of neoclassical economic theory and an important marker distinguishing neoclassical economics from classical economics. The proposal and application of the concept of utility marked the transition of neoclassical economics from the objective value theory system of classical economics to subjective value theory, and also marked the shift of the focus of economic research from value production theory to demand theory. In the logical system of neoclassical economics, the concept of value is no longer applicable to detailed analysis of consumer behavior. Therefore, utility, as an indicator measuring consumer benefits, entered the field of economics and eventually evolved into the logical basis of neoclassical economics.

Z. Wang, *Trading Economics*, Contributions to Economics,
https://doi.org/10.1007/978-981-99-9875-3_5

The concept of utility was proposed almost simultaneously by three founders of neoclassical economics in roughly the same period, in three different countries, and in three different languages. In 1871, the young British economist William Stanley Jevons published *The Theory of Political Economy* in English; in the same year, Austrian economist and founder of the Austrian School, Carl Menger, published *Principles of Economics* in German; in 1874, French economist Léon Walras published *Elements of Pure Political Economy* in French. Although the theories of the three masters each have their own emphasis, they share many common points in their analytical methods, all based on marginal analysis and starting with utility as the logical analysis. The three masters elevated the concept of utility to an unprecedented height, believing that the source of commodity value is not labor, but utility; the factor determining commodity price is not cost but utility.[1]

The concept of utility has undergone a gradual process from random use to becoming a standard concept in economics. Before the work of the three masters, a group of scholars began to use the concept of utility. In 1837, W. F. Lloyd in his *Lecture on the Notion of Value*; in 1844, Jules Dupuit in his article *On the Measurement of the Utility of Public Works*; in 1854, German economist Hermann Heinrich Gossen in his work *Development of the Laws of Human Relationships*; in 1855, Richard Jennings in his *Nature Elements of Political Economy* all used the concept of utility in different ways.[2]

Regarding the evolution of the concept of utility, the famous American economist, economic historian, and 1982 Nobel laureate in economics, George Joseph Stigler, made this brilliant comment: The statement of this ordinary matter first appeared by chance; it did not have importance in the development of economics, and did not grant its author intellectual prestige. Only when this statement was logically developed, or explicitly applied to economic problems, did it gain attention. And only when a considerable number of economists were persuaded to incorporate it into their analysis, did it gain importance.[3]

5.1.2 The Meaning and Expression of the Concept of Utility

The concept of utility was introduced into the neoclassical economic theory system to explain the motives of consumers' trading, and it necessarily centers on consumer behavior. In Paul A. Samuelson's classic economics textbook *Economics (18th Edition)*, the concept of utility is defined as follows: Utility refers to how consumers rank different goods and services... We can understand utility as the subjective enjoyment or usefulness that a person gets from consuming a good or service... Utility is a scientific concept, economics uses it to explain: how rational consumers allocate their limited resources to the various goods that can bring them the most satisfaction.[4] From Samuelson's definition, it can be seen that the essence of the concept of utility is the measurement of people's sense of satisfaction.

On the surface, the concept of utility is easy to understand. People are always living in a state of satisfaction and dissatisfaction. For a specific good or service, the utility it can bring to consumers exists as a precise value, just like weight. This is the representative view of cardinal utility theory. The main representatives include the founder of neoclassical economics and the founder of general equilibrium theory, French economist Walras, and the founder of welfare economics, British economist Pigou. Pigou believes that utility can not only be measured, but also compared interpersonally. His welfare economics is also built on such a logical basis. The cardinal utility theory once became the mainstream view in the field of economics and lasted until the 1930s.

In 1932, British economist Robbins published a widely influential work—*An Essay on the Nature and Significance of Economic Science*, which comprehensively criticized Pigou's cardinal utility. From then on, the economic community began to turn to ordinal utility theory, believing that utility cannot be accurately measured, but can only be ranked. Consumers can choose between different goods based on the order of utility. Ordinal utility theorists have built a decision-making system for trading agents with the help of utility indifference curves. People call the welfare economics based on ordinal utility theory as new welfare economics, and Pigou's welfare economics as old welfare economics.

Entering the 1940s, John von Neumann and Oskar Morgenstern published the classic work *Theory of Games and Economic Behavior*, and the situation reversed again. In *Theory of Games and Economic Behavior*, the authors analyzed the cardinal theory of utility and the ordinal theory of utility, and found that the two expressions of utility are essentially the same. If utility can be expressed in ordinal terms, it can certainly be expressed in quantitative terms. "If the individual's preferences are all comparable, then we can even obtain a (uniquely defined) numerical utility with renders the indifference curves superfluous."[5] The authors found that the concept of utility, as a description of people's preferences, can have countless different systems of numerical expressions, but they all satisfy the relationship of linear transformation and are in the same group of linear transformations. In other words, there is a one-to-one correspondence between the utility of the trading agent and the group of linear transformations. The authors used axiomatic form to express the conditions that the utility index must meet, including the axiom of complete order; the axiom of order and combination; the axiom of combination algebra, etc., a total of three groups of eight conditions. These conditions were later summarized into more concise expressions of the axioms of order, continuity, and independence.[6] Through rigorous mathematical proof, the author proved that any ordered data system of utility axioms has the properties of utility indicators.

Around the same time, American economist Paul A. Samuelson came to almost the same conclusion. He realized that the essence of utility is the preference ranking of different trading strategies, and whether utility is assigned an ordinal or cardinal number is not important and will not affect the conclusion of the study. In *Foundations of Economic Analysis* published in 1947, he argued that in any case, there obviously exist countless ways to choose a specific utility index and define it as the true cardinal measure of utility. Therefore, a line can be drawn from the origin through any point representing a combination of goods and services. Any point on this line to the origin can serve as a utility index and can be given a unique name.[7]

In von Neumann's utility axioms, the axiom of continuity requires that there can be countless preferences in the middle of any two different levels of preference, so that the preference assignment shows continuous characteristics; the axiom of independence requires that the decision-maker has complete independence in the choice of two preferences and will not be interfered with by other preferences. Further research on utility axioms found that as long as the axioms of order and continuity are met, a utility index system can be established in the trading space, and the restrictions added by the axiom of independence further enhance the stability and certainty of utility assignment. The behavioral economics that has emerged in recent years has proven through a large number of experimental studies that the axiom of independence does not hold in many real scenarios,[8] but this does not affect the status of "utility" as a decision-making measure.

Von Neumann's achievements brought two changes to the field of economics: one was to change people's view that the two expressions of utility are mutually exclusive. Because the numerical expression of utility is more convenient to use, the cardinal theory of utility has revived. The other change is to broaden people's understanding of the concept of utility. People no longer narrowly understand utility as the degree of satisfaction of consumer, but regard utility as a decision-making indicator system with logical consistency. In the utility decision-making system, there can be countless isomorphic indicator systems. These data-unequal, unit-varied indicator systems have completely equivalent functions for decision-makers. Under such a scenario, utility is no longer limited to the description of consumer behavior, and all trading agents, including manufacturers, can be unified in the theoretical framework of utility description. In the 100 years after the neoclassical revolution, this theory has been greatly improved. For example, when talking about utility and utility functions, contemporary economists no longer talk about "individuals trying to maximize some subjective feelings". "Utility" is just another way to talk about "preferences".[9]

5.1.3 Expected Utility Theory

The introduction of the concept of utility has solved the basis of trading decision-making and laid the logical foundation for the construction of economic theory. But this is only the first step to solve all the problems. The next problem is that when people face an uncertain world, for a mixed result that contains two possible events, the trading agent will inevitably face the challenge of utility assignment. Therefore, how to assign utility to mixed events in an uncertain world has become a theoretical problem that economics must solve. The solution of economists is to use the expected utility model.

The Expected Utility Theory was first proposed by Daniel Bernoulli, a famous mathematician, physicist, and member of the famous Swiss mathematician family, in 1738. The concept of expected utility was proposed to solve a famous problem at the time, that is, what price should a gambler pay to participate in a gambling game? At that time, people generally believed that the price paid by the gambler should be equal to the expected gain, but this was far from the actual situation. Bernoulli proved that the gambler's expected gain is almost infinite, but the actual situation is that the gambler only paid a small price when entering the gambling game. In order to resolve the contradiction between "theory" and reality, Daniel Bernoulli introduced the probability of different gambling results and successfully solved it using the method of expected utility. Although the expected gain is high, the probability of the result is very low, so the calculated expected value is still a small value. Daniel Bernoulli therefore concluded: The price of entering the gambling game is not equal to the gambler's expected gain, but equal to the expected gain. Although the Expected Utility Theory preceded the concept of utility into economics, Bernoulli's achievements did not attract the attention of economists for more than 200 years until von Neumann proposed the utility axioms.[10]

The generalized statement of the expected utility model is as follows: Assume that for the trading agent s that considers the trading strategy E_v, the utility generated in different situations is $\{u_1, u_2 \dots u_n\}$, the probabilities of realizing the corresponding utilities are $\{p_1, p_2 \dots p_3\}$. The calculation of expected utility of the trading strategy s is as follows:

$$U(s) = \sum_{1}^{n} p_i u_i \tag{5.1.1}$$

In Eq. (5.1.1), the probability p_i of each situation occurring is the objective probability known to the trading agent a_i; the utility u_i can be either the traditional sense of consumer satisfaction or the specific value of monetary gains. The Expected Utility Theory believes that the trading agent pursues the principle of utility maximization, and when choosing among different trading strategies, it will always choose the strategy with the greatest expected utility.

As of today, the Expected Utility Theory is still the standard model for mainstream economics to deal with uncertain trading situations. With the deepening of behavioral economics research, it has been found that the expected utility model does not coincide with the actual behavior of the trading agent in some aspects. Sometimes, the strategy chosen by the trading agent is not the one with the greatest expected utility.[11]

5.1.4 Prospect Theory

Prospect Theory was a decision-making theory proposed jointly in the 1980s by American behavioral economist and 2002 Nobel laureate in economics, Kahneman, and his collaborator Tversky. Through a large number of economic behavior experiments, Kahneman and Tversky found systematic deviations between the standard decision-making model of mainstream economic theory—the Expected Utility

Theory—and actual decision-making behavior. The deviations mainly manifest in three aspects: First, sensitivity deviation. The Expected Utility Theory believes that people will make decisions based on the expected value of absolute utility, the higher the utility level, the greater the contribution to expected utility. However, economic behavior experiments do not support this view, empirical evidence shows that people are not sensitive to the level of utility, but show strong sensitivity to changes in utility level; Second, preference orientation deviation. The Expected Utility Theory believes that in the face of uncertainty, people will show consistent risk aversion characteristics, which determines the concave nature of utility. But experiments have found that people adopt different strategies in different scenarios of gains and losses. In the face of positive income scenarios, people show risk aversion characteristics; while in the face of loss scenarios, people's preferences will reverse, showing risk preference characteristics; Third, probability value deviation. Expected utility is the utility mean calculated with various possible probabilities as weights. The lower the objective occurrence probability of an event, the smaller the weight in the calculation of expected utility. But a large amount of empirical evidence shows that low-probability events often play a significant role in decision-making, and there is a tendency for low-probability events to be systematically overestimated.

Based on the above findings, Kahneman revised the Expected Utility Theory, introducing the value function v, reference point r, and weight function π on the basis of the Expected Utility Theory. This constructs the decision model of Prospect Theory:

$$U(x_1, x_2, \ldots, x_n) = \sum_i \pi(p_i)v(x_i - r) \tag{5.1.2}$$

In Eq. (5.1.2), x_i represents a possible gain, with a corresponding probability of p_i, satisfying the probability condition $\sum_i p_i = 1$; π represents a non-linear weight function, usually an S-shaped function, which takes larger values at small probabilities and smaller values at high probabilities; v represents the value function, which is a concave function when $x_i - r > 0$ and a convex function when $x_i - r < 0$; r represents the value reference point, which is the decision reference system chosen by the trading agent.[12]

Prospect Theory believes that people will edit the information they receive before making decisions. Decisions are made based on the edited information, and both the weight function π and the value function v are the results of people's editing of the corresponding information. The characteristics of the editing function originate from the cognitive structure features formed by humans in the long evolutionary process. Behavioral economists have revealed the editing programs in different scenarios through a large number of empirical experiments.

Compared with the Expected Utility Theory, the prominent feature of the Prospect Theory is that it adds the subjective factors of the decision-maker, namely the so-called editing process, on the basis of the objective variables p_i and x_i. This reflects more subjective factors in the decision-making process, paves the way for solving the heterogeneity problem of the Expected Utility Theory, and shows a stronger explanatory power than the Expected Utility Theory.

5.2 Expected Return Function

5.2.1 Expectation and Return

In human cognitive activities, expectations play a very important role. Expectations are not only a form of cognitive activity, but also an important part of participation in cognition. In the process of constructing perception, people usually pre-play the phenomena they recognize based on the knowledge representation stored in their memory. The participation of expectations improves the efficiency of pattern recognition and enhances the adaptability of human. This effect is called the expectation effect of knowledge representation in psychology. When we see the English letter Q, we first think that the letter U may follow. The knowledge that generates this guess may be explicit or implicit.[13] Expectations can be formed at the conscious level, as well as at the subconscious or unconscious level. Expectations play a very critical role in decision-making under uncertain situations. In a rapidly changing world, decisions must be based on a reasonable assessment of all possibilities to increase the probability of correct decisions. Naturally, "expectation" has become one of the basic concepts of economics.

In order to maximize the accuracy of expectation, people fully mobilize all experiences and knowledge as well as various information from the surrounding environment in the process of expectation formation, which is an extremely complex psychological process. In economics, there are various theories about expectation formation. The most influential theories are the rational expectation theory and the adaptive expectation theory. Rational expectation refers to the expectation generated by logical inference on a complete information set. Methodologically, rational expectation requires a solution based on a set of behavioral equations; the rational expectation theory assumes that the trading agent fully understands the economic structure and its operating rules, and can calculate reasonable expected results based on a full grasp of complete information. Adaptive expectation is the expectation formed by the trading agent based on the historical change pattern of variables, especially the characteristics of recent changes.

Compared with rational expectations, the main feature of adaptive expectations is experience-led. Although rational expectations and adaptive expectations have their own characteristics and reflect some features of expectation formation, in fact, the process of human expectation formation is much more complex, and the existing theories cannot yet provide us with a comprehensive and correct picture.

Expectations have the characteristic of time structure, and expectations in different time intervals vary greatly. Short-term expectations and long-term expectations have their own focuses. The longer the term, the more uncertainty factors the situation contains, and the more open it is. The time structure corresponding to expectations is called the valuation time domain. Each expectation is generated on the corresponding valuation time domain.

The concept of "return" in accounting refers to the wealth brought by an economic activity, without considering the cost paid for the economic activity, it is a unilateral concept. In accounting, the concept that fully reflects the results of economic activity income and expenditure is "return". If the discussion scope is extended to the family domain, the concept of return seems inappropriate. After all, the central task of the family organization is no longer production, and economic activities have been reduced to a subordinate position. In order to cover the economic activities of different types of trading agents under a unified concept, it is necessary to introduce a broader and clear concept, which is the concept of "return" in a broad sense. The so-called broad-sense "return" refers to the results that trading activities can bring to the agent that are conducive to survival and development. Return can be the return of an enterprise, or the improvement of liquidity structure; it can be the expansion of market share, or the increase in the diversity of asset structure; return can be reflected in the current period, or in the long term.

5.2.2 Expected Return Function

One of the important manifestations of the scientific nature of economics is to explain as many phenomena as possible with as few assumptions as possible. However, the rationality of economic assumptions must withstand empirical tests. Before the rise of behavioral economics, the correctness of economic theory assumptions could only be achieved through indirect verification methods. However, the effectiveness of indirect proof is very limited. When the conclusions of economics diverge from the actual situation, it cannot be determined where the problem lies, so it will fall into a protracted academic dispute.

The empirical experiments of behavioral economics are mostly to simulate the decision-making process of humans in laboratory scenarios, and then draw conclusions based on the experimental statistical results. This still has a certain gap with the real reality scenarios. Due to the significant dependence of human decision-making on scenarios, when the social scenarios switches to the laboratory scenarios, people's decision-making behavior will inevitably undergo some degree of distortion, and the conclusions drawn on this basis also have the risk of "distortion". For example, Kahneman, Knetsch and Thaler conducted a famous experiment on coffee cup pricing among students at Cornell University. A group of students was randomly divided into two groups, one of which was given a coffee cup per person, and the other was not. Then, both the cup holders and those without cups were asked what they thought the reasonable price for the cup should be. The median price for the cup holders was \$5.25, while the median price for those without cups was \$2.25, a difference of nearly 2 times. This experiment simulated a real trading scenario, although all the elements of trading were present, the participants in the experiment were more playing a role, without a real intention to trade. In fact, agents in different trading phases naturally have different expectations for the price of the target, which is a basic rule of trading pricing. The difference in asking prices between the two parties still exists even after excluding endowment factors. Of course, we do not doubt the conclusion that the endowment effect exists, but show that behavioral experiments themselves may distort information.

Trading economics, when constructing decision models, fully considers the above situation, based on expected utility, borrows some ideas from the Prospect Theory of behavioral economics, and constructs an expected return function. The expected return function uses the accounting matrix of the trading agent as a measurement framework, the expected net return that the trading strategy may bring and the subjective probability of the corresponding situation as weights, and the expected return of the trading strategy as the function value.

Suppose a_i is any trading agent in the trading system, the accounting matrix at time step t is A, and the net assets are x; s is any strategy on the trading strategy set S of the trading agent a_i, that is, $s \in S$. Under the action of strategy s, the accounting matrix A is transformed into $A(s)$. According to the changes in the trading situation, $A(s)$ has two possible valuations: the trading situation friendly g achieves the maximum net asset value Y_g; the trading situation unfriendly b achieves the worst net asset value Y_b. The prior probabilities of the two trading situations g and b, are b and q, and satisfy the probability identity $p + q = 1$. under the above circumstances, the expected return value $E(s)$ evaluated by trading agent a_i for strategy s is:

$$E(s) = p(y_g - x) + q(y_b - x) \tag{5.2.1}$$

For the trading agent a_i, the above function establishes a single mapping between the strategy set S and the real numbers, that is, a function on the trading strategy set S, we call this function the expected return function of the trading agent a_i.

The construction of the expected return function conforms to the basic characteristics of human decision-making. Before taking actions, people always evaluate the best and worst possible outcomes, predict the probability of both scenarios, calculate the approximate result of the action, and make decisions based on this. The expected return function is also composed of two parts: the first item represents the best outcome; the second item represents the worst outcome, and the expected return value is obtained by the weighted average of subjective probabilities.

Compared with the expected utility, the expected return function has two differences: first, the probability weights and net asset values in the expected return function are subjective estimates, while the probabilities and asset values in the expected utility function are objective values known to the trading agent; second, the value average weighted by probability in the expected return function is based on the relative return of the original accounting matrix net assets, while the expected utility is the average of the absolute value of utility.

Compared with Prospect Theory, the expected return function also adopts the construction of value reference points. The x in the expected return function is equivalent to the value reference point r in the prospect model. The difference is that the expected return function omits the weight function and value function, and directly uses the expected valuation to replace the weight function and value function. This construction is based on two considerations: one is that the two editing functions are only used to describe the information processing of the trading agent, which is a psychological activity of the trading agent, and the final output still reflects the subjective judgment of the trading agent; the second is that the double-layer structure of Prospect Theory increases the complexity of the later theoretical deduction, and does not have much impact on the substantive results of the theoretical deduction. Directly using the expected variables to calculate the expected return changes that the trading strategy may bring can simplify the theoretical deduction process to the greatest extent.

In the expected return function, the probability estimates p and q, as well as the return estimates Y_g, Y_b and x, are all results after the trading agent's information editing. This structure determines that the expected return function can accommodate the empirical findings of behavioral economics, including the utility of value reference points, risk preference reversal, and overestimation of small probabilities, etc., thus it can explain all "strange" phenomena that behavioral economics can explain while expected utility cannot explain under the theoretical framework.

The trading agent's valuation of expected returns is usually very vague, only predicting the general trend of the market, and it is impossible to give a clear price evolution path, and the same is true for the judgment of market demand. The expected return function is also a function of rough values. The above discussion on the expected return function can only show the logical structure of the decision-making process.

The construction characteristics of the expected return function indicate that the path of net asset value changes is not important. No matter how the net asset value evolves, even if the return value of the trading strategy may decline over a period of time, as long as it realizes the optimization of the accounting matrix in some periods within the valuation time domain, it can become a possession strategy. In the valuation time domain, even if the net asset value may fall after reaching the peak, it will not affect the decision-maker's choice. The trading agent has a way to "lock in" the value through trading means when the net asset value curve reaches the highest point.

The expected return function, as the objective function of the trading agent, brings about the diversification pursued by the trading agent. Some trading agents may pursue the appreciation of tangible assets; while others focus on reputation enhancement. These agents pay more attention to social impact and relatively downplay wealth goals. More commonly, families place great importance on their children's education, enhancing the family's human capital stock by improving their children's education level. It can be seen that the expected return function can cover a wider range of trading behavior.

When facing liquidity difficulties, trading agents need to improve asset liquidity through trading. In this case, the performance of the expected return function is that the net assets x of the original accounting matrix A will shrink sharply in the upcoming valuation time domain, and the trading strategy s to improve asset liquidity may not necessarily bring the best Y_g, Y_b, but compared with the continuously shrinking value reference point x, it will still generate a larger expected return. This shows that the expected return function can cover the decision-making process under different trading motives.

The motive for asset diversification trading can also be reflected in the expected return function. When trading agents implement trading under the motive of asset diversification, they will systematically overestimate the value of the missing assets in the balance sheet, forming a significant trading utility. In this case, even if the new assets have the same market value as the original assets, in the expected valuation of the accounting matrix, the valuations of Y_g and Y_b will also be higher than the value of x in the original accounting matrix, achieving the expected return function $E(s) > 0$.

5.2.3 Utility Axiom Proof

Theoretically, any measurement system that satisfies the von Neumann utility axiom conditions can be used as a measure of utility. In other words, the theory established according to the measurement system that satisfies the utility axiom has isomorphic properties in logic with the mainstream theory established based on the concept of psychological utility.

We will prove that the preference order established on the trading strategy set S of the trading agent a_i based on the value of the expected return function of the trading strategy satisfies the utility axiom conditions. Assume s_1, s_2 are any two strategies on the trading strategy set S, s_1, s_2 can be either two pure strategies or mixed strategies; the corresponding expected return function values are $E(s_1)$ and $E(s_2)$. The rule we establish a preference order on the trading strategy set S according to the expected return function is: only when $E(s_1) > E(s_2)$, the trading strategy s_1 is superior to strategy s_2, denoted as $s_1 \succ s_2$; only when $E(s_1) = E(s_2)$, the preference order of trading strategy s_1 and s_2 is equivalent or indifferent, denoted as $s_1 \sim s_2$. Based on this agreement, we will prove that the expected utility function fully satisfies the three sets of conditions of the utility axiom.

First, we prove that it satisfies the two conditions of the axiom of order, namely the completeness condition and the transitivity condition.

(1) Proof of completeness: Assume that s_1, s_2, s_3 are any three strategies on the strategy set S of any trading agent a_i, with $\cdot\ s_1 \in S, s_2 \in S, s_3 \in S$. According to the definition of the expected return function, the three strategies can get corresponding real number assignments through the expected return function, which are $E(s_1)$, $E(s_2)$, $E(s_3)$. According to the properties of real numbers, for any two strategies s_1, s_2 in S, the value of the expected return function can only appear once in the following three relationships, and it is impossible to appear in two relationships at the same time:

$$E(s_1) > E(s_2) \quad (5.2.2)$$

$$E(s_1) < E(s_2) \quad (5.2.3)$$

$$E(s_1) = E(s_2) \quad (5.2.4)$$

When relationship (5.2.2) appears, we can define the preference order between trading strategies s_1 and s_2 as $s_1 \succ s_2$; when relationship (5.2.3) appears, we can define the preference order of the two strategies as $s_1 \prec s_2$; when relationship (5.2.4) appears, we can define the preference relationship of the two strategies as indifferent, that is, $s_1 \sim s_2$.

Since s_1 and s_2 are any two trading strategies on the strategy set S, the above demonstration shows that for any agent a_i in the trading system, a complete preference order can be established on its trading strategy set through the expected return function. This proves that the expected return function satisfies the preference completeness condition of the utility axiom.

(2) Proof of transitivity: Assume that the trading strategies s_1, s_2, s_3 have the following preference relationships, $s_1 \succ s_2$, $s_2 \succ s_3$, according to the definition of the expected return function, the relationship of the expected return function values of the three trading strategies can be inferred as follows:

$$E(s_1) > E(s_2), E(s_2) > E(s_3) \quad (5.2.5)$$

According to the property of real numbers satisfying the transitive relationship, we can get:

$$E(s_1) > E(s_3) \quad (5.2.6)$$

According to the agreed rules of trading strategy preference order, it can be inferred that the preference relationship between trading strategy s_1 and s_2 satisfies:

$$s_1 \succ s_3 \quad (5.2.7)$$

∴ The preference order defined by the expected return function satisfies the transitivity condition of the utility axiom.

Through the arguments of (1) and (2), we can conclude: On the set of trading strategy set S, the preference order established according to the expected return function satisfies all conditions of the axiom of order.

(3) Proof of the axiom of continuity: Assume that the trading strategies s_1, s_2, s_3 satisfy the preference relationship $s_1 \succ s_2 \succ s_3$. According to the rules of preference order defined by the expected function, the expected return function values of the three strategies have the following relationship:

$$E(s_1) > E(s_2) > E(s_3) \tag{5.2.8}$$

Since the real number system satisfies the continuity condition, we can find a set of positive real numbers p, q, less than 1, and $p + q = 1$, satisfying the following equation:

$$pE(s_1) + qE(s_3) = E(s_2) \tag{5.2.9}$$

The left side of Eq. (5.2.9) is the expected return function value of the pure strategies s_1, s_2 under the mixed strategy with a probability structure of (p, q). Therefore, the above equation is equivalent to the following equation:

$$E(s_1, s_3; p, q) = E(s_2) \tag{5.2.10}$$

According to the agreed rules, the mixed strategy $(s_1, s_1, s_3; p, q)$and strategy s_2 have an indifferent preference relationship, that is:

$$(s_1, s_3; p, q) \sim s_2 \tag{5.2.11}$$

This proves that the preference order defined by the expected return function satisfies the conditions of the axiom pf continuity.

(4) Proof of the axiom of independence: Assume that s_1, s_2, s_3 are three arbitrary strategies on the strategy set S of the trading agent a_i, s_1, s_2 satisfy the preference relationship $s_1 \succ s_2$, (p, q) is any probability pair, satisfying $p + q = 1$; From this, two mixed strategies $(s_1, s_3; p, q)$ and $(s_2, s_3; p, q)$ can be generated, and the expected return function values of the two mixed strategies are:

$$E(s_1, s_3; p, q) = pE(s_1) + qE(s_3) \tag{5.2.12}$$

$$E(s_2, s_3; p, q) = pE(s_2) + qE(s_3) \tag{5.2.13}$$

$$\because s_1 \succ s_2$$

$$\therefore E(s_1) > E(s_2) \tag{5.2.14}$$

$$\therefore E(s_1, s_3; p, q) > E(s_2, s_3; p, q) \tag{5.2.15}$$

$$\therefore (s_1, s_3; p, q) \succ (s_2, s_3; p, q) \tag{5.2.16}$$

This proves that the preference relationship defined by the expected return function satisfies the axiom of independence.

Based on the proofs of the axioms of order, continuity, and independence, we can conclude: The preference order established by the expected return function on the strategy set of the trading agent satisfies all conditions of the utility axiom and has the attributes of describing the trading agent's decision system, and the theoretical system established on this basis has logical consistency and completeness.

5.2.4 Logical Basis of the Expected Return Function

The argument in Sect. 5.2.3 includes the basic logical assumption of the expected return function, that is, the trading agent has the ability to accurately assign values to each strategy in the trading strategy set. In fact, this hypothesis is not fully applicable to trading agents with bounded rationality. The concept of bounded rationality was proposed by American economist Herbert Simon, who first introduced bounded rationality into economics, and gradually gained more and more recognition from economists. There are two core elements of bounded rationality: first, the limited nature of the information held by the trading agent, who is in a state of incomplete possession of information. Since the collection of information requires the payment of various costs, the information held by each trading agent is incomplete. This determines that the decision-making of the trading agent can only be carried out under uncertain conditions. Secondly, the ability of the trading agent to process information is limited. The trading agent's ability to use and discern information is limited, therefore, various cognitive errors are mixed in the cognition of the trading agent.[14]

Bounded rationality does not deny the rational assumption of trading behavior, but emphasizes that trading decisions are made in accordance with rational rules under the premise of incomplete limited information. In other words, the assumption of bounded rationality is a further constraint on the behavior of trading agents under the premise of rational assumptions, and rationality is the premise of bounded rationality. The assumption of rational trading behavior is at the bottom of economic theory and is an indispensable foundation for building a logical system. In economic theory, the standard of rational behavior includes two aspects: first, the preferences of the trading agent are complete. When the trading agent a faces any strategy s_i, s_j, there must be $s_i \succ s_j, s_i \prec s_j, s_i \sim s_j$, one of the three relationships is established, that is, strategy s_i is superior to strategy s_j; strategy s_i is inferior to strategy s_j; strategy s_i and strategy s_j have equal preference. One of the three must be chosen, and two relationships cannot be established at the same time. Second, the preferences of the trading agent are transitive. For three arbitrary trading strategies s_i, s_j and s_k, if the trading agent a prefers strategy s_i over strategy s_j, and prefers strategy s_j over strategy s_k, then the trading agent a must prefer strategy s_i over strategy s_k. When the above two conditions are met, we say that the behavior of the trading agent a is rational.[15] Obviously, the two assumptions about rationality are very basic and also build the premise of trading theory. Although behavioral economics has found that people's decisions in reality do not always strictly follow the rules of preference transitivity, there often appears the preference for strategy s_i is preferred over strategy s_j, the preference for strategy s_j is preferred over strategy s_k, but the preference for strategy s_i is worse than strategy s_k. Considering the delicate balance between the self-consistency of theoretical logic and the simplicity of theory, we regard the preference reversal that occurs in special scenarios as a specific phenomenon and exclude it from the theoretical perspective.

Trading agents with bounded rationality have a finite set of strategies. Trading agents will not implement trading strategies they do not know or understand, and strategies outside the trading agent's strategy set are irrelevant to the trading agent's decision. From this, we can prove that the logical basis of the expected return function is valid.

Assume s_i is any trading strategy on the trading strategy set s of the trading agent a, that is, $s \in S$, which means that the trading agent a_i must understand the possible gains and losses brought by s_i.

If the trading agent a_i cannot assign an expected return to the trading strategy s_i, it indicates that the trading agent a_i does not have sufficient knowledge about the trading strategy, and the trading strategy s_i belongs to the strategies that the trading agent a_i does not understand.

According to the conditions satisfied by the trading strategy set, the trading strategy s_i does not belong to the strategies in the trading strategy set, that is, $s_i \notin S$. Obviously, the conclusion contradicts the setting of $s \in S$. This proves that the trading agent a_i has the ability to assign values to all strategies in the trading strategy set.

In reality, although we often face difficult decisions, we will eventually make a choice after some effort, which also verifies the existence of the logical basis of the expected return function in reality.

The weight probabilities p and q in the expected return function are the results of the trading agent's subjective editing, fully reflecting the trading agent's preference characteristics in the face of uncertainty under different backgrounds, and have stronger descriptive characteristics. The preference order constructed by the expected return function does not require the condition of preference consistency as a prerequisite, and therefore will not encounter the dilemma of the Allais Paradox.

5.2.5 Institutional Basis of the Expected Return Function

The process of trading agents constructing the expected return function cannot be separated from the real social and economic environment, among which, the property right system and property right protection constitute the most important institutional basis of the expected return function.

5.2.5.1 Property Right System

Property rights are a prerequisite for trading, and trading promote the deepening of the property right system. No one is willing to trade for a ray of sunlight in the sky, because it is impossible to define the boundary of the right to this ray of sunlight, and there is a lack of effective means to maintain and hold this property right. Only when the sunlight is linked to a specific spatial structure and building, is it possible to conduct trading involving sunlight.[16] It can be seen that the property right system is an important institutional basis for defining the expected return function, which is also the core essence of the Coase theorem.[17]

In institutional economics, property rights are divided into two basic types: absolute property rights and relative property rights. Absolute property rights refer to the rights that an actor has over a valuable asset, including the right to occupy, the right to return, and the right to dispose. Absolute property rights have complete exclusivity, and any third party's use, possession, and disposal without the permission of the rights holder are infringements and need to be punished by law. The exclusivity of absolute property rights is not specifically targeted and has an absolute meaning that encompasses everything. These rights are directly based on civil law and do not require any additional agreements or contracts signed with third parties. Relative property rights are based on contracts signed by the trading parties. Although these rights are also protected by law, the specific rights need to be stipulated through contracts.

In the trading system, due to the diversity of asset endowments, the corresponding property rights also take various forms, including absolute property rights, relative property rights; private property rights, common property rights; common property rights can be further divided into collective property rights and state-owned property rights. These different types of property rights form the property rights structure of the trading system at a specific time. Corresponding to the property right structure of the trading system, a structural relationship will also be generated among different interests within the property right, and the rights of use, return, and disposal show a dynamic relationship of one diminishing and the other growing in application scenarios. The property right structure of the trading system belongs to the macro-structure category, while the internal structure of property rights belongs to the micro-structure category. The property right structures at these two levels together constitute the complete information of the property right structure of the trading system.

The property right structure of the trading system evolves with the trading system. As human society evolves from traditional forms to modern forms, three basic evolutionary trends are presented in the property right structure: first, the property right structure is becoming increasingly complex, and the scope of the relationship among property rights is becoming wider. Second, under the support of a perfect legal system, with more and more diversified trading modes, increasingly subdivided relative property rights are released within property rights, and different levels of rights are formed on the basis of subdivided relative property rights. The trading of various financial derivatives is the result of property right subdivision, and futures, options, swaps, etc. are typical examples of such relative property rights. Third, among all forms of property rights, the importance of relative property rights is increasing, and it is the main driving force for the complexity of the property right structure of the trading system. Relative property rights are both the result of trading promotion and the cause of trading activities, and have a close accompanying relationship with trading activities. With the expansion of trading activities and the complexity of modes, the rise of the importance of relative property rights in the trading system is inevitable.

The continuous deepening of the property right system is an important manifestation of the development of human society and the result of the evolution of the trading system. The structure of property rights continues to evolve in the direction of becoming more detailed, clearer, and more complex. The evolution of the property right system should match the evolution of the trading system. The construction of the property right system must meet the needs of the trading agent to define the expected return function. Otherwise, the lack of a property right system will become an obstacle to economic development. However, if the deepening of the property right system precedes the pace of the evolution of the trading system, it will instead increase trading costs, suppress trading activities, and also hinder economic development. The depth of the property right system determines the scope of trading activities, trading activities dictate the depth of the property right structure, and the expected return function defines the boundary of property right definition.

Different types of property rights play different roles in the operation of the trading system. They cooperate and compete with one another and are an indispensable basis for the effective allocation of resources in the trading system. Absolute property rights are the basis of relative property rights. Without absolute property rights, relative property rights lose their basic support. Private property rights have clear equity boundaries and clear incentive orientation. Trading activities induced by private property rights will not conflict with objectives. They can stimulate the trading enthusiasm of trading agents, maximize the potential of trading agents, and are the cornerstone of the efficient operation of the trading system. Various forms of common property rights play an important role in reducing the overall operating costs of the trading system and enhancing the resilience of the trading system. They are an indispensable part of the property right structure in the trading system. Taking the urban traffic network as an example, if private property rights are adopted, it may be more efficient than common property rights just from the perspective of maintenance and management of the traffic network. Due to the monopolistic characteristics of the traffic network, the attribute of private property rights pursuing maximum return will inevitably charge high tolls. The company owning the property rights of the traffic network will naturally have stable and substantial returns, with high investment efficiency. However, from the macro perspective of the entire city's operation, due to the high transportation costs, the efficiency of all trading activities in the city will decline, the city's competitiveness will be damaged, and it will ultimately hinder the healthy social and economic development of the city. Obviously, there is a conflict between micro-efficiency and macro-efficiency in the property right arrangement of the urban traffic network. In this case, public property rights become an effective institutional arrangement.

Each property right system has its own advantages and disadvantages. Absolute property rights have a solid value basis, but there is a risk of underdevelopment and waste of idle resources. Relative property rights can fully exploit the value resources of absolute property rights, but overuse and imbalance with absolute property rights may lead to the risk of bubble. Efficiency is the advantage of private property rights, but polarization is its most difficult problem to solve. Common property rights have the advantage of maintaining the overall stability of the trading system, but due to the many social functions of common property rights, there is a risk of internal conflict of behavioral objectives, and low efficiency is its intractable problem. Only when various types of property rights form a balanced structure that complements one another, can the advantages of each form of property rights be maximized, and their respective defects can be overcome by the coordination and complementarity among property rights, ultimately achieving the efficient operation and healthy development of the trading system.

Although there is competition among different property right systems, they are not mutually substitutable, let alone one property right system eliminating another. They complement one another and are prerequisites for one another. Due to the balancing role of common property rights, the social chronic disease of polarization induced by private property rights can be alleviated to a large extent. Conversely, due to the existence of private property rights, common property rights have an efficiency reference, which can also alleviate the loss of common property rights to a certain extent.

The organization of property rights, especially the design arrangements for relative property rights, will have a direct and profound impact on the behavioral strategies of trading agents. Take the trading of relative property right of land leasing as an example, a farmer leases a piece of farmland from a landlord. If the contract between the two parties simply stipulates the lease term and land rent, the lessee, in pursuit of maximizing return, will definitely try to obtain as much benefit from the land as possible within the agreed lease term. Since the land ownership belongs to the landlord, any land appreciation resulting from any long-term investment in the land belongs to the landlord. The farmer will not make any long-term investments that benefit beyond the lease term, neither will he invest in long-term use of water facilities, nor will he invest in soil improvement to maintain the long-term value of the land. The optimal strategy is to exhaust all the fertility of the farmland when the lease expires. To avoid such a result, the landlord has to supervise the lessee's use of the land and pay the trading cost of maintaining his own property right. Obviously, from the perspective of the entire trading system, trading costs are a waste of resources. For example, lease contract includes an appraisal value clause for the farmland, stipulating that at the end of the lease, the appraisal value of the land exceeding the market average belongs to the lessee, and the value below the market appraisal average is compensated by the lessee. The lessee will have another behavioral strategy, he will care about the long-term value of the land and choose economically effective ways to improve the long-term value of the land. The new property right design has successfully internalized the externality of the trading with the help of market forces, effectively reducing trading costs. It can be seen that using the market to reduce the externality of trading is an important way to improve the efficiency of the trading system.[18]

The rationality of the property right structure determines the operating efficiency of the trading system and also determines the growth performance of the economy. In 1950, South Korea's per capita GDP was less than 82% of Sri Lanka's; after 13 years of hard work, South Korea's per capita GDP was close to Sri Lanka's, reaching 97% of Sri Lanka's per capita GDP; another 10 years later, by 1973, South Korea's per capita GDP had surpassed Sri Lanka's, being 1.86 times that of Sri Lanka's per capita GDP; by 1983, South Korea's per capita GDP had far surpassed Sri Lanka's, being six times as much. The fundamental reason for the reversal of the strength and weakness of the two economies in economic development in just 33 years is the different evolution of the property right structure. The South Korean economy has grown rapidly due to the optimization of the property right structure, while the Sri Lankan economy has stumbled due to the deterioration of the property right structure.[19]

Trading costs not only affect the valuation of the expected return function, but more importantly, they affect the certainty of the expected return function. The higher the trading costs, the worse the expected stability of the expected return function, and the more severe the suppression of the trading agent's trading intention. In reality, the more backward the economy, the more complex the process of property right setting, especially the setting of relative property rights, which not only requires the trading agent to consume a large amount of financial costs, but also consumes a large amount of time costs of the trading agent. Whether it is absolute property rights or relative property rights, a considerable part needs to be established through government department authorization. The extremely low work efficiency and bureaucrat of government departments are often important reasons for the high trading costs.

The property right structure becomes more complex and refined with the evolution of the trading system, which is the basis for improving the efficiency of the trading system. If the co-evolution of the property right structure is artificially interfered with, the development of the trading system will be hindered, economic vitality will be suppressed, and the economy will lose its growth momentum and fall into a quagmire of stagnancy.

5.2.5.2 Property Right Protection

An effective property right system provides institutional guarantees for trading agents to construct expected return functions, while full and comprehensive property right protection provides security guarantees for trading agents to realize the returns of expected return functions.

Property right protection includes two levels of meaning, the first is the protection of property rights from infringement, which is the basic meaning of property right protection; the second is the protection of the integrity of property rights, that is, property rights are not interfered with by third parties outside the rights holders during the use and disposal process. We can imagine, if the results of the trading agent's efforts are not effectively protected, and are easily confiscated or requisitioned by others or organizations, what attitude will the trading agent take towards trading opportunities? The enthusiasm of the trading agent for trading opportunities will be completely lost, the attention of the trading agent will turn to how to protect the existing wealth, and there will be no more interest in how to create more new wealth. In this regard, the government of Sri Lanka in the sixties and seventies of the last century provides us with a very persuasive case. The failure of Sri Lanka may largely be attributed to the Sri Lankan government's public declaration that its policy was to reduce private property rights. Until 1977, successive Sri Lankan governments were formulating various policies to centralize economic rights, interfere widely with the market, and push the country towards a fully planned economy. Private property was threatened and confiscated, creating an atmosphere of uncertainty about the future.[20]

Respecting property rights and protecting the integrity of property rights are equally important. If the government interferes too much with the use of property rights by trading agents, it actually plays a negative role in diluting property rights, which is also an infringement of property rights. In modern society, although the government is paying more and more attention to the protection of property rights, including various intellectual property rights, and the relevant laws and regulations are becoming more and more perfect, and the crackdown on various illegal infringements is getting stronger, the phenomenon of interfering with the use of property rights and infringing on the integrity of property rights is very common. Real estate purchase and sale restrictions, rent control policies are everywhere, and various property rights intervention not only appears in developing countries, but is also common in developed economies. Most of these policies are launched under macro-prudential management, which may achieve the expected results at the time, but fundamentally weaken the foundation of the effective allocation of resources by the trading system, which is very detrimental to the long-term development of the economy. When owners are not allowed to charge tenants the full rent for the house, you will see a change in the behavior of the owners. The number of houses maintained and available for public rental decreases, owners rent houses to relatives and friends, and use houses for commercial or other uncontrolled purposes. The result of rent control is that property rights are only partially transferred from the owner to the current tenant group, and finally crowded slums appear.[21]

5.2.6 Advantages of the Expected Return Function

Compared with the standard expected utility function of neoclassical economics, the expected return function has the following four advantages:

First, the expected return function is based on accounting, which logically connects with modern economic management, thereby strengthening the realistic basis of economic theory. Accounting is the basic management means of economic behavior, the task of economic theory is to reveal the internal logic of economic behavior, the expected return function as the basis for trading decisions, effectively connects accounting with trading decisions, which is an important advantage of the expected return function;

Second, the expected return function unifies the decision-making mechanisms of two different agents, consumers and manufacturers, and unifies the trading agents to the objective function of maximizing the expected return function, changing the relatively fragmented situation of neoclassical economic consumption theory and supply theory;

Third, the expected return function evaluates the effects of different trading strategies based on the accounting matrix, measures the returns of different strategies with monetized measurement units, the results are very intuitive and easy to understand;

Fourth, the conflict between behavioral empirical results and mainstream economics reflects the deviation of the subjective judgment of the trading agent from the objective situation. The expected return function is the subjective assignment of the trading agent to different trading strategies, including the return estimation and subjective estimation of the occurrence probability of the trading strategy, effectively avoiding the conflict between theory and empiricism. At the same time, the expected function retains the concise form of the expected utility function, which also provides conditions for the simplification of theoretical deduction.

5.3 Trading Valuation Time Domain

Value is a manifestation of time and space, and the value of the expected return function needs to be realized in a specific time interval. The valuation time domain is the time concept that matches the expected return function. In mainstream economic theory, the issue of time is usually set as self-evident. Utility maximization does not explicitly stipulate the corresponding time, which is usually assumed to be immediate maximization.

5.3.1 Concept of Trading Valuation Time Domain

The trading valuation time domain is the time interval used by decision-makers to determine the expected returns of trading strategies.[22] Neoclassical economists believe that businesses and consumers make decisions based on the immediate comparison of the returns of different trading strategies, without considering the time effects of the trading strategies, which follows the rule of intermediate future. In fact, real-world decision-makers need to evaluate returns over a certain duration, following the rule of expectation.

When making decisions, businesses need to consider three aspects: the risk of the trading, the return, and the enterprise's image. Although these factors will ultimately be reflected in the enterprise's returns, they require a relatively slow transformation process. When multinational companies arrange production, they do not put all production resources in the region or country with the lowest production costs, but put some in places with higher costs, which is obviously unreasonable from the rule of immediate future. Only by examining the decision-making behavior of companies over a certain length of time in the valuation time domain can the rationality of this layout be discovered. Multinational companies set up production bases in multiple countries, considering not only production costs but also risk control. If a country experiences political unrest, worker strikes, or natural disasters, other production bases can make up for it in time, so as not to cause a complete interruption of the supply chain; producing in countries with higher costs helps maintain and enhance the product image. Whether it is for risk management considerations or image management needs, it is for the realization of long-term returns of the company.

In family decision-making, for trading that involve large amounts and have a significant impact on family life, long-term planning is also required. Take the purchase of real estate as an example, the family trading agent will evaluate many factors such as the future trend of house prices and life arrangements over a period of time.

In summary, whether it is an enterprise or a family, the evaluation of trading returns is based on a specific time interval. The valuation time domain is the evaluation time interval chosen by the trading agent when making decisions. The length of the valuation time domain has a very significant impact on the expected return function. The length of the valuation time domain determines the way the agent expresses information. Take stock market investors as an example, for the same market situation, long-term investors and short-term investors may have completely different views. Reflected in the expected return function, there will be a big difference, and then form completely different trading strategies. Investors with a shorter valuation time domain mainly consider the short-term effects of policies. Tightening monetary policy will increase the financing costs of listed companies and reduce income in the short term, and stock prices will decline. Investors with a short-term valuation time domain will decide to reduce stock holdings. In the view of investors with a longer valuation time domain, macro-control is conducive to the healthy operation of the macro economy and helps improve the business environment. Based on this judgment, long-term investors will buy when short-term investors sell stocks, resulting in a market clearing outcome. The choice of the valuation time domain not only has a significant impact on the decision-making of the trading agent in stock investment, but also plays an indispensable role in almost all trading activities.

The situation is the same for businesses. Enterprises with a shorter valuation time domain, cost control and return targets are tightly managed throughout the business operation. Enterprises with a longer valuation time domain will adopt a dynamic flexible strategy. To gain an advantage in long-term competition, they may choose to incur losses during a specific period. Some foreign banks, seeing the potential of the Chinese market, will set up branches in China, but in the first two years of operation, these new branches require substantial investment and do not make money. In the short term, this is not a desirable strategy; but in the long term, it is undoubtedly a decision with strategic vision. The situation of enterprises is very complex, each enterprise faces different circumstances, which determines that their trading valuation time domains are necessarily very different.

The reason why an enterprise continues to operate despite losses, rather than ceasing operations or closing down, is because the entrepreneur still has expectation of turning the situation around. If the enterprise closes down, the cost of resetting the business would be very high. The modern economy is a credit economy, and enterprises are woven into a complex network of creditors and debtors. Once an enterprise stops operating, it sends negative information to creditors, who will then come to collect debts. At this point, it is usually difficult for the enterprise to repay its debts through financing, and it is very likely to end in bankruptcy.

It is not to say that the longer the valuation time domain, the wiser the decision-maker's decisions will be. When the valuation time domain is stretched too long, uncertainty rapidly increases. The information support required by the decision-maker greatly increases, and the difficulty of decision-making increases rapidly with the expansion of the valuation time domain.

There are three main factors that influence the length of the valuation time domain of the trading agent: one is the risk or uncertainty of the trading; the greater the uncertainty, the more the valuation time domain tends to be short-term. In the face of unstable expectations, the trading agent will reduce the difficulty of decision-making by shortening the valuation time domain. Conversely, the more stable the trading environment, the smaller the uncertainty risk, the longer the valuation time domain chosen by the trading agent. The second is the lifecycle of the traded object, mainly referring to the length of the valuation time domain that the traded goods may have impact on the trading agent. Generally speaking, the longer the impact of the traded object, the longer the valuation time domain of the trading. Compared to buying a car, buying a piece of clothing has a short-term impact on people, so the valuation time domain for clothing is much shorter than that for cars. The third is the expected lifespan of the trading agent. As age increases, the agent's valuation time domain also shortens. The younger the trading agent, the more adventurous it is and the more inclined it is to choose a longer valuation time domain.

Whether it's an enterprise or a family, the valuation time domain is of limited length. This is because markets, technology, and economic conditions are always changing. Under conditions of bounded rationality and incomplete information, the foresight length of trading agents into the future is also very limited.

5.3.2 Short-Term Phenomenon of Valuation Time Domain

The varying lengths of the trading agents' valuation time domains form a specific time structure in the market, which has a significant impact on market operations.

Generally speaking, the time structure that moves towards the far end, the market tends to be more stable, and the corresponding liquidity will be weaker. The time structure of the real estate market is much longer compared to the stock market, therefore, the prices in the real estate market are much more stable than in the stock market, and there is also a significant difference in liquidity compared to the stock market.

The phenomenon of short-term valuation is characterized by a large number of trading agents shortening their valuation time domain in the trading system. The characteristic of short-term valuation is that trading agents pursue short-term returns, even one-time returns. In the commodity market, enterprises will fully exploit the advantage of information asymmetry, not hesitating to damage their own image and reputation, and peddle counterfeit and inferior products; in the capital market, speculative motives dominate the market, investors do not care about the industry characteristics of the enterprise, nor do they care about the level of business management, and they even do not care whether they are losing or making returns. As long as there is a story, they will hype it up and run away when they make money. This attitude of investors in turn indulges listed companies in fraud and opportunism. There is a lack of trust among trading agents in the market, and the entire economy operates inefficiently under a crisis of trust.

Although short-term valuation is inefficient, it is a highly stable state. When the majority of trading agents in the market adopt a short-term trading strategy, choosing a long-term valuation time domain will become a disadvantageous strategy. This is because once the short-term strategy dominates the market, the time that market opportunities can persist will shorten. The short-term strategy is a Nash equilibrium of the market. To break this situation, trading agents must assume that other trading agents will adopt a long-term strategy, otherwise they will adopt a short-term strategy. This forms a self-circulating situation, limiting the market strategy to its original position.

Short-term valuation not only affects the efficiency of economic operation, but even affects the entire social ethos and value orientation. Under this influence, impetuousness, focusing on returns, and declining moral standards have become increasingly prominent problems. The phenomenon of short-term valuation is very common in the early stages of market development, and it is very easy to fall into the trap of short-term valuation during the economic take-off period.

5.3.3 Valuation Time Domain and Time Preference

Time preference is an important concept introduced by the Austrian School into economic theory, which is used to describe the characteristics of saving behavior and investment behavior, manifested as aversion to delayed consumption. As the main representative of the Austrian School, Mises, pointed out, time preference is an absolutely necessary factor in human behavior. We cannot imagine a behavior that is not more satisfying in the near term than later. If a person does not regard near-term satisfaction as more important than long-term, he will never consume for satisfaction. He is always accumulating and not consuming enjoyment. He does not consume today, nor does he consume tomorrow, because when tomorrow comes, he does the same decision he made before.[23]

The concept of time preference plays an important role in intertemporal choice theory. In Paul Samuelson's *Discounted Utility Model* published in 1937, the time preference of the trading agent is manifested as the discount rate for future utility. Samuelson's intertemporal choice model is not only a standard example of public choice, but also a template for mainstream economics to describe economic behavior.[24] Behavioral economics research has found that time preference has significant internal inconsistency. As time extends, the discount rate shows a downward trend, that is, hyperbolic discount; the discount rate of returns is greater than the discount rate of losses; the discount rate of small amount returns is greater than the discount rate of large amount returns, etc.[25] Nevertheless, time preference remains a very useful concept in describing the characteristics of trading behavior, and its status in economic theory has not been diminished as a result.

Time preference and valuation time domain are both concepts related to time, and they are closely related. Generally speaking, trading agents with strong time preferences will also choose a shorter valuation time domain; conversely, trading agents with a clear short-term valuation time domain will usually have a strong time preference.

Although there is a certain connection between the two concepts, the difference between them is obvious. First, the emphasis of the concepts is different. Consumer time preference focuses on describing the overall characteristics of the trading agent. Theoretically, the time preference of the trading agent is relatively stable; while the valuation time domain corresponds to the trading strategy and changes with the choice of trading strategy. Second, the expressions of the two are different. The expression of consumer time preference is the time discount rate. The stronger the time preference, the higher the discount rate, and the greater the discount of future utility valuation; the expression of the valuation time domain is the time interval, and the length of time is used to measure the valuation time domain. The last and most important point is that time preference reflects the subjective wishes of the trading agent; while the valuation time domain reflects the rational choice of the trading agent.

Notes

1. Harry Landreth, David C. Colander (2014) History of Economic Thoughts (trans: Wen ZHOU), 4th edn. Posts & Telecom Press, Beijing, p 236–237.
2. Harry Landreth, David C. Colander (2014) History of Economic Thoughts (trans: Wen ZHOU), 4th edn. Posts & Telecom Press, Beijing, p 234.
3. Harry Landreth, David C. Colander (2014) History of Economic Thoughts (trans: Wen ZHOU), 4th edn. Posts & Telecom Press, Beijing, p 235.

4. Paul A. Samuelson, William D. Nordhaus (2008) Economics (trans: Shen XIAO), Posts & Telecom Press, Beijing, p 73.
5. John von Neumann, Oskar Morgenstern (1953) Theory of Game and Economic Behavior, 3rd edn. Princeton University Press, Princeton, p 20.
6. Colin F. Camerer, George Loewenstein, matthew Rabin (2010) Advances in Behavioral Economics (trans: Jingtong He, Zifeng SONG, Jidong YANG), People's University Press, p 128.
7. Paul A. Samuelson (2006) Foundations of Economic Analysis (trans: Yao HE), Dongbei University of Finance & Economics Press, p 104.
8. Colin F. Camerer, George Loewenstein, Matthew Rabin (2010) Advances in Behavioral Economics (trans: Jingtong He, Zifeng SONG, Jidong YANG), People's University Press, pp 130–134.
9. Daniel Hausmann (2007) The Philosophy of Economics (trans: Jiangfeng DING), Shanghai People's Publishing House, Shanghai, p 31.
10. Colin F. Camerer, George Loewenstein, Matthew Rabin (2010) Advances in Behavioral Economics (trans: Jingtong He, Zifeng SONG, Jidong YANG), People's University Press, p 127.
11. Jingtong HE, Yi NA (2015) Behavioral Economics—Selection, Intercommunication and Macro Behavior, People's University Press, pp 57–61.
12. Colin F. Camerer, George Loewenstein, Matthew Rabin (2010) Advances in Behavioral Economics (trans: Jingtong He, Zifeng SONG, Jidong YANG), People's University Press, p 176.
13. Ranlin PENG, Biying ZHANG (2004) Cognitive Psychology, Zhejiang Education Press, pp 60–68.
14. Chaoyuan YUE (2005) Decision-making theory and methods, China Science Publishing House, Beijing, pp 140–143.
15. Daniel Hausmann (2007) The Philosophy of Economics (trans: Jiangfeng DING), Shanghai People's Publishing House, Shanghai, p 227.
16. The relationship of light between neighbouring buildings is a factor to be taken into account in real estate property trading. Under other condition being equal, real estate property with sufficient light will be welcomed by more buyers; while those with obstructed light will lose value as a result.
17. Although Coase Theorem does not directly address the relationship between the property rights system and trading activities, nor does it address the content of the expected return function, it expresses the importance of property rights for trading activities in one way. The Coase theorem holds that, compared to the effectiveness of the property rights system, the ownership of property rights itself is not important. An effective property rights system is the fundamental factor in the efficiency of resource allocation in trading systems.
18. Eirik G. Furubotn, Rudolf Richter (2015) New Institutional Economics—A Paradigm of a Transaction Cost (trans: Jiangqiang JIANG, Changyuan LUO), Gezhi Publishing House, Shanghai, p 63.
19. James A. Dorn, Steve H. Hanke, Alan A. Walters (2014) The Revolution in Development Economics (trans: Zuhui HUANG, Wenhua JIANG), Gezhi Publishing House, Shanghai, p 91.
20. James A. Dorn, Steve H. Hanke, Alan A. Walters (2014) The Revolution in Development Economics (trans: Zuhui HUANG, Wenhua JIANG), Gezhi Publishing House, Shanghai, p 95.
21. James A. Dorn, Steve H. Hanke, Alan A. Walters (2014) The Revolution in Development Economics (trans: Zuhui HUANG, Wenhua JIANG), Gezhi Publishing House, Shanghai, p 95.
22. Anticipation has two meanings, one of which refers to the prejudgement or prediction of the development and change of things. In English, the corresponding word is forecasting. The other meaning refers to the agent's expectation and conception of the results of the development of things. Corresponding to the English word expectation. According to the division

of subjective and objective attributes, anticipation in the first layer of meaning is contained in the agent's knowledge of the objective laws and trends of change, with more objective components; in the second layer of meaning, it mainly involves people's aspirations based on the cognition of the development of things, which contains more subjective components. In the logic of human behavior, prejudgement generates expectation and expectation determines behavior. anticipation must be formed under the dominance of cognitive abilities. Due to the differences in cognitive ability and the quality and completeness of the information possessed by people, the anticipation formed by people will vary greatly in terms of clarity and precision. Generally speaking, due to the ambiguity and roughness of human language, these two features systematically affect people's trading decision-making behavior, resulting in people's trading behavior with great uncertainty and individual differences. In order to overcome the ambiguity and roughness of anticipation, people will rely on the support of beliefs, which makes the trading decision-making behavior more or less gambling in many cases. Based on the characteristics of anticipation, it is often difficult to formulate the expected return function of trading as a deterministic function.

23. In terms of process, anticipation formation takes place in about five stages, starting with the initial perception formation stage. This is a hazy, fuzzy, rough-around-the-edges judgement. At this stage, anticipation is not yet finalized and is highly variable. The second stage is the stage of initial reinforcement of anticipation. Further information and evidence is needed to reinforce the hazy anticipation, and this process is mostly done subconsciously. The third stage is the stage of anticipation corroboration. In this stage, anticipation starts to become clearer from being hazy. This process has entered the conscious level. The fourth stage is the stage of anticipation interaction. Every person lives on a huge social network, which generates mutual influence and interaction through social network relationships. When one's anticipation is clarified, one tries to influence those around him or her, and is also influenced by others. Through the process of mutual influence, mutual infection, mutual questioning, mutual verification and mutual support, the formation of anticipation is finally completed. The fifth stage is the stage of anticipation determination. After going through the above four stages, people have formed a relatively stable and clear anticipation. However, the adjustment of anticipation does not come to an end, and people will still adjust their anticipation if there are any challenges to their existing anticipation. This, however, requires a longer process.
24. Ludwig von Mises (2015) Human Behavior, Shanghai Academy of Sciences Press, p 450.
25. Colin F. Camerer, George Loewenstein, Matthew Rabin (2010) Advances in Behavioral Economics (trans: Jingtong He, Zifeng SONG, Jidong YANG), People's University Press, p 193.

Chapter 6
Principle of Maximizing of Expected Return

The maximization of expected return is the basic principle of trading economics, the basic rule for trading agents to make decisions, and the basis for logical deduction and model construction of trading economics return.

6.1 Three Dimensions of Trading Motivation

Trading motivation is the direct inducement that triggers the action of the trading agent. It is located in the middle position between trading behavior and the ultimate goal of the trading agent in the logical structure, and plays a connecting role in the trading dynamics system.

Once we establish the concept of trading on the accounting matrix, the trading motivation of both household agents and enterprises will immediately become clear. To sum up, there are three types of trading motivations for trading agents here below.

The first is the profit-seeking motive. The direct purpose of the profit-seeking motive is to increase asset return through trading. Investment and production trading are usually carried out under this motive. From the direct purpose of trading, stop-loss trading can also be classified under the profit-seeking motive. Stop-loss trading is a trade that stops wealth loss by reducing held assets, including selling falling stocks and real estate; selling off inventory backlog products at low prices; stopping production of loss-making products.

The second is the asset diversification motive. The trading agent optimizes the structure of the accounting matrix by increasing asset diversity. The asset diversification motive is an original motive for trading. One can imagine the scene when people first tried trading, their trading motive was to increase asset diversity. A family with sheep wants to get cattle, and a family with cattle wants to get sheep. The first trade in human history may have been carried out under this original motive.

Z. Wang, *Trading Economics*, Contributions to Economics,
https://doi.org/10.1007/978-981-99-9875-3_6

Thirdly, the liquidity motive. Trading agents enhance their payment ability by improving the liquidity of the accounting matrix. Liquidity is so important in modern economic activities that all enterprises and households must pay great attention to liquidity management, investing a large amount of trading resources in liquidity needs.

The three types of motives correspond to the three dimensions of asset value, asset structure, and asset liquidity on the accounting matrix. The trading motives between household agents and enterprise agents have an interactive relationship. In response to the diversification motive of household assets, enterprises will strive for product innovation to meet consumers' demand for trying new products.

6.2 Principle of Maximizing Expected Return[1]

Maximizing expected return is a restatement of the principle of maximizing utility and maximizing manufacturer profits in the context of transaction economics. The net value of the accounting matrix changes over time, and decision-makers choose as far as possible the most ideal trading strategy and timing to achieve the maximum growth of asset net value. This is a basic rule that all trading agents abide by. We call this rule the principle of maximizing expected return[2]: Traders always hope to improve their financial situation as much as possible through trading. Except for random trading as an approximate treatment, trading agents always choose the best timing and optimal strategy to implement trading within the allowed range of trading time, in order to maximize expected return.

The principle of maximizing expected return excludes random trading. Random trading refers to trading with relatively small amounts, which are trading that decision-makers can ignore in terms of the effect on optimizing the accounting matrix. Trading agents determine the upper limit of random trading based on the scale of assets they own. When the trading amount is less than the upper limit of random trading, decision-makers no longer pay attention to its trading effect and no longer include it in the normal decision-making process.

The principle of maximizing expected return emphasizes the role of trading time limit. The trading time limit is a time constraint that trading agents must face. Like liquidity constraints and regulatory constraints, it imposes restriction on the strategy choices of trading agents. The stronger the time limit constraint, the less room for strategy choices for trading agents. Point-in-time trading has almost no room for choice. Despite this, the maximization principle still unifies all trading to the maximization mode. The maximization principle requires trading agents to make maximization choices within the range of transaction time, which allows dominant strategies to incur losses during a certain period, as long as they can ultimately achieve maximum return in the valuation time domain. This gives trading agents the flexibility to make decisions in the face of actual situations.

Essentially, the principle of maximizing expected return is a different expression of the efficiency rule. In layman's terms, efficiency is to achieve as much gain as possible with as little payment as possible. The maximum efficiency rule governs all activities in the universe, whether in the micro or macro world. This rule is expressed in many theories and disciplines in different ways. Evolutionary selection theory believes: In a system where disorder gradually becomes a natural law, complex organisms (including humans, and more broadly, social organizations) can only persist by acting in a way that increases their probability of survival and self-replication. Therefore, evolutionary-selection theory proposes that individuals tend to maximize the expected value of a variable that measures their survival and reproductive adaptability or success rate.[3]

It should be pointed out that maximizing profits does not guarantee consistency with the principles of maximizing happiness. This is not merely due to differences in measurement units and calculation methods, but more importantly, differences in inherent logic. In consumer trading, people tend to experience happiness as much and as long as possible, the more repetitions of happiness, the better; but the attitude towards pain is just the opposite, regardless of the size of the pain, always hoping that the pain will end as soon as possible, preferably once and for all. The structural difference for happiness and pain distorts people's pursuit of maximizing profits to some extent. Taking the two interchangeable options of buying a private car and taking a taxi as an example, from an accounting perspective, taking a taxi is far more economical than buying a private car without reducing comfort and convenience. From the principle of maximizing expected return, taking a taxi is a possession strategy. However, in reality, people still prefer to buy private cars as their first choice for travel arrangements.

The study of behavioral economics reveals the causes behind the deviation of the trading agent from the principle of maximizing expected return have been revealed. Behavioral economics has found that each trading corresponds to a different mental account, and these accounts are separate and cannot be equivalently substituted. The reason for non-"rational" behavior that deviates from the principle of maximizing expected return is due to the existence of payment isolation in trading decisions. When payment behavior is temporally and spatially isolated from each consumption behavior, it largely eliminates the pain of people's payments, thereby obtaining more pleasure in the consumption process. For example, in the case of a buffet, the accommodation fee of a star-rated hotel usually includes the breakfast buffet fee, but because the breakfast consumption is temporally and spatially isolated from the accommodation fee payment, the entire fee that includes the breakfast fee is corresponded to the accommodation account, while the mental account of breakfast consumption does not make a payment. Therefore, guests will have a sense of pleasure in eating breakfast without spending money. Although consumers also know the truth that wool comes from sheep, they still prefer such payment arrangements. The same is true when buying a house to live in, people will record the cost of buying a house on the mental account of the property, forming a corresponding relationship between assets and costs, while the mental account of living consumption does not generate payment or only a small amount of payment for living, which is completely different from the feeling of renting.

In fact, payment isolation is only part of the reason for the apparent deviation of trading behavior from the principle of maximizing expected return. It is also common for people to buy some useless goods in pursuit of trading utility. The so-called trading utility, also known as trader surplus, refers to the difference between the actual trading price and the "expected value". Trading driven by trading utility are what people often call "taking advantage" behavior, although people all understand the truth of "taking small advantages and suffering big losses", but many times people still find it hard to resist its temptation.[4]

The principle of maximizing expected return can only be regarded as an approximate rule followed by trading activities. Fortunately, in a large number of trading activities in the trading system, the phenomenon of trading behavior deviating from the principle of maximizing profits caused by the separation of mental accounts only accounts for a very small proportion, and will not generate a subversive change to the overall operation rules of the trading system.

Compared to the principle of profit maximization in neoclassical economics, expected maximization is the result of the subjective judgment of the trading agent based on the information it holds, and does not represent the objective trading result. Due to the strength in constraint conditions, different information possession situations, and differences in information processing capabilities, trading agents will naturally have different choices in dominant strategies.

The principle of maximizing expected return only expresses the subjective desire of the trading agent to achieve the best result, not the actual result. Whether the trading agent can realize its initial desire depends on many uncertain factors. In reality, the results of trading often deviate from expectations, and in most cases, the situation is not as good as expected. Through the evaluation of the trading results, decision-makers will continuously revise and improve their decision parameters, and continue to self-adjust and optimize. We call trading agents with these characteristics limited rational decision-makers, to distinguish them from the "economic man" in mainstream economics.

In fact, it is impossible for trading agents with limited rationality to truly maximize profits or utility, and economists have long noticed this. Economist Xiaomin Liang wrote in the preface to the Chinese version of Thaler's "*Misbehaving*": Take myself as an example, I can talk about utility maximization and marginal analysis, but how many times have I thought about these principles in actual consumption? And in retrospect, many of my consumptions are definitely marginal utility zero, or even negative. These irrationalities have occurred many times in many people. Even those who created these theories, would they make choices completely rationally? It seems that this flashlight of economics is used to illuminate others, but in the end, no one has been illuminated.[5] Thaler pointed out the same problem: When ordinary people encounter optimization problems, they often cannot solve them, and they are far from finding solutions. Even if they go to a medium-sized grocery store to shop, there are countless combinations of goods they can buy within their budget. Have they really made the best choice? Of course, compared to shopping, we will encounter more difficult problems, such as choosing a profession, type of loan, or spouse. Given the failure rate we observe in these areas, it is hard to say that all the choices people make are optimal. In retrospect, it can be said that almost no one can truly achieve the optimal result, but this does not mean that people are willing to accept bad results.

From the definition of the expected return function, it is clear that trading under all three motives can be covered under the principle of maximizing expected return. It is clear that trading under the profit motive must necessarily aim at maximizing expected return; and the cases of the asset diversification motive and the liquidity motive are no exception. In either case, the trading must result in some improvement in the accounting matrix of trading agents. According to the definition of "gain" in trading economics, the improvement in the accounting matrix will inevitably reflected in the net value of the accounting matrix. Therefore, we also refer to the principle of maximizing expected returns as simply the trading principle.

Notes

1. All human activities can be divided into two basic types if they are classified according to the motives for their behavior: one type of game behavior is aimed at the promotion of interests; the other type is aimed at the protection of one's own interests from being infringed upon. The first type of behavior is aggressive in character; the second type of behavior is defensive in nature. The former can be called aggressive game; the latter can be called defensive game. Most of the game strategies we usually study belong to the category of aggressive games. The research on defensive game behavior is mainly concentrated in the military field, and the famous "The Art of War" can be regarded as a case of defensive game research.

   Due to the difference in game motivation, the two game behaviors obey completely different laws. The objective function of aggressive game is to obtain as much revenue as possible, in this kind of game mode, the two sides of the game in accordance with the principle of maximum expected return to choose, formulate strategies to win–win results for the common acceptance of the end game, to achieve the equilibrium of the game. The defense game is a behavioral mode initiated in a situation where one's own interests are threatened. In this mode, the behavioral objective function is no longer to increase revenue, but to maximize the protection of one's vested interests. In terms of strategy selection, the difference with the aggressive game is that the optimal strategy criterion of the defensive game is no longer how much to increase the gain, but how to cause as much harm as possible to the other party at the smallest cost to itself, so as to break down the fighting spirit of the other party, eliminating or reducing the potential threat to its own interests. Because of these characteristics, the defense game does not have a win–win equilibrium ending, but will show the spiral upward trend of the game cost. Both sides of the game step by step to raise the game budget, increase the destructive force of the attack, until there is a party's chips are consumed. When the game party can not afford the cost of the other side may produce, the loss is far beyond the ability to pay the game budget, the participating parties have to withdraw from the game until.

   For the whole society, the result of aggressive game is to create wealth and achieve win–win situation; while the result of defensive game is to consume wealth and waste resources. People always hope that all interpersonal interactions will be carried out under the aggressive game mode, and as far as possible, no defensive game behaviors will occur. Unfortunately, in the real world, defense games are always frequent. Once people feel their interests are threatened, they will instinctively activate the defensive game mode. This suggests that the trading system in a real world scenario is the result of a mixture of two game modes rather than a single behavioral mode dominated by the principle of maximizing expected return. This implies that the operational state of trading systems may be far more complex than the theories we have constructed, and the uncertainty in the evolution of trading systems is often far beyond our imagination.

Observed from the evolution of human society and transaction system, the probability of occurrence of defense game shows an overall decreasing trend. People have effectively reduced the frequency of defensive games through the construction of the rule of law, rule-making, and strengthening of regulation. Even so, in different fields and at different levels of human society, defense games—wars—that cause great losses to human society occur from time to time. The development of human civilization still has a long way to go.

2. The principle of maximizing expected return is an approximate description of profit-seeking behavior by human. In reality, people are not always in a state of rational thinking, and the measurement of various gains and losses is often disturbed by emotional fluctuations, the extent of which is sometimes even decisive. Under the effect of strong emotions, people are even willing to choose strategies that are unfavorable to them and willingly accept losses. Sometimes, however, people are influenced by their emotions to overestimate the benefits and losses of certain events.

We call the expected return of the trading strategy s corrected by the effect of emotions as the comprehensive valuation, which is represented as E_v, and use $finx(s)$ indicates the index of the emotional intensity of the trading agent induced by the strategy s. $finx(s) > 0$ means that the emotions induced by the strategy s are positive, including pleasure, sanctity, desire, etc.; the larger the value of $finx(s)$, the higher the intensity of the emotion. $finx(s) < 0$ means that the strategy s induces negative emotions, including resistance, pain, loss, self-blame, etc.; $finx(s) = 0$ means that the trading strategy s does not induce any emotional response, and the decision-making process is not significantly disturbed by emotions.

The distribution of the sentiment index $finx(s)$ shows that people's emotions always fluctuate around rationality. The resulting behavior obeys the law of large numbers, and rational behavior, as the expected mean of the law of large numbers, is the limit of a large number of emotionally disturbed behaviors. For trading strategy s, if the expected return under the rational state of the trading agent is $E(s)$, the composite valuation and the expected return satisfy the following relationship:

$$E_v(s) = (1 + finx(s))E(s)$$

The above equation shows that people tend to overestimate the value of a strategy that triggers a positive emotional response, while they tend to underestimate the value of a strategy that triggers a negative emotional response. The above relationship can explain people's decision-making choices when facing the same event, their self-sacrificing behaviors in specific situations, and their idiosyncratic behaviors that are detrimental to others and to themselves. Since the decision-making process is often disturbed by emotions, all kinds of complex phenomena in human society are the result of the intertwining of rationality and emotions. In essence, the principle of maximizing expected return is based on the rule of ranking the advantages and disadvantages of trading strategies based on the size of the value of the expected return function. The larger the value of the expected return function, the higher the ranking of the corresponding strategies. The strategy with the largest expected return function is at the top of the priority list. Aggregate return valuation with the addition of sentiment perturbation provides a different priority ranking than the expected return function, and the difference between the two rankings reflects the degree to which sentiment perturbs the decision. The greater the difference between the two rankings, the more pronounced is the disturbance of sentiment on the decision-making of trading agents. In this case, the gap between economic theories constructed based on rationality or limited rationality and the state of reality is also larger.

3. Roger B. Myerson (2001) Game Theory—Analysis of Conflict (trans: Yin YU, Jianping FEI), China Economic Publishing House, p. 2.

4. Colin F. Camerer, George Loewenstein, Matthew Rabin (2010) Advances in Behavioral Economics (trans: Jingtong He, Zifeng SONG, Jidong YANG), People's University Press.
5. Richard H. Thaler (2018) Misbehaving: The Making of Behavioral Economics (trans: Jin WANG), CITIC Press, Beijing.

Part II
Birth and Structural Evolution of Trading Network

This part consists of seven chapters, covering topics such as the trading community and the creation and structural evolution of a trading network.

Driven by profit motives, trading agents spontaneously seek potential trading partners in a trading community; this forms the seed of a trading network. For greater efficiency, trading agents would constantly invent new trading strategies, creating a widening range of trading phases and an ever more financialized and information-driven trading system.

The structure of a trading network is a natural result of placing certain constraints on the otherwise free-ranging profit motives. As the trading system evolves, the trading network would produce increasingly complex organizational structures, including the layered structure, the phase structure, and the aggregation structure. The "compactness" of the trading system also improves, with the dynamic and nonlinear characteristics increasing day by day.

This topic touches on many branches of the mainstream economics, including market organization theory, industrial organization theory, monopolistic competition theory, and spatial economics. Trading economics not only provides a refreshing theoretical perspective compared with the mainstream theories but also draws richer conclusions. These results show us the strong explanatory and theoretical unification power of trading economics.

Chapter 7
Trading Community

The trading network evolved from the community. Community members have close contacts and naturally become the embryo of the initial development of the trading network.

7.1 Concept of Trading Community

A trading community refers to a relatively stable community of trading agents that are geographically close, have close information exchanges, and have relatively dense trading connections. The trading community is a self-organized community where people establish close information contacts with each other for the purpose of cooperation and exchange, and the degree of aggregation is significantly higher than areas out of the community. Diversity and commonality are two characteristics that the trading community possesses at the same time. Diversity meets trading needs; commonality provides a basis for cooperation.

Within the trading system, the disintegration and reconstruction of the trading community are ongoing at all times. The evolution and changes of cities and changes in the external environment will lead to the disintegration of the original trading community; as long as conditions permit, new trading communities will re-emerge and form new trading network aggregations.

The trading community not only appears in the form of life, such as natural villages and urban communities, but also in the form of industrial clusters and industrial parks. A large number of trading agents with the same phase and highly related phases quickly gather together in a certain place to form an industrial cluster with a dense internal trading network, which is a typical form of a trading community. Within the industrial cluster, the degree of aggregation is usually very high, even far higher than the degree of ordinary trading communities. Industrial parks are another common form of trading community. Each industrial park usually has a theme, and

Z. Wang, *Trading Economics*, Contributions to Economics,
https://doi.org/10.1007/978-981-99-9875-3_7

trading agents in the park usually have the same trading phase. Although there are not many trading between trading agents, they will share the park's infrastructure and market information, thereby forming a strong competitive advantage.

The trading community is open, and new trading agents will move in at any time, and old agents will move out. The openness of the trading community is not only the basis for the expansion and development of the trading community, but also the condition for the interconnection between trading communities to form a trading network.

In the trading community, neighbors can become potential trading partners. The larger the trading community, the easier it is for community residents to find trading partners among their neighbors. As the number of agents on the same phase in the trading community increases, market competition will become more intense, and the trading efficiency of the community will also improve.

Trading of residents in the trading community is not limited to within the community, many of the trading need to be completed across communities. Despite this, the trading community is still an important support for residents to conduct trades. They obtain information from the trading community and form their own judgments to the trading situation; some basic, high-frequency trades usually need to be completed within the community.

The community members change due to migration, and the relationships between residents will also adjust accordingly. The trading community is a form of life, its evolution goes through the life cycle of embryonic development, growth and development, prosperity and expansion, and aging and degeneration.

The trading community is the basic unit of the trading system, and it is the smallest and most primitive trading system. No matter how large the trading system is, it is formed by the aggregation of trading communities. The trading community provides us with a small trading system template, limiting research to a single community can greatly simplify the research process.

7.2 Trading Community Capacity

Trading communities vary in size, and we use community capacity to measure their scale. The so-called community capacity refers to the number of trading agents that the trading community can accommodate. If S represents the trading community, the trading community capacity is represented by $|s|$. If the community has N trading agents, we denote it as:

$$|S| = N \tag{7.2.1}$$

Community capacity depends on conditions such as information dissemination efficiency of the community and transportation convenience. The more advanced the information technology and the more convenient the transportation, the lower the cost for the community to achieve close contact between members, and the larger the scale of the trading community. Generally speaking, the size of the community capacity is adapted to the stage of social development. The more advanced the society, the larger the trading community capacity.

Capacity has a significant impact on the characteristics of the trading community. Due to the limitation of the group size, low-capacity communities receive relatively less information from the outside and also respond relatively slowly to external information. Remote mountainous areas and peripheral small towns are usually areas where low-capacity communities live, where community residents live peaceful and their lifestyle remains almost unchanged. The situation in large-capacity communities is just the opposite. Due to the large number of residents, each trading agent is an information channel. The community receives a large amount of information from the outside and can respond to the external environment changes in a timely manner.

7.3 Community Openness

Community openness refers to the intensity of the trading community's connection with the outside world, measured by the proportion of residents involved in cross-community trades in the community. If the number of residents in the community involved in cross-community trades is n, and the community capacity is N, then the community openness is:

$$Op = \frac{n}{N} \tag{7.3.1}$$

Op represents the community openness, with a value between 0 and 1. If Op is 0, it means that the trading community is completely closed; if the openness s is 1, it means that the community is in a completely open state, and all community residents participate in cross-community trades. Usually, only a part of the members in the trading community will participate in cross-community trades, some residents' trades are completed within the community, and the openness of the trading community is between 0 and 1.

The openness of the trading community is constantly improving with social development. Tracing back to the early human society, the openness of the trading community was very low. In traditional societies, a few neighboring villages formed a trading community, with little contact with the outside world, almost like an isolated island in the trading community. In modern society, almost every community is highly open, even in remote villages, the openness has been greatly improved.

Although the increase in community openness is a basic trend in the evolution of the trading system, it is not the case that the higher the openness, the better for society. When the community completely loses its trading function, it will give rise to many social problems, including a decrease in the convenience of life, urban traffic congestion, and a slack social organizational structure, etc. To maintain the basic trading function of the community, it is necessary to keep the community openness at an appropriate level.

7.4 Agglomeration of Trading Communities

The community agglomeration is an indicator used to describe the network structure of the trading community, and it is defined as follows. We first define the agglomeration of any resident a_i in the community Ω. Suppose there are k neighbors in the community with trading links to a_i, among the k residents with trading links to a_i, there are M trading links, and the agglomeration of the trading agent a_i is defined as:

$$\delta_i = \frac{2M}{k(k-1)} \tag{7.4.1}$$

On the basis of trading agent a_i at agglomeration δ_i, we can calculate the agglomeration of the trading community Ω as:

$$\delta = \frac{\sum_{i=1}^{N} \delta_i}{N} \tag{7.4.2}$$

The agglomeration δ of the trading community Ω is the average value of the residents' agglomeration. In communities with high agglomeration, the trading connections between residents are relatively close. High-agglomeration communities form clear boundaries with neighboring communities, which is a relatively stable organizational structure. The rural areas of traditional society are typical examples of high-agglomeration communities.

The value of agglomeration δ is between 0 and 1. If the agglomeration value is close to 0, it means that the trading links of the trading community are concentrated on a few agents, and there are no trading links between other residents. This is an extreme situation meaning that the community structure no longer exists and no longer has community functions. The trading community can neither provide an environment for information sharing and communication among residents, nor can it build an effective constraint mechanism on residents' behavior, and can only be regarded as a loose group.

When the community agglomeration value is close to 1, it means that the members of the trading community have very close trading relationships, belonging to a super-agglomeration community. Residents of super-agglomeration communities have high behavioral consistency. Under the condition of incomplete information, the super-agglomeration community provides conditions for residents to observe and learn from each other, and the behavior of community residents is easy to become consistent.

Behavioral consistency is a double-edged sword. When community members have not yet accepted a new idea or technology, super-aggregated communities can become a fortress preventing new ideas and technologies from entering. Once a minority of residents in the community begin to accept, with the mechanism of high mutual influence of community residents, the original fortress will quickly become a hotbed of propagation, becoming a demonstration area for new ideas or technologies. Remote rural areas are the rich zones of super-aggregated communities, where the community is almost closed, and new ideas and technologies are difficult to penetrate. High aggregation has become an important reason for these areas to fall into long-term poverty.

The community is the common cornerstone of the trading system and the social system. If the community lacks sufficient aggregation, it will make the seemingly strong social system exceptionally fragile, with even a small external shock, it will fall into a state of panic and chaos. Excessively low aggregation will cause the trading community to lose its self-organizing ability, and it is difficult for the social system to obtain its due resilience.

7.5 Stability of Trading Community

As a part of society, the trading community always maintains dynamic exchanges with the outside world in terms of information, goods, and personnel. The stability of the trading agents constitutes an important feature of the trading community.

If the capacity of the trading community Ω at time step t is N, where there are N' agents inherited from time step $t-1$. The stability index of the trading community Ω is defined as follows:

$$S_t = \frac{N'}{N} \tag{7.5.1}$$

According to (7.5.1), the stability index S_t of the trading community Ω ranges from [0,1]. When $S_t = 0$, it indicates that the trading community Ω is in an absolutely unstable state, belonging to a completely new community. When $S_t = 1$, it indicates that the trading community Ω is in a highly stable state, belonging to a fully mature community. Generally, the stability of the trading community Ω is between the two extremes, that is, $0 < S_t < 1$, there are some old residents in the community, and some are new immigrants.

The stability of the trading community has a significant impact on the formation of community customs and the maintenance of traditions. Generally speaking, the higher the community stability index, the better the customs and traditions of the community are maintained; on the contrary, the lower the community stability index, the faster the community's customs changes. For those that were once regarded as classics by community residents can easily be lost in the reorganization process of community residents and form a new community appearance.

From the perspective of the evolution process of the social system, when the community is in a period of rapid development, the stability of the trading community is generally low; when society enters a period of stable development, the stability of the trading community rises accordingly. Certainly, for a turbulent society, the stability of the trading community will be destroyed, and this is an extreme situation.

Chapter 8
Generation of Trading Networks

Trading networks are topological structures spontaneously organized by a large number of trading agents driven by the motives of chasing profits, diversifying assets, and liquidity. Undoubtedly, the study of the development, evolution, and operation of trading networks will become a key to revealing the laws of human social and economic activities.

8.1 Generative Mechanism of Barter Network

The networking process of trading networks is a self-organizing process made by trading agents in the pursuit of maximizing their own interests, and it is also a process of effective resource allocation in the trading system.

8.1.1 Initial Form of Trading Networks

Let $\{a_i\}$ be the set of residents of the trading community Ω, and $\{A_i\}$ be the corresponding set of accounting matrices. $a_k \in \{a_i\}$ is any agent in the community, with the accounting matrix A_k. Since the accounting matrices of each trading agent are not identical in structure, through trading, traders can obtain the assets they wish to have, achieving a win–win result. In order to achieve the purpose of trading, agents will release its own trading information to its neighbors. The residents of the community will choose the best trading partner based on the information they have. If a_k chooses a_j as a trading object, the original accounting matrix A_k will be transformed into A_k^j, with an expected return of $E\left(A_k^j\right)$.

In the environment of barter trade, the phases of the trading parties are completely symmetrical. Each party is both a buyer and a seller, with completely identical trading

Z. Wang, *Trading Economics*, Contributions to Economics,
https://doi.org/10.1007/978-981-99-9875-3_8

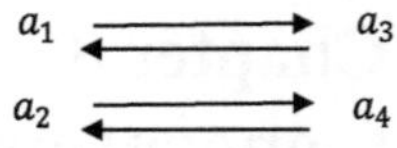

Fig. 8.1 The initial form of trading network

status. a_k is a trading agent in the community Ω. Based on the understanding of the community neighbors, he exchanges goods with his neighbor a_j at a certain rate. According to the principle of maximizing expected return from trading, if a deal is made between the trading agents a_k and a_j, the following two sets of conditions must be met:

$$E(A_k^j) > E(A_k^i) \quad i \neq j,\ i \neq k,\ j \neq k \tag{8.1.1}$$

$$E(A_j^k) > E(A_j^i) \quad i \neq j,\ i \neq k,\ j \neq k \tag{8.1.2}$$

Under the circumstance of barter, the probability of both parties meeting their trading conditions is very low. The goods that a_j needs happen to be what a_k wants to exchange; and the goods that a_j wants to exchange are what a_k needs. The matching of goods types is key to making the deal. Although the exchange rate of goods is also important, it can be agreed upon through bargaining. Due to the stringent trading conditions, under the barter mechanism, the community's trading activities are relatively rare, and the trading network during this period is relatively sparse, as shown in Fig. 8.1.

To overcome this situation, people reached a tacit understanding within the trading community, that is, at a fixed time and place, those willing to trade would gather together to trade, in order to increase the efficiency of reaching a trade agreement and to reduce the search cost of trading.

8.1.2 Evolution of Trading Network Patterns

Through the accumulation of experiences over a long period of time, people gradually form some consensus: which items are easy to find trading partners for, and which items are not, thus forming the concept of trading assets. a_i, a_j, a_k are three residents in the trading community, where, a_j and a_k wish to give up their items, but the items they are willing to exchange do not match, a_j needs the goods of a_k, but a_k needs the goods of a_i. In this case, although a_i does not have an urgent desire to exchange, if he can benefit from giving a hand to a_k and a_j to meet their trading needs, a_i will participate in this transaction. a_i first trades with a_k, then uses the items exchanged from a_k to trade with a_j. After two transactions, a_j has obtained the items of a_k and a_k has obtained the items of a_i. Both parties have satisfied their trading desires, and optimized allocation of resource has been achieved at the trading system level.

In this process, although the item a_i obtained from a_j is not what he needs, but since the item of a_j is a commonly accepted tradable asset in the community, there

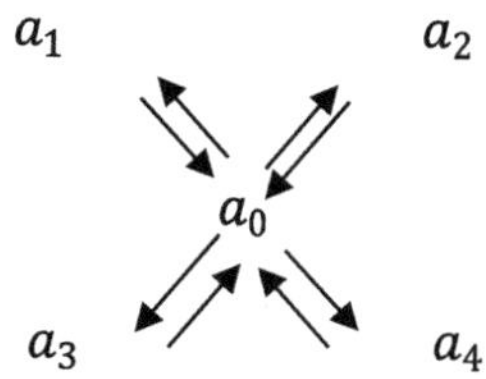

Fig. 8.2 The evolution of trading network form

will be others in the community who need it. As long as the following condition is met, a_i will be willing to help a_j and a_k satisfy their trading desires, that is:

$$E(A_i^k) > E(A_i) \tag{8.1.3}$$

$$E(A_i^j) > E(A_i^k) \tag{8.1.4}$$

According to the requirements of conditions (8.1.3) and (8.1.4), the accounting matrix achieved after the trade between a_i and a_k is optimized, and the accounting matrix is also optimized after the trade between a_l and a_j. The structure of trading network formed by the above transactions is as follows (Fig. 8.2).

In the above exchange network, in order to highlight the special position of the middleman, it is represented by a_0 to distinguish it from other trading agents. In the above trading, the middleman is not for obtaining a specific commodity, but for realizing his own wealth gains by serving other agents. Once the role of the middleman is evolved in the trading system, the matching efficiency will significantly improve, and trading activities will become more active. However, since the trade still remains at the level of barter, the wealth achieved by the middleman has a great uncertainty. If the middleman is left with many sheep and cows, the wealth will suffer a great loss in the event of a plague or wolf attack. It can be imagined that the middleman, facing many huge uncertainties, will undoubtedly be greatly limited in its role as a trading bridge.

8.2 The Generative Mechanism of Monetary Trading Network

When money enters the trading system, the original symmetry between the trading parties is broken. According to the flow of money, trading is divided into forward trading and reverse trading. The reverse trading agent spends money to obtain the desired commodity assets. When evaluating the trading, it needs to assess the cost-effectiveness of the asset, the usefulness of the commodity and the matching of the commodity features, etc.; while the situation of forward trading is much simpler. Due to the homogeneity of money, as long as the trading price is agreed upon, the trader hopes for more forward trading opportunities. It can be seen that the reverse traders are more cautious, and the trading conditions are relatively strict; while the forward traders are more aggressiveness and are on the active side.

Assuming a_k is in the reverse phase in the transaction, under the motivation of maximizing profits, the trading agent a_k hopes to choose a trading object that can realize the maximum expected return. Suppose the community neighbor a_j can meet the requirements of a_k, that is:

$$E(A_k^j) > E(A_k^i) \quad i \neq j \tag{8.2.1}$$

Comparing the conditions that need to be met in barter trade, it can be found that for reverse traders, the trading conditions under the monetary environment have not fundamentally changed from those under the barter environment, and the conditions for optimizing the accounting matrix are exactly the same. The change occurs in the forward traders a_j. For the forward trading agent, the profit can be accumulated continuously through trading, and the goal of maximizing profit does not need to be achieved by a single transaction, but by continuous trading that maximizes trading opportunities. Under such logic, the transaction with a_k only needs to meet the profit condition, that is:

$$E(A_j^k) > E(A_j) \tag{8.2.2}$$

To sum up, under the conditions of monetary trading, as long as any two trading agents in the community Ω, a_k and a_j can simultaneously satisfy the following conditions, a transaction will occur:

$$E(A_k^j) \geq E(A_k^i) \quad i \neq j \tag{8.2.3}$$

$$E(A_j^k) \geq E(A_j) \quad j \neq k \tag{8.2.4}$$

Compared with the conditions of barter (8.1.3) and (8.1.4), it can be seen that the conditions under monetary trading (8.2.3) and (8.2.4) are much looser. The forward trader has few requirements for the trading partner, as long as the trading price is above the break-even line.

The trading agent has an instinct to optimize the accounting matrix, and trading is an effective way to achieve the optimization of the accounting matrix. As time evolves, the conditions of monetary trading undoubtedly create more and more trading opportunities for community residents, and the trading network becomes increasingly dense.

Theoretically, there is a certain matching probability more or less between any two residents in the trading community. The larger the community scale, the higher the probability of the trading agent meeting his trading needs. In reality, cities and villages provide typical cases of the contrast of community scale effects. Compared with urban communities, rural communities are much smaller in scale, and the frequency and scale of trading within the community are much smaller than those in urban communities. The impact of community scale on matching probability determines the tendency of the trading community to expand continuously.

8.3 Improvement of Trading System Efficiency

Under the mechanism of barter, the probability of realizing a trade is much lower than that of monetary trading. Although the defects of the barter mechanism can be partially overcome by introducing the role of middleman, the improvement of trading efficiency is still very limited. We compare the differences between the two trading mechanisms from the perspective of matching probability, thereby revealing the mechanism of trading system efficiency enhancement.

8.3.1 *Matching Efficiency of Barter*

Under the barter mechanism, the efficiency of the two parties in matching trades is directly related to the types of tradable goods in the trading community. The more types of goods, the lower the probability of matching in each transaction. Suppose there are M types of tradable goods in community Ω. For simplicity, we assume that the same type of goods are completely homogeneous; and different types of goods have the same trading frequency. Taking the trade matching process of a_k and a_j in the community as an example, a_k wants to exchange his goods g_k while a_j hopes to exchange his goods g_j. A successful trade matching can only occur if both parties just happen to need each other's goods. From a probability perspective, g_j benig exactly what a_k needs has a probability of $\frac{1}{M}$; and g_k being what a_j needs has the same probability of $\frac{1}{M}$, then the probability of a successful matching between the two parties is $\Pr = \frac{1}{M} \times \frac{1}{M} = \frac{1}{M^2}$.

The matching probability reflects the operating efficiency of the trading system. The matching probability of the barter mechanism rapidly decreases as the number of tradable goods M increases (Fig. 8.3).

Barter is a low-efficiency trading mechanism. As the number of tradable goods increases, the problem of low trading efficiency becomes more prominent, eventually

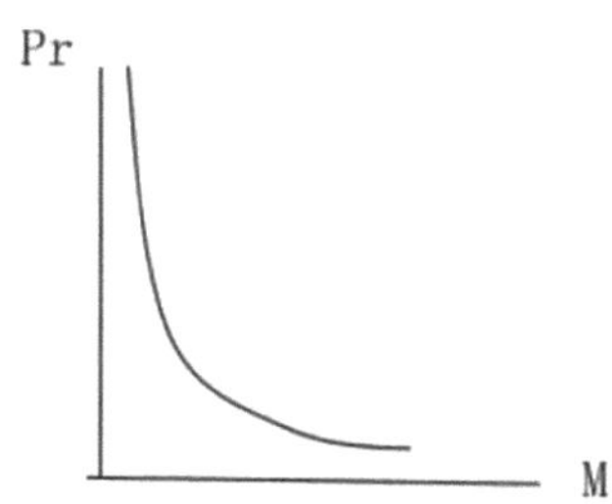

Fig. 8.3 The matching efficiency curve of barter system

becoming an insurmountable obstacle to the evolution of the trading system. For human society to develop, it is necessary to break through the bottleneck that restricts trading efficiency, and introduce a monetary trading mechanism.

8.3.2 Matching Efficiency of Monetary Trading Mechanism

After the introduction of the monetary trading mechanism, the matching process of the trading parties is simplified. The symmetry between the parties' status is broken, thus the complexity of the trading evaluation is reduced, and the matching efficiency of the trading system is greatly improved.

For simplicity, assume that the currency circulated in the trading community Ω is unique. Assume that the trading agent a_k is in the inverse phase and a_j is in the forward phase; there are M kinds of tradable goods in the trading community Ω, and the probability that a_k, who is in the inverse phase, needs a_j to sell the goods g_j is $\frac{1}{M}$; for a_j who is in the forward phase, due to the uniqueness of the currency, the probability of accepting the monetary assets is 1, thus a_k and a_j has a matching probability of $\Pr = \frac{1}{M} \times 1 = \frac{1}{M}$.

Under the monetary trading mechanism, the matching probability curve in the trading system is as follows (Fig. 8.4).

Compared with the barter system, the matching efficiency of monetary trading also shows a downward trend as the variety of goods increases, but the decline is much slower, and the matching efficiency of the two trading mechanisms differs by M times. The larger the trading base of the trading system, the more obvious the advantage in monetary trading efficiency.

In fact, the introduction of the monetary mechanism not only greatly improves the matching efficiency of the trading system, but also fundamentally changes the value orientation of the trading system. Under the barter mechanism, the purpose of trading is to meet certain life needs of the trading agent, and the value orientation is to obtain the use value or utility of goods; while under the monetary trading mechanism, value is abstracted by money, and the low holding cost creates conditions for the shift of trading motive from obtaining utility to accumulating wealth. Money ultimately

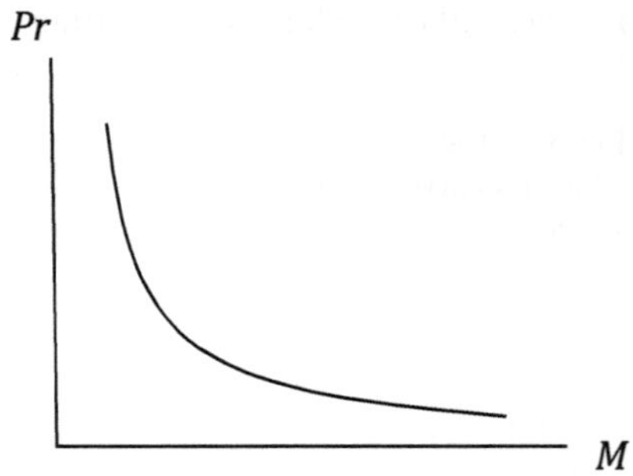

Fig. 8.4 The matching efficiency curve of monetary exchange system

becomes a symbol of wealth. The change in the value orientation of the trading system undoubtedly has a profound impact on the evolution of human society.

8.3.3 Improvement of Matching Efficiency

The matching efficiency of the trading system is an important factor affecting and restricting trading activities. With the development of human society, people continue to innovate, introduce new trading mechanisms, improve the trading environment, and continuously improve the matching efficiency of trading.

After the introduction of money, although the matching efficiency of the trading system has greatly improved, the matching efficiency of the monetary trading mechanism is still $\frac{1}{M}$. In many cases, the low matching efficiency remains an important factor in high trading costs, which to a certain extent suppresses the prosperity of the trading system.

In order to further improve the matching efficiency of trading, the role of middleman has evolved in the trading system. The emergence of intermediaries has further improved the matching efficiency of the trading system.

Assume a_k and a_j are two trading agents in the trading community Ω, where a_k is a general consumer, a_j is a middleman; the community Ω has M types of tradable goods, a_j owns m types of them, the probability of a_k matching a trade with a_j is:

$$\Pr_{kj} = \frac{m}{M} \tag{8.3.1}$$

It is clear that the introduction of middleman further enhances the matching efficiency of the trading system. From the matching probability formula (8.3.1), it can be concluded that the larger the scale of commerce, the more obvious the efficiency improvement effect it brings to the trading system, the lower the search cost of trading, and the greater its role in promoting economic growth. Therefore, the expansion of the scale of commercial organizations and the increase in market concentration are indispensable for improving the efficiency of the trading system.

Restricted by the cost of capital occupation and the scale of the trading community, no mall can provide all goods. To further improve the trade matching efficiency, a new mechanism must be introduced. The e-commerce platform built with the help of Internet technology provides consumers with a fast and convenient channel for collecting information, reducing the search cost of trading to an almost negligible level, and the improvement of the trading system efficiency is unprecedented.

Even so, we cannot assert that the matching efficiency of the trading system has reached its limit. Sometimes, people still need to spend a lot of time in offline markets for on-site selection, investigation, and first-hand experience. In terms of buying a house, furniture, or even a set of clothes, online trading is still not entirely satisfactory. Any trading involving goods with complex quality parameters still poses significant challenges to the e-commerce pattern. With the introduction of artificial intelligence and metaverse technology, we can expect potentially better solutions to the efficiency issues of complex goods transactions.

As the role of internet e-commerce platforms in trading activities becomes increasingly important, the openness of the trading community has greatly increased, bringing about widespread and profound social effects. Based on the further strengthening of interdependence among people, the trend of trading network compactness is more apparent. While the efficiency of the trading system is improving, the vulnerability of the social system will also be exposed, reflecting the contradictions in the evolution of human society.

In the evolution of the trading system, the essential attributes of trade have never changed with or without the participation of trading media. The trading network is always a self-organization process made by the trading agent. Trading agents in the same phase compete with one another, and once they fail, they will be excluded from the trading sequence. Each trading agent must start from satisfying its own desires, with the premise of satisfying the desires of others. Only on the basis of obtaining abundant trading resources to accumulate wealth. This is the operating mechanism of Adam Smith's "invisible hand" and the self-organizing mechanism of the trading network.

8.4 The Enhancement of Trading System Functions

The enhancement of trading system functions is an important aspect of its evolution, mainly reflected in the specialized division of labor, financialization of trade, and informatization, etc. The trading system improves efficiency and enhances resource allocation capabilities through function enhancement.

8.4.1 Specialization of the Trading System

The specialized division of labor makes the structure of the trading network increasingly complex and dense. To discuss the generation of the trading network, we needs to first analyze the process of specialization. Specialization is an inevitable result of the trading system evolution and a necessary path to improve efficiency. Under the barter mechanism, the introduction of middleman may induce a lower level of specialization, but due to the constraints of the matching efficiency of the trading system, specialization cannot be deepened. Therefore, we directly discuss the specialized division of labor under the monetary trading mechanism.

In the monetary trading system, wealth accumulation can only be achieved through forward trading. Enterprises separated from families to take on the main role in the foward phase, and their basic function is to provide people with tools for wealth creation and accumulation. In the discussion of specialization, we mainly focus on forward trading. Suppose $a_i \in \Omega$ is a trading agent in the trading community Ω, $\{g_k\}$

is the set of tradable goods in the trading community Ω. Here, g_k is used to represent both a tradable good and a trading strategy. $E_i(g_k)$ represents the expected return of trading agent a_i when executing the forward trading strategy g_k. If for the trading agent a_i, the trading strategy g_k yields a return that exceeds other trading strategies after repeated implementation, that is:

$$\frac{E_i(g_k)}{t \to \infty} > \frac{E_i(g_l)}{t \to \infty} \quad k \neq l \qquad l = 1, 2, 3 \ldots \tag{8.4.1}$$

For trading agent pursuing maximum profit, a_i will definitely choose and stick to the strategy g_k, continuously repeating the trading strategy g_k, which forms the specialty of the trading agent a_i in production or operation. All trading agents $\{a_i\}$ in the trading community Ω are all follow the above principle, carrying out long-term, repetitive trading activities to achieve their maximum expected return. In this process, the trading community Ω has formed a pattern of specialized division of labor.

According to the above mechanism, we examine the stable equilibrium state of the evolution of division of labor in the trading community. Suppose a and b are any two residents in the trading community, they each have two strategies to choose from, which are to participate in division of labor and cooperation Y and to continue to work alone N; suppose the proportion of residents in the community who choose to participate in division of labor and cooperation is p, and the proportion of residents who choose to work alone is q, the payoff matrix of the game in division of labor in the trading community Ω is as follows.

In the payment matrix, Table 8.1, $E(b, a)$ represents the expected return of trading agent b when cooperating with trading agent a, $E(a, b)$ represents the expected return of trading agent a when cooperating with trading agent b; $E(a)$ represents the expected return of trading agent a under the strategy of working alone, $E(b)$ represents the expected return of trading agent b under the strategy of working alone. Obviously, under this payment structure, when the two inequalities $E(a, b)p > E(a)$, $E(b, a)p > E(b)$ are both satisfied, the division of labor and cooperation strategy (Y, Y) is the Nash equilibrium solution to the game in the division of labor; if any of these conditions are not met, the strategy of working alone (N, N) becomes the Nash equilibrium solution of the aforementioned game.

Table 8.1 Division of Labor Payoff Matrix

		a	
		Choose division Y	Choose to work alone N
b	Choose division Y	$E(b, a)p$,$E(a, b)p$	0,$E(a)$
	Choose to work alone N	$E(a)$, 0	$E(a)$,$E(b)$

We can prove that both solutions are stable evolutionary equilibria. First, let's look at the division of labor strategy as an invasive strategy in the trading community. When the working alone strategy N is in a dominant position, at this time, for $E(a,b)p < E(a)$ and $E(b,a)p < E(b)$, at least one of the inequalities holds. Suppose $E(a,b)p < E(a)$ holds, in this case, we can always find a sufficiently small coefficient δ, which still satisfies $E(a,b)(p+\delta) < E(a)$, ensuring that the working alone strategy N continues to dominate in the community.

Similarly, when the division of labor strategy Y has already occupied the trading community Ω, $E(a,b)p > E(a)$, $E(b,a)p > E(b)$ both can be established, we can find a small invasion amount δ, so that $E(a,b)(p+\delta) > E(a)$, $E(b,a)(p+\delta) > E(b)$ continue to hold.

For the trading community Ω, the threshold for Y and N to switch dominance is $p^* = \frac{E(a)}{E(a,b)}$. Since the initial state of the trading community is N dominant, the division of labor strategy Y, as an invading strategy, must break through the threshold p^* to ultimately become the dominant strategy. However, the invasion strategy Y cannot reach the threshold in the trading community Ω through progressive accumulation. When the proportion of division of labor strategy Y is low, it cannot bring good return to the residents, and therefore cannot become a strategy option for the community residents. This falls into the logical cycle dilemma of the chicken and the egg. The only way out of the dilemma is mutation, that is, residents quickly change their working alone strategies and accept the division of labor strategy in a short period of time.

In fact, the trading community has the conditions to brew mutations. Due to long-term neighboring, in the limited-scale trading community, information sharing among residents forms a complete information game environment. Residents understand each other's skills. In such an environment, even during the period when the working alone strategy is dominant, the division of labor strategy can still quietly accumulate strength. After slow technical accumulation, when some residents' technical expertise significantly exceeds others, community residents will form a consensus on their technical expertise, and some residents will choose to give up working alone and seek to trade with residents with expertise. The threshold for specialized division of labor may be quickly broken.

We can imagine the life scene of a traditional community, where every household makes wine, and within the community, neighbors know the wine flavor of each household. Technology is a continuous accumulation process, and early technology is the basis for later accumulation. After a long time of technology accumulation, the gap among the brewing technologies of community residents gradually widens, until more and more residents give up brewing at home and buy the best wine from the best brewing household. Because it is profitable, the residents with the best brewing technology will also take brewing as a profession, specifically brewing for neighbors. This story vividly illustrates that specialized division of labor requires the community to provide special basis, and stable neighbor relations are the prerequisites for division of labor. Once the division of labor strategy becomes the dominant strategy in a few communities, it will quickly break through the original dominant trading mode of the trading system through the spread among communities and become the dominant trading strategy.

It should be noted that the threshold for the division of labor strategy in the trading community p^* will change with the change in the structure of the payment matrix. The higher the payment received by the division of labor strategy, the lower the evolutionary threshold p^*; and the payment of the division of labor strategy $E(a, b)$ is proportional to the efficiency advantage of the division of labor strategy. The more obvious the advantage, the larger the value of $E(a, b)$. The efficiency of division of labor is closely related to the technical advantages of the dividers. The more prominent the technical expertise, the more obvious the advantages of division of labor efficiency. This logical relationship shows that with the continuous dominance of working alone strategy, the technical expertise accumulated by residents becomes more prominent, and the threshold for the dominance of division of labor strategy p^* will show a continuous downward trend. With the help of time, the evolution of the trading system towards specialized division of labor is inevitable.

The difference in the accounting matrix of the trading agents is the premise of trading activities. The initial trade in the trading community appears based on the initial difference in the accounting matrix. The initial difference in the accounting matrix may come from the natural environment in which the trading agents live, or it may come from personal abilities and interests. The initial difference in the accounting matrix promoted the initial trading activities of the community, and trading further promoted specialized division of labor. Specialized division of labor in turn will expand the difference in the accounting matrix of trading entities, forming a continuously strengthening positive feedback process. The accounting matrix structure of blacksmiths and carpenters must be clearly differentiated, with the blacksmith's main assets concentrated on iron products and related raw materials and the carpenter's asset allocation concentrated on wooden products and timber. Other industries, such as tailors, doctors, herdsmen, farmers, etc., have their own unique accounting matrices, and the unique accounting matrix promoted by specialization has strengthened the mutual dependence of trading agents, providing a demand basis for intensified division of labor and cooperation. The positive feedback mechanism of trade and division of labor is shown in Fig. 8.5.

After specialized division of labor, the trading phase of the trading community presents a diversified trend. The trading agent $\{a_i\}$ $i = 1, 2 \ldots N$ is differentiating into more and more phases, and different specialties correspond to different

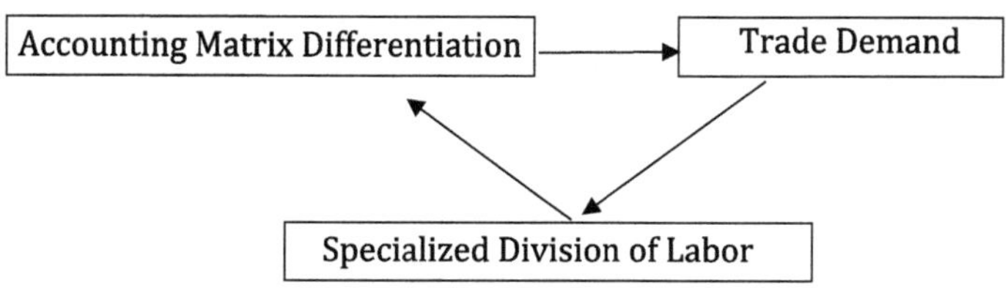

Fig. 8.5 The forward feedback mechanism of trading and division

phases. $\{a_i(g_k)\}$ represents the set of trading agents with commodity g_k as the specialty, representing the corresponding phase group in the trading community Ω. Thus, a corresponding relationship is formed between the phase group of the trading community Ω and the trading base, that is: $\{a_i(g_k)\} \leftrightarrow \{g_k\}, k = 1, 2 \ldots M$.

In the process of the division of labor evolution in the trading system, each agent has to consider not only its own constraints and endowment advantages, but also the division of labor choices of other agents in the trading community, to avoid the situation of excessive crowding in a certain phase, imbalance between supply and demand, and excessive competition. The process of specialization selection and professional skill cultivation of trading agents always follow the principle of maximizing profits, and hence the process of specialized division of labor in the trading system is spontaneously adjusted, maintaining the dynamic balance pattern of trading. Once the division of labor conditions of a certain industry are no longer met, the trading agent a_i will withdraw from the original phase and enter into a new phase, the original division of labor balance in the community Ω will be changed, and a new division of labor balance will be sought through market game.

8.4.2 Progressive Division of Labor in the Trading System

The specialized division of labor in the trading system is not completed at once, but presents a progressive evolutionary pattern. Driven by the profit motive, the trading agents continuously accumulate their own advantages in order to make their comparative advantages more prominent in competition.

With the improvement of the trading institutions, the trading cost gradually decreases. The uncertainty of the trading process is improved, and the production process originally completed by a single company may be broken down into several links, the direct consequence of which is the expansion of the trading base.

Assuming that community Ω further progresses the division of labor based on the original division of labor $\{a_i(g_k)\}$ $k = 1,2\ldots M$, the production process of commodity g_k is broken down into m parts or production links:

$$g_k = \{g_k^l\} \quad l = 1, 2 \ldots m \tag{8.4.2}$$

$a_i(g_k)$ is any agent in the industry set of g_k $\{a_i(g_k)\}$, when the profit realized from focusing on a single production link is greater than that from completing all production processes by itself, that is:

$$E_i(g_k^l) > E_i(g_k) \tag{8.4.3}$$

If in $\{a_i(g_k)\}$ there exists an agent a_j that is complementary and superior to a_i, and its profit structure satisfies the following condition:

$$E_j(g_k^{-l}) > E_j(g_k) \tag{8.4.4}$$

g_k^{-l} represents the remaining process in addition to g_k^l in the production process of g_k. When the industry set $\{a_i(g_k)\}$ shows the above matching relationship, the progression of division of labor will occur. We call the above matching condition the division of labor progression condition.

When the division of labor progression condition is met, the trading agent, in pursuit of maximizing profits, will spontaneously seek trading partners with matching relationships and form a division of labor and cooperation relationship, leading to the deepening of the division of labor. The trading agent a_i focuses on the production of g_k^l, giving up the production of g_k^{-l}; a_j gives up the production of g_k^l and focuses on g_k^{-l}, both sides play their comparative advantages, and through cooperation they elevate the production efficiency of g_k^l and g_k^{-l} to a higher level, thereby gaining larger profits and achieving stronger competitiveness.

Noodle shops on the streets of Tokyo rarely produce their own noodles. They buy noodles from businesses that specialize in noodle production. The location of the noodle shop is very important, they usually choose busy streets where the rent is expensive. Buying noodles from outside can save a lot of shop space and reduce the use of employees. Noodle manufacturers can produce in places where the rent is cheap. The division of labor and cooperation between the noodle shop and the noodle supplier is beneficial for both parties to reduce costs and provide high-quality and inexpensive products to the market.

In the division of labor progression condition, there are two implicit prerequisites: one is that each party involved in the division of labor has a clear comparative advantage in their further refined division of labor, which ensures that efficiency can be improved after the progression of division of labor; the second is that the subdivided market $M(g_k^l)l = 1, 2, 3\ldots$ must be large enough to ensure the producers of g_k^l have a sufficiently large profit margin. These prerequisites indicate that the division of labor is a gradual process, requiring a foundation in both technical reserves and market development. This explains why different trading systems have significant differences in the intensity of division of labor, and explains the gap between urban and rural markets in terms of division of labor.

Due to the constraints of the division of labor progression condition, each large-scale division of labor progression in the trading system requires a long period of accumulation. During the cycle of the division of labor progression, trading agents accumulate experience in continuous iterations of trade and production, form their own comparative advantages, and accumulate strength to meet the next progression of division of labor.

Use g_k to represent the intermediate goods of the initial division of labor; g_k^i to represent the intermediate goods after the second division of labor; $g_k^{i,j}$ to represent the intermediate goods after the third division of labor; …; $g_k^{i,j,\ldots l}$ to represent the goods after multiple divisions of labor, these intermediate goods at different levels have a subordinate relationship, that is:

$$\begin{aligned} g_k &= \{g_k^i\} \quad i = 1, 2, 3 \ldots \\ g_k^i &= \{g_k^{i,j}\} \ j = 1, 2, 3 \ldots \\ &\ldots\ldots \end{aligned} \tag{8.4.5}$$

On different levels of segmented markets, the market capacity decreases step by step:

$$M(g_k) > M(g_k^i) > M(g_k^{i,j}) > \cdots > M(g_k^{i,j \cdots l}) \tag{8.4.6}$$

In the sequence (8.4.6), $M(g_k^i)$ represents demand for the trading target g_k^i, that is, the market capacity of g_k^i. Due to the characteristic of decreasing market capacity in segmented markets, the levels of division of labor in any market are necessarily finite. The relative price of each industry's final product in the trading system and the scale of investment required for organizing production determine the maximum level of division of labor. Suppose the market capacity corresponding to the product g is $M(g)$, the minimum effective scale for maintaining independent production is Q_0, then the maximum level of market division of labor must satisfy the following condition, that is:

$$M(g) > M(g^i) > M(g^{i,j}) > \cdots > M(g^{i,j \cdots l}) > Q_0 \tag{8.4.7}$$

The gradual shrinking of market segmentation is the result of static analysis. Because the division of labor can effectively improve the production efficiency of the industry, the production cost continues to decrease during the division of labor, which will promote the price decrease and lead to market expansion.

In Fig. 8.6, D represents the market demand curve, S_1 and S_2 represent the supply curves before and after the progression of division of labor. With the progression of the division of labor, production efficiency is improved, and both producer surplus and consumer surplus will increase. The supply curve is pushed downward from S_1 to S_2. Under the condition that the demand curve D remains unchanged, the market capacity expands from M_1 to M_2, which provides conditions for further progression of the division of labor.

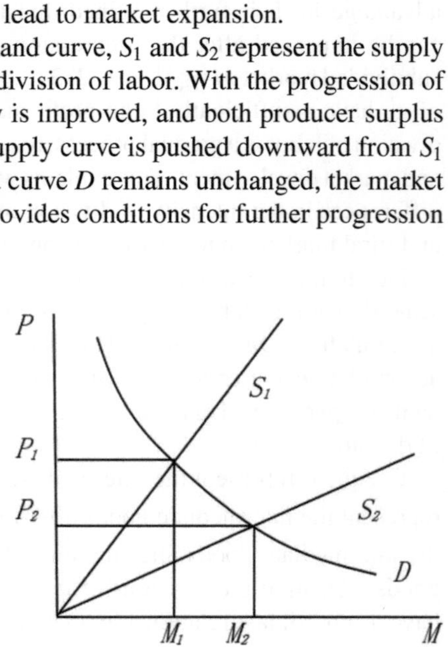

Fig. 8.6 Change of supply and demand due to the labor division advancement

Market capacity is a key constraint on the progression of division of labor, and to enhance the depth of division of labor, it is necessary to break through the constraints of market capacity. There are two ways to do this: one is to increase the openness of the trading community, expand the trading radius of the trading agents, and engage in more cross-community, cross-regional, and cross-border transactions, breaking through the limitations of original community scale. Various market barriers, including market access restrictions, trade barriers, etc., are obstacles to the openness of the community in the trading network. How to break down market barriers and achieve market connectivity is a key measure to increase market capacity and promote the progression of division of labor. The inherent logic of globalization stems from the trading system's ultimate pursuit of the progression of division of labor. Regardless of how international geopolitical relations evolve, the trading system's pursuit of efficiency will not change, and the trend of global integration will not change. According to the above analysis, the positive feedback mechanism of the progression of division of labor in the trading system is shown in the following figure.

In the feedback relationship shown in Fig. 8.7, dismantling trade barriers is the most difficult. Dismantling trade barriers brings a great impact on the existing interest pattern, which will be inevitably resisted by vested interest groups. The increase in social welfare may not promote the dismantling of trade barriers successfully. The current trend of anti-globalization thinking confirms this.

The second effective way to break through the constraints of market capacity is standardization. By standardizing product parts, different industries and products can share part of the supply chain, expanding the originally narrow upstream market to meet the conditions for further progression of division of labor. Its feedback relationship is shown in the following (Fig. 8.8).

Since industrialization, the standardization of production has been continuously advancing, leading to the continuous deepening of the division of labor, and the complexity of the trading network has also reached an unprecedented level.

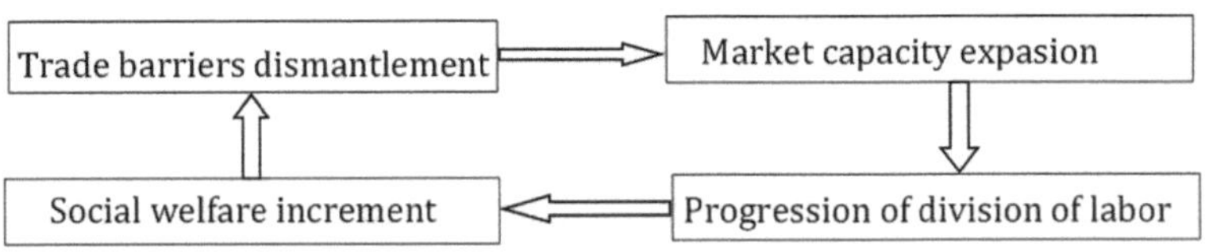

Fig. 8.7 The feedback loop of progression of division of labor

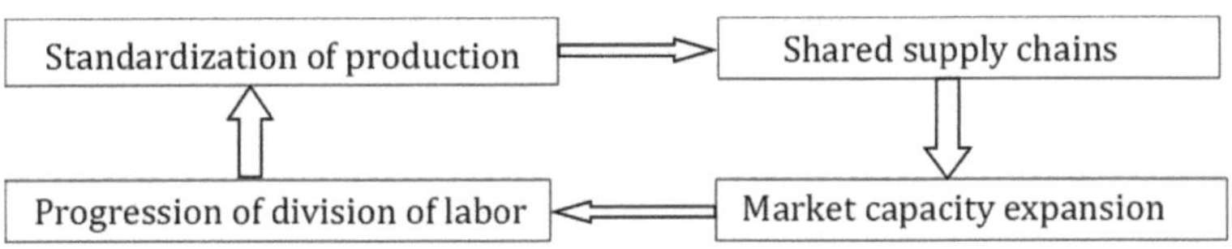

Fig. 8.8 The feedback loop of progression of division of labor

Comparing the two ways of division of labor progression, it is not difficult to find that compared to the unified market plan, the implementation of the standardized production plan faces less resistance. Advancing the standardization of production will not significantly touch the interests of vested interest groups, and all types of groups in the trading system will benefit from it. At the macro level, the efficiency of the trading system is improved, and the ability to utilize resources is further enhanced, which is a typical Pareto improvement process.

8.4.3 The Emergence of Government

Every trading agent has the motive to minimize costs and maximize profits, which determines that the trading network will inevitably choose an efficiency-first evolutionary orientation. Everyone wants to surpass others to become a winner and does not want to become a victim of others' plunder. The inherent conflict of trading motives accompanies the entire process of human social evolution. The prerequisite for the effective operation of the trading network is that each trading agent makes independent decisions under the guidance of real information and in a voluntary state. This requires the trading system to maintain a good trading order. Order is the greatest public demand in human society, and the government was born out of this demand. It is the inevitable result of the evolution of the trading system from simplicity to complexity. The more complex the trading system, the more frequent the trading and the larger the scale of trading, the more prominent the importance of trading order.

As a form of organization, the government needs a considerable amount of input to maintain its operation. Only when the trading system has developed to a sufficiently large scale, the cost of the government to maintain the order of trading becomes worthwhile. The relationship between cost and benefit determines that the demand for government public services always grows with the evolution and upgrade of the trading system. The services provided by the government to the public must match the stage of evolution of the trading system, neither excessive nor insufficient. In the early days of mankind, the scale of the trading system was very limited and the public demand for order was very limited, thus the corresponding government functions were very simple. By today's standards, it can at most be considered as the budding state of the government. From the overall development trend of human society, the trading system is undoubtedly evolving towards the direction of continuous expansion and increasing complexity, and accordingly, the scale and functions of the government will inevitably become larger and more important.

8.5 Financialization of the Trading System

When money enters the trading system, financialization becomes an inevitable process, which is the inevitable result of the trading agent pursuing the maximization of profits. The financialization of the trading system refers to the process in which the proportion of financial assets in the total assets of the system continues to rise. The role of financialization is to release the willingness to trade, enhance the ability of the trading system to allocate resources, and achieve the improvement of trading efficiency. On a micro level, financialization enhances the trading ability of the trading agent and maximizes the function of the trading agent pursuing return.

According to the principle of maximizing expected return, we can deduce the conditions for the emergence of financialization in the trading system, and construct the micro-mechanism of financialization in the trading system. Let a_i and a_j be two trading agents in the trading community Ω, and the trading strategy sets of the two agents at time t are S_i and S_j respectively. Assume the funding gap of a_i executing the trading set S_i is ΔC, the trading set that the existing funds can support is $S_i' \subset S_i$, the difference set between the two trading sets is $\Delta S_i = S_i - S_i'$; unlike the case with a_i, a_j has a surplus of funds ΔC when executing the trading set S_j; $E(S_i)$, $E(S_j)$, $E(\Delta S_i)$ respectively represent the maximum expected return of the three strategy sets.

If a_i is required to pay interest I by financing ΔC in some way to a_j, and the probability of achieving the expected return $E(\Delta S_i)$ by implementing ΔS_i through financing is p^*. The condition for a_i being willing to raise funds is:

$$E(\Delta S_i)p^* - I > 0 \tag{8.5.1}$$

For a_j who provide funds, it is necessary to consider both the safety of the principal and the rate of return. If the performance probability of a_i is p, and the default probability is q, the condition for a_j being willing to finance is:

$$pI - q\Delta C > 0 \tag{8.5.2}$$

Therefore, we get the payment matrix of the financing trading for a_i and a_j as follows (Table 8.2).

Table 8.2 Financing trading payment matrix

		a_j	
		Y	N
a_i	Y	$E(S_i') + E(\Delta S_i)p^* - I$ $E(S_j) + pI - q\Delta C$	$E(S_i') + E(\Delta S_i)p^* - I$ $E(S_j)$
	N	$E(S_i')$ $E(S_j) + pI - q\Delta C$	$E(S_i')$ $E(S_j)$

In the payment matrix, Y represents the financing strategy, and N represents the strategy without financing. The payment matrix shows that when $E(\Delta S_i)p^* - I > 0$ and $pI - q\Delta C > 0$ are both met, (Y, Y) is the only Nash equilibrium of the game.

When either $E(\Delta S_i)p^* - I \leq 0$ or $pI - q\Delta C \leq 0$ is met, (N, Y) or (Y, N) is a Nash equilibrium; when $E(\Delta S_i)p^* - I \leq 0$ and $pI - q\Delta C \leq 0$ are both met, the Nash equilibrium of the game is (N, N). Financial trading only occur in the trading system when the strategy combination (Y, Y) is a Nash equilibrium. Therefore, the condition for financial trading to occur in the trading system is $E(\Delta S_i)p^* - I > 0$ and $pI - q\Delta C > 0$, rearranged to get:

$$E(\Delta S_i)p^* > I \tag{8.5.3}$$

$$I > \frac{q}{p}\Delta C \tag{8.5.4}$$

Combine (8.5.3) and (8.5.4):

$$E(\Delta S_i)p^* > I > \frac{q}{p}\Delta C \tag{8.5.5}$$

From (8.5.5) we get:

$$E(\Delta S_i)p^* > \frac{q}{p}\Delta C \tag{8.5.6}$$

Let $r = \frac{E(\Delta S_i)}{\Delta C} - 1$, representing the expected return of the trading ΔS_i, which is a capital return indicator in accounting, substituting it back into (8.5.6) we get:

$$(1+r)p^* - \frac{q}{p} > 0 \tag{8.5.7}$$

Rearranging (8.5.7) gives the financialization condition of the trading system:

$$(1+r)p^* > \frac{1-p}{p} \tag{8.5.8}$$

Equation (8.5.8) contains the conditions for the emergence of financialization in the trading system. As can be seen from (8.5.8), under the principle of maximizing expected return, financial trading activities will inevitably emerge in the trading system.

The financialization condition (8.5.8) consists of two parts. The left side of the inequality represents the expected return condition of the borrower, and the right side of the inequality represents the risk level of the lender. The logic expressed by the financialization critical equation is that the lower the financial security of the trading environment, the higher the conditions required for the emergence of financialization. Return and safety are the two dimensions of the emergence of financialization. Only when the return can offset the potential losses caused by risk will financial activities occur.

The financing trading in the financialization conditions can be bond financing, loan financing, or equity financing. For equity financing, the expected dividends serve as the return on the investment of principal. The probability of the invested company going bankrupt is equivalent to the probability of principal loss, and other situations are exactly the same as bond financing.

The financialization condition (8.5.8) indicates that in the monetary trading system, financial trading have probabilistic characteristics. As long as the conditions are met, financial trading will occur. There are two key parameters in the financialization condition (8.5.8), which are the probability of successful trading p^* and the performance probability p. p^* reflects the certainty of the trading environment. The more stable the trading environment and the higher the certainty, the greater the probability of successful trading; the more unstable the trading environment and the higher the uncertainty, the lower the probability of successful trading. The performance probability p not only contains the behaviour characteristics of a_i, but also reflects the credit level of the trading environment. Only when both stability and credit level reach a certain standard, financial activities may emerge in the trading system and gradually evolve into a financial industry.

In the financial trading payment matrix, although (N, Y) and (Y, N) are both Nash equilibrium solutions with no actual significance, they have great enlightening significance in our understanding of the financial evolution process of the trading system. They represent a transition stage. For the two sets of conditions $E(\Delta S_i)p^* - I > 0$, $pI - q\Delta C \leq 0$ and $E(\Delta S_i)p^* - I \leq 0$, $pI - q\Delta C > 0$, once any set of conditions is met, the trading system enters the early stage of financialization. Through the bargaining between the trading parties, when one party with strong trading desires is willing to make concessions, the financialization conditions $E(\Delta S_i)p^* - I > 0$, $pI - q\Delta C > 0$ can be expected to be met. Taking the set of conditions $E(\Delta S_i)p^* - I > 0$, $pI - q\Delta C \leq 0$ as an example, the trading agent a_i is the main beneficiaries of financial trading, with a strong willingness to trade, but trading can only be implemented after finding a partner. If a_j has surplus funds, a_i as the party with a strong willingness to trade will find a_j and offer attractive conditions. For example, a_i is willing to pay a higher interest rate I, in order to reduce a_j 's concern about default, and is willing to provide guarantees or collateral to increase a_j 's trust in it. In this case, a_i's performance probability p increases and default probability q decreases accordingly, thus satisfying a_j's trading conditions, that is $pI - q\Delta C > 0$.

If conditions $E(\Delta S_i)p^* - I \leq 0$, $pI - q\Delta C > 0$ hold in the trading system, it indicates that the trading conditions of a_j are satisfied, showing a strong willingness to trade, while the trading conditions of a_i are not met. If a_j concedes to a_i by reducing the interest rate I until the trading conditions of a_i satisify $E(\Delta S_i)p^* - I > 0$, the financing trading will be achieved.

Based on the combination of trading conditions, we can divide the financial evolution process of the trading system into three stages:

The first stage is the non-financialization period of the trading system. Both conditions for financialization are not met, that is, $E(\Delta S_i)p^* - I \leq 0$, $pI - q\Delta C \leq 0$, the system stays on the (N, N) equilibrium solution. During this period, even if the trading system has entered the stage of monetary trading, money is only an auxiliary means of trading and has not become the trading object. The characteristics that may be presented during this period are social instability, lack of mutual trust among trading agents; the market size is small, and the scale of wealth accumulation is small. In the history of human social development, this period corresponds to the long early period of agricultural society.

The second stage is the early stage of financialization of the trading system. During this period, the conditions for financialization have been partially met, that is, $E(\Delta S_i)p^* - I > 0$, $pI - q\Delta C \leq 0$ or $E(\Delta S_i)p^* - I \leq 0$, $pI - q\Delta C > 0$ holds. As the operation time of the trading system accumulates, money continues to precipitate in the trading system, the accounting space of the trading system begins to differentiate, some trading agents accumulate more money, and the financial conditions of the trading system gradually mature. Compared with the non-financialization period, the early stage of financialization is relatively short. We have argued that as long as one party meets the financialization conditions, it will become a booster for the other party to meet the financialization conditions. Once financial activities emerge, driven by the profit motive, trading agents will inevitably imitate one another, financial trading strategies will quickly spread in the trading system, and eventually evolve into stable strategies in the trading system.

The third evolution stage of the trading system is the financialization stage. The financialization conditions are fully met, that is, $E(\Delta S_i)p^* - I > 0$, $pI - q\Delta C > 0$ are both satisfied. Once the process of financialization begins, the ability of the trading network to allocate resources will greatly enhance, and the efficiency of the trading system will rapidly increase. This period corresponds to the industrialization age of human society.

The conditions of financialization not only clarify the mechanism of financial trading emergence, but also reveal the conditions for the deepening of the financial system. With the evolution of the trading system, the stability of the trading environment continues to improve, the level of credit continues to enhance under the support of an increasingly improved legal environment, and the degree and depth of participation in financial trading by trading agents will be strengthened. When financial trading enter the historical stage of specialized division of labor, financial institutions, in order to achieve the goal of maximizing profits, will inevitably strive to accelerate the deepening of the financial system. The profit-seeking motive of financial institutions will drive them to develop more financial products to meet customer needs for financing, risk avoidance, and capital investment. On the other hand, due to the increase in the supply of various financial products, the price of financial products decreases, making it easier for trading agents to meet the conditions of financialization, providing more trading opportunities. Trading agents can use the support of various financial products to release liquidity constraints, obtain more profits, and achieve a win–win situation for finance and trading.

8.6 Informationization of the Trading System

In order to achieve the maximum profits, trading agents hope to capture as many opportunities as possible to obtain trading profits. The expansion of the information set is an important way to maximize profits. Driven by this motive, the demand for information in the operation of the trading system is constantly increasing, and the informationization of the trading system is inevitable. The informationization of the trading system refers to the process in which the importance of information in the trading system is enhanced and the proportion of trading related to information in the total trading volume is constantly increasing.

Suppose a_i is any agent in the trading community Ω, and the information set he owns is I_t, the set of trading strategies induced by the information set is S_t; after information enhancement, the obtained information set is I_i^*, and the induced strategy set is S_i^*, where, S_i corresponds to the maximum expected return $E(S_i)$, S_i^* corresponds to the maximum expected return $E\left(S_i^*\right)$. Obviously, the following relationship holds:

$$I_i \subset I^*,\ S_i \subset S_i^*,\ E(S_i) < E(S_i^*) \tag{8.6.1}$$

Based on the principle of maximizing expected trading return, a_i, in order to maximize expected return, will try to enhance its information set as much as possible. Due to the limitation of information cost, whether a_i will enhance the information set depends on the relationship between information cost and derived return.

Assume $I_i^* = I_i \cup \Delta I_i$, ΔI_i represents the part of information enhancement, $C(\Delta I_i)$ represents the cost that the trading agent a_i needs to pay to obtain ΔI_i, including time cost and monetary cost. According to the principle of maximizing expected return, the necessary condition for the trading agent a_i to enhance information is:

$$E(S_i^*) - E(S_i) > C(\Delta I_i) \tag{8.6.2}$$

The condition of information enhancement indicates that as long as information can bring benefits, the trading agent will be willing to pay for the information. Thus, there is a potential information market in the trading system. As long as the market mechanism exists, the market will evolve in two directions: one is specialized division of labor. The repeated iteration of trading will inevitably lead to specialized division of labor and continue to deepen with the progression of division of labor; the other is market expansion. Market expansion and specialized division of labor complement and promote each other. Specialized division of labor not only improves the quality of information supply but also reduces information costs, stimulating trading agents to release more information demand, promoting the rapid expansion of the information market, and guiding the information upgrade of the trading system.

The informatization of the trading system will produce two results: one is to enhance the information basis of trading and improve the ability of the trading network to allocate resources; the other is the increasingly close internal connections of the trading system, and the trading network will become more compact with the support of informatization. With the advancement of the informatization of the trading system, the supply of information will continue to improve. On this basis, trading behavior continues to optimize, the mode of production organization continues to upgrade, and the mode of social management continues to improve.

8.7 Increase in Trading Phases

Once the trading network is formed, driven by the profit-seeking motive of the trading agent, the trading system will emerge more and more trading phases with the densification of the trading network. The tendency of spontaneous increase in trading phases will accompany the entire evolution process of the trading system.

8.7.1 Trading Phases

Each trading agent, according to its link characteristics on the trading network, can determine its position in the entire trading network structure, which we call the trading phase of the trading agent. Each trading agent has his own trading phase, just like every organism in the ecosystem has its own ecological niche.

Agents in the same phase share limited trading resources, forming a competitive relationship with one another. The congestion of each phase on the trading network varies, some trading phases are highly competitive, while some phases have relatively low competition intensity.

The concept of trading phase can be generalized to refer to the relative position of the agent on the trading network, or the relative position in a specific society. The generalized phase is a broad concept, which can refer to the position of industrial division, the position under a specific business model, the role in information transmission, or even the position under a specific interest pattern.

The concept of trading phase is widely used in network analysis. It can be used to analyze market competition relationships and changes in industrial structure, and can also be used for issues in institutional evolution, interest game, technological progress, etc. The trading phase is a relative concept, and the same trading agent has different trading phases in different trading activities.

Phase order and phase constraints play a significant role in trading activities, representing two crucial characteristics of the trading phase. Phase order describes the status of the trading phase in the process of price negotiation. Phases with bargaining advantages are referred to as high-order phases, while those in a disadvantageous position are called low-order phases. The higher the phase order, the more apparent the bargaining advantage in the trade. Each trading phase has its own order, determined by the supply and demand relationship faced by the trading phase. The supply and demand relationship is dynamically evolving, and in different scenarios and periods, the supply and demand relationship of trade is always changing, and the order of the trading phase will change accordingly. Despite this, the order of each trading phase in the trading system still has high stability. This is because the formation of the supply and demand pattern depends on the phase structure, and the phase structure of the trading system is relatively stable. For example, the trading phase occupied by farmers is usually low-order. Although the supply and demand relationship in the grain and food market is highly dynamic, closely related to climate change and the spread of pests and diseases, the basic characteristics of the low-order phase of farmers have not changed. The key is that farmers, as suppliers of grain and food, are numerous, while grain dealers, as demanders, are far fewer in number. Each farmer has limited choices of dealers, while grain dealers have a large choice of farmers, which inevitably leads to a disparity in bargaining positions between the two parties.

Traditional industries usually occupy a lower trading phase, while modern service industries and technology-intensive industries occupy a higher trading phase. Globally, the dominant industries of Western developed countries usually occupy the high-end phase of the global value chain, while the industries of developing countries are basically distributed at the low-end phase. Whether within the trading system or globally, the distribution of the order of trading phases directly affects the pattern of wealth distribution. The higher the order of the trading phase, the greater the advantage in the process of wealth distribution. That is why hard-working farmers can never catch up with bankers in terms of income.

Phase constraints refer to the common constraints faced by all trading agents on the trading phase. Taking the farmer's phase as an example, the farmer's phase faces two constraints: firstly, the constraint of arable land resources. Each farmer must be limited by the possession of arable land resources, and all production activities must be based on the support of arable land resources; secondly, all agricultural production activities are subject to the constraints of crop production seasons and growth cycles. This means that there is a rigid upper limit to agricultural production output within a unit of time. In contrast, the constraints of the industrial phase are much weaker. Theoretically, the production scale of industrial manufacturing enterprises can expand indefinitely, and efficiency can be continuously improved through technology progress. This is even more the case for the financial trading phase, where a bank's asset scale can expand from 10 billion yuan to 100 billion yuan, and as long as it meets the regulatory requirements on capital adequacy ratio, the expansion target can be easily realized.

In the trading system, for a low-order trading phase with strong phase constraints, the industry has low competitiveness. Agriculture is a case in point. On this weak phase, farmers are disadvantaged groups in almost all economies, requiring special policy protection. Conversely, the financial industry, due to the combined effect of its higher phase order and relatively fewer phase constraints, it occupies an almost incomparable advantageous position in the wealth distribution of the trading system. For this reason, the government needs to impose strict regulation on the financial industry and restrict its trading activities to a certain extent. This not only prevents the financial sector from plundering the real economy but also avoids the occurrence of systemic risk crises that threaten the safety of the trading system.

Due to the differences in trading phase orders, trading agents always hope to ascend to higher order trading phases through their own efforts, thereby gaining greater competitive advantages. From the perspective of the evolution of the trading system, the pursuit of higher order trading phases by trading agents is an important way for the trading system to achieve efficiency improvement and hierarchical evolution.

8.7.2 Increase in Trading Phases

The number of phases in the trading system is directly related to the evolution of the division of labor in the trading system. Generally speaking, the higher the order of evolution of the trading system, the more complex the network structure of the trading system, the more trading phases it carries, and the higher the operating efficiency of the trading system.

Trading phases are the ecological niches of the trading system, which comply with the distribution principle of ecological niches in the evolutionary system, that is, the system has a tendency to spontaneously generate new ecological niches. In the trading system, through market competition and cooperation, more and more trading phases will also be spontaneously created. As the trading system evolves, the number of trading phases will continue to increase.

The continuous evolution of the trading network provides more and more phase choices for trading agents. Under the agricultural economic form, the trading phases are very simple, mainly including a few countable trading phases such as land management, agricultural production, handicraft manufacturing, and commercial trade. After entering the industrial economic form, the division of labor and cooperation becomes more and more detailed, the market becomes wider and wider, the market radius continues to extend, and the trading phases increase rapidly. In fact, the evolution and development process of the trading system is inevitably accompanied by an increase in trading phases. We call this evolutionary law of the trading system the principle of phase increase in the trading system.

Within the trading system, there are two different types of division of labor. One is the division of labor within the enterprise. The division of labor that Adam Smith first discussed in *The Wealth of Nations* is of this type. He detailed the division of labor within a company producing pins. In the production process of a simple product—a pin—it can be divided into five processes: wire drawing, straightening, cutting, sharpening, and pillow installation. Adam Smith believes that division of labor can improve production efficiency. In his thoughts, division of labor allows the same number of workers to complete much more work, as the proficiency of workers is improved due to division of labor, the time lost due to exchange among jobs is reduced, and the invention of machinery provides convenience for labor, simplifies work, and greatly increases the workload of workers.[1] In Adam Smith's view, division of labor is not only the reason for the increase in corporate production efficiency, but also an important cause of the difference between poor and rich countries. Division of labor allows various products to be manufactured and increased exponentially. In an orderly society, each worker has a large amount of labor products for sale in addition to meeting his own needs. This phenomenon is common in all classes. Due to the great abundance of labor products, they can be provided to the lowest class of people. Therefore, all classes of society become generally affluent.[2]

In addition to internal division of labor, there is another form of division of labor, which does not occur among workers, but among different enterprises. If the first type of division is called internal division, the latter should be called external division or social division. In *The Wealth of Nations*, Adam Smith also discussed the situation of external division, closely linking external division with people's trading behavior. He believes that since most of the help people need is through contracts, exchanges, and buying or selling, it can be seen that the division of labor originally arose from this tendency of human exchange. In the book, he illustrated the relationship between the two with an example: For example, in hunting or nomadic tribes, good bow and arrow makers often exchange livestock or game with others with their bows and arrows. He found that what he got from exchanging with others was more than what he hunted himself. Therefore, for his own benefit, he made bow and arrow making his main job, and thus became a weapon maker. After that, there appeared specialized house builders, blacksmiths or coppersmiths, nitrate makers or leather makers, etc., for the same reason. In this way, everyone exchanges the surplus part of their labor production with others for what they need; thus encouraging people to devote themselves to a specific profession, and to hone and perfect the unique talents or abilities of that profession.[3]

The two different types of division of labor play different roles in the economic system. Both internal division and external division play a positive role in improving the efficiency of the economic system, and both drive the increasement of trading phases.

In the evolution process of the trading network, the differences in the development of different societies or tribes are reflected in the characteristics of the trading network. The speed of the evolution of the trading network ultimately determines the survival of this country or tribe. The principle of trading phase increase can be realized in a wider geographical range through the extremely cruel way of network merger. American historian Jared Diamond provided such a case in his book *Guns, Germs, and Steel: The Fates of Human Societies*: "On the Chatham Islands, 500 miles east of New Zealand, centuries of independence came to brutal end for the Moriori people in December 1835. On November 19 of that year, a ship carrying 500 Maori armed with guns, clubs, and axe arrived, followed on December 5 by a shipload of 400 more Maori. Groups of Maori began to walk through Moriori settlements, announcing that the Moriori were now their slaves, and killing those who objected.

An organized resistance by the Moriori could still then have defeated the Maori, who were outnumbered two to one. ... Over the course of the next few days, they killed hundreds of Moriori, cooked and ate many of the bodies, and enslaved all the others, killing most of them too over the next few years as it suited their whim."[4]

From the description of the story, the most direct reason is the differentiation of trading network structure. A troop of 800 people, trekking long distances to conquer another tribe twice their size, relies on the advantage of organizational management, which is supported by a relatively developed trading network. The Moriori, who occupy geographical and human advantages, did not organize effective resistance, the key is the sparsity of the trading network, failing to organize in the face of sudden external invasion. According to Jared Diamond, "What makes the Maori-Moriori collision grimly illuminating is that both groups had diverged from a common origin less than a millennium earlier. Both were Polynesian people. The modern Maori are descendants of Polynesian farmers who colonized New Zealand around A.D. 1000. Soon thereafter, a group of those Maori in turn colonized the Chatham Islands and became the Moriori. In the centuries after the two groups separated, they evolved in opposite directions, the North Island Maori developing more-complex and the Moriori less-complex technology and political organization. The Moriori reverted to being hunter-gatherers, while the North Island Maori turned to more intensive farming."[5]

Comparing the two economic forms, agriculture shows obvious advantages in wealth accumulation and social division of labor than hunting and gathering, thus developing a complex trading network. Comparing the trading networks of the two tribes, it is not difficult to find that the Maori trading network is denser and more efficient; while the Moriori trading network is relatively sparse, and the connection relationship is relatively single.

In examining the evolution and development of the entire Polynesian society, Jared Diamond found a close relationship between population density and scale and the evolution of trading networks, especially the specialization of trading phases. This reveals that the development of trading networks is accompanied by the evolutionary law of the trading phase increase. As he described, "Economies remained simplest on islands with low population densities (such as the hunter-gatherers of the Chathams), low population numbers (small atolls), or both low densities and low numbers. In those societies each household made what it needed; there was little or no economic specialization. Specialization increased on larger, more densely populated islands, reaching a peak on Samoa, the Societies, and especially Tonga and Hawaii. The latter two islands supported hereditary part-time craft specialists, including canoe builders, navigators, stone masons, bird catchers, and tattooers."[6]

All transactions carried out by the trading agent are completed on specific phases. Agents on the trading network must achieve survival and development through continuous trading activities, which determines that the trading agent must simultaneously enter multiple trading phases to complete different types of transactions. If a certain trading phase cannot bring him profits, the trading agent will choose to exit this phase to ensure that all trading phases entered by the trading agent can bring him profits. As a trading agent pursuing maximum profits, there are two ways to achieve the goal of maximizing profits: one way is to carry out as many transactions as possible to gain profits from the transactions; the other way is to enter as many trading phases as possible to gain profits through as many channels as possible. Generally speaking, for the tested profitable trading phases, as a pursuer of maximum profits, the trading agent will not easily exit, but will increase transactions as much as possible to gain more profits.

Among the various phases that contribute to the profits of the trading agent, some phases contribute more, while others contribute less. In general, because the penetration of information on the trading network takes time, the longer the trading phase exists, the more trading agents will enter, the more intense the competition among the agents on the same phase, and the phase order will gradually decline inevitably. Restricted by the supply–demand relationship, the phase crowded with many trading agents can bring less profits. On the contrary, the newer the trading phase, the fewer trading agents will enter, the less intense the competition, and the higher the phase order. Driven by the profit motive, every trading entity hopes to discover new trading phases and achieve more profits through new trading phases.

We can summarize the above analysis in concise mathematical language: let $a_i \in \Omega$ be any trading agent in the trading community, at time step t, it enters m_t different trading phases to carry out trading, the trading results are reflected on the accounting matrix A_i, the corresponding amount of net asset is $|A_i|$. There is a causal correspondence between the total amount of trading phases m_t and the accounting matrix A_i. To express this relationship, the accounting matrix is denoted as $A_i(m_t)$. At time step $t + 1$, if there are m_{t+1} trading phases that can bring profits to a_i, the following relationship is satisfied:

$$m_{t+1} > m_t, \ |A_i(m_{t+1})| > |A_i(m_t)| \tag{8.7.1}$$

then a_i will enter m_{t+1} and carry out trading in more trading phases. This proves that the trading agent has the motive to try more trading phases.

For enterprises, trading phases are closely related to industrial development and business models. New industries and business models supported by new technologies will create new trading phases, and companies will inevitably create new trading phases while innovating and trying new business models. Families are responders and participants of business models. By participating in new trading phases, they provide market support for new industries, new technologies, new products, and new models, so that new industries and new models can survive and develop better.

Analysis shows that in the evolution process of the trading system, phase increase has a solid micro-foundation, and the profit motive is the driving force for trading agents to continuously create new trading phases. At the macro level, phase increase improves the efficiency of the trading system in allocating resources. By accommodating more trading agents into the trading system to achieve larger scale synergy, so as to enhance the trading system's ability to utilize resources and create value. Phase increase has a foundation at the micro level and a positive feedback at the macro level, and inevitably accompanies the evolution of the trading system.

8.7.3 Trading Phase Restructuring

Schumpeter put forward the innovation theory with distinctive features in his book *The Theory of Economic Development*, elaborating the view that technological innovation is the fundamental driving force for economic development. Schumpeter believes that technological innovation is intermittent and abrupt, and will have a certain degree of impact on the original economic structure, and uses the term "creative destruction" to describe this impact effect.

In real life, we can truly feel the tremendous impact of "creative destruction." E-commerce is a subversion of traditional business models, with unparalleled advantages in improving transaction matching efficiency and reducing transaction costs. Entering this century, e-commerce has risen in China, and then swept all the way, occupying the mainstream in business in a very short time, while the traditional business model that has lasted for centuries can only be relegated to the second line, playing a supporting role in E-commerce. Take Tmall as an example, the transaction volume of the "Double Eleven" online shopping festival in 2009 was only 50 million yuan; 2 years later, in the "Double Eleven" shopping festival in 2021, the transaction volume broke through 540 billion yuan, with an average annual growth rate of up to 117%. The vigorous momentum of E-commerce shows how vulnerable traditional business models are to the competition of e-commerce! In 2021, under the double attack of the "COVID-19" epidemic and E-commerce platforms, nearly 10 million physical stores in China closed, including both small street shops and large business entities. This is a vivid example of "creative destruction."

With the widespread application of technological innovation, new business models form a large-scale substitution for existing business models. In this process, the phase structure of the trading system will be reconstructed, and we call this process the phase restructuring of the trading system. During the phase restructuring process, some phases in the trading system will disappear, making room for new trading phases, and the network structure of the trading system will also be reconstructed. Since the newly born trading phase has higher efficiency, it usually replaces the old phase with fewer phases, resulting in a contraction effect of phase restructuring. Still taking E-commerce as an example, due to the strong scale effect of E-commerce, those who win out can grow into a business giant that includes all kinds of business models in a short time. A single E-commerce platform can almost replace thousands of different types of physical businesses. The phase structure of traditional business divided by industry, wholesale + retail, is replaced by the direct link model of E-commerce. JD.com, Taobao, Amazon, etc., are among the few winning e-commerce platforms.

In the evolutionary process of the trading system, the phase reconstruction triggered by technological innovation will terminate the trend of phase proliferation. The number of phases in the trading network will not only stop proliferating, but will also shrink for a period of time. However, the disturbance of the phase reorganization to the trend of phase proliferation is only temporary. After the redundant phases in the trading network are deleted, the original trading agents will seek business opportunities in the new trading environment, either by integrating into the trading network through phase migration or by finding new trading phases through innovative trading models. After digesting the redundant phases, the trading system will start a new round of phase proliferation. It is certain that the process of the trading system absorbing redundant phases is a time-consuming and laborious painful process, usually involving large-scale unemployment and bankruptcy, and it is an inevitable link in the upgrade and evolution of the trading system.

Notes

1. Adam Smith (2008) The Wealth of Nations, People's Publishing House, p 6–7.
2. Adam Smith (2008) The Wealth of Nations, People's Publishing House, p 8.
3. Adam Smith (2008) The Wealth of Nations, People's Publishing House, p 10–11.
4. Jared Diamond (1997) Guns, Germs, and Steel—the Fates of Human Societies, W. W. Norton, p 53.
5. Jared Diamond (1997) Guns, Germs, and Steel—the Fates of Human Societies, W. W. Norton, p 54.
6. Jared Diamond (1997) Guns, Germs, and Steel—the Fates of Human Societies, W. W. Norton, p 63.

Chapter 9
Expression of Trading Network

The trading network is an abstract network, and the expression of relationships is the essence of the trading network. In order to accurately understand the organizational characteristics of the trading network, we need to introduce an indicator system that reflects the characteristics of the trading network.

9.1 Trading Network Capacity

The capacity of the trading network refers to the number of nodes on the trading network, including the total number of households and businesses, also known as the capacity of the trading system, represented by N.

The capacity of the trading network is a key resource of the trading system. The larger the capacity of the trading network, the stronger the potential for growth of the trading system. Whether the potential of the trading system can be released is very critical to the trading environment. When the trading cost is high, the trading willingness of the trading agents will be suppressed, and the capacity of the trading network will become a floating variable, which will not have an active impact on the trading cycle, but will become a burden on society. Under normal circumstances, only when the trading cost is reduced to an acceptable range, the capacity of the trading network will become a motivating factor to promote the trading cycle. The larger the capacity of the trading system, the stronger the potential economic growth.

In the existing national economic statistics, the number of business agents and household agents are both counted, and we can directly add the two to get the indicator of trading network capacity.

Z. Wang, *Trading Economics*, Contributions to Economics,
https://doi.org/10.1007/978-981-99-9875-3_9

9.2 Node Degree

Assume a_i is any agent in the trading system, its node degree is defined as the total number of trading links with other trading agents on the trading network. If the trading agent a_i has k_i conditions, including forward and reverse trading links, at time step t, then the node degree of trading agent a_i at time step t is k_i. The node degree of the trading agent will change over time, but generally, the fluctuation of the node degree will usually be limited to a relatively stable range. Some trading agents will always have a high node degree, while others may have a low node degree.

Essentially, the node degree reflects the intensity that trading agent participate in the economic cycle. The higher the node degree, the deeper the participation of a trading agent in the economic cycle, and the greater the role it plays in the self-organization process of the trading network. We will observe later that the node degree of the trading agent is a key factor in determining its trading potential.

9.3 Degree Distribution Function

The node degree is a description of the connection of a single node. By putting together the degrees of all nodes in the trading network, we can see the distribution characteristics of the node degrees. We use the degree distribution function to describe it, denoted as $P(k)$.

The degree distribution function depicts important global characteristics of the trading network, and some dynamic properties of the trading network are closely related to the degree distribution function. According to the characteristics of the degree distribution function $P(k)$, the trading network can be classified as a random network or a scale-free network.

The degree distribution of the trading network is very uneven, usually a few agents have a very large node degree, while most agents are at an average but relatively low level, and it is a typical feature of scale-free networks. In the market, the degree distribution reflects the trading structure of the market. In a market where the degree distribution function $P(k)$ is relatively flat, trading opportunities are more balanced; if the degree distribution function $P(k)$ is steeper, it indicates that there is a monopoly in the market. The more severe the monopoly, the steeper the degree distribution function $P(k)$ will be.

For markets that have neither layers nor market makers, the node degree distribution function $P(k)$ is usually quite average. Generally, the node degree of market makers is much higher than that of general market participants. Markets with market makers usually have a steeper degree distribution function, and if it is a market maker market with multi-level layers.

9.4 Trading Network Density

The density of the trading network is an indicator reflecting the degree of evolution of the trading system. Comparing urban and rural trading networks can illustrate the issue. Urban communities have complete infrastructure and dense population, creating an ideal environment for trading, with detailed division of labor and prosperous markets, and a dense trading network; while rural areas have scattered residences and inconvenient transportation, high trading costs, and the trading network is much sparser compared to cities. The more developed the economy, the denser the trading network; the more backward the economy, the sparser the trading network.

For a trading network, if the maximum theoretical number of connected edges is Z, and the actual number of connected edges is M, the network density ω is defined as:

$$\omega = \frac{M}{Z} \tag{9.4.1}$$

For a trading network with a capacity of N, the maximum theoretical value of trading links is $Z = \frac{N(N-1)}{2}$, from which we can get the value of trading network density:

$$\omega = \frac{2M}{N(N-1)} \tag{9.4.2}$$

As can be seen from (9.4.2), the value range of network density ω is [0, 1]. When $\omega = 0$, it means that there is no connection between nodes, but merely a group of isolated points; when $\omega = 1$, it means that all nodes are connected, formed the maximum connection of the trading network.

Network density ω reflects the degree of division of labor in the trading system from one side, and is an important sign of the evolution of the trading system. From the trend of human society, the trading network is always evolving towards increasing density.

For the trading system, the trading network density ω is a dynamic variable, which will show the characteristics of seasonal and economic cycle changes. From a macro scale, the trading network density ω is relative stability. Although we cannot directly obtain the statistical data of the trading network density ω in the current national economic statistical system, we can obtain indirect data from the occupation statistics of national economic. Theoretically speaking, the trading network density ω is positively correlated with the amount of occupational divisions of labor, that is, the more classification, the greater the value of the trading network density ω. Based on this relationship, we can roughly infer the trend of the trading network density ω from the amount of occupational divisions and its changes.

9.5 Trading Network Circulation Rate

The trading network circulation rate is a measure of the degree to which the trading flow is maintained in the trading network cycle, similar to the conductivity index of a circuit. The trading circulation rate is both a dynamic indicator reflecting short-term changes in the trading network and an indicator reflecting the characteristics of the trading network and long-term evolution trend of the trading system.

The trading network cycle is realized through the interaction of a large number of trading agents. Over a period of time, the income flow and expenditure flow are the flow indicators of the trading agent participating in the trading network cycle, and the ratio of the two flow reflects the characteristics of the trading network cycle. We can use the ratio of expenditure flow to income flow over a period of time as an indicator to measure the participation of trading agents in the trading network cycle. Assuming that at time step t, the trading agent a_i has income I_t, and the expenditure is E, then the circulation rate ϑ_t is:

$$\vartheta_t = \frac{E_t}{I_t} \tag{9.5.1}$$

In the calculation formula (9.5.1) of the circulation rate, the income item I_t refers to various incomes of the agent, including labor income, investment income, and the sum of financing. The expenditure item E_t includes both the cash flow supported by income and the cash flow supported by liabilities, and bank deposits are not considered as the agent's expenditure. Under this definition, the circulation rate ϑ_t can be less than 1, greater than 1, but always greater than 0.

There is often a time lag between expenditure and income. The shorter the time examined, the more unstable the circulation rate. If it is calculated on a daily basis, the circulation rate ϑ_t can be infinite, while at other times the circulation rate ϑ_t drops to 0. If it is calculated on a monthly basis, the circulation rate ϑ_t becomes much more stable. If calculated annually, the circulation rate ϑ_t will be even more stable.

Generally speaking, a high circulation rate of the trading system is conducive to active trading and promotes rapid economic growth. If the trading circulation rate is very low, the trading flow on the trading network will be greatly hindered, any injection of trading flow will quickly decay, and the speed of economic growth will inevitably slow down.

In the trading system, the average circulation rate of all trading agents represents the circulation rate of the trading network, that is:

$$\theta = \sum_i \kappa_i \vartheta_i \tag{9.5.2}$$

In (9.5.2), the weight K_i represents the proportion of the trading agent's assets in the total assets of the trading system. Formula (9.5.2) shows that the main factors determining the circulation rate of the trading network are the high-income group and the business agents with a certain scale of assets. They occupy a higher asset weight in the trading system and are the main force determining the circulation rate of the trading network.

In terms of household agents, the circulation rate of the low-income class is higher than that of the high-income class. This is because the low-income class needs to take out a higher proportion of their income to for various expenditure. The circulation rate of enterprises generally does not change with income, but is mainly affected by the macro situation of the trading system. In the perspective of medium and long term, household agents are the determining force of the trading network circulation. The polarized distribution pattern is a key factor in suppressing the circulation rate of the trading network, when the polarization of the trading system exceeds a certain level, the economic cycle will fall into stagnation, and the economy will lose its growth momentum completely.

Income expectations are short-term factors affecting the circulation rate. When income expectations rise, even if the income of households does not change, expenditure behavior may adjust in advance, and the circulation rate increases accordingly. The same is true for enterprises. When income expectations (market expectations) rise, the response of enterprises is to increase productivity or increase investment to expand productivity, thereby stimulating circulation rate. For the trading system, the circulation rate of the trading network changes with changes in income expectations, and the direction of change is the same as the direction of income expectations.

Among the many factors affecting the circulation rate, whether the financial market is developed and whether corporate financing is satisfied have a great impact on the circulation rate of corporate agents. Since the assent scale of enterprises is generally much larger than that of households, any change in the circulation rate of enterprises is obvious to the circulation rate of the trading network. The more developed the finance market, the weaker the inhibitory effect of liquidity constraints on trading, and the greater the choice space for trading agents to make elastic expenditures.

The social security system, tax system, and trading environment will all have an impact on the circulation rate of the trading network. A good social security system, lower consumption tax, and higher inheritance tax are all very helpful for maintaining a higher circulation rate of the trading network.

9.6 Trading Efficiency

Trading efficiency is an indicator to measure the ability of trading activities to create value. At the micro level, we can calculate trading efficiency by the ratio of output benefits to trading volume:

$$e = \frac{v}{s} \tag{9.6.1}$$

In (9.6.1), e represents trading efficiency, s represents trading volume, v represents the value brought by the trading. It should be noted that the value here is not the profit obtained by the trader from the trading, but the national economic value created for the trading system, excluding the component of value transfer.

At the macro level, the overall operating efficiency of the trading system can be measured by the average value of all trading behaviors. With the proportion of each trading in the total trading volume of the trading system as the weight, the trading efficiency μ of the trading system is equal to the weighted average of all trading efficiency values over a certain length of time:

$$\mu = \sum_i \lambda_i e_i \tag{9.6.2}$$

In (9.6.2), λ_i represents the weight of a trading in the trading system.

The above definition is based on the micro foundation. In actual operation, we can use a simpler method to calculate the trading efficiency of the trading system, that is, directly calculate the ratio of output value Y to the total trading volume T of the trading system, that is:

$$\mu = \frac{Y}{T} \tag{9.6.3}$$

From (9.6.3), we can further discuss the relationship between trading efficiency μ and economic growth rate.

Taking the natural logarithm on both sides of (9.6.3) gives:

$$\ln \mu = \ln Y - \ln T \tag{9.6.4}$$

Rearranging (9.6.4) gives:

$$\ln T = \ln Y - \ln \mu \tag{9.6.5}$$

Differentiating both sides of (9.6.5) gives:

$$\frac{dT}{T} = \frac{dY}{Y} - \frac{d\mu}{\mu}$$

Let $dT = \Delta T, dY = \Delta Y, d\mu = \Delta\mu$ substitute into (9.6.5) to get:

$$\frac{\Delta T}{T} = \frac{\Delta Y}{Y} - \frac{\Delta\mu}{\mu} \tag{9.6.6}$$

Let $\frac{\Delta T}{T} = r_T, \frac{\Delta Y}{Y} = Gr, \frac{\Delta\mu}{\mu} = r_\mu$

From (9.6.6) we get:

$$r_T = Gr - r_\mu \tag{9.6.7}$$

It is known that the economic growth rate Gr and the rate of change of trading efficiency r_μ show a reverse trend. When $Gr > 0$, $r_\mu < 0$. From (9.6.7) we know that when $Gr > 0$, the following relationship holds:

$$r_T = Gr + |r_\mu| \tag{9.6.8}$$

When $Gr < 0$, the following relationship holds:

$$r_T = Gr - |r_\mu| \tag{9.6.9}$$

Equations (9.6.8) and (9.6.9) state a fact that in the trading system, whether it is economic growth or economic recession, the change in total trading volume is always greater than the rate of economic growth. When the economy is in an expansion cycle, trading grows at a faster rate; when the economy enters a contraction cycle, trading contracts at a faster rate. We call this phenomenon the leading effect of trading. The leading effect of trading will inevitably affect the moderation of money supply in the trading system. Some scholars have found that both the Cambridge school of monetary theory and the modern quantity school of money underestimate the real demand for money, which may lead to some degree of distortion of monetary policy.[1]

In the long run, trading efficiency reflects the operating quality of the trading system. With increasingly globalization in today's economy, trading efficiency is key to national competitiveness. Economies with high trading efficiency will undoubtedly be in a favorable position in global competition and will occupy the high end of the global supply chain. The evolution of the trading system is highly path-dependent, and in the grand scheme of global competition, today's position is the starting point for tomorrow's competition.

9.7 Trading Network Connectivity

Trading network connectivity is an indicator to measure the efficiency of trading network connectivity. In the trading network, the shorter the link between any two nodes, the higher the connectivity of the trading network. To define the connectivity more accurately, we need to introduce the concept of network distance.

In the trading network, any two nodes may have multiple link paths, and the path with the fewest nodes is called the geodesic between the two nodes. The number of nodes on the geodesic is referred to as the distance between the two nodes. It is obvious that the denser the trading network, the more selections of paths linking two nodes, the shorter the geodesic may be, and the closer the distance between the two nodes. The traffic network in the city is a typical example. How to build a network with the shortest traffic distance between any two points is key to improving urban traffic efficiency.

Assume the trading network has N nodes, its connectivity is defined as follows:

$$\xi = \frac{2}{N(N-1)} \sum_{ij\ i \neq j} \frac{1}{d_{ij}} \tag{9.7.1}$$

In (9.7.1), d_{ij} represents the distance between node i and node j; for two nodes that are not connected, the distance is considered infinite, that is, $d_{ij} = +\infty$. Obviously, the higher the connectivity of the trading network, the more direct and faster the connection between nodes. Compared with the trading network formed by E-commerce and traditional business, the E-commerce trading chain based on the Internet is shorter, the trading is more direct, many intermediate links are reduced, the trading circulation cost is also reduced, and the efficiency of the trading network is improved as a whole.

From an evolutionary point of view, the higher the evolutionary level of the trading system, the higher the connectivity of the trading network. At the early stage of the evolution of trading system, the connectivity of the trading network is usually at a very low level. Along with the evolution of the trading system, the connectivity of the trading network maintains an increasing momentum.

Trading network connectivity is an important organizational structure parameter of the trading system, which reflects the ability and efficiency of resource allocation of the trading system, embodies the evolutionary rank characteristics of the trading system, and has a close relationship with the trading efficiency indicators. Generally speaking, the higher the connectivity of the trading network, the higher the trading efficiency of the trading system; and vice versa, the higher the trading efficiency of the trading system, the higher the connectivity of its trading network.

9.8 Reconnection Rate of Trading Network

The reconnection rate of the trading network refers to the proportion of reconnected trade chains on the trading network within a unit time. According to the needs of the study, we can calculate the reconnection rate of the entire trading network, or the reconnection rate of the trading community, a local area in the trading network, or a specific market.

The reconnection rate is used to depict the game characteristics of the market. In markets with a high reconnection rate, the characteristics of repeated games are obvious, and the strategic choices of trading agents in these markets are generally more cautious and pay more attention to their reputation in the market; the situation is different in markets with a low reconnection rate, these markets have prominent features of random trading, the external constraints of trading agents are less, and the speculative atmosphere in the market is stronger.

In the trading system, the reconnection rate of the consumer goods market and the production goods market is higher, while the reconnection rate of the investment market is relatively lower. From the perspective of single trading amount, the trading amount of markets with a high reconnection rate is usually smaller, while the trading amount of markets with a low reconnection rate is higher.

The reconnection rate of the trading network is a relatively stable characteristic indicator, which is determined by the type of trading in the trading system. Generally speaking, in the early stage of the evolution of the trading system, the level of reconnection rate is relatively low; as the trading system gradually matures, the reconnection rate will show a slow upward trend.

Note

1. Yudong YAO, Zhuhuai XIE, Zeyu KONG (2017) The Theory of Money Demand base on the Perspective of Payment.

Chapter 10
Layered Structure of Trading Network

As a manifestation of complex organizational forms, the trading network has multiple dimensions of organizational structure. The layered structure is an important organizational form formed by the trading network under structural constraints, which has a significant impact on the operation and evolution process of the trading system.

10.1 Layered Structure Induced by Supply Constraints

The layered structure of the trading network is the result of specific constraints. On different layers of the trading network, the focus points of competition for trading agents vary. Trading constraints are a reality that trading agents must face, dictating the choices of trading agents' behavior. There are many types of trading constraints, including liquidity constraints, regulatory constraints, and technical constraints, but the main factors that directly influence the evolution of the trading network's layered structure are supply and trading time limit constraints. For convenience of expression, we collectively refer to these two types of constraints as structural constraints.

Within a specific time limit, the supply capacity of an enterprise is limited. In agricultural and livestock production, the supply constraint mechanism is relatively easy to understand. Whether it is grain supply or meat, egg, and milk supply, suppliers have an upper limit on their supply capacity.

In addition to agriculture, almost all industries that depend on natural resources have supply constraint issues. Industries that use oil, coal, and various ores as raw materials are all strongly constrained by supply capacity. Even manufacturing industries that are relatively distant from resource constraints have an upper limit on their supply capacity within a certain time limit.

The issue of supply constraints is more prominent in pre-industrial societies. The primary factor limiting the supply capacity of family workshops is labor. Family members are always limited, and even if apprentices can be recruited to supplement

Z. Wang, *Trading Economics*, Contributions to Economics,
https://doi.org/10.1007/978-981-99-9875-3_10

manpower, it is still difficult to significantly increase production capacity in a short period of time. The second main factor causing supply constraints in family workshops is space. In traditional societies, expanding homesteads is a very tricky issue, especially in towns.

The main target of supply constraints is manufacturers. The main target of time limit constraints is households. Some trading demands have strict time limits, and almost all trading demands related to food, clothing, housing, and transportation have a certain degree of time limit. People planning to travel need to buy plane or train tickets and book hotels within the planned time period; the transactions required for three meals a day also have clear time limits. Trading time limits mainly constrain reverse trading, and through the interaction of trading, they will inevitably affect forward trading behavior, ultimately affecting the formation of market structure.

10.1.1 Layering of Community Trading Networks

For commodity g, assume that the demand group on trading community Ω is $\{a_i\}_n$, the supplier group is $\{b_j\}_m$ and each supplier has a supply limit; the supply limit of supplier b_j is Q_j.

Assume that the value of the goods provided by supplier b_j is Z_j then it can be expressed as the following structure:

$$Z_j = \overline{\varsigma} - \varsigma_j \tag{10.1.1}$$

where, $\overline{\varsigma}$ represents the average value, ς_j represents the value surplus that supplier b_j can bring to consumers. When the value of the goods provided by supplier b_j exceeds the average level, the consumer surplus $\varsigma_j > 0$; when the value of the goods is below the average level, the consumer surplus $\varsigma_j < 0$; if the value of the goods is exactly equal to the average level $\overline{\varsigma}$, then $\varsigma_j = 0$.

In the goods provided by the supplier $\{b_j\}_m$, if we sort them according to the size of their value, we can get the following sequence:

$$Z_1 \geq Z_2 \geq Z_3 \geq \cdots \geq Z_m \tag{10.1.2}$$

In (10.1.2), Z_1 has the highest value and corresponds to the supplier b_1; then in order are b_2 corresponding to Z_2, b_3 corresponding to Z_3, and so on. Among many suppliers, because Z_1 can provide the most consumer surplus, demanders will inevitably flock to the supplier b_1. Due to the supply limit Q_1, b_1 cannot meet all the needs of $\{a_i\}_n$. In this case, price is the effective means of allocation, b_1 will raise the price until the total demand formed by customers who accept the price P_1 is limited within the supply limit Q_1. After b_1 raise price, the consumers squeezed out by the price will flock to the supplier with the second highest value b_2. b_2 will also raising prices until the remaining purchasing power is not greater than the supply limit Q_2.

According to the above logic, all suppliers will adjust their prices according to the value of their goods until all goods are allocated among the demanders.

In the above price adjustment process, suppliers who provide more consumer surplus to the market get higher value returns, thus establishing an effective market incentive mechanism. At the same time, consumers who are willing to pay higher prices can get higher quality goods and services, and a reasonable match between the value of goods and the payment price is achieved, and the market is cleared.

According to the above market allocation logic, the final market equilibrium structure is formed:

$$\frac{Z_1}{P_1} = \frac{Z_2}{P_2} = \cdots = \frac{Z_m}{P_m} = \lambda \tag{10.1.3}$$

In (10.1.3), Z_j represents the value of the goods of supplier b_j, P_j represents the pricing of supplier b_j for its goods, and λ is the market equilibrium price ratio. The market finds the position of the equilibrium price ratio through constant trial and error. In the trial and error process, consumers will shift from suppliers with lower price-performance ratios to those with higher ones; while suppliers with higher price-performance ratios will raise prices, and those with lower ones will appropriately reduce prices. The formation process of the equilibrium price ratio is both a process of information dissemination and a process of adjustment by trading agents, which takes some time, and this is the lag effect of market equilibrium. The lag of the market reaching equilibrium depends on the speed of information dissemination in the trading community. High-aggregation communities have an advantage in information dissemination, and the lag of market equilibrium is shorter.

At equilibrium pricing, the maximum trading resources obtained by b_j is Q_j, and the realized business income is:

$$V_i = P_i Q_j \tag{10.1.4}$$

According to the price-performance ratio equilibrium relationship, we get:

$$P_j = \frac{Z_j}{\lambda} \tag{10.1.5}$$

Substituting into the income function (10.1.4) we get:

$$V_i = \frac{Z_i}{\lambda} Q_j \tag{10.1.6}$$

In (10.1.6), Q_j and λ are both fixed parameters, so the size of an enterprise's profit depends on how much consumer surplus it provides to the market. The more consumer surplus a supplier provides, the greater the profit realized. The market incentivizes high-quality suppliers with more profit, guiding market participants to contribute more value and achieve maximum social welfare.

Equation (10.1.3) indicates that supply constraints are a key factor leading to market layering. The greater the gap in supply constraints between suppliers of different qualities, the more obvious the market layering, and the more disparate the equilibrium prices in different market tiers. Generally speaking, there is an inverse relationship between quality and quantity, the higher the quality of the goods, the lower the supply limit. From this, we can infer that there will be a progressive magnification structure in the market supply limit.

$$Q_1 < Q_2 < \cdots < Q_m \tag{10.1.7}$$

When supply limits of adjacent layers Q_j and Q_{j+1} exist large gap, it implies that there is also a large gap in the value of the corresponding goods Z_j and Z_{j+1}, as:

$$Z_j >> Z_{j+1} \tag{10.1.8}$$

According to the cost-performance equilibrium relationship (10.1.3), we can get:

$$P_j = \frac{Z_j}{\lambda} >> P_{j+1} = \frac{Z_{j+1}}{\lambda} \tag{10.1.9}$$

Equation (10.1.9) reveals the basic law of market layering evolution: the more dispersed the distribution of supply constraints, the more disparate the supply limits of goods of different qualities, the greater the price gap in layered markets. This law is evident in many markets. The labor market is a typical case. Top-tier actors, famous singers, excellent entrepreneurs, etc., are highly scarce resources in the labor market with huge market value. Their market remuneration is far higher than that of ordinary workers. Despite being a very small group, they can significantly influence the structure of social income distribution.

The same is true in the collectibles market, the fewer the number of artworks in existence, the higher the price. The relationship between price and existence is usually not linear, but is presented in a non-linear exponential relationship. In fact, the pricing distribution of all supply-constrained markets follows the inverse exponential law of the constraint limit.

10.1.2 Cross-Community Market Arbitrage Mechanism

We have discussed the process of achieving equilibrium in community markets under supply constraints, but trading communities are not isolated islands, they are part of a closely connected trading network. There are a lot of information connections between trading communities and cross-community trading.

A trading community is both a relational concept and a geographical spatial concept. Between two adjacent communities, since there are many related information between each other, when the price difference in the community market exceeds a certain limit, cross-community trading will occur. Even in supply-constrained markets, if there is a large price difference between adjacent communities, cross-community trading activities are inevitable. With the increase in cross-community trading, the re-balancing of community markets is realized.

In cross-community trading, the trading costs generated by distance and time consumption are key obstacles, therefore, the price difference between different community markets may always exist.

Assume Ω_1 and Ω_2 are two adjacent communities, their equilibrium states are as follows:

$$\frac{Z_1}{P_1^1} = \frac{Z_2}{P_2^1} = \cdots = \frac{Z_m}{P_m^1} = \lambda_1 \tag{10.1.10}$$

$$\frac{Z_1}{P_1^2} = \frac{Z_2}{P_2^2} = \cdots = \frac{Z_m}{P_m^2} = \lambda_2 \tag{10.1.11}$$

where, λ_1 is the community Ω_1 of cost-effectiveness; λ_2 is the community Ω_2 of cost-effectiveness. Assume Ω_1 cost-effectiveness is lower than Ω_2 cost-effectiveness, that is:

$$\lambda_1 < \lambda_2 \tag{10.1.12}$$

We can rewrite (10.1.12) as:

$$\lambda_2 = \lambda_1 + \Delta\lambda \quad \Delta\lambda > 0 \tag{10.1.13}$$

For any goods Z_i in the market of Ω_1 and Ω_2, the cost-effectiveness in the two community markets are:

$$\begin{aligned} \frac{Z_i}{P_i^1} &= \lambda_1 \\ \frac{Z_i}{P_i^2} &= \lambda_1 + \Delta\lambda \end{aligned} \tag{10.1.14}$$

$$\begin{aligned} \therefore P_i^1 &= \frac{Z_i}{\lambda_1} \\ P_i^2 &= \frac{Z_i}{\lambda_1 + \Delta\lambda} \end{aligned} \tag{10.1.15}$$

$$\therefore P_i^1 - P_i^2 = Z_i \frac{\Delta\lambda}{\lambda_1(\lambda_1 + \Delta\lambda)} \tag{10.1.16}$$

Assume the cross-community trading cost is C, cross-community trading activities must meet the following conditions:

$$P_i^1 - P_i^2 = Z_i \frac{\Delta\lambda}{\lambda_1(\lambda_1 + \Delta\lambda)} > C \tag{10.1.17}$$

Organize the above inequalities to get the condition for cross-community trading:

$$\frac{\Delta\lambda}{\lambda_1} > \frac{C\lambda_1}{Z_i - C\lambda_1} \tag{10.1.18}$$

The condition for cross-community trading (10.1.18) indicates that due to the existence of transaction costs, price differences are allowed between communities. Cross-community transactions will only occur when the cost-effectiveness gap between community markets is large enough.

Looking at the structure of the condition for cross-community trading (10.1.18), the trading cost appears in both the numerator and the denominator, with opposite signs. This structure indicates that the hindrance of trading costs to cross-community trading is not a linear relationship. As trading costs increase, the hindrance to cross-community trading does not rise proportionally, but rises at an exponential acceleration rate. This is easily confirmed in reality, a slight increase in distance will cause a very obvious change in trading volume. Even in the same mall, there is a big difference in sales performance just because of the difference in counter locations.

In condition (10.1.18), trading cost C includes two parts, one part is the transportation cost generated from spatial distance. The farther the two trading communities are, the larger the gap in cost-effectiveness may be. It can be seen that the improvement of transportation conditions will greatly benefit cross-community trading activities.

The other part of trading cost C comes from the time cost that may be generated from cross-community trading. Time cost has a strong relativity. The same time consumption, in the eyes of different trading agents, its cost estimation will have a big difference. Generally speaking, the stronger the economic strength of the trading agent, the higher the value of time, and the larger the time cost consumed in the trading. For this reason, even if the distance between two communities with a large wealth gap is not far, the price gap between the two markets can still be large. In a community with good conditions, because residents have higher time valuation, they will not spend time on cross-community trading to save money, and this results in the equilibrium pattern of expensive commodity prices with good conditions and cheap commodity prices with poor conditions in communities.

The relativity of time cost determines that even among trading agents in the same community, there will be different time cost estimates. The main body of cross-community trading is usually residents with relatively low time costs in the community, retired elderly people are often the main force of cross-community trading.

In the condition for cross-community trading (10.1.18), it also contains another piece of information: the higher the value of the goods, the more cost the trading entity is willing to pay for cross-community trading. In other words, the higher the value of the goods, the larger the market radius. This is easy to understand. People are willing to walk much further to buy a car than to buy vegetables. From this, it can be inferred: low-value goods have a smaller market radius and market segmentation is more common; high-value goods have a larger market radius and are more likely to form a large market pattern.

10.2 Time Constraint Induced Layered Structure

The time limit constraint is an important force in shaping the layered structure of the trading network. Network structures such as industrial clusters and community markets have a very close relationship with the time limit constraint.

10.2.1 Layered Trading Model

Assume $\{a_i\}_N$ is a group of consumer agents (reverse traders) on the trading community Ω, $\{b_j\}_M$ are a group of supplier agents (forward traders) on Ω. Due to the characteristics of the time limit constraint, when the consumer agents choose trading objects, distance and the accompanying trading certainty are key factors in decision-making. A closer distance not only ensures the completion of trading in a shorter time, but also is less affected by uncontrollable factors such as traffic and weather, of which, greatly reducing the uncertainty of trading. In addition, a closer distance allows consumers to easily obtain dynamic information from the other party, which also plays a positive role in reducing trading uncertainty.

According to the above analysis, when consumer a_i chooses a trading object, they first consider the distance of the other party. The closer the distance, the greater the probability that the manufacturer will get the trading opportunity. Therefore, the probability $P_{i,j}$ that supplier b_j is chosen by the trading agent a_i is related to their transportation distance $r_{i,j}$ as follows:

$$P_{i,j} \propto \frac{1}{r_{i,j}^2} \tag{10.2.1}$$

It should be noted that the concept of transportation distance is different from spatial distance. Even trading agents that are spatially adjacent may be far apart in terms of transportation. For example, under the condition of neither bridge nor tunnel, trading agents on both sides of the Huangpu River is difficult to trade even though they are across the river.

As the distance increases, the probability of the manufacturer getting the trading opportunity drops rapidly. The stronger the time limit constraint, $P_{i,j}$ decays faster with the increase of distance $r_{i,j}$. For situations where the time limit constraint is particularly strong, the decay rate may reach to level $P_{i,j} \propto \frac{1}{r_{i,j}^3}$, or even to level $P_{i,j} \propto \frac{1}{r_{i,j}^4}$. Here, we choose the second derivative of the transportation distance $r_{i,j}$

just to reflect a more common situation. In fact, no matter what decay rate is chosen, it does not change the conclusion of the derivation.

Since the probability $P_{i,j}$ has a value limit, that is, $0 \leq P_{i,j} \leq 1$, in order to meet the requirement for probability, the adjustment coefficient α is introduced, $P_{i,j}$ is expressed as follows:

$$P_{i,j} = \alpha \frac{1}{r_{i,j}^2} \tag{10.2.2}$$

In the above formula, changes of $r_{i,j}$ can be any real number greater than zero. The value size α depends on the value of the traded goods. The higher the value of the traded goods, the larger the value of α; on the contrary, for low-value traded goods, α has a smaller value.

For the convenience of deduction, $r_{i,j}$ is limited to natural numbers on $[1 + \infty)$, representing the unit of travel distance. The unit of travel distance can be adjusted according to convenience, it can be 1, 5, 10 km; or it can be a 10-min walk, 30 min; or it can be a 10-min drive, 20 min, 30 min, etc.

Now, let's calculate the total trading opportunities obtained by the supplier in the trading community Ω. For convenience, we assume that the number of trading agents within 1 traffic unit from b_j is n_1, the number of trading agents between 1 traffic unit and 2 traffic units is n_2, and so on, n_3, n_4, etc. According to the characteristics of time-limited trading, the total number of customers obtained by the supplier b_j is C_j:

$$C_j = \alpha \sum_{r_{i,j}} \frac{n_r}{r_{i,j}^2} \tag{10.2.3}$$

For convenience, assume that the agents in the trading community Ω follow a uniform distribution, and the density of the agents is denoted as ρ, from which we get the number of customers obtained by b_j:

$$C_j = \alpha \sum_{r_{i,j}} \frac{\pi \left\lfloor (r_{i,j} + 1)^2 - r_{i,j}^2 \right\rfloor \rho}{r_{i,j}^2} \tag{10.2.4}$$

Rearrange (10.2.4) to get:

$$C_j = \alpha \sum_{r_{i,j}} \frac{\pi (2r_{i,j} + 1)\rho}{r_{i,j}^2} \tag{10.2.5}$$

$$\because r_{i,j} \geq 1$$
$$\therefore C_j > 3\alpha\rho\pi \sum_{r_{i,j}} \frac{1}{r_{i,j}(r_{i,j} + 1)} \tag{10.2.6}$$

Assume that the farthest distance that b_j can reach customers is R_j beyond the range of R_j, the probability of b_j getting customers will become very small and can be ignored. R_j is related to the traffic convenience of the community where b_j is located, and also related to the influence of the industry where b_j is located. We might as well call R_j the trading radius of the trading agent b_j. Considering that the trading radius is mainly related to the traffic of the community, and has little to do with the ability of a single supplier, we can uniformly denote R_j as R_0.

Expand the right side of the above inequality to get:

$$C_j > 3\alpha\rho\pi\left(1 - \frac{1}{R_0}\right) \tag{10.2.7}$$

Due to the constraint of the lowest operating cost, each supplier must have a minimum number of customers to maintain normal operation. For this reason, Walter Christaller, a German geoeconomist, the founder of the "Central Place Theory" proposed the concept of "service threshold", defining the service threshold as the minimum service range to maintain the survival of the enterprise.[1]

Assume that the service threshold of b_j is C_j^0, b_j's location in the trading community must meet the following conditions:

$$C_j > 3\alpha\rho\pi\left(1 - \frac{1}{R_0}\right) \geq C_j^0 \tag{10.2.8}$$

From this, we can derive the density condition of the trading community:

$$\rho \geq \frac{C_j^0 R_0}{3\alpha\pi(R_0 - 1)} \tag{10.2.9}$$

Inequality (10.2.9) indicates that community density is key to the existence of a time-limited trading market. The greater the community density, the higher the probability of supplier survival; the lower the community density, the lower the probability of supplier survival. The trading of family agents are mostly time-limited, and the corresponding suppliers, including restaurants, supermarkets, convenience stores, etc., must adhere to the density law stated in (10.2.9) in their layout. In densely populated urban centers, more outlets can be set up; in suburban communities, due to the lower population density, whether it is restaurants, supermarkets, or convenience stores, only a limited number of outlets can be set up.

The community density condition (10.2.9) indicates that the emergence of cities is an inevitable choice to cater to trading needs. By increasing population density, urban communities create trading opportunities far higher than those in rural areas. The increase in trading opportunities further promotes urban scale expansion, and the positive feedback mechanism which promoting each other forms the driving force for continuous urban growth.

Time-limited constraints and supply constraints of trading induce two different layered forms in the trading network. The layered structure induced by supply constraints is represented as market price stratification. Within the same area, there can be markets with different prices and different qualities, forming different grades of market stratification. The layered structure induced by time-limited constraints is mainly manifested as a spatial structure, forming a pie-shaped distribution market in the trading network. Each pie-shaped market is centered on a trading agent aggregation area, forming a radiation area with different radii.

10.2.2 Christaller's Central Place Theory

Walter Christaller, a German geoeconomist, was the earliest scholar who studied market layering structure in history. In 1933, Christaller published *The Central Places in Southern Germany*, proposing a city-level theory centered on the concept of central places, known as the Central Place Theory in urban economics. The Central Place Theory has a foundational historical significance for the development of urban economics.

Christaller first analyzed the market spatial structure of a single product. Assuming that consumers are uniformly distributed in space and adhere to the principle of maximizing utility. Under the condition of no difference in supplier products, consumers always choose the supplier closest to them to achieve the minimum cost and maximum utility. Influenced by this, each supplier can only serve consumers within a circle with a fixed radius centered on its location. The numerous suppliers in the market each have their own circular service range, and these circles with the same radius will cover the entire city market.

There are areas not covered between adjacent circles, which will inevitably be divided by suppliers through market competition. Under the assumption of perfect market competition, there is no difference in the competitive strength of suppliers. Adjacent suppliers will equally divide the area between the service circles, and the city market will eventually form a hexagonal division structure. Due to the constraint of production costs, there is a minimum scale for the hexagonal service range. Below the minimum scale, the supplier will not be able to survive. Christaller called the minimum service range the service threshold of the supplier. The service threshold depends on the average production cost of the industry and determines the total number of suppliers that the city market can accommodate.

Different products have different production costs, so there are different service thresholds, and the market is divided into different layers, each layer corresponding to a category of products with the same production costs. The market is stratified from low to high, the higher the service threshold, the larger the scale of the urban market required, otherwise the supplier cannot survive. The number of market layers is closely related to the scale of the urban market. The larger the city scale, the more layers it can accommodate, and the more abundant the goods and services offered by the market; conversely, the smaller the city scale, the fewer market layers, and the narrower the spectrum of goods and services that the market can provide. These conclusions are basically consistent with the conclusions obtained from the layering trading model, and the differences between the two are mainly reflected in the analysis methods and logical basis. In the Central Place Theory, the main cause of market layering comes from the service threshold stipulated by trading costs; in the layering trading model, the main driving force for market layering evolution comes from time-limited constraints of trading. Despite the different analysis methods and basic logic, we have reached basically consistent conclusions, which strongly confirms the inevitability of market layering evolution.

10.3 Industrial Cluster Formation Induced by Synergistic Constraints

Since Harvard University professor and strategic management master Michael E. Porter deeply discussed the role of industrial clusters in national competitiveness in the 1990s, the proposition of industrial clusters has become a hot topic in economic theory research and economic policy formulation. Michael Porter defines industrial clusters as, in a specific field, a group of geographically adjacent, interactively related enterprises and related legal institutions, connected by their commonality and complementarity.[2] In his book *On Competition*, Michael discussed in detail the operating mechanism of industrial clusters and the process of its emergence, development and decline. Regarding the question of where industrial clusters will emerge, Michael Porter explained in his work *The Competitive Advantage of Nations* that whether a region can have industrial clusters depends on four elements: the first is the spatiotemporal background of corporate strategy and competition, including business rules, incentives and standards that regulate corporate competition and intensity. The so-called spatiotemporal background of corporate strategy and competition is the business environment, including policies, regulations, and the government's awareness of serving enterprises; the second is demand conditions, mainly referring to the local market size and the pickiness of the consumer group. We can call it the local demand environment; the third is related and supportive industries, that is, the supply environment; the fourth is the conditions of production factors, mainly referring to natural resources, human resources, financial resources, tangible infrastructure, information infrastructure, and technical research and development conditions. We can simplify it as the natural environment.[3] The above four elements constitute the specific endowment conditions of each region, determining the growth conditions of industrial clusters. The region with superior endowment conditions is more likely to have industrial clusters. Michael Porter's industrial cluster theory has the typical characteristics of strategic management and has strong practical significance to operate. It points out a clear path for macro policy makers to build efficient industrial clusters, but lacks the logical support of mainstream economic theory.

In the late 1990s, represented by American economist Paul R. Krugman, the Spatial Economics. Spatial economics, within the logical framework of neoclassical economics, focuses on the distribution of economic activities, with industrial clusters being an important research topic. The core idea of Paul R. Krugman's industrial cluster model is that when the internal correlation within an industry is greater than the correlation between industries, and transportation costs become a significant factor in business operating costs, businesses within the same industry will cluster in a certain area, forming an industrial cluster. The basic logic of Paul R. Krugman's model is that efficient industries support high wages in the industry, high wages attract labor to efficient industries; under the condition of limited labor supply, a region (or country) can only accommodate a specific industrial cluster.[4]

From the perspective of trading economics, the main driving force for industrial clustering comes from manufacturers pursuing maximum expected return, not from the household sector supplying labor. The essence of industrial clusters is the refined division of labor within the industry, that is, the high correlation within the industry. The motivation for refining the division of labor within the industry is the pursuit of efficiency by enterprises, both to achieve cost reduction and increased return, and to increase the certainty of trading. Under the stipulation of dual goals, the process of refining the division of labor within the industry inevitably has the characteristic of time-limited constraint. Suppliers must deliver products to downstream enterprises according to the plan, they must get parts and raw materials from upstream suppliers within a specified time. This time-limited constraint forms a tight production rhythm coupling relationship between upstream and downstream enterprises, we call this special form of time-limited constraint as synergy constraint. Under synergy constraints, upstream and downstream enterprises must be as close as possible, eventually forming industrial clusters that both highly specialized in division of labor and highly concentrated spatially.

Between two enterprises, whether industrial division of labor can be formed, the speed of synergy and trading costs are two key variables, and both variables are closely related to distance. In terms of synergy, whether it is the adjustment of production scale or product innovation, it must get a quick response from upstream enterprises, otherwise, downstream enterprises cannot achieve production goals. The premise of synergy is the support of effective and sufficient information flow, which not only includes the official information flow between enterprises but also includes the unofficial information flow formed by the contact between employees of enterprises. The more sufficient the information flow between enterprises, the faster the synergy response, and the higher the synergy quality. Personnel exchanges are inversely proportional to the distance between them, the closer the distance, the lower the cost of communication, and the higher the probability of communication. Use $v_{i,j}$ to represent the synergy speed of a_i and b_j, $r_{i,j}$ represents the transportation distance between the two enterprises. According to the above analysis, the two have the following relationship:

$$v_{i,j} \propto \frac{1}{r_{i,j}} \tag{10.3.1}$$

The factors that constitute trading costs are very complex, distance becomes the main factor affecting trading costs between enterprises with frequent trading. For frequent trading, the accumulated transportation costs over time are not negligible. Use $C_{i,j}$ to represent the trading cost of a_i and b_j, the relationship between it and the distance $r_{i,j}$ is as follows:

$$C_{i,j} \propto r_{i,j} \tag{10.3.2}$$

Considering factors such as trading matching, synergy speed, and trading costs. The expected returns function for trading agent a_i in $\{a_i\}_N$ who chooses trading partners b_j in $\{b_j\}_M$ is as follows:

$$E(a_i, b_j) = f\left(E(s_{i,j}), v_{i,j}, C_{i,j}\right) \tag{10.3.3}$$

where, $s_{i,j}$ is the strategy trading agent a_i use for choosing the supplier b_j, $E(s_{i,j})$ is the trading strategy $s_{i,j}$ use to bring expected return to a_i. When $E(s_{i,j}) > 0$, it represents the supply b_j and a_i are matched in structure, meaning b_j belongs to the adjacent upstream of a_i in the industrial cluster; when $E(s_{i,j}) = 0$, it means b_j does not structurally matched with a_i, and b_j does not belong to the adjacent upstream of a_i, or it does not belong to the industrial cluster where a_i is located. The value range of $E(s_{i,j})$, on the one hand, reflects the structural relationship between a_i and b_j ; on the other hand, it reflects the cost-performance ratio of a product that b_j provides. For the structure-adapted supplier b_j of the trading agent a_i, the higher the cost-performance ration of the product, the greater the value of $E(s_{i,j})$.

$v_{i,j}$ and $C_{i,j}$ are two highly correlated variables. When $C_{i,j}$ increases, the synergy speed $v_{i,j}$ will decrease; conversely, when $C_{i,j}$ decreases, $v_{i,j}$ will increase. The two variables wax and wane, and having a nonlinear multiplication and division relationship in mathematics. According to the inference of the two variables on the direction of the expected return function, under the condition that $E(s_{i,j})$ remains unchanged, the expected returns function of the trading agent a_i is as follows:

$$E(a_i, b_j) \propto \frac{v_{i,j}}{C_{i,j}} \tag{10.3.4}$$

Combining (10.3.1) and (10.3.2), we can get:

$$E(a_i, b_j) \propto E(s_{i,j}) \frac{\frac{1}{r_{i,j}}}{r_{i,j}} = \frac{E(s_{i,j})}{r_{i,j}^2} \tag{10.3.5}$$

From (10.3.5), we can get the expected return function of the trading agent in the division of labor of the industry:

$$E(a_i, b_j) = k \frac{E(s_{i,j})}{r_{i,j}^2} \tag{10.3.6}$$

In (10.3.6), $k > 0$ is a regulating constant. From (10.3.6) we can get:

$$\frac{E(a_i, b_j)}{E(a_i, b_l)} = \frac{E(s_{i,j})}{E(s_{i,l})}\frac{r_{i,l}^2}{r_{i,j}^2} \tag{10.3.7}$$

When $E(s_{i,j}) = E(s_{i,l})$,

$$\frac{E(a_i, b_j)}{E(a_i, b_l)} = \frac{r_{i,l}^2}{r_{i,j}^2} \tag{10.3.8}$$

If $r_{i,j} < r_{i,l}$, then:

$$\frac{E(a_i, b_j)}{E(a_i, b_l)} = \frac{r_{i,l}^2}{r_{i,j}^2} > 1 \tag{10.3.9}$$

$$E(a_i, b_j) > E(a_i, b_l) \tag{10.3.10}$$

According to the principle of maximizing expected return, will inevitably abandon the supplier b_l but choose b_j. As a result of such choice, suppliers will naturally choose to produce as close as possible to downstream enterprises, thus forming a highly concentrated trading community and giving birth to industrial clusters. This also explains why the distribution of industries in the trading network always presents a block-like feature, rather than a uniform or discrete distribution state. Whether in a city or a region, the distribution of industries always presents a clustering feature. Most of the technology innovation companies in the U.S. are concentrated in Silicon Valley on the west coast, including global giant technology companies such as Apple, Google, Facebook, Oracle, Intel, HP, Microsoft, Cisco. It is certain that Silicon Valley is more about the dwarfs behind the giants, with a large number of small companies playing an important supporting role in the technology industry cluster in Silicon Valley. Similarly, many enterprises in China's gold jewelry manufacturing industry are concentrated in a region called Shuibei in Cuizhu subdistrict, Luohu District, Shenzhen, forming an industry cluster with innovative vitality and strong competitiveness.

The core logic of (10.3.6) is driven by corporate interests. The basic principle followed by downstream enterprises in the industrial chain in choosing upstream enterprises is precisely the pursuit of profits and efficiency by enterprises, which promotes the formation of industrial clusters around downstream terminal enterprises as the center, forming a very close regional spatial layout. In the formation process of industrial clusters, downstream enterprises in the reverse trading phase are the key shapers. Their choices of upstream enterprises located in different geographical locations determine key parameters such as, where the industrial clusters form, what kind of geographical layout they have, and how large the clusters are. This forms a stark contrast with the basic logic of Paul R. Krugman's industrial cluster model, and the conclusions drawn from the model also have their own emphasis.

The complexity of reality always far exceeds theory. When upstream enterprises are subject to strict geographical constraints, the choices of downstream enterprises will be limited. Although the right to choose is still in the hands of the downstream leading enterprises, after a comprehensive assessment of the distance cost of raw materials to the market, the terminal downstream enterprises may still choose to be close to the upstream resource-based enterprises, eventually forming an industrial cluster centered on the upstream enterprises. Textile industry clusters, metallurgical industry clusters, etc. usually belong to this situation.

Equation (10.3.6) reveals the layered characteristics of the industrial clusters. In industrial clusters, terminal enterprises first form the core of the industrial cluster, and construct the first level of the industrial cluster around the core. The first level of trading agents is located at the sub-terminal position on the industrial chain, belonging to the adjacent upstream of the terminal enterprises. Sub-terminal enterprises also choose their adjacent upstream partners according to the principle of distance priority, forming the second layer of the industrial cluster; and so on, forming the third layer, the fourth layer... of the industrial cluster. The construction of industrial clusters is a process of building from the inside out, from downstream to upstream, layer by layer, eventually forming a large-scale, efficient, and highly competitive organizational structure.

The principle of industrial cluster expressed by (10.3.6) indicates that the scale of any industrial cluster is inevitably finite. Due to the finiteness of the progressive levels of industrial division, and the spatial distance between each level is limited, the scale of the industrial cluster is necessarily confined within a certain spatial area, only in this way can the competitiveness of the industrial cluster be maximized. This explains why in large economies, even within the same industry, several industrial clusters distributed in different regions will form. The biotech industry clusters in the United States are distributed in Boston in the Northeast, the San Francisco Bay Area, and San Diego in California. In China, automotive industry clusters are also distributed in several different regions, including Chongqing in the west, Shanghai in the east, Anhui in the central region, and Jilin in the northeast.

10.4 Network Form Under Non-structural Constraints

Assume Ω is a trading community in the trading network, for the market with the target g, the potential demand agents within the trading community Ω are $\{a_i\}_n$, and the potential supply agents are $\{b_j\}_m$. Trading is a continuous process, after each transaction, the trading agents will evaluate the results of trading for reference in the next trading decision; considering the information exchange environment in the community, residents will share some information. The situation is the same for supply manufacturers, they continuously accumulate experience in the production iteration process, continuously improve production processes, and improve product quality. The more a manufacturer sells, the more production iterations there are, the more product quality information feedback is obtained from the market, and the more opportunities there are for product improvement.

Now, let's examine the evolution of the probability distribution of any agent a_i choosing $\{b_j\}_m$ in the demand group $\{a_i\}_n$ in the trading community Ω.

$b_j \in \{b_j\}$ is any manufacturer, assume at time step t, the prior probability of a_i choosing b_j is $P_t^{i,j}$, considering the coherence of the trading agent's cognition and the consistency of the inherent logic, $P_t^{i,j}$ has a positive correlation with the prior probability $P_{t-1}^{i,j}$ at the previous time step $t-1$, that is:

$$P_t^{i,j} = \chi P_{t-1}^{i,j} \quad \chi > 0 \tag{10.4.1}$$

In (10.4.1), χ represents the adjustment factor, the size of χ reflects the trading experience at time step $t-1$. If a_i achieved the expected choice at $t-1$, χ will be greater than 1, that is, $\chi \le 1$; if a_i did not achieve the trading expectation, χ will be less than 1, that is, $\chi < 1$. In summary, the larger the expected returns $E(a_i, b_j)$ of a_i choosing b_j as the trading object, the larger the value of χ at the next time step; the smaller the value of $E(a_i, b_j)$, the smaller the value of χ at the next time step. χ reflects the trading agent's experience results, we can call it the experience factor of trading agent. The trading experience changes with time, and the experience factor χ will also change with time, use χ_t represents the experience result of trading agent a_i to the previous trading. Therefore, the prior probability recursion formula expressed by (10.4.1) can be further described as:

$$P_t^{i,j} = \chi_t P_{t-1}^{i,j} \quad \chi_t \ge 0 \tag{10.4.2}$$

From the supply side, the more trading resources b_j obtained, the more opportunities for product optimization will be, and the more consumer surplus provided to customers. In the trading community Ω, trading agents in the same phase are always in competition. Whoever can provide more consumer surplus can get more trading opportunities.

Suppliers can increase trader surplus through various ways. Improving product quality, beautifying product packaging, improving styling design, adding product functions, improving after-sales service, enhancing customer awareness through advertising, price reduction promotions, and many other measures are effective ways to increase consumer surplus. The size of the consumer surplus provided by the supplier to the customer reflects the efficiency level of its productivity. Enterprises that provide more trader surplus to customers have a more obvious advantage in peer competition. Use $\varsigma_t^{i,j}$ represents the consumer surplus that trading agent a_i obtained from b_j at time step t. It is obvious the experience factor χ is an increasing function of the trader surplus ς, that is:

$$\frac{d\chi}{d\varsigma} > 0 \tag{10.4.3}$$

Therefore, Eq. (10.4.2) can also be described as:

$$P_t^{i,j} = \chi_t\left(\varsigma_{t-1}^{i,j}\right)P_{t-1}^{i,j} \tag{10.4.4}$$

Next, let's look at the clustering effect in the trading community Ω, that is, the effect caused by the mutual influence of trading behaviors among neighbors in the community. Because there is information exchange in the trading community, community members can observe each other's trading behaviors. Assume that the trading agent a_i observed that at time step $t - 1$, there were K neighbors in the community who chose supplier b_j as a trading counter party, at time step t, the probability of a_i choose b_j as a trading counter party is a conditional probability $P_t[a_i|\{a_l\}_K]$, according to Bayes' theorem:

$$P_t^{i,j}\left[a_i|\{a_l\}_K\right] = \frac{P_t^{i,j}P_{t-1}\left[\{a_l\}_K|a_i\right]}{P_{t-1}\left[\{a_l\}_K\right]} \tag{10.4.5}$$

Expand (10.4.5) to get:

$$P_t^{i,j}\left[a_i|\{a_l\}_K\right] = \frac{P_t^{i,j}\prod_{l=1}^{K}P_{t-1}(a_l|a_i)}{\prod_{L=1}^{K}P_{t-1}^{l,j}} \tag{10.4.6}$$

Community member a_l observing the trading behavior of trading agent a_i, will impose an impact on his prior probability, let's call this impact factor $\gamma \geq 1$, that is:

$$P_{t-1}(a_l|a_i) = \gamma P_{t-1}^{l,j} \quad l = 1, 2, 3, \ldots \tag{10.4.7}$$

In the trading community, the mutual influence between members depends on the network structure of the community. The higher the community's cluster degree δ, the greater the mutual influence between members, therefore, the impact factor γ is a function of the community cluster degree δ. For simplicity, assume the function relationship is as follows:

$$\gamma = 1 + \delta \tag{10.4.8}$$

Substitute (10.4.7) and (10.4.8) into (10.4.6) to get:

$$
\begin{aligned}
P_t^{i,j}(a_i|\{a_l\}_K) &= \frac{P_t^{i,j}\prod_1^K (1+\delta)P_{t-1}^{l,j}}{\prod_1^K P_{t-1}^{l,j}} \\
&= (1+\delta)^K P_t^{i,j}
\end{aligned}
\tag{10.4.9}
$$

For trading agent a_i those choose b_j at time step $t - 1$ has the prior probability $P_{t-1}^{i,j}$, the probability of choosing b_j at time step t is:

$$
\begin{aligned}
P_t^{i,j}(a_i|\{a_i\}_K) &= (1+\delta)^K P_t^{i,j} \\
&= \chi_t(1+\delta)^K P_{t-1}^{i,j}
\end{aligned}
\tag{10.4.10}
$$

As the time step t passes, the members of the trading community gradually converge to the minority of suppliers of $\{b_j\}_m$ through continuous trading attempts, and eventually form an extremely polarized outcome. In (10.4.10), the experience factor χ, community cluster degree δ, and the distribution of previous trading resources K are the key parameters determining the choices made by the trading agent at time step t. The larger the value of the experience factor χ, the higher the probability that the trading agent will maintain the previous trading resource allocation pattern. The key factor determining the value of the experience factor χ is the amount of consumer surplus ς obtained by the trading agent during trading. The more consumer surplus obtained, the better the trading experience, and the larger the experience factor χ. From the perspective of enterprise evolution, the amount of trader surplus provided by the trading agent b_j is positively correlated with the trading resources K it obtains. The larger the K, the more the iterations b_j will get. For both technology improvement, market promotion, and after-sales service, there will be more evolution opportunities, and it is possible to provide more consumer surplus to the market. From the experience factor χ to the trader surplus ς, and then to the transaction opportunity K, the three form a positive feedback loop (Fig. 10.1).

The size of the community cluster degree δ depends on the strength of information exchange and trading contacts among community members. The community is a neighborhood relationship, and the relationship between community members is a self-organizing process from raw to mature. The community cluster degree δ grows with time t. In a relatively stable community, the cluster degree δ is an increasing function of time t. When the community cluster degree δ continues to increase, the

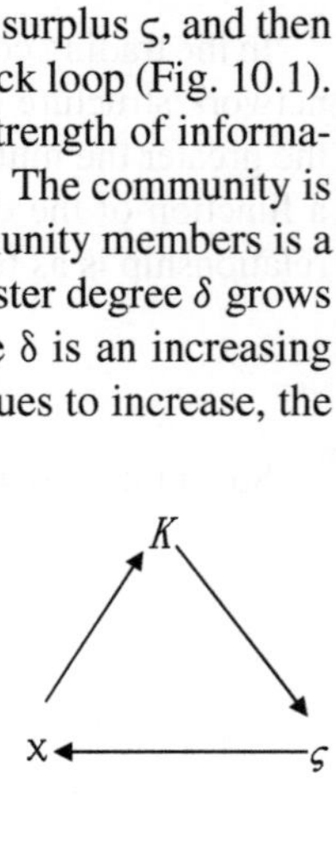

Fig. 10.1 The feedback loop of trading agent evolution

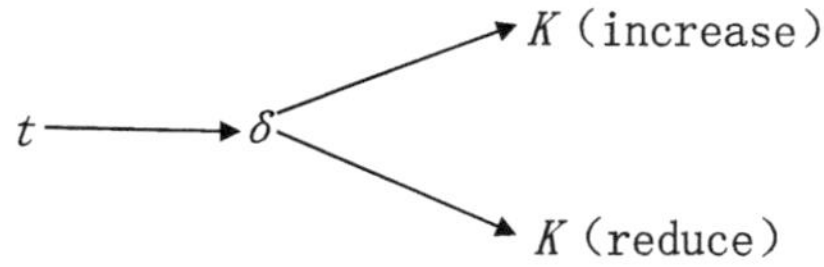

Fig. 10.2 The diagram of a two-tier evolutionary trend of the trading agent

mutual influence of community members during trading will also increase, the evolution speed of the community trading network will also accelerate, and the community trading resources will accelerate the pattern of polarization. Once b_j obtains more than the average level of trading resources $\{b_j\}_m$, the trading resources will converge towards b_j, and K will further increase, correspondingly; on the contrary, if K is less than the average level $\{b_j\}_m$, b_j will gradually lose trading resources, and K will become smaller and smaller. Under the effect of time t, the distribution of community trading resources will show a two-tier evolutionary trend (Fig. 10.2).

In the trading community, the speed of two-tier differentiation of trading resources depends on the clustering degree δ of the community. The higher the clustering degree δ of the community, the faster the differentiation speed of the trading resources K under the mutual influence of the trading agents. Since the clustering degree of most trading communities evolves from low to high, it is not difficult to infer that the differentiation speed of community trading resources must show an accelerating trend.

To summarize the above analysis, the structural evolution process of the trading community unfolds under two mechanisms: first, the positive feedback mechanism. The feedback loop composed of the three variables of the experience factor χ, trader surplus and trading opportunity K; second, the self-organizing differentiation mechanism. Through the spontaneous strengthening mechanism of information association among community members, it guides the continuous rise of community cluster degree. Under the demonstration mechanism, the distribution of community trading resources shows a polarized trend. The above two mechanisms converge on the trading resource K, forming a mutually reinforcing effect (Fig. 10.3).

Under the dual mechanism, the trading network without structural constraints shows a trend of spontaneous concentration of trading resources, and the trading agents who win in the competition will occupy more and more trading resources. The process of trading resource differentiation is the result of the efficiency competition

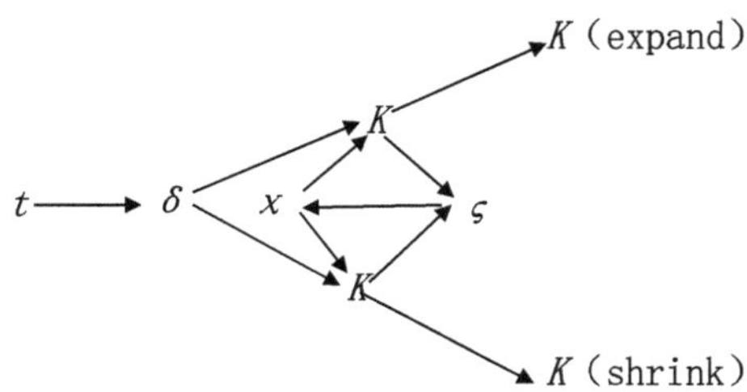

Fig. 10.3 The diagram of a two-tier evolutionary trend of the trading agent

of trading agents, and it is also the process of continuous optimization of resource allocation in the trading system.

For markets with distinct characteristics of a target, the situation is slightly different. Due to the differences in individual preferences of the trading agents, there will be trading that have a high consumer surplus in the eyes of a_i, but the situation is exactly the opposite in the view of a_2, resulting in the following outcome:

$$P_t^{i,j}(a_i|\{a_i\}_K) = \chi_t^{i,j}(1+\delta)^K P_{t-1}^{i,j} \tag{10.4.11}$$

$$P_t^{k,j}(a_k|\{a_i\}_K) = \chi_t^{k,j}(1+\delta)^K P_{t-1}^{k,j} \tag{10.4.12}$$

In Eqs. (10.4.11) and (10.4.12), the differences in the distribution of trading resources at time step t – 1 are diluted by individual preferences. The advantage of the trading agent b_j in the market share K is offset by the difference in the experience factors $\chi_t^{i,j}$ and $\chi_t^{k,j}$, making it difficult to quickly concentrate trading resources towards the dominant agent.

As manufacturers b_j and b_l providing personalized products to the market, they each have market shares $\{a_i\}_{Kj}$ and $\{a_i\}_{Kj}$, both can provide a higher consumer surplus for their customer base, $P_t^{i,j}$ and $P_t^{i,l}$ both maintain a high level. Despite this, the evolution of the trading community structure will still develop towards a gradually converging trend. The only difference is that the direction of convergence is no longer just one, but a few manufacturers. In a market structure with multiple leading manufacturers, distinct personality characteristics are an important means for suppliers to maintain customer relationships, which determines the evolution trend of the market. Suppliers need to follow the evolution of their customer group's traits to develop products, guiding the market towards an increasingly prominent direction of personalization.

The above discussions are all limited to a single trading community. In fact, due to the connectivity of the trading network, trading agents with strong competitive advantages, once they gain competitive advantages in their communities, they will compete in the adjacent trading communities. The advantages accumulated by the trading agents in the original community will assist them to participate in the competition in other communities. For each additional winning community, trading resources will further expand, providing ample opportunities for continuous production iteration and product optimization, which is beneficial for gaining advantages in the subsequent competition. By expanding the market radius of competition from near to far, enterprises that gain competitive advantages in the trading community will eventually go international. This is almost the path of evolution of all multinational enterprises.

In conclusion from the above analysis: for non-structural constraint trading markets, the trading network structure has a spontaneous concentration evolution trend. The process of trading resource concentration is also a process of trading agents competing and continuously improving operational efficiency, and it is also

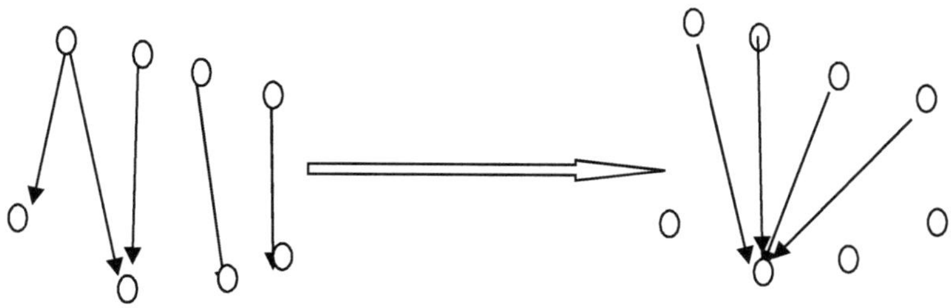

Fig. 10.4 The diagram of trading system evolution

a process of maximizing welfare in the trading system. The evolution process is intuitively shown in the Fig. 10.4.

10.5 The Nature of the Evolution of the Layered Structure of the Trading Network

Under the promotion of trading, the trading network structure shows the characteristics of layered evolution. The non-structural constraint market is at the top of the trading network, with the characteristics of global networking. On the non-structural constraint market, after fierce competition, only a few trading agents can win and obtain a monopoly dominant position. The scale-free structure of the trading network is precisely the result of the evolution of non-structural constraint trading.

The trading network with structured constraint presents a localized structure, divided the trading community into varying sizes of sub-communities. Despite the existence of cross-community trading, intra-community trading remains the mainstream. Compared to the global networking characteristics of non-structured constraint trading, structured constraint trading shows relatively mild competition characteristics in the evolution of market structure. Although there is a certain intensity of competition within the market, the intensity and nature of the competition are not as fierce as in non-structured constraint markets, and will not immediately manifest as a matter of life and death.

In terms of the manifestation of competition, trading with different constraint characteristics has its own emphases. The focus of competition in supply-constrained markets is product quality; the higher the product quality, the more substantial the profits obtained by the enterprise. The core of competition in time-limited constrained trading markets is the position of the trading network, that is, the rationality of the layout of business outlets, which is the key to success or failure. For industrial clusters, an enterprise's position in the cluster depends on whether it can establish a solid trust relationship with other enterprises in the supply chain, and minimize each other's trading cost and uncertainties. Behind all this, in addition to the enterprises' strength, the choice of location still plays an important role.

The layered evolution characteristics of the trading network and the differentiated competition mechanism ensure that the trading system operates efficiently while meeting diverse scenarios and trading needs. However, the evolution process of the trading system contains an alienation mechanism of self-restraint of efficiency. The spontaneous evolution of the global market inevitably ends in monopoly. Once a monopoly occurs, competition among enterprises disappears, and the market loses its efficiency basis in resource allocation. Monopoly enterprises will transform from innovators to obstructers of market innovation, using their super trading power to seize excessive profits.

In community markets, the result of competition in supply-constrained markets is resource monopoly; time-limited trading markets will artificially create entry barriers, forming market segmentation; the efficiency of industrial clusters is constrained by their own life cycle, each industrial cluster from emergence to growth, and then to decline, the industrial cluster eventually disintegrates. In the life cycle of an industrial cluster, the efficiency of the cluster evolves along the path of a parabola. The efficiency of the entire industrial cluster depends on the terminal companies of the cluster. Once the efficiency of the terminal enterprises declines, the entire industrial cluster loses its efficiency advantage. Whether it is a global market or a community market, without external intervention and market management, the trading system will eventually lock in an ineffective equilibrium state. Once this happens, not only does the evolution of the trading system stagnate, but the evolution of the social system also stagnates.

The trading system constituted by the self-organization of the trading network will not maintain permanent efficient spontaneous operation. The evolution process of the trading system from small to large, from simple to complex, has brought about the emergence of government management mechanisms. By giving the government increasingly powerful public functions, managing and intervening in the spontaneous evolution process of the trading system is a necessary requirement for the healthy evolution of the trading system. Whether it is the emergence of the government or the expansion of government functions, they have become an integral part of the evolution process of the trading system.

Whether it is the layered evolution mechanism of the trading network or the spontaneous termination mechanism of the competition efficiency of the trading system, these mechanisms provide us with a more multi-dimensional and deeper understanding of the market. The characteristics of the layered evolution of the trading network puts forward higher requirements for the government to manage the market. Only by deeply understanding the characteristics of different layered markets can we effectively manage different types of markets and maintain the efficient operation of the trading system. According to the characteristics of the layered evolution of the trading network, the government should accurately implement policies according to the characteristics of the object when managing the market. For structurally constrained local markets, price intervention and quality supervision should be the focus of management; for non-structurally constrained global markets, the focus of government management should be to prevent corporate alliances and avoid market monopolies.

The evolution trend of the trading network spatial layout is block aggregation. Under the motivation trend of reducing trading cost and maximizing the acquisition of trading resources, the population gathers from dispersed rural areas to spatially narrow cities, forming a highly aggregated urban structure; enterprises in the same industry will also gather in the same area, forming an industry cluster with a dense internal structure. Whether it is a city or an industry cluster, it is a form presented under the same force, that is, the pursuit of trading efficiency and maximization of return by the trading agent.

Notes

1. Roberta Capello (2022) Regional Economic (trans: Husen AN), 2nd edn. Economic Management Press, Beijing, p 75.
2. Michael Porter (2003) On Competition (trans: Dengdi GAO, Mingxuan LI), Citic Press, p 210.
3. Michael Porter (2003) On Competition (trans: Dengdi GAO, Mingxuan LI), Citic Press, p 224.
4. Paul R, Krugman's key criterion for industrial clusters is the following equation: $\left(\frac{w^2}{w^1}\right)^{\beta} = T^{-(\alpha-\gamma)}\left[\left(\frac{1+\alpha-\gamma}{2}\right)T^{1-\sigma} + \left(\frac{1+\gamma-\alpha}{2}\right)T^{\sigma-1}\right]^{1/\sigma}$

   The model focuses on two countries, each with two industries, where, w^1, w^2 denote the wage rates that the two industries are able to pay, respectively; α represents the share of inputs to each of the two industries that comes from within the industry, β represents the share of inputs to each of the two industries that comes from the labour force, and γ represents the share of inputs to each of the two industries that comes from another industry; σ represents the elasticity of substitution coefficients of the two commodities; and T represents the cost of transport, using the "iceberg" method introduced by Von Thunen and Samuelson, that is, using the number of units of goods that need to be sent out from the place of origin to deliver one unit of goods to the destination of the goods as transport costs. When $\left(\frac{w^2}{w^1}\right)^{\beta} < 1$ or $\left(\frac{w^2}{w^1}\right)^{\beta} > 1$, industrial cluster emergences; when $\left(\frac{w^2}{w^1}\right)^{\beta} \approx 1$, the role of spatial distance in industrial layout disappears, and different industries show random heterogeneous distribution. See also Masahisa Fujita, Paul Krugman, Anthony J. Venables (2013) The Spatial Economy: Cities, Regions and International Trade (trans: Qi LIANG), 1st edn. China Renmin University Press, Beijing, p 255.

Chapter 11
Trading Network Phase Structure

The phase structure is a structure formed by trading relationships, which determines the basic characteristics of market games.

11.1 Polycentric Phase Configuration

The multi-phase configuration is a phase structure in which multiple suppliers of comparable strength share the market. In a polycentric market, each supplier has a relatively stable customer base.

The polycentric phase configuration corresponds to a monopoly competition market and an oligopoly market in real scenarios, and these two market models occupy a dominant position in modern trading systems. The economic community has conducted very in-depth research on polycentric markets and has formed a large number of research literatures. After the polycentric trading model, we will introduce four representative monopoly models separately. These models are unique in both analysis perspective and analysis paradigm, and are very helpful for us to understand the characteristics of polycentric markets.

11.1.1 Polycentric Trading Model

In a polycentric market, each supplier has a relatively stable customer base, and the trading network form is as follows (Fig. 11.1).

In a polycentric market, the goals pursued by suppliers mainly include two aspects: one is to stabilize the existing customer base; the other is to strive to attract more customers from other suppliers. The competition in the polycentric market is also carried out on these two dimensions.

Z. Wang, *Trading Economics*, Contributions to Economics,
https://doi.org/10.1007/978-981-99-9875-3_11

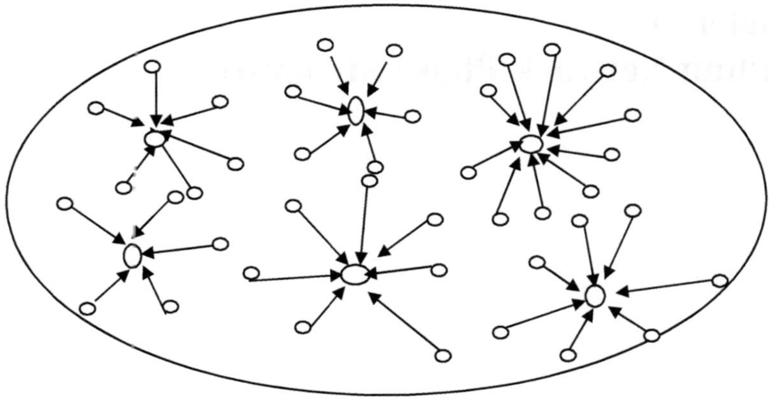

Fig. 11.1 The diagram of polycentric trading model

In a polycentric market, the demand group $\{a_i\}_N$ is divided into M groups by the supplier $\{b_j\}_M$, and we denote the customer group that chooses the supplier b_j as $\{a_i\}_N$. For technical reasons, we set the trading volume of each consumer trading as a unit of goods. In a polycentric market, the expected return function of consumer $a_i \in \{a_i\}_j$ is:

$$\begin{aligned} E(a_i, b_j) &= Z_j - P_j \\ &= Z_j - \frac{Z_j}{\lambda_j} \\ &= Z_j\left(1 - \frac{1}{\lambda_j}\right) \end{aligned} \tag{11.1.1}$$

Equation (11.1.1) shows that the size of consumer return is positively correlated with the value of goods provided by the supplier and the price-performance ratio. Under the premise of unchanged value, the expected return of consumers is mainly determined by the price-performance ratio. The higher the price-performance ratio, the greater the consumer's return. The relationship between the price-performance ratio λ and the expected return E is shown in Fig. 11.2.

Fig. 11.2 Expected return curve chart

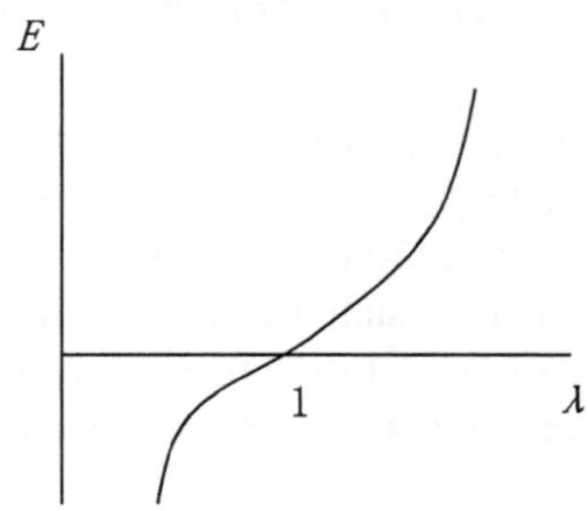

According to the principle of maximizing expected return, consumers always seek suppliers with the highest price-performance ratio in the market. We assume that there are information channels among consumers in the market, and we get to know the price-performance ratio of each supplier.

In the polycentric phase configuration market, the return of b_j is affected by various factors such as the scale of the customer group, the efficiency of the production organization, and the price-performance ratio of the goods provided.

$$E\left(b_j, \{a_i\}_j\right) = \left(P_j - C_j\right)M_j \tag{11.1.2}$$

In (11.1.2), the production cost C_j of the supplier b_j is proportional to the value of the product Z_j, and inversely proportional to production efficiency. The production efficiency is a measure of the supplier's efficiency in various aspects from product production to market marketing, to internal organizational management, which we represent with η.

Based on the above relationship, we can get:

$$C_j = \frac{Z_j}{\eta_j} \tag{11.1.3}$$

Substitute (11.1.3) into (11.1.2) and combine with (10.1.5), we can get:

$$\begin{aligned} E\left(b_j, \{a_i\}_j\right) &= \left(\frac{Z_j}{\lambda_j} - \frac{Z_j}{\eta_j}\right)M_j \\ &= \left(\frac{1}{\lambda_j} - \frac{1}{\eta_j}\right)Z_j M_j \end{aligned} \tag{11.1.4}$$

Equation (11.1.4) shows that the supplier's income is proportional to the customer size, the larger the customer size, the more the income; on the other hand, the lower the cost-performance ratio of the product, the greater the supplier's income under the premise of unchanged customer group. Therefore, the supplier must find a balance between the cost-performance ratio and customer size to maximize its own income.

Because the customer volume M_j of b_j is an increasing function of its cost-performance ratio λ_j, for simplicity, we assume $M_j = k\lambda_j$, substitute into (11.1.4) to get:

$$E\left(b_j, \{a_i\}_j\right) = kZ_j\left(1 - \frac{\lambda_j}{\eta_j}\right) \tag{11.1.5}$$

Equation (11.1.5) fully shows the contradictory role played by the cost-performance ratio between suppliers and consumers. For consumers, the higher the cost-performance ratio, the greater the expected benefits of the trading; for suppliers,

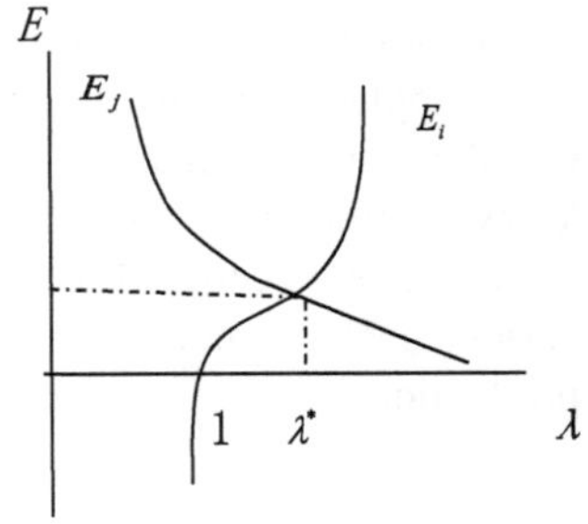

Fig. 11.3 Cost-performance balance diagram

the higher the cost-performance ratio, the greater the cost. Both parties reach a mutually satisfactory result through mutual game, and find the market equilibrium point of the cost-performance ratio value λ^* (Fig. 11.3).

In a polycentric market, enterprises have two strategies to choose from: one is to lower prices, improve the cost-performance ratio of goods to attract more customers. This is a commonly used short-term strategy by manufacturers; another strategy is to improve production efficiency, reduce production costs, achieve income growth without reducing the cost-performance ratio of goods, or improve the cost-performance ratio without reducing marginal income to gain a larger customer group.

Compared with the first strategy, the second strategy is obviously more strategic. The two strategies represent two directions of market evolution, one is vicious competition of price reduction promotion; the other is benign competition of efficiency improvement and cost reduction. Since vicious competition will lead to a lose-lose result and is not sustainable, benign competition is inevitably the evolution destination of the polycentric market.

In a polycentric market, once the cost-performance ratio gap between suppliers exceeds a certain threshold, customers will switch from suppliers with low cost-performance ratio to suppliers with high cost-performance ratio. Suppose the customer a_i of b_j finds that another supplier b_l has a higher cost-performance ratio, that is:

$$\lambda_j = \frac{Z_j}{P_j} < \frac{Z_l}{P_l} = \lambda_l \tag{11.1.6}$$

Before a_i deciding whether to switch from b_j to b_l, the first thing to consider is the conversion cost Cm. Conversion cost is a comprehensive cost, including transportation cost, time cost, product adaptation cost, and barrier crossing cost. Transportation cost is easy to understand; when consumers switch from the original supplier to a new supplier, it usually means that they need to travel from one place to another, and it is natural to incur transportation costs. Time cost refers to the time consumers spend investigating new suppliers. When consumers abandon the original supplier and switch to a new supplier, they need to carefully investigate the new supplier, and the time spent is a cost that cannot be ignored. Product adaptation cost refers to the cost of time spent learning and adapting when consumers use new products. The more complex the product, the higher the adaptation cost that needs to be paid when changing suppliers.

From the above analysis, it can be seen that customer transfer must meet the following conditions:

$$E(a_i, b_l) - E(a_i, b_j) > Cm \tag{11.1.7}$$

Expanding (11.1.7) we get:

$$E(a_i, b_l) - E\left(a_i, b_j\right) = (Z_l - P_l) - \left(Z_j - P_j\right) \tag{11.1.8}$$

Substituting (10.1.5) into (11.1.8) we get:

$$E(a_i, b_l) - E\left(a_i, b_j\right) = \left(Z_l - Z_j\right) - \left(\frac{Z_l}{\lambda_l} - \frac{Z_j}{\lambda_j}\right) \tag{11.1.9}$$

Let $\lambda_l = \lambda_j + \Delta\lambda$, $\Delta\lambda > 0$, $Z_l = Z_j + \Delta Z$, $\Delta Z > 0$
Rearranging (11.1.9) we get:

$$E(a_i, b_l) - E\left(a_i, b_j\right) = \Delta Z + \frac{Z_j \Delta\lambda}{\lambda_j\left(\lambda_j + \Delta\lambda\right)} - \frac{\Delta Z}{\lambda_j + \Delta\lambda} \tag{11.1.10}$$

$$\frac{Z_j \Delta\lambda}{\lambda_j\left(\lambda_j + \Delta\lambda\right)} > 0 \tag{11.1.11}$$

$$\therefore \quad E(a_i, b_l) - E\left(a_i, b_j\right) > \Delta Z - \frac{\Delta Z}{\lambda_j + \Delta\lambda} \tag{11.1.12}$$

From this, we get the condition for customers a_i to migrate from b_i to b_j:

$$E(a_i, b_l) - E\left(a_i, b_j\right) > \Delta Z - \frac{\Delta Z}{\lambda_j + \Delta\lambda} > Cm \tag{11.1.13}$$

After rearranging (11.1.13), we get the customer migration condition:

$$\Delta\lambda > \frac{\Delta Z}{\Delta Z - Cm} - \lambda_j \tag{11.1.14}$$

In condition (11.1.14), supplier b_j plays the role of a market benchmark. To clearly show this role, let $\lambda_j = \overline{\lambda}$ represent the average cost-performance ratio of the market, and substitute it into (11.1.14) to get the following formula:

$$\Delta\lambda > \frac{\Delta Z}{\Delta Z - Cm} - \overline{\lambda} \tag{11.1.15}$$

Migration condition (11.1.15) indicates that the higher the market transfer cost Cm, the more stable the polycentric market, the less likely the customer group is to migrate, and the supplier will have a larger cost-performance ratio selection margin, and the space for profit realization will be larger.

Equation (11.1.15) also shows that for high cost-performance ratio markets, consumers are more sensitive to cost-performance ratio; in markets with lower cost-performance ratio, consumers are less sensitive to cost-performance ratio. Apparently, this conclusion seems to contradict the general rule described by the law of diminishing marginal utility. In fact, the level of cost-performance ratio reflects the market supply and demand relationship. The higher the cost-performance ratio, the more sufficient the market supply, and the more picky the customers; the lower the cost-performance ratio, it means that the market supply is more tense, customers lose the price bargaining advantage, and it is difficult to be too picky about suppliers.

From (11.1.15), we know that as long as the supplier's cost-performance ratio adjustment amount $\Delta\lambda$ stays within the interval $\left[0, \frac{\Delta Z}{\Delta Z - Cm} - \overline{\lambda}\right]$, the customer group will continue to remain stable and there will be no customer transfer phenomenon. Since the supplier's income is inversely related to the cost-performance ratio, $\Delta\lambda = 0$ is the supplier's dominant strategy. At this time, the average cost-performance ratio of the polycentric market $\overline{\lambda}$ is the Nash equilibrium point of the market. As suppliers continue to iterative production, efficiency differences will accumulated in supplier $\{b_j\}_M$, and when a certain enterprise meets the conditions (11.1.15), it will take the lead in launching an attack on the market, expanding its customer base by improving the cost-performance ratio of its products, and the market equilibrium will be broken immediately. Under this circumstance, other suppliers will be forced to improve their cost-performance ratio, otherwise, customers will shift. Then, the market will enter a new stable range e$\left[\frac{\Delta Z}{\Delta Z - Cm} - \overline{\lambda}, +\infty\right]$. In this range, the new equilibrium of cost-performance ratio is higher than the previous equilibrium. For convenience, we denote the previous equilibrium $\left[0, \frac{\Delta Z}{\Delta Z - Cm} - \overline{\lambda}\right]$ as $\overline{\lambda_\theta}$; and the new equilibrium e$\left[\frac{\Delta Z}{\Delta Z - Cm} - \overline{\lambda}, +\infty\right]$ as $\overline{\lambda_1}$, the relationship between the two equilibrium satisfies $\overline{\lambda_0} < \overline{\lambda_1}$. With the continuous evolution of the polycentric market, we can obtain a sequence of cost-performance ratio equilibrium points, that is:

$$\overline{\lambda_0} < \overline{\lambda_1} < \overline{\lambda_2} < \cdots \tag{11.1.16}$$

From sequence (11.1.16), a set of intervals can be constructed, which is the stable interval sequence of the polycentric market:

$$\left[0, \overline{\lambda_0}\right], \left[\overline{\lambda_0}, \overline{\lambda_1}\right], \left[\overline{\lambda_1}, \overline{\lambda_2}\right] \cdots\cdots \tag{11.1.17}$$

The polycentric market presents a discontinuous intergenerational evolution from low to high along the sequence (11.1.17). On each stable interval, after a period of accumulation in experience, skills, and knowledge, the market equilibrium cost-performance ratio will jump to a new height and enter the next stable interval. The new equilibrium cost-performance ratio will form at the left endpoint of the stable interval.

From (11.1.15), we know that the higher the conversion cost Cm of the polycentric market, the more difficult it is for the market to transition, and the slower the speed of market intergenerational evolution. From the consumer's perspective, the faster the market evolves, the more benefits consumers get; but from the supplier's perspective, the faster the market evolves, the greater the pressure on suppliers. Therefore, suppliers always hope to maintain a certain intensity of transfer costs. Maintaining market transfer costs can not only alleviate the competitive pressure on suppliers but also is the basis for companies to realize profits. Among the components of market transfer costs, the only part that suppliers can effectively control is product adaptation costs. In order to maintain the existence of market transfer costs, suppliers will undoubtedly choose to strengthen product features and pursue a differentiated development strategy.

In reality, the intergenerational evolution of market transitions is achieved through product upgrades. enterprises accumulate experience and technology through iterative production and continuously optimize products based on user feedback, forming a product sequence. Take the iPhone as an example. After Apple released the first iPhone in January 2007, it released the second generation of iPhone in June 2008, a year and a half later, and the third generation of iPhone a year later. Since then, the iPhone has been updated almost every year. Each upgrade significantly improves the performance of the phone, but the selling price changes little. The price of the first-generation iPhone when it was launched in the United States in 2007 was $599; 15 years later, in 2021, the price of the iPhone 13 when it was launched in the United States was $799. After excluding inflation, it can be said that the price has basically not changed. The upgrading of Huawei and Xiaomi phones is roughly the same, with new models constantly being launched, but the price is basically stable. It can be seen that the process of product upgrades is usually also the process of market cost-performance ratio jumping, and it is the process of market intergenerational evolution.

11.1.2 Cartel Alliance Behavior

For the polycentric market, suppliers have another strategy that can achieve excess return at a lower cost, which is to establish a cartel alliance mechanism through supplier collusion.

The difficulty of establishing a cartel is directly proportional to the number of suppliers. In a cartel, every supplier has a motive to default, and when the majority of suppliers abide by the alliance agreement, the defaulting manufacturer can gain more market resources from the default. The larger the scale of the cartel, the stronger this default motive will be. Therefore, the more suppliers there are in the market, the higher the coordination costs and difficult it is to establish and maintain a cartel.

We can quantify the above qualitative analysis: suppose b_j is any manufacturer in the market manufacturer set $\{b_j\}_M$, participating in cartel A can bring b_j a profit of $ExtrA$. At the same time, participating in an alliance requires a lot of time for coordination and a part of the alliance operating costs, we record these collaboration costs as Ch; since cartels in the market are often seen as illegal behavior, once investigated, participants will face huge fines, we record the illegal costs as Ca; suppose the probability of the cartel being discovered is p.

According to the principle of maximizing expected return, The key for manufactures to take action is the contrast between the cost of participating in the alliance and the potential benefits. Only when participating in the alliance brings a larger net profit to the manufacturer, the manufacturer may participate in the alliance.

Based on the above analysis, we can get the alliance conditions:

$$\text{Extr}A > \text{Ch} + p \times \text{Ca} \tag{11.1.18}$$

Since there is a direct proportion relationship between the number of suppliers M and the coordination cost Ch, we can get:

$$Ch = kM \tag{11.1.19}$$

where, k is a positive real number greater than 0. Substitute (11.1.19) into (11.1.18) to get the condition for the alliance to appear:

$$\text{Extr}A > kM + p \times Ca \tag{11.1.20}$$

Equation (11.1.20) shows that the number of suppliers M existing in the market is the key variable determining whether a cartel will appear. Under the premise of fixed illegal costs and collaboration costs, the critical value for the alliance to appear in a polycentric market is:

$$M < \frac{1}{k}(\text{Extr}A - p \times Ca) \tag{11.1.21}$$

Equation (11.1.21) shows that the lower the illeagal cost of the alliance, the lower the threshold for market alliance. Even if there are many suppliers in the market, a cartel may still appear.

Obviously, the illegal cost is the key to preventing manufacturers from forming alliances. The higher the illegal cost, the less likely the alliance is to appear. It should also be noted that the excess profits brought by the alliance are the main motivation for manufacturers to break the legal bottom line. When the excess profits are huge, even with strict laws, it is still difficult to prevent manufacturers from forming alliances in some covert form.

Equation (11.1.21) provides us with such a scenario, when the number of manufacturers M in the market is small, the cost of alliance will drop significantly. In this case, it is very easy for manufacturers to form alliances.

11.1.3 Cournot Oligopoly Competition Model

At the beginning of the nineteenth century, French mathematician, economist, and philosopher Antoine Augustin Cournot first proposed the oligopoly competition model in his work "*Research on the Mathematical Principles of Wealth Theory*", which pioneered the study of oligopoly markets. In the Cournot oligopoly competition model, there are two suppliers in the market, supplying homogeneous products, the quantity is the decision variable of the supplier's game, and the price is determined by the total supply of the market.

Assume b_1, b_2 are the two suppliers, q_1, q_2 are the quantities chosen by b_1, b_2; the market price P is a decreasing function of the total supply, the price function is $P = Q - q_1 - q_2$, where Q is the market capacity limit. Assume b_1, b_2 have the same marginal cost, denoted as c.

The profits of suppliers b_1, b_2 depend not only on their own quantities but also on the reactions of the other party. The expected profit functions of both parties are:

$$E_1(q_1, q_2) = Pq_1 - cq_1 \tag{11.1.22}$$

$$E_2(q_2, q_1) = Pq_2 - cq_2 \tag{11.1.23}$$

Substitute the price function into (11.1.22), (11.1.23) respectively to get:

$$E_1(q_1, q_2) = q_1(Q - q_1 - q_2 - c) \tag{11.1.24}$$

$$E_2(q_2, q_1) = q_2(Q - q_1 - q_2 - c) \tag{11.1.25}$$

According to the principle of maximizing expected return, b_1, b_2's optimal production strategy must satisfy the first-order derivative condition of the expected profit function:

$$\frac{\partial E(q_1, q_2)}{\partial q_1} = 0 \tag{11.1.26}$$

$$\frac{\partial E_2(q_2, q_1)}{\partial q_2} = 0 \tag{11.1.27}$$

Expand (11.1.26), (11.1.27) to get:

$$(Q - q_1 - q_2 - c) - q_1 = 0 \tag{11.1.28}$$

$$(Q - q_1 - q_2 - c) - q_2 = 0 \tag{11.1.29}$$

Organize to get the optimal response function of suppliers b_1, b_2:

Fig. 11.4 Market supply equilibrium diagram

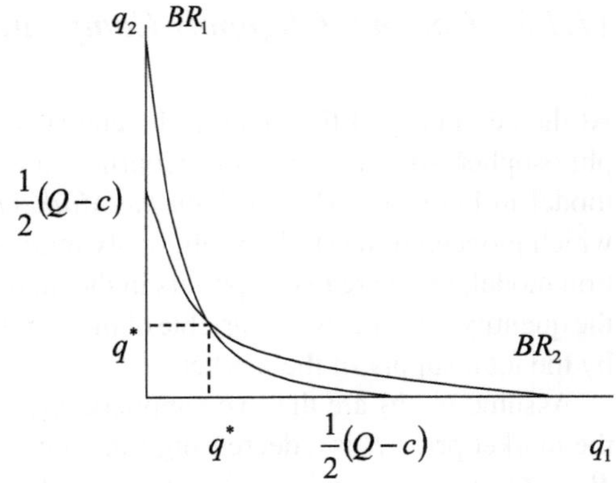

$$BR_1 = \frac{1}{2}(Q - q_2 - c) \tag{11.1.30}$$

$$BR_2 = \frac{1}{2}(Q - q_1 - c) \tag{11.1.31}$$

The above set of equations shows that the optimal output of b_1, b_2 needs to respond according to the decisions made by the other party. In the coordinate system with q_1, q_2 as the coordinate axes, the optimal response curves of the two manufacturers are shown in the following figure.

Figure 11.4 shows that after the game between b_1, b_2, the market will eventually form a Nash equilibrium at point (q^*, q^*). From (11.1.30), (11.1.31), we can solve the specific location of the market equilibrium point.

As can be seen from Fig. 11.4, the market equilibrium point is on the intersection of the optimal response curves of b_1, b_2. q^* satisfies the following equation:

$$q^* = \frac{1}{2}(Q - q^* - c) \tag{11.1.32}$$

Solve q^* from (11.1.32):

$$q^* = \frac{1}{3}(Q - c) \tag{11.1.33}$$

Substitute (11.1.33) into (11.1.24), (11.1.25) respectively to get b_1, b_2 Profits at the equilibrium point:

$$E_1^*(q_1, q_2) = \frac{1}{9}(Q - c)^2 \tag{11.1.34}$$

$$E_2^*(q_2, q_1) = \frac{1}{9}(Q - c)^2 \tag{11.1.35}$$

$$\because \quad Q \gg c \quad \therefore \quad E_1(q_1, q_2) = E_2(q_2, q_1) > 0$$

Under Cournot conditions, manufactures in an oligopolistic competition market have positive profits, and the lower the marginal cost, the higher the profits.

In the Cournot market, the profits realized at the equilibrium solution are not the potential maximum profits. If both parties reach an agreement and appropriately reduce production, both parties can achieve greater profits. According to (11.1.24) and (11.1.25), if b_1 and b_2 form alliance A to set a common pricing strategy, the profits realized by both parties when choosing the optimal output q are as follows:

$$E_1^M(q, q) = q(Q - 2q - c) \tag{11.1.36}$$

$$E_2^M(q, q) = q(Q - 2q - c) \tag{11.1.37}$$

According to the differential condition of the extremum, we can get the first-order equation about the optimal output q:

$$\frac{\partial E_1^M}{\partial q} = \frac{\partial E_2^M}{\partial q} = Q - 4q - c = 0 \tag{11.1.38}$$

Solve the optimal output from (11.1.38):

$$q = \frac{1}{4}(Q - c) \tag{11.1.39}$$

Under the optimal output, the maximum profit realized by the supplier is:

$$E_1^M = E_2^M = \frac{1}{8}(Q - c)^2 \tag{11.1.40}$$

Comparing the maximum profit with the equilibrium profit, we can get:

$$E_1^M - E_1^* = \frac{1}{8}(Q - c)^2 - \frac{1}{9}(Q - c)^2 = \frac{1}{72}(Q - c)^2 \tag{11.1.41}$$

From this, we get that the excess profit generated by cartel A is:

$$\text{Extr}A = \frac{1}{72}(Q - c)^2 > 0 \tag{11.1.42}$$

Equation (11.1.42) shows that the equilibrium pattern spontaneously formed in the Cournot market is unstable. In the absence of effective supervision, manufactures have a strong motivation to form alliances, eventually forming a cartel monopoly pattern. The larger the market capacity Q, the more excess profits the supplier obtains through the alliance, and the stronger the motivation to form an alliance. For markets with rigid supply constraints, the emergence of tangible or intangible cartel alliances is almost an inevitable phenomenon. The OPEC organization in the international oil market is a typical case.

11.1.4 Bertrand Oligopoly Model

The Bertrand oligopoly model was established by French economist Joseph Bertrand in 1883. The main difference between the Bertrand model and the Cournot model lies in the choice of decision variables. The decision variable of the Cournot model is output, while the decision variable of the Bertrand model is product price. In terms of market competition, Bertrand market competition is more intense, and the dominant strategy of firms is the break-even point. In the Bertrand market, not losing money is already the best result for manufactures.

Assume b_1 and b_2 are two suppliers in the market, providing homogeneous products, with product prices of p_1 and p_2 respectively; the marginal cost is c. Assume the market's transfer cost is $Cm = 0$, when b_2 prices higher than b_1, no customers continue to stay at b_2, all are transferred to b_1, at this time, sales volumes of b_1 and b_2 are:

$$q_1 = Q - p_1 \tag{11.1.43}$$

$$q_2 = 0 \tag{11.1.44}$$

If supplier b_1 prices higher than b_2, the same situation will occur, the sales volumes obtained by b_1, b_2 are as follows:

$$q_1 = 0 \tag{11.1.45}$$

$$q_2 = Q - p_2 \tag{11.1.46}$$

If suppliers b_1, b_2 choose the same price p, they will share the market equally, and the sales volumes achieved are as follows:

$$q_1 = q_2 = \frac{Q - p}{2} \tag{11.1.47}$$

In the Bertrand market, because b_1, b_2 both hope to squeeze the other out of the market, monopolize trading resources, and the dominant strategy is to always price lower than the other. Driven by this strategy, market prices continue to fall until they reach the bottom line of marginal cost c. If either party chooses $p_i < c$, they must bear the result of a loss. For profit-maximizing enterprises, this is an unwise choice. In the Bertrand market, the result of oligopoly game has only one equilibrium, that is, both parties choose the marginal cost c as the product price, that is:

$$p_1 = p_2 = c \tag{11.1.48}$$

At the equilibrium point, the profit of Bertrand market suppliers is zero, that is:

$$E_1(p_1, p_2) = E_2(p_2, p_1) = \frac{Q-c}{2}c - \frac{Q-c}{2}c = 0 \tag{11.1.49}$$

The equilibrium point of the Bertrand market is also unstable. As organizations pursuing profit, suppliers b_1, b_2 cannot be satisfied with zero profit results, they will inevitably choose some strategy to break the no-profit equilibrium pattern. In front of b_1, b_2, there are two possible strategies to choose from: one is to endure temporary losses, squeeze the other out of the market, and finally achieve a completely monopolistic market position; the other is to collude with the other party to form a cartel monopoly.

11.1.5 Hotelling's Oligopoly Competition Model

Hotelling's oligopoly competition model was proposed by American economist Harold Hotelling in 1929. Unlike the Cournot model and the Bertrand model, the Hotelling model introduces two factors, supplier differences and transfer costs, and therefore, it also yields richer conclusions than the Cournot model and the Bertrand model.

Assuming there are two oligopolistic suppliers in the market, we still mark them as b_1, b_2, and customers are evenly distributed on a straight line. The Hotelling model simplifies supplier heterogeneity into location differences; customer transfer costs are simplified into transportation costs. Assume that b_1 is located at the end of the line, with coordinates marked as 0; b_2 is located at the other end of the line, with coordinates marked as 1; customers are evenly distributed in the interval [0, 1], each customer has a coordinate identifier, $a_i \in \{a_i\}_M$ is any customer in the customer group, and the location coordinate is represented by x. In the distribution interval, a_i to b_1 is at a distance of x, and the distance to b_2 is $1 - x$. In the above spatial layout, the trading cost between customers and suppliers is reflected in transportation costs, with a unit transportation cost of T.

In the Hotelling market, b_1, b_2 provide completely homogeneous products, and the differences between suppliers are mainly reflected in product pricing and customer transportation costs. Therefore, customers distributed in the interval [0, 1] will choose their trading partners based on the product prices of b_1, b_2 and the distances to themselves. Since the goals of the customers are completely consistent, they will choose the supplier with the highest return and the lowest comprehensive cost, and a segmented pattern will appear in the customer interval, with a certain point in the interval becoming the dividing point between the two suppliers' customers. To the left of the dividing point, all customers choose supplier b_1; to the right of the dividing point, all customers choose supplier b_2.

Assume that the product price of b_1 is P_1, and the product price of b_2 is P_2, and the customer's trading volume is one unit of goods. For any customer a_i, when choosing supplier b_1, the total payment for the trading is:

$$Pa_i^1 = P_1 + xT \tag{11.1.50}$$

The total payment for choosing supplier b_2 is:

$$Pa_i^2 = P_2 + (1 - x)T \tag{11.1.51}$$

If a_i is at the critical point, the total payments of the two suppliers are equal, and we get the critical point equation from this:

$$P_1 + xT = P_2 + (1 - x)T \tag{11.1.52}$$

From (11.1.52), we get the position of the Hotelling market's critical point x^*:

$$x^* = \frac{P_2 - P_1 + T}{2T} \tag{11.1.53}$$

According to the market critical point position (11.1.53), we can calculate the expected return of suppliers b_1 and b_2 respectively. Assume that the two suppliers have the same marginal cost C. The supplier has the following expected profit function:

$$E_1(P_1) = \frac{P_2 - P_1 + T}{2T}P_1 - \frac{P_2 - P_1 + T}{2T}C \tag{11.1.54}$$

$$E_2(P_2) = \frac{P_2 - P_1 + T}{2T}P_2 - \frac{P_2 - P_1 + T}{2T}C \tag{11.1.55}$$

According to the principle of maximizing expected return, suppliers will optimize their pricing strategies to achieve maximum return. From this, we can get the first-order differential conditions for the extreme values of E_1 and E_2:

$$\frac{\partial E_1}{\partial P_1} = \frac{P_2 - 2P_1 + T + C}{2T} = 0 \tag{11.1.56}$$

$$\frac{\partial E_2}{\partial P_2} = \frac{P_1 - 2P_1 + T + C}{2T} = 0 \tag{11.1.57}$$

From (11.1.56) and (11.1.57), we can get the optimal reaction functions of the pricing strategies of b_1 and b_2:

$$BR_1(P_1) = \frac{P_2 + T + C}{2} \tag{11.1.58}$$

$$BR_2(P_2) = \frac{P_1 + T + C}{2} \tag{11.1.59}$$

From the perspective of both parties' optimal response functions, any price adjustment behavior of one party will inevitably cause a follow-up response from the other party. When one party wants to attract more customers by lowering prices, the other party will respond in the same way, and the price reduction effect will be completely offset. In the Hotelling market, suppliers achieve the optimal price that both parties can accept through mutual game, that is, the Nash equilibrium price. We use P^* to represent this equilibrium price, which satisfies the following relationship:

$$BR_1(P_1) = P^* = BR_2(P_2) \tag{11.1.60}$$

Substitute (11.1.58), (11.1.59) into (11.1.60) to get:

$$P^* = \frac{P^* + T + C}{2} \tag{11.1.61}$$

From (11.1.61) we get:

$$P^* = T + C \tag{11.1.62}$$

From (11.1.62) we can conclude: In the Hotelling market, the equilibrium price is the sum of marginal transportation cost and marginal production cost. At this equilibrium price, the maximum revenue obtained by suppliers b_1 and b_2 is:

$$E_1(P_1) = E_2(P_2) = \frac{T}{2} \tag{11.1.63}$$

From (11.1.63) we get the most important conclusion of the Hotelling model: In the oligopolistic competition market, due to the non-zero trading cost caused by transportation factors, there is a positive equilibrium profit for suppliers. The size of the equilibrium profit depends on the level of transportation cost (transfer cost). The higher the transportation cost, the higher the equilibrium profit of the supplier.

In the Hotelling model, transportation cost represents the market transfer cost, and location represents the difference between suppliers. We know that there is a positive correlation between supplier differentiation and market transfer cost. The more significant the differentiation of suppliers, the higher the adaptation cost for customers to transfer between suppliers. The Hotelling model reveals the motivation for suppliers to pursue differentiation.

11.1.6 D-S Monopolistic Competition Model

The D-S monopolistic competition model was first proposed in the paper "*Monopolistic Competition and Optimum Product Diversity*" published jointly by Indian economist Avinash K. Dixit and American economist and Nobel laureate Joseph E. Stiglitz in 1977. The distinctive feature of the D-S model is its modeling method, which uses the typical neoclassical economic equilibrium analysis framework. The assumptions of the model are relatively loose, and the conclusions are rich. Currently, the D-S model has become a basic tool in the fields of new trade theory, economic growth theory, and spatial economics.

The model divides the trading system into two parts, one part is the market under focus, there are n suppliers in the market, denoted as $\{b_i\}_n$, where, any supplier in the market $b_i \in \{b_i\}_n$ has the product price p_i, and the marginal cost is constant, denoted as c. Obviously, this market has a polycentric phase configuration and belongs to a monopolistic competition market; the remaining part of the trading system is classified as another part, with one of its suppliers as the representative, denoted as b_o, and its product price is used as the price reference of the trading system, it is agreed that $p_o = 1$. In a monopolistic competition market, products from different suppliers have constant elasticity of substitution σ.

Assume a is any trading agent in the trading system, representing consumers, with a CES utility function:

$$u = U\left(x_0, \left\{\sum_1^n x_i^\rho\right\}^{\frac{1}{\rho}}\right) \tag{11.1.64}$$

Due to the law of diminishing marginal utility, the function $y = \left\{\sum_1^n x_i^\rho\right\}^{\frac{1}{\rho}}$ must have convex characteristics, therefore, the substitution elasticity must satisfy $\rho < 1$. To avoid infinite singular values, it is required that $\rho > 0$. As an important structural parameter of the D-S model, ρ reflects the diversity preference of consumers, the larger the value of ρ, the stronger the diversity preference of the trading agent; at the same time, ρ also reflects the size of the substitution elasticity between goods, and has the following relationship with the substitution elasticity σ:

$$\rho = 1 - \frac{1}{\sigma} \tag{11.1.65}$$

From (11.1.65) it can be seen that ρ and σ have the same directional change relationship. Therefore, ρ is also known as the substitution elasticity parameter, and is highly related to the substitution elasticity σ. The larger the substitution elasticity σ, the larger the ρ.

The condition of constant elasticity of substitution means that in the decision-making of the trading agent, the demand elasticity for different goods is exactly the same. The size of the demand elasticity depends on the level of constant elasticity of substitution. The stronger the constant elasticity of substitution, the greater the demand elasticity, and the higher the sensitivity of consumers to price.

Obviously, the size of the substitution elasticity parameter ρ also indirectly reflects the intensity of the personalized features of different manufacturers' products. The more obvious the personalized features, the lower the substitutability between products, and the smaller the substitution elasticity parameter ρ; on the contrary, the higher the degree of product homogeneity, the larger the value of ρ.

The trading agent a complies with the following budget constraint:

$$x_0 + \sum_{1}^{n} x_i p_i = I \tag{11.1.66}$$

In (11.1.66), x_0 represents the quantity of products consumed by the trading agent a from supplier b_0; x_i represents the quantity of products consumed by the trading agent a from supplier b_i; I represents the current income of the trading agent a.

According to the objective function (11.1.64) and constraint condition (11.1.66) of the trading agent, we can get the Lagrange function of the trading agent:

$$L = U(x_0, y) - \lambda\left(x_0 + \sum_{1}^{n} x_i p_i - I\right) \tag{11.1.67}$$

According to the principle of maximizing expected return, the trading agent a will inevitably determine the value of the consumption x_i according to the marginal utility brought by each supplier's product and budget constraints, so as to reach the utility extremum at the value of x_i under the condition that other conditions remain unchanged. From this, we get the following extremum conditions:

$$\frac{\partial L}{\partial x_i} = \frac{\partial U(x_0, y)}{\partial x_i} - \frac{\partial}{\partial x_i}\left[\lambda\left(x_0 + \sum_{1}^{n} x_i p_i - I\right)\right] = 0 \tag{11.1.68}$$

Expand (11.1.68) to get:

$$\frac{\partial U(x_0, y)}{\partial y}\frac{\partial y}{\partial x_i} - \lambda p_i = 0 \tag{11.1.69}$$

Further expand the derivative of (11.1.69) to get:

$$\frac{\partial U(x_0, y)}{\partial y}\left[\frac{1}{\rho}\left(\sum_{1}^{n} x_i^{\rho}\right)^{\frac{1}{\rho}-1}\right]\rho x_i^{\rho-1} - \lambda p_i = 0 \tag{11.1.70}$$

Organize (11.1.70) to get:

$$\frac{\partial U(x_0, y)}{\partial y}\left[\left(\sum_1^n x_i^\rho\right)^{\frac{1}{\rho}}\right]^{1-\rho} x_i^{\rho-1} - \lambda p_i = 0 \tag{11.1.71}$$

Substitute $y = \left\{\sum_1^n x_i^\rho\right\}^{\frac{1}{\rho}}$ into (11.1.71) to get:

$$\frac{\partial U(x_0, y)}{\partial y} y^{1-\rho} x_i^{\rho-1} - \lambda p_i = 0 \tag{11.1.72}$$

Solve the optimal consumption quantity of the trading subject a for the supplier b_i product from (11.1.72):

$$x_i^* = y\left(\frac{1}{\lambda}\frac{\partial U(x_0, y)}{\partial y}\right)^{\frac{1}{1-\rho}}\left(\frac{1}{p_i}\right)^{\frac{1}{1-\rho}} \tag{11.1.73}$$

Equation (11.1.73) shows that in the consumption list of trading agents, the optimal consumption quantity of a commodity is inversely proportional to the price of the commodity.

Substitute (11.1.73) into (11.1.66) to get the optimal consumption quantity of the trading agent a for the supplier b_0:

$$x_0^* = I - y\left(\frac{1}{\lambda}\frac{\partial U(x_0, y)}{\partial y}\right)^{\frac{1}{1-\rho}} \sum_1^N \left(\frac{1}{p_i}\right)^{\frac{\rho}{1-\rho}} \tag{11.1.74}$$

According to (11.1.73), we can calculate the price elasticity of the trading agent a for the supplier b_i product demand:

$$E_p = -\frac{\Delta x_i}{\Delta p_i} / \frac{x_i}{p_i} = -\frac{\partial x_i}{\partial p_i} / \frac{x_i}{p_i} \tag{11.1.75}$$

Substitute (11.1.73) into (11.1.75) to get:

$$E_p = \frac{1}{1-\rho} \tag{11.1.76}$$

Affected by the price elasticity of demand, the supplier will adjust the price downwards for each additional product supplied to the market, otherwise, the matrket will not be able to reach equilibrium. For each additional product on any price p_i, the proportion of price reduction is $\frac{1}{E_p(p_i)}$. Therefore, the final marginal benefit of the product is:

$$MR = p_i\left(1 - \frac{1}{E_p(p_i)}\right) \tag{11.1.77}$$

From the condition of profit maximization, it can be known that when the marginal benefit is equal to the marginal cost, the supplier b_i reaches the optimal production scale and achieves the maximum profit.

From the assumption, it can be known that the marginal cost is constant:

$$MR = c \tag{11.1.78}$$

From this, the supplier's optimal production strategy is obtained:

$$p_i\left(1 - \frac{1}{E_p(p_i)}\right) = c \tag{11.1.79}$$

Substitute (11.1.76) into (11.1.79) to get:

$$p_i(1 - (1 - \rho)) = c \tag{11.1.80}$$

From (11.1.80), the optimal pricing of b_i can be obtained:

$$p_i^* = \frac{c}{\rho} \tag{11.1.81}$$

Equation (11.1.81) shows that under the condition of constant marginal cost, the optimal pricing of monopoly competition market suppliers is inversely proportional to the substitution elasticity parameter. The lower the substitution elasticity parameter, the higher the optimal pricing. The substitution elasticity parameter is closely related to the transfer cost. Generally speaking, under the same conditions, the lower the substitution elasticity parameter of the product, the higher the consumer transfer cost. It seems that the conclusion of the D-S model about the relationship between substitution elasticity and optimal pricing is basically consistent with the conclusions of the trading model and the Hotelling model.

Considering the symmetry of the supplier's status in the utility function, whether it is the supplier's optimal pricing p_i^* or the consumer's optimal consumption quantity x_i, they all have equal values, that is:

$$p_i^* = p^*, i = 1, 2 \dots n \tag{11.1.82}$$

$$x_i^* = x^*, i = 1, 2 \dots n \tag{11.1.83}$$

Substitute (11.1.82) and (11.1.83) into (11.1.67) to get:

$$L = U\left(x_0, x^* n^{\frac{1}{\rho}}\right) - \lambda(x_0 + x^* p^* n - I) \tag{11.1.84}$$

Due to budget constraints, there is a certain upper limit to consumer diversification. The maximum number of product types can be solved from (11.1.84):

$$n^* = (\lambda p^* \rho)^{\frac{\rho}{1-\rho}} \left(\frac{\partial U}{\partial y} \right)^{\frac{\rho}{1-\rho}} \tag{11.1.85}$$

In order to determine the relationship between product substitution elasticity and diversification in a monopolistic competition market, according to (11.1.85), we derive n^* with respect to the substitution elasticity parameter ρ. For technical reasons, we first take the logarithm of both sides of (11.1.85):

$$\ln n^* = \frac{\rho}{1-\rho} \left[\ln(\lambda p^* \rho) - \ln \frac{\partial U}{\partial y} \right] \tag{11.1.86}$$

Take the derivative of both sides of (11.1.86) with respect to ρ:

$$\frac{\partial \ln n^*}{\partial \rho} = \frac{1}{(1-\rho)^2} \left[\ln(\lambda p^* \rho) - \ln \frac{\partial U}{\partial y} \right] + \frac{\rho}{1-\rho} (\frac{1}{\rho}) \tag{11.1.87}$$

If the following condition is met:

$$\rho \geq \frac{1}{\lambda p^*} \frac{\partial U}{\partial y} \tag{11.1.88}$$

Then the following inequality holds:

$$\frac{\partial \ln n^*}{\partial \rho} > 0 \tag{11.1.89}$$

If the following condition is met:

$$\rho < \frac{1}{\lambda p^*} \frac{\partial U}{\partial y} \tag{11.1.90}$$

Then the following inequality holds:

$$\frac{\partial \ln n^*}{\partial \rho} < 0 \tag{11.1.91}$$

Equations (11.1.89) and (11.1.90) indicate that there is a bifurcation phenomenon in the monopolistic competition market, and the market critical point is near $\rho = \frac{1}{\lambda p^*} \frac{\partial U}{\partial y}$. On the left side of the critical point, the optimal number of product types is inversely related to the substitution elasticity parameter. The lower the substitution elasticity parameter, the greater the market's capacity for monopolistic suppliers. On the right side of the critical point, the market's capacity for monopolistic suppliers is directly related to the substitution elasticity parameter. The higher the product substitution elasticity, the greater the number of suppliers the market can accommodate. However, since the substitution elasticity parameter is inversely related to the market equilibrium price, as the substitution elasticity parameter increases and the quality becomes similar, the market equilibrium price will continue to fall. Therefore, the process of product convergence is necessarily temporary and unstable equilibrium; only when the market enters another bifurcation area, and suppliers begin to pursue product characteristics, and product substitution elasticity begins to decline, will the market enter a virtuous cycle. In fact, these are two stages that the market evolution must go through; the first stage is in the early stage of market development; the second stage is when market has entered maturity.

11.1.7 Overview of Polycentric Market Properties

The polycentric phase configuration is the dominant market mode of modern trading systems. We have conducted multi-dimensional research on the game characteristics and evolution rules of polycentric markets from different perspectives through five models, which has given us a deeper understanding of the characteristics of polycentric phase structure markets.

Firstly, the polycentric market is an unstable phase structure. In continuous competition, suppliers eliminate suppliers with low competitiveness through cost-performance leaps. After round after round of market elimination, the ultimate destination of market structure evolution is that the number of suppliers continues to decrease, and eventually converges to a monocentric monopoly or oligopoly structure.

Under the above evolution convergence rule, there is a small probability that the competitiveness of multiple suppliers in the market is very close, and after many rounds of competition, the original market pattern cannot be broken. In this case, suppliers will reach some kind of explicit or implicit alliance method, coordinate with each other, and form an alliance monopoly pattern.

Secondly, the transfer costs in a polycentric market tend to self-enhance. In a polycentric market, the higher the transfer cost, the larger the profit margin for suppliers. Driven by the motive of profit, suppliers enhance product differentiation through various means to maintain their own profit margins. Looking at the entire lifecycle of market evolution, in the early stages of market formation, suppliers are in a phase of experience accumulation, and mutual learning and imitation are typical characteristics of suppliers at this stage. Through the process of mutual learning and imitation among suppliers, the market gradually converges towards standardization and normalization. Once market standardization is completed, the market will enter a reverse process—the differentiation process. In this stage, suppliers shift from the aggressive strategy of the first stage to a steady offensive strategy. On the one hand, they aim to stabilize the customer base by highlighting individual characteristics and strengthening product features; on the other hand, they attract more customers by upgrading and replacing products, thereby launching attacks on competitors. In the two stages of market evolution, the evolution speed of the standardization stage is faster; while the differentiation and personalization stage evolve relatively slowly.

The number of suppliers decreases significantly in the standardization stage, and although the number of suppliers that can enter the differentiation stage is limited, their competitive strength is generally strong. These conclusions are confirmed in the trading model, Hotelling model, and D-S model.

Thirdly, the evolution process of the polycentric market usually shows the evolutionary characteristics of intergenerational leaps. The evolution of the cost-performance ratio in the polycentric market presents a leapfrog pattern. After a period of power accumulation, suppliers will have significant improvements in production efficiency, product design, and production technology, and these changes will be concentrated on the cost-performance ratio of the product. In the intergenerational leap evolution of the polycentric market, the cost-performance ratio changes in the direction of a stepwise increase. As the dominant market mode of the modern trading system, the evolutionary mode of intergenerational leaps in the polycentric market determines the basic characteristics of the evolution of the trading system, that is, the wave-like characteristics of evolution of acceleration–deceleration–acceleration.

The five models discussed in this section have their own emphasis and have corresponding market prototypes in reality. The Cournot model focuses on quantity game, which is highly consistent with the international crude oil market. The key conclusion derived from the Cournot model is: for large-capacity markets, it is inevitable for suppliers to form a cartel alliance. The Bertrand model focuses on price game, corresponding to a fully competitive market with numerous suppliers and highly homogeneous products in reality, which has typical characteristics of the early stage of market evolution. The Hotelling model focuses on supplier differentiation and the role of transfer costs, and can find more appropriate application scenarios in the later stage of market evolution, that is, mature markets. Compared with the above models, the D-S model has stronger universality and is suitable for market analysis at any stage of development. The model uses the equilibrium analysis method of neoclassical economics, uses product substitution elasticity as the key indicator to describe the polycentric market, and is logically rigorous, making it easy for quantitative analysis applications.

Compared with the above four monopoly competition models, the polycentric market trading model is more relaxed in terms of condition setting. It not only allows for product differentiation among suppliers, but also assumes the existence of transfer costs in the market; suppliers can compete not only in price, but also in quality and performance. Such trading model is more in line with the real situation of competition between enterprises and has a broader application scenario.

In terms of model construction methods, including the trading model, the Cournot model, the Bertrand model, and the Hotelling model, all have adopted game theory as the basic framework, and all trading agents adhere to the principle of maximizing expected return. The difference lies in that the game variable in the trading model is the product's cost-performance ratio. Compared with price, output, and other game variables, the meaning of cost-performance ratio is more comprehensive, and the game strategy implied in the conclusion is also richer.

Looking at the conclusions drawn from the models, the conclusions of the polycentric trading model are richer, not only containing all the conclusions of the other four models, but also having stronger dynamic evolution characteristics, thereby deepening our detailed understanding of the market evolution process.

11.2 Monocentric Phase Configuration

From a mathematical perspective, any natural number n can be seen as the result of adding up1 repeatedly, but such logic cannot be extended to the relationship between polycentric models and monocentric models. In the polycentric trading model, the focus of market game is between manufacturers in the same phase; while in the monocentric trading model, the focus of market game is between customers and manufacturers in different phases. Because of this, the monocentric trading model cannot be derived as a special case from the polycentric trading model, but needs to be independently constructed.

11.2.1 Monocentric Trading Model

The monocentric phase configuration is a market structure completely monopolized by a single supplier. Compared with the polycentric phase configuration market, the probability of a monocentric market appearing in modern trading systems is extremely small, and can only occur under extremely special circumstances. Despite this, as a phase configuration that may appear on the trading network, it is still necessary for us to study its operating mechanism.

In the monocentric market, there is only one supplier in the entire market, and customers have no other choices, belonging to a completely monopolistic market structure. The network relationship of the monocentric phase configuration is shown in Fig. 11.5.

Once the market forms a monopoly pattern, the monopolistic manufacture gains a super trading momentum, and the market has formed a de facto entry barrier. Under

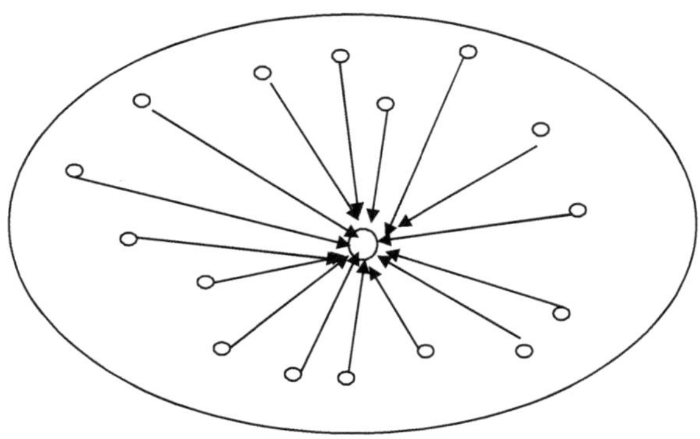

Fig. 11.5 The monocentric phase configuration diagram

such circumstances, the main tasks of the monopoly enterprise are only two: one is to maintain the basic satisfaction of the customer group to avoid market shrinkage; the other is to ensure legal operation to avoid government regulatory penalties. Based on this logic, we construct a monocentric trading model.

Assume that the monopoly manufacturer's initial pricing for the product is P, the corresponding sales volume is Q, and the marginal production cost is C; now the manufacturer plans to raise the price from P to $P + \Delta P$, $\Delta P > 0$. The manufacturer knows that a price increase may bring two consequences: one is that the market will respond to the price increase by reducing demand; the other is to attract the attention of the regulatory authorities and be punished by the regulatory authorities. Assume that the loss from being punished is Ca, and the probability of being punished is Pr. Under these circumstances, the expected return function of the manufacturer choosing the price increase strategy is as follows:

$$E(\frac{\triangle P}{P}) = (P + \triangle P)(Q + \triangle Q) - C(Q + \triangle Q) - (PQ - CQ) - \Pr \times Ca \tag{11.2.1}$$

After rearranging, we get:

$$E\left(\frac{\triangle P}{P}\right) = PQ\left(\frac{\triangle Q}{Q} + \frac{\triangle P}{P} + \frac{\triangle P}{P}\frac{\triangle Q}{Q} - \frac{\triangle Q}{Q}\frac{C}{P}\right) - \Pr \times Ca \tag{11.2.2}$$

Let $\pi = \frac{\Delta P}{P}, \alpha = -\frac{\Delta Q}{Q}/\pi$.

Substitute into (11.2.2) to get:

$$E(\pi) = PQ\left(\pi - \alpha\pi - \alpha\pi^2 + \alpha\pi\frac{C}{P}\right) - \Pr \times Ca \tag{11.2.3}$$

According to the principle of maximizing expected return, the manufacturer will only choose the price increase strategy when the price increase brings more than 0 return to the manufacturer. From this we get:

$$PQ\pi\left(1 - \alpha - \alpha\pi + \alpha\frac{C}{P}\right) - \Pr \times Ca > 0 \tag{11.2.4}$$

Organizing (11.2.4) we get:

$$PQ\pi\left(1 - \alpha - \alpha\pi + \alpha\frac{C}{P}\right) > \Pr \times Ca \tag{11.2.5}$$

Considering that price adjustments in reality are usually mild, without affecting the generality of the conclusion, we assume $\pi < 1$, from which we get the following results:

$$PQ\left(1-\alpha-\alpha\pi+\alpha\frac{C}{P}\right)>PQ\pi\left(1-\alpha-\alpha\pi+\alpha\frac{C}{P}\right)>\Pr\times Ca \quad (11.2.6)$$

$$\therefore PQ\left(1-\alpha-\alpha\pi+\alpha\frac{C}{P}\right)>\Pr\times Ca \quad (11.2.7)$$

$$\therefore \left(1-\alpha-\alpha\pi+\alpha\frac{C}{P}\right)>\frac{\Pr\times Ca}{PQ} \quad (11.2.8)$$

$$\therefore 1-\alpha\left(1-\frac{C}{P}\right)-\frac{\Pr\times Ca}{PQ}>\alpha\pi \quad (11.2.9)$$

$$\therefore \pi<\frac{1}{\alpha}-\frac{\Pr\times Ca}{\alpha PQ}-\left(1-\frac{C}{P}\right)<\frac{1}{\alpha}-\frac{\Pr\times Ca}{\alpha PQ} \quad (11.2.10)$$

$$\therefore \pi<\frac{1}{\alpha}\left(1-\frac{\Pr\times Ca}{PQ}\right) \quad (11.2.11)$$

Now, let's examine the conditions that the optimal pricing of a monopoly firm satisfies in the absence of effective market regulation.

Assuming $\Pr = 0$, we get from (11.2.3):

$$E(\pi)=PQ\left(\pi-\alpha\pi-\alpha\pi^2+\alpha\pi\frac{C}{P}\right) \quad (11.2.12)$$

According to the differential conditions of the extremum, the manufacture's optimal pricing satisfies the following equation:

$$\frac{\partial E(\pi)}{\partial\pi}=0 \quad (11.2.13)$$

From (11.2.13) we get:

$$1-\alpha-2\alpha\pi+\alpha\frac{C}{P}=0 \quad (11.2.14)$$

From (11.2.14) we get the optimal pricing strategy of the monopoly firm:

$$\pi^*=\frac{1}{2\alpha}-\frac{1}{2}\left(1-\frac{C}{P}\right) \quad (11.2.15)$$

Comparing (11.2.11) and (11.2.15), we can see the difference in pricing strategies of the monopoly firm under two different market environments:

$$\pi^*-\pi>\frac{1}{2\alpha}-\frac{1}{2}\left(1-\frac{C}{P}\right)-\frac{1}{\alpha}\left(1-\frac{\Pr\times Ca}{PQ}\right) \quad (11.2.16)$$

Organizing, we get:

$$\pi^* - \pi > \frac{1}{\alpha}\left(\frac{\Pr \times Ca}{PQ} - \frac{1}{2}\right) - \frac{1}{2}\left(1 - \frac{C}{P}\right) \tag{11.2.17}$$

From (11.2.17) we get the condition for $\pi^* - \pi > 0$:

$$\frac{1}{\alpha}\left(\frac{\Pr \times Ca}{PQ} - \frac{1}{2}\right) - \frac{1}{2}\left(1 - \frac{C}{P}\right) > 0 \tag{11.2.18}$$

Organizing, we get:

$$\alpha < \frac{2\Pr \times Ca - PQ}{PQ - CQ} \tag{11.2.19}$$

When (11.2.19) holds, it means that the market demand is relatively rigid. Under the constraint of effective market regulation, the monopoly manufacturer will adopt a pricing strategy lower than that of the free market environment:

$$\pi^* - \pi > 0 \tag{11.2.20}$$

Equation (11.2.11) shows: In a monopoly market, market price elasticity and government regulation are key factors determining corporate pricing behavior. The greater the price elasticity of the market, the more cautious the monopoly enterprise is about raising prices; the stricter the government's market regulation, the more significant the constraint effect on the monopoly enterprise. It is particularly worth noting that the enterprise's subjective judgment of the possibility of being punished plays a very important role in its pricing decision. This shows that the efficiency of government market regulation is very critical. Strict regulations alone are not enough. Even if theoretically Ca value is very large, if law enforcement efficiency is low, the probability of a monopoly enterprise being punished for violations Pr is low, the actual effect of the law will be greatly reduced.

From (11.2.15) we can see that when market demand is relatively rigid, the value of demand elasticity system α is very small, the market itself has weak price constraints on monopoly enterprises, and monopoly manufacturers tend to raise product prices, achieving excess monopoly profits by infringing consumer interests.

In addition, (11.2.19) and (11.2.20) also provide us with more information about the pricing strategy of monopoly manufacturers. For markets with high demand elasticity, the market itself will become an external constraint on the pricing behavior of monopoly manufacturers, and market regulation should focus on product quality and after-sales service; for markets with high demand rigidity, price regulation should be the primary task of government management departments.

11.2.2 Milgrom-Roberts Monopoly Model

In the study of firm behavior in a monocentric market, the Milgrom-Roberts model has significant influence. The Milgrom-Roberts model was developed by 2020 Nobel laureate in economics and American economist Paul R. Milgrom and economist John Roberts. The model was proposed by Milgrom and Roberts in 1982. This model is the first application of signal transmission game in industrial organization theory. The main conclusion of the model is: under the environment of information asymmetry, monopoly firms tend to limit the product price below the monopoly equilibrium price to prevent the entry of potential competitors. For this reason, the Milgrom-Roberts monopoly model is also known as the monopoly limit price model.

Assume b_1 is the only supplier in a monocentric market, and in a complete monopoly position; b_2 represents any potential competitive supplier. The Milgrom-Roberts model focuses on the pricing strategy adopted by the monopoly supplier b_1 to prevent b_2 from entering. The pricing behavior in two consecutive periods is examined. In the first period, b_1's pricing strategy will directly determine whether b_2 enters the market in the second period. Assume b_1's price in the first period is P_1.

Suppose b_1 has two possible types, the high-cost type is denoted as H, and the low-cost type is denoted as L, ϑ represents any type, which can have two different values, $\vartheta = H$ or $\vartheta = L$. In an asymmetric information market, b_2 does not know the exact type of b_1, and can only infer based on the observation of b_1's pricing behavior. Use $\mu(L)$ to represent the probability that b_2 infers b_1 is a high-cost type; use $\mu(L)$ to represent the probability that b_2 infers is a low-cost type. Obviously, the two should satisfy the probability identity: $\mu(H) + \mu(L) = 1$.

Use P_1^{ϑ} to represent the optimal monopoly price of b_1 when the type is ϑ; use $E_1^{\vartheta} = E_1^{\vartheta}(P_1^{\vartheta})$ to represent the expected revenue corresponding to the optimal monopoly price. Different types of monopoly prices and expected revenues satisfy the following relationship: $P_1^H > P_1^L$; $E_1^H < E_1^L$. Use δ to represent the market discount factor.

In the second period, if b_2 chooses to enter, the market will form a duopoly structure. In order to resist invasion of b_2, b_1 will try to suppress the price as much as possible until the price is close to the cost of production. If b_1 is of the low-cost type, the price will be suppressed very low, so that b_2 cannot bear it. In this case, the inference of b_2 with respect to b_1 type is a key parameter in the entry decision. If $\mu(H) \gg \mu(L)$, b_2 will enter; if $\mu(H) \ll \mu(L)$, b_2 will decide to give up entry.

Assuming under the duopoly structure, b_1 and b_2 expected profit functions are D_1^{ϑ} and D_2^{ϑ} respectively. According to the above analysis, we can reasonably assume:

$$E_1^{\vartheta} > D_1^{\vartheta} \tag{11.2.21}$$

$$D_2^H > 0 > D_2^L \tag{11.2.22}$$

Obviously, if b_1 is of the low-cost type, b_1 does not need to disguise, b_2 can judge the result of $\vartheta = L$ based on the pricing behavior of b_1, and thus actively give up the decision to enter the market. When b_1 is of the high-cost type, in order to prevent potential competitors from entering the market, b_1 will choose to send false signals $\vartheta = L$ to the market, as long as the following conditions are met:

$$E_1^H(P_1^L) + \delta E_1^H(P_1^L) > E_1^H(P_1^H) + \delta D_1^H \tag{11.2.23}$$

b_2 will choose a P_1^L lower than the optimal monopoly price, choosing to exchange temporary losses for greater long-term benefits, setting the price P_1 equal to or lower than the monopoly price of the low-cost type, that is:

$$P_1 \le P_1^L \tag{11.2.24}$$

Regardless of the type of b_1, the pricing strategy given by (11.2.24) is the dominant strategy of b_1. This is the key conclusion of the Milgrom-Roberts limit pricing model: that is, in order to prevent potential competitors from entering the market, the monopoly firm will actively choose to price the product lower than the optimal monopoly price, which explains the cause of the discrepancy between the theory and the actual situation of monopoly pricing.[1]

Whether it is a monocentric trading model or the Milgrom-Roberts limit pricing model, they both give very similar conclusions: even in a completely monopolistic market, suppliers will not indiscriminately raise prices, and they will not set the product price as high as possible. Monopoly suppliers face many external constraints, including market demand elasticity, government regulation, the coveting of potential competitors, etc., all of which play a role in limiting the monopoly supplier's price increase to a certain extent.

11.3 Random Trading Configuration

Both polycentric phase configurations and monocentric phase configurations are market types defined by stable phase structures, while random trading configurations are defined from the perspective of the stability of trading network links or network reconnection rates.

Trading relationships in random trading configurations are extremely volatile and highly randomized. In the random trading market, customers have no accumulation of past trading information, and there is no information transmission between customers. Marketplaces of traditional society and flea markets of modern society belong to this type of market configuration.

Although the random trading market is gradually declining in the modern trading system, this type of market still plays a certain role, especially in special scenarios and special fields, and even plays an irreplaceable role. The flea market is a good example. Even in economically advanced Western countries, flea markets as a cultural symbol still play an indispensable role in enriching residents' lives. Taking Europe as an example, France has Clignancourt flea market, Chatou flea market, Les Andelys flea market; Belgium has Brussels flea market; the Netherlands has Amsterdam flea market; Italy has Arezzo flea market; in the United States, there are many famous flea markets, such as Daytona flea market in Miami Beach, Shipshewana flea market in Indiana, and Springfield flea market in Ohio. In China, Beijing Panjiayuan Antique Market is a representative flea market, with more than 3000 stalls, covering an area of 50,000 m^2. The market operators come from more than 20 provinces, cities, and autonomous regions across the country; they operate old folk goods, crafts, collectibles, antique furniture, Buddhist artifacts, ethnic clothing, and daily necessities. In addition, Guangzhou Likang Second-hand Market, Shenzhen Sanhe Second-hand Market, Shunde Second-hand Market, Guangxi Nanning Hengde Second-hand Market, etc., all have a certain scale and influence. These markets operate a wide variety of goods, with values ranging from small items worth a few dollars to collectibles worth tens of thousands or even hundreds of thousands; the quality of goods is mixed. In modern metropolises, these flea markets are not only places for trading, but also shoulder the cultural responsibility of attracting tourists for sightseeing and tick off. They are vivid samples for understanding the livelihood customs, historical evolution, and cultural features of a city or even a country.

The typical feature of the random trading configuration is the instability of the trading relationship. We use a dotted line to represent the unstable trading relationship, and the corresponding trading network is shown in Fig. 11.6.

In the random trading market, there is a great asymmetry of information between the two trading parties, and the selection of trading object is completely random. In order to attract customers, sellers will fully utilize the advantage of information asymmetry to create illusions of quality or price for customers.

Assume $\{a_i\}_N$ is a group of random consumers, $\{b_j\}_M$ is a group of sellers. In the random market, consumers have no knowledge about suppliers, no past trading experience; there is also no information communication among consumers, they can only infer the cost-effectiveness of goods based on the appearance of goods and the sales information of sellers. Assume the real cost-effectiveness of the goods of seller b_j is λ_j, and a_i estimates it as $e(\lambda_j)$, consumers make their own choices based on

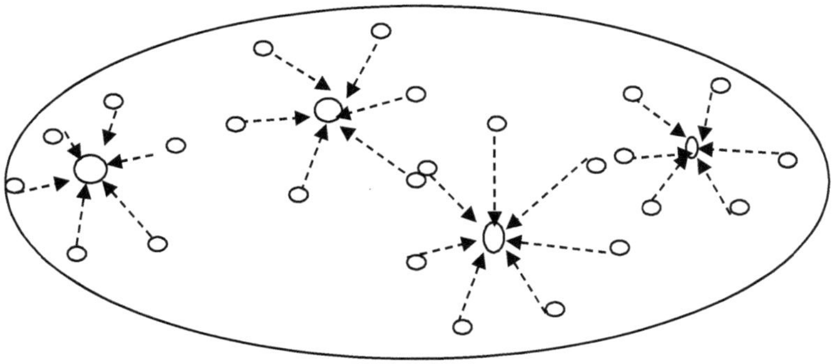

Fig. 11.6 The random trading configuration diagram

their valuation of the cost-effectiveness of various goods. For technical convenience, we still assume that the consumer's trading volume is one unit of goods each time.

Assume the expected return of a_i when choosing b_j as the trading object is:

$$E_i(b_j) = Z_j - P_j \tag{11.3.1}$$

According to the agreement, the trading agent a_i can only value the commodity value of the seller b_j based on the information they have:

$$\because\ Z_j = p_j e(\lambda_j) \tag{11.3.2}$$

$$\therefore E_i(b_j) = P_j e(\lambda_j) - P_j = P_j(e(\lambda_j) - 1) \tag{11.3.3}$$

Without any trading experience to refer to, consumers can only make judgments based on the limited information they get from the seller and choose the supplier with the highest expected cost-effectiveness for trading.

In a random market, only the sellers knows their real cost-effectiveness. In this case, the expected profit function of the supplier b_j is:

$$E_j = (P_j - C_j)N_j \tag{11.3.4}$$

Usually, there is a proportional relationship between the seller's purchase cost C_j and the real value of the goods. The higher the value of the goods, the greater the cost C_j the seller needs to pay. This relationship can be expressed by a function:

$$C_j = \alpha Z_j \tag{11.3.5}$$

Since the seller must gain profit from the trading, α must be less than 1; the size of the seller's customer base N_j depends on the size of the cost-effectiveness valuation formed by the seller's inducement. The higher the cost-effectiveness valuation of its goods by the seller's boasting, the larger the customer base. From this we get:

$$N_j = \beta e(\lambda_j) \tag{11.3.6}$$

In (11.3.6), β is a parameter greater than 1, substituting (11.3.5), (11.3.6) into (11.3.4) we get:

$$E_j = (P_j - \alpha P_j \lambda_j)\beta e(\lambda_j) \tag{11.3.7}$$

Organize (11.3.7) to get:

$$E_j = \beta P_j e(\lambda_j)(1 - \alpha\lambda_j) \tag{11.3.8}$$

From the structure of (11.3.8), the higher the cost-effectiveness valuation that the seller in the random market creates for consumers, the greater the benefit it brings to itself; and the lower the real cost-effectiveness, the more beneficial it is to the supplier. Due to the lack of a repeated game information feedback mechanism in the random market, the seller has no scruples about the consequences of fraud, which leads to the tendency of flea market sellers to sell counterfeit goods.

In a random market, if the seller does not create illusions, but shows the real cost-effectiveness to consumers, its profit function is as follows:

$$E_j = \beta P_j \lambda_j (1 - \alpha \lambda_j) \tag{11.3.9}$$

Compared with (11.3.8), we can get the seller's rent-seeking profit:

$$\Delta E_j = \beta P_j [e(\lambda_j) - \lambda_j](1 - \alpha \lambda_j) \tag{11.3.10}$$

The growth rate of rent-seeking profit is closely related to the effect of creating illusions:

$$\frac{\Delta E_j}{E_j} = \frac{e(\lambda_j) - \lambda_j}{\lambda_j} \tag{11.3.11}$$

Equation (11.3.11) shows that in a random market, sellers have a strong motivation to counterfeiting and will use all possible means to mislead consumers; of course, consumers will always try to discern the seller's information in order to protect their own interests. Usually, they will comparing goods in the market, and obtaining the other party's real information through bargaining, thereby increasing their ability to evaluate cost-effectiveness.

In the trading system, markets with a lower reconnection rate will show some characteristics of a random market, and both parties to the trading will also play a game of fraud and debunking.

11.4 Supply Chain Hub Configuration

We now turn to industrial organization, analyzing the trading characteristics induced by different organizational structures within the industry.

The hub configuration of the supply chain refers to a special configuration in the supply chain where a trading agent is at the central hub of the supply chain, and other upstream and downstream enterprises are connected to it in different phase modes. This configuration structure is shown in Fig. 11.7.

On the supply chain of products with higher added value, due to constraints such as technical constraints and huge investment scale, it is easy to form a hub configuration of the supply chain structure. Supply chains for smartphones, home appliances, cars, airplanes, etc., where the upstream is a large number of spare parts suppliers, and

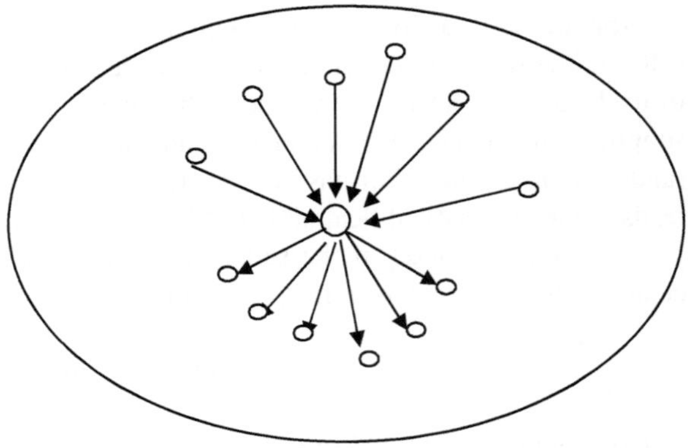

Fig. 11.7 The hub configuration of the supply chain

the downstream is a large consumer group, thus forming a hub configuration of the trading network. In fact, the hub may not only appear at the position of the terminal product, but also at any position in the supply chain, such as chip suppliers are at the hub position of many supply chains including smartphones, cars, home appliances, etc.

The trading agent at the hub position has unique trading advantages, it usually has super trading potential and strong bargaining power, and can influence the overall competitiveness of the market to a certain extent.

For the convenience of analysis, we denote the manufacturer at the hub position as b_0, the upstream partner as $\{b_j\}_M$; and the downstream customer as $\{a_j\}_N$. We focus on the structure and trading strategy of the expected profit function of the hub manufacturer E_0.

On the supply chain of the central hub configuration, the downstream enterprises basically have no bargaining power. Due to the relative stability of the supply chain organization, downstream enterprises will not change the trading relationship due to the price adjustment of the hub manufacturer. Therefore, we have reason to assume that the customer group N of the hub manufacturer is a constant, and has a stable demand quantity Q_0.

If the product pricing of b_0 is P_0, and the marginal cost is C, then the expected profit function is as follows:

$$E_0 = (P_0 - C)Q_0 \tag{11.4.1}$$

The marginal cost C is mainly composed of parts cost, labor cost, and fixed asset depreciation cost. Under other conditions unchanged, the marginal cost C is directly proportional to the average price of parts $\overline{P}$:

$$C = k\overline{P} \tag{11.4.2}$$

where, $k > 0$, the value depends on the marginal cost structure, that is, it depends on the proportion of various components including labor cost, fixed asset depreciation cost, energy consumption cost, and raw material cost. The higher the proportion of raw material costs, $k > 0$ the larger the value.

Substitute (11.4.2) into (11.4.1) to get:

$$E_0 = \left(\frac{Z_0}{\lambda_0} - k\frac{\overline{Z}}{\overline{\lambda}}\right)Q_0 \tag{11.4.3}$$

In (11.4.3), Z_0 represents the value of b_0 product, λ_0 represents the cost-effectiveness of b_0, $\overline{Z}$ and $\overline{\lambda}$ represent the average value and cost-effectiveness of upstream parts respectively.

Equation (11.4.3) shows that, under the condition of a given product performance, the hub manufacturer b_0 tend to lower their own cost-effectiveness, pressuring upstream manufacturers to improve cost-effectiveness. In practical operations, b_0 maintain a higher pricing for their own products, suppressing the price of upstream components. In the long run, although hub manufacturers have the ability to influence or even control upstream pricing, they still have the motivation to improve product performance from the perspective of consolidating market position, b_0 still motivated to improve product performance and as long as they can maintain stable cost-effectiveness, they can still benefit from product optimization.

For industries with a central hub configuration, the hub manufacturer is the key to the efficiency of the entire industry. Through its pressure on upstream manufacturers, upstream enterprises must continuously improve their own efficiency and increase the cost-effectiveness of their products. In this process, the hub manufacturer, in order to maintain its long-term interests, will transfer a part of the consumer surplus to downstream customers, but a considerable part of the consumer surplus provided by upstream enterprises will still be intercepted by the hub manufacturer. Therefore, in the central hub configuration, the manufacturer in the hub position is the profit center and has the most substantial benefits.

11.5 Supply Chain Layered Configuration

Compared with the hub configuration, the layered configuration is a more common trading network form on the supply chain. The layered configuration refers to a network configuration composed of multiple suppliers on each layer according to the trading phase on the supply chain. Between different levels, the upper level is in the forward trading phase, and the lower level is in the reverse trading phase. The trading relationship between upstream and downstream agents is relatively stable, but not unique. The network relationship is shown in Fig. 11.8.

On the supply chain with a layered structure, each layer is composed of multiple trading agents, which are in a competitive relationship with each other in the same phase, and this competitive relationship is the basis for ensuring the efficiency of the supply chain.

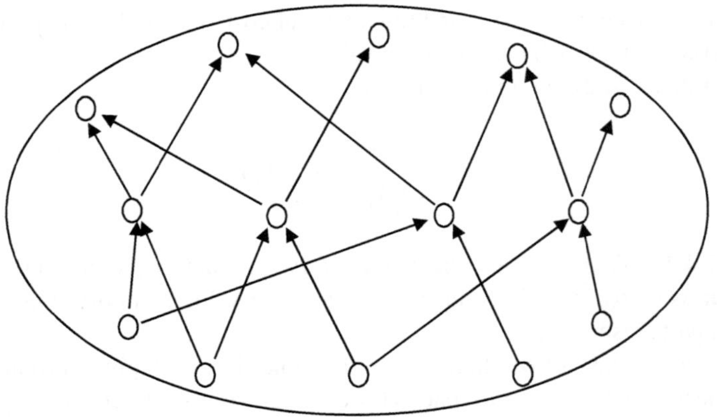

Fig. 11.8 The layered configuration of supply chain

The supply chain can have a multi-layer structure, but the game mechanism between the adjacent trading agents on each layer is exactly the same. Here, we only analyze the game process of a group of adjacent layers, as a summary of the entire supply chain operation mechanism.

Assume $\{a_i\}_N$ is a collection of trading agents at the same layer in the supply chain, $\{b_j\}_M$ is adjacent to $\{a_i\}_N$, $\{a_i\}_N$ is in the reverse phase, $\{b_j\}_M$ is in the forward phase. On different levels of the supply chain, the phase characteristics are relative. For $\{a_i\}_N$, $\{b_j\}_M$ is in the forward phase; for trading agents above $\{b_j\}_M$, $\{b_j\}_M$ is in the reverse phase; the same is true for $\{a_i\}_N$.

Let's examine the game process of $\{a_i\}_N$ and $\{b_j\}_M$. The trading agent $a_i \in \{a_i\}_N$ is any consumer, and the expected profit function has the following structure:

$$E(a_i, b_j) = (Z_j - P_j)Q_i = Z_j(1 - \frac{1}{\lambda_j})Q_i \tag{11.5.1}$$

In (11.5.1), Z_j and λ_j are the value and cost-effectiveness of the product of any supplier $b_j \in \{b_j\}_M$; Q_i is the trading volume of a_i. According to the principle of maximizing expected return, if a_i finds a supplier in the set $\{b_j\}_N$ with a cost-performance ratio higher than b_j, it will consider to transfer trade. Since a_i is in the supply chain, ensuring production stability becomes a major constraint for trade transfer. Changing upstream trading partners not only requires negotiation costs but also takes time to establish trust with new partners. Therefore, a_i must consider the transfer cost of trade relations Cm when considering changing trading partners. Trade transfer will only be profitable if potential trading partners meet higher conditions. For technical convenience, we assume that a_i trades one unit of goods each time.

According to the principle of maximizing expected return, the trading agent a_i needs to meet the following conditions to adjust trading partners:

$$E(a_i, b_l) - E(a_i, b_j) > Cm, i \neq j \tag{11.5.2}$$

Assume that ba_j is a supplier with a higher cost-performance ratio than b_j, and $Z_l > Z_j$.

$$\Delta E = (Z_l - P_l) - (Z_j - P_j) = (Z_l - Z_j) - (P_l - P_j) \tag{11.5.3}$$

The cost-performance ratio formula gives:

$$\Delta E = (Z_l - Z_j) - \left(\frac{Z_l}{\lambda_l} - \frac{Z_j}{\lambda_j}\right) \tag{11.5.4}$$

$$\because Z_l > Z_j$$

$$\begin{aligned} \therefore\ \Delta E &< (Z_l - Z_j) - \left(\frac{Z_l}{\lambda_l} - \frac{Z_l}{\lambda_j}\right) \\ \Delta E &< (Z_l - Z_j) - Z_l\left(\frac{1}{\lambda_l} - \frac{1}{\lambda_j}\right) \\ \Delta E &< (Z_l - Z_j) - Z_l\left(\frac{\lambda_j - \lambda_l}{\lambda_l \lambda_j}\right) \end{aligned} \tag{11.5.5}$$

Let $\Delta Z = Z_l - Z_j$ and $\Delta\lambda = \lambda_l - \lambda_j$, substitute into the above formula to get:

$$\Delta E < \Delta Z + \frac{Z_l}{\lambda_l}\left(\frac{\Delta\lambda}{\lambda_j}\right) \tag{11.5.6}$$

$$\because \frac{Z_l}{\lambda_l} = P_l$$

$$\therefore\ \Delta E < \Delta Z + P_l\left(\frac{\Delta\lambda}{\lambda_j}\right) \tag{11.5.7}$$

From (11.5.7), we can get the condition for a_i to implement trade transfer:

$$Cm < \Delta Z + P_l\left(\frac{\Delta\lambda}{\lambda_j}\right) \tag{11.5.8}$$

Arrange (11.5.8) to get another expression of the trade transfer condition for a_i:

$$\frac{\Delta\lambda}{\lambda} > \frac{Cm - \Delta Z}{P_l} \tag{11.5.9}$$

Equation (11.5.9) shows that when the conversion cost is large, it is very difficult for the downstream trading agent to transfer trades. Only when the new trading partner can provide a much higher cost-performance ratio than the original partner, will trade transfer occur.

For the upstream supplier b_j, the profit function has the following structure:

$$E_j = (P_j - C_j)N_j \tag{11.5.10}$$

where the marginal cost C_j is determined by the product value and production efficiency, the three have the following relationship:

$$C_j = \frac{Z_j}{\eta_j} \tag{11.5.11}$$

The size of the customer group $\{a_i\}_N$ depends on the cost-performance ratio of the product provided by b_j to customers. The two have the following relationship:

$$N_j = k\lambda_j \tag{11.5.12}$$

Parameter k is constrained by the following relationship:

$$\sum_1^M k\lambda_j = N \tag{11.5.13}$$

From this we get:

$$k = \frac{N}{\sum \lambda_j} \tag{11.5.14}$$

Substitute (11.5.11), (11.5.12), and (11.1.5) into (11.5.10) to get:

$$E_j = kZ_j\left(1 - \frac{\lambda_j}{\eta_j}\right) \tag{11.5.15}$$

According to the cost-performance ratio relationship, from (11.5.15) we get:

$$E_j = kP_j\lambda_j\left(1 - \frac{\lambda_j}{\eta_j}\right) \tag{11.5.16}$$

In the supply chain, due to the stable cooperation relationship between upstream and downstream enterprises, it is difficult for upstream enterprises to adjust prices. Therefore, it is agreed that $P_j = \overline{P}$ represents the industry average price, substitute into (11.5.16) to get:

$$E_j = k\overline{P}_j\lambda_j\left(1 - \frac{\lambda_j}{\eta_j}\right) \tag{11.5.17}$$

In order to examine the relationship between expected return and cost-performance ratio, we derivate on both sides of (11.5.17) of λ:

$$\frac{\partial E}{\partial \lambda} = k\overline{P}_j\left(1 - \frac{2\lambda_j}{\eta_j}\right) \tag{11.5.18}$$

From (11.5.18), we know that when $\lambda_j > \frac{\eta_j}{2}$:

$$\frac{\partial E}{\partial \lambda} < 0 \tag{11.5.19}$$

Equation (11.5.19) indicates that under fixed price conditions, the supplier's expected profit is a decreasing function of the cost-performance ratio. Therefore, when the price and production efficiency remain unchanged, the supplier will not adopt a strategy to improve the cost-performance ratio.

Let's examine the relationship between the production efficiency η and the expected profit. The derivative of Eq. (11.5.17) with respect to η is:

$$\frac{\partial E}{\partial \eta} = k\overline{P}_j\frac{\lambda_j^2}{\eta_j^2} \tag{11.5.20}$$

The above equation shows that the expected profit of b_j is an increasing function of the production efficiency η. In any case, if the supplier improves its own production efficiency, it will achieve the effect of increasing profits.

The above analysis shows that although the internal hierarchical structure of the supply chain has high stability, it does not mean rigidity and inefficiency. All participants in the supply chain have strong motivation to improve efficiency, which ensures the continuous evolution of the entire industry.

Note

1. Weiying ZHANG (2012) Game Theory and Information Economics, Shanghai, Gezhi Publishing House, p 320.

Chapter 12
Aggregation Structure of Trading Networks

The distribution of trading agents on the trading network is not uniform, but presents various patterns of aggregation. At different levels of the trading system, trading agents choose different forms of aggregation. Layered aggregation is a common feature of complex systems. The more complex the system, the more layered aggregation structures there are. Each additional layered structure will promote the synergy within the system, and the efficiency of the system will be greatly improved as a result.

12.1 Function of Aggregation Structure

With the evolution of the trading network, the aggregation form evolves from small to large, from simple to complex, gradually evolving a multi-level aggregation structure. In the evolution process, for each layer added in the structure, the capacity of the trading network will make a big leap. The trading network accommodates a huge number of trading groups through this layered aggregation structure.

The layered aggregation structure is not a simple function overlay, but conducting division of functions between different levels. The trading community at the bottom of the trading network aggregation is responsible for carrying out high-frequency, small-amount trading to ensure the convenience and low cost of trading. The basic function of city aggregation is to provide economical, stable, and convenient public product services, including city water supply, electricity supply, road maintenance, medical care, education, judiciary, public safety and other extensive basic guarantees, to ensure the smooth and orderly conduct of a huge number of trading.

Each time the aggregation structure is promoted, the frequency of cross-level trading will drop by an order of magnitude, while the trading amount will increase by an order of magnitude. That is to say, trading with small amounts and high frequency are preferably realized on the lower level aggregation form of the trading network, while trading with large amounts and low frequency can be realized on the higher level

Z. Wang, *Trading Economics*, Contributions to Economics,
https://doi.org/10.1007/978-981-99-9875-3_12

aggregation form. The trading system maintains a balance between system operation efficiency, trading cost, and trading certainty through the division of functions of aggregation levels.

In the layered aggregation structure of the trading network, the aggregation density shows a decreasing trend level by level. The trading community, as the bottom layer of aggregation, is the aggregation form with the highest concentration in the trading network and is the basic construction of the trading network. Above the city, the intensity of aggregation forms such as city clusters or economic belts is significantly weaker than the aggregation intensity within the city. The international aggregation form is at the top of the trading network aggregation structure and is the weakest organizational form of aggregation strength, mainly relying on bilateral or multilateral agreements to constrain the trading behavior of all parties. The density of the trading network is much weaker than the trading network within the country.

12.2 Aggregation Form of Trading Network

The aggregation form at different levels of the trading network is the product of trading network evolution. In the evolution process of the trading network, the earlier the aggregation form appears, the closer it is to the bottom of the trading network aggregation.

12.2.1 Community Aggregation

The trading community is the initial form of the trading network in human society and the source of the evolution of the modern trading network. When humans transitioned from a nomadic state to an agricultural settlement form, villages began to appear, and several nearby villages formed a relatively close trading community. Regularly held markets are the early form of community trading. Over time, markets gradually evolved into small towns, taking on the function of centralized trading in the surrounding communities. In towns, trading can be carried out all year round, and towns are born and grow in trading. With the continuous expansion of trading, the scale of towns is also expanding, more and more villages gradually merge into the town's territory, and eventually grow into today's super cities.

In the modern trading system, the trading community still plays a very important basic role. Trading agents live in their own communities, no matter how wide the trading links of the trading agents are, and how large the trading momentum is, they must be supported by the trading community. The basic trading that maintain the operation of the main body are almost completed in the community. This is true for household agents, and it is no exception for corporate agents. No matter how large the scale of the enterprise is and how large the market radius is, the basic trading of the enterprise's operations, including employee life, property management, water, electricity, natural gas and other trading, must be completed in the trading community. From the perspective of market organization evolution, in order to achieve efficient operation, enterprises must aggregate with upstream and downstream enterprises in a very limited trading community to minimize trading costs and achieve the effect of industrial synergy.

Community aggregation is the basis for the operation of the entire trading network and the fulcrum of the operation of the trading network. The reason why a wide-ranging and complex trading network can operate efficiently is precisely due to the support of countless trading communities. The efficiency of the operation of the trading community ultimately determines the operating efficiency of the trading network. The resilience of the organization of the trading community ultimately determines the ability of the trading network to withstand shocks.

12.2.2 City Aggregation

The city is the product of trade, and profit-seeking trading behavior attracts originally dispersed people to aggregate into cities in a relatively intensive space. Looking at the evolution process of the city, those originated from small-scale aggregated towns, after a long and continuous scale expansion, will eventually grew into larger cities. Some cities with locational advantages continue to expand on their original basis and eventually grow into central cities or super cities that radiate the surrounding areas.

Cities aggregate numerous trading communities, connecting previously segmented markets and creating ample conditions for the progression of division of labor. The deepening of the progressive division of labor further strengthens the functional and efficiency advantages of cities. Cities form a mutually reinforcing feedback mechanism between aggregation scale and function, efficiency.

The emergence of cities has promoted the dissemination and exchange of information, reduced trading costs, improved transportation conditions, increased the convenience of trading, and created unprecedented market prosperity in human history.

The emergence of cities has greatly increased the number of phases in the trading network. Various municipal management and urban public services are trading phases that only appear after the city is established. The city is like a large-scale machine, and the trading community is like the modules of this giant machine. The modules coordinate and cooperate with each other, making this machine operate efficiently day and night.

Historically, human society had already seen the form of urban aggregation as early as 3000 BC, which has a long history of over 5000 years. The Phoenicians traded with Mediterranean merchants using fast sailing ships, and the main commodities traded included dyes, food, textiles, and jewelry. These Phoenicians established numerous cities along the Mediterranean coast (today's Lebanon). Around 500 BC, Athens had become a regional trade center, trading goods including household handicrafts, olive products, food, and various raw materials.[1]

In the aggregation structure of modern trading networks, ancient village communities can be regarded as the periphery of the city. The urban aggregation form has a core area, a peripheral radiation area, and rural communities constitute the transition area of different urban aggregations.

12.2.3 Economic Belt Aggregation

Within the city group, there is also some form of aggregation. The aggregation formed by a group of geographically adjacent cities with closely linked industrial divisions is called economic belt aggregation.

Within a country, there will be several economic belts as the main pillars of the national economy. Cities within the economic belt have close industrial divisions, efficient market organizations, and strong external competitiveness. No matter how large the economic scale of a country is, the number of economic belts it can accommodate is usually limited. China has three major economic belts, namely the Yangtze River Delta city group or economic belt, the Pearl River Delta economic belt, and the Bohai Sea economic belt, which occupy an absolutely important position in China's economy. The United States has three major metropolitan areas, including the Greater New York area, the Great Lakes area, and the Greater Los Angeles area, accounting for nearly 70% of the US economy. Japan has three major metropolitan areas, including the Tokyo metropolitan area, the Nagoya metropolitan area, and the Osaka metropolitan area, its economic output accounting for 70% of the Japanese economy.

Economic belt aggregation is a product of the economic system evolution to a certain extent. As the trading system gradually develops, cities as trading platforms can no longer meet the trading needs of trading agents. Trading agents need a larger market radius and more trading partners. Economic belt aggregation emerged in this context. Each upgrade of the aggregation structure represents the expansion of the trading network. The increase in aggregation levels represents the trend of the trading network structure towards complexity and is a reflection of the powerful organization function of the trading network and the upgrade of trading efficiency.

12.2.4 National Aggregation

The nation represents a relatively independent trading system and is an important boundary of the trading network, playing an undeniable important role in the organization and management of the trading network. However, the aggregation form of the nation as a layer of the trading network may appear earlier in the evolutionary order than the economic belt aggregation layer, and even earlier than the emergence of the city aggregation layer. The aggregation of the nation as a special case of the trading network evolution does not prove that the evolution of the trading network is chaotic and disordered, but indicates that the nation, as an organizational form coexisting in the social system and trading system, has a misalignment in function and time. In other words, the nation is first a concept of the social system, and its existence as an organization of the social system predates the trading system.

In the aggregation structure of the trading network, the nation plays a dual role. The nation first represents the organizational management boundary of the trading network. The trading inside and outside the boundary have significant differences in terms of trading costs, trading methods, and trading rules. Secondly, the nation represents the role of the trading network manager, including responsibilities such as trading order management, trading system formulation, and implementation of macro-control. Looking at the evolution process of the trading network, trading network management accompanies the evolution of the trading network at all times. Even in the early stages of evolution, trading within the trading community also need order and management, but the management at that time mainly came from the self-discipline organization of the community. When the trading network evolved to the city form, the management needs further increased and carried out in more dimensions and levels, including community management, industry associations, city management, etc. The emergence of the nation as a trading network manager represents that the trading network has reached a high level in both scale and structure. In modern society, the systematic management of the trading network and the macro-control of the trading system have been elevated to an unprecedented height.

12.2.5 International Aggregation

International aggregation is the highest aggregation form of the world trading system and the weakest aggregation form in the modern trading system. With the evolution of the world trading system, the aggregation strength of the international aggregation form will gradually strengthen. The establishment of more and more regional trade cooperation mechanisms is strengthening international aggregation, enhancing the function of international aggregation, and promoting the integration of trading networks between countries. This not only represents the inevitable trend of human social evolution, but also the inevitable choice for human society to improve efficiency and achieve development.

In the evolution process of the trading network, the aggregation agent at each layer will continue to expand in scale. The trading community is constantly expanding with the convenience of transportation and the progress of information technology. Cities are also expanding, expansion requires resources, including human resources, economic resources, etc. The expansion of the city will inevitably lead to competition between cities. The larger the city, the stronger the attraction. A large number of immigrants are attracted from small cities, the squeezed and exploited small cities inevitably forced to decline. The national border cannot naturally expand, but it can eventually break through the link of the trading network, forming a trading network integration between countries. Various regional trade agreements are evidence that the trading network is moving towards integration.

In the evolution process of the trading network, the evolutionary order of different layers is not strictly rigid. The real situation is that the five different aggregation forms are in a synchronous evolution pattern. Even today, community aggregation as an ancient aggregation form is still evolving vigorously. Cities are either growing or declining, and regional economic belts are still on the road to evolution and reshaping.

Looking at the evolution of human society, the further strengthening of international aggregation is the basic trend of the evolution of the world trade network. The evolution of international aggregation has just begun, and the final pattern of human future still awaits further development at the international aggregation level. In this sense, the evolution of human trade networks is still not fixed.

12.3 Review of Urban Aggregation Model

The phenomenon of aggregation in trade networks, especially the phenomenon of urban aggregation, has long attracted the attention of economists and geographers, who have proposed numerous models and theoretical doctrines in an attempt to reveal the causes behind the aggregation phenomenon. In modern regional economics and spatial economics, this part of the theory is known as location theory. In order to better understand the intrinsic connection between the aggregation theory of trade economics and location theory, we will introduce three representative models here.

12.3.1 Thunen Model

The Thunen model is the first mathematical model in history to study urban location theory and is a pioneer in location theory. The Thunen model was proposed by German economist Johann Heinrich Von Thunen in 1826. Thunen is also known as the founder of economic geography and agricultural geography. The Thunen model is based on the following seven assumptions[2]:

1. There is a uniform space, with the same fertility of land and comparable transportation conditions;
2. Infinite demand, location equilibrium is solely determined by the supply side;
3. There is a single urban center, all goods are traded in the city;
4. Production factors are evenly distributed;
5. Each agricultural product has a specific production function, with constant return to scale;
6. Perfect market competition;
7. All product transportation costs are the same and remain constant.

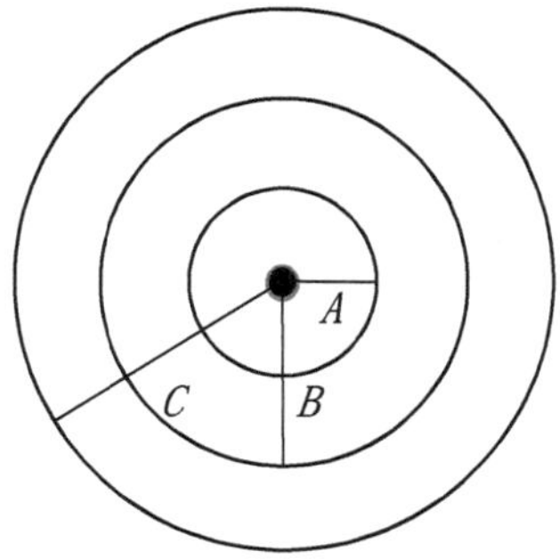

Fig. 12.1 Diagram of land rent distribution

In addition, Thunen assumes that land rent comes from the surplus of land production and is determined by the product sales price, production cost, and transportation cost. Let x be the quantity of product on a unit of land; c be the unit production cost; p be the product price; τ be the unit transportation cost; r be the land rent rate.

According to Thunen's understanding of the nature of land rent, the rent rate r can be expressed as the following function:

$$r(d) = (p - c - \tau d)x \tag{12.3.1}$$

where, d represents the distance from the land to the central city.

According to (12.3.1) the land rent forms an equivalent distribution ring centered on the city:(Fig. 12.1)

According to the distance from the city, the rents of the three rings A, B, and C rages high to low, forming three steps.

Taking the derivative of the rent function with respect to distance d, we get the marginal rent rate:

$$\frac{\partial r}{\partial d} = -\tau x \tag{12.3.2}$$

Equation (12.3.2) indicates that for each marginal unit increase in the distance from the land to the city, the rental rate will decrease by τx units.

The Thunen model links the land rental rate with the spatial distribution of land, providing an explanation for rent pricing that differs from Ricardo's, broadening people's perspective on the mechanism of land price formation.

12.3.2 *Alonso Model*

The Alonso model, developed by Argentine-American economist William Alonso based on the Thunen model, was published in 1964. The Alonso model greatly expands the application scenarios, from only applying to the analysis of agricultural areas outside towns, to including various situations such as urban location analysis.

The modifications of the Alonso model to the Thunen model mainly focus on two aspects. The first is the definition of land rent. The Alonso model adds a term for expected business profits to the Thunen land rent; the second is to expand transportation costs to production costs including transportation costs. The modified main rent function is:

$$r(d) = [p - \pi - c(d)]x(d) \tag{12.3.3}$$

In (12.3.3), $c(d)$ represents the marginal production cost closely related to the distance d from the city center, which includes the direct cost of goods production, the direct cost of transportation, and the indirect cost of transportation time consumption; π is the expected profit of the enterprise; $x(d)$ represents the enterprise output affected by the location distance d.

The sensitivity of Alonso's rent to location is expressed in the following formula:

$$\frac{\partial r}{\partial d} = [p - \pi - c(d)]\frac{\partial x}{\partial d} - \frac{\partial c}{\partial d}x(d) \tag{12.3.4}$$

Equation (12.3.4) indicates that the more sensitive the enterprise output is to the location, that is, the larger the value of $\frac{\partial x}{\partial d}$, the more easily the enterprise will accept the high rent of the city center location; if the enterprise production is completely insensitive to the location, that is., $\frac{\partial x}{\partial d} = 0$, the city will not form a tiered spatial structure of land rent.

From this, we can conclude: radiating from the city center to the periphery, the land rent forms a tiered decreasing distribution pattern. Enterprises will choose the most cost-effective area for their business according to their own operating characteristics, thus forming a balanced spatial distribution in the city. The rent in the city center area is the most expensive, but it can bring higher return for some enterprises, including businesses, finance, culture, intermediary services, etc., will all get more customers because of the city center, achieving maximum return. For manufacturing enterprises, the city center will not bring more customers, but increase the cost of land rent, under the condition of convenient transportation, these enterprises will choose to locate in the outskirts of the city or suburban areas.

Alonso also analyzed the location choice of households, using the following utility function to describe the family's decision-making goal:

$$U = U(d, z, q) \tag{12.3.5}$$

In (12.3.5), U represents the amount of utility obtained by the family; d denotes distance of residence from urban centers; z represents the set of goods consumed by the family; q represents the living area of the family.

The family budget constraint function is as follows:

$$y = pz + r(d)q + \tau d \tag{12.3.6}$$

In (12.3.6), τ Represents the marginal comprehensive transportation cost. The marginal comprehensive transportation cost is composed of two parts, one part is the direct transportation cost, and the other part is the indirect cost of time consumption.

Based on (12.3.5) and (12.3.6), we can construct the Lagrange function as follows:

$$L = U(d, z, q) - \lambda(y - pz - r(d)q - \tau d) \tag{12.3.7}$$

According to the requirements of the conditional extremum, we get:

$$\begin{aligned} \frac{\partial L}{\partial d} &= 0 \\ \frac{\partial L}{\partial q} &= 0 \\ \frac{\partial L}{\partial z} &= 0 \end{aligned} \tag{12.3.8}$$

From (12.3.8) we get:

$$\begin{aligned} \frac{\partial U}{\partial d} + \lambda\tau &= 0 \\ \frac{\partial U}{\partial q} + \lambda r &= 0 \\ \frac{\partial U}{\partial z} + \lambda p &= 0 \end{aligned} \tag{12.3.9}$$

From (12.3.9) we can get:

$$\lambda = -\frac{\partial U}{\partial d}/\tau = -\frac{\partial U}{\partial q}/r = -\frac{\partial U}{\partial z}/p \tag{12.3.10}$$

$$\therefore \ \frac{U'_d}{U'_q} = \frac{\tau}{r} \tag{12.3.11}$$

Equation (12.3.11) shows that when the marginal comprehensive transportation cost τ is very small, the marginal utility of distance will decrease, and the marginal utility of housing area will increase accordingly. Under this structure, the agent family agent will choose to buy property in areas far from the central city, replacing the location advantage of the city center with a larger living area. This shows that the more convenient the city transportation and the lower the trading cost, the more willing the household residents are to choose to live away from the central city, which leads to a decrease in urban residential density. The evolution of modern cities has proven this conclusion.

12.3.3 Christaller's Central Place Theory

In 1933, German economic geographer Walter Christaller proposed the urban hierarchy theory centered on the concept of central place in monograph "*Central Places in Southern Germany*", which was later referred to as the central place theory.

Christaller first analyzed the market distribution of a single product, assuming that consumers are evenly distributed in space. Due to the constraint of transportation costs, each supplier can only serve customers within a limited range in space. This forms a circular area centered on the supplier, which is the market range of the supplier. Markets outside this area will be occupied by other suppliers. This forms a market structure occupied by many suppliers.

Each ring in Fig. 12.2 represents the market range of a supplier. The supplier is located in the center of the corresponding circular area to provide the lowest trading cost service for the market. The supplier located in the center of the entire market has the highest efficiency, occupies the highest quality area in the city, and has the largest market range. Radiating from the central place, the efficiency of the suppliers decreases in turn, and the market range gradually decreases. In Christaller's theory, for market formed by urban aggregation, its efficiency ranking from low to high according to the distance from the city center. The entire city market is allocated to different suppliers according to the efficiency rule. This is the main reason why Christaller's theory is called the central place theory. In Christaller's theory, a city can have multiple central places. The higher the city level, the more central places it can accommodate.

In the early stage of market formation, there are certain gaps around adjacent markets. Suppliers who pursue maximum profit will never miss such trading opportunities. After market competition, the market will eventually form a combination structure of many hexagonal sub-markets. As shown in the figure below:

Figure 12.3. shows the final structure of a single commodity market. Due to the variety of commodities in the market, each commodity market will have a minimum

Fig. 12.2 Market structure in early stage

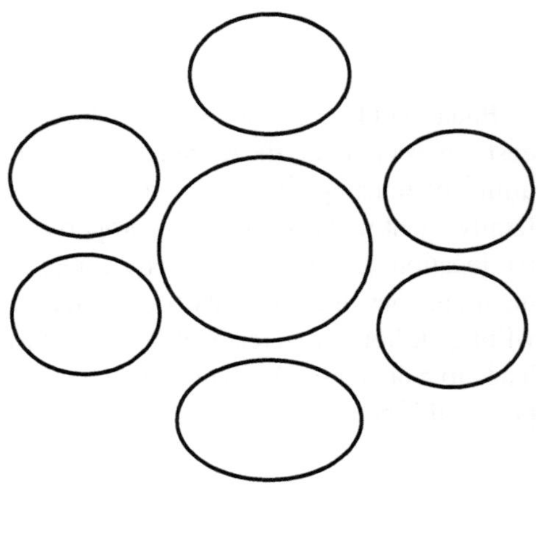

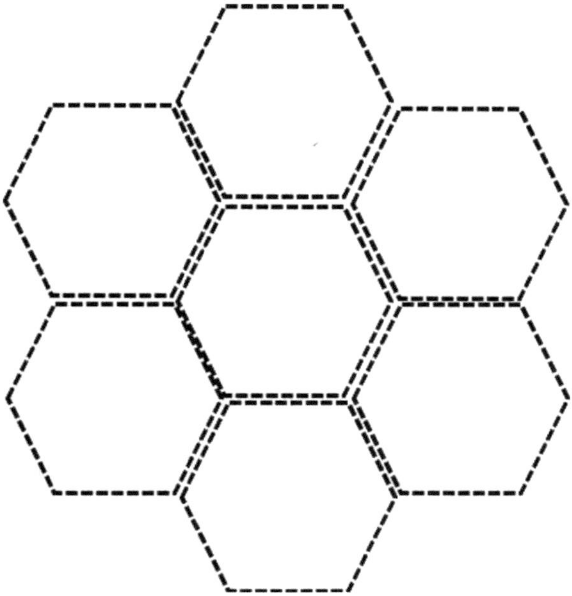

Fig. 12.3 Market structure in later period

market scale determined by production costs, technological thresholds, etc. Only when the minimum market scale of the supplier is met can an enterprise maintain its operation and stay in the market. This market segmentation scale determined by the characteristics of the goods inevitably leads to the emergence of a market layered structure. The market at the bottom has the lowest entry threshold (the smallest scale maintained by the supplier), and the market entry threshold increases layer by layer from low to high, with the market at the top having the highest entry threshold. The market layered structure is shown in the following Fig. 12.4.

Based on the understanding of the market structure, Christaller classified cities. The higher the rank of the city, the more market levels it accommodates, and the richer the goods and services it provides to consumers. On the contrary, the lower the rank of the city, the fewer market levels, and the poorer the types of goods and services it provides to consumers.

Christaller applied his theory to the cities in southern Germany, dividing the cities into seven levels based on market stratification and the number of central places. Christaller's research results are shown in the following Table 12.1.

Christaller's central place theory has a typical historical significance for the development of urban economics, but today, the theory has the obvious simplicity of a startup theory. It is not a model that shows a causal relationship. We better understand it as a classification outline, a method that can organize our thoughts and data. At best, it is a description of the economic spatial structure, not an explanation.[4]

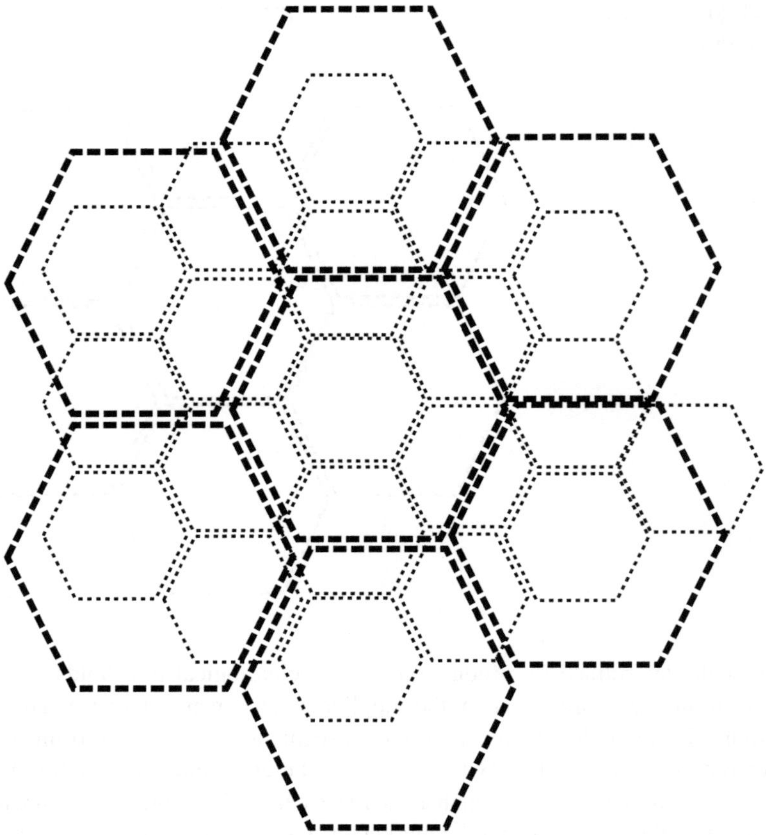

Fig. 12.4 Market layered structure

Table 12.1 Empirical results for cities in southern Germany[3]

Layer	1	2	3	4	5	6	7
Theoretical number of central places	1	2	6	18	54	162	486
Observational number of central places	1	2	10	23	60	105	462

12.4 Urban Aggregation Trading Model

Urban aggregation is an important form of spatial organization of the trading network. The fundamental force driving urban aggregation comes from the pursuit of maximum self-interest by trading agents, and urban aggregation is the result of the choice of trading agents. Based on this logic, when we construct the urban aggregation model, we use the trading equation as the basis, combined with the characteristics of the location choice of the trading network to complete the modeling.

12.4.1 Urban Aggregation Trading Model

The derivation process of the trading equation will be unfolded in Chap. 14, and we directly use the conclusion of the trading equation here. The trading equation describes the trading agents using a probabilistic method, calculates the execution probability for each strategy on the strategy set of the trading agents. The higher the probability of the trading strategy being executed, the greater the possibility of being implemented. Using this method, we have established a priority order for execution on the trading strategy set, and the trading strategy with the highest ranking is executed first.

Assume a_i is any agent on T of the trading system, $s \in S_i$ is any strategy on the strategy set S_i, the trading equation gives the probability of a_i implementing strategy s:

$$\Pr(s) = 1 - R_g(s)\frac{q}{p}\mu^n \tag{12.4.1}$$

In (12.4.1), R_g represents the risk-return index of trading strategy s, which is a measure of the relationship between risk and return of the trading strategy. The specific expression is $R_g = \frac{e_g - e_b}{e_g - e_0}$, where, e_g is the ideal state return, e_b represents the profit or loss in the worst-case scenario, e_0 represents the expected average market return, the value threshold. p represents the prior probability that trading agent a_i behaves ideally with respect to the trading situation H. q represents the prior probability that the trading situation H behaves in an undesirable state. The two probability parameters satisfy $p + q = 1$. μ represents the behavior characteristic of a finite rational trading agent, which has relative stability. n is the number of agent when trading agent a_i synergistically implement strategy s.

In the trading network, city aggregation forms the pulse values of agglomeration and trading network density, making the spatial distribution of the trading network highly uneven. Within the city agglomeration, there are usually multiple agglomeration centers, including cultural and commercial centers, scientific research and education centers, industrial manufacturing centers, trade and logistics centers, etc. During the growth and development of the city, various agglomeration centers will be nurtured. These agglomeration centers will experience a life cycle from non-existence to existence, from small to large, from prosperity to decline, and finally extinction.

The growth and development process of the agglomeration center is driven by the spontaneous choice of a large number of trading agents. In the selection process of the trading agent, it needs to consider its own special circumstances and constraints, as well as the selection behavior of other trading agents. Due to the exclusive feature of spatial locations, at each time step t, the trading agent can only choose one location. As long as we can depict the selection mechanism of the trading agent at the time step t, we can also give a complete picture of the city aggregation process.

Suppose $a_i \in \{a_i\}_N$ is any trading agent on the trading system T, it needs to choose a property location on the space covered by the trading network at the time step t. Assume that the trading agents on the trading system T have the right to freely choose the property location. Ω is any agglomeration center in the trading system T, it can be a city agglomeration, a certain agglomeration center within the city, or a natural village agglomeration, etc. Using the trading equation, we can calculate the probability of the trading agent a_i choosing the agglomeration center Ω as the property location. On the agglomeration center Ω, we first establish the location coordinates (x, y). The coordinate (x, y) takes the center point of Ω as the origin, the east–west direction as the χ axis; the north–south direction as the y axis. Assume a_i is the property acquisition costs $Lc(x, y)$ that need to be paid at the chosen location (x, y). The size of the property acquisition costs $Lc(x, y)$ depends on the land price and rental price of (x, y), and it also depends on the size of the space demand of the trading agent a_i. Under the condition that the land price and rent remain unchanged, the larger the space demand, the higher the cost of choosing the trading location. $\rho(x, y)$ represents the population density at location (x, y).

Assuming that the aggregation center Ω is distributed on a circular disc with a radius of R, the property location chosen by the trading agent a_i at (x, y) is within the circular disc, and it is:

$$\frac{\sqrt{x^2 + y^2}}{R} = r \tag{12.4.2}$$

According to the distribution law of urban land prices, the property acquisition costs of the trading agent $Lc(x, y)$ are affected by two factors: first, the distance between the trading agent's location and the aggregation center Ω. The closer the distance to the aggregation center, the higher the land price. Under the condition of unchanged space usage intensity, the property acquisition cost of the trading agent a_i is higher. Second, the average land price of the aggregation center Ω. The difference in land prices between different cities is huge, the larger the city scale, the higher the land price. The city land price usually shows an exponential growth relationship with the scale of the aggregated population or the scale of the trading agent m. From this, we can get the following relationship:

$$Lc(x, y) = \frac{\Gamma\left(m^\beta\right)}{\left(\left(x^2 + y^2\right)^{\frac{1}{2}}\right)^2} \tag{12.4.3}$$

In (12.4.3), $\Gamma\left(m^\beta\right)$ represents the cost coefficient. The cost coefficient $\Gamma\left(m^\beta\right)$ is positively correlated with the space usage intensity of the trading agent and the average city land price, $\beta > 0$ is the sensitivity parameter of city land price to aggregation scale, β usually takes a value between 0 and 1, that is, $0 < \beta \leq 1$.

According to the density distribution function of the aggregation center Ω, we can get:

$$\iint \pi R^2 \rho dx dy = m \tag{12.4.4}$$

For simplicity, we assume that the density function $\rho(x, y) = \rho$ is a constant, (12.4.4) can be simplified to:

$$\pi R^2 \rho = m \tag{12.4.5}$$

Rearrange to get:

$$R = \sqrt{\frac{m}{\pi \rho}} \tag{12.4.6}$$

Substitute (12.4.2) into (12.4.6) to get:

$$\left(x^2 + y^2\right)^{\frac{1}{2}} = r\sqrt{\frac{m}{\pi \rho}} \tag{12.4.7}$$

Substitute (12.4.7) into (12.4.3) to get:

$$\begin{aligned} Lc(x, y) &= \frac{\Gamma\left(m^{\beta}\right)}{r^2 \frac{m}{\pi \rho}} \\ &= \frac{\Gamma\left(m^{\beta}\right)\pi \rho}{r^2 m} \end{aligned} \tag{12.4.8}$$

The benefits of attracting trading agents to choose the aggregation center Ω for property acquisition come from two aspects: first, the agglomeration effect of Ω. Due to the agglomeration effect, the trading cost of a_i will be significantly reduced, and it can obtain competitive advantages in technology and cost with related trading agents, including forming adjacency effects with upstream and downstream enterprises. Second, sharing endowed natural resources owned by Ω, including various types of mineral resources and regional advantages of geographical location. Various types of transportation resources, including rivers, ports, and transportation hubs, all belong to different types of transportation resources. We can understand resource endowment as an exogenous phenomenon of geographical extremes. The introduction of the concept of geographical extremes is to emphasize the uneven distribution of resource endowments. Each city aggregation is formed on different types of geographical extremes.

Due to the regulations of trading types and their own characteristics, the trading agent a_i has differences in the degree of sharing the advantages of the aggregation center Ω. For the aggregation center Ω, some trading agents may have a higher degree of sharing, for other trading agents, the ability to share Ω advantages may be very limited.

Based on the above analysis, we assume that the trading agent a_i shares the benefits of the agglomeration effect from the aggregation center Ω as $\kappa(r)m^{\alpha}$, where, $\kappa(r) \geq 0$ is the sharing coefficient of the trading agent a_i for the agglomeration effect. The value of $\kappa(r)$ depends on two factors: one is the sensitivity of the trading agent to the agglomeration effect. There is a great difference in the sensitivity of trading agents to the agglomeration effect, which is mainly determined by the trading type of the trading agent. Generally speaking, trading agents provide service products have a higher sensitivity to the agglomeration effect, and trading agents provide manufactured products have a relatively lower sensitivity to the agglomeration effect. The second is the property location chosen by the trading agent. The farther the property location from the aggregation center, the lower the degree of sharing of the agglomeration effect by the trading agent. Under other conditions unchanged, the closer the property location is to the aggregation center, the higher the degree of sharing of the agglomeration effect by the trading agent. Therefore, the sharing parameter of the trading agent for the agglomeration effect $\kappa(r)$ is a decreasing function of the distance between the property location of the trading agent and the aggregation center, satisfying $\frac{\partial \kappa(r)}{\partial r} < 0$. m is the total number of trading agents carried by the aggregation center Ω, $\alpha > 0$ is the agglomeration effect parameter of the aggregation center Ω. The larger the value of α, the more significant the agglomeration effect produced by the aggregation center Ω. the value of α depends on various factors such as the industrial structure of the aggregation center, the urban spatial layout, and the level of urban management. Generally speaking, the closer the urban industrial structure, the more reasonable the spatial layout, the higher the efficiency of urban management, the more significant the city's agglomeration effect, the larger the value of α.

The trading agent a_i shares the benefits of natural endowments from the aggregation center Ω as τv, where, $\tau \geq 0$ represents the sensitivity of trading agent a_i to natural endowments of the aggregation center Ω. The larger the value of τ implies that the trading agent a_i is more dependent on the natural endowment of the aggregation center Ω and shares more revenue from natural endowment of the aggregation center Ω. The value of τ is also related to the number of trading agents in the aggregation center Ω that are involved in sharing endowment resources. The more agents participating in sharing, the smaller the share of endowment resource value each trading agent can share. For simplicity, we assume that all trading agents in the aggregation center Ω participate in sharing endowment resources. The sensitivity parameter of endowment resources τ can be expressed as a function $\tau(m)$ and has $\frac{\partial \tau}{\partial m} < 0$. v represents the value of natural endowments owned by the aggregation center Ω, which is a price estimation of natural resources.

Based on the analysis of the benefits and costs of the property location choice of trading agent a_i, we can calculate the main parameters in the trading equation. We denote the property location strategy of a_i as S, and the return under the ideal trading situation are:

$$e_g = \kappa(r)m^{\alpha} + \tau v - Lc(x, y) \tag{12.4.9}$$

The gains from decision-making under the adverse trading situation are:

$$e_b = -Lc(x, y) \tag{12.4.10}$$

Since the market average expected return level e_0 is a constant, it plays a role as a decision reference in the decision-making of the trading agent. To simplify the calculation process, we might as well set $e_0 = 0$, this special treatment will not affect our derivation conclusion.

Based on the above calculations, we can obtain the return risk index of the trading agent a_i:

$$R_g = \frac{e_g - e_b}{e_g - e_0} = \frac{\kappa(r)m^\alpha + \tau v}{\kappa(r)m^\alpha + \tau v - Lc(x,y)} \tag{12.4.11}$$

Substitute (12.4.8) into (12.4.11) to get:

$$\begin{aligned} R_g &= \frac{e_g - e_b}{e_g - e_0} = \frac{\kappa(r)m^\alpha + \tau v}{\kappa(r)m^\alpha + \tau v - \frac{\Gamma(m^\beta)\pi\rho}{r^2 m}} \\ &= \frac{\kappa(r)m^{\alpha+1}r^2 + \tau v m r^2}{\kappa(r)m^{\alpha+1}r^2 + \tau v m r^2 - \Gamma(m^\beta)\pi\rho} \end{aligned} \tag{12.4.12}$$

Substitute (12.4.12) into (12.4.1) to get the execution probability of the property location strategy S:

$$\Pr(s) = 1 - \frac{\kappa(r)m^{\alpha+1}r^2 + \tau v m r^2}{\kappa(r)m^{\alpha+1}r^2 + \tau v m r^2 - \Gamma(m^\beta)\pi\rho}\frac{q}{p}\mu^n \tag{12.4.13}$$

Equation (12.4.13) provides the probability function of the trading agent's property location decision, describing the basic rules of trade network aggregation, which we call the aggregation trading model.

In order to reveal the basic characteristics of the property decision function, we further analyze the property decision function. We derive the scale of the aggregation center m and the derivative of the value of endowed resources owned by the aggregation center v, respectively, to reveal the role of scale and endowed resource value in the process of trade network aggregation.

$$\begin{aligned} \frac{\partial \Pr(s)}{\partial m} &= \frac{q}{p}\mu^n \\ &\times \left\{ -\frac{\kappa(r)(\alpha+1)m^\alpha + \tau' v m r^2 + \tau v r^2}{\kappa(r)m^{\alpha+1}r^2 + \tau v m r^2 - \Gamma(m^\beta)\pi\rho} \right. \\ &\left. + \frac{\left[\kappa(r)m^{\alpha+1}r^2 + \tau v m r^2\right]\left[\kappa(r)(\alpha+1)m^\alpha r^2 + \tau' v m r^2 + \tau v r^2 - \Gamma' \beta m^{\beta-1}\pi\rho\right]}{\left[\kappa(r)m^{\alpha+1}r^2 + \tau v m r^2 - \Gamma(m^\beta)\pi\rho\right]^2} \right\} \end{aligned} \tag{12.4.14}$$

Arrange to get:

$$\frac{\partial \Pr(s)}{\partial m} = \frac{q}{p}\mu^n \times \left\{ \frac{\kappa(r)m^\alpha r^2\pi\rho\left[(\alpha+1)\Gamma\left(m^\beta\right) - \Gamma'\beta m^\beta\right] + vr^2\pi\rho\left[\tau' m\Gamma\left(m^\beta\right) + \tau\Gamma\left(m^\beta\right) - \tau\Gamma'\beta m^\beta\right]}{\left[\kappa(r)m^{\alpha+1}r^2 + \tau v m r^2 - \Gamma\left(m^\beta\right)\pi\rho\right]^2} \right\} \tag{12.4.15}$$

If the following conditions are met:

$$(\alpha+1)\Gamma\left(m^\beta\right) - \Gamma'\beta m^\beta > 0 \tag{12.4.16}$$

$$\tau' m\Gamma\left(m^\beta\right) + \tau\Gamma\left(m^\beta\right) - \tau\Gamma'\beta m^\beta > 0 \tag{12.4.17}$$

Then there is:

$$\frac{\partial \Pr(s)}{\partial m} > 0 \tag{12.4.18}$$

In order to get a more concise condition, add (12.4.16) and (12.4.17) to get the following inequality:

$$\tau' m\Gamma\left(m^\beta\right) + (\alpha+\tau+1))\Gamma\left(m^\beta\right) - (\tau+1)\Gamma'\beta m^\beta > 0 \tag{12.4.19}$$

$$\therefore (\tau+1)\Gamma'\beta m^\beta < \left(\tau' m + \alpha + \tau + 1\right)\Gamma\left(m^\beta\right)$$

$$\because \tau' < 0, m \geq 1$$

$$\therefore (\tau+1)\Gamma'\beta m^\beta \leq \left(\alpha + \tau + \tau' + 1\right)\Gamma\left(m^\beta\right)$$

$$\therefore m^\beta \leq \frac{\left(\alpha+\tau+\tau'+1\right)\Gamma\left(m^\beta\right)}{(\tau+1)\Gamma'\beta}$$

$$\therefore m \leq \left(1 + \frac{\alpha+\tau'}{\tau+1}\right)^{\frac{1}{\beta}} \left(\frac{\Gamma\left(m^\beta\right)}{\Gamma'\beta}\right)^{\frac{1}{\beta}} \tag{12.4.20}$$

Equation (12.4.20) indicates that there is a threshold for the attractiveness of the aggregation center Ω to the trading agents' property placement. Only when the scale is below the threshold, the attractiveness of the aggregation center to the trading agents' property placement will increase with the increase of scale; when the scale of the aggregation center exceeds the threshold, the increase of scale will instead reduce the attractiveness of the aggregation center. This conclusion explains the fact that globally, regardless of the process of urbanization, the equilibrium scale of cities will always be limited within a certain range, rather than expanding indefinitely.

Let's examine the impact of resource endowment on the attractiveness of the aggregation center:

$$\begin{aligned}\frac{\partial \Pr(s)}{\partial v} &= \frac{q}{p}\mu^n \\ &\times \left\{-\frac{\tau m r^2}{\kappa(r)m^{\alpha+1}r^2 + \tau v m r^2 - \Gamma\left(m^\beta\right)\pi\rho}\right. \\ &\left.+\frac{\left[\kappa(r)m^{\alpha+1}r^2 + \tau v m r^2\right]\tau m r^2}{\left[\kappa(r)m^{\alpha+1}r^2 + \tau v m r^2 - \Gamma\left(m^\beta\right)\pi\rho\right]^2}\right\}\end{aligned} \tag{12.4.21}$$

Arranging (12.4.21) we get:

$$\frac{\partial \Pr(s)}{\partial v} = \frac{q}{p}\mu^n \frac{\tau m r^2 \Gamma\left(m^\beta\right)\pi\rho}{\left[\kappa(r)m^{\alpha+1}r^2 + \tau v m r^2 - \Gamma\left(m^\beta\right)\pi\rho\right]^2} > 0 \tag{12.4.22}$$

Equation (12.4.22) indicates: The value of the resource endowment possessed by the aggregation center and the attractiveness of the aggregation center always maintain a positive correlation. The greater the value of the resource endowment possessed by the aggregation center, the stronger the attractiveness to the trading agents' property placement. This conclusion reveals the important role of resource endowment in the formation process of urban aggregation. Among cities of different scales, the difference in resource endowment is an important cause of different aggregation scales.

12.4.2 *Origin of Urban Aggregation*

The aggregation trading model (12.4.13) can reveal the cause of the origin of urban aggregation. We can assume that the initial spatial distribution of the trading network is uniform (in fact, the spatial distribution of the trading network shows an aggregated state at different levels from the beginning. The assumption of uniform distribution is just for the convenience of discussion). Due to differences in natural resources and geographical conditions, trading agents first gather at places with superior natural endowments, forming the initial aggregation point of the trading network, and the uniform distribution state of the trading network is broken. Resource endowment advantages can be classified into two types: one type is mineral resource endowment, including salt resources, coal resources, forest resources, and metal mineral resources. Natural resource advantages have become the cause of the origin of many cities, the most famous representative city of which is San Francisco in the United States. In 1776, Spanish missionaries built a fortress in San Francisco, marking the beginning of the city's development history. In the 1840s, San Francisco was still a small town with only a few hundred people scattered in the fields. With the discovery of gold, the population quickly reached 250,000 in just a few years, becoming an important city on the west coast of the United States. Today, San Francisco, the location of the famous Silicon Valley, has long become synonymous with technological innovation. There are many similar cities, such as Daqing in China is also a typical city that quickly aggregated due to the discovery of oil.

Another type of resource endowment advantage is superior geographical location, that is, convenient transportation. Cities that have arisen due to the aggregation of this type of resource endowment are more numerous, and most of the famous cities in the world are located near ports, rivers, and transportation hub. Shanghai, New York, Paris, Amsterdam, London, etc., all these cities are born and grow due to superior geographical locations.

The origin of each city can be found in the advantages of natural resource endowment and geographical location. These advantages have different characteristics, thus defining the unique process of the origin of urban aggregation. Once the city has completed the initial aggregation, the resource endowment advantage has completed its basic mission. In the subsequent development and growth process, the agglomeration effect becomes the key factor in the growth of the city.

Of course, it is not objective to regard resource endowment as an exogenous phenomenon of the trading system. The ability of humans to utilize resources is always improving with technological progress. When the technological conditions are not available, some resources have no value to humans and are not considered resources. For example, before the advent of radio communication technology, radio frequency bands could not be seen as valuable resources by people, and even the concept of radio frequency bands did not exist. Similarly, before the advent of flight technology, people would not regard air routes as economic resources. In traditional societies, the sky was only a place to reflect sunlight and generate rain and snow, and had no other value. However, when air travel became an increasingly common mode of transportation, air routes became very important valuable resources. It can be seen that resources are a relative concept, and resource endowments are not constant.

From this, the value of resource endowment is also a dynamic variable, but the change cycle is relatively long. The evolution of the value of resource endowment will inevitably change the aggregation structure of the trading network and promote the aggregation to move from the original equilibrium point to a new equilibrium point.

12.4.3 Urban Expansion Mechanism

Once urban aggregation forms the initial clustering at a location with obvious locational advantages and outstanding resource endowments, the clustering effect begins to play a role, thereby initiating the rapid expansion of urban aggregation. In the process of urban aggregation, for the clustering effect to play a role, there must first be an initial aggregation reaching the critical scale m_0. Only in this way, the clustering effect m^α will be large enough, so that the attraction $\kappa(r)m^\alpha$ of the trading agents will be large enough to guide the trading agents to make location selection decisions. In the early stage of urban evolution, whether the initial aggregation scale can reach the critical level m_0, can rely on the attraction of the value of resource endowment υ. Only when the value of resource endowment υ is large enough, can it attract enough trading agents, and can it push the evolution process of urban aggregation onto the track of the positive feedback mechanism dominated by the clustering effect. The actual situation also confirms this point, in cities that have spontaneously aggregated, the advantage of resource endowment is usually significantly stronger than that of surrounding small towns.

The agglomeration effect and the resource endowment effect are not completely isolated and do not affect each other; there are ways in which they interact. First, resource endowment is the basis of the agglomeration effect and the first driven force of the formation of the agglomeration effect. Second, as the agglomeration effect drives the city to aggregate on an increasingly larger scale, the demand for infrastructure will also increase accordingly. Demands such as road network construction, railway network construction, airline network construction, airport construction, and port construction will be put on the agenda. As these infrastructures continue to improve, the city's share in the national and even global transportation network and trade network increases, and the advantage of resource endowment becomes more prominent. Taking the international metropolis Shanghai as an example, Shanghai is located at the mouth of the Yangtze River, facing the East China Sea, with the golden waterway Huangpu River running across the city, forming a natural advantage for inland and overseas trade, and possessing superior resource endowment. As the city continues to expand, the existing infrastructure resources become increasingly strained. Therefore, more highways are being built; the airport has been expanded from one to two, and a third airport is also in the planning. The number of high-speed railway lines is also increasing, the port has been expanded from the original Wusongkou terminal to the Waigaoqiao terminal. After entering the twenty-first century, the Yangshan deep-water port terminal was built, and by 2018, the Yangshan deep-water port terminal has become the largest container terminal in the world. Obviously, the construction of these infrastructures further strengthens the relative advantage of Shanghai's resource endowment, and then strengthens the original agglomeration effect advantage of Shanghai. The mutually reinforcing relationship between resource endowment advantage and agglomeration effect will eventually continue to widen the gap in scale between different cities, forming a Matthew effect of the strong getting stronger and the weak getting weaker.

Equation (12.4.20) shows that once the aggregation scale exceeds the critical value, the effect of aggregation begins to decay, the speed of urban expansion begins to slow down, and finally reaches the limit scale, entering the equilibrium state of urban evolution.

The size of the agglomeration effect is determined by the industrial structure of the city, and the industrial structure is part of the evolution of the trading system, which is always in a state of constant evolution. This fact indicates that the equilibrium scale of the city will change with the evolution of the trading system, constituting the evolutionary direction of whether the city expands or decays. If a city's industrial structure is highly dependent on resource endowment, when the endowment value v is on the verge of exhaustion, the city will decline. The evolutionary history of many resource-based cities has proven this point.

In traditional societies, rural aggregation structures are usually based on natural villages, which can be regarded as both a trading community and an aggregation center. The size of a natural village is mainly determined by the degree of land resource concentration. The more abundant the land resources, the larger the scale of the natural village; the more scarce the land resources, the smaller the scale of the natural village. Comparing the scale of natural villages in the south and north of China can clearly show this difference. Generally speaking, the population density in the southern China is high and land resources are relatively scarce, so the scale of natural villages in the south is generally smaller; while the population density in the north is relatively low, and compared with the south, land resources are relatively abundant, so the scale of natural villages in the north is much larger than that in the south.

Comparing the aggregation of natural villages with urban aggregation, it is not difficult to find that land resources are the key factor supporting the aggregation of natural villages, while the main driving force of urban aggregation is the agglomeration effect. Resource endowment and aggregation scale have a linear relationship, while the agglomeration effect and aggregation scale have a nonlinear relationship based on positive feedback. The differences in the determining mechanisms behind the two types of aggregation are the key reasons for the huge scale difference between the aggregation of natural villages and urban aggregation.

12.4.4 Main Structural Features of Urban Aggregation

The aggregation trading model indicates that information plays a very important role in the process of aggregation in the trading network. The understanding of the destination Ω by the trading agents is the basis for forming the prior probability p and q of the trading agents a_i. As the organizational form of the trading network, the trading community is the main channel for the source of information for trading agents. The trading community is not only the basis for the collection of information for trading agents, but also the basis for the construction of the state coordination set. This logical relationship also determines the main structural features of urban aggregation.

One of the main structural features of urban aggregation is the clustering of trading agents in the same phase. Trading agents in the same industry often gather together, chemical enterprises will gather in a certain city area, textile enterprises will gather in another area, commerce and catering, although constrained by spatial distribution, still show a certain degree of clustering, such as city business centers will gather a large number of retail businesses, a food street will usually gather many catering businesses. Cities around the world basically follow the same layout of trading agents. This is not only the effect of aggregation at work, but also the result of the state coordination set playing a role in the decision-making of trading agents. From the aggregation trading model, we can know that the demonstration factor of the state coordination set μ^n plays a very key role. Even if the aggregation effect α of the aggregation center Ω is very low, as long as the number of demonstration agents on the state coordination set n is large enough, the probability of the trading agent a_i choosing Ω as a place to settle $\Pr(s)$ may still be very large.

Another significant feature of urban aggregation in terms of main structure is the zonal distribution of trading agents with certain similar characteristics. The rich in the city will gather in a certain area without agreement; the middle class will also gather in an area without agreement; and poor or relatively poor families will also gather in a certain specific area. These are the zonal distributions of different classes; similarly, families from a certain region or country will tend to choose a certain specific area, forming a community with the same cultural background. For example, Chinatowns scattered around the world are usually the first choice for Chinese immigrants to settle or live. After the reform and opening up, a large number of farmers went to the city to work, and when people from the same village went out to work, they usually went together, choosing the same city, and even the same industry and the same company.

12.4.5 Formation of the Urban Layered System

In modern society, every country has a large number of cities of various sizes, each playing different functional roles in the national industrial system. These cities form a layered system of division and cooperation. There is no universal standard for classifying cities in the world, and the city systems of each country are different. The methods of division also vary, and they are constantly adjusted with changes in economic development stages and population scale. Between 1830 and 1870, the United States divided cities into three levels: first-tier cities with a population of over 1.3 million, mainly represented by New York at the time; second-tier cities with a population between 130,000 and 1.3 million; third-tier cities with a population between 30,000 and 130,000. In 1870, the population of the United States was only 39 million; by 2021, the population of the United States had reached 333 million. After 150 years of development, the population of the United States has increased by 7.5 times. Obviously, the city division standards of 1870 cannot be applied to the current United States. In the 2000 census, the U.S. Census Bureau defined the concepts related to cities as follows[5]:

1. Urban areas. These are defined as fixed geographical areas with a population of no less than 2500 and a population density of no less than 500 people per square kilometer. In the 2000 census, there were 3756 urban areas in the United States;

2. Metropolitan areas. These are defined as core areas with a large population and their economically integrated neighboring communities. The population is no less than 50,000. In the 2000 census, the United States had 361 metropolitan areas;
3. Micropolitan areas. These are smaller urban areas than metropolitan areas, with a population generally between 10,000 and 50,000. In the 2000 census, the United States had 559 micropolitan areas;
4. Principal cities. These are defined as the largest autonomous cities within each metropolitan or micropolitan area. Each autonomous city has an autonomous body through which local governments exercise political power and public services, such as sewage treatment, crime control, and firefighting activities.

In China, cities are usually divided into four levels: first-tier cities, represented by Beijing, Shanghai, Guangzhou, and Shenzhen, which belong to the category of super-large cities; second-tier cities, represented by provincial capital cities in the economically developed eastern regions and some provincial capital cities in large provinces in the central and western regions, such as Nanjing, Hangzhou, Chengdu, Zhengzhou, Jinan, Tianjin, etc., which belong to the category of metropolises; third-tier cities, mainly represented by prefecture-level cities, including Ningbo, Shaoxing, Jiaxing, Wuxi, Anyang, Baoding, Langfang, etc., which belong to the category of medium-sized cities; fourth-tier cities, mainly represented by county-level cities, such as Kunshan, Yuzhou, Gu'an, etc., which belong to the category of small cities.

In fact, if cities are classified according to their population size, there can be more classification criteria, and the situation in each country is different, making it difficult to form a unified standard. If cities are classified according to their functional positioning, the situation will change. In a country's urban system, regardless of the size of the city, all cities can be divided into two basic types based on the role each city plays in the urban system. One type is the central city; the other type is the satellite cities surrounding the central city. Central cities are distributed at geographical poles, have outstanding resource endowment advantages, either have certain mineral resources, are located at convenient transportation junctions, or are in the center of vast agricultural hinterlands; while satellite cities can be seen as the spillover results of the resource endowment advantages and agglomeration effects of central cities, sharing the externalities of central cities and enjoying relatively low property costs. The central city and its satellite cities together form a higher level of aggregation structure—the city cluster.

The reason for the emergence of city cluster is due to the differences in the sensitivity to agglomeration effects and the intensity of land use by trading agents. By classifying trading agents based on the two dimensions of sensitivity to agglomeration effects and intensity of land use, the following results can be obtained.

Table 12.2 shows the results of trading agents classification on two dimensions. According to (12.4.12), the return risk index on return of the trading agents are as follows:

$$R_g = \frac{\kappa(r)m^{\alpha+1}r^2 + \tau v m r^2}{\kappa(r)m^{\alpha+1}r^2 + \tau v m r^2 - \Gamma\left(m^\beta\right)\pi\rho} \tag{12.4.23}$$

According to (12.4.23), we can evaluate the return risk indices R_g of the property strategies of the four types of trading agents. Type I trading agents have a high sensitivity to agglomeration effects, that is, the agglomeration effect sensitivity coefficient $\kappa(r)$ is relatively large, and they are sensitive to the property location r, the closer the location is to the city center, the larger the sensitivity coefficient $\kappa(r)$. Another important feature of type I trading agents is that the intensity of land use is relatively low, that is, the value $\Gamma\left(m^\beta\right)$ is relatively small, and the sensitivity to the city aggregation scale m is relatively low. From this, we can infer that the return risk index of type I trading agents is very close to 1, as $R_g \approx 1$. For these trading agents, the larger the scale m of the aggregation center Ω, the closer the return risk index is to 1. Therefore, the larger the scale m of the aggregation center or city, the smaller the return risk index R_g of type I trading agents. According to (12.4.13), type I trading agents prefer cities or aggregation centers with larger scales. Due to the characteristics of high sensitivity to agglomeration effects and low intensity of land use, these trading agents tend to choose the main urban area of the central city as their property location.

In reality, type I trading agents usually include financial institutions, cultural service enterprises, luxury business institutions, high-end catering enterprises and other tertiary industry institutions with high added value characteristics. Among family agents, the higher the income, the more likely they are to choose areas and regions rich in public resources (education resources, medical resources, etc.), and usually, areas rich in public resources are concentrated in the central urban area. Compared to type I trading agents, type II trading agents also have a high sensitivity to the agglomeration effect, but due to the high intensity of land use, if they choose the main urban area of the central city, the cost of property placement will be higher. To resolve this contradiction, type II trading agents usually choose the peripheral areas or suburbs of the central city, which retains the benefits of being close to the central city while avoiding excessively high property placement costs. Type II agents mainly include logistics enterprises, automobile trade enterprises, etc., and technology-intensive enterprises usually also belong to type II trading agents, choosing the suburbs of the central city facilitates the recruitment of the required technical personnel.

Table 12.2 Classification of the trading agents

Classification	High sensitivity to agglomeration effects	Low sensitivity to agglomeration effects
Land use intensity—low	I. High sensitivity, low strength	III. High sensitivity, high strength
Land use intensity—high	II. High sensitivity, high strength	IV. Low sensitivity, high strength

Type II household agents are mainly trading agents employed by type I enterprises, with relatively low household income. These households need to choose property placement in the central city due to employment, but they cannot afford the high property placement costs in the central urban area, so the peripheral urban areas of the central city become the best choice for these households.

Type III trading agents have characteristics of lower sensitivity to the agglomeration effect and lower intensity of land use, which means that the agglomeration effect sensitivity coefficient $\kappa(r)$ has a smaller value, and is not very sensitive to the property placement location r; the land use intensity coefficient $\Gamma(m^{\beta})$ has a smaller value, and is not sensitive to the city aggregation scale m. For the above characteristics of type III trading agents, if a central city with a larger aggregation scale is chosen as the property placement location, the return risk index R_g will have a higher value, while choosing the neighboring satellite city of the central city, the return risk index R_g has a smaller value; if a smaller peripheral satellite city is chosen as the property placement location, because these trading agents do not have high land use intensity, they will not save a considerable amount of cost from the property placement cost, but will cause a loss of agglomeration effect income due to the distance from the central city, which is not worth the loss. Therefore, the neighboring satellite city will be the first choice for type III trading agents.

Type III trading agents include manufacturing enterprises with relatively small production scales and relatively low technology added value; service industries with low entry thresholds and intense competition, and household agents employed in these industries.

The basic characteristics of type IV trading agents are lower sensitivity to the agglomeration effect and higher land use intensity. Obviously, it is the best choice for these trading agents to choose peripheral satellite cities far away from the central city and with the smallest aggregation scale as the property placement location.

As can be seen from (12.4.8), the property placement cost can be calculated as follows:

$$Lc(x, y) = \frac{\Gamma(m^{\beta})\pi\rho}{r^2 m} \tag{12.4.24}$$

For type IV trading agents, if they choose the central city or neighboring satellite city, because the central city and neighboring satellite city are much larger in scale and density than the peripheral satellite city, the property placement cost will also be much higher than the peripheral satellite city; on the other hand, due to the low sensitivity of type IV trading agents to the agglomeration effect, the benefits obtained from the central city or neighboring satellite city are not much higher than those from the peripheral satellite city, which inevitably leads to the return risk index R_g of choosing the central city or neighboring satellite city will be higher than the result of the peripheral satellite city. According to the aggregation trading model (12.4.13), type IV trading agents will inevitably choose the peripheral satellite city as the property placement location.

Type IV trading agents are mainly composed of manufacturing enterprises with relatively low technology added value and large production scales, as well as household agents employed in these enterprises.

In the trading system, the formation process of the urban stratification is a self-organizing behavior spontaneously chosen by a large number of trading agents. The urban system will contain varying numbers of urban groups, and the size of each urban group depends on the radiation intensity of the central city. The more obvious the agglomeration effect produced by the central city, the greater the value of the resources it possesses, the stronger the radiation it produces, the more satellite cities it can attract, and the larger the urban group it ultimately forms. Although the urban stratification system has great stability once formed, it is not immutable. Technological progress is the basic force driving the evolution of the trading system, and it is also the driving force for the evolution of the urban system. The agglomeration effect of each city depends on the stage of the life cycle of the dominant industry. If the dominant industry of the central city is in the rising cycle, the agglomeration effect of the city will continue to strengthen, and the city scale tends to expand; the urban group led by the central city will also be in the expansion cycle; on the contrary, if the dominant industry of the central city has entered the sunset cycle, the agglomeration effect of the city will continue to decline, and more and more trading agents will move out and choose cities with greater agglomeration effects and more vitality for their businesses. The scale of the city that migrates out will continue to shrink, and the urban group it is in will gradually move towards disintegration and reconstruction.

12.5 Evolution of Trading Network Aggregation Structure

The structure at each aggregation level is in continuous evolution. The basic force driving the evolution of the aggregation structure is the competition between aggregates. The evolution driven by competition follows a common law, that is, the centralization of resource allocation. The evolution of the aggregation structure also develops in the direction of centralization, and the equilibrium structure of the original aggregate is gradually broken. Accompanied by one or several aggregates winning in the competition, resource allocation gathers towards the winners, becoming the center of the aggregation layer. This evolutionary trend is no exception, whether it is at the community aggregation level, the city aggregation level, the economic belt aggregation level, or the national aggregation level.

For aggregates that do not have independent decision-making capabilities, such as communities, economic zones, international trade cooperation regions, etc., the common feature of these aggregates is that the coordination between internal members is spontaneously realized. The competitive behavior of such aggregates is determined by the coordination efficiency between the internal members of the unit. The higher the coordination efficiency of the aggregate, the more prominent the competitive advantage in the competition of the aggregation layer. For aggregates with decision-making capabilities, the competition between units will be more direct, and the means of competition will be more diversified, and the competition will be more brutal.

The behavioral characteristics of the aggregate depend on the decision-making mechanism and the interest orientation of the decision-maker. Each aggregate has its own unique interest stratification structure, its own unique way of behavior, and its own distinct personality characteristics. This is true for aggregates at all levels, whether they are aggregates with clear decision-making mechanisms, such as cities and countries, or aggregates without clear decision-making mechanisms, such as communities and economic zones. The country is the most complex aggregate form with the most decision-making agents. Among the five levels of aggregation stratification, the behavioral characteristics of the national aggregate are also the most complex and the most difficult to figure out. There is no uniform national behavior pattern. The behavior pattern of each country is determined by the decision-making mechanism and the interest structure behind it. Just as there are no two identical leaves in nature, there are no two countries in the world with exactly the same behavior patterns. Only by understanding these can we understand the peculiar characteristics of the evolution of the world's international pattern.

In the trading system, aggregates at the same level compete with each other. Once an aggregate gains an absolute advantage, it becomes the information hub of its level. Information plays a crucial role in the modern economy, and the information hub will give the dominant aggregate a greater competitive advantage. Accompanying the information center are roles such as the technology innovation center, education and talent cultivation center, cultural communication center, and financial center. The positive feedback mechanism of competition between aggregates will undoubtedly further strengthen the centripetal evolution trend of the trading system.

Just like market evolution, once a monopoly forms, market efficiency will severely decline. The monopolistic enterprise will use its advantage to control the market, ultimately becoming an obstacle to the effective allocation of market resources. In the global trading system, once a country gains an absolute advantage, it will suppress competing countries. At the international level, due to the lack of strong external constraints, a unipolar international game cannot achieve the optimal Nash equilibrium for all parties. When the dominant position of a unipolar country is challenged, it will inevitably choose a competitive strategy that betrays the best interests of all humanity, objectively becoming a stumbling block to the progress of human society. At this point, the trading system once again shows its self-alienating characteristics.

In the evolution process of the trading network, the aggregate structure also presents dynamic changes, among which the reconstruction of the aggregate structure is a very eye-catching phenomenon. In the process of aggregate structure reconstruction, some aggregates expand rapidly, while others gradually decline and wither. During industrialization, urbanization attracted a large number of farmers to move from rural areas to cities, restructuring the aggregate structure under the agricultural economic form. Since post-industrialization, regional aggregate structures have been restructured. Once prosperous industrial areas began to decline, such as the north-eastern United States—the Great Lakes region before the 1970s was a heavy industry agglomeration area, Germany's Ruhr area, London's industrial area in the UK, are typical examples. These once prosperous industrial city agglomeration areas, with the adjustment of industrial structure, a large number of enterprises closed or relocated, a large population loss, corresponding to the migration movement to the Sunbelt. It can be seen that the aggregate structure presents periodic reconstruction, and the basic force driving the reconstruction of the aggregate structure is migration, the migration of enterprises and families. Whether it is the reconstruction of the aggregate structure in the process of urbanization or the reconstruction of the aggregate structure in the process of industrial structure adjustment, the migration of trading agents is the main cause.

The competition among aggregates at the same aggregation level for trading agents is manifested as the cross-aggregate migration of trading agents. Trading agents always migrate from aggregates with relatively low trading network density to aggregates with high network density. The trading network density represents both market prosperity and the level of economic development, as well as the opportunity for trading agents to realize profits. As profit-motivated trading agents, migrating from areas with low trading network density to areas with high trading network density aligns with the basic value orientation of trading agents. Whether it is migrating from rural areas to cities, from small towns to metropolises, or from economically backward areas to economically developed areas, trading agents always migrate along the gradient vector of trading network density.

Drawing on the basic principles of the population migration model proposed by American economist Michael P. Todaro in the 1970s,[6] combined with the structural characteristics of the trading network, we derive the aggregate reconstruction model of the trading network.

Let Ω_k and Ω_l are two aggregates on the same level, which can be two trading communities in same city, two different cities, or two different economic zones or countries. Suppose the network densities of Ω_k and Ω_l are ρ_k and ρ_l respectively, and the cost of moving into the aggregate Ω_l is m_l^c; $a_i \in \Omega_k$ is any trading agent on Ω_k, with a net asset scale of z_i, the probability of a_i moving from Ω_k to Ω_l is $\Pr(a_i|\Omega_k - \Omega_l)$.

The motivation for the migration of trading agents is directly proportional to the migration benefits. The greater the expected benefits of migration, the stronger the motivation for migration. It is inversely proportional to the cost of migration. The higher the cost of migration, the weaker the motivation for migration. Since each trading agent has different abilities to bear costs, those with stronger abilities are more likely to overcome the obstacle of resettlement costs. However, those with weaker abilities cannot realize migration even if there is a large expected migration benefit.

Based on the above analysis, we can infer that the probability of a_i moving from Ω_k to Ω_l $\Pr(a_i|\Omega_k - \Omega_l)$, which can be expressed as follows:

$$\Pr(a_i|\Omega_k \to \Omega_l) = k\frac{z_i}{m_l^c}\frac{\rho_l}{\rho_k} \tag{12.5.1}$$

where k is the adjustment coefficient, satisfying $k > 0$. For different types of trading agents, the value of k can vary. Household agents and enterprise agents will have different emphases in migration decisions, and different types of enterprises will also have different emphases in site selection, all of which are reflected in the value of k.

The migration model (12.5.1) can accurately describe some phenomena in the reconstruction of the trading network aggregate structure, explain why big cities are getting bigger and small towns are getting smaller. It can also explain why residents in poor areas on the edge of the trading network are reluctant to leave their hometowns, gradually evolving into almost closed areas; and it can explain the differentiation mechanism between communities in the same city.

The migration formula also reveals the differentiation mechanism of network communities. The higher the trading potential order, the greater the probability of migration of trading agents under the same conditions. High-order trading agents are always the active factors in the reconstruction of the trading network aggregate. Under the continuous action of migration activities, the trading network eventually forms a pattern of high-order agents gathering in communities with excellent environments; while weak trading agents will stay in the original community, forming a trend of the strong getting stronger and the weak getting weaker. This differentiation mechanism not only exists in the reconstruction process of trading communities, but also in the evolution of cities and countries.

In the migration probability formula, it includes the self-restraint mechanism of the dominant aggregations attracting resources from other aggregations, thereby achieving a new equilibrium structure in the process of aggregation structure reconstruction. As the dominant aggregation attracts more and more trading agents to migrate in, the network density will further increase, which will undoubtedly increase its attractiveness; at the same time, as more and more trading agents gather together, the scarcity of resources will become more and more prominent, including housing, land, road traffic resources, etc., which will become more scarce, inevitably leading to price increases, various restrictions increase, etc., all of these will increase the resettlement cost of migration. In countries around the world, the prices of houses and land in big cities are far higher than those in small and medium-sized cities; big cities also have more restrictions on traffic than small and medium-sized cities, all of which will become factors preventing more trading agents from migrating in.

Notes

1. Arthur O'Sullivan (2015) Urban Economics (trans: Jingkui ZHOU), 8th edn. Peking University Press, Beijing, p 18.
2. Roberta Capello (2022) Regional Economic (trans: Husen AN), 2nd edn. Economic Management Press, Beijing, p 46.
3. Roberta Capello (2022) Regional Economic (trans: Husen AN), 2nd edn. Economic Management Press, Beijing, p 78.
4. Masahisa Fujita, Paul Krugman, Anthony J. Venables (2011) The Spatial Economy: Cities, Regions and International Trade (trans: Qi LIANG), China Renmin University Press, Beijing, p 21.
5. Arthur O'Sullivan (2015) Urban Economics (trans: Jingkui ZHOU), 8th edn. Peking University Press, Beijing, p 18.
6. Jun TAN, Yueping SUN (2016) Applied Welfare Economics, Economic Management Press, Beijing p 254.

Chapter 13
Compactness of Trading Systems

The non-linear characteristics of the trading system stem from the interaction between trading agents. In the continuous evolution process, the non-linear features of the trading system become increasingly prominent. To describe and measure the intensity of the non-linear characteristics of the trading system, we introduce the concept of compactness and use compactness to measure the intensity of the compactness of the trading system.

13.1 Concept of Compactness[1]

Non-linearity is a basic characteristic of complex systems. Complex systems have two typical characteristics, namely the close association between components and the positive feedback mechanism based on interaction. The association of system components needs to be expressed through interaction between components; while the positive feedback mechanism requires specific behavior patterns of each component as support. Based on this understanding, we can find an effective measure of the non-linear strength of the trading system.

13.1.1 Interaction Mechanism of Trading Entities

The closeness of internal connections in the system is a key indicator of the stage of system development.[2] The higher the level of system evolution, the more significant the role of internal connections in system operation. If ignoring the internal connection of the system is a simplification method of system research, and is only effective in the initial stage of system evolution; for complex systems that have entered a high

Z. Wang, *Trading Economics*, Contributions to Economics,
https://doi.org/10.1007/978-981-99-9875-3_13

level of evolution, the connection has become an indispensable characteristic of the system.

In the trading system, the interaction between trading agents mainly refers to the process which one agent's decision and trading behavior have an impact on another agent's decision and return. According to the mechanism of action, the interaction between agents can be divided into two types: one is trading action. Trading agents realize interaction through the trading network and spread this effect outward. On the closely connected trading network, the decision of the trading agent will inevitably affect the return of other agents, such as the debtor's ability to repay and the trading decision that affects the ability to repay, will undoubtedly affect the result of the creditor's realization of rights and interests to a certain extent. The interaction formed by trading agents through trading is the basis of internal connection in the trading system, and other types of actions are extensions of this type of action.

Another type is the role of information. In the trading community, information spreads quickly among neighbors. Residents observe the income situation of their neighbors, and this information becomes a factor influencing their decisions. Under conditions of insufficient information, people always enhance their information by observing the decisions and consequences of others' actions to reduce decision-making risks. Against the backdrop of increasing information flow and dissemination speed, the radius of information influence is growing. With the open channels of the trading network, information spreads quickly in the trading system, with an extremely wide range of influence. In the trading system, the "butterfly effect" can only be realized with the wings of information.

The two mechanisms between trading agents will tightly connect the numerous trading agents into an organic whole, ultimately profoundly affecting the operation and evolution of the trading system.

13.1.2 Visualization of the Concept of Compactness

Compactness refers to the closely related state within the system. The phenomenon of compactness is very common and is commonplace in our daily life. Cars driving on the road seem independent, but they are interconnected, and this interconnection is constantly changing. When the road is wide and there are few cars, the vehicles on the road have a low degree of correlation, and the speed of each car can almost change freely. When the number of vehicles on the road increases, the vehicles must look ahead and behind, and the correlation between them suddenly increases. When the road is congested, the speed of each car will strictly depend on the speed of the car in front. As long as the car in front moves, the car behind will follow closely, and the long line of cars on the entire road suddenly becomes closely related, and the road system tends to be highly compact.

Trading are the fundamental source of correlation within a trading system, and the strength of the correlation formed by different types of trading varies. For example, when one agent is indebted to another, or one party holds the equity of another, these equity trading can directly transmit the economic status of one party to the other, affecting many aspects of the other party's risk and return, etc. This relationship forces the equity holder to pay close attention to the other party's economic status and trading. Compared with equity trading, the correlation strength formed by ordinary commodity trading is much weaker. After the trading is completed, the correlation between the two parties will quickly decrease.

13.1.3 Axiomatic Definition of Compactness

Compactness is a measure of the compactness of a trading system. Due to the complexity of the components, it is almost technically impossible to accurately express the size of various elements' effects using explicit formulas. To solve this problem, we need to use the method of axiomatic definition to give the conditions that compactness needs to satisfy. The axiomatic method not only avoids the difficulty of specific calculations but also facilitates the design of more practical quantitative indicators in various application scenarios.

Establish a single mapping relationship ϕ between the state set of the trading system Σ and the semi-open interval of real numbers $[0, +\infty]$, if ϕ satisfies the following conditions, then ϕ is the compactness on the state set Σ of the trading system:

1. For all states of the trading system, there is $\phi \geq 0$;
2. For any two states of the trading system, if state 1 shows stronger internal correlation than state 2, then ϕ satisfies the relationship: $\phi_1 > \phi_2$;
3. When agents in the trading system are independent of each other and their influence on each other can be ignored, the state corresponding to ϕ satisfies $\phi = 0$.

According to the above axiomatic regulations, we can use interpolation to establish an indicator system for the compactness of the trading system. In actual operation, several states can be pre-selected, their compactness ranked, and values assigned first to the state with the highest compactness, then assigned in order according to axiom 2. Through repeated operation of the above procedure, we can continuously increase the number of states and gradually establish a relatively complete compactness indicator value system.

When measuring the compactness of a trading system, it is relatively easy to handle trading systems with relatively uniform evolution, and it is difficult to calculate the compactness of trading system that with a high degree of structural localization. For example, when the trading system shows a dense local network and sparseness elsewhere, this situation often occurs during the structural adjustment period of the trading system, and large-scale industrial transfers may result in such outcomes. In this case, the compactness measurement of the entire trading system needs to be comprehensively evaluated based on the size of local weights.

Based on the compactness metric, we can divide the trading system into two basic types: compact state and relaxed state. Trading systems that are in the compact state, the interactions between agents play a significant role in the operation of the trading system, and prominent non-linear characteristics. Trading systems that are in the relaxed state, the internal correlation has little impact on system behavior. At this time, the trading system can be regarded as the linear superposition of the behaviors of a large number of trading agents, suitable for linearization.

13.2 Factors Influencing Compactness

A trading chain is a chain that closely links several trading agents through related trades in the trading network. Supply chains, debt chains, equity chains, etc., are common forms of related trading chains. The more trading chains generated in the trading network, and the longer they are, the higher the degree of compactness of the trading system.

13.2.1 Trading Network Density

The density of the trading network implies the degree to which trading agents in the trading network share nodes and information. The denser the trading network, the higher the node degree of the agents in the trading network. This means that the agent has more trading associations and information exchanges with more agents, it also means that the interconnections within the system are more compact.

On the other hand, the density of the trading network also reflects the degree of division of labor within the system. The more developed the division of labor in the trading system, the denser the trading network. The case of the shoe industry's division of labor can well illustrate the close relationship between the self-organizing process of division of labor and the densification of the trading network. In the era of manual workshops, there is usually no division of labor within the shoe industry, and each workshop independently completes production. The products of different merchants are similar, whether in function, design, or market reputation, there is not much difference. Each workshop has its own customer base, neither needs innovation nor needs to compete with other peers. While producing batches of shoes, these workshops also cultivate batches of technically qualified shoemakers from apprentices, promoting more and more shoemakers to set up their own businesses. As the number of peers increases, each workshop gradually feels the market competition pressure. Under this background, there will be smarter shoemakers who no longer sell shoes, only make soles, and sell the soles to other shoe-making workshops. Initially, only a few workshops used the bought soles to make shoes, and found that this business model was cheaper than making shoes independently. These merchants, with the cost advantage, quickly expanded their market share. When more and more shoe-making workshops abandoned the traditional production model, and buy soles from the sole workshops, the first division of labor within the shoe industry appeared. Similar situations also occurred when the leather workshops separated from the shoe-making workshops, the shoelace workshops separated from the shoe-making workshops.

As the sole workshops focus on producing soles, continuously improving the process, and beginning to try various materials, developing soles with different performances, such as soles with good elasticity, soles with good wear resistance, etc. The shoe-making workshops, under the dual effects of technology and competitive pressure, will continuously introduce new technologies, transition from manual to industrial manufacturing, and the original manual workshops gradually transform into modern factories. At the same time, the market is segmented, and shoe companies develop shoes with different functions, such as dress shoes, casual shoes, basketball shoes, climbing shoes, tennis shoes, etc. Some companies will focus on shoes of a certain function, and there will be sports shoe companies, and leather shoe companies, etc.

As market competition intensifies, division of labor will become further refined. Some shoe manufacturers have started to seek help from specialized design companies, injecting more technical content into shoe styles and performance, hiring professional advertising companies to advertise for them, and employing professional market research companies to conduct market demand surveys, etc. At this stage, after completing internal division of labor and market segmentation, the shoe industry has begun to extend its cooperative relationships beyond the shoe industry, cooperating with an increasingly wide range of related industries, including research departments, sports industry, film and entertainment industry, etc., ultimately weaving itself into an increasingly dense network.

The above process of division of labor evolution clearly shows us that in the process of continuous division of labor, each agent's external trading have increased. In the past, the main trading partners of each shoe workshop were textile workshops and shoe-buying customers. With the progression of division of labor, shoe companies need to trade with many cooperating manufacturers, from advertising to design, from market research to production equipment, almost every link requires trading. Compared to before, the number of trading partners and the content of trading have increased exponentially, the density of the trading network has increased, and the interconnectivity between trading agents has been strengthened.

The densification of the trading network not only enhances the demand for information by trading agents, but also provides channels and carriers for information circulation. With the improvement of information dissemination technology, each trading agent receives more information than before, and while gaining more trading opportunities, each agent will also feel an increasingly large impact from the external environment.

13.2.2 Leverage Ratio of the Trading System

The density of the trading network reflects the connection characteristics between agents from a topological perspective, but the connotation of compactness is not limited to this. The nature of trading will also affect the compactness of the trading system. Compared with simple commodity trading, financial trading cause a closer connection between agents and have a more direct and significant impact on the compactness of the trading system.

For business-type trading agents, the leverage ratio refers to the ratio of liabilities to equity capital. For household-type trading agents, the leverage ratio refers to the ratio of total household debt to household income. For the entire trading system, the leverage ratio can be calculated by the ratio of total liabilities to total assets or the ratio of total liabilities to GDP.

In financial analysis, the leverage ratio is often used to measure the debt risk of an enterprise. The higher the leverage ratio, the greater the debt risk of the enterprise. In economic analysis, the significance of the leverage rate goes far beyond this. The leverage ratio represents the state of the trading amplification mechanism. The higher the leverage ratio, the stronger the trend of the expansion of the trading system, and it also means that the risk contained in the trading system is higher.

There are many ways to increase leverage, and the most common leveraged trading is to increase trading volume through debt. It can also be done through margin trading, installment payments, credit card payments, leasing, etc., all of which are types of leveraged trading. Leveraged trading is a very important system in the modern economy and is an important mechanism supporting economic operations. Changes in the leverage ratio, whether increases or decreases, will have a significant impact on the economy. Bank credit volume is a major factor affecting the leverage ratio. Faced with changes in business risks, commercial banks continuously adjust their credit strategies, resulting a constantly changing leverage ratio in the trading system.

The higher the leverage ratio, the stronger the compactness of the trading system. Equity relationships closely link trading agents, and what happens to one agent quickly affects another related trading agent. A trading system with a high leverage ratio can easily trigger a trading ring phenomenon. Before a financial crisis erupts, the leverage ratio of the trading system will continue to rise. After the crisis erupts, the leverage ratio will quickly drop, triggering violent fluctuations in compactness.

13.2.3 Debt Structure of the Trading System

The leverage ratio of the trading system measures the average level of amplification in the trading system', and is calculated on the basis of asset-liability ratio of a single trading agent, without considering the specific situation of the structure of creditor's rights. In fact, the length and structure of the debt chain also affect the compactness of the trading system.

$$a \longrightarrow b \quad \text{and} \quad b \longrightarrow c$$

Fig. 13.1 The creditor relationship of a, b, c

$$a \longrightarrow b \longrightarrow c$$

Fig. 13.2 The diagram of a debt chain

Let a, b, and c be three arbitrary trading agents in the trading system. If a has a creditor relationship with b, and b has a creditor relationship with c, this relationship can be represented with arrows (Fig. 13.1).

The above relationship forms a cohesive relationship between creditor's right and debts, which we call a debt chain, and express it in the following form (Fig. 13.2).

In the modern economy, banks play a key role in shaping the debt structure of the trading system. After banks enter the debt chain, the structure of the debt chain begins to become more complex, it can be summarized as the following multi-layer structure. We use small dots to represent general trading agents, large dots to represent banking institutions, and the direction of the arrows to represent the direction of equity.

Figure 13.3 shows the structural characteristics of the debt chain after the bank joins. In addition to the creditor relationship between banks and non-financial customers, there is also a creditor relationship between banks. In fact, the complexity

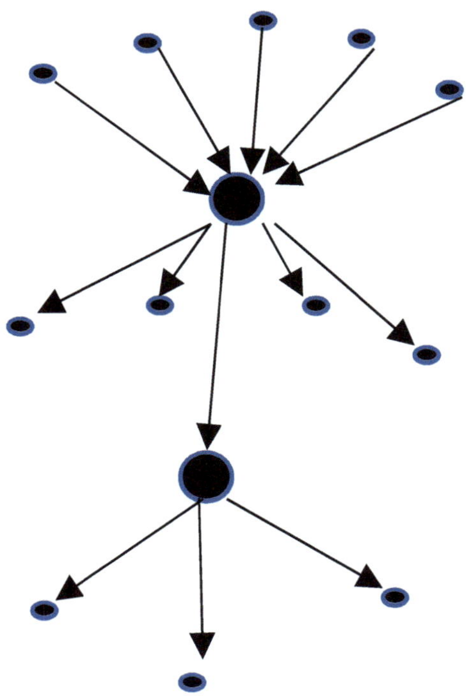

Fig. 13.3 The diagram of debt chain structure

of real-world debt relationships far exceeds Fig. 13.3, the application of accounts payable and commercial bills is much more widespread than bank credit. There is a common creditor relationship of accounts payable between enterprises; there is a debt relationship of bills payable between households and public service enterprises. Commercial bills are a liability tool often used by large and medium-sized enterprises, inevitably further increasing the complexity of the debt chain structure. After accounts payable and commercial bills are added to the debt chain, Fig. 13.3 will evolve into the following shape.

After corporate credit is added, the debt chain structure evolves towards a debt network, and it is in line with the evolution law of the trading system (Fig. 13.4). The higher the evolution stage of the trading system, the more complex the debt chain structure. In this case, we still use the term "debt chain" to name such debt relationships because creditor's right and debts in these debt relationships are unidirectional. In fact, creditor's right and debts in bidirectional relationships are very common. Enterprises that borrow from banks usually open deposit accounts in the lending banks, forming a bidirectional creditor relationship between the bank and the borrowing enterprise. Under the concept of the debt chain, bidirectional creditor relationships should belong to two different debt chains.

The trading system contains a large number of debt chains. The number of agents contained in the debt chain is called the length of the debt chain; the total debt on the debt chain is called the equivalent of the debt chain. In the trading system, the average length of the debt chain and the average equivalent of the debt chain represent the strength of the debt association in the trading system.

Fig. 13.4 The evolution of the debt chain

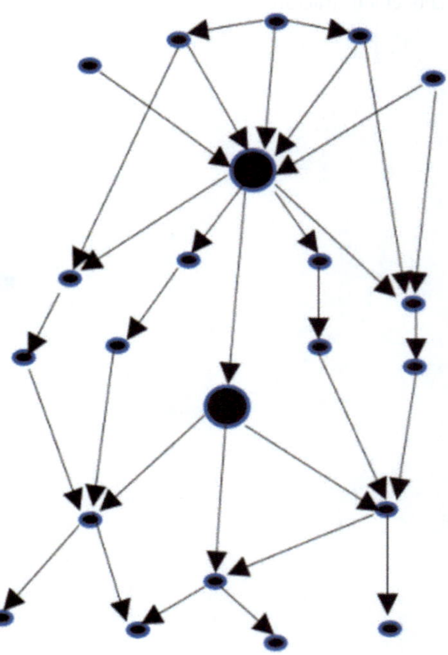

There is a positive correlation between the strength of debt association and the compactness of the trading system, that is, the higher the strength of debt association, the stronger the compactness of the trading system; conversely, the lower the strength of debt association, the weaker the compactness of the trading system. For the trading system, having an appropriate strength of debt association is necessary, otherwise it cannot effectively organize production, let alone achieve the expansion of trading scale. When the economic debt association strength exceeds a certain limit, the trading system will face huge vulnerability risks. On a debt chain with high connectivity, if one debtor has a problem, it will quickly spread to the entire trading system through the debt chain.

In the 1980s, the United States relaxed financial regulation, and various financial services continued to converge, with banks, securities, and insurance gradually moving towards mixed operations. Asset-backed securitization products developed rapidly, becoming a type of asset widely held by various financial institutions. Taking subprime loans as an example, commercial banks issued mortgage loans to families with weaker repayment capabilities and higher credit risks. This was originally a very traditional bank credit business, and the debt chain was very short. After securitization, these assets circulated widely in the investment market, becoming the target of various institutions such as banks, insurance companies, securities companies, and hedge funds. After being recombined and packaged by investment banks, the spread of subprime bonds further increased, not only circulating in the United States, but even spreading to Europe and Asia. When the continuous decline in U.S. house prices led to a significant shrinkage of subprime debt assets, the debt chain supported by subprime loans became a highway for the spread of financial risks, eventually leading to a global financial tsunami.

13.2.4 Equity Structure of the Trading System

In the trading system, according to the equity relationship, we can divide the trading agents into several groups, and there is an equity relationship between the trading agents in each group. These groups of agents with equity relationships can include both enterprise-type agents and family-type agents. We use the group with the most trading agents and the largest asset scale to represent the strength of the equity association of the trading system. The stronger the equity association, the higher the compactness of the trading system.

The strength of equity association has a significant impact on the operation of the trading system. Trading systems with different strengths of equity association show completely different adaptability. Trading systems with high-strength equity associations have the characteristics of shock resistance and good stability, but their response to market speed changes is slow, with Japan being a typical case; on the contrary, economies with low equity association have poor stability, but prominent market self-organization characteristics, strong adaptability to external changes, with the United States being a typical representative.

Among the four main factors affecting the compactness of the trading system, the density of the trading network stems from the evolutionary trend of division of labor; leveraged trading, equity trading, etc., are the accompanying phenomena of the financialization of the trading system. It can be seen that the main factors affecting the compactness of the trading system are variables from system evolution, and the compactness of the trading system is the inevitable result of its own evolution.

13.3 Compactness Oscillation

Compactness oscillation is a special phenomenon that occasionally occurs in the operation of trading systems, referring to the process where the compactness of the trading system suddenly increases in a very short time, and then quickly decreases. As a characteristic indicator of the evolution of trading systems, compactness is usually quite stable, but when the trading system is subjected to a large shock, compactness oscillation will occur. As a background parameter of system operation, compactness has a very wide impact on system operation. Once an oscillation occurs, it will cause great damage to the trading system, the efficiency of system operation will rapidly decline, and it may even induce a structural collapse of the trading network, leading to a crisis. This is like the gravitational structure in the universe, as the background structure of the universe's operation, gravitational waves that induce gravitational oscillations are often associated with catastrophic events such as supernova explosions or major celestial collisions.

There are mainly two types of causes for compactness oscillation: one is the occurrence of large-scale trading cascades in the trading system; the other is the outbreak of a crisis in the trading system. The crisis is both a cause and a result of compactness oscillation, the two are intertwined.

13.3.1 Trade Cascade

When society is controlled by a special atmosphere, the public's consistent behavior will cause the compactness of the trading system to skyrocket to an unprecedented level, a large number of trading agents enter a cascade state, and the trading system falls into chaos. Behind the sudden rise in compactness is group consistent behavior, the causes of which are multifaceted, including herd mentality, collective behavior, and panic.

Conformity is a psychological concept, meaning changes in behavior or beliefs made according to others.[4] According to the psychological characteristics behind conformity behavior, it can be divided into two types: compliance and acceptance. Conformity behavior that arises under reward and punishment mechanisms is compliance; acceptance is herd behavior that arises through accepting a viewpoint, through one's own value judgment. Both types of conformity are not due to external pressure, but are voluntarily chosen through cognition of the consequences of behavior.

From a motivational perspective, both normative motives and informational motives can produce herd behavior. Normative motivation is the desire to maintain consistency with the group in the face of group pressure, to avoid isolation and group retaliation. As social animals, humans have an instinctive psychological need for a sense of belonging to a social group, and maintaining consistency with the majority of the group is a natural way to gain recognition and achieve a sense of belonging. Informational motivation is the desire to obtain information from others' behavior. Usually, the more complex the situation faced, the greater the uncertainty, the easier it is for informational motivation to play a role. In the face of rumors, conformity behavior often appears more prominent than usual. In the operation of trading systems, informational motivation plays a more important role. In reality, many decisions are made under conditions of insufficient information, which is the basic background for conformity to arises. The informational motivation behind conformity is realized through social learning. Research has found that social learning plays a significant role in financial markets.[5]

Collective behavior refers to the consistent actions that people take in response to certain external stimuli. Spontaneous gatherings, demonstrations, racial conflicts, etc., fall within the scope of collective behavior. In the economic field, panic-induced buying frenzies, large-scale stock selling behaviors, etc., also belong to collective behavior. From the perspective of the implementation mechanism, conformity is a subsequent effect generated under the demonstration of others; while collective behavior is the consistent behavior of the group, the two have essential differences.

The main feature of collective behavior is that emotional contagion can quickly increase the connection between agents, enhancing the compactness of the trading system. Whether it is panic or optimism, both are important causes of collective behavior. When a strong emotion such as excitement or fear permeates the group, this emotion has a very strong contagion, and it will soon form a powerful force for consistent action in the group.

In reality, conformity behavior and collective behavior are intertwined. conformity contains the characteristics of collective behavior, and collective behavior is also involved in conformity, and it is difficult to distinguish between the two. Whether it is conformity behavior or collective behavior, for the trading system, they are all presented in the form of cascade trading, and a large number of consistent trades emerge in a short period of time, showing a high degree of consistency in both the trading target and the trading direction. The trading system belongs to the category of the ecosystem, diversity is the key indicator of the health of the ecosystem, once a large number of trading agents adopt a consistent trading strategy, it will break the carrying capacity of the trading system, leading to the collapse of the trading system.

13.3.2 Crisis Phenomenon

The destructive effect of a crisis in the trading system comes from the consistent behavior of a large number of trading agents, which is also the key to causing fluctuations in the compactness of the trading system. In the outbreak and escalation of a crisis, rumors and panic reinforce each other, forming a self-strengthening process. Panic provides an environment for the spread of rumors, and rumors in turn further intensify the public's panic. This mutually reinforcing relationship, while enhancing trading consistency, also pushes the crisis deeper and deeper. After the outbreak of the crisis, the trading network falls into a fragmented state, the compactness of the trading system drops rapidly, and the economy falls into recession or stagnation.

The oscillation of compactness due to various causes cannot be separated from special social psychological activities. The mutually stimulating psychological processes are like a nuclear fusion, and the energy released often exceeds people's imagination. However, any willing response, no matter how strong it was initially, will quickly fade, showing a strong impulsivity. This is also the root cause of the oscillation of the compactness of the trading system.

13.4 Evolution of Trading System Compactness

The compactness of the trading system is a dynamic variable that is constantly changing. A sudden event can cause the compactness of the trading system to rise sharply. When families and businesses adopt conservative strategies without prior agreement, the compactness of the trading system will decrease accordingly. The instability of compactness leads to the variability of macro-behavioral laws, which is a challenge and puzzle often faced by economists.

In the long-term evolutionary trend, the compactness of the trading system shows a very stable evolutionary trend, that is, the trend of continuously increasing compactness. We call this trend the compactification of the trading system.

Human has experienced two basic economic forms—agricultural economic form and industrial economic form.[6] In the era when agriculture dominated, each family was a unit of production and consumption, and the basic operating mode of the agricultural economic form was self-sufficiency. Under such an economic organization model, no matter how large the scale of the country is, each production unit—farm households are almost independent of each other.[7] Financial activities under the agricultural economic form are negligible, and if financial trading occur, they only appear sporadically, locally, and accidentally. In such a situation, it is usually impossible for a chain reaction of bankruptcy of a series of trading agents caused by the bankruptcy of one trading agent to occur.

In a self-sufficient dominated trading system, the production boundary of each production unit is its own consumption demand, and the limited consumption demand restricts the expansion of production; on the other hand, self-sufficiency also restricts production capacity. Each producer cannot allocate production factors through trading, and production can only be limited to the number of production factors they own, and the scale of production is also restricted. Under the agricultural economic form, the usual way for families to expand their production scale is to increase the number of children, which is why societies under the agricultural economic form, regardless of cultural background, share a common feature—a strong demand for the number of children in families. When trading becomes the bridge connecting the market and production, both demand and supply have the prospect of unlimited expansion. The means of production are no longer limited to everything owned by one's family; the demand for products is no longer limited to one's own needs. Through market marketing means, the production activities of trading agents can almost expand infinitely. This is the fundamental difference between the agricultural economic form and the industrial economic form.

Under the industrial economic form, production activities need to rely on division of labor and cooperation to complete. The operating characteristic of the industrial economic form is to rely on market forces for resource integration and allocation, and finance is an important link in resource integration and allocation. Under the industrial economic form, economic development is always accompanied by the continuous refinement of division of labor and the continuous expansion of the scope of cooperation. From trading agents to enterprises, from industries to countries, division of labor and cooperation are everywhere.

An important manifestation of human societal development is the increase in information exchange and the advancement of information technology. People move from rural areas to cities, shortening spatial distances, living in closer, narrower spaces, and the inevitable consequence of increased contact is the intensification of information connections. Due to the increase in information connections and the strengthened interdependence caused by division of labor, the possibility and frequency of people adopting consistent behaviors have greatly increased. From the beacon towers of early societies to the post stations of traditional societies, to the telegraphs and telephones of not long ago, to today's mobile phones and the Internet, the speed of information exchange and the breadth of connections are showing an exponential growth trend. These have greatly promoted the compactness of the trading system.

From a large-scale historical perspective, the compactness of the economy is always improving, which is a basic trend of human societal development. Behind this trend is the acceleration of global economic integration and the process of human society increasingly moving towards integration. The process of improving the compactness of human society first went through a slow rise during the agricultural period, from almost isolated states to small-scale market trading, and then to the early stages of urbanization, where connections between members of society were gradually established and slowly strengthened. After entering industrialization, the speed of compactness increased. During this period, whether it was the process of social division of labor or the speed of urbanization, there was an unprecedented increase. This is a period of rapid change in the face of human society and the fastest stage of compactness improvement.

The transformation of the economic form of human society has fundamentally changed the operating characteristics of the trading system. The trading system has changed from being linearly dominated to a super complex system that is nonlinear. The impact of this change is extremely profound, forcing us to completely change the views and ways of dealing with the world formed in traditional society. The modern world is made up of countless interconnected subsystems, and we must think about problems from these interconnected perspectives. In the past, this way of thinking about problems was not very important. What did the development of Los Angeles have to do with the ranchers in the Sacramento Valley 100 years ago? Nothing. But today, the irrigation canals running through north and south California have caused north and south California to constantly struggle for water. 40 years ago, what did the differences between Islamic sects have to do with us? Obviously nothing. But now the interconnections of the whole world make this dispute important to any place.[8] Dietrich Dorner pointed out when analyzing the major mistakes often made in modern society management: “Humans seem to have formed a tendency from a very early time, that is, there is a special basis for dealing with problems. Suppose our task at hand is to chop wood, to drive a herd of horses into a canyon, or to make a trap for hunting a huge beast, all these tasks are problems of the moment, and usually, it is meaningless to go beyond them. …The observation of problems must take into account that it is included in many other related problems, and the necessity of looking at problems in this way rarely appeared at that time. But for us, this is a principle rather than an exception.[9]

After industrialization, society entered a relatively stable period, but with the advancement of technology, especially information technology and transportation technology, the compactness of the trading system continues to increase. From the perspective of human history, the slow accumulation stage of the agricultural economy still occupies most of the historical period, and the stage of significant increase in compactness only occupies a small proportion of history. From this point of view, the process of increasing the compactness of human society is far from over.

The compactness of the trading system also manifests in the supervision of the behavior of trading agents and legal constraints. Basic information of each trading agent, trading status, ID card information, credit card information, internet browsing information, communication information, and travel information, etc., are increasingly being collected as a means to monitor and evaluate trading agents. People increasingly lament that life no longer has privacy. In fact, whether people are willing or not, this is the basic direction of the evolution of the trading system, and everyone is being woven more and more tightly into the huge social network.

13.5 The Compactness Effect of the Trading System

The result of the compactness of the trading system is that the interdependence of trading agents through the trading network is strengthened, and it inevitably triggers two changes: on the one hand, the continuously enhanced compactness improves the efficiency of the trading system. The expansion of the system's trading scale provides a continuous driving force for economic growth. On the other hand, with the compactness of the trading system, the trading chains on the trading network are constantly lengthening, and the requirements for mutual coordination are correspondingly increased, leading to an increase in the preconditions for the smooth operation of the trading system, and the vulnerability of the trading system increases. While compactness enhances the coordination of the trading system, the system's disturbance amplification mechanism also strengthens accordingly. Originally small, local fluctuations or disturbances, after being amplified by the trading network amplification mechanism will quickly extend to the entire trading system, forming an impact on the system that is several times the magnitude of the initial disturbance. This is an important reason for the frequent financial and economic crises after human society entered the industrial economic form.

13.5.1 Efficiency Enhancement Effect

The efficiency enhancement effect of compactness is obvious. The compactness of the trading system itself is the result of the continuous pursuit of efficiency by trading agents, the higher the compactness of the trading system, the higher the coordination efficiency between trading agents, and the more obvious the effect of $1 + 1 > 2$.

The compactness of the trading system promotes the efficiency improvement of the trading network in two dimensions: one is the improvement of the trading efficiency of the network. The density of the trading network is an important manifestation of compactness, and the density of the trading network inevitably accompanies the deepening of social division of labor. The progressive division of labor's efficiency-enhancing effect on production is a conclusion verified by history, and production efficiency is an important part of trading efficiency. The density of the trading network undoubtedly increases the convenience and timeliness of trading, and the ability to meet trading needs is stronger, these effects are ultimately reflected in the improvement of trading efficiency. The second is that increasing the financialization of the trading system to releases more trading potential of trading agents, and increases the liquidity of assets to expands both the extension and connotation of resource allocation in the trading system, thereby improving the efficiency of resource allocation.

13.5.2 Uncertainty Amplification Effect

The uncertainty of the trading system is reflected in two aspects: the uncertainty of asset prices and the liquidity of assets. According to the characteristics of asset sources and asset value formation, assets can be divided into two basic types: one is equity assets, including bonds and equity; the other is pricing assets, the value of which depends on market pricing. Although equity assets also need to be priced through market trading, the main determinants are the efficiency of asset utilization and the ability of risk management from the equity responsible party. The higher the efficiency of asset use and the stronger the risk management capabilities of the equity responsible party, the higher the price of the corresponding equity assets, and the greater the value of the assets of the equity beneficiary. The stock market and bond market are the main equity markets. Although asset prices are affected by many factors, the underlying logic of the market is mainly the performance and credit level of the equity responsible party.

Pricing assets refer to assets whose value is entirely determined by market prices, such as real estate, production equipment, furniture and appliances, all of which are pricing assets. Their value depends on the pricing formed by market trading and is no longer directly related to the characteristics of the trading agent. In summary, the value of equity assets depends on the quality of equity, while the value of pricing assets depends on trading pricing. The fundamental difference between the two types of assets lies in the value determination mechanism.

An increase in the density of the trading network is an important feature of the compactness of the trading system, which means that trading agents need to achieve survival and development through more frequent trading, and inevitably increases the dependence on asset liquidity. The basis of liquidity is trading, and the uncertainty of trading will affect the liquidity of assets. Once there is a significant decline in asset liquidity, trading constrained by liquidity will be hindered, and asset values will be damaged.

An increase in equity trading is another important feature of the compactness of the trading system, which means that the proportion of equity assets of the trading agent increases, and the result is inevitably that the dependence of asset value on the financial status of the equity responsible party increases. In an uncertain trading environment, the success or failure of trading is presented in a probabilistic form. The higher the proportion of equity assets of the trading agent, the greater the risk of asset loss it bears.

In summary, the uncertainty risks of trading agents have two main sources: one is the risk transmission caused by the failure of the trading of equity responsible party; the other is the decline in asset liquidity, and assets cannot be realized at the expected price, leading to a shrinkage in value.

In the process of market operation, trading failure and liquidity decline, as two independent events, trigger a mechanism between the risks of asset loss and liquidity, easily forming the following mutually reinforcing trading loop (Fig. 13.5).

The close relationship between trading failure and liquidity reduction further strengthens the association between the compactness of the trading system and uncertainty. Next, we will discuss the formation mechanism of the increase in the uncertainty of the value of equity assets caused by the compactness of the trading system:

Let a_i be any agent in the trading community Ω, according to the relationship of the equity responsible party of the equity assets he holds, form a set of equity responsible party directly or indirectly corresponding to equity assets of a_i, called

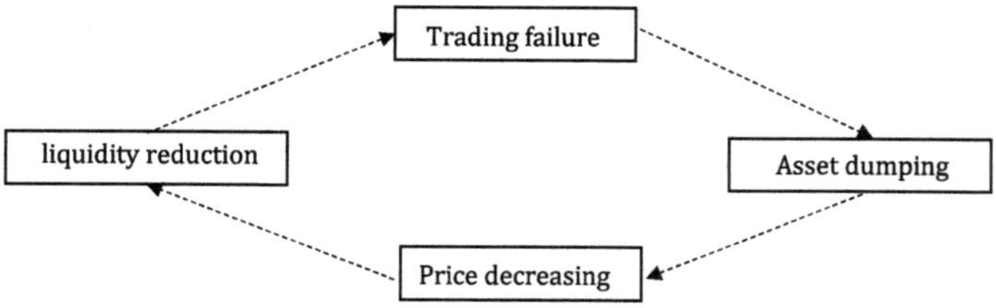

Fig. 13.5 Feedback loop of market stress

a_i's equity association set, represented by $A_i^c = \{a_j\}_N$, the superscript c of the capital letter A represents the equity association relationship. In the association set, the trading agent a_j is either the debtor of a_i, or equity responsible party of a_i, or the indirect equity liability party of a_i. The trading agents in A_i^c formed an equity relationship network around a_i.

In Fig. 13.6, the arrows represent equity relationships, the issuer of the arrow is the beneficiary of the equity, and the direction of the arrow is the equity responsible party. a_1, a_2, a_5 are the direct equity responsible parties of a_i, while a_3, a_4 are the indirect equity responsible parties of a_i, belonging to the equity-related parties. Figure 13.6 shows a very simple equity relationship network, but in reality, the equity relationship network is often very complex.

In the equity-related set A_i^c, according to the distance of the responsibility relationship with a_i, it is divided into first-level relationships, second-level relationships, and so on. The first-level relationship is the direct equity responsible party of a_i, the second-level relationship is the equity responsible party of the direct responsible party, and the third-level relationship is the second-level responsible party of the direct responsible party.

In the equity relationship shown in Fig. 13.6, if a_4 defaults on its debt, the assets of its creditors a_1 and a_2 will be damaged, thereby affecting their ability to repay

Fig. 13.6 Diagram of equity relationship network

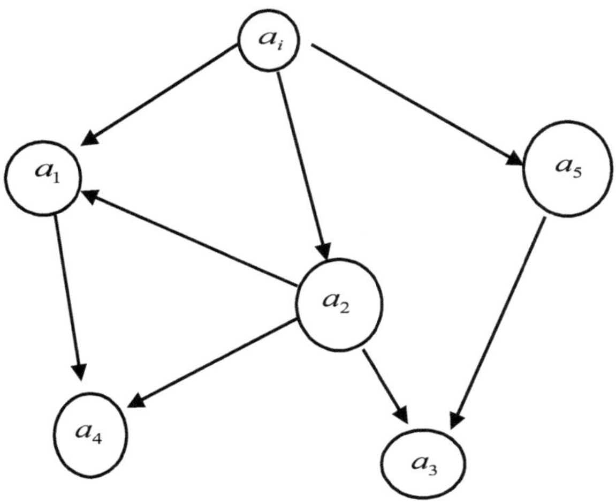

their debts to a_i. The increase in default risk for a_i does not mean that the default risk of a_4 will be directly transferred to a_i, but through a_1 and a_2 transmitted to a_i. In the default event of a_4, a_1 and a_2 play a risk buffering role for a_i. It can be seen that on the equity relationship network, the further away from a_i, the smaller the risk directed to a_i.

The situation with equity risk is the same. If a firm is poorly managed, resulting in a decline in profits or losses, it will affect the asset value and cash dividends of the equity beneficiaries. On the equity relationship network, whether it is a creditor relationship or an equity relationship, there is a risk transmission mechanism. We collectively refer to debt default and operating losses as trading failures.

The internal relationships of a_i within the equity-related set present a network form, which is part of the trading network. The risk of trading agent failure is transmitted upstream through the equity-related network, eventually converging to a_i. In this process, each trading failure probability of the agent has a superimposed relationship, which means that the larger the equity-related set, the greater the risk of trading failure will become after superposition through the equity-related network.

Assume $a_j \in A_i^c$ is any agent on the related set, located at k_j related level, the trading failure probability is P_j, the probability that a_i loss equity assets P_{LOS} can be calculated by the following formula:

$$P_{los} = \sum_{1}^{N} \frac{P_j}{k_j} \tag{13.5.1}$$

Equation (13.5.1) shows that under the condition that the overall risk level of the trading system remains unchanged, the probability of loss of equity assets of the trading agent a_i is directly proportional to the size of the equity-related set, and is closely related to the risk distribution of the related set level structure. The expansion of the scale of the equity-related set and the increase in the structure level are the main manifestations of the increased compactness of the trading system, which means that the compactness of the trading system will inevitably lead to a greater risk exposure of equity assets.

The uncertainty faced by pricing assets includes two aspects: on the one hand, the uncertainty of asset value; on the other hand, the uncertainty of asset liquidity. To analyze the uncertainty of the value of pricing assets, it is necessary to introduce the concept of market correlation. Market correlation refers to the correlation between different sub-markets in the same market in the formation of quotations and prices, which can be achieved through two different channels of supply and demand. On the supply side, different types of market correlation strengths vary greatly. For example, the vegetable market is a typical local market, where supply and demand are mainly affected by local weather conditions and supply scale. A rise in prices in a local vegetable market does not mean that other vegetable markets will also rise. With the advancement of logistics technology, vegetables have begun to be transported long distances across a wider area, and the correlation between different vegetable markets has accordingly increased. In contrast to vegetables is the grain market.

Because grain is easy to transport, the radius of the grain market is much larger than that of the vegetable market, so the correlation of the grain market is higher than that of the vegetable market.

On the demand side, the correlation of trading agents depends on the consistency of trading motives. For markets that meet basic household and corporate needs, trading motives are mainly focused on normal operation. The correlation of agents in this type of trading market is relatively low, and trading are closely related to their own needs. A family will not buy lobster just because the neighbors bought lobster. The situation on the stock market is completely different. Because trading agents have the same trading motive—to pursue investment gains, this determines that the decision-making information of trading agents has mutual reference value. Investors always refer to the strategies of other investors as much as possible when making decisions. This characteristic of the stock market determines that the correlation of trading agents is much higher than that of the vegetable market.

Assume that the trading agent a_i holds M types of pricing assets, the weighted average correlation of the corresponding pricing assets is calculated as follows:

$$\sigma = \sum_{1}^{M} \rho_j \sigma_j \tag{13.5.2}$$

In (13.5.2), σ represents the weighted average market correlation, σ_j represents the market correlation corresponding to the respective pricing assets, ρ_j represents the proportion of such assets in priced assets a_i. The market correlation σ_j ranges from 0 to 1. When $\sigma_j = 1$, it indicates that the corresponding market is in a non-correlated state, completely unaffected by external influences, and there is no mutual influence between trading agents; when $\sigma_j = 1$, it indicates that the corresponding market is in a strong correlation state, there is a close linkage between similar markets, and there is a high degree of synergy in the behavior of trading agents. The average market correlation calculated from this σ also ranges from 0 to 1.

As defined by compactness, in the trading system, there is a positive correlation between asset correlation σ and compactness ϕ. The higher the compactness of the trading system, the stronger the asset correlation, and their relationship can be expressed as follows:

$$\sigma = k\phi, \ k > 0 \tag{13.5.3}$$

Market fluctuations, including price fluctuations and liquidity changes, are extremely complex. Supply and demand relationships, policy factors, or sudden events can all become important influencing factors. However, the most common and intrinsic mechanism of the market is the internal correlation of the market. For markets with high correlation, it means that the interaction between related markets and trading agents has a significant impact on market trends. The higher the market correlation, the greater the degree of each market being affected by other markets, the more overlapping factors the market is affected by, the worse the stability, and the greater the uncertainty. If P_w represents the probability of significant fluctuations in priced assets, we can get:

$$P_w = \alpha\sigma \tag{13.5.4}$$

In (13.5.4), α is a parameter greater than 0. Substitute (13.5.3) into (13.5.4) to get:

$$P_w = \alpha k\phi \tag{13.5.5}$$

Let $\beta = \alpha k$, Eq. (13.5.5) can also be expressed as follows:

$$P_w = \beta\phi,\ \beta > 0 \tag{13.5.6}$$

Equation (13.5.6) indicates that the higher the compactness of the trading system, the greater the probability of fluctuations in asset value and liquidity. Admittedly, not all fluctuations necessarily cause losses to trading agents, and some fluctuations will bring asset appreciation and liquidity improvement to trading agents. Overall, due to the unpredictability of fluctuations, the increase in the frequency of fluctuations undoubtedly increases the probability of trading decision failure.

In summary, with the strengthening of the compactness of the trading system, trading agents not only face greater asset loss risks, but also face the challenge of increased decision-making difficulty. Due to the different trading phases and potentials of trading agents, the impact of uncertainty they bear is different. But overall, when the compactness of the trading system is enhanced, each trading agent will inevitably face greater uncertainty and higher trading risks. When the risk exceeds the range that the trading agent can bear, the trading agent will go bankrupt and exit the trading system. The self-organizing mechanism of the trading network is the basis for the trading system to modify itself. If a large number of trading agents fall into bankruptcy, the structure of the trading network will be severely damaged, presenting a fragmented situation, and the trading system will also lose its rapid self-repair ability.

The compactness process of the trading system not only increases the uncertainty at the micro level, but also increases the systemic risk at the macro level. Only when the government strengthens market supervision and enhances the effectiveness of macro-management and regulation while the trading system continues to compact, can it offset the challenges brought by the compactness of the trading system.

It should be noted that with the tightening of the trading system, the self-healing ability of the trading network is also correspondingly strengthened, and this change is reflected at both the micro and macro levels. At the micro level, the risks faced by trading agents inevitably translate into product demands for risk resistance and resolution, thereby giving rise to risk trading markets, which optimize the allocation of various types and different magnitudes of risks among trading agents, allowing those with strong risk resistance and a strong risk preference to bear more uncertainty while also gaining more risk return. Various insurance products and a wide range of financial derivative products play a role in risk diversification and optimal allocation to some extent. At the macro level, the macro-control system and social security and social assistance systems are becoming more and more perfect, macro-control means are becoming richer, control experience and control theory are gradually maturing, macro-prudential supervision continues to be strict, financial supervision is constantly strengthened, especially the proactivity of the central bank and financial departments in macro-management is increasingly evident, these measures make the trading system have a stronger resistance and more efficient self-healing ability when encountering shocks and when trading agents encounter trading failures. The enhanced self-healing ability can partially offset the negative impact of tightening on the trading system, enabling human society to gain more benefits from the process of tightening the trading system.

Notes

1. Tightness as an academic concept comes from topology and refers to a class of sets with a particular property. In topology, to say that a set is tight is to say that there exists a finite open set subcover of any open set cover of that set. Tight sets have the excellent quality of transforming infinite problems into finite ones and belong to the basic objects of topological study. The concept of tightness is derived from the word tightness in real life. In life, people use the word tightness to describe the compact qualities of organizational structures. For example, we say that the skin is tight, the structural layout of a painting is tight, and so on. Topological tightness is a concept obtained by abstraction on the basis of commonplace semantics. The notion we use here is a reduction of the semantics of tightness to describe the property of tight transactional links between trading agents within a trading system.
2. There are two relationships between the components of the system, one is competition. The so-called competitive relationship refers to the sharing of limited resources and the influence of component behavior on the results of resource allocation. The components with competitive relationship are usually in the same niche in the system, and the relationship corresponding to the competitive relationship is dependent relationship. A dependency is a relationship in which one component derives a benefit from the behavior of another component. Dependencies can be either unidirectional or bidirectional. Bidirectional interdependence is the interdependent relationship between two components, which belongs to symbiotic relationship.

   The competition relationship ensures the efficiency of the system in resource allocation, and the dependence relationship ensures the efficiency of the system in overall operation. Competition and dependence ensure the efficiency of the system at both the micro and macro levels. Synergy can be achieved not only in the competitive relationship, but also in the dependent relationship, and also in the coexistence of the two relationships.
3. The relationship between the components in the system is not fixed. In fact, even if the agent is in a competitive relationship, at a higher level, it will show a strong dependence. Thus it can be seen that the relationship between agents is not only changeable, but also hierarchical.
4. David Myers (2006) Social Psychology (trans: Yubo HO), 8th edn. Post and Telecom Press, p 153.
5. Juanjuan MENG, Longkai ZHAO, Yuzhen LIU (2013) Herd Mentality and Stock Market Participation in Decision Making, Financial Research, p 153–165.
6. Economic form is not only a concept of economic organization, but also a concept of time in a characteristic historical period. In terms of economic organization, the economic form is the characteristics of economic operation stipulated by the mainstream industrial mode; in terms of time, it refers to the specific period in the evolution of human society, specifically, the agricultural economic form refers to the society before the industrial revolution; and the industrial economic

form refers to human society since the industrial revolution. Although people sometimes refer to the current era as the information age, the dominant form of economic organization is still industry.

7. In fact, even in the form of agricultural economy, there are still a small number of transactions between farmers, but at this time the transaction does not occupy a dominant position in the family and agricultural society.
8. Dietrich Dorner (1995) The Logic of Failure (trans: Zhigang WANG), Shanghai Science and Technology Education Press, Shanghai, p 5.
9. Dietrich Dorner (1995) The Logic of Failure (trans: Zhigang WANG), Shanghai Science and Technology Education Press, Shanghai, p 5.

Part III
Mechanism of Interaction Among Trading Agents and Polarization of Trading Potential

This part comprises six chapters on the trading equation, trading ring, the distribution of trading potential, the equation of trading system evolution, and the evolution of trading space.

The trading equation reveals the micro-level workings of the interaction of trading agents in a trading network. The trading ring, in comparison, is a macro-mechanism that greatly impacts a trading system. Trading equation and trading ring work together and underpin the unique analytical methodology of trading economics.

The polarization of a trading system is demonstrated from two angles: the distribution of trading potential and the evolution of trading space. The evolution equation of trading system captures, in a clear and succinct form, the quantitative relationship between the polarization of trading potential, economic growth, and financialization of trading system. It further reveals the ultimate dilemma that human society must face—growth or polarization. The trading trajectory equation shows, intuitively, the mechanism of polarization and evolution of the trading space.

Chapter 14
Trading Equation

Trading agents are woven into the trading network, realizing interaction and connection through the trading network. The trading equation uses Bayesian games under incomplete information conditions as a tool to establish a mathematical equation of the interaction of trading agents, revealing the general law of trading agent behavior.

14.1 Trading Decision Model

In order to establish an equation that accurately describes the behavior characteristics of trading agents, we need to understand the basic structure of the decision-making process of trading agents.

14.1.1 Trading Situation

The trading system provides trading opportunities for trading agents, as well as the institutional rules that trading behavior must comply with, and provides variables for policy control. The trading system connects people and institutions with different resource endowments to form a huge trading network. The trading network is always in the process of growth, operation, and change through spontaneous organization. The trading situation is a collection of institutions, rules, technology, knowledge, and economic situation, a collection of business opportunities, and also a total set of all information, the mother set of the strategy set of trading agents. Trading agents must make decisions and trade under the trading situation.

Information connects the trading situation with the largest possible set of trading agent decision choices—the strategy set. The more extensive and complete the information possessed by the trading agent, the more possibilities can be mined from the

Z. Wang, *Trading Economics*, Contributions to Economics,
https://doi.org/10.1007/978-981-99-9875-3_14

trading situation. The trading situation is like a river, the strategy set is a lake that draws water from the river, and information is the channel that connects the river and the lake.

Usually, the decision-making of trading agents will not have a perceptible impact on the trading situation. In this case, the decision-making process is actually a static process; when the behavior of trading agents has a perceptible impact on the trading situation, the game between trading agents and the situation evolves into a dynamic one.

When the trading momentum of the trading agent[1] is large enough to have an impact on the entire economy, the decision-making process of trading agents enters into dynamic game theory. Multinational corporations and large companies in strategic industries have such capabilities.

Trading agents must assume that the situation is in a certain state in order to make decisions. This assumption is a belief that plays a very important role in decision-making. Incorrect beliefs will inevitably lead to incorrect decisions, and the correctness of beliefs depends not only on whether the information is sufficient, but also on the cognitive model of the decision-maker.

14.1.2 Trading Strategy Set

The essence of decision-making is choice. Trading agents, based on the information they have, obtain various possible trading alternative strategies from the trading situation, and we simply refer to the set formed by alternative strategies as the trading strategy set. The trading strategy set provides the greatest trading possibility for traders and is the basis of trading decisions.

For the convenience of expression, we use S_i to represent the strategy set of the trading agent a_i, and the strategy set S_i is expanded as follows:

$$S_i = \{s_1, s_2 \dots s_n\}$$

where, s_i represents a trading strategy of the trading agent a_i. In the trading strategy set S_i, the trading strategy s_i not only contains trading content, but also information such as trading quantity and trading direction.

The trading strategy set can be seen as a result induced by the information set of the trading agent. Under the same trading situation, due to different information sets, the strategy sets of trading agents will have their own characteristics. Individual differences are everywhere, even in the same city, not all drivers will choose exactly the same driving route, due to the influence of factors such as information, habits, preferences, and subjective judgments of traffic conditions. In the trading system, individual differences lead to the diversification of market demand.

14.1.3 Strategy Mother Set of the Trading System

The union of all agent strategy sets in the trading system is called the strategy mother set of the trading system. The strategy mother set is the basis for the operation of the trading system and is constantly changing with the evolution of the trading system. Whether it is the change in the economic operation situation, economic system reform, or the change in the mentality of the trading agent, it will be reflected through the change in the strategy mother set of the trading system. When analyzing the medium- and long-term growth potential in the economy, parsing the structure and scale changes of the strategy mother set of the trading system is a very effective qualitative analysis method.

From an evolutionary perspective, the size and structure of the strategy set represent the decision-making space and preferences of the trading agent, and the resource allocation capability of the trading system. The larger the strategy set, the larger the decision-making space of the trading agent, the more choices available to the trading agent, and the stronger the resource allocation capability of the trading system.

The influences of property rights system, economic system, management regulations, etc., will eventually be mapped onto the strategy set of the trading system. Under the planned economic system based on the completely public property rights system, the scale of the trading agent's strategy set is very limited, the trading agent has almost no freedom of choice, and the strategy set of the trading system is of a very small scale; but under the market economic system, the scale of the strategy set is much larger, and the structure is also greatly enriched. From the trend of social development, the strategy set is always developing in the direction of increase to ensure the potential possibility for economic growth. If the strategy set of the trading system suddenly shrinks, it will inevitably have a very serious impact on the operation of the trading system. The evolution of the trading system will stagnate, and even a retrogression phenomenon may occur.

14.1.4 Trading Constraint Set

Constraints refer to the restrictions faced by the trading agent in realizing a certain desire or maximizing its own potential. Decision-making is actually a choice under constraints. Without constraints, decision-making loses its meaning.

Trading agents usually face three types of constraints, namely liquidity constraints, technical constraints, and regulatory constraints. Liquidity constraints are the restrictions of the trading agent's limited payment means on unlimited trading desires. Liquidity constraints restrict the trading activities of the trading agent at a specific point in time.

Technical constraints mainly refer to the constraints that technology imposes on the specific transactions of the trading agent. In complex financial transactions, technology becomes a constraint for many non-professionals, who need to delegate it to others. More often, this occurs in enterprise production activities. Although people know that manufacturing chips and advanced fighter jets are profitable, most companies are blocked from the industry due to technical constraints.

Regulatory constraints are mainly the constraints generated by government or industry self-regulatory organizations on market regulation. In economic activities, there are many entry constraints, such as telecommunications services, financial services, medical services, etc., most of which need to obtain qualifications from government regulatory departments to enter.

Compared with traditional trading systems, modern trading systems regulate their members more, almost to the point of ubiquity. The regulations in modern trading systems cover all aspects, broadly divided into economic regulation, safety regulation, and anti-monopoly regulation, etc. Various types of regulations, to varying degrees, from different sides, and through different mechanisms, will ultimately affect the decisions of trading agents, and also the size and structure of the strategy set of the trading system, among which, the impact of entry and exit regulation is the most direct.

Constraint conditions are not absolutely rigid. Under certain conditions, constraint conditions can be overcome by trading agents, thus losing their constraining effect. For example, in the case of technical constraints, companies can obtain the required technology through technical research and development, or eliminate technical constraints by purchasing patents; facing regulatory constraints, trading agents can create conditions to meet regulatory qualification requirements; liquidity constraints can be overcome by incurring debt or implementing forward transactions to raise the required funds. However, overcoming constraint conditions inevitably incurs costs and assumes corresponding uncertain risks. For example, in the case of technical constraints, overcoming technical constraints requires the investment of corresponding funds, but it does not guarantee that the required technology can definitely be obtained. Whether a company invests funds in the research and development of new technology depends on whether this technology can bring enough expected benefits to the company. The more expected benefits, the more enthusiastic the company is about developing new technology.

14.2 Approximate Decision Rule

When humans face a large amount of information and complex evaluations, they must make approximate processing to ensure decision-making efficiency. Experiments in behavioral economics show that people often use analogy methods in the decision-making process, looking for approximate cases as references from past experiences or examples around them, and making judgments and decisions based on experience. This is a typical method of approximate decision-making.

Approximate decision-making is a specific application of the bounded rationality assumption of trading agents. On the surface, approximate decision-making is a denial of the principle of maximizing expected returns in some sense, but from a broader perspective, approximate decision-making is precisely a wise move for trading agents to pursue maximum returns. Only by ensuring decision-making efficiency can trading agents possibly capture valuable trading opportunities and achieve maximization of returns in the sense of accounting matrix calculation, rather than maximizing returns on a specific transaction. According to Paul A. Samuelson, in real life, people can only make decisions based on incomplete information or analysis. Pursuing complete profit or utility maximization takes too much time. Consumers cannot spend a day looking for the cheapest lettuce; a company cannot spend millions of dollars hiring econometricians to study the price elasticity of thousands of products. ...In some cases, using 'snap judgment' (simple decision principle) is the most economical decision-making method.[2]

Approximate decision-making mainly manifests on two levels. On the one hand, in order to improve decision-making efficiency, simplified alternative methods are used under complex situations, that is, decision-making methods are approximate. Case analogy decision-making or inferring the whole from a small sample are relatively common approximate decision-making methods; on the other hand, in the decision-making process, the approximate processing used when estimating expected returns, that is, decision-making quantity is approximate.

In fact, it is difficult for trading agents to achieve the goal of maximizing profits. This is caused by multiple constraints: first, the constraint of incomplete information. Real-world trading decisions are often made under conditions of incomplete information, and the trading results carry a certain degree of uncertainty. Trading agents cannot absolutely determine which trading strategy can truly achieve the maximum profit, and the element of luck cannot be eliminated in the decision-making process. This determines that trading agents can only accept a profit evaluation within a certain approximate range. Second, the constraint of decision-making time. Many real-world trading opportunities have specific time window, and it is impossible to allow people to collect information and calculate accurately without limit. Take the purchase of home appliances as an example, buyers can roughly compare different appliances, but due to the numerous auxiliary functions of appliances, the study of many details such as price, performance, brand, after-sales service, etc., takes a long time. In the context of inflation, by the time the buyer has figured it out, the price has already changed. These examples show that trading opportunities, like commodities, are scarce, which is the root of the time constraint on decision-making. Third, the constraint of decision-making cost. The evaluation of profits requires the collection of a large amount of information and time, all of which are decision-making costs that cannot be ignored. It is hard to imagine that a person who cares about the subtle differences in profit evaluation can completely ignore the decision-making costs generated by the evaluation itself.

In actual decision-making, trading agents can only perform calculations with a limited time step. If the problem is too complex, they can only rely on intuition to choose an approximate solution as the strategy. Due to the constraints of incomplete information and decision-making costs, it is impossible for trading agents to evaluate all strategies. The experience and habits of trading agents, as well as recent events around them, play a very important role in the decision-making process. If an event that occurs in the trading community can serve as a successful reference or a lesson to avoid failure, the trading agent will take this event as a priority reference for decision-making.

Approximate decision-making improves decision-making efficiency, but approximate decision-making must follow certain rules. Simply put, the approximate order of magnitude is only accepted by trading agents when it is lower than the trading order of magnitude. Every trade has a specific order of magnitude. Generally speaking, the order of magnitude of enterprise tradings is much larger than that of family tradings; the order of magnitude of investment transactions is larger than that of consumption transactions. In decision-making, at which quantity level the trading agent begins to pay attention depends on the order of magnitude of the transaction amount and the order of magnitude of the assets owned by the trading agent. Common sense tells us that the wealthy class is not very concerned about the price when consuming, and the low-income class will spend a long time comparing even small transactions. This is mainly caused by the difference in asset order of magnitude.

Behavioral economics has found that people's trading decisions are made on multiple segmented mental accounts. Different mental accounts cannot be converted to each other, the budget for watching movies and the budget for buying clothes belong to different mental accounts. If people lose their movie tickets on the way to the movies, and the money in the movie budget account is already used up, people will give up the idea of watching the movie instead of taking money from other budget accounts to buy tickets again. When making trading decisions, people's responses to external changes are mainly based on the accounting results of the corresponding mental accounts. The prospect theory of behavioral economics believes that what decision-makers value is not the absolute amount, but the degree of deviation from the value reference point. The expected transaction amount often serves as the transaction value reference point, and the ignored amount becomes a measure of the degree of deviation from the value reference point as a proportion of the expected transaction amount.[3]

In the decision-making process of the trading agent, considering that the actor has a tendency to pursue efficiency, we call the approximation treatment paradigm in the decision model and expected return valuation as the approximate decision rule of the trading agent, and apply it to the behavior analysis of the trading agent.

The approximate decision rule is an important supplement to the principle of maximizing expected trading returns. The principle of maximizing expected trading returns stipulates the general principles that decision-makers follow when choosing between different schemes, while the approximate decision rule provides the criteria for scheme selection in the decision-making process, which can maximize expected returns and ensure the efficiency of decision-making. Through the approximate decision rule, the trading agent can minimize the probability of decision-making errors in the face of numerous decision-making demands.

14.3 Trading Equation

Let $\{a_i\}_N$ be the set of trading agents in the trading community Ω, $a_i \in \{a_i\}_N$ is any agent in community Ω. According to our analysis of decision patterns, a_i's trading decision is made under uncertain trading situations, and information is the key element of decision-making. In a world of information asymmetry, observing the behavior of other agents is an important way for trading agents to obtain information.

Assume s is any strategy on the strategy set S_i of the trading agent a_i, whether the return that strategy s can bring to the trading agent a_i depends on the state of the trading situation H. The trading situation H has two possible states, one is the state that can bring ideal returns to s, which we call a friendly state, represented by g; and the state that causes the return of the trading strategy s to deteriorate, which we call an unfriendly state, represented by b. In this case, a_i's decision is actually a mixed game with a virtual opponent—the trading situation H.

Faced with the uncertainty of the trading situation H, the trading agent a_i can implement the trading strategy s or give it up. We use Y and N to represent the two different choices. For the trading strategy s, the trading agent a_i has the following payoff matrix (Table 14.1).

In payoff matrix 14.3.1, e_g, e_b are respectively the expected returns when the trading strategy s responds to two different situations. e_g represents the expected return when the situation H is in a friendly state, and e_b represents the expected return when the trading situation H is in an unfriendly state. e_b may take positive or negative values. When e_b takes a negative value, it means that implementing s may bring losses, to the trading agent a_i.

The expected return valuation is affected by the length of the valuation period. Generally speaking, as the length of the valuation period increases, the expected return valuation of the trading strategy s may increase. However, the length of the valuation period is a double-edged sword. As the valuation period extends, the difficulty of the trading agent in judging the situation increases, the uncertainty increases, and the risk faced by the trading agent also rises. This is a problem that the trading agent a_i needs to weigh when making decisions.

Table 14.1 Payoff matrix in situation game

Strategy \ Situation		Trading Situation H	
		g	b
a_i	Y	e_g	e_b
	N	0	0

The trading situation H has a great deal of uncertainty, and the trading agent can only assign the two states of the trading situation with different probabilities. At the beginning of the decision, a_i gives a prior inference value for the probabilities of the two states of H based on the information and past experience it has. Suppose the prior probability of g occurring is p, and the prior probability of b occurring is q, the two satisfy $p + q = 1$.

Before the implementation of the trade, a_i will also observe the trading behavior of community neighbors and related phase agents on the trading chain, infer relevant information from their decisions, and then correct the prior probability. We call the set of associated trading agents observed by the decision maker a_i to enhance confidence in judging the trading situation the state coordination set of the trading agent. The state coordination set of the trading agent is based on the community Ω, mainly composed of same-phase neighbors, and trading agents closely related to the return of the trading strategy s outside the community Ω, including upstream and downstream trading agents on the trading chain and same-phase friends in the social circle. Social interaction is an important channel for trading agents to obtain information. For trading agents in the same trading community, due to differences in social capabilities, the size and structure of the state coordination set may vary greatly.

The state collaboration set is a reference for decision-making and has a significant impact on the decision-making of the trading agent. American economist and Nobel laureate in economics, Robert J. Shiller, also affirmed this conclusion. According to Shiller, "The conventional media—print media, television, and radio—have a profound capability for spreading ideas, but their ability to generate active behaviors is still limited. Interpersonal and interactive communications, particularly face-to-face or word-of-mouth communications, still have the most powerful impact on our behavior."[4] The members of the state collaboration set mainly come from the community where the trading agent is located or the social circles. These people mainly convey information to the decision-makers through face-to-face communication or what they see with their own eyes.

Figure 14.1 intuitively describes the internal structure of the trading agent's state collaboration set.

Fig. 14.1 State collaboration set

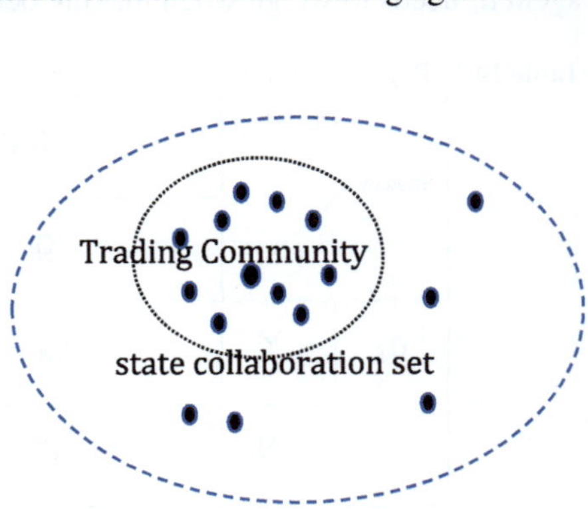

To mark the correspondence between the decision-maker a_i and the state collaboration set, we denote the state collaboration set of a_i as $A_i^c = \{a_j\}_{N_i}$, a_j represents the trading agent in the state collaboration set of a_i; N_i represents the number of agents in the state collaboration set.

Assume that during the observation window period, a_i observes the number of agents implementing the trading strategy s on the state collaboration set A_i^c as n, according to Bayes' theorem[5] we know that the result of a_i correcting the prior probability after observing the behavior of other agents is:

$$\Pr(g|n) = \frac{\Pr(g) \times \Pr(n|g)}{\Pr(n)} \tag{14.3.1}$$

Known:

$$\Pr(g) = p \tag{14.3.2}$$

$$\Pr(n) = \Pr(g) \times \Pr(n|g) + \Pr(b) \times \Pr(n|b) \tag{14.3.3}$$

Based on the assumption of limited rationality of trading agents, in a friendly trading situation, trading agents do not always seize the opportunity to implement the strategy s; on the contrary, in an unfriendly trading situation, trading agents may implement the strategy s due to misjudgment of the situation. We assume that the decision probabilities of limited rationality trading agents are:

$$\Pr(s|g) = \eta \tag{14.3.4}$$

$$\Pr(s|b) = \lambda \tag{14.3.5}$$

On the trading network, although the decision-making of trading agents is influenced by all parties on the network, the decision-making process is still independent, which is the basic condition for judging trading agents. We therefore assume that the decision-making behavior of trading agents is an independent event,[6] and we can get the following results:

$$\Pr(n|g) = \eta^n \tag{14.3.6}$$

$$\Pr(n|b) = \lambda^n \tag{14.3.7}$$

Substitute (14.3.2), (14.3.3), (14.3.6), (14.3.7) into (14.3.1) respectively to get:

$$\Pr(g|n) = \frac{p \times \eta^n}{p\eta^n + (1-p)\lambda^n} \tag{14.3.8}$$

After rearranging, we get:

$$\Pr(g|n) = \frac{p}{p\left(1 - \left(\frac{\lambda}{\eta}\right)^n\right) + \left(\frac{\lambda}{\eta}\right)^n} \tag{14.3.9}$$

This is the result of the trading agent a_i correcting the prior probability of the situation state after obtaining the action information of the state collaboration set. Based on this result, combined with the payoff matrix of the game, we can get the expected returns of the trading agent a_i implementation strategy s:

$$E(s) = \Pr(g|n) \times e_g + \Pr(b|n) \times e_b \tag{14.3.10}$$

Substituting (14.3.9) into (14.3.10) we get:

$$E(s) = e_g \frac{p}{p\left(1 - \left(\frac{\lambda}{\eta}\right)^n\right) + \left(\frac{\lambda}{\eta}\right)^n} + e_b\left(1 - \frac{p}{p\left(1 - \left(\frac{\lambda}{\eta}\right)^n\right) + \left(\frac{\lambda}{\eta}\right)^n}\right) \tag{14.3.11}$$

Rearranging (14.3.11) we get:

$$E(s) = \left(e_g - e_b\right)\frac{p}{p\left(1 - \left(\frac{\lambda}{\mu}\right)^n\right) + \left(\frac{\lambda}{\eta}\right)^n} + e_b \tag{14.3.12}$$

In reality, trading agents form reasonable expectations of trading returns by understanding the trading situations of other agents and their own past experiences, which we represent with e_0. Reasonable expected returns e_0 reflect the trading environment of the community Ω where the trading agent a_i is located, and indirectly reflect the overall quality of the trading system. Reasonable expected returns play a very important role in trading decisions, like a threshold. Only when the expected returns can enter the value threshold will the trading agent consider the trading strategy. Based on these characteristics, we also call reasonable expected returns e_0 the value threshold of the trading agent.

When the returns brought by the trading strategy s can cross the value threshold e_0, it will have a greater attraction to the trading agent, inducing the trading agent to implement the trade. According to the principle of maximizing expected returns, trading agents always choose strategies with the highest possible returns. The more a strategy exceeds the expected return level, the greater the probability of its implementation. The part that exceeds the reasonable return, we call it the trader's surplus.[7] Let's calculate the surplus return rate brought by the trading strategy s for the trading agent a_i:

$$r = \frac{E(s) - e_0}{e_0} \tag{14.3.13}$$

According to the principle of maximizing expected returns, the probability of the trading agent a_i adopting the strategy s is proportional to its surplus return rate. The higher the surplus return rate, the greater the probability of implementation of strategy s. If the probability of the trading agent a_i implementing the strategy s is $\Pr(s)$, we can get:

$$\Pr(s) = \beta \times r \tag{14.3.14}$$

In (14.3.14), β is the balancing coefficient, r is the surplus return rate. Substituting (14.3.13) into (14.3.14) we get:

$$\Pr(s) = \beta \frac{E(s) - e_0}{e_0} \tag{14.3.15}$$

Substituting (14.3.12) into (14.3.15) we get the result:

$$\Pr(s) = \beta \left[\frac{1}{e_0} \left(e_g - e_b \right) \frac{p}{p\left(1 - \left(\frac{\lambda}{\eta}\right)^n\right) + \left(\frac{\lambda}{\eta}\right)^n} + \frac{e_b}{e_0} - 1 \right] \tag{14.3.16}$$

The trading agent a_i use Eq. (14.3.16) to evaluate trading strategies on the strategy set, and a ranking of the merits and demerits of trading strategies is formed. With allowable liquidity constraint, trading strategies are selected from high to low. The higher the ranking of the trading strategy, the higher the priority level for implementation, and the greater the tilt of the trading agent's allocation of liquidity resources. In fact, even strategies with higher probability estimates may not necessarily be implemented. If there are strategies with higher probability estimates on the strategy set, the trading agent will first consider strategies with higher probability estimates subject to liquidity constraints. The action probability $\Pr(s)$ is merely the possibility of the trading agent implementing the strategy, not the absolute result. Based on the principle of maximizing expected returns, the trading agent will make the most of liquidity resources and arrange as many trading strategies as possible that bring surplus returns to the accounting matrix.

To determine the pending parameters β of (14.3.16), we agree that all reference agents of a_i in its state synergy set A_i^c fully implement s, then the probability of a_i implementing the trading strategy s is 1, that is:

$$\text{when} \quad n = N_i, \quad \Pr(s) = 1 \tag{14.3.17}$$

Substitute the boundary condition (14.3.17) into (14.3.16) to get:

$$\beta \left[\frac{1}{e_0} \left(e_g - e_b \right) \frac{p}{p\left(1 - \left(\frac{\lambda}{\eta}\right)^{N_i}\right) + \left(\frac{\lambda}{\eta}\right)^{N_i}} + \frac{e_b}{e_0} - 1 \right] = 1 \tag{14.3.18}$$

Rearrange to get:

$$\beta = \frac{e_0\left[p\left(1-\left(\frac{\lambda}{\eta}\right)^{N_i}\right)+\left(\frac{\lambda}{\eta}\right)^{N_i}\right]}{(e_g-e_b)p+(e_b-e_0)\left[p\left(1-\left(\frac{\lambda}{\eta}\right)^{N_i}\right)+\left(\frac{\lambda}{\eta}\right)^{N_i}\right]} \tag{14.3.19}$$

Substitute (14.3.19) into (14.3.16) to get:

$$\begin{aligned}\Pr(s) = &\frac{(e_g-e_b)\left[p\left(1-\left(\frac{\lambda}{\eta}\right)^{N_i}\right)+\left(\frac{\lambda}{\eta}\right)^{N_i}\right]}{(e_g-e_b)p+(e_b-e_0)\left[p\left(1-\left(\frac{\lambda}{\eta}\right)^{N_i}\right)+\left(\frac{\lambda}{\eta}\right)^{N_i}\right]}\frac{p}{p\left(1-\left(\frac{\lambda}{\eta}\right)^{n}\right)+\left(\frac{\lambda}{\eta}\right)^{n}}\\ &+\frac{\left[p\left(1-\left(\frac{\lambda}{\eta}\right)^{N_i}\right)+\left(\frac{\lambda}{\eta}\right)^{N_i}\right]e_b}{(e_g-e_b)p+(e_b-e_0)\left[p\left(1-\left(\frac{\lambda}{\eta}\right)^{N_i}\right)+\left(\frac{\lambda}{\eta}\right)^{N_i}\right]}\\ &-\frac{e_0\left[p\left(1-\left(\frac{\lambda}{\eta}\right)^{N_i}\right)+\left(\frac{\lambda}{\eta}\right)^{N_i}\right]}{(e_g-e_b)p+(e_b-e_0)\left[p\left(1-\left(\frac{\lambda}{\eta}\right)^{N_i}\right)+\left(\frac{\lambda}{\eta}\right)^{N_i}\right]}\end{aligned} \tag{14.3.20}$$

According to the assumption of bounded rationality, we know that $\frac{\lambda}{\eta} \ll 1, N_i \gg 1$, $\left(\frac{\lambda}{\eta}\right)^{N_i}$ can be ignored. Let $\left(\frac{\lambda}{\eta}\right)^{N_i} \approx 0$, substitute into (14.3.20) to get:

$$\Pr(s) = \frac{e_g-e_b}{e_g-e_0}\frac{p}{\left[1-\left(\frac{\lambda}{\eta}\right)^{n}\right]p+\left(\frac{\lambda}{\eta}\right)^{n}} - \frac{e_0-e_b}{e_g-e_0} \tag{14.3.21}$$

In Eq. (14.3.21), $\Pr(s)$ can be seen as the formal solution of the Nash equilibrium between the trading agent a_i and the virtual participant situation H. $\Pr(s)$ provides a measure of the possibility of the trading agent a_i choosing trading strategy s under a specific situation. The higher the value of $\Pr(s)$, the greater the possibility of a_i implementing s, and vice versa.

In Eq. (14.3.21), $\frac{e_g-e_b}{e_g-e_0}$ and $\frac{e_0-e_b}{e_g-e_0}$ represent the expected relationships under different situations. When $e_g - e_b \gg 0$, the prior probability (p) or the quantity of the reference agents on the state synergy set (n)have crucial impact on the trading agent a_i's decision making. If the trading agent is confident in its judgment of the situation, p value is high, then the trading behavior of the reference agent becomes insignificant. On the contrary, if p value is not high, the trading behavior of the reference agent will play a key role in the decision-making of a_i. If few people implement s by the reference agent, a_i will wait for further information; and if the number of people implementing s by the parameter agent n is relatively large, the amount of information held by the trading agent a_i and the size of the prior probability are no longer important. Even if p value is small, it will not hinder a_i from following the reference agent to implement the strategy s.

When the expected return difference between two different situations is not large, that is, when $e_g - e_b \leq u_0$, u_0 represents a quantity that can be approximately ignored in the decision-making context. In this case, the uncertainty of the situation H itself is no longer important, information and judgment about the situation are no longer important, and the information conveyed by the trading behavior of the reference agent is also no longer important. The key factor affecting the decision-making of a_i is the comparison between the expected return e_b realized when the situation H enters a bad state b and the reasonable return e_0. If the difference in returns can maintain a positive value and the difference is large, a_i will implement the strategy s; otherwise, a_i will abandon the trading s.

To simplify the above equation, let $\frac{e_g - e_b}{e_g - e_0} = R_g$. R_g reflects the profit gap formed by the trading strategy s under different situations, and we call it the profit risk index. The larger the profit risk index, the higher the uncertainty of implementing the strategy s. If the trading agent misjudges the situation, it will cause a large loss. Let $\frac{e_g - e_b}{e_g - e_0} = R_g$, this indicator reflects the gap between the profit formed by the trading strategy s under adverse conditions and the agreed profit.

Substitute the above two indicators into Eq. (14.3.21) to get:

$$\Pr(s) = R_g \frac{p}{\left[1 - \left(\frac{\lambda}{\eta}\right)^n\right] p + \left(\frac{\lambda}{\eta}\right)^n} - R_b \tag{14.3.22}$$

$$\because R_g - R_b = 1$$

$$\therefore \Pr(s) = R_g \frac{p}{\left[1 - \left(\frac{\lambda}{\eta}\right)^n\right] p + \left(\frac{\lambda}{\eta}\right)^n} - (R_g - 1) \tag{14.3.23}$$

Organize (14.3.23):

$$\Pr(s) = 1 + R_g \left(\frac{p}{\left(1 - \left(\frac{\lambda}{\eta}\right)^n\right) p + \left(\frac{\lambda}{\eta}\right)^n} - 1 \right)$$

$$\Pr(s) = 1 + R_g \left(\frac{p - \left(1 - \left(\frac{\lambda}{\eta}\right)^n\right) p - \left(\frac{\lambda}{\eta}\right)^n}{\left(1 - \left(\frac{\lambda}{\eta}\right)^n\right) p + \left(\frac{\lambda}{\eta}\right)^n} \right)$$

$$\Pr(s) = 1 + R_g\left(\frac{p - p + \left(\frac{\lambda}{\eta}\right)^n p - \left(\frac{\lambda}{\eta}\right)^n}{\left(1 - \left(\frac{\lambda}{\eta}\right)^n\right)p + \left(\frac{\lambda}{\eta}\right)^n}\right)$$

$$\Pr(s) = 1 + R_g\left(\frac{\left(\frac{\lambda}{\eta}\right)^n (p - 1)}{\left(1 - \left(\frac{\lambda}{\eta}\right)^n\right)p + \left(\frac{\lambda}{\eta}\right)^n}\right)$$

$$\Pr(s) = 1 - R_g\left(\frac{\left(\frac{\lambda}{\eta}\right)^n (1 - p)}{p - \left(\frac{\lambda}{\eta}\right)^n p + \left(\frac{\lambda}{\eta}\right)^n}\right)$$

$$\Pr(s) = 1 - R_g\left(\frac{\left(\frac{\lambda}{\eta}\right)^n (1 - p)}{p + \left(\frac{\lambda}{\eta}\right)^n (1 - p)}\right)$$

$$\Pr(s) = 1 - R_g\left(\frac{\left(\frac{\lambda}{\eta}\right)^n q}{p + \left(\frac{\lambda}{\eta}\right)^n q}\right) \tag{14.3.24}$$

$$\because q < 1, \frac{\lambda}{\eta} < 1$$

$$\therefore \left(\frac{\lambda}{\eta}\right)^n q << 1$$

Omit the denominator item $\left(\frac{\lambda}{\eta}\right)^n q$ in (14.3.24) to get:

$$\Pr(s) = 1 - R_g\left(\frac{\left(\frac{\lambda}{\eta}\right)^n q}{p}\right) \tag{14.3.25}$$

Rearranging (14.3.25) yields:

$$\Pr(s) = 1 - R_g \frac{q}{p}\left(\frac{\lambda}{\eta}\right)^n \tag{14.3.26}$$

To further simplify Eq. (14.3.26), let $\mu = \frac{\lambda}{\eta}$. The size of μ reflects the rational structure of the trading agent. The higher the degree of rationality, the smaller the value of μ. On the contrary, the larger the irrational component of the trading agent, the larger the value of μ. The rational structure of the trading agent has a high degree of stability, and μ is usually a constant parameter. According to the assumption of limited rationality of the trading agent, the rational structure parameter satisfies $0 < \mu < 1$.

Substituting the rational structure parameter into (14.3.26) yields a more concise form of the equation:

$$\Pr(s) = 1 - R_g \frac{q}{p} \mu^n \tag{14.3.27}$$

Equation (14.3.27) describes a basic model for evaluating trading strategies with different profit expectations and risks when the trading agent uses information from various aspects of the trading network in the face of uncertain trading situations H. Given that (14.3.27) comprehensively reflects the interconnections and characteristics of the trading situation judgment, trading strategy profit evaluation, and the interaction mechanism of the trading agents in the decision-making of the trading agents, it has a high universality. We call (14.3.27) the trading equation.

The trading Eq. (14.3.27) indicates that the larger the profit risk index, the more cautious the trading decision. In order to reduce decision-making risks and increase final profits, decision-makers need to observe the behavior of other trading agents around them. The larger the profit risk index, the more important the behavior information of the reference agent.

Prior judgment is also very important in decision-making. Even in the case of high profit risk, if the decision-maker has a high prior probability of a friendly situation p, it can also offset the concerns when implementing strategy s. This is what people often call the impression effect.

Demonstrations from trading agents on the state coordination set also play a crucial role in trading decisions. Each demonstrator is a probe into the uncertainty of the trading environment. When multiple demonstrators appear on the state coordination set, these demonstrators form a filter network for trading risks. For the decision-maker a_i, the role of demonstration behavior is risk filtering. When the number of demonstrators n is large enough, the value of μ^n will become very small, meaning that the demonstrators have successfully filtered the risks in the trading environment. The more significant the risk filtering effect, the higher the execution probability $\Pr(s)$ of the decision-maker a_i.

Formally, the trading equation is a typical nonlinear equation, which is very consistent with the nonlinear characteristics of the trading system. The trading equation accurately describes the characteristics of open interaction in the trading network, presents the interaction relationships between the community and the trading network through the number of demonstrator agents in the state coordination set n, and reflects the essence of nonlinearity and limited rationality in trading economics.

Notes

1. We will discuss the concept of trading potential in detail in Chap. 17.
2. Paul Samuelson, William Nordhaus (2008) Economics, (Chief Trans: Xiao Chen), 18th edn. Beijing: Posts and Telecommunications Press, p 168.
3. Dong Zhiyong (2005) Behavioral Economics, Peking University Press, Beijing.
4. Robert J. Shiller (2004) Irrational exuberance (Trans: Liao Li), China Renmin University Press, Beijing, p 172 (in Chinese).
5. Bayes Criterion is challenged by cognitive psychology, and the doubts mainly come from two aspects: First, Bayes criterion requires the evaluation of new information independently of existing information. However, people need to encode new information before accepting it, and only the encoded information will enter people's evaluation system. However, the coding process is closely related to the existing information, which often leads to selective attention and people can only see what they want to see. Therefore, the evaluator's use of new information cannot be independent of the existing information. Second, Bayes criterion requires that the order in which information enters the evaluator's field of view does not affect the evaluation of new information. In fact, since new information cannot be independent of existing information, it is determined that the order of information will inevitably have an impact on information evaluation. Based on the above questions, some scholars have revised Bayes criterion and proposed quasi-Bayes criterion, adding the coding part of evaluator to the standard Bayes criterion. Undoubtedly, quasi-Bayesian criteria can more accurately describe people's behavior in processing information, but it also adds further complexity to the model. We continue to use the standard Bayes criterion here, mainly due to consideration of the balance between the accuracy and brevity of the model.
6. In fact, the decision-making process of the trading agent in the trading network is bound to be affected by other trading agents. In order to simplify the model, we have simplified the interaction mode of the trading agent.
7. The concept of consumer surplus, first introduced into economics by Marshall, refers to the difference between the maximum price that the demand side is willing to pay for a transaction and the actual price. Trader surplus, deriving from the concept of consumer surplus which is only applicable to the demand side of the trading, applies to both the buyer and seller in the trading.

Chapter 15
Interpretation of Trading Phenomena

The interpretation of phenomena is not only the basic method of testing economic theory, but also the basic responsibility of economic theory. We choose five types of trading phenomena with different specificities as a test for the trading equation. Very common in social and economic life, these five phenomena have indispensable impact on social and economic operations. However, mainstream economics has not given them sufficient attention and in-depth explanation.

15.1 Phenomenon of Trading Cascades

Trading cascades are a phenomenon that often emerges in the operation of the trading system, which has a significant impact on the operation of the trading system and can even change the evolutionary direction of the trading system. The phenomenon of trading cascades has multiple levels of causes, and its underlying logic is rooted in human cognitive patterns. No matter how the information environment improves, we can never eliminate the cascade phenomenon from the trading system. As long as certain conditions are met, trading cascades will emerge.

The literal meaning of "cascade" refers to multi-level waterfalls. When applied to the field of computer science, it refers to the mapping relationship among multiple objects. When the initiator performs an operation, other associated objects will also perform the same operation. After the concept of "cascade" is adopted in the economic field, it is used to vividly describe the specific trading behavior of the trading agent, referring to the trading phenomenon where the trading agents on the trading network form a high degree of consistency in decision-making through mutual influence. The phenomenon of trading cascades, commonly known as herd effect or following the trend, is referred to as conformist behavior or information cascade in some academic works, which are all results caused by different translations of the English word "cascade".[1]

Z. Wang, *Trading Economics*, Contributions to Economics,
https://doi.org/10.1007/978-981-99-9875-3_15

15.1.1 Current Status of Research on Trading Cascade

As early as the 1930s, the phenomenon of trading cascades had attracted the attention of some economists. The great British economist John Maynard Keynes had already paid attention to the phenomenon of trading cascades in his epoch-making monograph "The General Theory of Employment, Interest and Money". He believed that the daily fluctuations in investment returns obviously involved some inexplicable group bias, even a ridiculous emotion affecting the market.[2] However, due to the lack of compatibility between the phenomenon of trading cascades and the "economic man" assumption of neoclassical economics, although market fluctuations caused by trading cascades occurred from time to time in the following half a century, the issue of trading cascades had not received due attention from economists. Mainstream economics simply regarded it as an irrational phenomenon and excluded it from the theoretical system. Keynes called the behavior of investors being greedy and blindly following the trend the animal spirits.[3] Former Chairman of the Federal Reserve, Alan Greenspan, sighed deeply when talking about the inscrutable animal spirits. "I had long been aware of such "spirits" and their quirkiness; in 1959, as a young economist, I had my first taste of being impressively wrong in a public prediction when I worried in the pages of Fortune magazine of investors' "over-exuberance" at what would prove to be very far from the top of a roaring bull market. The point isn't that I and other economic forecasters didn't understand that markets are prone to wild and even deranging mood swings that are uncoupled from any underlying rational basis. The point is rather that such "irrational" behavior is hard to measure, and stubbornly resistant to any reliable systematic analysis."

Even so, Greenspan still staunchly defends the mainstream economic system based on the "economic man". "I seek to identify specific behavioral imperatives—spirits—such as euphoria, fear, panic, optimism, and many more—and explore how they, and the cultures they foster, interact with rational economic behavior and spur important market outcomes. This isn't to say that we should throw Homo economicus out with his dirty bathwater: Despite ample evidence of persistent irrational market behavior, the data indicate that over the long run, rational economic judgments still guide free economies. But, of course, the long run can, famously, take a very long time."[4]

Robert J. Shiller is equally puzzled by the "irrational prosperity" caused by unpredictable trading cascades. "In 2000 I thought that most people I met, from all walks of life, were puzzled over the apparently high levels of the stock market. It seemed that they were unsure whether the market levels made any sense, or whether they were indeed the result of some human tendency that might be called *irrational exuberance*. They wondered whether the high levels of the stock market might have reflected unjustified optimism, an optimism that might have pervaded our thinking and affected many of our life decisions. They seemed unsure what to make of any small market downturn, wondering whether the previous market psychology could ever return. After expressing his worries and confuse, He had this to say about then Federal Reserve Chairman Alan Greenspan: "Even Alan Greenspan seemed unsure. ……

A modern version of the prophets who spoke in riddles, Greenspan likes to pose questions rather than make pronouncements. In the public exegesis of his remarks it was often forgotten that, when it comes to such questions, even he did not know the answers."[5]

With the emerging and deepening research of behavioral economics, the research on trading cascades has changed, and people have gradually unveiled the trading cascades and herd effects. Behavioral economics categorizes the causes of trading cascades into three types: trading cascades based on information asymmetry, trading cascades based on reputation maintenance, and trading cascades based on return correlation. The so-called information asymmetry trading cascades is due to the lack of complete investment information by investors. In order to reduce investment risks, they hope to obtain supplementary information from the decisions of other investors. The motivation of the trading agent to enhance information eventually forms a trading cascade under the effect of Bayesian learning mechanism. The so-called reputation maintenance type trading cascade means investors will start follow-up investment when they lack sufficient confidence. Doing so can at least maintain average performance and not damage their professional reputation. The so-called return-related trading cascade refers to the situation in the entrusted agency market where the remuneration of investment agents is linked to the relative performance of their peers. If it is better than the average level of peers, the agent will receive higher than the average remuneration; if it is lower than the average level of peers, the agent will get very low remuneration, and may even be fired. In this case, the agent chooses the safest trading strategy to follow the crowd, which does not need to bear the risk of lagging behind and can get a good return. Obviously, the follow-the-crowd strategy is the most cost-effective investment strategy.

Although behavioral economics has conducted in-depth research on trading cascades, people have already understood the initiation conditions of trading cascades at many levels such as decision-maker psychology, market organization structure, and market operating environment. However, within the framework of mainstream economics, there is still a lack of logically consistent theoretical expression for the phenomena of trading cascades.

15.1.2 Existence of Trading Cascades

We use the trading equation to prove the possibility of trading cascades in the operation of the trading system, and thereby reveal the key causes of the trading cascade phenomenon.

Assume a_i is any trading agent in the trading community Ω, S is the trading strategy that the trading agent a_i intends to implement. If a trading cascade occurs on a_i, it means that a_i implements the trading strategy S under the influence of community neighbors in the case of a lower prior probability p (assuming $p \leq 0.5$).

Assuming the minimum execution probability is p_0, we now prove that there is a cascade threshold n^* in the community Ω. As long as the number of people implementing the trading strategy S on the state coordination set reaches the threshold requirement, a_i will implement the strategy S. Hence, the cascade phenomenon occurs in the trading community Ω.

According to the assumption, if any subject a_i in the community Ω implements a cascade trading, the following conditions need to be met:

$$\Pr(s) = 1 - R_g \frac{q}{p} \mu^n \geq p_0 \tag{15.1.1}$$

Based on the cascading trading conditions given in (15.1.1), we can calculate the threshold n^* for cascading trades to occur in community Ω.

$$R_g \frac{q}{p} \mu^n = 1 - p_0 \tag{15.1.2}$$

Taking the logarithm of both sides of Eq. (15.1.2), we get:

$$\ln R_g + n \ln \mu + \ln \frac{q}{p} = \ln(1 - p_0) \tag{15.1.3}$$

After rearranging, we get:

$$n \ln \mu = \ln(1 - p_0) - \ln \frac{q}{p} - \ln R_g \tag{15.1.4}$$

$$\therefore n = -\frac{\ln R_g - \ln(1 - p_0) - \ln \frac{p}{q}}{\ln \mu} \tag{15.1.5}$$

The n obtained from (15.1.5) is a positive real number. Considering the practical meaning of the cascade threshold, we take the value $n^* = [n]+1$, in which $[n]$ represents the integer part of n. As a universally representative assumption, we assume the prior probability $p = q = 0.5$. We assume that the rational structure parameter of the trading agent μ follows the 2/8 distribution principle, that is, 80% of the behavior of the trading agent meets the requirements of rationality, and 20% of the behavior has irrational characteristics. We assume the return risk index $R_g = e = 2.7183$, which means that the return risk index R_g is at a high level, indicating that the trading strategy S is of a high-risk type.

Under the above conditions, the value of n calculated by (15.1.5) is:

$$n = -\frac{\ln R_g - \ln(1 - p_0) - \ln \frac{p}{q}}{\ln \mu} = \frac{1 - (-1.6)}{1.3} = 2 \tag{15.1.6}$$

According to the relationship between the trading community threshold n^* and n, we get the threshold n^* as follows:

$$n^* = [n] + 1 = 3 \tag{15.1.7}$$

Equation (15.1.7) shows that in a general sense, the threshold for a trading cascade in the trading community Ω to occur is 3. Even for riskier trading strategies S, as long as there are 3 neighbors implementing it, more neighbors will follow. This shows that the conditions for cascading trades to occur in the trading system are easily met.

The result expressed by Eq. (15.1.7) is highly symbolic. In the Chinese cultural system, the number "3" has a special meaning. As Laozi stated in the *Tao Te Ching*, one gives birth to two, two gives birth to three, and three gives birth to all things. In Chinese proverbs, there are sayings like "three people make a crowd", and "three people make a tiger", which vividly describe the effect of behavior accumulation. The calculation result of Eq. (15.1.7) just confirms the collective wisdom of the Chinese culture.

Equation (15.1.7) shows that the threshold for cascading behavior to occur in the trading community is actually very low. Cascading phenomena should be very common in trading systems, and we should often observe them in reality, but the actual situation is not the case. This is because most cascading behaviors are local phenomena, or even individual behaviors, and only a few cascading trades that meet special conditions will eventually brew into wave-like group phenomena. The so-called special conditions refer to when the return risk index R_g of the trading strategy S and the number of trading agents involved n form a close negative correlation, and the trading cascade and the trading ring stimulate each other, then it is possible to form a huge volume of cascading trading phenomena.

In more open communities, due to the larger resident status synergy set, the diversity of the trading agents on the synergy set is more prominent in terms of information possession and trading status, which easily meets the threshold requirements for cascading. For relatively closed communities, the resident status synergy set is smaller, and its main composition comes from the community itself. The homogeneity of the reference subject status is high, and there are fewer people willing to take the risk for high-risk trading strategies, usually failing to meet the threshold conditions for trade cascading. This forms the regional characteristics of the trading network: in network regions formed by more open communities, the propagation of information and trading strategies is relatively rapid; and in more closed areas of the trading network, the island effect of the trading community is very obvious, which does not easily follow the rhythm of the outside world, and their development will be relatively slow.

It is generally believed that the herd effect is an irrational manifestation of the trading system. Greenspan attributed the herd behavior to the animal spirits in humans, and attributed the various asset bubble phenomena driven by the herd behavior and the destruction caused by the bursting of bubbles to irrational factors such as frenzy and fear. He believes "A significant part of stock price dynamics is driven by the innate human propensity to intermittently swing between euphoria and fear, which, while heavily influenced by real economic events, nonetheless has a partial life of its own."[6] Undeniably, irrational factors such as frenzy and fear play an indispensable role in the process of cascading trading, but essentially, rationality is still the dominant factor in the cascading process.

The above analysis shows that **the phenomenon of trade cascading or herd effect is rational human behavior, the result of people pursuing maximum returns, and has nothing to do with animal spirits.** The emergence of cascading phenomena in the trading systems is fundamentally due to the uncertainty of the trading system and the asymmetry of information among trading agents. The uncertainty of the trading system is a companion of the dynamic evolution of the trading system. As long as the trading system is in development and evolution, uncertainty cannot be eliminated.

Information asymmetry is reflected in two aspects: on the one hand, trading agents have their own information sets, and there is usually a considerable difference among the information sets of different agents; on the other hand, there is a difference between the information held by trading agents and that transmitted by behavior, which is a phenomenon of information mutation between the actor's information and the interpretation of behavior.

Whether it is the uncertainty of the trading system or the asymmetry of information between trading agents, both are inherent attributes of the trading system and cannot be completely eliminated. Information asymmetry is not only due to the interest game of trading agents, but also due to the characteristics of human cognition. No matter how advanced information technology is and how low the cost of information is, it is impossible to eliminate the asymmetry of information. If the trading system cannot eliminate the uncertainty in operation, and the trading agents cannot eliminate the asymmetry of information between each other, the phenomenon of trade cascading will inevitably occur, no matter how excellent the economic management and macro-control measures are.

From an evolutionary perspective, with the continuous compaction process of the trading system, the association between trading agents through the trading network becomes more closely linked, and the division of labor progresses, the degree of financialization increases, all of which will make the trading chain on the trading network longer. The state coordination set of trading agents will evolve in two directions—expansion of scale and enhancement of diversity, which makes it easier for the cascade threshold in the trading community to be met, the probability of trading cascades increases, and the phenomenon of trading cascades will affect a larger range as the trading system becomes more compact. In fact, larger, wider, and more frequent trading cascade phenomena are precisely the characteristics of the overall strengthening of the system caused by the compaction of the trading system.

15.1.3 Trading Cascade Process

Cascade phenomena do not always end in tragedy. Trading cascades can often become a strong driving force for economic growth. From consumer upgrades to enterprise transformation, trading cascades play an indispensable role. Only when cascade behavior reaches a phenomenal level in the operation of the trading system, will it have a negative impact on the stability of the trading system.

The problem is that not all trading strategies can trigger cascade phenomena. Only when the excess return of the trading strategy $u_2 = e_g - e_0$ is positively correlated with the number of participating agents n, the return gap $u_1 = e_g - e_b$ is inversely proportional to the number of agents n, and the cascade can spread across communities in the trading network, can it possibly become a sufficient equivalent of trading cascade phenomena.

The emergence of cascade phenomena has a complete process, usually going through multiple links: brewing—emotion formation (optimism or fear)—cascade formation—maintenance and reinforcement—growing doubt—fear appears—stampede event occurs—cascade ends. The above eight links actually include two cascading strategies: one is the contrarian trading strategy S; the other is the dual strategy of S, i.e. $-S$. Usually, the first half of the cascade cycle is dominated by the contrarian strategy S, while the second half is dominated by the dual strategy $-S$. We will discuss the two stages separately.

First, let's discuss the cascade process of the contrarian trading strategy S. Assume Ω_1 is any community in the trading network, initially agents n_0 have a high prior probability for the contrarian trading strategy S in the community, satisfying $p \geq p_0$, and implementing this strategy. Under their influences, trading agents with their prior probability reaching p_0 level in the trading community Ω_1 will satisfy the condition of strategy S, which is $\text{pr}(g|n) \geq p_0$ when their posterior probability is adjusted. Once entering this stage, it means the cascade trading in the community Ω_1 initiates, and the number of agents implementing S will increase from the initial n_0 to n_0', meeting $n_0' > n_0$. When the trading strategy S meets the conditions of $u_2(n_0') \geq u_2(n_0)$, that is, the excess return is positively correlated with the number of agents implementing the trade, which means that the return risk index R_g decreases as the number of participants n increases. From the cascade threshold formula (15.1.5), it can be seen that the threshold $n_1'^*$ corresponding to n_0' is less than the threshold n_1^* corresponding to n_0, that is, $n_1'^* \leq n_1^*$. Therefore, a self-reinforcing feedback mechanism is formed among the three variables: the number of agents implementing the trading strategy S, the excess return $u_2(n)$, and the threshold n_1^*. That is, the more agents implementing the trading strategy S, the higher the excess return, the lower the cascade threshold, and more trading agents enter the cascade state, choosing to implement the trading strategy S.

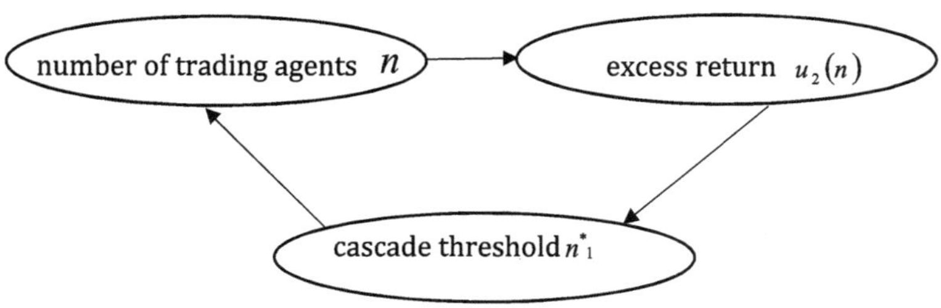

Fig. 15.1 Self-reinforcing feedback loop

In the process of cascade self-reinforcement, due to the continuous increase in excess returns, the risk preference of trading agents in the trading community Ω_1 continues to strengthen, and they increasingly choose an aggressive state. In this scenario, the expected probability of a worsening trading situation decreases, the risk of potential losses also decreases, and the value of returns under a worsening situation $e_b(s)$ will significantly increase. Its increase rate keeps in sync with $e_g(s)$, or even exceeds the growth rate of $e_g(s)$. In this case, the profit gap $u_1(n)$ will narrow as the number of agents n implementing s increases, that is, $u_1(n_0') \leq u_1(n_0)$. This process will undoubtedly accelerate the decline of the return risk index R_g, the trend of the cascade threshold decline is strengthened, and the self-realization characteristics of cascade trading continue to increase (Fig. 15.1).

The cascade behavior of the trading strategy S in the trading community Ω_1 will quickly spread to the neighboring community Ω_2 through cross-community trading. Affected by the community Ω_1, the cascade threshold of the community Ω_2 starts directly from n_1^*. A lower threshold means that the cascade process of Ω_2 will be faster than the initial community Ω_1, and the excess returns u_2 will also increase at a faster rate. The result is that after the trading strategy S spreads in the community Ω_2, the cascade threshold is further reduced, that is $n_2^* \leq n_1^*$.

The situation in the community Ω_2 will spread in two directions: one is to return to the initial community Ω_1. As the cascade threshold value decreases, more trading agents in Ω_1 will enter the cascade process; the other is to spread forward from Ω_2 to the adjacent community Ω_3. In the community Ω_3 the cascade process of Ω_2 will replay, but the starting threshold is lower and the cascade speed is faster, which means $n_3^* \leq n_2^*$. After extensive community spread, the trading strategy S will eventually trigger a new round of cascade phenomena in the trading system.

Stocks and real estate are two types of markets that are prone to cascade phenomena. The total amount of stocks on the stock market is limited, and the phase transition of trading on the stock market is almost zero constraint, which can be converted from the selling phase to the buying phase at any time. The convenience of phase transition on the stock market makes it very easy to form a one-sided supply or demand pattern. Once the expectation of rising or falling is formed, there will be a situation where off-market investors want to enter the market to buy, and on-market investors want to continue to increase their holdings; or in the opposite scenario, on-market wants to sell, off-market waits and watches. This characteristic of the stock market determines the high correlation between price trends and the number of dominant phase agents n.

In the real estate market, the numerous complicated procedures determine the long supply cycle of new houses, and the real estate's requirements for the location of the plot add a strong time constraint to the supply of real estate. This determines that supply and demand relationship in the real estate market has limited self-regulation ability and relatively slow adjustment speed, thus forming the positive correlation between price increases and the number of home buyers n. The Chinese real estate market is a typical cascading transaction market. With the continuous rise in housing prices, real estate investment has almost become the first choice for Chinese household residents. The motivation behind the investment is irrelevant to whether there is a need for housing. Every family wants to buy a house, and everyone is discussing housing prices, forming a super cascading transaction phenomenon. By the first 20 years of the twenty-first century, from first-tier cities such as Beijing and Shanghai, to provincial second-tier cities, and then to regional and county-level third and fourth-tier cities, housing prices across the country had almost doubled. The increase in housing prices in first-tier cities even exceeded 20 times, and the crazy housing prices not only buried huge risks for the Chinese economy, but also greatly increased the operating costs of the Chinese economy and weakened the international competitiveness of the Chinese economy.

The reason why the Chinese real estate market can form such a large-scale and long-lasting super cascading transaction is mainly due to China's unique land supply mechanism and real estate development system, as well as the imperfect tax system and other multiple factors leading to the expectation of rising housing prices. The return gap of the real estate investment strategy u_1 is almost 0. On the other hand, the continuously rising housing prices have led to an excessive return on real estate investment that remains high, and the cascading threshold has almost dropped to 0. Under such circumstances, cascading trading can happen at any time and anywhere. During the most severe period of property speculation, people even didn't ask whether they would own property rights, whether the prices were reasonable, whether the location of property had advantages, whether the house design is suitable, or even whether the house was built on the ground. Even if it was underground with bad lighting, as long as it was a house, someone would rush to buy it.

In the process of gradual decrease of the cascading threshold after the initial high level, the peak of the cascading intensity corresponds to the lowest point of the cascading threshold. Subsequently, the threshold gradually rises again until it returns to the level before the start of the cascade. At this point, the cascading process of the trading strategy S ends. Usually, the final stage of the cascade of the trading strategy S is always accompanied by the beginning of the dual strategy $-S$ cascade, entering the second half of the cascade cycle.

Now, let's discuss the cascading process of the dual strategy $-S$. When a part of the trading agents obtain excess returns from S that reach or exceed the expected target, their trading status will begin to change from the original aggressive state to conservative one, becoming more sensitive to the risk of market decline. Against this background, a part of the trading agents in the market will switch from the strategy S to the dual strategy $-S$, and the market supply and demand relationship will start the initial fine-tuning. The momentum of continuous expansion of $u_2(s)$ begins to slow down. As the number of agents joining the dual strategy $-S$ increases, $u_2(s)$ will eventually stop growing. At this point, the cascading process of the dual strategy $-S$ formally begins.

Theoretically speaking, although as an independent trading strategy, $-S$ has the same logic with S in terms of the mechanism of cascade occurrence. However, due to different trading phases, corresponding adjustments need to be made in the relationship between the trading situation and the corresponding expected returns. The high returns of the trading strategy s correspond to the friendly state of the trading situation g; whereas it is just the opposite with the dual strategy $-s$. It is

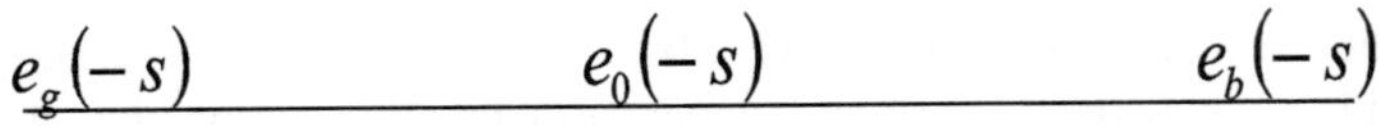

Fig. 15.2 The relationship of expected returns of the dual strategy

when the trading situation changing from good to bad that implementing $-s$ can achieve high returns. Therefore, for the trading situation states g and b, the expected returns of strategy $-s$ are $e_g(-s)$ and $e_b(-s)$ respectively. Since the dual strategy $-s$ is a defensive strategy, the agreed return is not to lose money, that is, $e_0(-s) = 0$. The three expected returns of the dual strategy $-s$ are just the inversion of the corresponding relationship of the trading strategy s, that is:

The meaning expressed by Fig. 15.2 is that when the trading situation is in the g state, implementing the dual strategy $-s$ to sell assets means losing more profit opportunities. The trading agent is considered a loss caused by the execution of strategy $-s$, and $e_g(-s)$ takes a negative value; on the contrary, if the situation is in the b state, the trading agent implementing the dual strategy $-s$ will reduce losses and preserve the profits of s, and $e_b(-s)$ takes a positive value. From this, we can calculate the profit gap and excess return on the dual strategy $-s$:

$$u_1(-s) = e_b(-s) - e_g(-s) \tag{15.1.8}$$

$$u_2(-s) = e_b(-s) - e_0(-s) = e_b(-s) \tag{15.1.9}$$

When the market expectation changes from good to bad, $e_g(-s)$ quickly approaches 0 from a negative value, and the profit gap $u_1(-s) = e_b(-s) - e_g(-s)$ converges to $u_2(-s) = e_b(-s)$; on the contrary, as the trading situation worsens, the excess return of strategy of $u_2(-s)$ begins to rise. Under the action of the above two forces, the return risk index $R_g \to 1$.

From the above analysis, it can be seen that the corresponding relationship of trading strategy s and the two states g and b of situation H is just the opposite to that of the dual strategy $-s$. The corresponding relationship of p, q and the states of situation H is also mutually inverted. The prior probability p is the chance judgment of the implementer of the dual strategy $-s$ about the occurrence b of trading situation H; q is the prediction of the implementer of the dual decision $-s$ about the occurrence g of the trading situation H.

From the threshold formula (15.1.5), we know:

$$n = -\frac{\ln R_g - \ln(1 - p_0) - \ln \frac{p}{q}}{\ln \mu} \to -\frac{\ln(1 - p_0) + \ln \frac{p}{q}}{\ln \mu}$$

When the expectation of trading situation reversal p continues to strengthen, $\frac{p}{q} \to +\infty$.

With the constant In$(1 - p_0)$ and $\frac{p}{q} \to +\infty$, n will turn from positive to negative.

$$\because\ n^* = [n] + 1$$
$$\therefore\ n^* = [n] + 1 \to 1 \qquad (15.1.10)$$

As the cascade threshold of the dual strategy $-s$ approaches 1, it means that the cascade channel of the dual strategy $-s$ opens, and almost all agents holding s assets will accept $-s$ trading strategy. Correspondingly, because the cascade threshold of s is getting higher and higher, the cascade channel of the trading strategy s is basically closed, and only a small number of agents may carry out s strategy trading. The scattered trading behavior of strategy s cannot compete with the flood-like $-s$ strategy, and the huge disparity in supply and demand will inevitably cause a sharp drop in prices.

Comparing the cascade process of the dual strategy pair $(s, -s)$, the cascade threshold $n^*(s)$ of strategy s is a gradually declining process, and the number of trading agents entering the cascade state shows a stepwise increase. When the cascade threshold $n^*(s)$ is reduced to a certain extent, the number of trading agents that meet the cascade state will show a blowout growth, and at this time the cascade channel of the dual strategy $-s$ is in a closed state, which forms a situation where the quantity of hope to buy is far higher than the willingness to sell, pushing the trading price to rise sharply. Although the price rises due to the mismatch in the number of supply and demand, the volume of successful matching transactions is not high, and the transaction volume will not increase significantly. In this situation, among the, there are still a large number of trading agents that implement strategy s have not realized their purchase intentions; the cascade process has not ended, and the trading price continues to rise. This situation may only change when the trading agents holding assets s start to worry about the risk of price drops. When a portion of the trading agents holding assets s begin to shift towards the dual strategy $-s$, the market trading volume begins to increase. However, the trading price at this time is still high, and may even still be rising. As the trading intention of the strategy s has been cleared, the cascade process of the strategy s ends here. At the same time, as the number of agents implementing $-s$ increases, gradually meeting the cascade threshold conditions, the dual strategy $-s$ cascade officially takes over when the strategy s cascade ends.

Compared to the cascade process of strategy s, that of strategy $-s$ is faster, the cascade threshold $n^*(-s)$ will quickly approach the extreme, the market will see a large amount of selling under the drive of panic, and prices will plummet, creating a situation similar to an avalanche. On this point, Alan Greenspan commented "fear induces a far greater response than euphoria. Accordingly, asset prices and other fear-sensitive financial variables move far more rapidly when falling than they do when rising."[7]

The contrast in cascade behavior of the dual strategies $(s, -s)$ is determined by human cognitive characteristics. Generally speaking, people need to verify and gradually accept optimistic emotions, and only after repeated verification will they accept optimistic emotions. Panic emotions are different. People are infected with panic emotions faster, with fewer links. People's first reaction is usually to run away, without any verification process. The difference in acceptance speed of the two emotions is a survival strategy explored by humans in hundreds of thousands of years of evolution filled with death risks, and is deeply engraved in human genes. It can be imagined that in the dangerous wilderness, being cautious about optimism can avoid many dangers, and the price paid is just a little less gain. Group panic emotions carry dangerous information, and a quick response must be made, or any negligence can cost lives. Even if the final check is a false alarm, the price paid is at most a little more running.

The start of the dual strategy $-s$ cascade marks the beginning of a rapid drop in trading prices, and the price bottom must appear under the condition of volume-price cooperation, so as to completely clear the trading intention under the cascade state of $-s$. When new trading agents enter the market to take over the assets sold by $-s$, it marks the end of the cascade process of the dual strategy $-s$, and also marks the end of the cascade cycle induced by strategy $(s, -s)$.

The contrast in cascading behavior of the strategy pair $(s, -s)$ is reflected in the trend of trading prices, showing an asymmetric structure of cascading trajectories, that is, the short-tail structure of the price curve.

Figure 15.3 shows that the cascading price curve induced by the strategy pair $(s, -s)$ is an asymmetric parabola on the time axis, with a steeper curve on the downside of the price, which constitutes a significant feature of the cascading trading price trend. When we observe the stock price index curve, we will find such configurations on the fluctuating price curve. Each configuration unit represents a cascading process of a strategy pair that has occurred in the market, and they are the historical archives of the stock market's tidal movement.

It should be pointed out that when the cascading process of the dual strategy $-s$ is restricted for some reason, the price trajectory dominated by the strategy pair $(s, -s)$ will show completely different characteristics. The real estate market is a typical example. Because real estate has both investment and residential functions, there is a significant asymmetry in the effects of the two strategies in the strategy pair $(s, -s)$. For the buying strategy s, the dual functions of real estate will not be any constraint. When the expectation of rising house prices is formed, both speculative demand and rigid demand will join the home buying. On the contrary, when the expectation of falling house prices is formed, holders for investment purposes

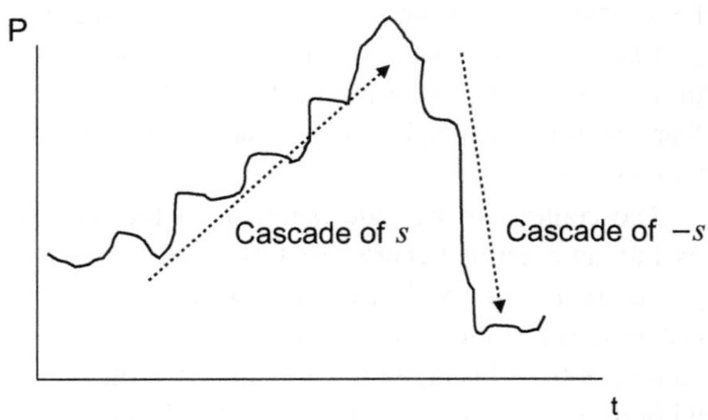

Fig. 15.3 Trend of cascading trading prices

will quickly implement the dual strategy $-s$, while holders for residential purposes will not. In this case, the cascading process of the dual strategy $-s$ is hindered by residential demand, and the cascading intensity will be weakened. The result is that the speed of decline in real estate prices slows down, forming a special pattern of rapid rise and slow fall in house prices.

15.2 Technological Innovation

Innovation is the driving force for the evolution of the trading system and the path for its expansion. Innovation is everywhere—technological innovation, process innovation, business model innovation, enterprise management innovation, marketing means innovation and financial innovation, all belong to the innovative category leading the evolution of the trading system.

15.2.1 Technological Innovation from the Perspective of Mainstream Economics

Technology and technological innovation occupy a very important position in the theoretical system of mainstream economics and are the basic variables that constitute the production function and total output function. The most commonly used Cobb–Douglas production function (abbreviated as C-D function) has the following form:

$$Y = AK^{\alpha}L^{\beta},\ \alpha, \beta > 0 \tag{15.2.1}$$

In (15.2.1), K is the capital stock, L is the labor input, A is the technology level. The basic idea expressed by the $C - D$ function is that after excluding the contributions of capital and labor, technology is the determinant of value output. Under the condition of constant factor input, technological progress determines economic growth.

Robert M. Solow proposed the method of calculating technological progress by using growth rate residuals based on the $C - D$ function. The specific derivation process is as follows:

Take the natural logarithm on both sides of (15.2.1):

$$\ln Y = \ln A + \alpha \ln K + \beta \ln L \tag{15.2.2}$$

Differentiate both sides of (15.2.2):

$$\frac{dY}{Y} = \frac{dA}{A} + \alpha\frac{dK}{K} + \beta\frac{dL}{L} \tag{15.2.3}$$

Approximate the three differential variables respectively:

$$
\begin{aligned}
dY &= \Delta Y \\
dK &= \Delta K \\
dL &= \Delta L
\end{aligned}
\tag{15.2.4}
$$

Substitute (15.2.4) into (15.2.3) to get:

$$
\frac{\Delta Y}{Y} = \frac{\Delta A}{A} + \alpha \frac{\Delta K}{K} + \beta \frac{\Delta L}{L} \tag{15.2.5}
$$

Equation (15.2.5) expresses the relationship between capital stock, labor input, technological progress, and economic growth rate. Based on this, we get:

$$
\frac{\Delta A}{A} = \frac{\Delta Y}{Y} - \left(\alpha \frac{\Delta K}{K} + \beta \frac{\Delta L}{L} \right) \tag{15.2.6}
$$

Equation (15.2.6) is the Solow residual. The Solow residual has become a major tool for people to analyze economic growth, evaluate the speed of technological progress, and improve total factor efficiency. However, the Solow residual has also been questioned, including issues of statistical errors, measurement of capital and labor input, etc. The main problem is that as a residual term, it contains not only the single factor of technological progress, but also many factors that interfere with output growth, such as macroeconomic fluctuations and macro policy factors.

Among the different schools of mainstream economics, the Austrian school represented by Schumpeter attaches great importance to the contribution of technological progress to economic growth. Schumpeter believes that technological innovation is the main driving force for sustained economic growth; the pioneering spirit of entrepreneurs, willingness to take risks, and strong desire for success are the sources of technological innovation; enterprises are the main force of technological innovation. Schumpeter believes that large enterprises with a monopoly position are the main force of technological innovation due to their strong financial resources and the strength of technological innovation. Based on this judgment, Schumpeter challenges the almost unshakeable belief of economists—the perfectly competitive market is the most efficient and achieves the Pareto optimal market organization model. Schumpeter believes that the imperfectly competitive market is more innovative, more efficient than the perfectly competitive market, and has more growth potential. This is the famous Schumpeter hypothesis.[8]

According to Schumpeter, technological innovation is not only the main driving force for economic growth, but also the key promoter of the evolution of the trading system structure. He believes that while technological innovation brings new industries to the economy, it will have a substitution effect on old related industries, and may even cause destruction to existing industries. The structural destruction brought about by technological innovation is different from the structural adjustment caused by price competition. It is a process of large-scale elimination of old technologies and production systems and the establishment of new production systems. Schumpeter called this process "creative destruction".

Schumpeter believes that technological innovation is to establish a new production function, that is, to introduce a new production factor and production organization method into the production system. Based on this definition, Schumpeter divided technological innovation into five basic types: (1) introducing new products; (2) adopting new production methods; (3) opening up new markets; (4) introducing new sources of raw material supply; and (5) introducing new production organization methods.

Technological innovation activities, which appear to be highly random on the surface, still follow certain rules in their choice of direction. Specifically, changes in relative prices of factors will provide an incentive mechanism, pointing out the direction of technological innovation for enterprises. This is the idea contained in the neoclassical price incentive model. The basic concept of the model adheres to the tradition of neoclassical firm theory, believing that when enterprises arrange production, they tend to develop technologies that can use relatively expensive factors more economically or develop technologies that utilize relatively cheap factors, thereby achieving the goal of minimizing costs and maximizing profits. This motivation will guide the direction of technology development. When oil prices continue to rise, the market will compete to develop electric vehicle technology; when human capital becomes more and more expensive, artificial intelligence and industrial robot technology with human substitution functions will receive widespread attention and develop rapidly towards maturity. It is fair to say that the neoclassical price incentive model can explain most of the phenomena of technological innovation, but it omits the most common type of technological innovation. In Schumpeter's five types of technological innovation, product innovation ranks first, and product innovation does not involve changes in the relative prices of production factors and belongs to the category of neutral technological progress. The neoclassical price incentive model focuses on the mechanism of non-neutral technological progress.

15.2.2 Technological Innovation from the Perspective of Trading Economics

In the view of trading economics, innovation is not the result of the curiosity of the trading agent, but that of its profit-seeking motive. The trading agent can occupy a more advantageous trading position through innovation. It can be seen that technological innovation activities can also be included in the decision-making process of the trading agent.

We use the trading equation to explore the basic laws of the innovative behavior of trading agents in the context of the trading community. Among the two basic trading agents of the trading system, enterprises are the main force of innovation.

Although the innovation process cannot be separated from the participation of families, the pursuit of asset diversification by families is the underlying logic of corporate innovation, pointing out the direction for corporate innovation. However, this cannot change the fact that the enterprise is the main force of innovation. Therefore, we focus on the innovative behavior of enterprises here.

Innovation is a strategy of enterprises, and the decision-making process also follows the basic laws described by the trading equation. The cost and benefit of innovation, the entrepreneurs' confidence in innovation, and the innovative atmosphere of the trading community are the three key elements that affect corporate innovation.

Assume that b_j is an enterprise in the trading community Ω, s is the innovative strategy on the strategy set s, and the two states corresponding to the trading situation H are innovation success and innovation failure. Assume that the prior probability of b_j achieving the goal of s is p, and the prior probability of failure is q. For the trading strategy s, assume that the state coordination set of the trading agent b_j is B_j^c, and the number of subjects in B_j^c that successfully implement the innovation strategy is n. Under this decision-making framework, the execution probability of b_j implementing an innovative strategy $\mathrm{pr}(s)$ can be calculated by the trading equation.

The benefits that innovation brings to an enterprise can be measured in two ways: one is the operating income brought by innovation, and the other is the added market value that innovation brings to the firm. In comparison, an increase in operating income requires a slow marketing process, while changes in an enterprise's market value usually react very quickly. For a promising innovation project, even before the new product is launched, the capital market begins to react. Even for non-listed companies, the market value of the company is also an indicator that decision-makers attach great importance to. In view of this, we use the change in market value as a measure of the benefits of corporate innovation, ΔZ representing the expected increase in market value that the innovative strategy s brings for the trading agent b_j, and the expected return of successfully achieving the goal of the innovation strategy is $e_g = \Delta Z$. When innovation fails, there is no innovation income, and the innovation input becomes a sunk cost, so when innovation fails the return is $e_b = -C$, where C represents innovation input. Assume the reasonable expected return on investment in the trading community is e_0. From this, the risk index of the innovative strategy s is calculated as follows:

$$R_g(s) = \frac{\Delta Z - (-C)}{\Delta Z - e_0} \tag{15.2.7}$$

Substitute into the trading equation to get:

$$\Pr(s) = 1 - \frac{\Delta Z + C}{\Delta Z - e_0}\frac{q}{p}\mu^n \tag{15.2.8}$$

Generally speaking, the cost of innovation is proportional to the difficulty of innovation. Therefore, we need to introduce the concept of innovation intensity, represented by x. The so-called innovation intensity refers to the knowledge distance between innovation and existing technology or models. The farther the knowledge distance of the innovation project, the higher the innovation intensity. Innovation intensity $x = 0$ indicates that the trading strategy s does not contain any innovative elements, meaning that it is the direct application of mature technology. We agree that when the innovation intensity value is $o < x \leq 1$, it indicates that the trading strategy s is some improvement to mature technology; when $x > 1$, it represents the trading strategy contains a lot of new technology. The higher the innovation intensity of the innovative strategy s, the greater the development cost that needs to be invested. At the same time, the higher the innovation intensity, the lower the probability of success of the innovation strategy, and the smaller the number of leading agents in the state coordination set n. The above relationship can be expressed by the following function:

$$C = C(x),\ p = p(x),\ n = n(x) \tag{15.2.9}$$

Compared with the relationship expressed by Eq. (15.2.9), the relationship between the innovation market value effect ΔZ and the innovation intensity x is more complex. The market value effect brought by innovation does not strictly correspond to the intensity of innovation. Even if the strategy has a high intensity of innovation, it may not necessarily bring corresponding benefits to the enterprise. If it can hit the market hotspots, even if the intensity of innovation is not high, it can also bring good market value benefits to the enterprise. For example, in the context of the rampant COVID-19 pandemic, new drugs for treating COVID-19 may bring huge market value benefits to enterprises. Other new drugs, even if they have greater innovation intensity, may not necessarily outperform the market value effect of new drugs against the coronavirus. The key to determining the size of the innovation market value effect is the market prospect of technological innovation. This shows that the market also plays a very important role in guiding the allocation of innovation resources.

According to Eq. (15.2.9), the trading equation can be expressed as follows:

$$\Pr(s) = 1 - \frac{\Delta Z + C(x)}{\Delta Z - e_0}\frac{q(x)}{p(x)}\mu^{n(x)} \tag{15.2.10}$$

After simplifying the function, we get:

$$\Pr(s) = 1 - R_g(x, \Delta Z)\frac{q(x)}{p(x)}\mu^{n(x)} \tag{15.2.11}$$

In Eq. (15.2.11), the return risk index $R_g(x,\ \Delta Z)$ contains two variables with opposite effects. The intensity of innovation increases the return risk index, while the innovation market value effect ΔZ reduces the return risk index. Obviously, with other conditions being equal, the strategy with greater innovation intensity has a lower probability of implementation, while the innovation strategy with a more obvious market value effect has a higher probability of being implemented.

We assume that $\mathrm{pr}(s) \geq 0.8$ is the execution probability of the trading agent, and from Eq. (15.2.11) we get:

$$1 - R_g(x, \Delta Z)\frac{q(x)}{p(x)}\mu^{n(x)} \geq 0.8 \tag{15.2.12}$$

Arrange (15.2.12) to get:

$$R_g(x, \Delta Z)\frac{q(x)}{p(x)}\mu^{n(x)} \leq 0.2 \tag{15.2.13}$$

From (15.2.13), the necessary condition for the trading agent b_j to implement the innovation strategy s is as follows:

$$\frac{p(x)}{q(x)} \geq 5R_g(x, \Delta Z)\mu^{n(x)} \tag{15.2.14}$$

We assume that the bounded rationality of the trading agent satisfies the 2/8 rule, $\mu = \frac{1}{4}$, substitute into (15.2.14) to get:

$$\frac{p(x)}{q(x)} \geq 5R_g(x, \Delta Z)\left(\frac{1}{4}\right)^{n(x)} \tag{15.2.15}$$

Arrange (15.2.15) to get:

$$\frac{p(x)}{q(x)} \geq \frac{5}{4}\frac{R_g(x, \Delta Z)}{4^{n(x)-1}} \tag{15.2.16}$$

From (15.2.16), we get:

$$\frac{p(x)}{q(x)} > \frac{R_g(x, \Delta Z)}{4^{n(x)-1}} \tag{15.2.17}$$

Equation (15.2.17) indicates the necessary conditions for the trading agent to participate in innovation. If the strategy s cannot meet the conditions given by (15.2.17), it means that the execution probability will be below the level of 0.8. There is a high risk of failure to execute such a strategy, which does not conform to the basic principle of maximizing expected returns.

In the innovation condition (15.2.17), $p(x) = q(x) = 0.5$ is the critical point of phase change. When $p(x) < 0.5 < q(x)$, $\frac{p(x)}{q(x)} < 1$, as $p(x)$ is further from 0.5, $\frac{p(x)}{q(x)}$ decreases faster, and the gap to meet the innovation condition is larger. On the contrary, if $p(x) > 0.5 > q(x)$, $\frac{p(x)}{q(x)} > 1$, as $p(x)$ increases, $\frac{p(x)}{q(x)}$ will grow at a faster rate. This shows that near $p(x) = 0.5$, there is an innovation threshold effect. Crossing the 0.5 threshold from either the left or the right, The prior probability $p(x)$ will cause a significant change in innovative behavior.

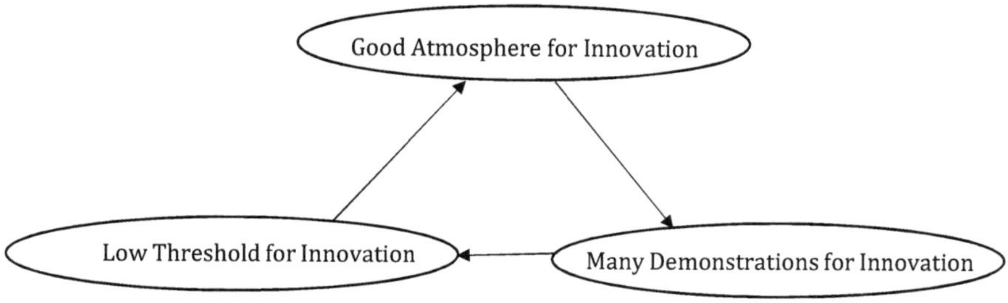

Fig. 15.4 Feedback loop for innovation stimulation

We can draw the following conclusions from Eq. (15.2.17):

First, the higher the intensity of innovation in trading strategies, the larger the value of the return risk index $R_g(x, \Delta Z)$, the smaller the number of leading demonstration agents $n(x)$, and the higher the conditions for trading agents b_j to implement innovative strategies, the lower the possibility of implementing innovative strategies. Therefore, innovative activities in the trading community must proceed in order from low to high intensity of innovation. Innovation is a continuous process with significant path dependence. For trading systems, whether it is technological innovation, conceptual innovation, or management model innovation, it cannot be achieved overnight. Countries with originally low levels of innovation find it difficult to completely change the situation of technological backwardness in a short time and need a long process of accumulation and trial and error (Fig. 15.4).

Second, the community atmosphere plays a very important role in innovation activities. In communities with a strong atmosphere of innovation, residents have a higher enthusiasm for innovation, which will produce more innovative results, further encouraging more residents to participate in innovation. This positive feedback mechanism inevitably leads to the island phenomenon of innovation activities: innovation activities within the trading system present a block distribution feature, and there is a huge gap in the innovation capabilities among different regions. In the trading system, innovation capabilities cannot be evenly distributed.

Third, closure is not conducive to innovation. In communities with a high degree of closure, residents have less contact with the outside world in trading, the state coordination set of community residents has a higher tendency towards homogenization, and there are relatively fewer trading agents playing a leading role, so it is more difficult to meet the conditions for innovation. Even if some innovative activities occur, they can only be at a lower level of innovation intensity.

Fourth, the main obstacles to innovation by trading agents in the trading system are the problems of excessively high innovation risk and cost. The excessively high return risk index is the main reason restricting the innovation power of most countries. Developing capital markets and risk investment systems are effective measures to enhance the market value effect of innovation and reduce the cost of innovation. Developed capital markets can provide enterprises with a responsive and fair market value evaluation system, and risk investment can effectively diversify innovation risks and reduce the innovation costs of innovative enterprises. Developed capital markets are the fertile ground for the development of risk investment systems, and efficient risk investment systems provide strong momentum for the development of capital markets. Both are mutually beneficial and promote each other, and neither can be lacking. In general, finance has given wings to innovation, and modern finance is the cornerstone of a country's innovation capability.

Fifth, a consumer market with sufficient depth and breadth is the fertile ground for technological innovation. The ultimate destination of all products is consumption. A consumer market with enough depth and breadth provides a tempting profit prospect for technological innovation. Theoretically speaking, market depth and breadth are inversely related to the return risk index R_g. The greater the market depth and the wider the breadth, the better the trading agents' expected the benefits e_g and e_b that technological innovation may bring, which helps to reduce the return risk index of technological innovation by trading agents R_g, increasing the enthusiasm for technological innovation in enterprises. It is not difficult to find empirical cases closely related to the economic volume and technological innovation. The United States is the most innovative country in the world and the economy with the deepest consumer market. The coexistence of both in one economy is not a mere coincidence.

Sixth, the compactness of the trading system is conducive to accelerating the speed of technological innovation. In the process of the increasingly compact trading system, the internal trading chain of the system is constantly extended, and the scale of the state coordination set of the trading agent is expanded accordingly. At the same time, the continuously extending trading chain will cross more and more trading communities, absorbing diverse community residents into the state coordination set, forming a companion relationship between the scale expansion and diversity of the state coordination set, which plays a role in lowering the threshold of innovation. This drives the innovation activities of the trading system to be more frequent and widely distributed, and innovation shows an accelerating trend.

15.3 Community Poverty

From the perspective of trading economics, the fundamental cause of poverty is that the trading agent is isolated from the mainstream of the economic cycle for some reason. Community poverty refers to the special phenomenon of group poverty in the trading system. Compared with individual poverty, community poverty poses a greater threat and drag to economic development and social harmony, and deserves more attention. The community in community poverty can be one in the narrow sense, a vast area, or a sovereign country.

In the trading system, trading failures occur, causing the assets of the trading agent to shrink or even go bankrupt and exit the trading network. The losses brought to the trading agent and the impact on the quality of life of the members are obvious. This is a random phenomenon that can never be avoided in the operation of the trading system. Trading failure is not a structural or social issue, but a random occurrence and scattered distribution phenomenon.

15.3.1 *Mainstream Economics Research on Poverty Phenomenon*

For a long time, people had regarded poverty as a social problem, and economists had not paid much attention to it until the 1950s and 1960s.

After World War II, the world economy experienced more than a decade of rapid growth, further widening the gap between developed economies and developing countries, and poverty became more prominent. In 1965, Schultz, the famous American economist and Nobel laureate in economics, had an article published in the *American Economic Review* titled "The Economics of Poverty—Investing in Poor People: An Economist's View", calling for economists to include poverty issues in the research agenda of economics. He evaluated the current state of economic research and said that although economists had done a lot of analysis and research on economic stability and economic growth, there was still a lack of specialized research on poverty issues with theoretical significance in economics. Despite all the statistical data pointing out the distribution of individual income, as well as the age, gender, and family structure of low-income earners and those below a certain standard of consumption, many writings discussing the characteristics of the poor could be easily found. However, these writings had not used economic knowledge to integrate these data into a unified theoretical framework, nor had they proposed any economic hypotheses to explain poverty. Some people's empirical research work was very valuable, but it had not been able to form a unified analysis method to determine the decisive factors of individual income and wealth distribution. However, those who provided statistical data should not be blamed, because economists had not been able to form a theory to guide the organization and analysis of poverty data. Although statisticians had not provided corresponding theories, if someone must have been blamed, it should be economists, because they had not included the theory of poverty issues in the research field of economics.

He also said that it had not always been the case. Malthus established a theory of the causes of poverty and drew a far-reaching pessimistic conclusion based on what he considered to be a normal population growth pattern. Marx established a theoretical system that believed that the wealth created by society was owned by capital owners. Marshall's concept of enterprise included the accompanying relationship between economic progress and poverty eradication; Pigou supplemented this concept with a welfare plan. However, modern economists had not yet found interest in studying poverty. There was a time when there was concern about individual distribution issues, but this enthusiasm had long since faded. Recently, the exquisite social welfare function had become fashionable, but its purpose was not to analyze poverty, and it was useless for explaining and analyzing poverty.

Schultz believed that the reason why economists held such an attitude lied in the basic logic and beliefs of mainstream economics. He thought thatpeople would usually respect such a natural law: poverty would naturally disappear. The few people who were still poor in affluent societies were mostly due to their preferences or circumstances. It was not surprising that there was no place for poverty in the modern economic system.[9]

The causes of poverty are extremely complex, involving institutional, cultural, and historical reasons, as well as economic, financial, and technological factors. There are both external objective factors and personal factors. These numerous reasons are intertwined and interdependent, shrouding the phenomenon of poverty in a fog. To this day, scholars have not reached a consensus on the causes of poverty. Economists can be divided into two groups: one group believe that poverty is the result of social and economic conditions. They emphasize that malnutrition, poor schools, broken families, discrimination, lack of job opportunities, and dangerous environments are key factors determining the fate of the poor.[10] The other group believe that poverty arises from bad personal behaviors—these behaviors are the responsibility of the individual and should be corrected by the poor themselves. In the past few centuries, proponents of laissez-faire have insisted that the poor are those who are not thrifty, are lazy, and drunkards.[11]

The above two viewpoints, emphasizing the external objective factors and internal subjective factors leading to poverty, are two sides of the same coin and cannot be completely separated. However, for a considerable period, the internal cause of poverty has dominated academia. People instinctively believe that poverty is only the business of the poor, individual poverty is the result of laziness and incompetence, and is the loser of competition, while community poverty or national poverty is due to cultural and institutional backwardness, and is caused by ignorance. Whether it is individual poverty or collective poverty, it should be the responsibility of the poor themselves. Harvard professor and economist George Gilder is a supporter of the internal cause. In his *Wealth and Poverty*, he emphasized the necessity of poverty for maintaining the efficient operation of the capitalist economic system: poverty plays a crucial role in maintaining the efficient operation of the economy under the capitalist system. It is the fear of falling into poverty that drives people to work hard and fully utilize all their potential. Wealth will be continuously created, eventually achieving the result of eliminating poverty. Therefore, capitalism is the perfect combination of people's moral aspirations for freedom, fraternity and equality, and the ideal of eliminating poverty and increasing wealth. Gilder believes that an economic thought emphasizing fair distribution is poisoning the capitalist system, and high welfare and high taxes will bring disastrous consequences to the United States, because the interaction between wealth and poverty in capitalist society—poverty can make people work hard to create wealth—has been distorted.[12]

After years of debate, people are increasingly recognizing that although poverty is not unrelated to personal factors, external conditions are the main reason why the poor cannot extricate themselves from the quagmire of poverty. In terms of poverty reduction, the government can not only do something, but it is also obligatory. In September 2000, at the United Nations Summit, 189 member states jointly signed the "United Nations Millennium Declaration", pledging to halve the global poverty level by 2015 (based on the level of 1990).[13] This is the largest international poverty reduction action led by governments in human history, and it can also be seen as the manifestation of the results of economic studies on poverty in real life.

15.3.2 Analysis of Poverty Phenomenon by Trading Economics

The typical characteristics of poverty are that the scale of assets of the trading agent is far below the average level of the trading system, the liquidity of assets is poor, and the financing means are lacking; they are at the edge of the trading network, the trading space is small, and there is a stubborn intergenerational inheritance. After all, the essence of poverty is the lack of trading opportunities, and the manifestation of poverty is the small scale of wealth. Tradings are the way to accumulate wealth, and the lack of trading opportunities will inevitably lead to poverty. Based on this understanding, we will prove the existence of poverty in the trading system through the trading equation, and reveal that the key to structural poverty is community closure.

Suppose Ω_0 is a closed community, a_i are the residents of Ω_0, S_i is the strategy set of the trading agents a_i, $s \in S_i$ is the trading strategy of the trading agents a_i, p_0 and q_0 are respectively the prior probabilities of the situation status of the trading agents a_i about the trading strategy s; R_g is the return risk index of the trading strategy s, A_i^c is the state synergy set of a_i, and μ is the rational structure parameter.

$\because$ Ω_0 is a closed community

$\therefore$ $A_i^c \subset \Omega_0$, that is, the state synergy set of a_i all comes from the community where it is located, and belongs to the subset of Ω_0.

According to the trading equation, the execution probability of the trading strategy s is:

$$\Pr(s) = 1 - R_g \frac{q_0}{p_0} \mu^n \tag{15.3.1}$$

The state synergy set in the closed community has a high tendency to homogenize, and the trading behavior of the reference agent usually has a high consistency. In this case, we can assume that the demonstration parameter of the reference agent $n = 0$, Eq. (15.3.1) simplifies to the following form:

$$\Pr(s) = 1 - R_g \frac{q_0}{p_0} \tag{15.3.2}$$

Suppose $\mathrm{pr}(s) \geq 0.8$ is the necessary condition for executing the trading, that is:

$$1 - R_g \frac{q_0}{p_0} \geq 0.8 \tag{15.3.3}$$

Arrange (15.3.3) to get:

$$R_g \frac{q_0}{p_0} \leq 0.2 \tag{15.3.4}$$

From (15.3.4) we get:

$$\frac{p_0}{q_0} \geq 5R_g \tag{15.3.5}$$

$$\because p_0 + q_0 = 1$$

$$\therefore p_0 \geq 5R_g - 5p_0R_g \tag{15.3.6}$$

Arrange (15.3.6) to get:

$$p_0(1 + 5R_g) \geq 5R_g \tag{15.3.7}$$

$$\therefore p_0 \geq \frac{5R_g}{1 + 5R_g} \tag{15.3.8}$$

Inequality (15.3.8) indicates the trading conditions for residents of a closed community. These are very stringent trading conditions. Even if the trading strategy s has no loss risk, satisfying $e_b(s) = e_0$, and the return risk index shrinks to $R_g = 1$, it is still quite difficult to meet the trading conditions. For the trading agent a_i to execute a risk-free trading strategy s, its initial prior probability p_0 must meet:

$$p_0 \geq \frac{5R_g}{1 + 5R_g} = \frac{5}{6} \approx 0.833 \tag{15.3.9}$$

Condition (15.3.9) indicates that even for risk-free trading strategies, the trading agent must have enough information to execute the trade, and the initial prior probability—that is, the confidence of success must exceed 80%, which is a quite high level of confidence. In a closed community, it is not difficult to infer that the possibility of implementing strategies with a slightly larger return risk index is almost zero. This is a typical characteristic of residents in a closed community, showing a high degree of risk aversion.

In the trading network, each trading agent is part of the trading environment, and its behavior will become a force shaping the trading environment. When the residents of the closed trading community generally show strong risk aversion and are willing to implement very few trades, it means that the trading opportunities that the residents of the closed community can get are also very few. Therefore, the size of the residents' trading strategy set is much smaller than that of the residents of the open community.

We assume that Ω_1 is an open community, a_j is a resident of community Ω_1, S_j is the strategy set of a_j, $s \in S_j$ is the same strategy as a_i; the prior probabilities about the trading situation are p_1 and q_1, A_j^c is the state coordination set of trading agent a_j. We assume that community Ω_1 and community Ω_0 have the same rational structure parameters.

Now, let's examine the execution probability of the same trading strategy s by the trading agent a_j in the open community Ω_1. According to the trading equation, the execution probability of a_j for the trading strategy s is as follows:

$$\Pr(s) = 1 - R_g \frac{q_1}{p_1} \mu^n \tag{15.3.10}$$

Similarly, if the minimum action condition of a_j is $\text{pr}(s) \geq 0.8$, we get from (15.3.10):

$$1 - R_g \frac{q_1}{p_1} \mu^n \geq 0.8 \tag{15.3.11}$$

After rearranging (15.3.11), we get:

$$R_g \frac{q_1}{p_1} \mu^n \leq 0.2$$

$$\frac{p_1}{q_1} \geq 5 R_g \mu^n$$

$$\because\ p_1 + q_1 = 1$$

$$\therefore\ p_1 \geq \frac{5 R_g \mu^n}{1 + 5 R_g \mu^n} \tag{15.3.12}$$

From Eqs. (15.3.8) and (15.3.12), we can derive the ratio of the minimum prior probability of trading in closed community to that in open community when the same trading strategy s points to trading:

$$\frac{Min(p_0)}{Min(p_1)} = \frac{\frac{5R_g}{1+5R_g}}{\frac{5R_g\mu^n}{1+5R_g\mu^n}} \tag{15.3.13}$$

Organizing (15.3.13):

$$\frac{Min(p_0)}{Min(p_1)} = \frac{5R_g\left(1 + 5R_g\mu^n\right)}{5R_g\mu^n\left(1 + 5R_g\right)}$$

$$\frac{Min(p_0)}{Min(p_1)} = \frac{1 + 5R_g\mu^n}{\mu^n\left(1 + 5R_g\right)}$$

$$\frac{Min(p_0)}{Min(p_1)} = \frac{1 + 5R_g\mu^n}{\mu^n + 5R_g\mu^n} \tag{15.3.14}$$

$\because\ 0 < \mu < 1, \therefore$ with n increases, $R_g\mu^n << 1$

$$\therefore\ \frac{Min(p_0)}{Min(p_1)} \approx \frac{1}{\mu^n} \tag{15.3.15}$$

According to the rational structure parameters generally accepted by people, we can get more specific results from (15.3.15):

$$\frac{Min(p_0)}{Min(p_1)} \approx \left(\frac{\eta}{\lambda}\right)^n = \left(\frac{0.8}{0.2}\right)^n = 4^n \tag{15.3.16}$$

The prior probability condition represents the threshold of trading execution. The higher the trading threshold, the fewer trades the trading agent can implement. Equation (15.3.16) reflects the difference in trading opportunities between closed and open communities, with a ratio of up to 4^n, indicating that the trading opportunities in open communities are several times that of closed communities. The more open the community, the more frequent the cross-regional trading activities of community residents, the longer the trading chain, the more significant the diversity of the state coordination set, and the number of demonstrations of the state coordination set n increases accordingly. The trading opportunities in open communities further increase, and the distance from closed communities will be even greater.

The trading set of community residents is the result of the joint creation of community residents. When all residents are in a state of high-risk aversion, it is impossible to have sufficient trading opportunities within the community. There is a mutual mapping relationship between trading opportunities and the trading set of residents. According to Eq. (15.3.16), we can analogize the comparison of the scale of strategy sets of two types of community residents:

$$\frac{|S_0|}{|S_1|} \approx \frac{1}{4^n} \tag{15.3.17}$$

In Eq. (15.3.17), $|S_0|$, $|S_1|$ represents the scale of the trading strategy set $|S|$, that is, the number of strategies carried. Equation (15.3.17) shows the huge gap between the trading strategy set of closed community residents and that of open community residents. What is even more surprising is that the open community is in a process of rapid evolution, while the closed community will be locked in a high stability state. As time goes on, the gap in trading opportunities between the two will rapidly widen. When the demonstration parameter of the open community is $n = 1$, the gap in trading opportunities between the two types of communities is 4 times; when the demonstration parameter of the open community is $n = 2$, the gap in trading opportunities between the two types of communities quickly expands to 16 times; and when the demonstration parameter of the open community is $n = 3$, the gap in trading opportunities between the two types of communities is as high as 64 times; if the demonstration parameter of the open community is $n = 4$, the gap in trading opportunities between the two types of communities is as high as 256 times, and the trading opportunities of closed community residents are only 1/256 of that of open community residents. How rapid is the acceleration of the gap between closed and open communities!

A graph can more intuitively show the evolution of the gap in trading opportunities between the two types of communities (Fig. 15.5).

Fig. 15.5 Multiple curve of trading opportunities

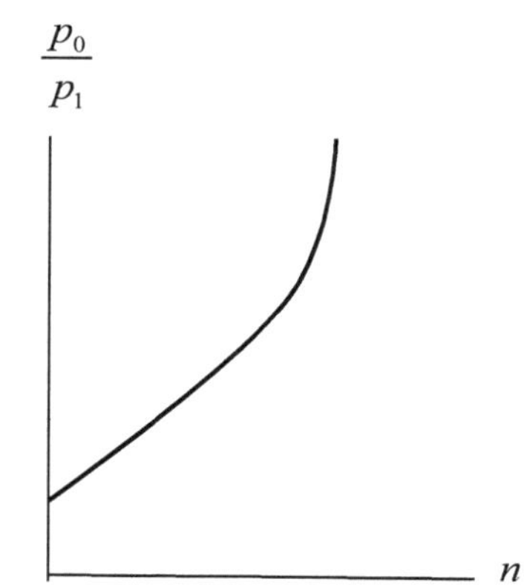

Trading is the source of wealth. The fewer trading opportunities, the poorer the residents. Equation (15.3.17) reveals how the phenomenon of community poverty appears in the evolution process of the trading system. It proves a profound conclusion: **Isolation is the fundamental cause of poverty in communities. Isolated communities are segregated from the mainstream trading system, completely detached from the main course of the evolution of the trading system, forming a self-stabilizing micro-environment. Isolation leads to the characteristic of residents being highly risk-averse, and the stubborn conservative state determines that the demand for financial services in isolated communities is scarce, and the process of community financialization is much slower compared to that in open communities. This trading state derived from isolation limits the choice of trading agents, further strengthens the isolation of the community, and ultimately leads to a vicious cycle**. In this case, no matter how advanced the trading system evolves, if there is no external force intervention, the isolated community will still maintain a stable state, being locked in the poverty trap for a long time.

Looking at the situation in real society, most of the poor areas are in the peripheral far away from the economic center, isolated from the outside world. In the vast developing countries, including China, most of the poor population live in rural areas, especially in remote mountainous areas. The common geographical characteristics of poor areas are inconvenient transportation, very little per capita land that can be irrigated, low education level of residents, and poor health and medical conditions, forming an almost completely isolated survival state. Urban poverty does not conform to the general law of poverty on the surface, that is, it is isolated from the mainstream of the trading network and is in a relatively closed state. In fact, although living in the bustling city, the poor population in the city have nothing to do with high-income jobs and investment activities due to restrictions on their educational background, family savings, etc.. In Trading Economics, employment itself is also a kind of trading, wealth distribution is always tilted towards mainstream jobs, and low-income jobs represent the marginalization of trading agents. In modern society, family investment is a key way to share the growth of social wealth, and families without investment are destined to become the poor. The poor population in the city generally live in slums, forming closed "islands" in the city. The high crime rates and poor sanitation conditions are not conducive to the growth of children, and once they develop bad habits, they will become a further cause of poverty.

Behind the phenomenon of poverty is the positive feedback strengthening mechanism between poverty and information islands. Isolation leads to disconnection from the trading system, and trading with the outside world is decreasing day by day. With the decline in trading volume, the amount of information exchange with the outside world also decreases proportionally. The reduction of information, whether for a single trading agent or for a group, is fatal, leading to a series of information deficiency syndromes, from the shrinkage of the strategy set of trading, to the conservative trend of trading status, to the strengthening of a series of constraints, ultimately locking a region or country firmly in poverty. Poverty leads to the thinning of the trading network in a region, becoming an isolated information island in the trading network.

15.4 Gambler Behavior

Gambler behavior is widespread in all aspects of human social life, and it can even be said that gambler behavior deeply participates in, and to a certain extent, shapes the evolutionary process of human society. Whether it is economic activity or political decision-making, we often see the gambler behavior. However, in the logical system of mainstream economics, gambler behavior is regarded as a typical representative of irrationality. The results of gambler behavior often deviate from the goal of maximizing profits and almost always end in disaster. From the results, gambler behavior indeed seems crazy and contrary to common sense. This is also the main reason why mainstream economics classifies it as an "anomaly" and excludes it from the scope of research.

With the rise of behavioral economics, phenomena regarded as "anomalies" by mainstream economics, including gambler behavior, have gradually attracted the attention of behavioral economists. Behavioral economics uses various behavioral experiments to try to uncover the secrets hidden deep in the gamblers.

15.4.1 Explanation of Gambler Behavior by Behavioral Economics

Behavioral economics provides two explanations for gambler behavior, the first of which is the theory of mental accounting, which is a basic concept of behavioral economics, referring to a virtual account constructed psychologically by decision-makers for different trading activities. Despite its virtual nature, mental accounts have a significant impact on the decision-making of individuals. Behavioral economics believes that the reason why gamblers continue to bet after losing money repeatedly is that the corresponding mental account has not been closed. The mental account will only be settled after it is closed. Although the gambler lost money at the time, with the mental account still open, the gambler believes that the game is not over, and continuing to bet is to recover the loss.

Another characteristic of gamblers is that the more they bet, the bigger they get. The reason given by behavioral economics is that only by increasing the bet can the increasingly large losses be recovered. For the gamblers' wasteful nature, behavioral economics believes that gamblers have multiple mental accounts, with their own principal belonging to one account, and the money won through gambling belonging to another account. Gamblers see these as two completely unrelated accounts, not considering the money won from gambling as their own.

Another theoretical path of behavioral economics is the sunk cost theory, which first appeared in mainstream economics. As early as before 1900, economists began to use the concept of sunk costs. It was used in the 19th-century works on agriculture and railway management.[14] The classic textbook *Economics* written by Paul A. Samuelson and William D. Nordhaus in 1948 also discussed sunk costs. However, the concept of sunk costs did not have its own position in the framework of neoclassical economics. As Allan A. Schmid, author of *Institutional and Behavioral Economics* said, economics professors in universities would tell students that sunk costs should be ignored by decision-makers.[15] But in behavioral economics, sunk costs have found their own place, becoming a powerful tool for behavioral economics to explain many "anomalous" phenomena.

Sunk costs refer to the costs that do not change whether they are consumed or used. They are related to fixed costs, but there are differences between the two. Sunk costs are irrelevant to the profits of a company and the utility of consumers, which is the main reason why sunk costs are marginalized in mainstream economics.

Behavioral economics research has found that although sunk costs are useless in accounting, they often play an indispensable role in the actual actions of trading agents. The "sunk cost fallacy" is a powerful proof. It refers to the behavior of people continuing to invest additional funds to save sunk costs, resulting in greater losses. A typical case in this regard is the supersonic passenger plane jointly developed by France and the UK. The development process was very difficult, the costs were repeatedly added, and the only reason for the additional funds in the later period was the sunk costs that had already been invested in the early stage. This case is so typical that people also call it the "Concorde Paradox".

Behavioral economics believes that gambler behavior is a typical sunk cost fallacy. In order to recover the lost money, the sunk cost effect will drive the gambler to keep increasing the bet. "From the moment he lost his first bet, he couldn't help but want to get a return. So, he continued to invest, continued to invest… and in the end, he ended up bankrupt."[16]

The sunk cost effect not only works in casinos, but also in the stock market. Investors insist on increasing investment to recover the already sunk costs, which are all manifestations of the sunk cost effect.

Behavioral economics has found that the manifestation of gambling varies greatly among individuals. Even under the same circumstances, some people may quickly enter a gambler state, while others will not. The common reason for this difference comes from the Dunning-Kruger effect.[17] Those who are less capable but more confident are more likely to believe that they have better luck than others. They believe that they have mastered the mystery with a small sample observation when facing complex and disorderly phenomena.[18]

15.4.2 Explanation of Gambler Behavior by Trading Economics

Assume a_i is any agent in the trading system T, s is a strategy that the trading agent a_i can repeatedly implement, and ν_0 is the input required when implementing the trading strategy s, similar to the bet placed by the gambler. The initial state of the trading agent a_i when implementing the strategy s is that the situation H presents a friendly state g and an unfriendly state b with prior probabilities p, q both being $\frac{1}{2}$. When the situation H is friendly g, the trading agent will gain several times the input cost ν_0 in returns, that is, $e_g = k\nu_0, k > 1$, and k represents the odds of the bet in gambling activities. When the situation H is unfriendly b, the loss of the trading agent is the initial input ν_0, that is, $e_b = -\nu_0$. When the trading agent a_i repeatedly implements the trading strategy s, the input and return structure remains unchanged.

Assume that the reasonable return rate of the community Ω where the trading agent a_i is located is r_0. Given the universality of the law of diminishing marginal returns, it is assumed that the agreed return rate r_0 is a decreasing function of the initial cost ν_0, that is, $r_0 = r(\nu_0)$, $\frac{\partial r_0}{\partial \nu_0} < 0$. Thus, the agreed return is $e_0 = r(\nu_0)\nu_0$. Obviously, the basic condition that induces the trading agent to enter the gambler mode is that the expected return rate of the trading strategy s is much higher than the reasonable return rate r_0, that is, $k >> r_0$.

Now we analyze how the trading agent a_i will choose a trading strategy after repeatedly failing for m times and losing an amount of $m\nu_0$. According to the law of large numbers, the more the probability deviates from the central value, the greater the possibility of probability callback. Facing the trading situation H, the initial prior probability of the trading agent a_i is $p^1 = q^1 = \frac{1}{2}$. When the situation H continuously presents an unfriendly state for m times, the trading agent a_i has a reason to infer that the probability of the situation H presenting again an unfriendly state b will significantly decrease, while the probability of presenting a friendly state g will rapidly increase. The probability of the trading situation H presenting an unfriendly attitude for the $m + 1$ time is inversely proportional to the number of consecutive occurrences m of b. From this, we obtain the prior probability as follows:

$$q^{m+1} = \frac{1}{2m+2}, \ p^{m+1} = 1 - \frac{1}{2m+2} \quad m = 0, 1, 2 \ldots \tag{15.4.1}$$

Assume that the number of agents implementing trading strategy s in the community Ω where the trading agent a_i is located is n_0, and the rational structure parameter of the community is $\mu = \frac{1}{4}$.

Based on the above analysis, we can calculate the return risk index of the trading agent a_i when implementing the trading strategy s for the $m + 1$ time:

$$R_g = \frac{e_g - e_b}{e_g - e_0} = \frac{kv_0 - (-v_0)}{kv_0 - r(v_0)v_0} \tag{15.4.2}$$

Arrange (15.4.2) to get:

$$R_g = \frac{k+1}{k - r(v_0)} \tag{15.4.3}$$

According to the trading equation, we calculate the probability of the trading agent a_i implementing the trading strategy s for the $m + 1$ time:

$$\Pr^{m+1}(s) = 1 - R_g \frac{q^{m+1}}{p^{m+1}} \mu^{n_0} = 1 - \frac{k+1}{k - r(v_0)} \frac{\frac{1}{2m+2}}{1 - \frac{1}{2m+2}} \mu^{n_0} \tag{15.4.4}$$

Arrange (15.4.4) to get:

$$\Pr^{m+1}(s) = 1 - \frac{1}{4^{n_0}} \frac{k+1}{k - r(v_0)} \frac{1}{2m+1} \tag{15.4.5}$$

Gambler behavior has three distinct characteristics: one is the spirit of never admitting defeat, fighting more and more bravely despite repeated defeats. Even if they are repeatedly frustrated, gamblers always stick to their original trading strategies and gamble more as they lose. This is the most representative characteristic of gambler behavior, and is often seen as a manifestation of gambling addiction. The second is the greedy characteristic, only looking at profits and ignoring risks. Ignoring risks is a basic character trait of gamblers, and behind it is the unrestrained manifestation of human greed on gamblers. The third is the reckless style of gambling more and more, and sinking the boat. Gambler behavior is often more gambling as you lose, and more gambling as you gamble. After repeated failures, gamblers always fantasize about a lonely throw and turn the tide. However, it is this reckless style that ultimately leads to the tragic end of the gambler's family. In fact, the seemingly irrational characteristics of gambler behavior still conform to the logic of human rational behavior. The problem lies in the decision-maker's lack of deep understanding of the changes in the situation and the simplification of the random process. Based on the results given by Eq. (15.4.5), we can analyze the logic behind the characteristics of gambler behavior one by one.

From Eq. (15.4.5), we know that after the gambler has continuously failed for m times, the probability of continuing to implement the trading strategy s, that is, the probability of continuing to bet, is an increasing function of the number of failures

m. That is, the more failures m, the higher the probability of continuing to bet. This result is exactly the spirit of the gambler's repeated defeats and more bravery.

From Eq. (15.4.5), we know that the probability of the gambler continuing to bet is an increasing function of the odds k. The higher the odds k, the greater the temptation for gamblers, so regardless of the risk of failure, gamblers are willing to try their luck. This shows that the key reason for gamblers to ignore risks is the temptation of high returns, and the gambler's risky behavior is a rational decision after careful calculation.

In Eq. (15.4.5), the probability that tempts gamblers to continue betting is a function of the increase in stakes. In the eyes of gamblers, when the odds are in their favor, the rational decision should be to increase the bet as much as possible; only in this way can they fully utilize the odds to achieve maximum returns. After continuous losses, gamblers will increasingly believe in the law of large numbers that the next time is the opportunity to turn the tide, and will increase the bet. This is the basic logic of the gambler's reckless behavior.

In addition, Eq. (15.4.5) also explains why gambling behavior always presents in a congregated form, that is, the phenomenon of group gambling. From Eq. (15.4.5), it can be seen that when the demonstration parameter n_0 increases, the probability of the trading agent a_i participating in gambling will rapidly increase. In this regard, under the same conditions, we can calculate the increase in the probability of a_i participating in the game with each additional person on n_0.

According to Eq. (15.4.5), we can calculate the probability of a person entering the game for the first time under the demonstration of n_0 people:

$$\Pr(s) = 1 - \frac{1}{4^{n_0}} \frac{k+1}{k - r(v_0)} \tag{15.4.6}$$

When the demonstration parameter increases by 1 person, the probability of the trading agent a_i entering the game is:

$$\Pr'(s) = 1 - \frac{1}{4^{n_0+1}} \frac{k+1}{k - r(v_0)} \tag{15.4.7}$$

The marginal effect of the demonstration parameter is calculated from (15.4.6) and (15.4.7):

$$\Delta \Pr(s) = \frac{1}{4^{n_0}} \frac{k+1}{k - r(v_0)} - \frac{1}{4^{n_0+1}} \frac{k+1}{k - r(v_0)} \tag{15.4.8}$$

After rearranging (15.4.8), we get:

$$\Delta \Pr(s) = \frac{3}{4^{n_0+1}} \frac{k+1}{k - r(v_0)} \tag{15.4.9}$$

From (15.4.9), we can get the cumulative effect produced by the demonstration parameter $n_0 + 1$:

$$\sum \Delta \Pr(s) = \sum_{1}^{n_0} \frac{3}{4^{n_0+1}} \frac{k+1}{k - r(v_0)} \tag{15.4.10}$$

After rearranging (15.4.10), we get:

$$\sum \Delta \Pr(s) = \frac{1}{4}\left(1 - \frac{1}{4^{n_0}}\right) \frac{k+1}{k - r(v_0)} \tag{15.4.11}$$

Equation (15.4.11) shows the casino effect that the larger the casino, the more it can attract people. When a country becomes a casino, almost no one can resist the temptation of speculation. The tulip bubble event that occurred in the Netherlands in the seventeenth century is a strong evidence. Tulips were originally a kind of flower produced in Turkey. Introduced into the Netherlands in the early seventeenth century, they were subsequently regarded as a symbol of wealth and glory by the upper class. Speculators found business opportunities in it, hoarded a lot, and drove up prices. After a period of brewing and fermentation, the speculation of tulips had become a trend throughout the Netherlands by 1635. At the same time, the price also skyrocketed to a crazy level. After more than two years of madness, the tulip market suddenly collapsed, and the price fell by 90% in just six weeks. The tulip bubble is the first recorded bubble event in human history, and it is also a case of nationwide gambling in human society. The newly risen Dutch Empire also declined in this tumultuous bubble event.

The rigorous argument about gambling behavior shows that gambler behavior fully conforms to the paradigm of rational behavior, and it also explains that the gambler mentality is widely present in the decision-making process of trading agents. Of course, the three typical characteristics of gambler behavior do not always appear in people's decision-making process, but will appear and disappear from time to time with certain emphasis. In the stock market, investors often continue to add investment to stocks that are already deeply trapped, in order to dilute the cost per share and prepare for the rise in stock prices. This is the manifestation of the gambler's unyielding spirit in stock investment. In fact, when people face major interest choices, people often unconsciously enter the gambler behavior mode due to constraint by incomplete information. This is a helpless choice for people to maximize their interests, and it is also a wise move.

Through the explanation of the mechanism of gambler behavior, we can see the different logical paths chosen by trading economics and behavioral economics. Behavioral economics focuses on the psychological process of people's decision-making, providing an empirical psychological basis for gambler behavior. Trading economics starts from the general principles of trading, and through rigorous logical deduction, incorporates gambler behavior into the law system commonly followed by trading behavior. With their own characteristics and complementary to each other, the two theoretical systems have enriched people's cognitive levels of the gambler phenomenon.

15.5 The Phenomenon of Industrial Agglomeration

Industrial agglomeration is a key factor shaping the uneven distribution characteristics of the trading network industry, and has always received widespread attention from economists. Alfred Marshall and Michael E. Porter have very in-depth analyses in their works.[19] In Chap. 11 of their book, the theme of industrial agglomeration is also discussed in the "Industry Cluster Form Induced by Synergy Constraints". Here we try to use the trading equation to analyze the phenomenon of industrial agglomeration, in order to have a deeper and thorough understanding of the mechanism of its occurrence.

15.5.1 The Process of Industrial Agglomeration

Ω is any trading community in the trading system. Assume that at time step t, the industrial distribution of the trading community Ω is in equilibrium, with no industry having a clear advantage in the trading community Ω. b_i is any subject in the trading community that needs to choose an investment strategy, where, s_1, s_2 are any two investment strategies on the trading strategy set of b_i. Under the existing industrial distribution trend in the trading community Ω, the return risk indices of investment strategies s_1 and s_2 have no significant difference, that is:

$$R_g(s_1) \approx R_g(s_2) \tag{15.5.1}$$

According to the assumption of the trading community's industrial distribution trend, on the state synergy set of b_i, the nu.

mber of leading agents n_1 and n_2 of investment strategies s_1 and s_2 are also at a comparable level, that is:

$$n_1 \approx n_2 \tag{15.5.2}$$

In the trading community Ω, since there is no obvious tendency in the industrial distribution, we can infer that on the information set of the trading agent b_i, the information about investment strategies s_1, s_2 is roughly equivalent in terms of saturation and content direction, and the prior probabilities formed by this p_i and q_i do not have significant differences.

According to the trading Eq. (14.3.27), the probabilities of the trading agent b_i choosing investment strategies s_1, s_2 are as follows:

$$\Pr(s_1) = 1 - R_g(s_1)\frac{q_i}{p_i}\mu^{n_1} \tag{15.5.3}$$

$$\Pr(s_2) = 1 - R_g(s_2)\frac{q_i}{p_i}\mu^{n_2} \tag{15.5.4}$$

From the industrial distribution pattern of the trading community Ω, it can be seen that the probabilities of the trading agent b_i choosing investment strategies s_1, s_2 are roughly equivalent, that is:

$$\Pr(s_1) \approx \Pr(s_2) \tag{15.5.5}$$

If the trading situation H of the trading community Ω does not change significantly at time step $t + 1$, the trading community will continue to maintain a balanced distribution of industries. As time evolves, the industrial structure of the trading community Ω will fluctuate randomly around the balanced pattern.

At time step $t+1$, if the trading situation H changes significantly, according to the resource endowment characteristics of the trading community Ω, the change in the trading situation H will tilt towards the investment strategy s_1, causing a significant decrease in the return risk index of the investment strategy s_1, thereby changing the relationship between the investment strategies s_1 and s_2:

$$R_g(s_1) < R_g(s_2) \tag{15.5.6}$$

All other things being equal, the trading agent b_i will also tilt in the choice of investment strategies:

$$\Pr(s_1) = 1 - R_g(s_1)\frac{q_i}{p_i}\mu^{n_1} > 1 - R_g(s_2)\frac{q_i}{p_i}\mu^{n_2} = \Pr(s_2) \tag{15.5.7}$$

If the change in the trading situation H is strong enough to make the trading agent b_i meet the action conditions in the execution probability of the investment strategy s_1, that is:

$$\Pr(s_1) \geq P^* \tag{15.5.8}$$

In Eq. (15.5.8), P^* represents the minimum execution probability value of the action. When condition (15.5.8) is met, the trading agent b_i will be added to s_1 industry. At time step $t + 1$, due to the actions of the trading agent b_i, the industry distribution of the trading community Ω undergoes a slight change, the equilibrium relationship of (15.5.2) is broken, and a new relationship appears:

$$n_1 + 1 > n_2$$

The choice of the trading agent b_i has a very limited impact on the industrial structure of the trading community Ω, and it is easily obliterated by subsequent random fluctuations. After the passage of time, at time step $t + \tau$, the investors accumulated by the investment strategy s_1 increased from n_1 to $n_1 + k_1$, and the investors accumulated by the investment strategy s_2 increased from n_2 to $n_2 + k_2$. Under the continuous favorable effect of the trading situation H on the investment strategy s_1, the investment strategy s_1 forms a significant advantage in the industry distribution of the trading community, that is:

$$k_1 >> k_2$$

At time step $t + \tau$, we examine the probability of any investment agent b_j in the trading community Ω choosing strategy s_1 and s_2.

$$\Pr(s_1) = 1 - R_g(s_1)\frac{q_j}{p_j}\mu^{n_1+k_1} \quad (15.5.9)$$

$$\Pr(s_2) = 1 - R_g(s_2)\frac{q_j}{p_j}\mu^{n_2+k_2} \quad (15.5.10)$$

Obviously, under the current situation, the trading agent b_j will tend to invest in strategy s_1, that is:

$$\Pr(s_1) >> \Pr(s_2) \quad (15.5.11)$$

In the process of industrial agglomeration, if there is an agglomeration threshold K^*, and the following conditions are met:

$$k_1 \geq K^* \quad (15.5.12)$$

The investors in the trading community Ω are no longer disturbed by small random fluctuations when making investment decisions, ensuring that the execution probability of the investment strategy s_1 meets the action conditions:

$$\Pr(s_1) = 1 - R_g(s_1)\frac{q_j}{p_j}\mu^{n_1+k_1} \geq 1 - R_g(s_1)\frac{q_j}{p_j}\mu^{K^*} \geq P^* \quad (15.5.13)$$

When the industrial agglomeration condition (15.5.13) is met, the industrial distribution in the trading community Ω will no longer be disturbed by random disturbances, showing an accelerated agglomeration trend, and the scale of the industry s_1 rapidly expands in the trading community Ω.

Industrial agglomeration is usually composed of core enterprises and supporting service enterprises. The core enterprises of industrial agglomeration are at the center of the trading ecology, creating a demand market for supporting service enterprises. Accompanied by an increase in the number of core enterprises investing in s_1, the market demand for supporting services is also rapidly growing. Supporting service enterprises are distributed in many segmented markets, which we uniformly mark as s_1' for simplicity. Let b_l be any trading agent looking for investment opportunities in the trading community Ω. As the s_1' market expands, the corresponding return risk index $R_g(s_1')$ will show a continuous downward trend. As known from the trading equation, the probability of trading agent b_l choosing investment strategy s_1' increases as the return risk index decreases:

$$\Pr(s_1') = 1 - R_g(s_1')\frac{q_l}{p_l}\mu^{n_1'} \tag{15.5.14}$$

In Eq. (15.5.14), n_1' represents the number of trading agents in the trading community Ω that have already invested in strategy s_1'. All other things being equal, after the return risk index $R_g(s_1')$ drops to a certain level, the investment strategy s_1' will meet the action requirements of the trading agent b_l:

$$\Pr(s_1') \geq P^* \tag{15.5.15}$$

Over time, the trading community Ω will form an industry cluster with s_1 as the core and s_1' as supporting services. Within the industry cluster, the larger the scale of the core enterprise group, the more complete the supporting services, the higher the operation efficiency of the industry cluster, and the stronger the competitiveness released to the outside world.

15.5.2 Scale of Industrial Agglomeration

The scale of industrial agglomeration depends on the number of core enterprises, and the equilibrium number of core enterprises is exactly compatible with the demand provided by the trading system for this industry. At the micro level, companies within the industry cannot directly obtain total demand information, but can only perceive the market supply and demand situation through the valuation of the return risk index. With the increase in the number of core enterprises, the internal competition of industrial agglomeration becomes more and more intense, and the return risk index of each enterprise rises accordingly, becoming a barrier to prevent new investors from entering. The equilibrium scale of industrial agglomeration appears at the position where the probability of the trading agent's investment strategy execution is exactly equal to the critical probability P^*. Suppose the number of core enterprises in the trading industry cluster is N_1, b_k is any agent in the trading community Ω that has not entered the industry cluster, and the situation H that may be faced by the investment strategy s_1 has no clear tendency, then $p_k = q_k$. According to the trading equation, the execution probability of trading agent b_k regarding investment strategy s_1 is:

$$\Pr(s_1) = 1 - R_g(s_1)\frac{q_k}{p_k}\mu^{N_1'} \tag{15.5.16}$$

Substituting the known conditions into (15.5.16) we get:

$$\Pr(s_1) = 1 - R_g(s_1)\mu^{N_1'} \tag{15.5.17}$$

From the conditions of the trading agent's actions, it is known that when the execution probability of the trading agent b_k meets the following conditions, the trading agent b_k will invest in s_1 and join the ranks of the core enterprises.

$$\Pr(s_1) = 1 - R_g(s_1)\mu^{N_1'} > P^* \tag{15.5.18}$$

If the probability condition (15.5.18) is met, the industry agglomeration with s_1 as its core will continue to grow. From Eq. (15.5.18), it is known that the return risk index $R_g(s_1)$ needs to meet the following conditions:

$$R_g(s_1)\mu^{N_1} < 1 - P^* \tag{15.5.19}$$

After rearranging, we get:

$$R_g(s_1) < \frac{1 - P^*}{\mu^{N_1}} \tag{15.5.20}$$

Similarly, when the return risk index meets the following conditions, there will be no new investors entering, but there is a risk of loss from the existing core enterprises. In this case, the industry agglomeration centered on s_1 will stop expanding and fall into a state of contraction.

$$R_g(s_1) > \frac{1 - P^*}{\mu^{N_1}} \tag{15.5.21}$$

Combining conditions (15.5.20) and (15.5.21), we can obtain the equilibrium conditions of industry agglomeration.

$$R_g^*(s_1) = \frac{1 - P^*}{\mu^{N_1}} \tag{15.5.22}$$

In the above equation, $R_g^*(s_1)$ represents the equilibrium value of the return risk index of industry agglomeration.

In the process of industry agglomeration, the return risk index has a close relationship with the number of main bodies N_1 entering strategy s_1. Every market has a saturation point of supply and demand balance. Assuming that the market saturation point faced by s_1 is N_1^0, before the scale of industry agglomeration reaches the market saturation point, the expansion of the scale of industry agglomeration will inevitably drive the deepening of internal division of labor in the industry, thereby reducing the production cost of core enterprises and enhancing the external competitiveness of industry agglomeration. When the scale of industry agglomeration crosses the market saturation point, the internal competition pressure of the industry will rapidly increase, the expected return of the core enterprises will decrease, and the return risk index will increase.

When $N_1 < N_1^0$, $R_g(s_1)$ is a decreasing function of the number of entry agents N_1, satisfying:

$$\frac{\Delta R_g(s_1)}{\Delta N_1} < 0 \tag{15.5.23}$$

When $N_1 > N_1^0$, $R_g(s_1)$ is an increasing function of the number of entry agents N_1, that is:

$$\frac{\Delta R_g(s_1)}{\Delta N_1} > 0 \tag{15.5.24}$$

From the equilibrium condition of industry agglomeration (15.5.22), it is known that the equilibrium scale of industry agglomeration will appear on the right side of the market saturation point N_1^0, that is:

$$N_1^* > N_1^0 \tag{15.5.25}$$

According to the equilibrium condition (15.5.23) and the phase change relationship of the return risk index (15.5.23), (15.5.24), we can obtain the evolution trajectory of industry agglomeration.

Figure 15.6 intuitively shows that the size of the industry agglomeration scale N_1^* depends on the specific location of the market saturation point N_1^0. The higher the market saturation point of an industry, the larger the potential agglomeration scale. In addition, the scale of industrial agglomeration is also affected by the effective production scale. Constrained by the characteristics of production technology, the effective production scale of different industries varies greatly. Generally, the effective production scale of the heavy industry is larger. The effective production scale of industries such as petrochemicals, steel metallurgy, and automobile manufacturing is generally larger, while the effective production scale of light manufacturing such as clothing processing and other industries is relatively smaller. All other things being equal, the larger the effective production scale, the lower the market saturation point, and the smaller the industrial agglomeration equilibrium scale measured by the number of enterprises entering s_1.

The position of the market saturation point is subject to the total demand at two levels. The first is the total demand scale of the whole market. Obviously, if the trading system has very limited total demand for a certain industry, it is impossible to have a large scale of industrial agglomeration at any location in the trading network. The second is the demand scale of the local market. Due to the constraints of commodity circulation costs and information diffusion radius, the market within the trading system will be divided into several adjacent local markets, each covering a range limited within the radius allowed by technical conditions. Under the condition of uniform demand density distribution, the larger the market radius, the larger the

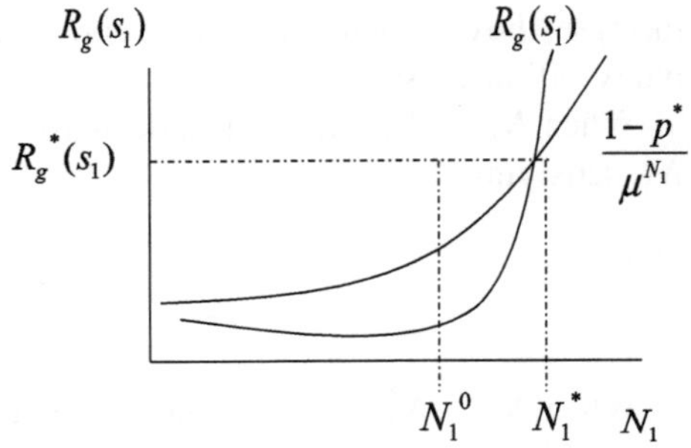

Fig. 15.6 Evolution trajectory of industry agglomeration

local market scale. The demand scale of the local market has a more direct impact on the position of the market saturation point. The larger the scale of the local market, the higher the position of the market saturation point.

The distance between the industrial agglomeration equilibrium point N_1^* and the market saturation point N_1^0 depends on the sensitivity of the return risk to the agglomeration scale $\frac{\Delta R_g(s_1)}{\Delta N_1}$. The greater the sensitivity of return risk, the more sensitive the return risk index within the industrial agglomeration is to the agglomeration scale. After crossing the market saturation point N_1^0, the return risk index will rise rapidly, intersect with the industrial agglomeration action curve $\frac{1-p^*}{\mu^{N_1}}$, and reach the equilibrium state of agglomeration scale. In this scenario, the distance between the industrial agglomeration equilibrium point N_1^* and the market saturation point N_1^0 is very close. On the contrary, the smaller the sensitivity of return risk, the lower the sensitivity of the return risk index of industrial agglomeration to the agglomeration scale, and the further the industrial agglomeration equilibrium point N_1^* is from the market saturation point N_1^0.

The sensitivity of return risk of industrial agglomeration reflects the efficiency of organizational synergy within the industrial agglomeration. The higher the efficiency of organizational synergy, the more obvious the offsetting effect of internal competition costs through synergy advantages within the industry. On the contrary, the lower the efficiency of internal organizational synergy in industrial agglomeration, the very limited internal competition costs that the synergy advantages of industrial agglomeration can offset, thus limiting the further expansion of the scale of industrial agglomeration. We can find that the scale of industrial agglomeration in some locations is very large, while the scale of similar industrial agglomeration in other locations is very limited. The efficiency of organizational synergy is the key factor causing this difference.

Equation (15.5.22) shows that the equilibrium state of industrial agglomeration has a high degree of dynamism. The equilibrium scale of industrial agglomeration highly depends on the changes in the trading situation H. When the trading situation H entering a continuously deteriorating channel, the return risk index of industrial agglomeration $R_g(s_1)$ will rise accordingly, and industrial agglomeration shows a gradually shrinking trend. When the trading situation H maintains a continuous improvement trend, the return risk index of industrial agglomeration $R_g(s_1)$ will decrease accordingly, industrial agglomeration will attract more investors, and the equilibrium scale will continue to expand.

When the trading situation is unfavorable for industrial agglomeration, the return risk index of industrial agglomeration will continue to climb along the rising channel. As can be known from the conditions of industrial agglomeration collapse (15.5.21), the scale of industrial agglomeration will fall into a continuous shrinking trend until the entire industrial cluster completely disperses. The process from prosperity to decline of the heavy industry cluster in the "Rust Belt" of the United States is a strong proof. The "Rust Belt" in the United States was centered around the Great Lakes, including western New York, Pennsylvania, West Virginia, Ohio, northern Illinois, eastern Iowa, and southeastern Wisconsin. This vast area was once the manufacturing center of the United States before the 1970s, covering steel metallurgy, automobile manufacturing, and heavy industry equipment manufacturing, attracting many enterprises to gather here. With the continuous rise in production costs, the once vibrant industrial cluster gradually lost its market competitiveness, and a lot of enterprises either went bankrupt or moved to countries with lower production costs abroad. In 1984, then Democratic presidential candidate Walter Mondale called this declining area the "Rusty Bowl". In the Great Lakes manufacturing center of the United States, Detroit was the most representative, known as the "Motor City" of the country. The world's three major automobile companies—General Motors, Ford Motor Company and Chrysler—were all headquartered here. The famous Fox Theatre, the largest department store in the United States, Hudson's Department Store, and Detroit's "Fifth Avenue" Woodward Avenue were all symbols of Detroit's past prosperity. Due to the decline of the industrial manufacturing industry, Detroit, then the second largest industrial city in the United States, eventually went bankrupt in 2013.

The equilibrium condition (15.5.22) shows that there is a large difference in the stability of industrial agglomerations of different scales. The smaller the scale of the industrial agglomeration, the smaller the equilibrium value of the return risk index, which means that the stability of the industrial agglomeration is worse, and any minor external disturbance may become an obstacle to the continued growth and development of the industrial agglomeration. On the contrary, the larger the scale of the industrial agglomeration, the larger the equilibrium value of the return risk index, and the stronger the resilience of the industrial agglomeration to external shocks.

The equilibrium condition (15.5.22) contains the positive feedback mechanism of industrial agglomeration. When the trading situation H continues to be friendly to the industry s_1, the return risk index $R_g(s_1)$ will show a continuous downward trend. Assume that at time step t, the return risk index is $R_g(s_1)_t$, and at time step $t+1$ the return risk index is $R_g(s_1)_{t+1}$. Due to the impact of trading situation H, the return risk index satisfies $R_g(s_1)_{t+1} \geq R_g(s_1)_t$. With other conditions remaining unchanged, it is known from the trading equation that the trading community Ω will have more trading agents joining the investment ranks of s_1, and the number of leading agents will increase from N_{1t} to N_{1t+1}, that is, $N_{1t+1} > N_{1t}$.

From the equilibrium condition (15.5.22), the condition for the industrial agglomeration to achieve equilibrium at time step t is:

$$R_g^*(s_1)_t = \frac{1 - P^*}{\mu^{N_{1t}}} \tag{15.5.26}$$

The equilibrium condition at time step $t + 1$ is:

$$R_g^*(s_1)_{t+1} = \frac{1 - P^*}{\mu^{N_{1t+1}}} \tag{15.5.27}$$

According to the assumption of bounded rationality,$0 < \mu < 1$

$$\begin{aligned} &\because N_{1t+1} > N_{1t} \\ &\therefore \frac{1 - P^*}{\mu^{N_{1t}}} < \frac{1 - P^*}{\mu^{N_{1t+1}}} \\ &\therefore R_g^*(s_1)_{t+1} > R_g^*(s_1)_t \end{aligned} \tag{15.5.28}$$

Equation (15.5.28) shows that when the trading situation H becomes more friendly, the equilibrium condition for the industrial agglomeration of s_1 is easier to satisfy, the industrial agglomeration will enter a process of accelerated expansion, and a new industrial cluster will quickly form.

When the trading situation H is unfavorable to s_1, it means that the return risk index $R_g(s_1)$ will rise, the original agglomeration equilibrium state will be broken, and the scale of industrial agglomeration will fall into a contraction trend. Assuming that at time step t, the return risk index is $R_g(s_1)_t$, and the return risk index at time step $t+1$ is $R_g(s_1)_{t+1}$. Due to the effect of the trading situation H, the return risk index changes and satisfies $R_g(s_1)_{t+1} \geq R_g(s_1)_t$. If the industrial agglomeration is in equilibrium at time step t, due to the change in the situation, the industrial agglomeration no longer satisfies the equilibrium condition (15.5.22) at time step $t + 1$, and enters the shrinking process, the number of demonstrations decreases,$N_{1t+1} < N_{1t}$.

From the industrial agglomeration equilibrium condition (15.5.22), it can be seen that the above changes will cause the industrial agglomeration equilibrium condition at time step $t + 1$ to increase, requiring s_1 to have a lower return risk index, and it is more difficult to achieve agglomeration equilibrium.

$$R_g^*(s_1)_{t+1} < R_g^*(s_1)_t \tag{15.5.29}$$

From Eq. (15.5.29), it can be inferred that the industrial agglomeration of s_1 will enter an accelerated shrinking process, forming a vicious cycle and leading to the rapid decline of industrial agglomeration.

The existence of positive feedback mechanisms indicates that the process of industrial agglomeration has a great deal of instability. The rise and fall of industrial clusters are highly sensitive to changes in the trading situation, and it is easy to see the rapid gathering and dispersing phenomenon of "its rise is vigorous, and its demise is also sudden."

15.5.3 Conclusions on Industrial Agglomeration Analysis

Through the analysis of the process of industrial agglomeration and the equilibrium scale, we can draw the following four conclusions:

1. Industrial agglomeration is the result of the coupling of the resource endowment characteristics of the trading community and the trading situation. Only when the coupling strength and duration reach a certain standard, the phenomenon of industrial agglomeration will emerge in the trading community. This shows that the phenomenon of industrial agglomeration cannot appear universally in the trading network, but presents a point distribution, emerging in a few trading communities.
2. The form of industrial agglomeration always follows the trajectory of changes in the trading situation and is always in the process of dynamic evolution. Industrial agglomeration inevitably goes through the process of rise and fall. New industrial agglomerations rise with the emergence of new technologies and decline with the replacement of new technologies. The rise and fall of industrial agglomeration constitute an important aspect of the evolution of the trading system;
3. The early process of industrial agglomeration is very fragile and is easily disturbed by external factors. If the government can formulate and implement industrial incentive policies in combination with characteristics of local resource endowment, it will play a very important role in accelerating the formation of industrial agglomeration.
4. Industrial incentive policies not only need to have clear and strong incentive guidance, but also need to be maintained for a long enough time to help industrial agglomeration cross the agglomeration threshold and enter a self-reinforcing virtuous cycle.

Notes

1. Robert J. Shiller (2004) Irrational exuberance (Trans: Liao Li), China Renmin University Press, Beijing, p 172 (in Chinese).
2. Dong Zhiyong (2005) Behavioral Economics, Peking University Press, Beijing, p 248.
3. In fact, greed does not come from animals, but is a unique human nature. Animals never need more than a full meal, nor do they ever need more than physical needs to possess. Only human beings, driven by the motive of trading, can conceive the infinite desire for the possession of wealth. It should be admitted that greed is a byproduct of human civilization. The reason why people are used to attributing their bad things to animals is that animals do not speak, let alone defend themselves.
4. Alan Greenspan (2014) The Map and The Territory (Trans: Yu Jiang), CITIC Press, Beijing.
5. Robert J. Shiller (2004) Irrational exuberance (Trans: Liao Li), China Renmin University Press, Beijing, p 172 (in Chinese).
6. Alan Greenspan (2014) The Map and The Territory (Trans: Yu Jiang), CITIC Press, Beijing, p 52.
7. Alan Greenspan (2014) The Map and The Territory (Trans: Yu Jiang), CITIC Press, Beijing, p 230.

8. As the research progressed, scholars found that the reality was far more complicated than Schumpeter's hypothesis. "In previous years, the vast majority of research and development costs were borne by large corporations. In the last decade, especially with the growing importance of the "new economy" and Internet companies, research and development funding for small businesses has also increased rapidly. Small businesses with fewer than 500 employees account for one-fifth of U.S. R&D spending, while the largest companies spend less than two-fifths. Research also shows that small businesses account for a certain percentage of inventions and innovations. When John Jewkes and his colleagues traced the most important inventions of the twentieth century, they found that less than half of them came from large corporate LABS." Paul Samuelson, William Nordhaus (2008) Economics (Chief Trans: Xiao Chen), 18th edn. Posts and Telecommunications Press, Beijing, p 171.
9. Schultz T W, Investing in poor people: An economist's view. The American Economic Review, 1965, 55(1/2): 510–520.
10. Paul Samuelson, William Nordhaus (2008) Economics (Chief Trans: Xiao Chen), 18th edn. Posts and Telecommunications Press, Beijing, p 343.
11. Paul Samuelson, William Nordhaus (2008) Economics (Chief Trans: Xiao Chen), 18th edn. Posts and Telecommunications Press, Beijing, p 343.
12. Yao Kaijian, Liang Xiaomin (2005) Introduction to the famous works of Western Economics, China Economics Press, Beijing, p 237.
13. Peng Gang, Huang Weiping (2018) Development Economics Course, China Renmin University Press, Beijing, p 323.
14. David R. Jaster (2021) Behavioral Economics (Trans: He Jingtong, Gao Linji), China Machine Press, Beijing, p 19.
15. Alain Smid (2004) Institutional and Behavioral Economics (Trans: Liu Can, Wu Shuirong), China Renmin University Press, Beijing, p 55.
16. Wang Fuyou (2020) Behavioral Economics: Insight into Irrational Behavior in economic life, China Workers Publishing House, Beijing, p 61.
17. In 1999, psychologists Dunning and Kruger published the paper "On How the lack of correct understanding ability leads to overevaluation of self", revealing the law of behavior in the crowd, that is, the lower the ability of people, the more likely to overestimate themselves and show overconfidence. A similar performance is that even people with strong abilities are prone to overconfidence in unfamiliar areas. This is called the Dunning–Kruger effect, after the two authors.
18. This tendency to exaggerate the representation of small samples in the population has been dubbed the decimal principle by Amos Tversky and Daniel Kahneman, referring to the erroneous tendency to violate the law of large numbers.
19. See also: Alfred Marshall (2012) Principles of Economics (Trans: Lian Yunjie), Huaxia Press, Beijing; Michael Porter (2003) Competition Theory (Trans: Gao Dengdi, Li Mingxuan), CITIC Press, Beijing.

Chapter 16
Trading Loop

The self-reinforcing process is a basic form of system circulation and an important force driving system evolution. In the trading system, the competition and survival of the fittest selection process among trading agents is a typical manifestation of the self-reinforcing mechanism. The trading loop is a feedback mechanism with self-reinforcing characteristics formed by the interaction among different trading phases in the trading system. The trading loop to the trading system is like the role of a typhoon cyclone in the meteorological system, which undoubtedly has a very important impact on the operation and evolution of the trading system.

16.1 Concept of Trading Loop

The trading feedback loop (feedback loop), or simply the trading loop, refers to the feedback mechanism with self-reinforcing characteristics formed by the interaction between multiple trading phases in the trading system. The trading loop is a common phenomenon in the operation of the trading system, and the most common trading loop appears in the investment market. Investment demand increases, asset prices rise, more trading agents flood into the bullish phase of the market, asset suppliers increase supply, market turnover amplifies, more trading agents flood into the bullish phase, asset prices rise further, and more potential investors are enticed to enter—this is a typical trading loop. The iterative cycle of the feedback mechanism drives the stock market to rise and fall, resulting in unpredictable market conditions.

The positive feedback mechanism not only dominates the stock market, but also governs the real estate market, bond market, foreign exchange market, and other markets. Even in ordinary consumer markets, trading loop phenomena may occur under certain expectations. When panic begins to wander in the market, the emergence of trading phenomena is not far off. First, prices quietly rise, a portion of highly sensitive consumers begin to increase their purchases, suppliers take the opportunity

Z. Wang, *Trading Economics*, Contributions to Economics,
https://doi.org/10.1007/978-981-99-9875-3_16

to raise prices, consumers' panic is initially confirmed by the market, and more consumers follow suit. As commodity prices continue to rise, market panic intensifies. Consequently, consumers begin to panic buy, and the market quickly descends into chaos. Panic buying often erupts unexpectedly, causing destructive impacts on the trading system.

The trading loop is a typical nonlinear phenomenon with highly dynamic characteristics. Driven by the positive feedback mechanism, both trading volume and trading prices can experience significant fluctuations. Trading loops can be guided by either trading volume or price. Trading volume and trading prices can either follow the same direction of change, i.e., increased trading volume and price rise, decreased trading volume and price fall, or they can follow the opposite direction of change, i.e., increased trading volume and price fall, or decreased trading volume and price rise. The initiation of trading loops can vary, but all trading loops follow the same pattern: trading volume first expands, then contracts; in terms of price, whether it is rising or falling, there will be a price regression process in the latter half of the trading loop. The parabolic trajectory is the basic operation mode of the trading loop.

Trading loops and cascade trading are two closely related trading phenomena, both of which can cause significant fluctuations in the trading system. They are phenomena generated by different mechanisms. Firstly, trading loops are interactive responses between different phases, while cascade trading is the interactive response of trading agents in the same phase. Secondly, the underlying logic of forming trading loops is the interest correlation of different phase agents, and these trading agents obtain the maximum possible benefits through coordinated actions. The underlying logic of cascade trading is the incomplete decision-making information of the trading agents, adopting a strategy to reduce decision-making risks by referencing the behavior information of others.

Trading loops and cascading trades often appear together. Trading loops often involve cascading trades, and cascading trades also rely on the promotion of trading loops. Taking the real estate market as an example, when a part of families with a strong risk preference increase their real estate investment, the market equilibrium is immediately disrupted, and house prices begin to rise. The phenomenon of cascading in the demand phase begins to appear. Early successful investment families have a demonstration effect, and more and more families flood into the demand phase, pushing house prices to rise further. On the other hand, real estate developers occupying the supply phase of the real estate market respond to changes in the demand phase, increase land purchases, and intensify new project development. Under this background, the greater the input of developers, the more trading opportunities they get, and the greater the returns. Following the pace of developers, local governments will also respond by increasing land supply. Steel companies, glass manufacturers, building materials manufacturers, home appliance manufacturers, furniture manufacturers, etc., many phases on the trading network will participate in the response, hoping to get a share of the prosperity of the real estate market. These suppliers from different industries respond to the real estate market situation, which will be reflected in the income of families, and ultimately form a feedback loop with many phases participating on the trading network. It can be seen that in the real estate trading loop, cascading trades not only play an important role in the initial stage of the trading loop, but also the power source of the trading loop.

Trading loops have the characteristics of self-realization and self-reinforcement. As a special phenomenon in the operation of the trading system, the trading loop injects a great deal of instability into the trading system. The self-realization characteristic of the trading loop comes from the synchronous expectations of the trading agents. Once the expectations of trading agents are synchronized, the trading loop will appear.

Robert J. Shiller, a professor of economics at Yale University in the United States and the laureate of the 2013 Nobel Prize in Economics, discussed the formation mechanism of trading loops in the financial market in his book *Irrational Exuberance*. Shiller described that "In feedback loop theory, initial price increases (caused, for example, by the kinds of precipitating factors described in the previous chapter) lead to more price increases as the effects of the initial price increases feed back into yet higher prices through increased investor demand. This second round of price increases feeds back again into a third round, and then into a fourth, and so on. Thus, the initial impact of the precipitating factors is amplified, resulting in much larger price increases than the factors themselves would have suggested." He believed that the repeated, carefully planned scams using pyramid structures in the financial market were controlled experiments that were difficult to replicate in the laboratory. This controlled experiment was a strong proof of the existence of trading loops. He cited the Ponzi scheme that occurred on Wall Street in 1920 (the scam planner was Charles Ponzi) and the Ponzi scheme that occurred in Albania in 1996–1997,[1] "Ponzi schemes, or pyramid schemes, by means of which hoaxers create positive feedback from putative current investment returns to future investment returns. These schemes have been perpetrated so many times that governments have had to outlaw them, yet they still keep popping up. They are particularly interesting since they are, in a way, controlled experiments (controlled by the hoaxer!) that demonstrate characteristics of the feedback that cannot be seen so plainly either in normal markets or in the experimental psychologist's laboratory." He believed that all market bubbles had the same formation mechanism as Ponzi schemes, all of which were amplification processes driven by feedback loops. He said that "It would appear, by extrapolation from examples like those given earlier, that speculative feedback loops that are in effect naturally occurring Ponzi schemes do arise from time to time without the contrivance of a fraudulent manager. Even if there is no manipulator fabricating false stories and deliberately deceiving investors in the aggregate stock market, tales about the market are everywhere. When prices go up a number of times, investors are rewarded sequentially by price movements in these markets, just as they are in Ponzi schemes. There are still many people (indeed, the stock brokerage and mutual fund industries as a whole) who benefit from telling stories that suggest that the market will go up further. There is no reason for these stories to be fraudulent; they need only emphasize the positive news and give less emphasis to the negative." Shiller believed that the trading loop was the key to unraveling the mystery of irregular market movements. "Feedback loop dynamics can generate complex and even apparently random behavior. ...... the apparent randomness of the stock market, the tendency it has to create sudden moves for no apparent reason, might not be so inexplicable after all. The branch of mathematics that studies nonlinear feedback loops, called chaos theory, may be applicable to understanding the complexity of stock market behavior."[2]

16.2 Typical Cases of Trading Loops

In reality, examples of trading loops are very common. For example, after the price of grain rises, the production costs of meat, eggs, and milk will all rise, eventually leading to a general rise in the price of food commodities, and the CPI index will rise. When the CPI increase exceeds a certain level, workers' wages need to be correspondingly increased, leading to an increase in the labor cost of industrial manufactured goods. At this point, the response among phases has not yet established a feedback loop. Only when the prices of agricultural inputs such as fertilizers, pesticides and seeds start to join the price increase sequence, forcing farmers to further raise prices, can the feedback trading loop be constructed, and the trading loop officially starts.

Once the price trading loop starts, it will push up prices faster and more forcefully. Post-World War I Germany provides a typical example of this.[3] In November 1918 when the armistice was declared, Prices in German were already 2.5 times those of the same period in 1914 before the war. The speed of inflation then accelerated, and hyperinflation broke out in 1923, the speed of price increases entering a galloping mode. At the peak of inflation, calculated with the pre-war price index as 100, the price index of 40 basic commodities reached an astronomical number of 143×10^{12}. If drawn out at a normal scale, this column would be as high as 2 million miles.

The spiral effect of chasing each other between price increases and currency demand has formed, so much so that even with the printing press running at full capacity, it could not meet the market's demand for cash. On October 25 in 1923, the cash issuance in just one day reached 120×10^{15} marks, while the demand for the day was 10^{18}, which was eight times the supply capacity. Prices and currency chased each other, and the supply of money was exploding. Correspondingly, the exchange rate of the German mark plummeted rapidly (Table 16.1).

Behind the crazy inflation was a constantly self-reinforcing trading loop. Price increases, currency issuance, exchange rate depreciation, and market speculation formed a mutually reinforcing and mutually promoting trading loop. War was the initial cause of price increases. To meet the needs of the war, resources were tilted towards the military industry. As prices rose, the trading system's demand for money increased, and the German central bank continued to issue money to meet the demand for money, which in turn further promoted price increases, forming the first trading loop of malignant inflation.

At the same time, another trading loop was quietly forming. Price increases and currency issuance led to the devaluation of the German mark. When the market formed a stable expectation of the devaluation of the currency, speculative activities were staged crazily. People borrowed German marks from banks to buy dollars, sold

Table 16.1 US dollar to German mark rate[4]

Year/month	Exchange rate
1914.7	4
1919.1	9
1916.7	14
1920.1	65
1920.7	40
1921.1	65
1921.7	77
1922.1	192
1922.7	493
1923.1	17,972
1923.7	353,412
1923.8	4,620,455
1923.9	98,860,000
1923.10	25,260,208,000
1923.11	4,200,100,000,000

dollars after the mark depreciates, repaid mark loans and obtained speculative profits. The more severe the devaluation of the mark, the higher the speculative profits. This process was replicated and iterated over and over again, with the scale expanding each time, forcing the banking system to rapidly increase the money supply, and further gathering the pressure of currency devaluation.

The third trading loop was formed between wages and prices. In the summer of 1923, under the joint efforts of desperate workers and unions, companies began to adopt a mechanism linking wages to the cost of living index. This added new forces to the already strong inflation trading loop, and the speed of inflation entered a crazier stage (Fig. 16.1).

The trading loop structure that brewed Germany's galloping inflation was very simple, but it had a huge amount of energy, which ultimately destroyed the post-war German economy and became an important inducement to reignite the World War.[5]

The trading loop has a strong power, but it is very fragile. In the trading loop, once a link is blocked, the entire trading loop will reduce its momentum until it stops running. Taking the trading loop of the German inflation as an example, the powerful trading loop consisted of four links: price increases, currency issuance, exchange rate depreciation, and market speculation. As long as any of these links was blocked, the momentum of the trading loop would weaken. If the German government could limit currency issuance or crack down on market speculation in time, the momentum of price increases would weaken.

The 2007 U.S. subprime crisis is another case that shows the powerful power of the trading loop. On March 13, 2007, the U.S. Mortgage Bankers Association announced that the default rate of subprime mortgages in the fourth quarter of 2006 rose from

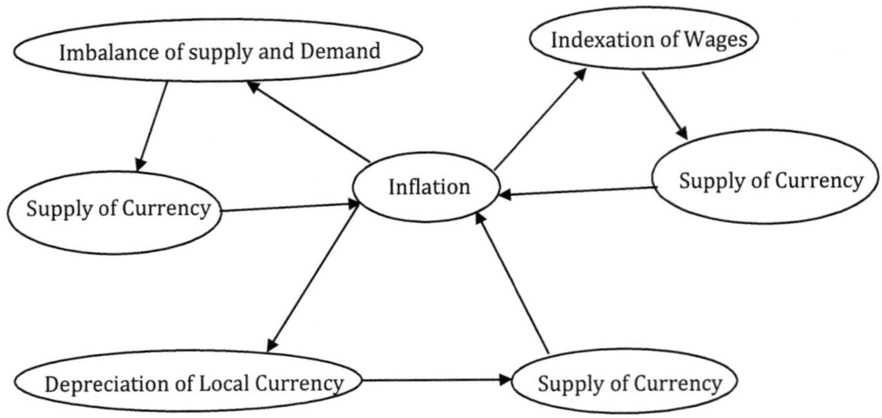

Fig. 16.1. The trading loop of galloping inflation

12.56% in the third quarter to 13.33%, a new high in four years, and the proportion of borrowers losing the right to redeem collateral set a historical record. As soon as the news was released, the Dow Jones Industrial Average fell 242.66 points, and global stock markets followed suit. This was the precursor to the financial tsunami. On April 4, the second-largest subprime mortgage lender in the United States, New Century Financial Corporation, filed for bankruptcy protection, and the subprime crisis officially began.

In the subsequent three months, more than 30 subprime mortgage companies in the United States went out of business or went bankrupt, and several hedge funds that invested in subprime bonds suffered heavy losses. Any financial institution involved in the securitization of subprime loans was severely hit on their balance sheets. On August 6, a US mortgage investment company applied for bankruptcy protection due to rapidly deteriorating loan quality. At this point, the crisis shock wave began to extend beyond the US borders, releasing destructive energy in Europe, Asia, and Australia. On July 30, Germany's IKB Deutsche Industriebank faced financing difficulties; on August 9, BNP Paribas, France's largest bank, announced the freezing of three of its investment funds, suspending subscriptions and redemptions; Union Investment and Frankfurt Trust in Germany also suspended fund redemptions; NIBC Bank in the Netherlands suffered a loss of 1.37 billion euros due to the US subprime crisis. The European financial market was quiet, with a short-term liquidity crisis.

In January 2008, financial institutions announced their operating performance for the fourth quarter of 2007 in succession, and the huge losses of major financial institutions further pushed the crisis to a deeper level. Citigroup lost $98.3 billion; Merrill Lynch lost $98 billion; Washington Mutual lost $18.7 billion. From January 21 to 22, global stock markets generally fell, with the Asia–Pacific stock market falling more than 3%, and the European stock market falling more than 5%.

On February 27, Fannie Mae announced a loss of $35.5 billion for the fourth quarter of 2007; on the 28th, Freddie Mac announced a loss of $24.5 billion for the fourth quarter. Affected by this, the stock prices of US mortgage institutions further shrank significantly. On March 16, Bear Stearns was announced to be acquired by JPMorgan Chase due to its inability to resolve the liquidity crisis.

In early July, Indymac Bank, a US residential mortgage institution, experienced a severe bank run. On September 15, due to severe losses in the subprime business and the failure of the equity sale plan, Indymac Bank was forced to apply for bankruptcy protection. On the same day, Merrill Lynch was acquired by Bank of America. The global financial market experienced a panic drop, with the US stock market opening sharply down 300 points. The Asia–Pacific stock market and the European stock market fell more than 3%.

In September, the American International Group encountered serious liquidity difficulties and was forced to seek assistance from the Treasury Department. At this point, the financial crisis that originated in the subprime loan market eventually evolved into a global financial tsunami.

Looking at the entire process of the international financial crisis, the financial crisis produced four large-scale, intertwined and mutually reinforcing trading loops: the trading loop formed between the real estate market and investment institutions; the trading loop formed between investment institutions and the money market; the trading loop formed between investment institutions and the stock market; and the trading loop formed between the real estate market, investment institutions, money market, and the stock market. Among them, the trading loop between the real estate market and investment institutions is the trigger loop; the real estate market, investment institutions, money market and stock market is the largest trading sub-loop. The composite trading loop composed of four trading sub-circles has a very high response intensity and releases a huge energy shock wave. This is the fundamental reason why a mini-market of just over 100 billion US dollars can produce a devastating financial crisis.

Information dissemination and expected spread play a crucial role in the formation of trading loops. When the U.S. stock market experiences a significant drop or rise, the European stock market tends to follow suit with changes in the same direction. Conversely, changes in the European stock market will also be transmitted to the U.S. stock market. The response mechanism between the two is not based on capital flows or cross-market arbitrage, but through mutual influence of information.

A trading loop is a broad interactive pattern. Its essence is the special reaction pattern between trading agents, and the connection between agents in the trading system is the basis for the emergence of trading loops. The tighter the trading system, the greater the probability of a trading loop occurring.

16.3 Operation Mechanism of Trading Loops

The operation mechanism of trading loops includes two types: trading linkage mechanism and trading demonstration mechanism. The trading linkage mechanism falls into the category of direct effects, while the trading demonstration mechanism falls into the category of indirect effects. The two mechanisms complement each other, forming the powerful impact and dynamic changes of trading loops.

16.3.1 Trading Linkage Mechanism

The so-called trading linkage mechanism refers to the trading response behavior between the upper and lower trading phases along the trading chain. The existence of a trading loop depends on the topological structure of multi-dimensional associations in the trading network. Trading agents, through extensive trading contact relationships, both accept influences from other trading agents and spread their own influences through the network structure. Adjacent phases in the trading loop usually have close trading links. Taking the real estate trading loop as an example, the trading behavior of families is directly transmitted to real estate developers, and the trading behavior of developers is transmitted to land suppliers and building material suppliers. Only when the trading agents in the subsequent phase somewhat respond to the previous phase can a trading be completed. The trading loop is formed through the trading linkage between phases. The linkage structure diagram of the real estate trading loop is as follows:

In Fig. 16.2, the solid line represents the forward trading direction, i.e., the direction of the flow of trading funds, including the flow of funds for purchasing goods and the flow of financing interest and equity dividends. The dashed line represents the flow of wages and salaries, which is a reflection of the employment relationship. The trading linkage mechanism defines the basic framework of the trading loop.

16.3.2 Trading Demonstration Mechanism

The trading network is not only a carrier of trading flows but also a carrier of information dissemination. Trading agents need to obtain supplementary information by observing the behavior of other trading agents based on their prior judgment, thereby verifying or modifying their prior judgment. The trading demonstration mechanism influences the decision-making of trading agents through information channels, thereby forming cascading trading behavior.

Trading demonstration is a key step in activating cascading trading. We can use the trading equation to prove this conclusion. Suppose a is any agent in phase i on the trading loop, and the probability of implementing trading strategy s on the trading

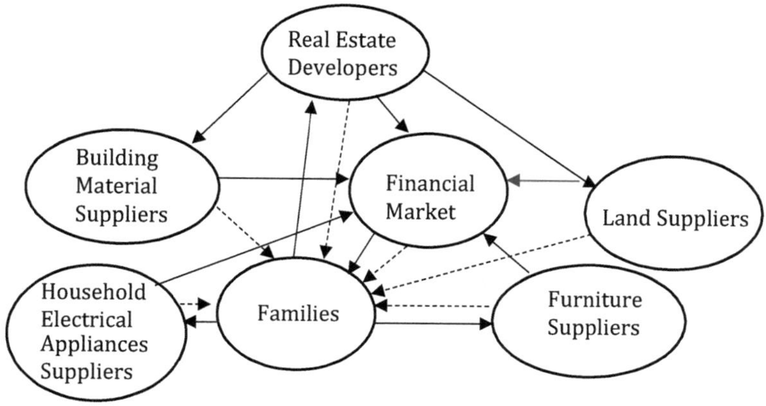

Fig. 16.2 The trading loop in real estate

loop is Pr(s), according to the trading equation, we know that:

$$\Pr(s) = 1 - R_g \frac{q}{p} \mu^n \tag{16.3.1}$$

The trading equation shows that, under the condition that the return risk index R_g of the trading strategy and the doubt index of the trading agent $\frac{q}{p}$ remain unchanged, as the number of demonstrations by trading agents in the same phase n increases, the risk filtering effect quickly intensifies, and the probability of the trading agents in the trading loop implementing strategies s will increase accordingly. Once the decision threshold is breached, cascade trading within the phase is activated. Cascade trading is an important part of the trading loop, and the activation of cascade trading adds powerful momentum to the trading loop.

In summary, in the two operating mechanisms of the trading loop, the trading linkage mechanism constructs the structure of the trading loop, while the trading demonstration mechanism provides power for the trading loop. The two operating mechanisms each have different carriers. The carrier of the trading linkage mechanism is the trading flow, and the different phases on the trading loop complete the coordinated response process through the connection of the trading flow. The carrier of the trading demonstration mechanism is the information flow, which achieves the result of indirect action through the propagation of information among trading agents. Compared with the trading linkage mechanism, the trading demonstration mechanism transmit much faster with the help of information dissemination. In times of panic, the trading demonstration mechanism often becomes the force determining the direction of the trading loop due to its efficient dissemination ability.

16.4 Description of the Trading Loop

The trading loop has two main dimensions, namely structure and scale. The structure of the trading loop is described by order, and the scale of the trading loop is described by equivalent.

16.4.1 *Order of the Trading Loop*

There are trading loops of various sizes in the trading network, such as real estate trading loops, stock market trading loops, and collectibles market trading loops. In addition to the differences in trading bases, an important indicator reflecting the characteristics of the trading loop is the number of phases that make up the trading loop. The more phases that make up the trading loop, the more complex the interaction and feedback mechanisms of the phases. For example, the real estate trading loop has more phases. Compared with the stock trading loop and the collectibles market trading loop, it involves more industries and the market operation is more unpredictable. Based on this, we call the total number of phases that make up the trading loop the order of the trading loop. Theoretically, the order of the trading loop can be infinite, but in most cases, the order of the trading loop is only a single digit, and trading loops exceeding 10 orders are relatively rare. We call trading loops with lower orders low-order trading loops, and those with higher orders high-order trading loops.

The order of the trading loop that can be generated in the trading system is closely related to the scale of the trading system. Generally speaking, the larger the scale of the trading system, the easier it is to produce high-order trading loops. The smaller the scale of the trading systems is, the lower the probability of emerging high-order trading loops will be.

16.4.2 *Trading Loop Equivalent*

The trading loop equivalent refers to the total amount of transactions realized on the trading loop at a unit time step, that is, the total amount of transactions of all trading agents on the trading loop with the trading base of the trading loop as the target. To avoid double counting, when calculating the trading loop equivalent, we only calculate the reverse transaction amount on each phase.

The important factors affecting the trading loop equivalent mainly include two aspects: one is the order of the trading loop. The higher the order of the trading loop, the larger the number of participating agents and the scale of the trading base, and the more transactions will be generated; the second is the unit value of the trading base. The values of different trading bases vary greatly. A set of real estate, a car, a washing machine, a piece of clothing, etc., can all be components of the trading base, but their values vary greatly. Real estate is usually in units of millions of RMB, cars in units of hundreds of thousands of RMB, washing machines in units of thousands of RMB, and clothing usually in units of hundreds of RMB, etc. Therefore, with different trading base compositions, the trading loop may generate a huge gap in trading equivalents.

The real determinant of the size of the trading loop equivalent is still the number of participants in the trading loop, that is, the capacity of the trading loop. A trading loop with a large capacity, even if it is supported by low-value transactions, can still generate a large equivalent trading. In this regard, the tourism trading loop is a good example. Although the tourism trading loop is only composed of a few trading phases such as transportation, accommodations, catering, and scenic spot tickets, the value of the trading base is not high, but due to the large capacity of the trading loop, the equivalent of the tourism trading loop is still very considerable.

The equivalent of the trading loop is a function of time, fluctuating with the time step t. If we use x_t^i to represent the trading volume of the m-th trading loop's i-th phase at time step t, and use X_t to represent the trading equivalent realized by the trading loop at time step t, the two have the following relationship:

$$X_i = \sum_1^m x_t^i \tag{16.4.1}$$

16.4.3 Trading Loop Equivalent Equation

The trading loop operates under the drive of two basic mechanisms, namely the self-feedback mechanism within the phase and the positive feedback mechanism between phases. The superposition of the two feedback mechanisms determines the direction of the trading loop. Based on this logic, we construct the equivalent equation of the trading loop.

Let x_t^i be the trading equivalent realized by the i-th phase of the trading loop at time step t. According to the operating principle of the trading loop, the trading equivalent x_t^i is the result of two different feedback mechanisms: part of it comes from the self-feedback within the phase, this part of the equivalent is $\alpha_i x_{t-1}^i$, where α_i is the internal feedback factor of phase i, satisfying $\alpha_i \geq 0$. The higher the self-feedback strength of the phase, the larger the value of α_i. Another part of the equivalent comes from the feedback between phases, where the feedback equivalent of phase i to phase j is $\beta_{ij} x_{t-1}^j$, where β_{ij} is the external feedback factor of phase i to phase j. Each phase has an internal feedback factor and $m - 1$ external feedback factors. In fact, the phases on the trading loop only feedback to specific phases and do not feedback to other phases. For phases with feedback response, the external feedback factor takes a value greater than zero, that is, $\beta_{ij} > 0$; for phases without feedback response, $\beta_{ij} = 0$.

The trading equivalent of phase i of the trading loop at time step t satisfies the following equation:

$$x_t^i = \alpha_i x_{t-1}^i + \sum_{\substack{j=1 \\ j \neq 1}}^{m} \beta_{ij} x_{t-1}^j \tag{16.4.2}$$

The feedback factor of the trading loop is an important structural parameter of the trading loop, determining the dynamic evolution characteristics of the trading loop. However, the feedback factor changes continuously in the operation of the trading loop, leading to more complex and variable operating characteristics of the trading loop. For simplicity, in the following discussion, we always assume that the feedback factor of the trading loop is a constant.

As a special trading phenomenon in the trading system, the trading loop is inevitably closely related to the properties of the trading system. Theoretically, the higher the compactness of the trading system, the larger the feedback factor of the trading loop, that is, the compactness of the trading system ϕ is positively correlated with the feedback factor of the trading loop α, β. In the evolution process of the trading system, with the increasing compactness of the trading system, the probability of the emergence of the trading loop continues to increase. The relationship between the feedback factor of the trading loop α, β and system compactness ϕ belongs to the function category. To reflect this relationship, the feedback factor α, β can be represented as $\alpha(\phi)$, $\beta(\phi)$ respectively.

On the trading network, the capacity of each phase is limited. The maximum trading volume that each phase can generate is also limited. Once it reaches its trading volume limit, the trading phase will lose its response capability and will not continue to generate new trades. In the stock market, once the bullish phase exhausts all its capital stock, it is impossible to continue to make more trades. The situation is the same for the bearish phase, which also has a short selling limit. Although the trading phase has more redundancy under the support of financing and short selling mechanisms, there is still a maximum trading limit.

The phases on the trading network are open, and the trading agents have a certain flexibility in choosing phases, and will decide which phase to enter according to the characteristics of the trading situation, thereby changing the capacity of the trading phase. The trading limit of the phase M_t^i is a function of phase capacity, and changes in phase capacity will inevitably cause changes in the phase limit. In the stock market, when the market is bullish, there will be a large number of investors rushing into the bullish phase, thereby pushing up the trading limit of the bullish phase. When the market is bearish, the situation will be reversed—investors will rush into the bearish phase, increasing the trading limit of the bearish phase.

The remaining trading resources of each phase change over time. The remaining trading resources of the trading phase i at time step t are determined by the limit

M_t^i and the trading volume of previous time steps. The larger the trading volume in the early stage, the more trading resources the trading phase i consumes, and the less remaining trading resources. Of course, since the capacity of the trading phase is dynamically changing, the remaining trading resources of the trading phase are not always decreasing with the increase of time t, but show a more complex change pattern.

It is relatively complex to accurately calculate the remaining trading resources of each trading phase. We can use the factor $1 - \frac{x_{t-1}^i}{M_{t-1}^i}$ to approximately reflect the proportion of remaining trading resources of the phase. When the current trading volume x_{t-1}^i is closer to the trading upper limit M_{t-1}^i, the closer the factor $1 - \frac{x_{t-1}^i}{M_{t-1}^i}$ value is to 0. If the previous trading volume x_{t-1}^i is far from the trading upper limit M_{t-1}^i, the factor $1 - \frac{x_{t-1}^i}{M_{t-1}^i}$ will take a positive number less than 1. If the previous trading volume $x_{t-1}^i = 0$, the factor $1 - \frac{x_{t-1}^i}{M_{t-1}^i}$. In the operation of the trading loop, $1 - \frac{x_{t-1}^i}{M_{t-1}^i}$ plays the role of a damping factor. The closer the trading volume x_t^i is to the trading upper limit M_t^i, the greater the resistance the damping factor produces to the trading loop, until the trading loop completely stops running.

We integrate the above factors into Eq. (16.4.2) to get a more comprehensive phase feedback equation:

$$x_t^i = \left(\alpha_i(\phi) x_{t-1}^i + \sum_{\substack{j=1 \\ j \neq 1}}^{m} \beta_{ij}(\phi) x_{t-1}^j \right) \left(1 - \frac{x_{t-1}^i}{M_{t-1}^i} \right) \tag{16.4.3}$$

Since the phase i is any phase on the m-order trading loop, the operation process of the trading loop can be described by a set of equations composed of m equivalent equations:

$$\begin{aligned} x_t^i &= \left(\alpha_i(\phi) x_{t-1}^i + \sum_{\substack{j=1 \\ j \neq 1}}^{m} \beta_{ij}(\phi) x_{t-1}^j \right) \left(1 - \frac{x_{t-1}^i}{M_{t-1}^i} \right), i, j = 1, 2 \ldots m \\ &\alpha_i(\phi) \geq 0 \\ &\beta_{ij}(\phi) \geq 0 \end{aligned} \tag{16.4.4}$$

Equation (16.4.4) is the equivalent equation we use to describe the trading loop.

For the m-order trading loop, the equivalent equation is composed of m nonlinear difference equations. When $m = 1$, the trading loop equation degenerates into a logistic map:

$$X_t = \alpha(\phi)X_{t-1}\left(1 - \frac{X_{t-1}}{M_{t-1}}\right) \tag{16.4.5}$$

As can be seen, we can regard the trading loop equation as a high-dimensional logistic map (Logistic Mapping).[6] The academic community has a deep research on the logistic map (or logistic equation). The logistic map has very complex characteristics, including stable states, unstable states, bifurcation phenomena, and chaotic phenomena. Undoubtedly, the high-dimensional trading loop equivalent equation will be more complex, meaning that the trading loop described by the equivalent equation may produce extremely complex trading phenomena, which is an important source of the nonlinear characteristics of the trading system.

16.5 Stability of the Trading Loop

For the m-order trading loop equivalent equation:

$$x_t^i = \left(\alpha_i(\phi)x_{t-1}^i + \sum_{\substack{j=1 \\ j\neq 1}}^{m} \beta_{ij}(\phi)x_{t-1}^j\right)\left(1 - \frac{x_{t-1}^i}{M_{t-1}^i}\right), i, j = 1, 2 \ldots m$$
$$\alpha_i(\phi) \geq 0$$
$$\beta_{ij}(\phi) \geq 0 \tag{16.5.1}$$

At the steady state point $X_f = \begin{pmatrix} x_f^1 \\ x_f^2 \\ \vdots \\ x_f^m \end{pmatrix}$, the following relationship is satisfied:

$$x_f^i = \left(\alpha_i(\phi)x_f^i + \sum_{\substack{j=1 \\ j\neq 1}}^{m} \beta_{ij}(\phi)x_f^j\right)\left(1 - \frac{x_f^i}{M_f^i}\right)$$
$$i, j = 1, 2 \ldots m \tag{16.5.2}$$

Arrange the above formula to get:

$$\left[\alpha_i(\phi)\left(1-\frac{x_f^i}{M_i}\right)-1\right]x_f^i-\left(\alpha_i(\phi)x_f^i+\sum_{\substack{j=1\\j\neq i}}^{m}\beta_{ij}(\phi)x_f^j\right)\left(1-\frac{x_f^i}{M_f^i}\right)=0$$
$$i,j=1,2\ldots m \tag{16.5.3}$$

From Eq. (16.5.3) we can get the steady state solution of the trading loop, where, $X_t=\begin{pmatrix}x_t^1\\x_t^2\\\vdots\\x_t^m\end{pmatrix}=0$ is a steady state solution of the trading loop. This steady state corresponds to the state before the trading loop starts, which is a common steady state for all trading loops, called the trivial steady state of the trading loop. In addition to the trivial steady state, the steady state solution of the trading loop is called the non-trivial steady state.

Let $X_f=\begin{pmatrix}x_f^1\\x_f^2\\\vdots\\x_f^m\end{pmatrix}$ be any steady state solution of the trading loop, which can be either a trivial steady state or a non-trivial steady state. According to the first method of Lyapunov, we analyze the stability of the trading loop in the vicinity of the steady state solution.

In the vicinity of any steady state solution $X_f=\begin{pmatrix}x_f^1\\x_f^2\\\vdots\\x_f^m\end{pmatrix}$, the equivalent equation of the trading loop can be linearized into the following set of equations:

$$\begin{pmatrix}x_t^1\\x_t^2\\\vdots\\x_t^m\end{pmatrix}=\begin{pmatrix}a_{11}&a_{12}&\cdots&a_{1m}\\a_{21}&a_{22}&\cdots&a_{2m}\\\cdots&\cdots&\cdots&\cdots\\a_{m1}&a_{m2}&\cdots&a_{mm}\end{pmatrix}\begin{pmatrix}x_{t-1}^1\\x_{t-2}^1\\\vdots\\x_{t-1}^m\end{pmatrix} \tag{16.5.4}$$

The coefficient matrix of the above linear equation is the Jacobian matrix, namely:

$$a_{ij}=\frac{\partial F_i}{\partial x_t^j}\Big|_{X_f} \tag{16.5.5}$$

where, $F_i\left(x_t^1,x_t^2\ldots x_t^m\right)=\left(\alpha_i(\varphi)x_t^i+\sum\beta_{ij}(\varphi)x_t^j\right)\left(1-\frac{x_t^i}{M_{t-1}^i}\right)$.

Obtained from (16.5.5):

$$a_{ij}(\phi) = \beta_{ij}(\phi)\left(1 - \frac{x_f^i}{M_f^i}\right), \quad \begin{matrix} i, j = 1, 2 \ldots m \\ i \neq j \end{matrix} \tag{16.5.6}$$

$$a_{ii} = \left[\alpha_i(\phi)\left(1 + x_f^i\right) + \sum_{\substack{j=1 \\ j \neq i}}^{m} \beta_{ij}(\phi) x_f^j\right]\left(1 - \frac{x_f^i}{M_f^i}\right) \tag{16.5.7}$$

The characteristic equation of the trading loop can be derived from Eqs. (16.5.6) and (16.5.7):

$$\begin{pmatrix} a_{11} - \lambda & a_{12} & \cdots & a_{1m} \\ a_{21} & a_{22} - \lambda & \cdots & a_{2m} \\ \cdots & \cdots & \cdots & \cdots \\ a_{m1} & a_{m2} & \cdots & a_{mm} - \lambda \end{pmatrix} = 0 \tag{16.5.8}$$

Expanding (16.5.8) yields the following *m*-order polynomial equation:

$$a_0\lambda^m + a_1\lambda^{m-1} + \cdots + a_{m-1}\lambda + a_m = 0 \tag{16.5.9}$$

The Routh-Hurwitz determinant is obtained from (16.5.9):

$$\Delta_1 = a_1$$

$$\Delta_2 = \begin{vmatrix} a_1 & a_0 \\ a_3 & a_2 \end{vmatrix}$$

$$\Delta_3 = \begin{vmatrix} a_1 & a_0 & 0 \\ a_3 & a_2 & a_1 \\ a_5 & a_4 & a_3 \end{vmatrix}$$

$$\Delta_4 = \begin{vmatrix} a_1 & a_0 & 0 & 0 \\ a_3 & a_2 & a_1 & 0 \\ a_5 & a_4 & a_3 & a_2 \\ a_7 & a_6 & a_5 & a_4 \end{vmatrix}$$

$$\cdots\cdots$$

$$\Delta_m = \begin{vmatrix} a_1 & a_0 & 0 & \cdots & 0 \\ a_3 & a_2 & a_1 & \cdots & 0 \\ a_5 & a_4 & a_3 & \cdots & 0 \\ \cdots & \cdots & \cdots & \cdots & \cdots \\ a_{2m-1} & a_{2m-2} & a_{2m-3} & \cdots & a_m \end{vmatrix}$$

According to the Routh-Hurwitz criterion, when the conditions $a_0 > 0$, $\Delta_i > 0$, $i, j = 1, 2 \ldots m$ are met, the steady-state solution of the trading loop equivalent equation is stable. Otherwise, the steady-state solution is unstable.

When the equivalent equation steady-state solution is stable, it means that the trading loop evolves within a bounded space. As time t increases, the trading loop always operates within a certain equivalent range. As can be seen from the Routh-Hurwitz criterion, the stability conditions of the trading loop are very strict, and the trading loop cannot meet the stability conditions in most cases.

In order to further analyze the stability of the trading loop, we choose the simplest second-order trading loop as the analysis sample.

Let $m = 2$, the trading loop equivalent equation group is as follows:

$$x_t^1 = \left(\alpha_1(\phi)x_{t-1}^1 + \beta_{12}(\phi)x_{t-1}^2\right)\left(1 - \frac{x_{t-1}^1}{M_{t-1}^1}\right) \tag{16.5.10}$$

$$x_t^2 = \left(\alpha_2(\phi)x_{t-1}^2 + \beta_{21}(\phi)x_{t-1}^1\right)\left(1 - \frac{x_{t-1}^2}{M_{t-1}^2}\right) \tag{16.5.11}$$

The Jacobian matrix corresponding to Eqs. (16.5.10) and (16.5.11) is:

$$J = \begin{bmatrix} \alpha_1(\phi)\left(1 - \frac{x_f^1}{M_f^1}\right) - \left(\alpha_1(\phi)x_f^1 + \beta_{12}(\phi)x_f^2\right)\frac{1}{M_f^1} & \beta_{12}(\phi)\left(1 - \frac{x_f^1}{M_f^1}\right) \\ \beta_{21}(\phi)\left(1 - \frac{x_f^2}{M_f^2}\right) & \alpha_2(\phi)\left(1 - \frac{x^2}{M_f^2}\right) - \left(\alpha_2(\phi)x_f^2 + \beta_{21}(\phi)x_f^1\right)\frac{1}{M_f^2} \end{bmatrix} \tag{16.5.12}$$

This gives the characteristic equation of the equivalent equation:

$$\begin{bmatrix} \alpha_1(\phi)\left(1 - \frac{x_f^1}{M_{f1}^1}\right) - \left(\alpha(\phi)_1 x_f^1 + \beta_{12}(\phi)x_f^2\right)\frac{1}{M_f^1} - \lambda & \beta_{12}(\phi)\left(1 - \frac{x_f^1}{M_f^1}\right) \\ \beta_{21}(\phi)\left(1 - \frac{x_f^2}{M_f^2}\right) & \alpha_2(\phi)\left(1 - \frac{x^2}{M_f^2}\right) - \left(\alpha_2(\phi)x_f^2 + \beta_{21}(\phi)x_f^1\right)\frac{1}{M_f^2} - \lambda \end{bmatrix} = 0 \tag{16.5.13}$$

Expand the left determinant of (16.5.12) to get the characteristic equation:

$$\left(\alpha_1(\phi) - 2\frac{\alpha_1(\phi)}{M_f^1}x_f^1 - \frac{\beta_{12}(\phi)}{M_f^1}x_f^2 - \lambda\right)\left(\alpha_2(\phi) - 2\frac{\alpha_2(\phi)}{M_f^2}x_f^2 - \frac{\beta_{21}(\phi)}{M_f^2}x_f^1 - \lambda\right)$$
$$- \beta_{12}(\phi)\beta_{21}(\phi)\left(1 - \frac{x_f^1}{M_f^1}\right)\left(1 - \frac{x_f^2}{M_f^2}\right) = 0 \tag{16.5.14}$$

Rearrange (16.5.13) to get:

$$\lambda^2 - \lambda\left[(\alpha_1(\phi) + \alpha_2(\phi)) - 2\left(\frac{\alpha_1(\phi)}{M_f^1}x_f^1 + \frac{\alpha_2(\phi)}{M_f^2}x_f^2\right) - \frac{\beta_{12}(\phi)}{M_f^1}x_f^2 - \frac{\beta_{21}(\phi)}{M_f^2}x_f^1\right]$$
$$+ \left(\alpha_1(\phi) - 2\frac{\alpha_1(\phi)}{M_f^1}x_f^1 - \frac{\beta_{12}(\phi)}{M_f^1}x_f^2\right)\left(\alpha_2(\phi) - 2\frac{x_f^2}{M_f^2} - \frac{\beta_{21}(\phi)}{M_f^2}x_f^1\right)$$
$$- \beta_{12}(\phi)\beta_{21}(\phi)\left(1 - \frac{x_f^1}{M_f^1}\right)\left(1 - \frac{x_f^2}{M_f^2}\right) = 0 \tag{16.5.15}$$

It is known that the general solution of the quadratic equation has the following form:

$$\lambda_1 = \frac{T + \sqrt{T^2 - 4\Delta}}{2} \tag{16.5.16}$$

$$\lambda_2 = \frac{T - \sqrt{T^2 - 4\Delta}}{2} \tag{16.5.17}$$

where, the two parameters in (16.5.16) and (16.5.17) are as follows:

$$T = \alpha_1(\phi) + \alpha_2(\phi) - 2\left(\frac{\alpha_1(\phi)}{M_f^1}x_f^1 + \frac{\alpha_2(\phi)}{M_f^2}\right) - \frac{\beta_{12}(\phi)}{M_f^1}x_f^2 - \frac{\beta_{21}(\phi)}{M_f^2}x_f^1$$
$$= \frac{\alpha_1(\phi)M_f^1 - 2\alpha_1(\phi)x_f^1 - \beta_{12}(\phi)x_f^2}{M_f^1} + \frac{\alpha_2(\phi)M_f^2 - 2\alpha_2(\phi)x_f^2 - \beta_{21}(\phi)x_f^1}{M_f^2} \tag{16.5.18}$$

$$\Delta = \left(\alpha_1(\phi) - 2\frac{\alpha_1(\phi)}{M_f^1}x_f^1 - \frac{\beta_{12}(\phi)}{M_f^1}x_f^2\right)\left(\alpha_2(\phi) - 2\frac{x_f^2}{M_f^2} - \frac{\beta_{21}(\phi)}{M_f^2}x_f^1\right)$$
$$- \beta_{12}(\phi)\beta_{21}(\phi)\left(1 - \frac{x_f^1}{M_f^1}\right)\left(1 - \frac{x_f^2}{M_f^2}\right) \tag{16.5.19}$$

$$T^2 - 4\Delta = \left(\frac{\alpha_1(\phi)M_f^1 - 2\alpha_1(\phi)x_f^1 - \beta_{12}(\phi)x_f^2}{M_f^1} - \frac{\alpha_2(\phi)M_f^2 - 2\alpha_2(\phi)x_f^2 - \beta_{21}(\phi)x_f^1}{M_f^2}\right)^2$$
$$+ 4\beta_{12}(\phi)\beta_{21}(\phi)\left(1 - \frac{x_f^1}{M_f^1}\right)\left(1 - \frac{x_f^2}{M_f^2}\right) \tag{16.5.20}$$

$$\because \beta_{12}(\phi) \geq 0, \beta_{21}(\phi) \geq 0, 1 - \frac{x_f^1}{M_f^1} \geq 0, 1 - \frac{x_f^2}{M_f^2} \geq 0$$

$$\because T^2 - 4\Delta \geq 0$$

It can be seen that the two characteristic roots of the trading loop equivalent equation are real numbers. The second-order trading loop equivalent equation has the following general solution:

$$\begin{aligned} x_t^1 &= c_{11}e^{\lambda_1 t} + c_{12}e^{\lambda_2 t} \\ x_t^2 &= c_{21}e^{\lambda_1 t} + c_{22}e^{\lambda_2 t} \end{aligned} \tag{16.5.21}$$

The four parameters in the general solution (16.5.21) $c_{ij} \geq 0$ are determined by the initial values of the trading loop equivalent equation.

The stability of the trading loop can be determined by the general solution (16.5.20). According to the form of the general solution (16.5.21), only when the two characteristic roots λ_1 and λ_2 are both smaller than 0, the solution of the trading loop is a bounded solution, and the trading loop will show stable characteristics. When at least one of the two characteristic roots λ_1 and λ_2 is greater than 0, the solution of the trading loop will show divergent characteristics, indicating that the trading loop will eventually enter an unstable state. Based on the above logic, we further analyze the relationship between the parameters of the trading loop equivalent equation and the stability of the trading loop.

(1) When $\Delta > 0$, the signs of the characteristic roots λ_1 and λ_2 depend on T. When $T > 0$, the characteristic roots λ_1 and λ_2 are both positive real numbers, that is, $\lambda_1 > 0$ and $\lambda_2 > 0$, the trading loop has instability. As time t increases, the trading volume X_t will tend to infinity.

For the second-order trading loop, if the feedback structure meets the following conditions:

$$\frac{\alpha_1(\phi)}{\beta_{12}(\phi)} > \frac{x_f^2}{M_f^1 - 2x_f^1}, \frac{\alpha_2(\phi)}{\beta_{21}(\phi)} > \frac{x_f^1}{M_f^2 - 2x_f^2} \tag{16.5.22}$$

The characteristic root equation of the trading loop satisfies $T > 0$.

According to the feedback condition (16.5.21), when the internal feedback factor in the trading loop is stronger than the external feedback factor, the trading loop will show unstable characteristics. This shows that the stability of the trading loop depends on the feedback structure characteristics of the trading loop.

When $T < 0$, the characteristic roots λ_1 and λ_2 are both negative real numbers, that is, $\lambda_1 < 0$ and $\lambda_2 < 0$, the trading loop shows asymptotic stability. As time t continues, the trading loop will inevitably converge to zero volume and eventually disappear.

When the feedback structure of the trading loop meets the following conditions:

$$\frac{\alpha_1(\phi)}{\beta_{12}(\phi)} < \frac{x_f^2}{M_f^1 - 2x_f^1}, \frac{\alpha_2(\phi)}{\beta_{21}(\phi)} < \frac{x_f^1}{M_f^2 - 2x_f^2} \tag{16.5.23}$$

The trading loop will satisfy $T < 0$, showing asymptotic stability. The feedback characteristics of such trading loops are dominated by external feedback, and the internal feedback mechanism is in a weak phase position.

Combining the above analysis, we can conclude that the cascading trading of the same phase main body in the trading loop is the key factor leading to the continuous amplification of the trading volume. Trading loops that are prone to cascading phenomena have unstable evolutionary tendencies. From an evolutionary perspective, in the early stages without cascading trading or herd effects, the trading loop is usually in a stable operation state, and the change in trading volume is relatively slow. Once a cascading trading phenomenon emerges, the volume of the trading loop will explode and quickly enter an out-of-control situation.

(2) When $\Delta \leq 0$, the stability of the trading loop is independent of the sign of T. Whether T is positive or negative, the trading loop shows saddle point characteristics, that is, it converges in one direction and diverges in another. Specifically, on the two phases of the trading loop, one phase operates stably, while the other phase is unstable. If phase 1 has stable characteristics, phase 2 must be unstable. At this time, the trading loop has the following feedback structure:

$$0 < \alpha_1(\phi) < \alpha_2(\phi), 0 < \beta_{12}(\phi) < \beta_{21}(\phi) \tag{16.5.24}$$

The feedback characteristics of such trading loops are that the feedback strengths of the two phases are asymmetrical, and the internal and external feedback factors of one phase are both greater than the two feedback factors of the other phase.

(3) When $T = 0$, subject to the nature of the second-order trading loop, it requires the structural parameters to satisfy $T^2 - 4\Delta \geq 0$. Under this constraint, Δ can only take non-positive values, that is, $\Delta \leq 0$. At this time, the two characteristic roots of the trading loop are real numbers with opposite signs, that is, $\lambda_1\lambda_2 < 0$. As can be seen from the previous analysis, such a trading loop will also show saddle point characteristics.

Due to the special nature of the second-order trading loop, the possibility of the characteristic roots λ_1, λ_2 being complex numbers is excluded. However, this situation is only a special case of the second-order trading loop. For trading loops of the third order and above, there is a complete possibility of complex characteristic roots. When the trading loop has complex characteristic roots, the trading loop will show an oscillating operating state. Under certain conditions, the trajectory of the trading loop in phase space may present a limit cycle pattern.

16.6 The Phenomenon of Trading Loop Bifurcation

In the quantity equations of the second-order trading loop (16.5.10) and (16.5.11), there are four structural parameters, namely internal feedback factors α_1 and α_2, and external feedback factors β_{12} and β_{21}, which determine the operating form of the trading loop. Within the range of structural parameter values, some sensitive points exist. As long as the structural parameters change slightly, the form of the trading loop will undergo abrupt changes, either from a stable state to an unstable state, or from an unstable state to a stable state. These sensitive points are bifurcation points of the trading loop, and other points in the structural parameter interval are normal points of the trading loop. The trading phenomena presented by the trading loop at the bifurcation points are called the phenomena of the trading loop bifurcation.

From the discussion in the previous section, we know that the bifurcation points of the second-order trading loop should appear in the two equations of $T = 0$ and $\Delta = 0$, namely:

$$\frac{\alpha_1(\phi)M_f^1 - 2\alpha_1(\phi)x_f^1 - \beta_{12}(\phi)x_f^2}{M_f^1} + \frac{\alpha_2(\phi)M_f^2 - 2\alpha_2(\phi)x_f^2 - \beta_{21}(\phi)x_f^1}{M_f^2} = 0 \tag{16.6.1}$$

$$\left(\alpha_1(\phi) - 2\frac{\alpha_1(\phi)}{M_f^1}x_f^1 - \frac{\beta_{12}(\phi)}{M_f^1}x_f^2\right)\left(\alpha_2(\phi) - 2\frac{x_f^2}{M_f^2} - \frac{\beta_{21}(\phi)}{M_f^2}x_f^1\right) - \beta_{12}(\phi)\beta_{21}(\phi)\left(1 - \frac{x_f^1}{M_f^1}\right)\left(1 - \frac{x_f^2}{M_f^2}\right) = 0 \tag{16.6.2}$$

Equations (16.6.1) and (16.6.2) both contain four structural parameters, and each equation has a large number of bifurcation points. Taking $T = 0$ as an example, the solution of the following equation group contains the bifurcation points of the trading loop:

$$\frac{\alpha_1(\phi)M_f^1 - 2\alpha_1(\phi)x_f^1 - \beta_{12}(\phi)x_f^2}{M_f^1} = 0 \tag{16.6.3}$$

$$\frac{\alpha_2(\phi)M_f^2 - 2\alpha_2(\phi)x_f^2 - \beta_{21}(\phi)x_f^1}{M_f^2} = 0 \tag{16.6.4}$$

Obviously, any point that satisfies the relationship $\alpha_1(\phi) = \frac{\beta_{12}(\phi)x_f^2}{M_f^1 - 2x_f^1}$, $\alpha_2(\phi) = \frac{\beta_{21}(\phi)x_f^1}{M_f^2 - 2x_f^2}$ is a bifurcation point of the trading loop. Assuming $\beta_{12} = k_1$, $\beta_{21} = k_2$, k_1 and k_2 are all non-negative real numbers, then the trading loop bifurcates at $\alpha_1(\phi) = \frac{k_1 x_f^2}{M_f^1 - 2x_f^1}$, $\alpha_2(\phi) = \frac{k_2 x_f^1}{M_f^2 - 2x_f^2}$. Among them, the trading loop shows structural stability in the $\alpha_1(\phi) < \frac{k_1 x_f^2}{M_f^1 - 2x_f^1}$, $\alpha_2(\phi) < \frac{k_2 x_f^1}{M_f^2 - 2x_f^2}$ region, and the structure loses stability in the $\alpha_1(\phi) > \frac{k_1 x_f^2}{M_f^1 - 2x_f^1}$, $\alpha_2(\phi) > \frac{k_2 x_f^1}{M_f^2 - 2x_f^2}$ region.

According to the rule of bifurcation point values, the bifurcation points of the trading loop will change with the movement of the external feedback factor.

Theoretically, there can be countless bifurcation points in the second-order trading loop.

As can be known from the properties of the logistic map, a system containing a large number of bifurcation points must have a channel leading to a chaotic state. The fact that the second-order trading loop contains countless bifurcation points indicates that the trading loop not only has high instability, but also the possibility of a chaotic state. For an m-order trading loop, the probability of chaos is even greater.

Each bifurcation of the trading loop is a denial of the rules built on a specific structure. When the trading loop operates in a bifurcation-dense area, and we cannot accurately predict the specific location of the bifurcation point, predicting market operations is like sailing in waters full of hidden reefs, with the danger of capsizing at any time. The bifurcation of the trading loop usually occurs against the backdrop of oscillations in the compactness of the trading system. The drastic changes in compactness have a huge impact on the feedback structure of the trading loop. After experiencing a massive structural change, the behavior of the trading loop becomes even more unpredictable. Under these circumstances, it is even more difficult to accurately predict the specific direction of the trading loop and the trading system.

Each outbreak of a crisis is the result of a large-scale bifurcation of the trading loop. On the eve of a crisis, the trading system is already at a bifurcation point leading to chaos, but people still view the evolution of the trading system with linear thinking that extrapolates smoothly, resulting in a complete lack of awareness of the impending crisis. The financial crisis that broke out in the United States in September 2008 is a good example. Up until the eve of the crisis in September 2008, not a single one of the many highly respected institutions, including the Federal Reserve and the International Monetary Fund (IMF), was able to detect any signs of the crisis. The IMF predicted in its spring 2007 report that "global economics risks [have] declined since … September 2006 …. The overall U.S. economy is holding up well... [and] the signs elsewhere are very encouraging." The highly respected JPMorgan Chase Bank even predicted three days before the crisis (September 21, 2008) that the U.S. economy would accelerate in the first half of 2009. Even less than 24 h before the crisis, there was still no consensus on the impending crisis, with the chairman of the President's Economic Advisory Council predicting that the unemployment rate would continue to decline in 2009. After the financial storm, former Federal Reserve Chairman Alan Greenspan was still puzzled when reviewing that shocking past. "What went wrong? Why was virtually every economist and policy maker of note so off about so large an issue?".[7]

In fact, the main reason that prevented people from detecting signs of the crisis was not the complex and mysterious mechanism of the crisis, but the linear thinking pattern that people had long been accustomed to. Greenspan also saw this point. "With the crisis less than twenty-four hours away, conventional wisdom had not yet coalesced around even the possibility of a typical recession, to say nothing of the worst economic crisis in eight decade."[8]

If people could abandon the linear thinking pattern and recognize the bifurcation characteristics of the trading loop and the possible structural changes brought about by the oscillation of the compactness of the trading system, they would see that this crisis was actually dominated by a trading loop with an exceptionally simple structure: enterprises go bankrupt and liquidity freezes, leading to more enterprises' bankruptcy and liquidity freeze on a larger scale. Each cycle of the trading loop gathers a larger volume. Once the volume of the trading loop crosses a certain threshold, the financial market will enter a liquidity freeze mode, the trading network will fall into paralysis, and the crisis will immediately erupt.

Notes

1. The Ponzi scheme was historically led by a man named Charles Ponzi's, an Italian-American Wall Street speculator. In 1919, he began scheming, promising investors annual returns of up to 40%. After attracting the first group of investors, a portion of the money was returned to the investors. Due to the fulfillment of investment commitments, more investors had subsequently been attracted to invest. The Ponzi scheme was sustained by a steady stream of investors. Ponzi managed to maintain the scheme for seven months, attracting as many as 30,000 investors. The scam was later uncovered and Ponzi was jailed for three years.
2. Robert J. Shiller (2004) Irrational exuberance (Trans: Liao Li), China Renmin University Press, Beijing, p 64–86 (in Chinese).
3. In fact, in the decade from 1937 to 1949, China also experienced a hyperinflation, the extent of which was even greater than that of Germany. However, the statistics were far less complete than those of Germany. See: [US] Don Pahlberg (1998) The History and Analysis of Inflation (Trans: Sun Zhong), China Development Press, Beijing, p 106–118 (in Chinese).
4. Don Pahlberg (1998) The History and Analysis of Inflation (Trans: Sun Zhong), China Development Press, Beijing, p 80 (in Chinese).
5. Don Pahlberg (1998) The History and Analysis of Inflation (Trans: Sun Zhong), China Development Press, Beijing, p 70–87 (in Chinese).
6. Logistic curve is a special curve first discovered by Belgian mathematician Verhulst, which is a typical case of simplicity resulting in complexity. It is usually used for such fields as group growth and population growth.
7. Alan Greenspan (2014) The Map and The Territory (Trans: Yu Jiang), CITIC Press, Beijing.
8. Alan Greenspan (2014) The Map and The Territory (Trans: Yu Jiang), CITIC Press, Beijing.

Chapter 17
Distribution of Trading Potential

The trading network connects many trading agents, which interact and influence each other through network links, forming the operating ecology of the trading system. However, the mutual influence and interaction between trading agents are neither uniform nor symmetrical, and the influence of different trading agents varies greatly. In the trading system, most trading agents have very limited influence, and only a few trading agents may have strong influence. They occupy a certain monopoly position, and have strong dominance in trading protocols and pricing rights. These advantages will eventually be converted into their high profits. Trading potential is an indicator used to describe the status and influence of trading agents in the trading system.

17.1 Trading Potential

When talking about free competition markets, people usually have a subconscious assumption that all market participants have roughly the same competitiveness and compete fairly on an equal footing. People always uphold this idea: equality is the basis of competition, without equality there can be no competition efficiency. But the cruel reality is that market participants are not always on an equal footing, and there are huge differences between trading agents in their competitiveness. This is a basic feature of the real world, and the trading system is no exception. To describe this gap, we need to introduce a new concept—trading agent potential, or trading potential for short.

Z. Wang, *Trading Economics*, Contributions to Economics,
https://doi.org/10.1007/978-981-99-9875-3_17

17.1.1 Concept of Trading Potential

Trading potential is an indicator used to describe the degree of advantage of trading agents in games with opponents and in phase competition. The higher the trading potential, the more obvious the advantage of the trading agent in the trading game. Trading potential is a concentrated reflection of various factors such as the phase order of the trading agent, market share, and the ability to prevent competitors from entering.

Trading agents are distributed at different phases of the trading network, with varying degrees of trading potential. Trading agents at the center nodes of the trading network usually have a strong ability to influence other trading agents. In contrast, most nodes on the trading network have very limited influence on other agents, almost negligible. These agents can only show a certain macro value through a large number of aggregations and behavior coordination.

In the trading system, the operating efficiency of super trading agents largely determines the efficiency of the entire system. When a company with super trading potential is inefficient but too big to fail, it will drag down the economy of the entire country. In a sense, those who have lost their efficiency advantage but have super trading potential have actually become the kidnappers of the national economy. The government often finds itself in a dilemma, unable to help their crisis, and yet can't ignore their inefficiency.

To illustrate this point, let's look back at some of the scenes when the financial tsunami swept the world at the beginning of this century. In the fall of 2008, two of the three major American car companies—General Motors and Chrysler—were on the verge of bankruptcy. Because the three companies had super trading potential,[1] the U.S. government ultimately decided to bail them out. In December 2008, the U.S. Treasury announced a $17.4 billion rescue plan for the two companies. However, this was just the beginning of the rescue, and the U.S. government had to pay a higher price to save the auto industry. When General Motors and Chrysler were able to raise funds on their own from the financial market to completely get rid of the operating crisis, and the stock prices in the capital market began to rise, the rescue funds used by the U.S. government reached $81.8 billion, 4.7 times the original rescue plan.[2]

17.1.2 The Origin of the Concept of Trading Potential

In the theoretical system of mainstream economics, in order to maintain compatibility with the perfect competition theory framework, both families and enterprises, the two types of trading agents, are treated homogeneously. Since Adam Smith, mainstream economics has always adhered to this tradition, known as the "Smith tradition". The "Smith tradition" regards the market monopoly phenomenon caused by the competitive differences of trading agents as a special case, which the government does not need to take special measures to intervene, and theoretically there is no need to conduct special research on the monopoly phenomenon.[3] In the "Smith tradition", the differences between trading agents, including huge disparities in competitiveness, are all ignored. Against this background, the concept used to describe the differences between trading agents—trading potential—has no room for survival.

Entering the era of neoclassical economics, the "Smith tradition" is still regarded as a standard by economists. Alfred Marshall, the leading figure of neoclassical economics, is also a fan of the "Smith tradition". However, his pragmatic academic style that values reality makes him not completely ignore the increasingly prominent monopoly phenomenon like other scholars. Although he clearly knows that the deep reason for the increasing gap between trading agents is the law of increasing returns, which is incompatible with the assumption of perfect competition, he still discussed the law of increasing returns in his classic textbook *Principles of Economics*. However, he eventually compromised with the "Smith tradition", attributing increasing returns and abnormal expansion of enterprise scale to the personal traits of entrepreneurs, and cleverly dissolved the logical conflict between the two in random fluctuations. According to his principle, it was quite obvious to see how each step in the development of a capable and enterprising manufacturer made the next step easier and faster. Therefore, if the owner was lucky and maintained abundant energy and was not afraid of hard work, his development was likely to continue. But these couldn't last forever; once these declined, his business was likely to be destroyed by the factors that made it prosper, unless he handed over the business to another capable person like he was in the past. It could be seen that the rise and fall of individual manufacturers might be regular, while a huge industry experienced long-term fluctuations and continued to develop. This was like the leaves undergoing a large amount of metabolism, while the trunk grew year after year.[4] In Marshall's view, the development of individual enterprises beyond the industry level is just a random phenomenon, just like random fluctuations eventually return to the average level.

In the 1930s, E.H. Chamberlin, a professor of economics at Harvard University, and Joan Robinson, a professor at Cambridge University, almost simultaneously had their respective monographs published—*The Theory of Monopolistic Competition* and *Economics of Imperfect Competition*, which immediately caused a huge response in the economic community. People began to accept the idea that the differentiation of trading agents is a norm of reality. The "Smith tradition" has since ended its dominant position in mainstream economics. Against this backdrop, the concept of trading potential, which describes the differences between trading agents, could emerge, and economists gradually began to use various concepts to describe these differences.

American economist and Nobel laureate Joseph E. Stiglitz used the term "market power" in his book *The Truth of America* to analyze the problems that had arisen in the American economy. He believes that the root cause of a series of problems such as the lack of vitality in the American economy, imbalance in market structure, corporate exploitation of consumers, and polarization of wealth distribution lies in the extremely uneven distribution of market power. Large corporations with super market power, by virtue of their huge competitive advantages, obtain excess profits, fundamentally subverting the efficiency basis of market resource allocation. In his believe, all industries, the number of competing companies was decreasing. Market sales shares were increasingly concentrated in the top two or three large companies. … As market concentration increased, market power strengthened. Companies used market power to raise the price of relative costs, the so-called "markup", and seized high profits through this process. The result was that large companies were taking an increasing share of the national income cake, and corporate profit margins were also hitting new highs, rising from 10 to 16% in recent years. It was estimated that in 2016, 28 companies covered by the S&P 500 index contributed 50% of all corporate profits, reflecting a more concentrated market power than in the past.[5]

Trading potential is a further deepening of the concepts of corporate monopoly and market power, and a refined description of the distribution of differences among trading agents. The introduction of the concept of trading potential lays the foundation for our in-depth analysis of the evolution of trading systems.

17.2 Measurement of Trading Potential

When we understand trading potential as the ability of trading agents to participate in competition and their influence on other trading agents, how to accurately measure trading potential becomes a very pressing task and is the basis for our analysis of the distribution of trading potential in trading systems.

17.2.1 Dimensions of Trading Potential

Trading potential can be defined from three dimensions, namely trading scale, pricing power, and the ability to prevent competitors from entering. The three dimensions are interrelated and reinforce each other. Agents with a larger trading scale usually also have stronger abilities in terms of pricing power and preventing competitors from entering. Similarly, agents with strong pricing power will fully utilize their bargaining power to strive for more benefits for themselves while also striving for as many trading resources as possible to increase their trading scale.

In the three dimensions of trading potential, trading scale includes both the forward trading of the trading agent and the reverse trading of the trading agent, covering all trading activities of the agent on the trading network. Trading scale is the basis of trading potential. Only with enough economic strength and a large trading scale can one control the market, influence the decisions of other trading agents, and achieve the goal of excess returns.

Pricing power is another dimension for measuring trading potential, and its connotation is not just the ability to determine prices, but also includes more content such as price discrimination, advantages on dispute resolution, etc. Theoretically, price discrimination is illegal, but it is very common in reality. Multinational companies, by fully utilizing the differences in the rigor of laws in different countries, will adopt different pricing strategies and different after-sales service terms for different countries and regions. Typically, multinational companies will offer more favorable prices and relatively generous after-sales service to economically developed countries, while for many developing countries, there will be significant discrimination in both price and after-sales service. The reason why multinational companies dare to do this and will not be punished by regulatory authorities is mainly because these multinational companies have strong influence.

The pricing power of a company is a very important aspect for investors, and even a key factor for investors to decide on investment. Warren Buffett once pointed out that the most important criterion to judge whether a company is doing well or not was whether the company had the pricing power of goods. If people had the ability to raise the price of goods while maintaining business dealings with competitors, they can do business better.[6]

In terms of preventing competitors from entering, the means used by companies are varied. In the 1990s, Microsoft Corporation, in order to consolidate its monopoly position in the personal operating system, would attack any company that could pose a threat to it. Netscape, was originally a very excellent American company in the field of Internet browsers, and did not directly compete with Microsoft's personal operating system, but Microsoft was still worried that it would become a competitor later. In order to defeat Netscape, Microsoft developed its own IE browser. Although it was not comparable in quality to Netscape's browser, Microsoft gave it away for free to customers, bundling IE with the operating system, and eventually defeated Netscape.

Preventing competitors from entering is also a key measure of a company's ability to control the market. Buffett likened this ability to a company's moat. What should be considered was the width of this moat and the company's ability to maintain its width, to ensure that it was difficult for other companies and operators to cross. And company managers were told that they were expected to widen this river every year.[7]

Patent rights are a common means for large companies to prevent competitors from entering. Patents, originally used to encourage innovation, often unfortunately become tools to prevent market competition and suppress technological innovation. Large companies use their huge financial advantages to acquire patents from inventors or small businesses. In order to obtain patents, they may even directly acquire companies that own certain patents, building a formidable patent barrier, making any potential entrants face costly, marathon-style endless litigation and back off.[8]

For families, the scale of trading is relatively easy to understand, and pricing power is mainly manifested as the ability to negotiate wages and the ability to negotiate investment. The ability to negotiate wages is directly related to the level of education of the worker and the market value of their skills. Generally speaking, the higher the level of education, the stronger the bargaining power in the workplace. The supply and demand relationship of skills in the workplace and the potential value that skills bring to the company's production determine the market value of the skills. The higher the value, the stronger the bargaining power of the job seeker. The ability of investment negotiation is manifested as the investor's impact on the process of how capital is used and the ability to negotiate the return on investment. Obviously, the wealthier the family, the stronger its ability to negotiate investment.

17.2.2 Trading Potential Function

In the three-dimensional measurement space of trading potential, the corresponding variables have a mutually reinforcing relationship. This kind of interaction and mutual restraint will present extremely complex external forms. For simplicity, we use an axiomatic method to define the trading potential quantitatively.

Assume ψ is a one-to-one mapping between the subject set of the trading system T and the set of real numbers $(-\infty, +\infty)$. At time step t, any trading agent $a_i \in \{a_i\}_N$ in the trading system T has a corresponding real number under this mapping. If $\psi(a_i)$ satisfies the following three conditions, then the mapping ψ is the trading potential function of the trading system T, and the value of $\psi(a_i)$ is the trading potential of the trading agent a_i:

I. For any trading agent a_i in the trading system T, there is $\psi(a_i) > 0$;
II. For any trading agents a_i and a_j in the trading system T, if there is a difference in their overall strength in the three-dimensional space of trading potential, then $\psi(a_i) \neq \psi(a_j)$. If a_i has stronger overall strength than a_j, then $\psi(a_i) > \psi(a_j)$, and vice versa;
III. If a_i and a_j have the same overall strength, then $\psi(a_i) = \psi(a_j)$.

According to the definition of trading potential, we can draw the following conclusion: if $\psi(a_i)$ is the trading potential function of the trading system T, for any constants $k > 0$ and $c > 0$, $k\psi(a_i) + c$ is also the trading potential function of the trading system T. We can prove the above conclusion.

$\because$ $\psi(a_i)$ is the trading potential function on T,

$\therefore$ any trading agents a_i, a_j will be assigned a trading potential value according to their respective comprehensive strengths, satisfying $\psi(a_i) > 0$, $\psi(a_j) > 0$; if a_i has a comprehensive strength superior to a_j, then $\psi(a_i) > \psi(a_j)$; if a_i has a comprehensive strength inferior to a_j, then $\psi(a_i) < \psi(a_j)$; if a_i, a_j have comparable comprehensive strengths, then $\psi(a_i) = \psi(a_j)$.

$$\because k > 0,\ c > 0$$

$\therefore k\psi(a_i) + c > 0$, satisfying the axiom conditions of the trading potential function I.

$\because$ When $\psi(a_i) > \psi(a_j)$, it also satisfies $k\psi(a_i) + c > k\psi(a_i) + c$;

When $\psi(a_i) < \psi(a_j)$, it also satisfies $k\psi(a_i) + c < k\psi(a_i) + c$;

When $\psi(a_i) = \psi(a_j)$, it also satisfies $k\psi(a_i) + c = k\psi(a_i) + c$;

$\therefore \psi(a_i) + c$ satisfies the axiom conditions of the trading potential function II and III.

$\therefore k\psi(a_i) + c$ is the trading potential function on the trading system T.

This shows that if $\psi(a_i)$ is the trading potential function on the trading system T, then all linear transformations of $\psi(a_i)$ are trading potential functions on T. All trading potential functions of the trading system T form a group of linear transformations. Each trading potential function on the trading potential transformation group assigns trading agents with varying trading potential values, but does not change the order of trading potential distribution among trading agents. All trading potential systems defined by all trading potential functions on the trading system T have isomorphic relationships.

The above conclusion indicates that the value of the trading potential is not important; the key is that the trading potential distribution determined by the trading potential function is unique. The distribution of trading potential is a very important structural parameter of the trading system, which not only has a significant impact on the operating status of the system, but also has a profound impact on the social system. The distribution of trading potential is a dynamic structure. As the trading system evolves, the trading potential will show a trend of polarization, which is an important feature of the evolution of the trading system.

In the trading system, we call the trading agents ranked high in trading potential as high-order trading potential agents, or simply high-order agents; we call the trading agents ranked low in trading potential as low-order trading potential agents, or simply low-order agents. We will later prove that at any stage of the evolution of any trading system, low-order agents always occupy the majority of the trading system, while high-order agents always belong to the minority. In the evolution of the trading system, the competition between trading agents will ultimately be reflected in the competition of trading potential. Each trading agent hopes to obtain a higher order of trading potential in order to occupy a competitive advantage.

17.3 Theorem of Trading Potential Polarization

In the evolution of the trading system, the trading potential always evolves towards greater differentiation, showing the Matthew effect of the strong getting stronger and the weak getting weaker. In fact, as a comprehensive indicator of the competitiveness of trading agents, differentiation is self-evident from the logic of competition.

17.3.1 Equation of Trading Potential Evolution

According to the characteristics of the hierarchical evolution of the trading network, the tendency of market concentration is mainly manifested in the non-structural constraint market, that is, the global market, and it is not prominent in the community market. Therefore, we choose the global market for the game analysis of trading potential evolution.

The source of trading potential for both families and enterprises is the same, namely trading resources. The more trading resources are occupied, the faster the strength accumulates, and the stronger the trading potential. In the subsequent proof, we will put families and enterprises together to prove the differentiation process of trading potential.

Assume that at time step t, the capacity of the trading system is N_t. As time t continues, N_t will change accordingly. $\{a_i\}_{N_t}$ is the set of agents in the trading system, including both families and enterprises, a_i and a_j are two arbitrary trading agents on $\{a_i\}_{N_t}$.

For the convenience of proof, without affecting the generality of the conclusion, assume that at each time step t, each trading agent only conducts one reverse trading. In the monetary trading system, reverse trading is constrained by liquidity, while forward trading is not. Due to the difference in constraints between forward and reverse trading, different strategies are formed for the two types of trading. The strategy of reverse trading focuses on the selection of trading objects, while the strategy of forward trading focuses on obtaining as many trading resources as possible.

According to the assumption of limited rationality of trading agents, reverse trading agents tend to choose those with higher trading potential when selecting trading partners. Decision-makers believe that trading potential is a characteristic of the agent that has been proven by the market, and choosing based on the trading potential of the other party is a safe and economical strategy. Under the guidance of this principle, the evolution of the trading system will follow the basic rule: the higher the trading potential, the easier it is for the trading agent to obtain trading resources.

Assuming a_i selects the object for reverse trading, a_j is any agent in the trading system, $P_{ij}(t)$ is the probability of a_i choosing a_j as a trading object at time step t, $\psi_j(t)$ is the trading potential of a_j at time step t, according to our analysis, the probability $P_{ij}(t)$ satisfies the following relationship:

$$P_{ij}(t) = \alpha_{ij}\psi_j(t) \tag{17.3.1}$$

In (17.3.1), $\alpha_{ij} \geq 0$ is the weight coefficient that trading agent a_i assigns to trading agent a_j. The weight coefficient α_{ij} reflects the selection preference of trading agent a_i and the expectation of the overall situation of trading agent a_j. It can be imagined that due to the limitations of the trading community size and the limited information set, the selection weight for most agents in the trading system is almost zero, that is, $\alpha_{ij} \approx 0$. Only a small number of trading agents can obtain a larger selection weight. For any trading agent a_i, the weight assignment to other trading agents is constrained by the finitenessof attention resources, satisfying the following idagent:

$$\sum_{j=1}^{N_t} \alpha_{ij} = 1 \tag{17.3.2}$$

The trading potential of trading agent a_j at time step $t+1$, $\psi_j(t+1)$, is determined by the trading flow obtained at the previous time step. The trading flow obtained by a_j depends on the selection probability given to it by other trading agents. From this we get:

$$\psi_j(t+1) = \beta \sum_{\substack{i=1 \\ i \neq j}}^{N_t} p_{ij}(t) \tag{17.3.3}$$

In (17.3.3), $0 \leq \beta \leq 1$ is the trading potential conversion coefficient. The size of the trading potential conversion factor β reflects the market's position in the trading system T. The larger the value of β, the more prominent the role of trading in determining the status of trading agents, and the higher the market's position in the resource allocation process of the trading system. On the contrary, the smaller the value of β, the smaller the role of trading activities in the process of establishing the status of trading agents, and it also indicates that the importance of the trading system in the social system is not strong.

Substitute Eq. (17.3.1) into (17.3.3) to get:

$$\psi_j(t+1) = \beta \sum_{\substack{i=1 \\ i \neq j}}^{N_t} \alpha_{ij} \psi_j(t) \tag{17.3.4}$$

After rearranging, we get:

$$\psi_j(t+1) = \left(\beta \sum_{\substack{i=1 \\ i \neq j}}^{N_t} \alpha_{ij} \right) \psi_j(t) \tag{17.3.5}$$

In (17.3.5), the parameter $\beta \sum_{\substack{i=1 \\ i \neq j}}^{N_t} \alpha_{ij}$ reflects the market recognition and comprehensive ability of the trading agent a_j, which determines the evolution of the trading potential of the trading agent a_j. We call it the trading potential feedback factor of a_j, and simplify it as follows:

$$\pi_j = \beta \sum_{\substack{i=1 \\ i \neq j}}^{N_t} \alpha_{ij} \tag{17.3.6}$$

Substitute (17.3.6) into (17.3.5) to get:

$$\psi_j(t+1) = \pi_j \psi_j(t) \tag{17.3.7}$$

We convert the difference Eq. (17.3.7) into a differential equation. Subtract $\psi_j(t)$ from both sides of (17.3.7) to get:

$$\psi_j(t+1) - \psi_j(t) = (\pi_j - 1)\psi_j(t) \tag{17.3.8}$$

Make the following idagent transformation to (17.3.8):

$$\frac{\psi_j(t+1) - \psi_j(t)}{(t+1) - t} = \left(\pi_j - 1\right)\psi_j(t) \tag{17.3.9}$$

Convert (17.3.9) into an equivalent differential form:

$$\frac{d\psi_j(t)}{dt} = \left(\pi_j - 1\right)\psi_j(t) \tag{17.3.10}$$

Equation (17.3.10) describes the basic law of the evolution of the trading potential of any trading agent a_j on the trading system over time t. We call it the trading potential equation.

In order to obtain the general solution of the trading potential function, we need to further transform (17.3.10):

$$\frac{d\psi_j(t)}{\psi_j(t)} = \left(\pi_j - 1\right)dt \tag{17.3.11}$$

Integrate both sides of (17.3.11):

$$\int \frac{1}{\psi_j(t)} d\psi_j(t) = \int \left(\pi_j - 1\right)dt \tag{17.3.12}$$

Integrate (17.3.12) to get:

$$\ln \psi_j(t) = \left(\pi_j - 1\right)t + c \tag{17.3.13}$$

$$\therefore \psi_j(t) = e^c e^{\left(\pi_j - 1\right)t} \tag{17.3.14}$$

Take $t = 0$ in (17.3.14) to get the initial condition of the equation:

$$\psi_j^0 = e^c \tag{17.3.15}$$

In (17.3.15), ψ_j^0 is the initial value of the trading potential of a_j.

Substitute the initial condition (17.3.15) back into (17.3.14) to get:

$$\psi_j(t) = \psi_j^0 e^{(\pi_j - 1)t} \tag{17.3.16}$$

Equation (17.3.16) is the general solution of the trading potential function. It shows that the trading potential is an exponential function of time t. This indicates that the trading potential has highly dynamic characteristics.

17.3.2 Trading Potential Polarization Theorem

As can be seen from the general solution of the trading potential function (17.3.16), when $\pi_j = \beta \sum_{\substack{i=1 \\ i \neq j}}^{N_t} \alpha_{ij} > 1$, the trading potential $\psi_j(t)$ will continue to increase with the passage of time t, that is:

$$\lim_{t \to +\infty} \psi_j(t) = \lim_{t \to +\infty} \psi_j^0 e^{(\pi_j - 1)t} = +\infty \tag{17.3.17}$$

When $\pi_j = \beta \sum_{\substack{i=1 \\ i \neq j}}^{N_t} \alpha_{ij} < 1$, the trading potential $\psi_j(t)$ will continue to decay with the passage of time t, and eventually tend to 0:

$$\lim_{t \to +\infty} \psi_j(t) = \lim_{t \to +\infty} \psi_j^0 e^{-(1 - \pi_j)t} = 0 \tag{17.3.18}$$

When $\pi_j = \beta \sum_{\substack{i=1 \\ i \neq j}}^{N_t} \alpha_{ij} = 1$, the trading potential $\psi_j(t)$ will enter a stable state, not changing with time t, and remain constant at the initial value:

$$\lim_{t \to +\infty} \psi_j(t) = \lim_{t \to +\infty} \psi_j^0 e^{(\pi_j - 1)t} = \psi_j^0 \tag{17.3.19}$$

As can be seen from the above derivation, any trading agent in the trading system a_i, there are three possible evolutionary trends for its trading potential: respectively, the trading potential $\psi(a_i)$ continues to increase, the trading potential $\psi(a_i)$ continues to decrease, and the trading potential $\psi(a_i)$ remains unchanged at the initial level ψ^0.

Since the attention weight of each trading agent is constrained by Eq. (17.3.2), there is a repulsive relationship between the feedback factors among the agents in the trading system. When the feedback factor of some trading agents in the trading system is greater than 1, i.e. $\pi_i > 1$, there must be some trading agents in the trading system with a feedback factor less than 1; and the larger $\pi_i > 1$ is, the smaller the feedback factor of other agents becomes after being squeezed by a_i. This is the inevitable result of attention as a finite scarce resource.

From this, we can conclude that in any trading system T, we can certainly find trading agents a_i with a feedback factor greater than 1 and trading agents a_j with a feedback factor less than 1.

According to the general solution of the trading potential function (17.3.16), take trading agents a_i and a_j as an example, we can calculate the general evolutionary trend of the trading potential distribution in the trading system. At time step t, the difference in trading potential $\psi_i(t)$ and $\psi_j(t)$ of trading agents a_i and a_j is:

$$\psi_i(t) - \psi_j(t) = \psi_i^0 e^{(\pi_i - 1)t} - \psi_j^0 e^{(\pi_j - 1)t} \tag{17.3.20}$$

Arrange (17.3.19) to get:

$$\psi_i(t) - \psi_j(t) = \psi_i^0 e^{(\pi_i - 1)t} \left(1 - \frac{\psi_j^0}{\psi_i^0} e^{-(\pi_i - \pi_j)t} \right) \tag{17.3.21}$$

$$\because \pi_i > 1, \pi_j < 1$$

$$\therefore \pi_i - 1 > 0, \pi_i - \pi_j > 0$$

$\therefore$ As the time step t continues to increase, the difference in trading potential of trading agents a_i and a_j will tend to infinity:

$$\frac{\lim}{t \to \infty} \psi_i(t) - \psi_j(t) = \frac{\lim}{t \to \infty} \psi_i^0 e^{(\pi_i - 1)t} \left(1 - \frac{\psi_j^0}{\psi_i^0} e^{-(\pi_i - \pi_j)t} \right) \to +\infty$$

$\because$ Trading agents a_i and a_j are any two representatives in the trading system T.

$\therefore$ The trading potential distribution of the trading system T will inevitably show a polarized evolutionary trend. We call this evolutionary trend of the trading system the Trading potential Polarization Theorem.

The trading potential polarization theorem indicates that the trend of trading potential polarization is an inevitable result in the evolution of the trading system, and it is a manifestation of the inherent nature of the trading system. The extended conclusion is that the speed of trading potential polarization must be closely related to some characteristic variable of the trading system. We will prove that the speed of trading potential polarization is positively correlated with the capacity of the trading system. The larger the capacity of the trading system, the faster the speed of trading potential polarization. Under equivalent conditions, the intensity of trading potential polarization in large-capacity trading systems is far higher than that in small-capacity trading systems.

Assuming the capacity of the trading system T is N, according to the structure formula of the trading potential feedback factor (17.3.6), the minimum theoretical value of the feedback factor π is $\pi = 0$, and the maximum theoretical value occurs when a trading agent owns all the resources of the trading system. At this time, the feedback factor is $\pi = \beta(N - 1)$. From this, it can be concluded that the distribution interval of the trading system feedback factor π is $[0, \beta(N - 1)]$. Obviously, under the condition that the trading agent's trading potential conversion ability parameter β_i remains unchanged, the larger the capacity of the trading system N, the larger the distribution interval of the feedback factor, and the larger the difference between the feedback factors on the trading system T, and from Eq. (17.3.20), the faster the differentiation speed of the trading system's trading potential.

The capacity of the trading network is a dynamic variable, reflecting people's views on the economic outlook to certain extent. The better the economic outlook, the faster the growth rate of the number of enterprises. On the contrary, if the macroeconomic situation is poor and the outlook is pessimistic, the number of enterprises may shrink.

Population is the basis of the capacity of the trading system. During the period of population growth, the capacity of the trading system will continue to expand. When society enters the aging stage, the momentum of population growth is suppressed, and severe aging usually accompanies population shrinkage. Based on the close relationship between population and the capacity of the trading system, we can infer that there is a certain causal relationship between the state of trading potential differentiation and population structure. In societies where the population structure is young, the population size is growing, the capacity of the trading system will also grow rapidly, and the trading potential shows a rapid differentiation trend. For societies where the population structure is aging, the speed of trading potential differentiation shows a slowing trend, and there may even be a reversal of trading potential differentiation.

17.3.3 Factors Influencing the Trading Potential Feedback Factor

As can be seen from the trading Eq. (17.3.16), the feedback factor of the trading agent determines its rise and fall in the trading system. The feedback factor of the family is mainly determined by the choice strategy of reverse trading, including whether the investment is appropriate, whether the structure of consumption and investment is reasonable, and the reserve of human capital. The feedback factor of the enterprise is mainly determined by three factors: the trading agent's ability of trading potential conversion, market preference structure, and market expectations. Among these three factors, the trading agent's ability of trading potential conversion and market preference structure are relatively stable factors, while market expectations are the main unstable factors.

The factors leading to changes in market expectations mainly come from two aspects: firstly, the expectation of technological changes. People always favor new technology products, not only because new technology products can bring new experiences to people, but more importantly, they will have an increasingly better application environment, while the application environment on which old products rely will gradually shrink and disappear. For example, when CD playback technology appeared, old-fashioned tape technology was forced to withdraw from the market, and users with old-fashioned tape machines would face difficulties in maintenance and nowhere to buy new film and television works. Technology is always in the process of continuous iteration and updating, and the market will respond as soon as new technology sprouts. Whether in the capital market or in the commodity market, new technology will always be sought after, while relatively old technology will be gradually neglected by the market. In wave after wave of technological revolution, due to the sudden change in market expectations, it often leads to the collapse of giant companies that originally had strong trading potential (in the wave of digital imaging technology, the former optical imaging giant Kodak collapsed, becoming a typical case of Schumpeter's innovative destruction theory), and small companies or start-ups representing the direction of new technology development may quickly grow into giants (Microsoft and Apple in the United States are typical representatives of such cases).

Secondly, it is the impact of bullish or bearish information. When a company is amid the tailwind of favorable policies, its market valuation will skyrocket, its financing ability will be enhanced, and its ability to convert trading potential will be strengthened. With the push of these favorable factors, the market's expectations for such companies will gradually increase. On the contrary, amid the headwind of bearish policies, companies will go through the exact opposite process. The increase in financing costs and the shrinkage of trading resources will follow. In addition, information on the company's conditions is also an important factor leading to changes in market expectations. Information on the company's financial situation, progress in technological innovation, and changes in the company team, etc., will all become important factors in changing market expectations.

Compared with technological innovation factors, the impact of information is more focused on agents that are already in a high level of trading potential, and the market's attention is usually focused on them. For a large number of low-level trading potential agents, the cost and benefit of attention are disproportionate, and the market invests less attention resources on them. It can be seen that the main driving force for the rapid growth of low-level trading potential agents is the power of technological change; and the cause for the fall of high-level trading potential agents can be both the power of technological change and the impact of information. Summarizing the above analysis, we can draw this conclusion: The faster the technological progress, the faster the distribution of trading potential in the trading system changes; the higher the monopoly of technology, the stronger the polarization of trading potential. Under the effect of this law, in modern society where the speed of technological progress is accelerating, the characteristics of trading potential evolution are: on the one hand, the speed of trading potential differentiation is accelerating; on the other hand, the speed of super trading potential agents changing positions is also accelerating. This situation gives people a feeling of sudden rise and sudden fall. In fact, this is a manifestation of the accelerated evolution of the trading system.

17.3.4 The Kuznets Curve

In his study of the distribution of income in the United States from 1913 to 1948, Simon Smith Kuznets proposed the "bell curve" of income disparity, later known as the "Kuznets Curve". Kuznets believed that in the process of industrialization, the phenomenon of income inequality inevitably developed along a curve that first expanded and then contracted. In the early stages of industrialization, the exacerbation of income inequality was due to the fact that only a small number of people benefited from the wealth brought about by industrialization, but the situation would change later, with more people sharing the wealth created by industrialization, thereby curbing the expansion of income inequality.[9] According to Kuznets' theory, polarization is only a temporary phenomenon in special historical development periods and will disappear with economic development. However, later data did not support Kuznets' conclusion, and the polarization of income and wealth did not converge, but became more prominent.

In fact, the appearance of the temporary "Kuznets" phenomenon is not necessarily due to the efficiency improvement brought about by the industrialization, but is likely to be the result of the periodic fluctuations in the capacity of the trading system. The sample taken by Kuznets happened to be during the two World Wars, which caused a large loss of population, huge economic damage, and many business failures, all of which would greatly affect the capacity of the trading system and ultimately affect the evolution of the trading system.

Let's take a look at the changes of the U.S. population growth over the 100 years from 1901 to 2000. We can find that during the sample interval selected by Kuznets, the growth rate of the U.S. population was at a historical low (Fig. 17.1):

In the first 12 years of the twentieth century, the average annual growth rate of the U.S. population was 16‰, while in the 36 years of the sample interval from 1913 to 1946, the average annual growth rate of the U.S. population was 12‰; in the 54 years after the sample interval, i.e., from 1947 to 2000, the average annual growth rate of the U.S. population was 12.8‰ (Fig. 17.2).

Although changes in population size can only indirectly reflect changes in the capacity of the trading system, as the basis of the capacity of the trading system, these changes can still explain some problems. During the sample interval of the Kuznets curve, the normal operation of the U.S. economy was disrupted by the sudden arrival of the two World Wars, which can also be seen from the huge fluctuations in the U.S. economic growth curve.[10]

In the derivation of trading potential polarization, for the convenience of technical processing, we limit the trading frequency of trading agents, and each agent has only one reverse trade in a time step. In this case, N_t not only represents the capacity of the trading system, but also the trading scale of the trading system. The growth

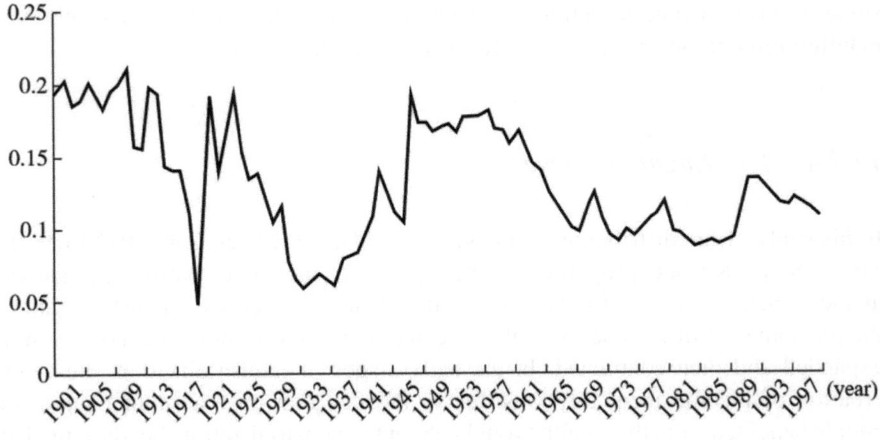

Fig. 17.1 The U.S. population growth curve

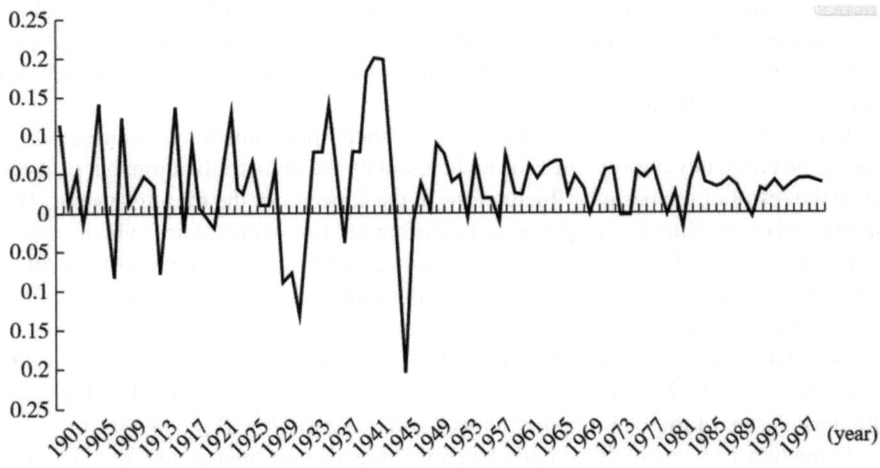

Fig. 17.2 The U.S. economic growth curve

of N_t represents the scale expansion of the trading system, that is, the expansion of capacity scale and trading scale. In the evolution process of the trading system, the expansion of trading scale is the fundamental driving force for the differentiation of trading potential. As the previous chapters have told us, the profit-seeking motive of trading agents drives the deepening of division of labor, the pace of the trading system's pursuit of efficiency will never stop, and the inevitable result is that the trading scale of the trading system will continue to expand. Thousands of years of human history have powerfully confirmed this conclusion.

Differentiation is an inevitable product of human societal progress. We can only slow down the speed of differentiation through continuous system reforms to avoid excessive differentiation leading to the collapse of the social system. However, we can never fundamentally eliminate the phenomenon of differentiation in human society. This is an inevitability determined by the inherent laws of the trading system.

17.4 The Power Law Distribution of Trading Potential

The theorem of trading potential polarization tells us that the distribution of trading potential in the trading system naturally shows a trend of differentiation. The gap in trading potential among trading agents will become larger and larger as the trading system evolves. However, we do not know how the trading potential is distributed in the trading system at a specific point in time. Accurately grasping the distribution law of trading potential has great practical significance for both system reform and the formulation of market supervision policies.

17.4.1 The Power Law Distribution Function of Trading Potential

Generally speaking, the distribution characteristics of indicators in a group depend on the behavioral characteristics behind the indicators. If the object reflected by the indicator is a group of unrelated individuals, the most common distribution form of such indicators is the normal distribution, such as the distribution of IQ or height in a population. In addition, binomial distribution, Bernoulli distribution, Poisson distribution, etc., are also common distribution forms, and they each have their own adaptive phenomenon characteristics. Binomial distribution is usually suitable for the probability distribution of a shooter hitting k times out of n shots; it can also be used as the probability distribution of n samples, k of which are defective; it can also be used as the probability distribution of n coin tosses, k of which show heads. The Bernoulli distribution can be used in n independent experiments, each of which has only two results, either A or B, in n experiments, k times A or k times B occur. The Poisson distribution can be used for the probability of rare events, especially for describing the event distribution where the probability of an event only depends on the time interval between two events, and is irrelevant to the specific time point. The main feature of such events is that there is no correlation between the number of events occurring in different time periods. For example, the number of protons emitted by radioactive materials, the probability of accidents, errors, failures, disasters, the probability distribution of the number of public facility service demands in a certain time period, etc., can all be described using the Poisson distribution.

When the measured values have a characteristic of "fashion" popularity, and the occurrence of events is associated with some kind of "following behavior", power law distribution dominates for these types of events. Compared to the normal distribution, the power law distribution has a fat tail as its main distribution feature, with the distribution density function declining at a relatively slow pace. For the distribution of World Wide Web links, websites with a large number of nodes are quite common, far exceeding the proportion of the same intensity indicators of the normal distribution.

In trading systems, in addition to a few agents with super trading potential, there are also a large number of trading groups with quite high trading potential. The middle class usually has a high trading potential in the society and is the largest group in a country. Among enterprise groups, small and medium-sized enterprises make up the absolute majority, apart from a few large and extra-large enterprises. Medium-sized enterprises have considerable strength in terms of quantity, market sales, enterprise asset scale, production capacity, and other aspects. They are the backbone of the economies of various countries and occupy a considerable proportion. These phenomena all conform to the "fat tail" characteristic of power law distribution, which indirectly verifies the possibility of trading potential distribution following the power law distribution.

In trading systems, in order to maximize the capture of trading opportunities and reduce decision-making risks, observing the trading behavior of other agents is an important way to obtain valuable information, and cascade trading is thus generated. Obviously, the characteristics of trading potential are very consistent with the conditions of the power law distribution phenomenon: firstly, the formation of trading potential is the result of trading agents pursuing maximum returns; secondly, in the accumulation process of trading potential, due to the constraint of incomplete information, the follow-up strategy is a strategy commonly adopted by trading agents. We can infer that the distribution of trading potential in the trading system should conform to the power law distribution.

Although we have sufficient reasons at the qualitative analysis level to determine that the distribution of trading potential conforms to the characteristics of the power law distribution, it is very difficult to give a complete proof at the quantitative level, and we can only provide quantitative proof through simplified models.[11]

To prove that the distribution of trading potential conforms to the power law distribution, we need to prove that in the trading system, the proportion of trading agents that satisfy $\psi \geq k$ in the trading system has a power law form, that is: $F(k) = \frac{c}{k^{\alpha}}$. Assume the capacity of the trading system T is t, and it grows uniformly with the increase of time step t, with only one trading agent added at each time step. The agent capacity at time step $t + 1$ is $t + 1$, of which t agents are previously accumulated agents, and the $t + 1$ agent is a new agent. According to the order of birth, we assign each agent a number. For the agent born at time step t, the number is t; for the agent appearing at time step $t + 1$, we assign $t + 1$ number.

Assume the probability of the trading agent $t + 1$ adopting a random trading strategy is p, randomly selecting trading objects from previously born trading agents; the probability of adopting a follow-up strategy (or optimal strategy) is q, based on each agent's trading potential, the higher the trading potential, the greater the probability that the trading agent $t + 1$ is selected. The probabilities of the two strategies satisfy the condition of $p + q = 1$.

In our preset conditions, despite the very strict restrictions on the growth of the trading system capacity, the freedom for trading agents to choose different strategies is still retained. They can adopt a mixed strategy composed of random selection and optimal selection, which ensures that while facilitating quantitative proof, the key features of the trading system are still retained, making the proof results meet higher universality requirements.

Under the random strategy, any agent i shares trading resources p from the newborn agent $t+1$. As a member of t, the trading resources that i can share are $\frac{P}{t}$. Assuming that i obtained a trading resource volume of $x_i(t)$ before the time step $t+1$, since all trading resources before the time step $t+1$ are t, the trading agent i owns a proportion of all trading resources $\frac{x_i(t)}{t}$. According to the allocation rules of trading resources under the follow-up strategy, the trading agent i can get a trading share of $\frac{x_i(t)}{t}q$ from the trading resources q of the newborn trading agent $t+1$. Adding the above two trading resource shares, we get the trading resources newly obtained by the trading agent i at the time step $t+1$ are $\frac{p}{t}+\frac{x_i(t)}{t}q$, that is, the growth of trading resources obtained by the trading agent i realized at the time step $t+1$ can be written as:

$$\Delta x_i(t)=\frac{p}{t}+\frac{x_i(t)q}{t} \tag{17.4.1}$$

Since the increase of each time step t is exactly 1, make an equivalent transformation of (17.4.1):

$$\frac{\Delta x_i(t)}{\Delta t}=\frac{p}{t}+\frac{x_i(t)q}{t} \tag{17.4.2}$$

Convert (17.4.2) into an equivalent differential form:

$$\frac{dx_i(t)}{dt}=\frac{p}{t}+\frac{x_i(t)q}{t} \tag{17.4.3}$$

Organize (17.4.3) to get:

$$\frac{dx_i(t)}{p+x_i(t)q}=\frac{dt}{t} \tag{17.4.4}$$

Integrate both sides of (17.4.4):

$$\int\frac{1}{p+x_i(t)q}dx_i(t)=\int\frac{1}{t}dt \tag{17.4.5}$$

From (17.4.5) we get:

$$\frac{1}{q}\ln(p+x_i(t)q)=\ln t+C \tag{17.4.6}$$

In (17.4.6), let $C=\ln c^{\frac{1}{q}}$, $c>0$, continue to organize to get:

$$p + x_i(t)q = ct^q \tag{17.4.7}$$

From (17.4.7) we get:

$$x_i(t) = \frac{ct^q - p}{q} \tag{17.4.8}$$

According to the preset boundary conditions, when i=t, the trading agent a_t does not have any accumulated trades in a new position close to a_{t+1}. According to the trading rules, at this time a_t cannot get the trading share under the following strategy of a_{t+1}, only the trading share under the random strategy of a_{t+1}, so there is $x_i(t) = \frac{P}{t}$, substitute it back into (17.4.8) to get:

$$c\frac{i^q}{q} - \frac{p}{q} = \frac{p}{t} \tag{17.4.9}$$

$$c\frac{i^q}{q} = \frac{p}{q} + \frac{p}{t} \tag{17.4.10}$$

Organize to get:

$$c = pq\left(\frac{1}{q} + \frac{1}{t}\right)i^{-q} \tag{17.4.11}$$

Substitute (17.4.11) back into (17.4.8) to get:

$$x_i(t) = \frac{pq\left(\frac{1}{q} + \frac{1}{t}\right)\left(\frac{t}{i}\right)^q - p}{q} \tag{17.4.12}$$

Further organize to get:

$$x_i(t) = p\left(\frac{1}{q} + \frac{1}{t}\right)\left(\frac{t}{i}\right)^q - \frac{p}{q} \tag{17.4.13}$$

According to the definition of trading potential, the trading potential of the trading agent is proportional to the total amount of trading resources obtained. The more trading resources the trading agent possesses, the higher the order of trading potential; the trading agent with a higher order of trading potential possesses more trading resources of the trading system. According to Eq. (17.4.13), we can get the trading potential $\psi_i(t)$ of the trading agent i:

$$\psi_i(t) = \beta x_i(t) = \beta p\left(\frac{1}{q} + \frac{1}{t}\right)\left(\frac{t}{i}\right)^q - \beta\frac{p}{q} \tag{17.4.14}$$

In Eq. (17.4.14), β is the trading potential conversion factor of the trading agent i.

According to Eq. (17.4.14), we can get the conditions that trading potential $\psi \geq k$ of the trading agent i:

$$\psi_i(t) = \beta x_i(t) = \beta p\left(\frac{1}{q} + \frac{1}{t}\right)\left(\frac{t}{i}\right)^q - \beta\frac{p}{q} \geq k \tag{17.4.15}$$

Organize (17.4.15) to get:

$$\beta p\left(\frac{1}{q} + \frac{1}{t}\right)\left(\frac{t}{i}\right)^q \geq k + \beta\frac{p}{q} \tag{17.4.16}$$

Continue to organize (17.4.16):

$$\left(\frac{t}{i}\right)^q \geq \frac{k+\beta\frac{p}{q}}{\beta p\left(\frac{1}{q}+\frac{1}{t}\right)}$$

$$\left(\frac{i}{t}\right)^q \leq \frac{\beta p\left(\frac{1}{q}+\frac{1}{t}\right)}{k+\beta\frac{p}{q}}$$

$$\frac{i}{t} \leq \left(\frac{\beta p\left(\frac{1}{q}+\frac{1}{t}\right)}{k+\beta\frac{p}{q}}\right)^{\frac{1}{q}}$$

$$\therefore i \leq \left(\frac{\beta p\left(\frac{1}{q}+\frac{1}{t}\right)}{k+\beta\frac{p}{q}}\right)^{\frac{1}{q}} t \tag{17.4.17}$$

Equation (17.4.17) gives the conclusion: in the trading system T, the trading agents with a birth order less than $\left(\frac{\beta p\left(\frac{1}{q}+\frac{1}{t}\right)}{k+\beta\frac{p}{q}}\right)^{\frac{1}{q}} t$ all meet the trading potential $\psi_i(t) \geq k$ conditions. It is known from the assumption that the total number of trading agents that meet the condition (17.4.17) in the trading system T is i. This gives the trading potential probability distribution function of the trading system T:

$$F(k) = \frac{i}{t} \tag{17.4.18}$$

From (17.4.18) we get:

$$F(k) = \left(\frac{\beta p(\frac{1}{q}+\frac{1}{t})}{k+\beta\frac{p}{q}}\right)^{\frac{1}{q}} \tag{17.4.19}$$

When $k \gg \beta\frac{p}{q}$, the term $\beta\frac{p}{q}$ can be omitted in the denominator of the above formula, and the simplified result of the trading potential function is obtained:

$$F(k) = \left[\beta p\left(\frac{1}{q} + \frac{1}{t}\right)\right]^{\frac{1}{q}} \frac{1}{k^{\frac{1}{q}}} \tag{17.4.20}$$

Let $c = \left[\beta p\left(\frac{1}{q} + \frac{1}{t}\right)\right]^{\frac{1}{q}}$, $\alpha = \frac{1}{q}$, substitute into (17.4.20) to get:

$$F(k) = \frac{c}{k^{\alpha}} \tag{17.4.21}$$

As shown by Eq. (17.4.21), the trading potential distribution function satisfies the power law distribution.

Looking at the structure of the power law distribution function of trading potential, we can draw the following conclusions: First, the differentiation characteristics of the trading system depend on the behavior type of the trading system. The more common the following strategy in the trading system, the more obvious the advantage accumulation effect, and the faster the differentiation of trading potential. On the contrary, the higher the proportion of random trading strategies, the weaker the differentiation of the trading system, and the more the distribution of trading potential tends to be uniform. In reality, for time-limited trading, due to the different constraints faced by each trading agent, the proportion of following strategies in such trades is very low. Time-limited trading markets usually correspond to community markets with relatively small transaction volumes. In contrast, non-structured constraint trades have larger amounts, more complex information structures, and higher uncertainty in expected returns. These characteristics of non-structured constraint trades determine that the frequency of use of following strategies is relatively high, and the power law distribution characteristics of trading potential distribution are also more obvious. Since non-structured trading is usually a global market, this once again shows that the global market is a market where trading potential polarization is very likely to occur.

Second, the trading potential conversion factor β plays a dual role in the trading potential function. On the one hand, the trading potential conversion factor β plays an amplifying role in the polarization process of the trading system through the feedback facto π. The larger the trading potential conversion factor, the faster the differentiation of the trading system; on the other hand, the trading potential conversion factor β also plays a role in generally increasing trading potential in the trading system. This is clearly shown in Eq. (17.4.20), where the trading potential conversion factor β is in the numerator of the coefficient c, intuitively showing that the larger the value of β, the more groups with high-order trading potential emerge in the trading system T, meaning that the trading system tends to be more average, which contradicts the conclusion drawn from the trading potential polarization theorem. This is the specific manifestation of the dual nature of the trading potential conversion factor β.

In fact, the trading potential polarization theorem and the trading potential distribution function have different meanings. The trading potential polarization theorem reveals the mechanism of advantage accumulation in the trading system. The trading potential conversion factor β inevitably plays a driving role in this process. The higher the trading potential conversion factor β, the faster the differentiation of trading potential, reflecting the relative relationship of trading potential in the evolution process of the trading system. The trading potential distribution function measures the proportion of trading agents with trading potential greater than a certain value. Although it also contains the relative relationship of trading agents, compared with the trading potential polarization theorem, the description of the difference in trading potential between different agents is more macroscopic. The distribution function only tells us the proportion of trading agents with trading potential greater than a certain value k in the system capacity, but does not further give the difference in trading potential of these agents. The different emphases of the trading potential polarization theorem and the trading potential distribution function in depicting differences are the main reasons for the seemingly contradictory role of the trading potential conversion factor β.

In the trading potential distribution function, the minimum trading potential k needs to satisfy the inequality $k \gg \beta\frac{p}{q}$. This relationship clearly shows that the trading potential conversion factor β plays a role in promoting efficiency improvement and general increase of trading potential in the evolution of the trading system T. Looking back at the history of human society, especially the more than three hundred years of development since the Industrial Revolution, in the process of rapid evolution of the trading system, people's lives have generally improved, and the trading potential of the trading agents is incomparable to the past. This shows that although the differentiation of the trading system is increasing, the public will still benefit from the evolution and development of the trading system. The theorem of trading potential polarization only tells us that the relative gap among trading agents is constantly widening, but this does not mean that the situation of the disadvantaged agents will get worse.

From the trading potential distribution function (17.4.20), we can also observe another result. When the trading potential conversion factor $\beta = 0$, the trading potential distribution function $F(k) = 0$, it indicates that the trading potential distribution function degenerates into a point at this time, and the trading potential of all trading agents is 0. In fact, this means that the trading system no longer exists, and trading activities no longer play any meaningful role in the process of people's status determination. In the real world, we can find such a scenario in the former planned economic model.

Third, in the power law distribution function of trading potential (17.4.21), time t is located at the denominator position of c. As time t continues, the coefficient of the distribution function c will continue to shrink, eventually approaching the limit value $c = \left(\frac{\beta p}{q}\right)^{\frac{1}{q}}$, and the trading potential distribution function approaches the limit value $F(k) = \left(\frac{\beta p}{q}\right)^{\frac{1}{q}} \frac{1}{k^{\frac{1}{q}}}$. This indicates that there is a steady-state structure in the distribution of trading potential in the trading system. On the surface, this result seems to contradict the theorem of trading potential polarization. In fact, the steady-state structure of trading potential distribution and trading potential polarization can coexist. Even if the trading system reaches a stable state of trading potential distribution, the gap between trading agents at different levels can continue to widen. The fact that the gap between the wealthy class and the middle- and low-income class in Western society today is constantly widening also confirms this.

The result of the trading potential distribution tending to a steady state implies this: as time goes by, the market concentration continues to increase, forming a situation where a few companies control the market, the trading system enters a stable state, and society subsequently falls into rigidity. The innovation ability and resource allocation efficiency of the trading system will further decline, and the trading system will operate in a low-efficiency state. Any trading system built by any system will inevitably become rigid as time goes by. Only by constantly improving and reforming the system, and timely adjusting the structure of the trading system, can the trading system keep maintaining its efficiency and vitality.

In the trading potential function $F(k)$, the variable t has three meanings, in addition to representing the never-ending time, it also represents the capacity of the trading system and the total volume of transactions in the trading system. The multiple meanings of t mean that the trading potential distribution function contains more content that needs to be interpreted. As the trading system expands in terms of agent capacity and total transaction volume, the differentiation trend of the trading potential of the trading system will become more prominent.

The above conclusion is drawn on basis of a highly simplified model of the trading system, which ties the evolution of trading to the expansion of the trading system's capacity. This results in a situation where, as time progresses, the capacity of the trading system is always in a state of continuous expansion. This does not always hold true. In many situations, not only does the number of trading agents not increase, but it may even decrease. However, the key factor driving the differentiation of trading potential comes from the logic of following strategic behavior and increasing trading opportunities. In reality, even if the capacity of the trading system decreases, as long as technological innovation continues, there is still huge potential for growth in trading opportunities. Therefore, despite the many simplifications made in the trading model, the logic of reality still exists. Therefore, the main conclusions derived from the power law distribution function of trading potential have great universality.

17.4.2 Calculation of Trading Potential Power Law Distribution

In order to intuitively display the trend of the trading potential function, we follow the 2/8 distribution principle of random strategy and following strategy, time step t=10, trading potential conversion factor $\beta = 0.8$, the critical values of trading potential grades are taken as $k = 0.1$, $k = 0.5$, $k = 1$, $k = 2$, $k = 3$, $k = 4$, $k = 5$, from which the distribution of trading potential is calculated as follows (Table 17.1).

Based on the obtained trading potential distribution data, we can draw a schematic curve of the trading potential distribution (Fig. 17.3).

Table 17.1 Trading potential distribution

$F(0.1)$	$F(0.5)$	$F(1)$	$F(2)$	$F(3)$	$F(4)$	$F(5)$
0.66	0.23	0.117	0.055	0.034	0.024	0.019

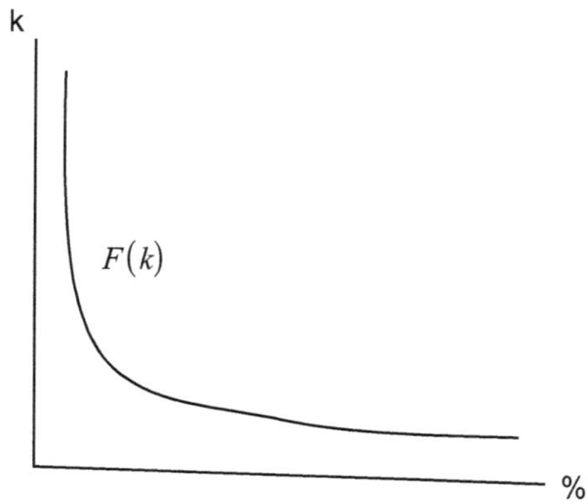

Fig. 17.3 Schematic curve of trading potential distribution

The above calculation results clearly show the polarization characteristics of trading potential. The number of agents with high trading potential is very low in the trading system, while most trading agents have a lower level of trading potential. In the above case, 77% of the trading agents in the trading system have a trading potential of $\psi < 0.5$; 34% of the trading agents have a trading potential of $\psi < 0.1$; trading agents with a trading potential of $\psi \geq 2$ only account for 5.5% of the trading system, and trading agents with a trading potential of $\psi \geq 5$ are even less, accounting for less than 2% of all trading agents.

In the above calculation, the trading system has already shown a highly differentiated pattern of trading potential in just 10 time steps. Only 2% of the high-order trading potential group in the trading system has a trading potential of up to 10 times compared with 77% of the trading agents, and the gap with the 34% low-order group is nearly 50 times. As time goes on, this gap will further widen.

Examining the density of trading potential distribution can also yield meaningful results. The distribution density of trading potential is calculated by the formula $\omega = \frac{\Delta n}{\Delta \psi}$, where Δn represents the proportion of agents between two trading potential grades, $\Delta \psi$ represents the difference between two adjacent trading potentials. In the above case, the distribution densities of the seven trading potential grades are as follows (Table 17.2).

Table 17.2 Distribution densities of trading potential

ω_1	ω_2	ω_3	ω_4	ω_5	ω_6	ω_7
3.4	1.075	0.226	0.062	0.021	0.01	0.005

The calculation results show that the low-order trading potential interval is a dense area of trading agents, with a large number of low-order trading potential subjects concentrated in this area. This also indicates that the low trading potential group has highly homogeneous characteristics. In the high-order trading potential interval, the higher the trading potential, the sparser the distribution, indicating that the individual characteristics of the trading potential subjects are distinct, and there are significant differences in trading potential.

From the perspective of the location of the trading agents' agglomeration, the agents of which the trading potential satisfies $0.1 \leq \psi < 2$ account for 60.5% of the total number of trading agents. This interval is in the middle of the trading potential distribution interval, indicating that the distribution of trading potential in the trading system also conforms to the olive-shaped distribution characteristics. With the evolution of the trading system, the majority of the middle agents occupying the trading system will shift. From the information revealed by the trading potential function, the position of the middle group will move downward, that is, evolve in the direction of polarization of the trading system.

17.5 The Intrinsic Mechanism of Trading Potential Differentiation

The theorem of trading potential polarization reveals an important law of the evolution of the trading system. From a deeper perspective, there are many reasons for the polarization of trading potential, including human social organization, human cognitive patterns, and interaction between trading agents.

17.5.1 The Micro-mechanism of Trading Potential Differentiation

In the trading system, the polarization of trading potential is manifested in both families and enterprises, but the mechanisms and forms presented by families and enterprises are quite different. Specifically, the differentiation of enterprise trading potential is the basis for the polarization of the trading system, and the differentiation process of family trading potential is mainly realized through the polarization of enterprise trading potential. From the perspective of evolutionary history, enterprises are a type of agents separated from family agents. The ultimate ownership of enterprises belongs to families, not to the enterprises themselves. There is no ultimate interest in enterprises. The rights and interests of enterprises as legal persons are merely an intermediate form of the ultimate interests of families. Therefore, enterprises are the promoters of family trading potential differentiation and play a key role in the trading system polarization. Based on this logic, our discussion on the micro-mechanism of trading potential polarization mainly focuses on the differentiation mechanism of enterprise trading potential.

Trading potential polarization refers to the severe polarization of trading potential distribution in a trading system, where a few trading agents have super trading potential, while most trading agents are in low-order positions. To simplify the demonstration process, we take the trading community as the object of study, and through a detailed analysis of the differentiation process of supplier trading potential, we reveal the micro-mechanism of trading system differentiation.

Let b_j and b_k be two in-phase suppliers in the trading community Ω. At time step t, the number of customers obtained by suppliers b_j and b_k on Ω are n_j and n_k respectively; a_i is a resident of the trading community Ω who trades with b_j and b_k for the first time.

Assume that a_i mainly learns about the situation of b_j and b_k from the trading choices of neighbors. Before the trading is implemented, the expected return of a_i is mainly focused on the product itself, without showing any expected difference between different suppliers, so there is $e_g(b_j) = e_g(b_k) = e_g$. In the face of commodity trading, if the trading situation is unfriendly, the corresponding expected return should be the real value of the supplier's product, that is, $e_b(b_j) = z_j$ and $e_b(b_k) = z_k$. Assume that a_i has no obvious preference for the prior probability of suppliers b_j and b_k, that is, $p(b_j) = p(b_k) = p$ and $q(b_j) = q(b_k) = q$.

According to the trading equation, at the time step t+1, the choice probabilities given by a_i to suppliers b_j and b_k are as follows:

$$\Pr(b_j) = 1 - R_g^j \frac{q}{p} \mu^{n_j} \tag{17.5.1}$$

$$\Pr(b_k) = 1 - R_g^k \frac{q}{p} \mu^{n_k} \tag{17.5.2}$$

According to the set parameters, we can calculate the return risk coefficients R_g^j and R_g^k respectively:

$$R_g^j = \frac{e_g - z_j}{e_g - e_0} \tag{17.5.3}$$

$$R_g^k = \frac{e_g - z_k}{e_g - e_0} \tag{17.5.4}$$

Under the condition of constant cost, the ability of suppliers b_j and b_k to assign value to products is proportional to the trading opportunities obtained by the suppliers. The more trading opportunities the suppliers get, the more times of production iteration, the more learning opportunities for technology and management, and the stronger the ability to assign value to products.

Based on the above logic, we assume that b_j and b_k have the same production function $z = l \cdot n$, where $l > 0$ is the manufacturer's learning ability factor, and n is the number of customers obtained by the manufacturer.

Substituting the production function into (17.5.3) and (17.5.4) respectively, we get:

$$R_g^j = \frac{e_g - z_j}{e_g - e_0} = \frac{e_g - \ln_j}{e_g - e_0} \tag{17.5.5}$$

$$R_g^k = \frac{e_g - z_k}{e_g - e_0} = \frac{e_g - \ln_k}{e_g - e_0} \tag{17.5.6}$$

In Eqs. (17.5.5) and (17.5.6), since e_g and e_0 are two relatively stable parameters, the number of customers acquired by b_j and b_k, represented by n_j and n_k, becomes the key factor determining the ratio of the profit gap to the trading income with a_i. The larger the number of customers, the smaller the return risk coefficient. Therefore, we can further express the return risk coefficient as the following function:

$$R_g^j = \frac{e_g - kn_j}{e_g - e_0} = \beta L^{-n_j} \tag{17.5.7}$$

$$R_g^k = \frac{e_g - kn_k}{e_g - e_0} = \beta L^{-n_k} \tag{17.5.8}$$

$\beta > 0$ is a balancing constant, and L represents the comprehensive learning ability of the manufacturer. Here, we assume that the trading agents have the same learning ability, and there is $L \geq 1$. When $L = 1$, it means that the trading agent has no learning ability. The larger L is, the stronger the learning ability. Substitute (17.5.7) and (17.5.8) into (17.5.1) and (17.5.2) respectively to get:

$$\Pr(b_j) = 1 - \beta L^{-n_j} \frac{q}{p} \mu^{n_j} \tag{17.5.9}$$

$$\Pr(b_k) = 1 - \beta L^{-n_k} \frac{q}{p} \mu^{n_k} \tag{17.5.10}$$

In (17.5.9) and (17.5.10), $\Pr(b_j)$ and $\Pr(b_k)$ are the probabilities of the trading agent a_i choosing to trade with suppliers b_j and b_K at time steP t+1. According to the probability relationship, we use $Q_j(t+1)$ and $Q_k(t+1)$ to represent the dual probabilities with $\Pr(b_j)$ and $\Pr(b_k)$, that is, the probability that a_i does not trade with the corresponding supplier. The above trading equation has the following transformation:

$$\beta L^{-n_j} \frac{q}{p} \mu^{n_j} = 1 - \Pr(b_j) = Q_j(t+1) \tag{17.5.11}$$

$$\beta L^{-n_k} \frac{q}{p} \mu^{n_k} = 1 - \Pr(b_k) = Q_k(t+1) \tag{17.5.12}$$

From (17.5.11) and (17.5.12) we can get:

$$\frac{Q_k(t+1)}{Q_j(t+1)} = \frac{\beta L^{-n_k} \frac{q}{p} \mu^{n_k}}{\beta L^{-n_j} \frac{q}{p} \mu^{n_j}} \tag{17.5.13}$$

Arrange (17.5.13) to get:

$$\frac{Q_k(t+1)}{Q_j(t+1)} = L^{n_j - n_k} \mu^{n_k - n_j} \tag{17.5.14}$$

From (17.5.14) we get:

$$\frac{Q_k(t+1)}{Q_j(t+1)} = \frac{L^{n_j - n_k}}{\mu^{n_j - n_k}} \tag{17.5.15}$$

Assume $n_j - n_k = \Delta n > 0$, Substitute into (17.5.15) to get:

$$\frac{Q_k(t+1)}{Q_j(t+1)} = \left(L \frac{1}{\mu} \right)^{\Delta n} \tag{17.5.16}$$

According to the 2/8 principle of finite rational structure parameters, we get from (17.5.16):

$$\frac{Q_k(t+1)}{Q_j(t+1)} = 4^{\Delta n} L^{\Delta n} \tag{17.5.17}$$

In normal cases, trading agents all have certain learning abilities, so $L > 1$. Equation (17.5.17) shows that the ratio of probabilities $Q_j(t+1)$ and $Q_k(t+1)$ is the exponential function of the difference in customer acquisition Δn. Given that $Q_j(t+1)$ and $Q_k(t+1)$ have a reverse mirror relationship with $\Pr(b_j)$ and $\Pr(b_k)$, the larger Q_k is, the smaller the value of $\Pr(b_k)$. From this, we can draw the conclusion that the trading agents have the characteristic of accumulating competitiveness in the market. The greater the early advantage, the further the advantage will be strengthened in the subsequent competition, and the competitiveness will widen the gap with other trading agents at an exponential rate. Given that the trading system is in continuous evolution, the learning ability of the trading agents is also constantly improving, and the gap in competitiveness between trading agents will expand at a higher acceleration.

In the micro-mechanism of trade differentiation, there are mainly two mechanisms: the first is the positive feedback mechanism of the competitiveness of trading agents. The competitive advantage of the trading agents at time step *t* will be brought to the time step *t*+1 by gaining more trading resources to enhance competitiveness;

and if they lose in the previous competition, it will weaken the competitiveness at the next time step. The second is the signal amplification mechanism. Through the mutual influence between trading agents in the trading community, the difference signal between suppliers is amplified, playing the role of an accelerator in the process of trade differentiation. This mechanism is realized through μ^n, and appears as an exponential function $4^{\Delta n}$ in the implementation probability. The two different mechanisms come from different phases of the trading parties. They reinforce each other, complement each other, and play a role in promoting the accelerated differentiation of the trading system.

17.5.2 The Social Logic of Trade Differentiation

Behind the polarization of trading potential, the real pusher is the "advantage accumulation effect" of the economic system. The principle of advantage accumulation was first proposed by American economist Brian Arthur in his *Complexity Economics*. The so-called "advantage accumulation effect" is that advantages can accumulate and become the advantage of the next round of competition, thus widening the gap in competition under the same rules. The key to the "advantage accumulation effect" lies in "accumulation". A random advantage is not important; once a certain advantage becomes a variable that can accumulate over time, no matter how insignificant the advantage, it will eventually show great power over time. The "advantage accumulation effect" is an inherent attribute of the trading network, which determines that the operation of the trading network will not be bound by the equilibrium state. Any equilibrium situation will eventually be broken, forming a wave-like development rhythm.

The "advantage accumulation effect" is manifested differently in different types of trading agents. For families, those with competitive advantages will inevitably obtain more wealth distribution. These families are usually diligent, smart, pay attention to information collection, decisive in trading decisions, and good at seizing investment opportunities without blind following suit.

Among the many factors leading to trade differentiation, the ability to collect information, accept information, and make correct decisions using information is the most critical. These abilities are summarized as information processing capabilities. In fact, the ability to handle things and overcome difficulties essentially belongs to the category of information processing capabilities. In the ocean of information, how to select, absorb information, and how to use experience information to build decision models are the key links in people's information processing. The stronger the ability to process information, the faster people can respond to new situations. Similarly, the stronger the ability to process information, the more solid the basis for decision-making, and the greater the likelihood of making correct decisions.

Once wealth distribution forms disparities among family groups, these differences will impact the next round of competition through several channels. Firstly, families with more wealth have a higher social status and a higher degree of nodes in social networks, giving them an information advantage due to their extensive social connections. This advantage will inevitably be converted into business opportunities in some way, and the abundant information provides a more solid basis for decision-making, ensuring a higher probability of correct decisions than others. Secondly, many transactions have certain prerequisites, including the scale of funds owned and the reputation of previous transactions. These prerequisites objectively divide family groups into two different categories, and families with more wealth are more likely to meet these prerequisites. Generally speaking, families with more wealth have a relatively larger set of trading strategies. The larger the strategy set, the more trading options available, and the more opportunities to gain profits than others. Finally, the impact of wealth differences spreads between generations, maintaining and widening the gap. Families with more wealth can provide better education for their children. Good education not only lays the foundation for children who are about to enter society to participate in competition, allowing them to compete in society with a better state and a higher starting point, but also ensures that they are in an environment of elite students while they grow up. These relationships with other students ultimately form an important part of their social network, providing social relationship resources for future competition.

The advantages of enterprises can also accumulate. The first is market advantage. Companies that have an advantage in competition will gain a larger market share and have a better market trading network. This advantage gives companies more dominance in pricing, thus there is still more profit space for the company; the second is financial advantage. Companies that have gained a competitive advantage can obtain more income from operations and obtain more and cheaper funds from the financial market than others. Ample funds give companies more investment options, which provide a very valuable initiative for the next competition; the third is technological advantage. Companies that have gained a competitive advantage have a greater ability to upgrade and transform technology, ensuring the company's leading advantage in technology; the fourth is talent advantage. Good market sales and strong financial strength are naturally the basis for companies to attract high-quality talents. The quality of the management team and the level of technical personnel are key to determining the success or failure of enterprise competition. Companies that have gained a market competitive advantage have proven the adaptability of existing products and technology and the effectiveness of internal management mechanisms, which provide a basis for further attracting talents. The addition of more talents will further expand the original advantages; the fifth is brand advantage. An important sign of a company gaining a competitive advantage is the establishment of a brand with high market recognition. The brand is the business card of the company and the ID card of the company in the market. There is a relationship of trust and loyalty between the brand and consumption. A brand with a good reputation is a huge intangible asset for the company, which can win more returns for the company under the same conditions.

The "accumulative effect of advantages" in a company is constrained by the "law of diminishing returns". As the scale of the company continues to increase, the rate of return on investment begins to decline. In today's increasingly automated production environment, the role of the "law of diminishing returns" gradually weakens, and the "economies of scale" effect becomes more and more apparent. After the capital intensity increases, the proportion of the company's fixed costs in the total costs increases, and as the scale of production expands, the unit cost decreases accordingly. However, there is definitelya limit to the scale of corporate management. When the scale of the company exceeds a certain limit, the efficiency of the company begins to decline, including the increase in information transmission links, the decline in decision-making efficiency, and the increasing rigidity of corporate management. To solve these problems, companies usually adopt a group model, and the companies within the group maintain a certain degree of independence. But the levels of the group cannot increase indefinitely. For each additional level, the efficiency of information transmission and decision-making will drop by one level. Today, multinational companies usually have three levels: the group level, the regional level, and the production company level, which are already close to the limit in terms of management levels.

Technological innovation is undoubtedly another major constraint on the "accumulative effect of advantages". Each major technological innovation inevitably produces a "lane changing" effect on the market and society. In the face of technological revolution, enterprises that can agilely seize opportunities are usually small and medium-sized ones. In the early stages of major technological emergence, the market risk is high and the market capacity is small. These characteristics often make giant companies that already have a great advantage easily overlook the latest trends in market development. On the other hand, it requires high costs for large companies with advantages to adjust their product structure and update their production equipment on a large scale. Large companies also face the dilemma of rigid management systems and low decision-making efficiency. These are the disadvantages that large companies show in the face of major technological innovations. In the trading network, there will be such a phenomenon where a batch of giant companies that have grown under the push of the "accumulative effect of advantages" are replaced by a batch of new companies that are constantly accumulating advantages in the new technology wave. As the old large companies fall, new large companies appear. This is also the embodiment of Schumpeter's "creative destruction". In the evolution of the trading system, each round of updates brings a new look to the trading system. The trading system evolves in the continuous alternation of super trading agents.

In a world full of uncertainty, opportunities or chances always present themselves in a probabilistic fluctuation. The uneven distribution of opportunities in time and space constitutes what people call luck. All human activities can never exclude the role of luck. There is a step effect in the evolution process of trading potential. If the opportunity is good and can be seized, the trading potential of the agent will jump a step. Since the distribution of trading potential is pyramid-shaped, the higher the trading potential, the fewer competitors, and the more resources that can be used. If the opportunity is seized to successfully ensure a higher step, it will lay the foundation for the transition to a higher trading potential.

Notes

1. The automobile industry was once a symbol of American industrial prosperity and had a huge influence on American employment, industrial chains and financial markets. In terms of employment, the U.S. auto industry lost 400,000 jobs in 2008, and if the three major companies went bankrupt, the number of job losses would have exceeded 1 million. If retired employees and health insurance workers were included, the number of people affected exceeded 2 million. General Motors (GM) alone supplied 12% of the world's passenger cars and trucks, employed 243,000 people and had production facilities and commercial locations in 140 countries. In the United States, GM has 207 production locations in 35 states and more than 500,000 contracts per year. In terms of the industrial chain, automobile manufacturers are the largest buyers of bulk commodities such as steel, aluminum, iron, copper, plastics and electronic chips in the United States, and steel purchases account for 30% of the total demand in the United States market. Automobiles and parts account for 10% of U.S. goods exports. In the financial markets, auto companies are important issuers of high-yield bonds, with market shares as high as 10%. The securitization of bank loans to auto makers is an important part of the U.S. financial market.
2. Through such a set of numbers, we can more intuitively understand the specific meaning of the super trading potential, and have more in-depth understanding of the importance of the super trading potential to the trading system. American President Dwight D. Eisenhower said during a congressional hearing that what's good for General Motors is good for America.
3. Steven Rattner, who helped engineer the auto bailout, described this story vividly in his book. See: Rattner S. Overhaul: An Insider's Account of the Obama Administration's Emergency Rescue of the Auto Industry. Boston: Houghton Mifflin Harcourt, 2010.
4. Zhu Fuqiang (2013) History of Economic Theory, Tsinghua University Press, Beijing.
5. Alfred Marshall (2012) Principles of Economics (Trans: Lian Yunjie), Huaxia Press, Beijing, p 369–370.
6. Joseph E. Stiglitz (2020) The Truth about America (Trans: Liu Binfu, Liu Yiming, Liu Jiamu), China Machine Press, Beijing, p 55.
7. Joseph E. Stiglitz (2020) The Truth about America (Trans: Liu Binfu, Liu Yiming, Liu Jiamu), China Machine Press, Beijing, p 48.
8. Joseph E. Stiglitz (2020) The Truth about America (Trans: Liu Binfu, Liu Yiming, Liu Jiamu), China Machine Press, Beijing, p 48.
9. Joseph E. Stiglitz (2020) The Truth about America (Trans: Liu Binfu, Liu Yiming, Liu Jiamu), China Machine Press, Beijing, p 60.
10. Thomas Piketty (2014) Capital in the 21st Century (Trans: Ba Shusong et al.), Citic Press, Beijing, p 14.
11. Angus Maddison (2009) Millennium Statistics of World Economy (Trans: Wu Xiaoying, Shi Faqi), Peking University Press, Beijing.
12. The following proof comes from the "deterministic approximation of the richer process" in Networks, Groups, and Markets: Revealing Behavioral Principles and Effect Mechanisms in a Highly Networked World. See: David Ellis, Jon Kleinberg (2011) Networks, Groups, and Markets: Revealing Behavioral Principles and Effect Mechanisms in a Highly Connected World (Trans: Li Xiaoming, Wang Weihong, Yang Yunli), Tsinghua University Press, Beijing, p 345–348 (in Chinese).

Chapter 18
Equation of the Trading System Evolution

The polarization process of trading potential is an important trend in the evolution of the trading system, which have a profound impact on the operation of the trading system. The polarization of trading potential is not an isolated process. In the evolution process of the trading system, there is a very close accompanying relationship between the polarization of trading potential and economic growth.

18.1 Measurement of Trading Potential Polarization

The theorem of trading potential polarization proves that the evolution of the trading system will inevitably lead to the polarization of trading potential. However, the accurate measurement of the degree of trading potential polarization is still a problem to be solved. Variance is the most commonly used measure of deviation from the mean in statistics, but it is not an ideal indicator for measuring trading potential polarization. In the calculation of variance, small sample groups with high deviation are ignored due to their extremely low proportion in the total sample, while trading potential polarization (including wealth distribution polarization) is precisely the deviation phenomenon of small samples.

Based on the characteristic that Trading potential follows a power law distribution, we use the commonly used Gini coefficient method to measure the intensity of polarization, and construct the trading potential polarization index of the trading system.

Figure 18.1 shows that the more severe the degree of trading potential polarization, the steeper the trading potential distribution curve, and the larger the area enclosed with the equal division diagonal line, both of which have the same direction of change. The measurement index of the degree of trading potential polarization can be constructed based on this.

Z. Wang, *Trading Economics*, Contributions to Economics,
https://doi.org/10.1007/978-981-99-9875-3_18

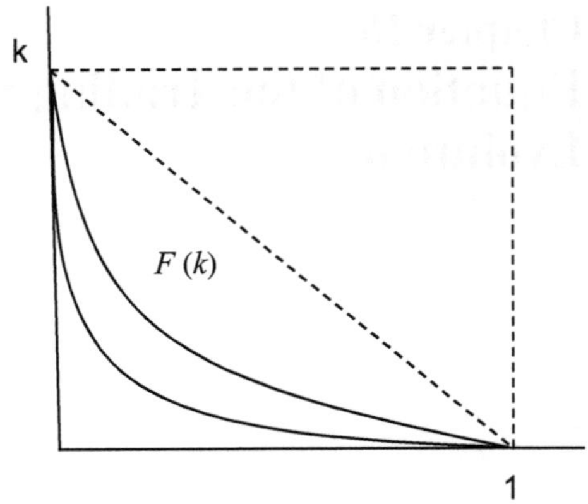

Fig. 18.1 Trading potential distribution curve

In Fig. 18.2, two sides of a rectangle are formed by two coordinate axes and two dashed lines, respectively K^* and 1. The height of the rectangle is K^*, representing the maximum value of K. The base of the rectangle represents the proportion oftrading agents that satisfy $F(a_i) > k$ in the trading system. S' represents the area enclosed by the distribution function curve $F(k)$ and the equal division diagonal line, and S represents the area of the triangle enclosed by the equal division diagonal line and the two coordinate axes. The Greek letter χ represents the trading potential polarization index, defined as follows:

$$\chi = \frac{S'}{S} \tag{18.1.1}$$

According to the definition of χ, the value range of χ is $0 \leq \chi < 1$; the larger the value of χ, the more uneven the distribution of trading potential in the trading system, and the more severe the degree of polarization; on the contrary, the smaller the value

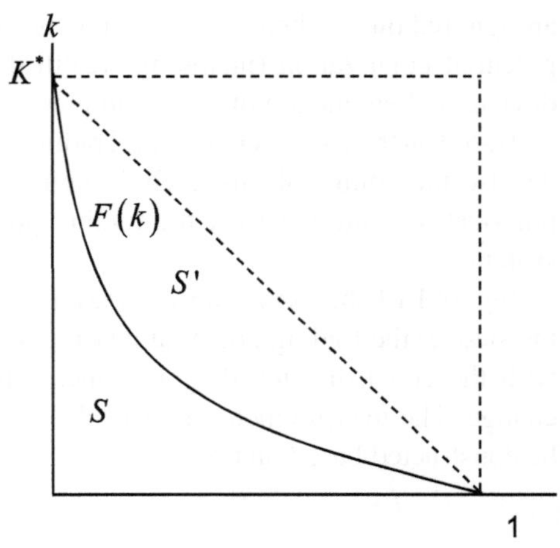

Fig. 18.2 Trading potential area distribution

of χ, the more even the distribution of trading potential. When the trading potential distribution function $F(k)$ completely coincides with the diagonal line, $S' = 0$. From Eq. (18.1.1), it can be seen that at this time $\chi = 0$, it corresponds to the absolute equality state of the trading system.

According to the definition of the trading potential polarization coefficient χ, the area enclosed by the distribution curve $F(k)$ and the diagonal line is:

$$S' = S - \int_0^{K^*} F(k)dk \tag{18.1.2}$$

As can be seen from Fig. 18.2, S is half the area of the rectangle, that is $S = \frac{K^*}{2}$, substitute it and (18.1.2) into (18.1.1) to get:

$$\chi = \frac{S'}{S} = 1 - \frac{2}{K^*}\int_0^{K^*} F(k)dk \tag{18.1.3}$$

Equation (18.1.3) shows that the trading potential polarization coefficient χ is determined by the trading potential distribution function. Once the trading potential distribution function is determined, the trading potential polarization coefficient χ is also determined.

We know that the trading potential distribution function changes continuously over time t. In order to illustrate the evolution characteristics of the distribution function, the distribution function $F(k)$ is rewritten as $F(k, t)$. Therefore, the formula for the trading potential polarization coefficient χ can be written in the following form:

$$\chi(t) = \frac{S'}{S} = 1 - \frac{2}{K^*}\int_0^{K^*} F(k, t)dk \tag{18.1.4}$$

18.2 Equation of the Trading System Evolution

We construct the equation of the trading system evolution to summarize the various factors that affect the process of trading potential polarization into clear quantitative relationships, providing effective tools for in-depth analysis of the differentiation process of the trading system.

18.2.1 Derivation of the Equation of the Trading System Evolution

The gap among trading agents is the result of gradual accumulation in the process of trading iteration. Each trade is a game of the trading agents, which will inevitably produce differences in payment. If the payments of the two sides of the game are always the same, there will be no game of trading agents, let alone the evolution and development of the trading system.

Starting from this logical point, we can conclude that t he differentiation of trading potential is the result of trading iteration accumulation. Trade promotes economic growth, and the speed of trading potential differentiation is necessarily proportional to the speed of economic growth. The faster the economic growth, the faster the frequency and scale of trading activities grow, and the speed of trading potential differentiation will inevitably accelerate.

While considering the expansion of χ with economic growth, we also need to consider the role of another important factor—the distribution ratio of the trading system. The promotion of economic growth to the differentiation of trading potential must be played through the distribution link. Distribution is the result of trade and the driving force of trade. From this perspective, the distribution relationship of the trading system is very important for the process of trading potential polarization. In the trading system, the most important distribution structure is the distribution relationship between capital and labor. Because the distribution of capital is extremely uneven, the more the distribution tilts towards capital, the faster the speed of trading potential differentiation. On the contrary, if the distribution tilts towards labor, the speed of trading potential differentiation under the same trading intensity will be relatively gentle.

Measuring the distribution structure of the trading system requires indicators from multiple aspects, including wages, capital returns, capital turnover rate, initial distribution, redistribution, as well as wage distribution and industry distribution of corporate returns, etc. For simplicity, we use the ratio of the average return on capital to the average wage rate per unit time as a substitute indicator for the distribution index of the trading system, called the distribution ratio of the trading system. Although this indicator omits distribution information, it can still well reflect the changes in the distribution pattern when continuously examining the evolution process of the trading system.

Use η to represent the distribution ratio of the trading system, the indicator is defined as follows:

$$\eta = \frac{pr}{w} \tag{18.2.1}$$

In (18.2.1), pr represents the capital profit rate, and w represents the average wage rate.

Based on the relationship between the speed of trade potential differentiation and economic growth and the distribution ratio of the trading system, we get the following relationship:

$$\frac{d\chi}{dt} = \alpha\eta Gr \tag{18.2.2}$$

In (18.2.2), Gr represents the economic growth rate, $\alpha > 0$ is the structural parameter of the trading system.

Given that the differentiation of trade potential is the result of accumulation, integrate both sides of the above equation over the time interval $[0, t]$ to get:

$$\int_0^t \frac{d\chi}{dt} dt = \alpha \int_0^t \eta Grdt \tag{18.2.3}$$

From (18.2.3) we get:

$$\chi|_0^t = \alpha \int_0^t \eta Grdt \tag{18.2.4}$$

Expand (18.2.4) to get:

$$\chi(t) - \chi(0) = \alpha \int_0^t \eta Grdt \tag{18.2.5}$$

We assume that at the starting point of the evolution of the trading system, the trade potential is in a state of absolute uniform distribution, and the trade potential polarization coefficient $\chi(0) = 0$. Substitute it into (18.2.5) to get:

$$\chi(t) = \alpha \int_0^t \eta Grdt \tag{18.2.6}$$

In modern society, another important driving force for the accelerated differentiation of trade potential comes from the financialization of assets, which is the process of strengthening the investment function and liquidity function of assets. The various assets held by trading agents can have two different functions, namely the investment function and the use function. Equity assets belong to investment assets, and production equipment belongs to functional assets. Some assets have both investment and use functions, such as real estate and land assets. When the part of the assets held by the trading agent has an investment function, we say that these assets have a certain degree of financialization. The liquidity of assets refers to the ability of the asset to be realized. The investment function of an asset must be based on a strong ability to realize. If there is a lack of realization ability or poor realization ability, no matter how the asset price changes, the actual investment significance is not great. For example, production equipment will also change in the replacement price with the change in demand and supply relationship, but due to the strong specificity and poor liquidity, few people hold a certain type of production equipment as an investment.

In the trading system, when the proportion of financialized assets in all assets reaches a certain level, the financialization of assets will become a catalyst for rapidly expanding the gap in trade potential. The higher the proportion of financialization in assets, the faster the speed of trade potential differentiation. Because the trading frequency of financialized assets is much higher than that of non-financialized assets. Through high-frequency trading, a limited scale of financialized assets can support a huge trading scale. The trading of financialized assets has greater uncertainty and is more likely to result in a situation where most people lose money and a few people make money.

Based on the above analysis, we can draw the following conclusion that in a trading system, the financialization rate of assets is directly proportional to the degree of trade potential differentiation. Use Fr to represent the asset financialization rate of the trading system (that is, the proportion of the total amount of financialized assets in the total amount of assets in the trading system), the following relationship exists:

$$\chi = \beta Fr \tag{18.2.7}$$

In (18.2.7), $\beta > 0$ is the structural parameter of the trading system.

Since there is no strict dependency relationship between asset financialization and economic growth, even if economic growth is slow, the asset financialization rate may continue to grow and maintain a high level. Therefore, the two forces driving the differentiation of trade potential—economic growth and asset financialization—have a superimposed relationship.

Based on the above judgment, we combine the two forces driving the differentiation of trade potential to get the following equation:

$$\chi(t) = \alpha \int_0^t \eta Gr dt + \beta Fr \tag{18.2.8}$$

Substitute (18.1.4) into (18.2.8) to get:

$$\alpha \int_0^t \eta Gr dt + \frac{2}{K^*} \int_0^{K^*} F(k, t) dk + \beta Fr = 1 \tag{18.2.9}$$

Equation (18.2.9) establishes a quantitative relationship between the distribution function of trading potential and such factors as economic growth, basic distribution relationships and the financialization rate of assets. It reveals the relationships between the main variables affecting the evolution of the trading system, which we call the equation of the trading system evolution.

18.2.2 Calculation of the Equation of the Trading System Evolution

We deduce based on the equation of trading system evolution, hoping to gain more knowledge about the evolution of the trading system.

Suppose the trading potential distribution function of the trading system T at time step t is $F(k, t)$, the level of financialization is $Fr(t)$, the economic growth function is $Gr(t)$, and the upper limit of trading potential is $K^*(t)$. According to the equation of the trading system evolution, the following equation holds:

$$\alpha \int_0^t \eta Gr(t)dt + \frac{2}{K^*(t)} \int_0^{K^*(t)} F(k,t)dk + \beta Fr(t) = 1 \tag{18.2.10}$$

At time step $t + 1$, the following relationship also holds:

$$\alpha \int_0^{t+1} \eta Gr(t)dt + \frac{2}{K^*(t+1)} \int_0^{K^*(t+1)} F(k,t+1)dk + \beta Fr(t+1) = 1 \tag{18.2.11}$$

Subtract the corresponding items on both sides of (18.2.10) and (18.2.11) to get:

$$\begin{aligned} &\alpha\left(\int_0^{t+1} \eta Gr(t)dt - \int_0^t \eta Gr(t)dt\right) \\ &+ \left(\frac{2}{K^*(t+1)} \int_0^{K^*(t+1)} F(k,t+1)dk - \frac{2}{K^*(t)} \int_0^{K^*(t)} F(k,t)dk\right) \\ &+ \beta(Fr(t+1) - Fr(t)) = 0 \end{aligned} \tag{18.2.12}$$

Arrange (18.2.12) to get:

$$\alpha \int_{t}^{t+1} \eta Gr(t)dt + \left(\frac{2}{K^*(t+1)} \int_{0}^{K^*(t)} F(k,t+1)dk + \frac{2}{K^*(t+1)} \int_{K^*(t)}^{K^*(t+1)} F(k,t+1)dk - \frac{2}{K^*(t)} \int_{0}^{K^*(t)} F(k,t)dk \right) + \beta(Fr(t+1) - Fr(t)) = 0 \tag{18.2.13}$$

According to the power law distribution of the trading potential distribution function $F(k,t)$, we know that

$$\int_{K*(t)}^{K^*(t+1)} F(k,t+1)dt \ll 1 \tag{18.2.14}$$

We can ignore this term on the left side of (18.2.13) to get:

$$\alpha \int_{t}^{t+1} \eta Gr(t)dt + \left(\frac{2}{K^*(t+1)} \int_{0}^{K*(t)} F(k,t+1)dk - \frac{2}{K^*(t)} \int_{0}^{K*(t)} F(k,t)dk \right) + \beta(Fr(t+1) - Fr(t)) = 0 \tag{18.2.15}$$

Let $\int_t^{t+1} \eta Gr(t) = \delta_1$, $Fr(t+1) - Fr(t) = \delta_2$, substitute into (18.2.15) to get:

$$\alpha\delta_1 + \left(\frac{2}{K^*(t+1)} \int_{0}^{K*(t)} F(k,t+1)dk - \frac{2}{K^*(t)} \int_{0}^{K*(t)} F(k,t)dk \right) + \beta\delta_2 = 0 \tag{18.2.16}$$

Continue to arrange to get:

$$\int_0^{K^*(t)} F(k,t+1)dk + (\alpha\delta_1 + \beta\delta_2)\frac{K^*(t+1)}{2} = \frac{K^*(t+1)}{K^*(t)} \int_0^{K^*(t)} F(k,t)dk \tag{18.2.17}$$

Let $\frac{K^*(t+1)}{K^*(t)} = 1 + \delta_3$, $\delta_3 \geq 0$ be real numbers. Substitute into (18.2.17) to get:

$$\int_0^{K^*(t)} F(k,t+1)dk + (\alpha\delta_1 + \beta\delta_2)\frac{K^*(t+1)}{2} = (1+\delta_3) \int_0^{K^*(t)} F(k,t)dk \tag{18.2.18}$$

Arrange (18.2.18) to get:

$$\int_0^{K^*(t)} [F(k,t+1) - F(k,t)]dk = \delta_3 \int_0^{K^*(t)} F(k,t)dk - (\alpha\delta_1 + \beta\delta_2)\frac{K^*(t+1)}{2} \tag{18.2.19}$$

If the result is:

$$\int_0^{K^*(t)} [F(k,t+1) - F(k,t)]dk < 0 \tag{18.2.20}$$

then

$$\delta_3 \int_0^{K^*(t)} F(k,t)dk - (\alpha\delta_1 + \beta\delta_2)\frac{K^*(t+1)}{2} < 0 \tag{18.2.21}$$

holds.

Arrange (18.2.21) to get:

$$\delta_3 < (\alpha\delta_1 + \beta\delta_2)\frac{K^*(t+1)}{2}\frac{1}{\int_0^{K^*(t)} F(k,t)dk}$$
$$\because \frac{K^*(t)}{2} \leq \frac{K^*(t+1)}{2} \tag{18.2.22}$$

$$\therefore \delta_3 \leq (\alpha\delta_1 + \beta\delta_2)\frac{K^*(t)}{2}\frac{1}{\int_0^{K^*(t)} F(k,t)dk} \tag{18.2.23}$$

When condition (18.2.23) holds, condition (18.2.22) is true. Therefore, (18.2.23) is a strong condition for (18.2.20) to hold.

According to the definition of the trading potential polarization coefficient, we know:

$$\chi(t) = 1 - \frac{2}{K^*(t)} \int_0^{K^*} F(k, t)dk \tag{18.2.24}$$

From (18.2.24) we get:

$$\frac{K^*(t)}{2} \frac{1}{\int_0^{K^*(t)} F(k, t)dk} = \frac{1}{1 - \chi(t)} \tag{18.2.25}$$

Substitute (18.2.25) into the strong condition (18.2.23) to get:

$$\delta_3 \leq (\alpha\delta_1 + \beta\delta_2)\frac{1}{1 - \chi(t)} \tag{18.2.26}$$

From this we conclude that when condition (18.2.26) is satisfied, the trading potential distribution function of the trading system T satisfies (18.2.20).

According to result of (18.2.20), we know that the trading potential distribution function of the trading system T at time step t is $F(k, t)$, and the trading potential function at time step $t + 1$ is $F(k, t + 1)$, the evolutionary relationship between $F(k, t)$ and $F(k, t + 1)$ is shown in the following figure.

Figure 18.3 intuitively shows the evolution trend of the trading potential distribution function of the trading system $F(k, t + 1)$. At time step $t + 1$, the trading potential distribution function becomes steeper. This means that with economic growth and the increase in financialization, the differentiation intensity of the trading system will continue to increase.

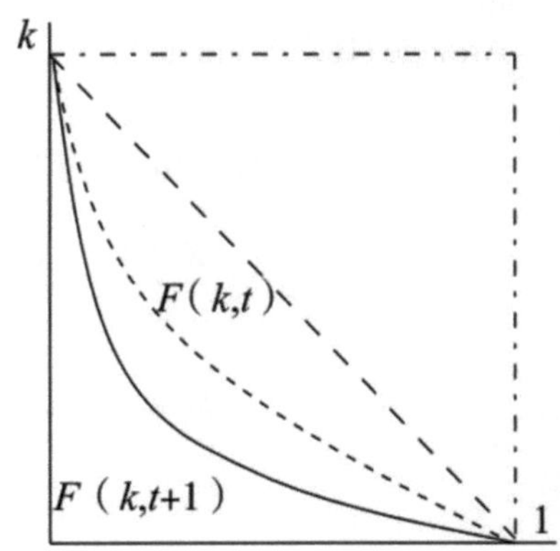

Fig. 18.3 The evolution trend of the trading distribution function

Condition (18.2.26) includes the cases of $\delta_3 = 0$, $\delta_1 > 0$ and $\delta_2 > 0$. In real scenarios, this means that the economy is growing, and the financialization process of the trading system is still ongoing. However, the trading agents at the super trading potential position do not have the ability to further expand their advantages. In this case, although the trading potential range of the trading system has not expanded, the degree of differentiation of the trading system is intensifying.

According to (18.2.19), we know:

If

$$\int_0^{K^*(t)} [F(k,t+1) - F(k,t)]dk > 0 \text{ holds,} \tag{18.2.27}$$

then

$$\delta_3 \int_0^{K^*(t)} F(k,t)dk - (\alpha\delta_1 + \beta\delta_2)\frac{K^*(t+1)}{2} > 0 \text{ holds.} \tag{18.2.28}$$

From (18.2.28), we get:

$$\delta_3 > (\alpha\delta_1 + \beta\delta_2)\frac{K^*(t+1)}{2}\frac{1}{\int_0^{K^*(t)} F(k,t)dk}$$
$$\because\ K^*(t) \le K^*(t+1) \tag{18.2.29}$$

$\therefore$ is the weak condition that holds true for (18.2.27).

$$\delta_3 > (\alpha\delta_1 + \beta\delta_2)\frac{K^*(t)}{2}\frac{1}{\int_0^{K^*(t)} F(k,t)dk} \tag{18.2.30}$$

From this, we get the equivalent form of the weak condition (18.2.30):

$$\delta_3 > (\alpha\delta_1 + \beta\delta_2)\frac{1}{1-\chi(t)} \tag{18.2.31}$$

From this, we conclude that when the trading system T satisfies the weak condition (18.2.31), the trading potential distribution function $F(k,t)$ may satisfy the following inequality:

$$\int_0^{K^*(t)} [F(k,t+1) - F(k,t)]dk > 0 \tag{18.2.32}$$

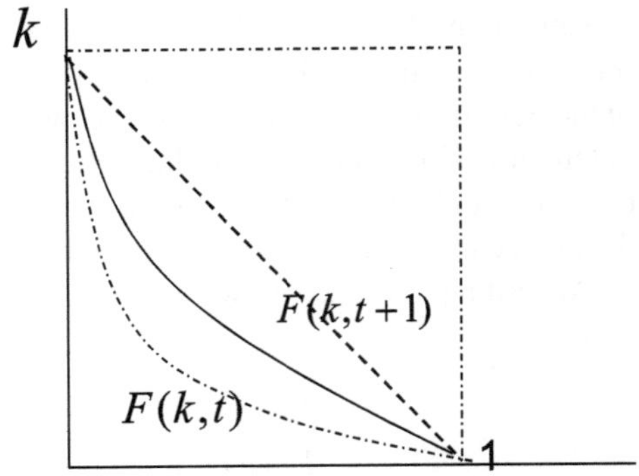

Fig. 18.4 The evolution trend of the trading potential distribution function

Figure 18.4 intuitively presents the evolution trend of the trading potential distribution function $F(k, t)$ expressed by (18.2.32):

Figure 18.4 shows an evolution trend opposite to that in Fig. 18.3, where the trading potential distribution function becomes flatter and closer to the diagonal line representing the equilibrium distribution. This means that the trading system T becomes more uniform in trading potential distribution while expanding the trading potential range. On the surface, the expansion of the trading potential range contradicts the uniformization of the trading potential distribution. The expansion of the trading potential range represents the further strengthening of the trading potential of the high-order trading potential group, and the gap between the low-order trading potential and the high-order trading potential in the trading system will become larger. In this case, this contradiction can only be resolved if a part of the low-order trading potential group in the trading system moves to the medium group while the strength of the high-order trading potential group continues to increase, forming an olive-shaped distribution of trading potential.

One extreme case contained in condition (18.2.31) is $\delta_1 < 0$ and $\delta_2 < 0$, which corresponds to the real scenario of economic recession and the regression of financialization. The degradation of the trading system can also reduce the differentiation intensity of trading potential. This indirectly shows a truth: differentiation is the result of evolution, and equality is not a sign of progress.

After calculating the equation of the trading system evolution, we can draw the following three conclusions: First, the trading system has a trend of accelerated differentiation. As can be seen from conditions (18.2.26) and (18.2.31), the larger the polarization coefficient of trading potential $\chi(t)$, the more difficult it is for the trading system T to meet the condition (18.2.31) required to reverse the continuous differentiation trend. On the contrary, the condition (18.2.26) for the trading system T continuing to increase the intensity of differentiation is easier to meet. Under this probability of evolutionary selection, for the trading system with more severe differentiation, it is a high probability event for the trading polarization coefficient $\chi(t)$ to continue to increase. This shows that the evolutionary path of the trading system T has an increasingly strong path dependence effect.

Secondly, economic development and the process of economic financialization are the basic driving forces pushing the trading system towards polarization. In the evolution process of the trading system, when the economy is in a period of rapid growth, it is often the period when the differentiation of the trading system is most obvious. The mechanism of financialization on the differentiation of the trading system is the same. From this, we can conclude that polarization is the price that human society must pay for pursuing economic growth. To prevent the trend of differentiation of the trading system means that the economy will fall into stagnation, or even the quagmire of regression. Differentiation and stagnation are the dilemma that human society cannot escape.

Thirdly, although only a small proportion of the trading system, high-order trading potential groups, especially super trading potential groups, play a very key leading role in the evolution process of the trading system. In a sense, the super trading potential agents can be regarded as the representatives of the characteristics of the times. The better the super trading potential agents develop, the more vitality the society will have. The whole society will benefit from the development of high-order trading potential groups.

18.3 The Differentiation Process of the Trading System

In the equation of the trading system evolution (18.2.9), two parameters α and β, reflecting the structural characteristics of the trading system, play an important role, defining the speed and intensity of trading potential differentiation in the face of economic growth and asset financialization for different countries. Behind these two parameters, the distribution system and trading rules play a decisive role. Tax system, redistribution system, labor pricing mechanism, minimum wage system, access rules of financialized asset market, financing rules, etc., will all be reflected in the structural parameters of the trading system through different channels. In addition, the property rights system will also have an impact on the values of α and β to a certain extent. The higher the degree of privatization, the larger the values of α and β. On the contrary, the lower the degree of privatization, the smaller the values of α and β.

In the evolution process of the trading system, the continuous differentiation of trading potential is the main theme in system evolution. However, under a specific economic structure, when the relationship between capital and labor in distribution changes, there is a possibility of reversal in the trend of differentiation of the trading system. In the period after the World War II, with the booming development of American manufacturing industry, the continuous expansion of labor demand increased the bargaining power of workers' wages. Many families entered the middle class through employment and wage income growth, which was the fastest growing period of the American middle class, and the Gini coefficient showed a downward trend. With the full unfolding of globalization, many manufacturing industries moved out to other countries, the American economic structure shifted from real economy to virtual economy, asset financialization rapidly increased against the backdrop of financial deregulation, and the Gini coefficient turned back up.

During different stages of the evolution of the trading system, the roles played by economic growth and financialization trends in the process of trading potential differentiation have a cyclical relationship of waxing and waning. In the early stages of economic development, economic growth is the main driver of trading potential differentiation. As the scale of assets accumulated by the trading system grows larger, the financialization of the trading system becomes inevitable. When the scale of assets held by people reaches a certain level, increasing asset liquidity and optimizing asset structure through trading will become an increasingly strong demand in society. Various asset trading markets will emerge one after another, and the process of asset financialization will begin to accelerate. After experiencing a period of rapid economic development, economic growth will inevitably slow down gradually, and the driving force of economic growth for trading potential differentiation will also gradually decline. At this point, asset financialization begins to accelerate and gradually takes over from economic growth as the main driver of trading potential differentiation.

The relationship between economics and finance in alternatingly driving trading potential polarization can be fully manifested in the U.S. capital market. Before the World War II, the wealthiest people in the United States were almost all entrepreneurs in the industrial sector. Rail transportation, steel smelting, petrochemicals, automobile manufacturing, and other industries were the main fields that created the world's richest people. After the World War II, especially since the 1990s, the world's richest people on the Wall Street became financial investors and technology elites, taking place of industrial entrepreneurs. Warren E. Buffett, Steve Jobs of Apple, and Elon Reeve Musk of Tesla are all part of this new generation of the world's richest people. The change in the world's richest people on the Wall Street clearly reflects the role change in driving the polarization of trading potential in the United States.

Asset bubbles are an important driver of accelerating trading potential differentiation. The distribution of financialized assets among trading agents is uneven, with about 70% of the Wall Street stocks in the United States held by a small wealthy class. This determines that when asset bubbles push up asset prices, only a minority of the market can benefit. After the appearance of asset bubbles, the ability to capture investment opportunities is not equal. Trading agents with high trading potential are much superior to lower-order agents in both financing ability or information processing ability. This determines that each bubble will inevitably further widen the existing gap in trading potential. Looking back at history, it is not difficult to find that each asset bubble, whether it was in the stock market or the real estate market, trading potential would go through a process of accelerated differentiation.

Measured on the scale of historical evolution, the differentiation process of the trading system caused by asset bubbles is often a deviation from the long-term evolution trend of the trading system. When an asset bubble is in an expansion cycle, the trading system will go through a process of accelerated financialization; and when an asset bubble enters a collapse cycle, the trading system will go through a process of rapid financialization adjustment. In this process, the polarization coefficient of trading potential in the trading system $\chi(t)$ fluctuates in resonance.

At different stages of the evolution of the trading system, the process of trading potential differentiation presents different characteristics. In general, trading potential polarization mainly goes through four evolutionary stages: The first stage is the early stage of industrialization. In the early stage of the transition from an agricultural economy to an industrial economy, capital is relatively scarce. The advantageous position of capital brings higher returns, and the distribution ratio of the trading system η is relatively high. From the perspective of economic development experiences around the world, the initial stage of industrialization is usually also the take-off stage of the economy, and the historical high of economic growth rate usually appears during this period. The speed of social stratification accelerates, and the polarization of income distribution and wealth distribution quickly emerges. Correspondingly, the coefficient of trading potential polarization χ rapidly increases. Trading potential polarization is not only reflected in the distribution of family wealth, but also in the accelerated increase in market concentration, and the differentiation within the enterprise group is also rapidly forming;

The second historical stage is the middle and late stages of industrialization. During this period, the scarcity of capital has declined compared to the early stage of industrialization, the phenomenon of labor surplus is becoming less, and the distribution ratio of the trading system η begins to decline. At the same time, the economic growth rate gradually slows down, the speed of differentiation of the trading system slows down, and even a reversal phenomenon may occur.

The third historical stage is the financialization period of the economy. In the middle and late stages of industrialization, the proportion of asset financialization gradually increases. By the late stage of industrialization, the rate of asset financialization usually reaches a high level, and another important force driving trading potential polarization—the financialization of the trading system—begins to play a role, and the coefficient of trading potential polarization χ begins to rise again.

The fourth historical stage is the era of digital economy. The digital economy may be the final economic form that humans will experience. The typical characteristics of the era are the widespread use of artificial intelligence and the high substitution rate of machines for production and services. In this period, capital once again becomes the dominant factor of the trading system, the demand for capital in the economy is almost unlimited, and the demand for labor begins to decline, and the distribution ratio of the trading system η will rise sharply again. In this period, human society will usher in an unprecedented process of polarization, and the coefficient of trading potential polarization χ will reach a historical high.

18.4 Social Fairness and Justice

The basis for the existence of the trading system is the order and stability of the trading system, which in turn must be based on fairness and justice; otherwise, the society will fall into the quagmire of chaos and turmoil.

18.4.1 The Essence of Fairness and Justice

In the theoretical cognition of economics, fairness and efficiency are regarded as two opposing concepts. It is believed that one cannot have both, and this is used as a standard to distinguish the views of fairness and justice into two opposing schools: namely, the fairness-first school and the efficiency-first school. However, if we return to the logical starting point of the concept of fairness and justice, and examine the logical context of the theory of fairness and justice, we will find that fairness should not only be regarded as the opposite of efficiency, but that the two are highly internally united, mutually dependent and supportive with each other.

Fairness and justice encompass many levels. We can evaluate whether a matter is fair and just, and also assess whether a person's actions conform to the principles of fairness and justice. These belong to the micro-level of fairness and justice. Rule fairness, system fairness, and social fairness belong to the macro category of the concept of fairness and justice. Regardless of the level, the logical basis for determining the standards of fairness and justice is to maintain the normal operation of the social cooperation system. If we further ask, why do people choose to cooperate instead of acting alone like Robinson? The reason is that cooperation can achieve efficiency far higher than individuals, it can release capabilities that individuals cannot match, and it can overcome difficulties and challenges that individuals cannot bear. Cooperation can achieve the effect shown in $1 + 1 > 2$, and cooperation is more efficient. The reason why people pursue fairness and justice is to maintain cooperative relationships with each other. People advocate for fairness and justice at the micro-level to achieve cooperative relationships within a smaller scope; and the human society pursues fairness and justice at the macro level to achieve widespread cooperation among people on a larger scale. People seek cooperative relationships of different levels and intensities in order to create higher productivity and work efficiency. When people feel unfair, they will lower the willingness to cooperate or deal with cooperation in a negative attitude. If the entire trading system falls into an unjust situation, the bedrock of social cooperation will be shaken, and the trading system based on cooperation will show cracks and even fall into a turbulent quagmire.

Based on the underlying logic of fairness and justice, we can be sure that any concept of fairness and justice must be based on achieving effective social cooperation and conducive to releasing social productivity. To objectively and accurately evaluate the efficiency of cooperation, we need to observe from two dimensions:

one dimension involves the enthusiasm for cooperation or the willingness to cooperate. If a concept of fairness and justice can arouse people's high enthusiasm for cooperation, we believe that this concept is legitimate and reasonable. The focus of this dimension is the current state of cooperation. Another dimension involves the sustainability of enthusiasm for social cooperation. Only when the efficiency conditions on both dimensions are met can we confirm the legitimacy and rationality of the concept of fairness and justice. From this, two secondary concepts—immediate efficiency and long-term efficiency of cooperation—are derived. The immediate efficiency of cooperation refers to the current efficiency of cooperation, while the long-term efficiency of cooperation the long-term effectiveness of social cooperation or the maintainability of current efficiency. A legitimate and reasonable concept of fairness and justice must become a bridge between immediate cooperation efficiency and long-term cooperation efficiency, not only able to stimulate the enthusiasm and efficiency of current social cooperation, but also to maintain the current cooperation efficiency as a norm of social cooperation.

The concept of fairness and justice expresses people's value expectations for participating in social cooperation. It is a value standard defined from one's own interests, which determines the distinct relativity of the concept of fairness and justice. The standards of fairness and justice of some people are often denied by others, and vice versa. Even among a group of people who hold the same fairness and justice relationship in some aspects, sharp oppositions may arise in other aspects. Due to the extremely wide range and multiple levels of the concept of fairness and justice, and its strong value orientation, even within a country, there may be significant differences in people's understanding of fairness and justice and the emphasis on it. Even in academia, there is no consensus on the understanding of fairness and justice, and opinions vary widely. Some scholars have made a rough count, and there are as many as 17 different definitions of fairness and justice in the existing literature.[1]

Despite the dazzling array of views on fairness and justice, the essential difference among different views lies in the choice of emphasis between short-term efficiency and long-term efficiency. The more emphasis on short-term efficiency in the concept of fairness and justice, the more emphasis on the development of individual potential and the importance of free competition; on the contrary, the more emphasis on the long-term efficiency of social cooperation, the stronger the tendency to limit distribution differentiation, and the more obvious the claim to limit the development of individual potential. Among the different schools of the concept of fairness and justice, those who emphasize equal opportunities and rule justice usually focus on short-term efficiency. They value the fairness of competition rules and emphasize equal opportunities in theory, but they ignore the differences in individual endowments, resource possession, and the reality of unequal wealth distribution. Those who emphasize result fairness and wealth distribution fairness hold the logic of prioritizing long-term efficiency. In order to avoid harming the foundation of long-term efficiency, they are willing to sacrifice short-term efficiency. They do not care about the fairness of wealth distribution rules, but only care about the results of distribution. The above two opposing views of fairness and justice are difficult to reconcile, and they cannot balance the relationship between short-term efficiency and long-term efficiency, which fundamentally violates the original intention of cooperation.

The long-term and short-term efficiency of social cooperation cannot be completely separated. Without the support of short-term efficiency, there is no basis for long-term social cooperation efficiency; similarly, if only the current efficiency is considered and competition is overly emphasized, it will lead to a polarized situation of wealth distribution, which is a conclusion we have proven in the theorem of trading potential polarization. When the polarization of wealth distribution continues to intensify, the foundation of social cooperation will be destroyed, and short-term efficiency cannot be maintained. The long-term and short-term efficiency of social cooperation must be unified within the tolerable limit of a specific stage of social development in order to maintain the normal operation of the social cooperation system.

The relationship between short-term and long-term efficiency must adapt to the stage of social development. In the evolution process of the trading system, the closer to the starting point of human social civilization evolution, the stronger the survival pressure people face, and therefore the more emphasis on current short-term efficiency; on the contrary, the higher the stage of human social evolution, the more emphasis on the sustainability of social cooperation efficiency, and the more important the status of long-term efficiency. Because the balance between short-term and long-term efficiency is constantly adjusted adaptively in the process of social development evolution, it also brings about the corresponding evolution of the concept of social fairness and justice. We call the concept of fairness and justice that emphasizes short-term efficiency as low-order fairness and justice, and the concept of fairness and justice that emphasizes long-term cooperation efficiency as high-order fairness and justice. As human society evolves from low to high, the concept of fairness and justice also undergoes a stage evolution from low to high.

There are three reasons why the concept of fairness and justice follows the evolutionary law from low to high: First, the importance of cooperation in the evolution of human trading systems is becoming more prominent. People's production and life are connected more closely, leading to a continuous increase in the compactness of the trading system. Second, in traditional societies with relatively low productivity, people only focus on the present and are not able to spare extra energy to care about the future. Only when the pressure of real-life survival is no longer the sole concern, will they care about long-term efficiency. Third, with the development of human society, the social cost of disrupting order and stability is getting higher. The essence of wealth is social relations, and social stability is the foundation of wealth accumulation. The more wealth, the more complex the superimposed social relations, and the higher the dependence on a stable social order. Wealth accumulation is the result of human social progress. With the rise of social evolutionary stages, social wealth accumulates rapidly at a geometric speed. Once the social order is disrupted, the wealth supported by stable social relations will vanish. Social turmoil is becoming an unbearable burden for humanity.

It is impossible for the concept of fairness and justice to blindly pursue higher levels when detached from the historical stages of social evolution; otherwise, the society will lose the motivation for progress and fall into utopian self-indulgence. As John Rawls pointed out in his *Theory of Justice* that the standard for distinguishing the merits of justice could not be judged by how beautiful and attractive the expressed wishes were, but should be judged from the broad results it induces.[2] If the result of a concept of fairness and justice is the loss of social productivity, poverty and backwardness, no matter how beautifully this concept is packaged, it will eventually be abandoned by the society.

18.4.2 Social Justice Measurement

When people evaluate justice, the core concern is whether the ratio of input to output is reasonable and within a tolerable range. If it is, people will conclude that the result is just; otherwise, they will conclude that the result is unjust. According to this logic, the trading potential polarization coefficient χ cannot meet the requirements of the justice index, and it is just a quantitative description of the objective situation of trading potential polarization. We need to rebuild a dedicated index to measure social justice.

When we start to quantify the fairness of the trading system, we will encounter some problems. Benefits are easy to understand and can be measured in money, but how to measure input is no small challenge. The primary problem is what is input. Is it the money spent, or the labor expended, or both? How is labor defined? Does it only refer to physical labor, or does it include the total of physical labor and mental expenditure? In mental expenditure, does it only include mental labor, or does it also include psychological pressure? Only when these questions are clarified can we accurately measure input.

In the human social system, people are undoubtedly the core. The fairness of the social system itself has a strong social ethical color, and to measure the fairness of the social system, we must return to the social ethical level.

Based on this understanding, we need to unify the concept of labor expenditure, including physical labor, mental labor, and the mental payment formed by psychological stress, under the concept of labor expenditure. The concept of expenditure does not include monetary payments, because money is the result of the distribution of the trading system, and fairness, as a measure of the rationality of the trading system in wealth distribution, if monetary payment is included in the concept of expenditure, it will return to the trading system, thus forming a logical cycle.

In order to accurately measure the intensity of labor expenditure, it is necessary to establish the concept of standard labor intensity units. The so-called standard labor intensity unit refers to the product of the statutory labor time length within a unit time such as a week or a month and the intensity of physical and mental labor expenditure. Standard labor intensity, as a unit of labor expenditure, if a person has expended two standard labor units, it means that his (her) labor time length or the intensity of physical or mental labor has reached twice the average. When standard labor intensity is used as a unit to measure the total labor expenditure of the trading subject, it takes into account both physical and mental expenditure. This means that the psychological experience of the laborer in the process of expenditure is also included in the labor expenditure. The higher the pain index of the psychological experience, the more standard labor intensity units included in the labor expenditure.

Labor intensity units will vary in different countries and at different stages of economic development. Generally speaking, the more developed the trading system, the smaller the standard labor intensity. Both the standard labor time length or the labor intensity within a unit time will decrease with economic development. The statutory labor time is constantly decreasing, and the labor intensity is also decreasing.

The fairness of the trading system is measured by the ratio of expenditure to income. We take expenditure W and income U as the horizontal and vertical axes respectively, and examine the spatial distribution of the trading system's income ratio, from which we can identify the degree of fairness of the trading system.

In Fig. 18.5, the income axis U and the expenditure axis W form the distribution space of the trading system. Each trading agent finds its position in the social distribution space based on its own trading potential, corresponding to a coordinate point in the distribution space. The trading system distribution space is divided into two by a 45-degree oblique line OF. On the line OF, the income to expenditure ratio of each distribution point is equal to 1, therefore, it represents an absolutely fair distribution relationship. In real life, since we can never achieve absolute fairness, there must be a certain tolerance for the attitude towards fairness, so there is a line on either side of OF, representing the degree of deviation from absolute fair distribution that people can tolerate under the social background at that time. The two deviation tolerance lines divide the trading system distribution space into three areas, which are s area, representing the socially acceptable appropriate distribution area; s_1 area, representing the strong distribution area with less expenditure and high income; and s_2 area, representing the weak distribution area with more expenditure and low income.

In the trading system, each trading agent can only correspond to one allocation coordinate point in the allocation space, and can only fall into one of the three distribution areas, which determines the relationship of mutual growth and decline

Fig. 18.5 Distribution relationship of the trading system

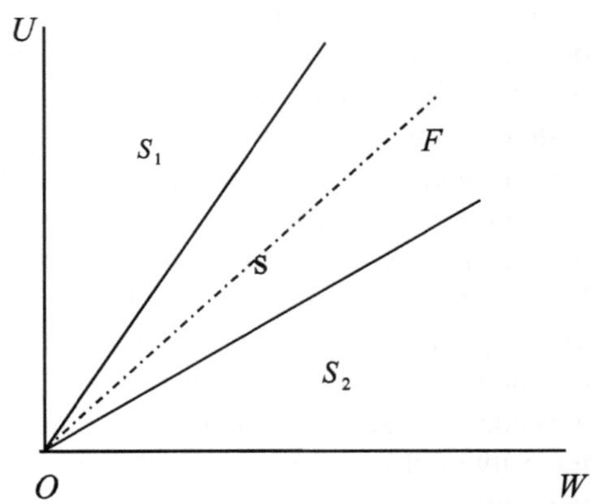

among the three areas of the distribution space s, s_1, and s_2. In the three areas of the distribution space, the more trading agents in the appropriate distribution area, the higher the fairness of the trading system's distribution; on the contrary, the fewer agents in the appropriate allocation area, the more severe the deviation of the trading system's distribution relationship from fairness. Based on this understanding, we define the fairness index of the trading system as follows:

$$fn = \frac{N_s}{N_1} \tag{18.4.1}$$

In Eq. (18.4.1), fn represents the fairness index of the trading system's distribution, N_s represents the number of families in the appropriate distribution area s, and N_1 represents the total number of families in the trading system, that is, the families in the trading system's capacity.

According to definition (18.4.1), the fairness coefficient of the trading system fn takes values between 0 and 1. The highest level of fairness in the trading system is $fn = 1$, and the theoretically lowest level of fairness is $fn = 0$. Although the fairness coefficient and the Gini coefficient $Gini$ have a close internal relationship, there is a fundamental difference in the core logic of the indicators. The Gini coefficient $Gini$ is mainly used to describe the distribution of wealth among people, which is an objective description of a phenomenon, while the fairness index fn uses the ratio of payment to income for measurement. Income and payment represent the result of distribution and the process of income, respectively. Including them in the calculation of the fairness index of the trading system can more comprehensively reflect the essential requirements of the concept of fair justice.

In the three areas of the distribution space, the dominant distribution area S_1 and the appropriate distribution area s have a strong repulsion relationship. The appropriate distribution area s is highly sensitive to changes in the dominant distribution area S_1. A slight increase in the number of agents in the dominant distribution area will cause the number of agents in the appropriate distribution area s to be compressed by multiples. This is because the trading agents lost from the appropriate distribution area s are multiples of the number of agents in the dominant distribution area. A considerable part of the agents originally in the appropriate distribution area are pushed into the weak distribution area due to the promotion of a few agents to the dominant distribution area. The reason why there is such a strong repulsion relationship between the distribution areas is mainly because the distribution of wealth is always carried out after the transaction is completed, and the total wealth has become a fixed value. For the distribution of fixed wealth, it is definitely a relationship of mutual growth and decline; in addition, because the wealth share owned by the trading agents in the dominant distribution area is much higher than that of the agents in the appropriate distribution area, which result in a multiple relationship between the changes in the agents in the dominant distribution area and the appropriate distribution area.

In the social distribution space, The size of the appropriate distribution area s. represents the society's tolerance for deviations from the absolute justice distribution line. The larger the area s is, the higher the society's tolerance for deviations

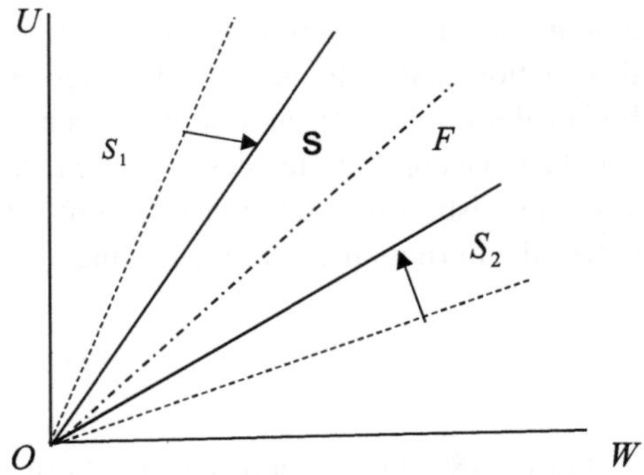

Fig. 18.6 Evolution of distribution relationship

from justice, and the stronger the demand for efficiency generated by competition; conversely, the smaller the area *s* is, the lower the society's tolerance for deviations from justice, and the stronger the consciousness of fairness and justice. As we concluded from our previous analysis, human society is always evolving in the direction of increasing consciousness of fairness and justice, which brings about corresponding changes in the structure of social distribution space.

Figure 18.6 intuitively shows the trend of evolution of the structure of social distribution space, that is, the evolution trend of the angle of deviation from justice line from large to small, and the appropriate distribution area *s* gradually narrows towards the absolute fair distribution line.

18.5 The Widespread Impact of Trading Potential Differentiation

The impact of trading potential differentiation on the trading system is widespread and profound. The main manifestations of trading potential differentiation are concentrated in three aspects, namely the enterprise, the family, and the trading system.

18.5.1 The Market Concentration Continues to Rise

The manifestation of trading potential differentiation in the enterprise is the continuous increase in market concentration. In reality, the market concentration presents a parabolic evolution process. In the early stages of market incubation and development, with small market capacity and few suppliers, the market concentration is high, which is the so-called blue ocean stage. As the market capacity gradually expands, more enterprises will enter, and the market competition will gradually enter the white-hot stage, which is the so-called red ocean period. After cruel and

Table 18.1 Sales concentration of the 5 largest beer manufacturers in US[3]

Year	5 largest beer manufacturers (%)	HHI
1647	19.0	140
1954	24.9	240
1964	39.0	440
1974	64.0	1080
1984	83.9	1898
1994	87.3	2641
2004	85.2	2924
2006	83.0	2785

intense competition, some enterprises are merged, some go bankrupt, and the number of surviving enterprises is decreasing, gradually forming a relatively stable market pattern, which is the so-called mature market stage.

The American beer market provides us with a very typical case. The first brewery in the U.S. was established in New York in 1625 (then New Amsterdam). Until the second half of the nineteenth century, restricted by preservation technology and transportation technology, the beer industry had a small marketing radius with each beer manufacturer selling within a very small range. National and regional markets were born after the emergence of preservation technology and transportation technology. In 1933, the United States lifted the Prohibition, and there were only 31 beer production enterprises in that year. It only took a year for the number of beer manufacturers to increase to 756. In the following decade, the American beer market entered a period of rapid development, with new enterprises constantly entering and the market concentration relatively low. But as the market matured, the market concentration began to gradually climb (Table 18.1).

Not only the beer market, almost every market will go through the above three stages, eventually forming a market structure with high concentration. Between 1997 and 2012, the market concentration of 75% of industries in the United States showed an upward trend, with the market sales share increasingly concentrated in the top 2 or 3 large manufacturers. In fields such as cable television, the internet, and telecommunications, there were only a few suppliers, and consumers hardly had much choice. In markets such as social networking sites, home decoration, pacemaker manufacturing, beer, etc., about 80% of the market share was occupied by 2 or 3 suppliers; in niche markets such as cat food, airline food, jelly, dog food, coffin, battery, etc., the trend of share concentration in a few enterprises was also not escaped.

The result of the continuous concentration of the market is the damage of competition, the basis for the existence of market efficiency, and it is replaced by the excess monopoly profits brought by monopoly for enterprises. In fact, companies must participate in brutal market competition in order to obtain the expected market position, and once they have obtained a dominant market position, competition becomes unimportant, even disdainful. Peter Thiel, the founder of Thiel Asset Management

Company in the United States, once made such an astonishing statement: Competition is for losers.[4]

18.5.2 Polarization of Wealth Distribution

In terms of families, the trading potential polarization is manifested as the polarization of wealth possession. French economist Thomas Piketty provided a large amount of data in his *Capital in the Twenty-First Century*, proving the fact that wealth distribution is becoming increasingly polarized (Tables 18.2, 18.3 and 18.4).

It should be seen that there are also some restrictive factors in the process of trading potential polarization. It is the existence of these restrictive factors that the process of trading system differentiation present a gradual spiral upward trend. Among them, the limited life span is the biggest constraint on the differentiation of the trading system. When the life of the main members of the family comes to an end, the family agent also goes to disintegration. At this time, the issue of intergenerational wealth transfer must be considered. Under different cultural backgrounds and different institutional arrangements, the impact of wealth accumulation in the process of intergenerational transfer is different. In traditional Eastern societies, when the father dies, the original family wealth needs to be evenly distributed among the male heirs. In Eastern societies, especially in traditional Chinese society, each family has many children, and wealth is interrupted after being evenly divided. Although wealth can be accumulated again in the hands of children, it will be split again in the next wealth transfer process. Considering that the average life expectancy of people in traditional societies was relatively short, wealth was constantly split at a high frequency. In addition, the split

Table 18.2 Labor income inequality at different time and in different space[5]

Ration of total labor income by different groups	Low inequality (= Scandinavia in 1970s–80s)	Medium inequality ($\approx$ Europe in 2010)	High inequality ($\approx$ U.S. in 2010)	Extreme inequality ($\approx$ U.S. in 2030)
Top 10% (upper class) (%)	20	25	35	45
Top 1% (ruling class) (%)	5	7	12	17
Next 9% (wealthy class) (%)	15	18	23	28
Middle 40% (middle class) (%)	45	45	40	35
Lowest 50% (lower class) (%)	35	30	25	20
Corresponding gini coefficient (comprehensive inequality index)	0.19	0.26	0.36	0.46

Table 18.3 Capital possession inequality at different time and in different space[6]

Ratio of total capital by different groups	Medium inequality (≈ Scandinavia in 1970–80s)	Medium to high inequality (≈ Europe in 2010)	High inequality (≈ U.S. in 2010)	Extreme inequality (≈ Europe in 1910)
Top 10% (upper class) (%)	50	60	70	90
Top 1% (ruling class) (%)	20	25	35	50
Next 9% (wealthy class) (%)	30	35	35	40
Middle 40% (middle class) (%)	40	35	25	5
Lowest 50% (lower class) (%)	10	5	5	5
Corresponding gini coefficient (comprehensive inequality index)	0.58	0.67	0.73	0.85

Table 18.4 Total income inequality at different time and in different space(labor and capital)[7]

Ratio of total income by different groups (labor and capital)	Low inequality (≈ Scandinavia in 1970s–80s)	Medium inequality (≈ Europe in 2010)	High inequality (≈ U.S. in 2010)	Extreme inequality (≈ U.S. in 2030)
Top 10% (upper class) (%)	25	35	50	60
Top 1% (ruling class) (%)	7	10	20	23
Next 9% (wealthy class) (%)	18	25	30	35
Middle 40% (middle class) (%)	45	40	30	25
Lowest 50% (lower class) (%)	30	25	20	15
Corresponding gini coefficient (comprehensive inequality index)	0.26	0.36	0.46	0.58

wealth is homogeneous, and the competitive advantage of wealth is discounted. This may to some extent explain why the modern capitalist system did not first appear in China.

18.5.3 Destruction of Social Justice

Based on the dynamic relationship of the three areas of social distribution space, it is not difficult to draw such a conclusion: the polarization of trading potential is very likely to lead to a decline in the fairness of the trading system. This is because the high-order trading potential group can easily use their strong influence on the market to obtain excess returns. The distribution coordinates of the high-order trading potential group usually fall in the dominant distribution area s_1. The renowned economist Joseph E. Stiglitz has extensively discussed this point in his works such as *The Price of Inequality* and *People, Power, and Profits: Progressive Capitalism for an Age of Discontent*.[8]

In fact, the causes of social justice destruction are far more than trading potential polarization. The bubble process of the trading system often causes great damage to the foundation of social justice. When the trading system falls into the bubble process, the social distribution process will change from the original primary distribution to the wealth redistribution dominated by speculative behavior. In the bubble-dominated trading system, the way to obtain high returns is no longer to compete for efficiency and create wealth through labor, but to rely on shrewd calculations and opportunistic speculative activities. Under the condition that the total social wealth remains basically unchanged, a large amount of wealth is transferred to successful speculators, and more speculative losers and trading agents who have not participated in speculative activities ultimately become the victims of speculative activities. Even if their wealth is not explicitly transferred, due to the relativity of wealth value, part of their wealth value will be transferred to successful speculators. The structure of social distribution space will undergo major changes in this process. Apart from a small number of trading agents moving from the appropriate distribution area s to the dominant distribution area, more trading agents will slide from the appropriate distribution area s to the weak distribution area s_2. The structure of social distribution space presents a fission trend, the appropriate distribution area s is hollowed out, and the social justice index drops.

It is not difficult to find that the trading system has once again fallen into the conflict of the "increasing paradox". On the one hand, as can be known from the theorem of trading potential polarization, with the continuous evolution of the trading system, the distribution of trading potential in the trading system presents an increasingly significant bipolarization trend, and the coefficient of trading potential polarization intensity χ continues to increase, causing the foundation of social justice to be increasingly eroded; on the other hand, as the trading system evolves to a higher order, the concept of fair justice also adjusts accordingly, and the tolerance for justice deviation will continue to decrease. In terms of the structure of social distribution space, it is the continuous shrinkage of the appropriate distribution area s, the standard for satisfying fair distribution is getting higher, and the difficulty of maintaining social justice is increasing. The higher the evolution stage of the human social system, the more prominent the internal logical conflict brought by the "increasing paradox", which leads to sharper social contradictions. In fact, the "middle-income trap" is also a manifestation of the "increasing paradox". Of course, at different stages of the evolution process of the trading system, the "increasing paradox" will have more manifestations.

If we use mathematical language to display the above two completely opposite evolutionary trends, we can get the following description:

$$\frac{\lim s}{t \to +\infty} = 0 \quad (18.5.1)$$

$$\frac{\lim Max\{\psi(a_i) - \psi(a_j)\}}{t \to +\infty} = +\infty \; 1 \le i, j \le N \quad (18.5.2)$$

Equations (18.5.1) and (18.5.2) respectively represent the two opposite evolutionary trends of the trading system. Equation (18.5.1) represents the trend of the social system's increasing difficulty in maintaining social justice; (18.5.2) represents the prospect of the economic development foundation being constantly eroded. This is the deepest contradiction that human society must face with the most profound impact. Whether this contradiction brought about by social and economic development can be effectively resolved has become a touchstone for testing the quality of the system.

Fortunately, modern human society has found an effective way to resolve the "increasing paradox", a contradiction that could lead to the disintegration of the social system. By establishing a social security system, the potential harm to the foundation of social cooperation caused by economic development is reduced, and the social justice index is maintained at a relatively high level. With the support of the social security system, trading agents in the disadvantaged distribution area can receive compensation for their earnings. Since social justice is measured by the ratio of income to expenditure, the marginal income effect of the justice index is particularly sensitive to low-income groups. A slight change in earnings can significantly alter the structure of social distribution. The social security system is very important for low-income groups, affecting their quality of life and personal dignity. In any country, low-income groups occupy a considerable proportion of society, and their experience of social justice is crucial in the overall evaluation of social justice.

The power-law distribution characteristics of trading potential show that the proportion of groups with super trading potential in the capacity of the trading system is very small, which means that only a small part of the trading agents can successfully enter the strong distribution area. This indicates that the structure formed by regions S_1 and s_2 is the key factor determining the justice level of the trading system. To successfully avoid the challenge of the "increasing paradox", the key is not to limit the super trading potential group, but to strengthen the middle power of trading power, that is, the middle class, and to create a favorable growth environment for small and medium-sized enterprises.

In alleviating the contradiction of the "increasing paradox", the role of the progressive tax system should not be underestimated. If the social security system can promote some trading agents from the weak distribution area to the appropriate distribution area, the progressive tax system plays a role in reducing the deviation of fair distribution from the strong distribution area. Through the progressively increasing tax rate, the progressive tax system levies a considerable part of the excess profits from the strong potential group, and pulls some trading agents from the strong distribution area into the appropriate distribution area, thus playing a positive role in promoting social justice.

All value orientations should be confined within a specific range. Once exceeding this range, they will turn into their opposites and fall into a predicament of self-denial. The social security system and progressive tax system used to promote social justice are no exception; they cannot exceed the boundaries set by the stage of social development and economic capacity. Once these boundaries are exceeded, the result will be counterproductive. In the distribution space, a large number of agents originally in the disadvantaged distribution area s_2 will, through the compensation mechanism of the social security system, cross the fair distribution area s and directly enter the dominant distribution area s_1. Agents originally in the fair distribution area s will be squeezed out and slide into the disadvantaged distribution area s_2, leading to new injustices. Undoubtedly, distorted distribution relationships will inevitably lead to a distortion of social value orientations, the efficiency of the trading system will be damaged, and social vitality will be significantly reduced.

18.5.4 Decline in Economic Vitality, Slow Growth

From the conclusions of the trading system evolution equation, we know that the evolution process of the trading system is difficult to avoid the trend of trade potential differentiation. However, each trading system, due to the differences in structural parameters α and β, will have a great disparity in the speed of differentiation. Excessive differentiation of trade potential not only makes it difficult to achieve resource allocation efficiency under fair competition, but also easily leads to social stratification and political instability. In a society with extreme differentiation of trade potential, the vested interest class will intentionally prevent economic openness to maintain and consolidate their own interests. They will exert influence on the government to enact some unfair policies at home. These indirect effects of trading potential differentiation will harm economic vitality in various ways.

When the structural parameters of the trading system lack rationality, and the speed of trade potential differentiation becomes too fast, the phenomenon of trading potential differentiation induced by economic growth will in turn damage the foundation for further economic growth, leading to economic stagnation or slow growth. Both the continents of South and North America have abundant natural resources and long coastlines along the Pacific and Atlantic Oceans, providing excellent trade conditions. In the early eighteenth century, the economies of the countries in South and North America were all in their infancy, with almost no difference in their levels of economic development. However, in the subsequent development process of more than 300 years, the economies of the South American countries have lagged far behind that of the North American countries, and the gap is getting wider and wider.

Table 18.5 clearly shows the gradual economic gap between Latin American countries and North American countries represented by the United States over the 300 years from 1700 to 2000. Over this period, although Latin American countries had also experienced continuous growth, with GDP per capita increasing by 11.27 times, the GDP per capita of the United States had increased by 53.38 times, and the income gap between the two had widened by 79 times.

In the half-century after the end of the World War II, the economic gap between the North and the South had not narrowed, and the gap in some countries had even further widened (Table 18.6).

The fact that there is such a huge disparity in economic development between two different regions on the same American continent has attracted the attention of many economists and sociologists. People seek the causes of the economic development gap between North and South America from various aspects, realizing that the causes are multifaceted. Institutional factors, cultural factors, economic policies, and excessive wealth gaps all bear responsibility for the economic backwardness of Latin American countries. Among them, the polarization of income distribution is a key factor causing the loss of economic vitality in Latin American countries, and the "growth backlash effect" is the main culprit of the Latin American phenomenon (Table 18.7).

The polarization of income distribution has long become an incurable chronic disease in Latin American countries. In the 1950s, Mexico's Gini coefficient was 1.36 times that of the United States, and the severe polarization situation did not improve in the following 40 years. The situation in Brazil was roughly the same.

Table 18.5 Comparison of GDP per capita in Latin American countries and the U.S.[9]

	1700	1820	1870	1930	2000
Brazil	459	646	713	1048	5556
Mexico	568	759	674	1618	7218
Latin America	521	701	756	1873	5844
U.S.	527	1257	2445	6123	28,129
Latin America/U.S.	0.99	0.56	0.31	0.31	0.21

(in U.S. Dollars)

Table 18.6 Ratio of GDP per capita in major Latin American countries to that in the U.S.[10]

	1950	2000
Argentina	0.52	0.30
Brazil	0.17	0.20
Chile	0.40	0.35
Columbia	0.23	0.18
Mexico	0.25	0.26

Table 18.7 Ratio of gini coefficient in Latin American countries to that in the U.S.[11]

Argentina	Brazil	Chile	Columbia	Mexico
1.28	1.45	1.40	1.41	1.31

(in 2000)

In the early 1980s, when the "Brazilian economic miracle" just ended, the Gini coefficient had already reached 0.579. Entering the twenty-first century, the Gini coefficient even reached an extremely polarized level of 0.591.

By comparing the situation of Latin American countries with the United States, we find that the trading potential polarization in Latin American economies is extremely sensitive to economic growth, and the social equity cost required for economic growth is far higher than that of the United States. Under such circumstances, Latin American countries cannot withstand the social costs that long-term economic growth may bring like the United States, and the decline in economic vitality and slowdown in economic growth are almost inevitable.

Notes

1. Wang Guisheng (2020) Welfare Economics, 2nd edn. China Labor and Social Security Press, Beijing, p 138 (in Chinese).
2. John Rawls (1988) A Theory of Justice (Trans: He Huaihong, He Baogang, Liao Shenbai), China Social Sciences Press, Beijing, p 6.
3. James W. Brock (2011) American Industrial structure (Trans: Luo Yu, Pan Biyue, Hu Shanbin), 12th edn. China Renmin University Press, Beijing.
4. The Herfindahl-Hirschman Index (HHI), or Herfindahl Index for short, is a composite index that measures the degree of industrial concentration. It refers to the sum of the squares of the percentages of total revenues or total assets of each market competitor in an industry, and is used to measure changes in market share, i.e., the dispersion of the size of vendors in the market. The larger the value of HHI, the higher the degree of market concentration and the higher the degree of monopoly.
5. Joseph E. Stiglitz (2020) The Truth about America (Trans: Liu Binfu, Liu Yiming, Liu Jiamu), China Machine Press, Beijing.
6. Thomas Piketty (2014) Capital in the 21st Century (Trans: Ba Shusong), CITIC Press, Beijing, p 251.
7. Thomas Piketty (2014) Capital in the 21st Century (Trans: Ba Shusong), CITIC Press, Beijing, p 252.
8. Thomas Piketty (2014) Capital in the 21st Century (Trans: Ba Shusong), CITIC Press, Beijing, p 253.
9. Joseph E. Stiglitz (2022) The Price of Inequality (Trans: Zhang Ziyuan), China Machine Press, Beijing.
10. Francis Fukuyama (2015) The Source of Backwardness: Interpreting the Development Gap between Latin America and the United States (Trans: Liu Wei), CITIC Press, Beijing, p 102.
11. Francis Fukuyama (2015) The Source of Backwardness: Interpreting the Development Gap between Latin America and the United States (Trans: Liu Wei), CITIC Press, Beijing, p 71.
12. Francis Fukuyama (2015) The Source of Backwardness: Interpreting the Development Gap between Latin America and the United States (Trans: Liu Wei), CITIC Press, Beijing, p 72.

Chapter 19
Evolution of Trading Space

Trading space is the projection of the trading system in geometric space and is the geometric expression of trading economics. When we continuously examine the trading behavior of trading agents in the trading space, we will find some laws of trading trajectory evolution and reveal some characteristics of the operation of the trading system.

19.1 Trading Space

All trading activities need to be carried out on a specific trading space domain. Therefore, we need to define the concept of trading space to lay the foundation for studying the behavior trajectory of trading subjects.

19.1.1 Trading Vector

Assume $G = \{g_1, g_2, g_3, \ldots, g_M\}$ is the trading base of the trading system, g_i represents a type of trading target in the trading system, we call the vector composed of trading goods, trading volume, and trading direction based on the trading base as the trading vector. The trading vector is in the following form:

$$X = \begin{pmatrix} x^1 g_1 \\ x^2 g_2 \\ x^3 g_3 \\ \vdots \\ x^M g_m \end{pmatrix} \tag{19.1.1}$$

Z. Wang, *Trading Economics*, Contributions to Economics,
https://doi.org/10.1007/978-981-99-9875-3_19

It can be simplified as:

$$X = \begin{pmatrix} x^1 \\ x^2 \\ x^3 \\ \vdots \\ x^M \end{pmatrix} \tag{19.1.2}$$

In the trading vector, x^i represents the trading corresponding to the first i goods in the trading base, the absolute value $|x^i|$ represents the trading amount of this trading, $x^i > 0$; indicates that the trading is a forward trading, that is, selling goods g_i; $x^i < 0$ indicates that the trading is a reverse trading, that is, buying goods g_i; $x^i = 0$ indicates that there is no trading under this target.

The trading vector changes over time, we mark it as X_t, that is:

$$X_t = \begin{pmatrix} x_t^1 \\ x_t^2 \\ x_t^3 \\ \vdots \\ x_t^M \end{pmatrix}$$

From an external observer's perspective, the trading behavior of the tradingagent agent a_i at time step t has typical characteristics of a stochastic process., and is influenced by many factors, including macro-environmental factors and factors related to the tradingagent agent itself. For the random variable X_t, the result of the transition from time step t to time step $t + 1$ will be determined by the transition probability of the trading vector X_t.

19.1.2 Trading Space

Based on the trading vector, we define trading space. For this, we need to establish the concept of a unit trading vector. The so-called unit trading vector is a trading vector generated by only one unit trading asset, as follows:

$$X_0^i = \begin{pmatrix} 0 \\ \vdots \\ 1 \times g_i \\ \vdots \\ 0 \end{pmatrix}$$

Any M dimensional trading vector X can be expressed as a linear combination of M unit vectors X_0^i, that is:

$$X = x^1 X_0^1 + x^2 X_0^2 + \cdots + x^M X_0^M = \sum_1^M x^i X_0^i$$

The vector set generated by M unit trading vectors is called the trading space of the trading system T, denoted by Ω. The dimension of the trading space Ω is equal to the trading base capacity M on the trading system T.

Based on the concept of trading space, we can re-describe the operation of the trading system T: The trading system T corresponds to a trading space Ω, and all trading activities of any tradingagent agent a_i can be described by the trading vector X_t. The trading vector X_t changes with time t, leaving a trading trajectory in the trading space Ω. The trading activities of the trading agent a_i will highly likely appear in a relatively stable area in the trading space Ω, and its trading trajectory moves randomly within this area.

Along with the evolution of the trading system T, the trading space Ω is also undergoing corresponding changes. The trading space Ω has three types of movements: one is the expansion movement of the space dimension M. Due to economic and technological progress and deepening social division of labor, The trading base of the trading system T is able to expand, and the dimensions of the trading space evolve from low to high; the second is the expansion of the active area in the trading space Ω. With economic growth, the capacity of the trading system T increases and the volume of trading s grows, the scope of trading activities will inevitably continue to expand; the third is the structural movement of the trading space Ω. With technological progress, some old commodities exit the trading base, new commodities enter the trading base, causing the trading space Ω to shrink in some dimensions and expand in new dimensions.

At the micro level, with the evolution of the trading system T, the active area of the trading agents in the trading space Ω gradually differentiates from the overlapping areas in the early stage of the evolution, forming reducible structures separated from each other in the trading space Ω.

19.1.3 Magnitude of Trading Vector

The trading vector X contains many trading items, each corresponding to different trading amounts. The sum of all trading volumes contained in the trading vector X is an important indicator of the trading vector, which we call the magnitude of the trading vector X. It is calculated using the following formula:

$$|X| = \sum_{1}^{M} |x_i| \tag{19.1.3}$$

Any trading vector X, Y on the trading space Ω has three possible relationships:

$$\begin{aligned} &(1)\ |X| - |Y| > 0 \\ &(2)\ |X| - |Y| < 0 \\ &(3)\ |X| - |Y| = 0 \end{aligned} \tag{19.1.4}$$

When relationship (1) holds, we say that the magnitude of the trading vector X is higher than the trading vector Y, or simply X is greater than Y; if relationship (2) holds, we say that the trading vector X is a low-magnitude vector, Y is a high-magnitude vector, or simply X is less than Y; if X, Y satisfy relationship (3), we call X, Y the same-magnitude trading vectors.

In the trading space, same-magnitude vectors are on the same hyperplane. In the M-dimensional trading space Ω, same-magnitude vectors correspond to the same $M - 1$ -dimensional hyperplane; in the 2-dimensional trading space Ω, all trading vectors with a magnitude of Q correspond to a square enclosed by four sides; in the 3-dimensional trading space, the entire vectors of the magnitude Q correspond to an octahedron formed by 8 triangular planes. We call these geometric bodies of varying magnitudes and closed structures as **trading magnitude rings.**

The trading space is divided into countless trading magnitude rings from small to large around the coordinate origin according to the magnitude. In the trading system T, agents with different trading potentials run on their corresponding magnitude rings. As shown in Fig. 19.1

Fig. 19.1 The diagram of trading magnitude rings

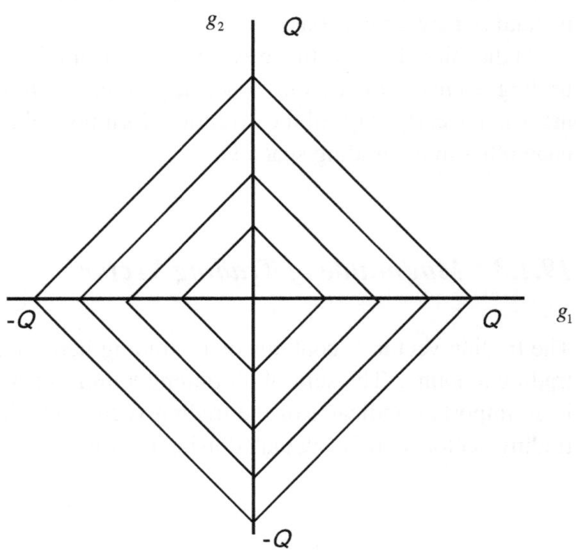

The trading activities of the trading agent a_i always unfold on a specific magnitude ring. Numerous trading agents in the trading system T operate in the trading space Ω, just like celestial bodies in the universe running along their orbits, forming a complex yet orderly trading space operation landscape.

19.1.4 Trading Space Distance

The trading vector X corresponds to a phase point in the trading space Ω. In the trading space Ω, we can establish the concept of distance between any two phase points.

According to the magnitude of the trading vector, we can define the distance between any two trading vectors X and Y in the trading space Ω. If D_{XY} represents the distance between X and Y in the trading space Ω, then we have:

$$D_{XY} = \| X | - | Y \| \tag{19.1.5}$$

According to definition (19.1.5), we can prove that D_{XY} satisfies the three properties of the "distance" concept:

(1) For any two trading vectors X, Y in the trading space, it satisfies $D_{XY} \geq 0$;
(2) For any two trading vectors X, Y in the trading space, it satisfies

$$D_{XY} = D_{YX}$$

(3) For any three trading vectors X, Y, Z in the trading space, it satisfies $D_{XZ} \leq D_{XY} + D_{YZ}$

Properties (1) and (2) are relatively easy to understand, while understanding property (3) is relatively difficult. Below we prove property (3):

Assume X, Y, and Z are three arbitrary vectors in the trading space Ω, their magnitudes are:

$$|X| = x, |Y| = y, |Z| = z$$

$$\because D_{XZ} = \| X | - | Z \| = |x - z|$$

$$\because \ |x - z| = |x - y + y - z|$$

$$\because x - y \leq |x - y| = D_{XY}$$

$$y - z \le |y - z| = D_{YZ}$$

$$\therefore\ |x - z| \le ||x - y| + |y - z|| = |x - y| + |y - z|$$

$\therefore D_{XZ} \le D_{XY} + D_{YZ}$ The inequality holds.

The above proof shows that D_{XY} fully satisfies the conditions of linear space distance and can serve as the distance of the trading space Ω; trading space Ω An order can be established with D_{XY} as the scale.

19.1.5 Trade Vector Liquidity Pressure

Each phase point in the trading space Ω corresponds to a set of trades, which require liquidity support of a certain scale to complete, creating a certain intensity of liquidity pressure on the trading agents. Due to differences in the financial status of trading agents, the same trade vector may generate vastly different liquidity pressures-on different agents. For agents with a higher trading potential, the liquidity pressure generated by a certain trade vector may be negligible, while for those with lower trading potential, it may be unbearable.

We use $lp_i(X)$ to represent the liquidity pressure formed by the trade vector X on the trading agent a_i. For any trade vector X, the trading agent a_i has two possible states: the first state is able to complete payments without increasing liabilities and will not affect the trading arrangements at time step $t + 1$; the second state requires liabilities to complete payments or it can complete payments without liabilities, but may affect the trading arrangements at time step $t+1$. For these two states, we assign values to $lp_i(X)$ as follows:

For the first state, $lp_i(X) = 0$;

For the second state, $lp_i(X) > 0$;

For convenience, we limit the value range of liquidity pressure $lp_i(X)$ to the half open interval $[0, +\infty)$. For the second state, if payments can be completed without debt financing at the expense of the trading arrangements at time step $t + 1$, $lp_i(X)$ takes a value close to 0; if debt financing is needed to complete payments. The more difficult the financing is to get, larger value $lp_i(X)$ takes; for the tradingagent a_i, if debt financing is almost impossible, then we agree to take the value $lp_i(X) = +\infty$.

Theoretically, liquidity pressure $lp_i(X)$ is inversely proportional to the agent's trading potential $\psi(a_i)$. For any trade vector X, with other conditions being equal, the greater the agent's trading potential $\psi(a_i)$, the smaller the value of $lp_i(X)$; conversely, the smaller the agent's trading potential $\psi(a_i)$, the greater the value of liquidity pressure $lp_i(X)$.Provided that trading potential is equal, the liquidity pressure $lp_i(X)$ is closely related to the payment ability of the trading agents a_i.

There are two factors affecting the payment ability of trading agents: one is the total amount of liquidity reserves of the tradingagent, that is, the scale of the held cash; the other is the liquidity of assets. In the accounting matrix of the trading agent, the higher the proportion of highly liquid assets, the stronger the ability of the tradingagent to convert liquidity, and the greater the payment ability it has. The payment ability of the tradingagent is closely related to the structure of the accounting matrix.

Asset liquidity is also closely related to the liquidity environment of the trading system. When the liquidity environment in the trading system is in an accommodative state, the asset liquidity of the tradingagent is also strong; on the contrary, when the liquidity environment in the trading system enters a tightening state, the asset liquidity of the tradingagent will weaken accordingly, and the payment ability will be affected, and the liquidity pressure will increase accordingly.

19.1.6 Expected Returns of Trading Vectors

The trading vector X corresponds to a definite expected return in the valuation time domain of the tradingagent, and we denote this expected return result as $E(X)$.

The expected return of the trading vector does not necessarily have a stable correspondence with the trading volume. High-volume trading vectors may not get more expected returns, and low-volume trading vectors may not only get less expected returns. In fact, even for trading vectors in the same trading volume environment, the expected returns may vary greatly. In the trading system, asset values and market demand are always changing. Although the trading volume is the same and consumes the same liquidity resources, the results of choosing different trading vectors may be vastly different, which fully reflects the complexity of trading decisions.

Although the trading volume cannot guarantee proportional returns, without a large enough trading volume, it is impossible to obtain a large value of returns. No one would expect to gain a return of 10,000 yuan from an investment of 1 yuan. Under most probable conditions, a certain level of trading has a maximum expected return. There is no trading strategy in the world that has an infinitely high return rate, which means to achieve greater returns, we need to increase the trading volume.

19.1.7 Transition Probability of Trading Vectors

When we regard the trading vector X as a random vector, the possible value of the trading vector X is called the state of X. The possible value set of the trading vector X in the trading space Ω is called the state domain of X, denoted as K. Because of the correspondence between the trading vector X and the trading agent a_i, the state domain K of the trading vector X, is also known as the state domain of the tradingagent a_i.

The transition probability refers to the probability of the state of the trading vector X from time step t state x_t Transitioning to time step $t+1$ state x_{t+1}. We use $P_{x_t x_{t+1}}$ to represent the transition probability from state x_t to state x_{t+1}:

$$P_{x_t x_{t+1}} = P\{X = x_{t+1} | X = x_t\} \tag{19.1.6}$$

Based on the definition of transition probability (19.1.6), we can further define the transition probability over a time span of n time steps, that is:

$$P^n_{x_t x_{t+n}} = P\{X = x_{t+n} | X = x_t\} \tag{19.1.7}$$

Given the initial value of the trading vector X and the transition probability $P_{x_t x_{t+1}}$, the probability distribution of the trajectory of the trading vector X will be uniquely determined.

19.2 Trading Space Structure

The trading space structure is formed by the interrelationships of the trading agents' state domains. Due to the differentiation trend of the trading system, the trading space will inevitably evolve into a division of numerous disconnected state domains.

19.2.1 State Connectivity

Assume x_1,x_2,x_3, are three arbitrary states on the trading space Ω. Within a finite time τ, if the transition probability between two states satisfies the condition $P_{x_1,x_2} > 0$; $P_{x_2,x_1} > 0$, we call x_1 and x_2 two connected states, denoted as:

$$x_1 \longleftrightarrow x_2 \tag{19.2.1}$$

State connectivity is an equivalence relation:

(1) $x_1 \leftrightarrow x_2$ then there is $x_2 \leftrightarrow x_1$
(2) $x_1 \leftrightarrow x_2, x_2 \leftrightarrow x_3$ then there is $x_1 \leftrightarrow x_3$

From the definition (19.2.1), the key to the connectivity of two trading states is that the transition probability is greater than 0. The transition probability is defined by the possibility of trading agents' behaviors and is defined according to various trading constraints. For lower-income families, due to liquidity constraints and accounting matrix scale limitations, trading activities are usually limited to necessities and essential services, therefore luxury consumption is basically not connected to their trading state domain.

The situation for enterprises is easier to understand. A company's trading activities are closely related to its operating scope. The trading state domain of a clothing company mainly includes textiles, clothing production equipment, employee recruitment, product advertising, sales agent trading s, etc., and has little connection with real estate development, shipbuilding, artificial intelligence development, and other trading state domains.

In fact, whether they're families or enterprises, all trading agents will form a relatively stable trading state domain in continuous trading activities. This is not only due to the stability of trading momentum, but also the relatively stable business scope and family preferences, and the significant role of trading habits.

When defining whether two states are connected, the time factor is very important. The key to determining whether two states are connected is to check if the time is limited to a certain range. If time is extended indefinitely, anything is possible. Enterprises may exits the industries, and the financial standing of families may also change, which would render the standard moot for determining whether states are connected.

19.2.2 State Closure

In the trading space Ω, according to the connectivity characteristics of the trading state domain, it can be divided into two basic types: open set and closed set. The so-called open set refers to the trading state domain K, which is connected with its complement $\Omega - K$. If the trading state domain K and its complement $\Omega - K$ are not connected, then K is called a closed set. We are mainly concerned with the situation where the trading state domain K belongs to the closed set. For this, we need to further refine the concept of state closure K.

Definition 1 In the trading space Ω, if the transition probability of any state in the state domain K to its complement $\Omega - K$ within a finite time τ is zero, then the state domain K is called a closed set within the time limit τ, also known as the relative closed set in the trading space Ω.

Definition 2 In the trading space Ω, if the transition probability of any state in the state domain K to its complement $\Omega - K$ is zero at any length of time, then the state domain K is called the absolute closed set in the trading space Ω.

Definition 3 In the trading space Ω, if the transition probability of any state x in a state domain K to the state y of its complement $\Omega - K$ satisfies the limit condition: $\lim_{\tau \to \infty} P_{xy}^{\tau} = 0$, then the state domain K is called the asymptotic closed set in the trading space Ω.

In order to facilitate the detailed description of the evolution of the state domain, on the basis of the concepts of several closed sets proposed earlier, we also need to introduce the concept of weak closure. The so-called weak closure refers to the state domain K where the transition probability of any state x to another arbitrary internal state y always satisfies the following relationship with the transition probability to the state z on the complement $\Omega - K$:

$$P_{xy} > P_{xz} \tag{19.2.2}$$

As a tool to describe the change of the tradingagent's state, the change of the closure itself reflects the behavioral characteristics of the trading agent, among which the contraction movement is a typical change of the state closure.

Definition 4 Closed set contraction refers to the process of continuously reducing the radius of the closed set ρ. The radius of the closed set refers to the maximum modulus among all states in the closed set, that is: $\rho = \text{Max}|x|, \quad x \in K$.

The state closed set can have different movement directions, it can either contract inward or expand outward. Closed set contraction usually occurs in situations where enterprises are struggling and families are falling into poverty. When the tradingagent faces difficulties, the pressure to repay debts increases, external financing becomes difficult, and under the squeeze of both sides, the accounting matrix enters a rapid contraction process, and the trading volume begins to shrink continuously. Closed set expansion occurs during the rising period of the trading agent, the development of the trading agent enters a virtuous cycle, the accounting matrix is in a sustainable expansion trend, and the state domain of the tradingagent shows a corresponding expansion momentum.

According to the definition of different types of closed sets, we can judge that the state domains on the trading space Ω all meet the weak closed set condition (19.2.2). Since the tradingagent is on the edge of its own state domain K, it has the ability to make certain flexible trading arrangements, but the range of flexibility is not infinite. According to the differences in the trading potential order of the tradingagent, the flexible range on the edge of the state domain K will also be different. In order to further refine the description of the characteristics of the state domain, we need to establish the concepts of finite weak closed set and closed set elasticity separately.

Definition 5 In the trading space Ω, the state domain K is a weak closed set, R is a closed set on Ω, and there is $K \subset R$, x, y are any two states on K, z is any state on the complement $R - K$, w is any state on the complement $\Omega - R$. If the following conditions are met:

$$P_{xy} > P_{xz}, P_{xw} = 0 \tag{19.2.3}$$

We then call K a finite weak closed set with an elasticity boundary of R. On this basis, we can define the concept of elasticity of the finite weak closed set.

Definition 6 In the trading space Ω, K is a finite weak closed set with an elasticity boundary of R, x is any state in the state domain K, y is any state in the state domain R. The finite weak closed set K Elasticity value k is defined as follows:

$$k = \frac{\max(|Y| - |X|)}{\max |X|} \quad (19.2.4)$$

Obviously, the higher the trading potential of the tradingagent, the stronger the ability to arrange flexibly, and the elasticity value k of the state domain K is larger. In the trading space Ω, each tradingagent has its own trading state domain K and corresponding elasticity k, forming a state domain distribution structure in the trading space.

The above 5 types of closed sets, including relative closed, absolute closed, asymptotic closed, weak closed, and finite weak closed sets, are collectively referred to as state closed sets. When the trading space Ω can be divided into two or more state closed sets, we call the trading space Ω decomposable or reducible. Otherwise, the trading space Ω is called irreducible. Obviously, when all states in the trading space Ω are interconnected, then Ω is an irreducible space. When the trading space Ω can be decomposed into two or more weak closed sets, we call Ω a weakly reducible space.

19.2.3 State Cycle

In the state domain of the tradingagent, the frequency of each state varies greatly. For example, food consumption is constantly occurring in the trading process, and clothing consumption is the same; but compared with it, the trading s of buying real estate or cars are much less. In a family cycle, the opportunity to buy a house is still very small, unless it is real estate speculation. In order to depict the difference in the frequency of visits to different states in the trading process, we introduce the concept of state cycle.

Definition 7 For the state x, the smallest time τ that makes the inequality $P_{xx}^{\tau} > 0$ hold is called the cycle of the state x.

The state cycle depends not only on the trading content on the state, but also closely related to the structure of the state domain of the tradingagent. The state cycle of the food trade is very short, as short as less than a day, and no more than a week. But the state cycles of car trading and real estate trading are much longer. For companies, the cycle of each state is directly related to the company's main business and business scope. Real estate development companies will frequently return to the states such as land trading and construction materials trading, and these state cycles are usually very short; similarly, car manufacturing companies will frequently return to engine, car parts, steel products and other types of trading.

In the state domain of each tradingagent, there are always some high-frequency cycle states. We call the subset composed of these states the core of theagent's state domain. Compared with other states in the state domain, the core is relatively stable, corresponding to the iconic trading content of the tradingagent, reflecting the habits and operational characteristics of the tradingagent, and also reflecting the order characteristics of the trading potential.

19.3 Trading Trajectory Equation

Transition probabilities are a very useful tool for examining the evolution of trading s. By analyzing transition probabilities, we can predict the direction of trading trajectories well.

19.3.1 Analysis of Factors Affecting Transition Probabilities

Each trading will have some impact on subsequent trading. Conversely, each trading is influenced by many completed trading s, and the behavior of the trading agent trading is largely constrained by the trajectory of past tradings.

The probability of a trading occurring is influenced by two types of factors, namely, reinforcing factors and inhibiting factors. Among them, reinforcing factors increase the probability of the trading vector turning towards the trading while inhibiting factors decrease the probability of the trading vector turning towards the trading.

The reinforcing factors of transition probabilities are constituted by trading that have a positive correlation with the trading in question, such as buying a car, which requires purchasing car liability insurance and third-party accident insurance. The car trading is a positive correlation trading for the insurance trading. If we observe the trading agent implementing a car trading at time step t, we can infer the probability of the insurance trading at time step $t + 1$ from this trading behavior.

Among the reinforcing factors, positive correlation is not only induced by functional correlation, but also by the liquidity constraints of the trading agent. Because reverse trading can put liquidity pressure on the trading agent, forcing the agent to implement positive trading s that increase liquidity. The larger the liquidity gap of the trading agent, the stronger the liquidity pressure induced by the reverse trading. For example, when buying a house, due to insufficient liquidity, the buyer needs to borrow from the bank. When a company makes an investment, in the lack of sufficient funds, it also needs to apply for a loan from the bank, or issue bonds, or issue additional shares, or sell old production lines, etc. These are all positive correlation trading induced by liquidity constraints.

Inhibiting factors mainly include trading that have a substitution relationship with the trading in question. For example, air conditioners and fans have a substitution relationship. When we observe the trading agent buying an air conditioner at time step t, we can infer from this that the probability of the subject buying a fan at time step $t+1$ will decrease. Unlike positive correlation factors, substitution relationships have symmetry. This is because the substitution relationship comes from the same or similar functions. For example, a car trading is a substitute trading for a motor-cycle trading, and vice versa. Of course, the specific situation depends on the overlap of the functions of the trading targets. When the functions of the two trading targets do not completely overlap, these two trading can only be considered as partial substitution relationships, not complete substitution relationships.

Like positive correlation relationships, substitution relationships can be functional substitutions of trading targets, or results induced by liquidity constraints. **Under hard constraints**, at adjacent time steps t and $t+1$, a strong substitution relationship will also form between two reverse trading. Whether in family life or corporate production arrangements, there are often situations where, due to tight funds, a choice must be made between two trading. For example, a family that has just bought a house. Under liquidity constraints, at time step $t + 1$, the likelihood of purchasing a car will decrease immediately afterwards. The same is true for enterprises. If a large investment has just been completed at time step t, it is unlikely that a new large investment will be made at time step $t + 1$. Therefore, the set of alternative trading should include two types of trading: one is trading the trading that has some degree of functional substitution relationship with the target; the other is trading the trading where the main body has roughly the same trading intention and requires a large amount of funds.

The substitution relationship decays rapidly over time. A car purchased in the first half of the year, after a few years, will see its ability to substitute decay completely. Each target has its own life cycle, which can provide a somewhat quality use function within the life cycle. Once the length of the life cycle is exceeded, the substitution relationship generated by function overlap will naturally disappear.

The evolution process of the trading vector X cannot be completely controlled by the influence of completed trading, otherwise the random variable X can only rotate in a closed state set. The trading vector X is a very sensitive random variable, very sensitive to external dynamic information, in that any changes in the trading environment will be reflected in the expected return function of X. When the liquidity constraints in the trading environment tend to be relaxed, the probability of the trading vector X jumping to a higher level will increase; on the contrary, if the liquidity constraints in the trading environment tend to be tight, the probability of the trading vector X jumping to a higher level will decrease. Similarly, economic climate, macroeconomic policies and related institutional arrangements can all affect the jumping behavior of the trading vector X from various aspects such as cost, return, and liquidity constraints. Lowering institutional costs will inevitably promote the trading vector to jump to a higher level. When the economy is in a boom, most trading agents are in an aggressive state, with a strong risk preference, and the probability of increasing the trading level will increase; when the economy enters into a depression, the risk preference of trading agents tends to be conservative, and the probability of the trading level decaying increases.

19.3.2 Trading Trajectory Equation

The analysis of the factors affecting the transition probability shows that the trading trajectory of the tradingagent has a certain pattern, both a strong path dependence and random fluctuations under the influence of external factors. Specifically for a certain trading agent, the determination of the transition probability requires a deep dive into the details of the trading structure, separating the promoting factors and inhibiting factors from the historical events of past trading. In order to reflect the core elements of the trading probability, we need to further summarize and simplify the influencing factors of the transition probability, which can be summarized into three aspects:

First, the magnitude difference between the target state trading x_{t+1} and the initial state x_t of the trading vector X. The larger the magnitude difference between the two states, the greater the amplitude of the trading transition, and the challenge to the trading agent increases from both the maintenance of behavioral inertia and the liquidity constraints and trading risks. Therefore, the larger the trading level transition, the transition probability $P_{x_t x_{t+1}}$ becomes smaller.

The second is the target state x_{t+1} of the trading vector X forming a popular pressure on the trading agent. All trading activities are subject to the constraints of the liquidity balance, and the trading arrangements of the trading agent must be limited within the allowed constraint ranges. The greater the liquidity pressure formed by the target state x_{t+1} on the trading agent a_i, the more liquidity resources areconsumed. Under the same conditions, the trading agent will try to avoid such arrangements and choose a target state with less liquidity pressure. Therefore, the greater the liquidity pressure, the smaller the probability $P_{x_t x_{t+1}}$ of the target state x_{t+1} to occur.

The third is the expected return value generated by the target state x_{t+1} of the trading vector X. All behaviors of the trading agent are ultimately for the pursuit of profit. The fundamental driving force for the trading agent to move from state x_t to state x_{t+1} is the expected return that the target state x_{t+1} may bring to the trading agent a_i. The higher the expected return of the target state x_{t+1}, the stronger the willingness of the trading agent a_i to move to state x_{t+1}. Within the range of liquidity constraint, the trading agent a_i always chooses the target state with the highest expected return x_{t+1}.

Among the three factors affecting the transition probability, the difference in trading volume and liquidity pressure constrain the trading choices of the trading agent a_i, while the expected return plays a guiding and promoting role in the decision-making of the trading agent a_i. The final decision of the trading agent a_i is a balance of two opposing forces.

Considering the individual differences of the trading agent t, in order to accurately depict the relationship between the leap of trading volume and the transition probability, it is necessary to introduce the sensitivity intensity index of the trading agent, which we represent with the Greek letter κ. The so-called sensitivity intensity of the trading agent refers to the sensitivity to the transition of trading volume determined by the adapting capacity of the trading agent a_i. The stronger the ability of the trading agent a_i to adapt and control new trading strategy arrangements, the less sensitive the response to the transition of trading volume, and the smaller the value of the sensitivity intensity κ. On the contrary, the weaker the ability of the trading agent a_i to control and adapt to new trading strategy arrangements, the greater the value of the sensitivity intensity κ. The trading agent a_i Sensitivity Intensity κ takes values in the semi-closed interval $[0, +\infty)$. When $\kappa = 0$, it indicates that the trading agent a_i does not react to trading transitions at all, has a very strong endurance, and belongs to the extreme case of the trading agent; when $\kappa = +\infty$ represents the trading agent a_i has no endurance, is extremely sensitive to trading transitions, and the sensitivity intensity is infinitely large, which also belongs to the extreme case.

The trading sensitivity intensity κ and the trading potential $\psi(a_i)$ of the tradinga-gent a_i are inversely proportional. The higher the trading potential $\psi(a_i)$, the lower the trading sensitivity intensity κ. Conversely, the lower the trading potential of the tradingagent $\psi(a_i)$, the higher its trading sensitivity intensity κ.

Based on the above analysis, we can conclude that the transition probability $P_{x_t x_{t+1}}$ of any tradingagent a_i on the time step t trading vector a_i from state x_t to state x_{t+1} is related to the magnitude difference of state x_t, x_{t+1} D_{t+1} as follows:

$$P_{x_t x_{t+1}} \propto \frac{1}{1 + \kappa D_{t+1}} \tag{19.3.1}$$

In Eq. (19.3.1), the denominator on the right side includes the constant 1 to avoid the occurrence of an infinitely large singularity when the denominator is 0, which is a technical processing requirement.

The transition probability $P_{x_t x_{t+1}}$ of the trading vector X from state x_t to the target state x_{t+1}, which is inversely proportional to the liquidity pressure formed by the target state $x_{t+1}\mathrm{lp}(x_{t+1})$. The greater the liquidity pressure $\mathrm{lp}(x_{t+1})$, the smaller the transition probability $P_{x_t x_{t+1}}$. The following expression is obtained from this:

$$P_{x_t x_{t+1}} \propto \frac{1}{1 + \mathrm{lp}(x_{t+1})} \tag{19.3.2}$$

Driven by the profit motive, the tradingagent agent always seeks the target state x_{t+1} that can bring as much profit as possible. When the trading magnitude remains unchanged, the trading agent will inevitably choose the state vector that can maximize the expected profit. Therefore, the transition probability $P_{x_t x_{t+1}}$ is directly proportional to the expected increase in the target state x_{t+1} $E(x_{t+1})$, that is:

$$P_{x_t x_{t+1}} \propto E(x_{t+1}) \tag{19.3.3}$$

Agent The transition probability $P_{x_t x_{t+1}}$ of the trading eAgent a_i from the state x_t to the target state x_{t+1} is a function of the above three variables. By integrating the quantitative relationship between the three variables and the transition probability $P_{x_t x_{t+1}}$, we can obtain the following results:

$$P_{x_t x_{t+1}} = \frac{\alpha E(x_{t+1})}{(1 + \kappa D_{t+1})(1 + \text{lp}(x_{t+1}))} \tag{19.3.4}$$

In Eq. (19.3.4), α represents the equilibrium constant to be determined. To eliminate the undetermined coefficient α, we set the following boundary conditions: when the target state x_{t+1} and the initial state x_t are at the same level, we assume that the liquidity pressure of the target state satisfies $lp(x_{t+1}) = 0$; according to the principle of maximizing expected returns, the target state x_{t+1} has a minimum return threshold requirement u_0, when $E(x_{t+1}) = u_0$, the state x_{t+1} can no longer be the pursuit target of the decision-maker, and can only cause the trading choice of concern to a_i, assuming that the transition probability at this time is $P_{x_t x_{t+1}} = 0.5$.

Substitute the boundary conditions into the transition probability Eq. (19.3.4) to get:

$$P_{x_t x_{t+1}} = \frac{\alpha u_0}{1 \times 1} = 0.5 \tag{19.3.5}$$

$$\therefore \alpha = \frac{1}{2u_0} \tag{19.3.6}$$

Substitute (19.3.6) into (19.3.4) to get:

$$P_{x_t x_{t+1}} = \frac{E(x_{t+1})}{2u_0(1 + \kappa D_{t+1})(1 + \text{lp}(x_{t+1}))} \tag{19.3.7}$$

Equation (19.3.7) organically links various factors such as trading volume transition, expected return, liquidity pressure, trading behavior path dependence, and the reaction characteristics of the tradingagent, revealing the evolution law of the trading trajectory, and can well explain how the tradingagent achieves the trading volume transition, and explains how the trading trajectory of the tradingagent bifurcates and gradually polarizes. We call (19.3.7) the trading trajectory equation.

According to the conventional definition of probability, the transition probability $P_{x_t x_{t+1}}$ must take values in the interval [0, 1]. Theoretically, in the state domain of the tradingagent a_i, there may exist alternative states with high expected returns, short transition distances, and small liquidity pressures; there may also exist alternative states with expected returns $E(y) < 0$. In this case, the trading trajectory Eq. (19.3.7) will result in transition probabilities $P_{x_t x_{t+1}} > 1$ or $P_{x_t x_{t+1}} < 0$. Although the above extreme situations do not affect the use of the trading trajectory equation, the results obtained from the trading trajectory equation can still provide a priority ranking for the alternative states in the state domain of the tradingagent. However, for the sake of logical rigor, we need to make the following stipulations for the trading trajectory Eq. (19.3.7):

when $\frac{E(x_{t+1})}{2u_0(1+\kappa D_{t+1})(1+lp(x_{t+1}))} > 1$.

The transition probability takes the value $P_{x_t x_{t+1}} = 1$;

when $\frac{E(x_{t+1})}{2u_0(1+\kappa D_{t+1})(1+\text{lp}(x_{t+1}))} < 0$.

The transition probability takes the value $P_{x_t x_{t+1}} = 0$;

when $0 \le \frac{E(x_{t+1})}{2u_0(1+\kappa D_{t+1})(1+lp(x_{t+1}))} \le 1$.

The transition probability takes the value $P_{x_t x_{t+1}} = \frac{E(x_{t+1})}{2u_0(1+\kappa D_{t+1})(1+\text{lp}(x_{t+1}))}$.

19.3.3 The Inherent Mechanism of State Field Differentiation

Along with the evolution of the trading system, the state field of trading agents shows a continuous trend of differentiation in the trading space. The trading trajectory equation can provide a good explanation for this. When trading agents achieve better returns through trading, the cash flow shows a gradually increasing trend. Under this situation, the liquidity pressure of the trading agents will gradually decrease, providing conditions and confidence for the leap in the scale of the trading agents. The leap in trading scale inevitably leads to the expansion of the accounting matrix and the increase in asset scale. A larger asset scale means that there is a larger cash flow match, which provides security for the further leap in the scale of the trading agents. This is a self-reinforcing mechanism, the premise of which is that the trading agents must maintain high efficiency in resource allocation and be able to satisfy the reasonable matching relationship between asset scale and cash flow. The flowchart showing this self-reinforcing mechanism is as follows.

In the trading trajectory equation, the sensitivity index of the trading agents κ acts as a filter, converting the transition distance of the trading scale ring into a risk pressure coefficient. The higher the trading momentum of the trading agents, the stronger the resistance to transition risk, and the smaller the resistance encountered; on the contrary, the lower the trading momentum of the trading agents, the weaker the resistance to risk, even for small changes in trading scale, there will be a strong reaction, eventually becoming an irresistible resistance to trading transition. The transition sensitivity intensity κ is a very personalized indicator, fully showing the individual differences among the trading agents in the trading system.

If the sensitivity intensity of the trading agents κ index is incorporated into the self-strengthening mechanism process, the positive feedback loop presented in Fig. 19.2 will become even stronger. When the liquidity of the trading agents is improved, they will expand trading driven by profit-seeking motives. If they can find a target vector with better expected returns, they will obtain more cash flow returns while expanding the accounting matrix, all of which will help to improve the trading agents' ability to withstand scale transitions, reduce sensitivity to liquidity pressure, and further enhance the willingness of trading agents to expand trading and implement scale transitions. The inclusion of sensitive intensity κ greatly enhances the strength and speed of the feedback loop.

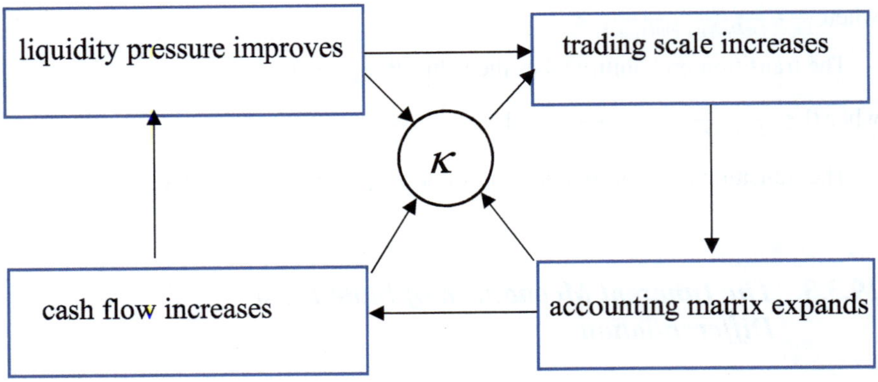

Fig. 19.2 The feedback loop of trading scale increases

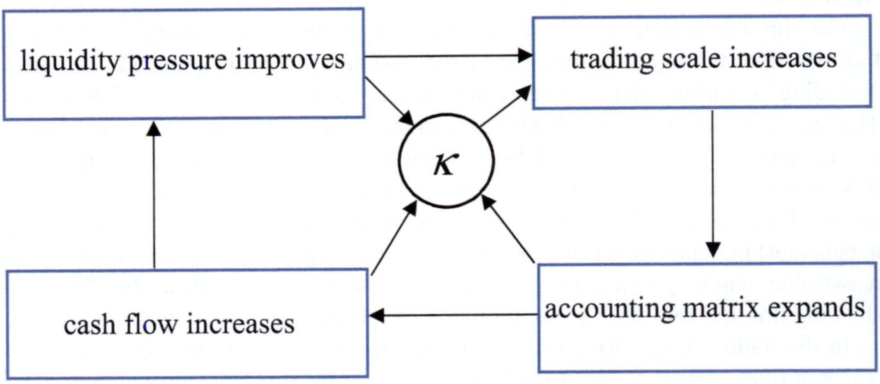

Fig. 19.3 The feedback loop of trading scale increases with the consideration of sensitive intensity

The feedback mechanism described in Fig. 19.3 will also present in the opposite feedback direction. Under the heavy pressure of liquidity, trading agents are forced to choose to reduce the scale of the accounting matrix and lower the trading scale to alleviate liquidity pressure. Cash flow is the result of the corresponding assets generating returns. The cash flow that can be generated after the asset scale shrinks will also decrease, laying the groundwork for reducing the trading scale in the next period. Once liquidity pressure increases, assets must be reduced again, forming a spiral decline in trading scale. The logical relationship of this self-strengthening mechanism is as follows:

In Fig. 19.4, the feedback process will also be strengthened with the factor of the sensitivity intensity κ of the trading agents is brought in. The new feedback process structure is as follows (Fig. 19.5).

The two self-reinforcing mechanisms correspond to two different resource allocation states, with the trading volume leap mechanism corresponding to an efficient resource allocation state; while the trading volume decay mechanism corresponds to

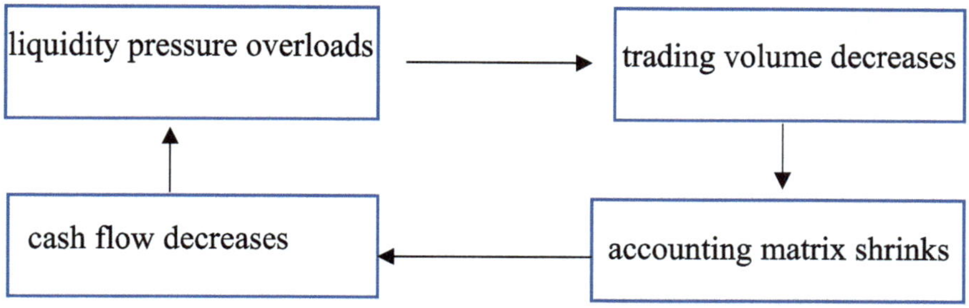

Fig. 19.4 The feedback loop of trading volume decreases

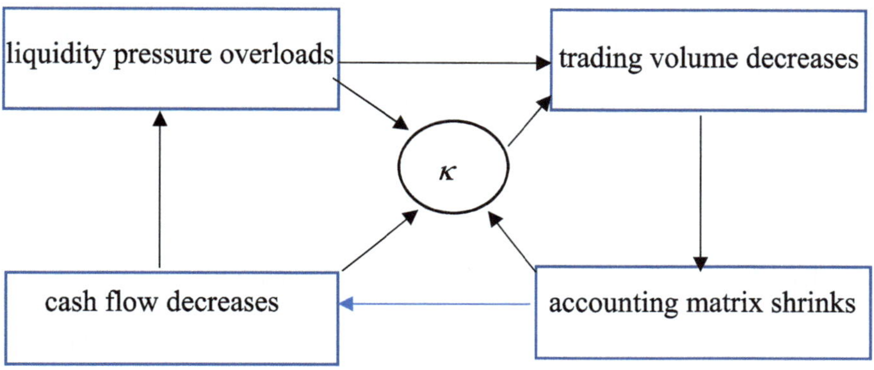

Fig. 19.5 The feedback loop of trading volume decreases with the consideration of sensitive intensity

an inefficient or low-efficiency resource allocation state. Under the influence of two self-reinforcing mechanisms of different nature, the evolution of the trading space maintains the operating efficiency of the trading system by adjusting the resource allocation structure. Decision-making accuracy and returns that meet expectations represent effective resource allocation. These agents gain more and more resource allocation opportunities through continuous trading volume transitions, and are in a continuous expansion trend in the trading space; while decision-making failures and poor benefits represent inefficient resource allocation. Unable to effectively convert resources in the accounting matrix into benefits and cash flow, the cash flow continues to run low, and they are forced to continuously reduce the trading volume. The opportunity for resource allocation gradually shrinks, and the final outcome is to exit the trading and be eliminated.

19.4 Evolution of Trading Space

In the evolutionary process of the trading system, the trading space is also evolving synchronously, and it shows significant characteristics in terms of scale and structure.

19.4.1 Expansion of Trading Space, the Inevitability of the Economic Globalization

In the evolutionary process of the trading system, driven by technological innovation, more and more new products are designed, manufactured and pushed to the market; on the other hand, due to the innovation of trading modes, more and more assets become tradable assets. The trading base continues to expand under the dual mechanisms of technological innovation and model innovation, providing more and more trading options trading for trading agents. The trading space is a space formed by the trading base. The expansion of the trading base will inevitably lead to an increase in the dimensions of the trading space.

19.4.1.1 Historical Evidence of Trading Space Expansion

In the early stages of human society, the trading space was very narrow. In primitive society, the tradable assets are nothing more than cattle, sheep and a few decorative items. Since the late Neolithic agricultural society, the tradable assets expanded from livestock and decorations to agricultural by-products, production tools, handicrafts, etc. As human society evolved from a nomadic form to an agricultural economic form, the trading space made a big leap. However, the real leap in the expansion of the trading space occurred after human society entered the industrial economic form. When trading promoted human society from an agricultural economic form to an industrial economic form, the dimensions of the trading space expanded rapidly. Up to today, the scale of trading base is difficult to accurately count, and the breadth of the trading space has reached an unprecedented level.

The Industrial Revolution was a time of great expansion in human society's trading space. The large-scale application of machinery in the production field and the development of new power represented by steam engines have made human production capabilities achieve a leap that was difficult to imagine before. "Once manufactured, these quantities of goods must be sold. Sale, resulting in profit, is the final goal of all industrial production. The immense stimulus given to production by the factory system immediately affects the distribution of commodities. The increased amount of goods on the market lowers prices, lower prices mean increased demand, and more business. Competition becomes more intense. As improvements in transport open an ever wider field to its activities, it extends from individuals to regions and to nations, more eager than ever in the pursuit of their material interests. Conflicts and economic wars are let loose, and the winner is he who succeeds in enlarging, in spite of his competitors, his sphere of operations, and in finding more and ever more new markets. The ambition of producers makes them daring, and the most distant countries, continents hardly yet explored, become their prey. The whole world henceforward is nothing but one immense market, where the great industries of all countries contend as on a battlefield. … obviously the consumer is now in a much more favorable position than he was before, goods have greatly increased in quantity, while prices have been, on the whole, considerably reduced. Many things, formerly expensive and hard to come by, are obtainable in localities and in circles where previously they were unknown."[1] This is how French historian Paul Mantoux described the process of the Industrial Revolution in England in his book The Industrial Revolution in the Eighteenth Century: An Outline of the Beginnings of the Model Factory System in England. From this, we can glimpse into the prosperity brought about by the Industrial Revolution.

Along with the expansion of the trading space dimension, the state domain of the trading agent is also continuously expanding. The trading process is also a process of wealth accumulation. The more wealth is accumulated, the larger the scale of the trading. This mechanism of mutual promotion between trading activities and wealth accumulation determines that the evolution of the trading system must be accompanied by the growth of the trading scale. When the average magnitude of the trading agents' participation in trading continues to rise, the state domain of the trading agent in the trading space is also continuously expanding, and the entire trading space is like an ever-expanding universe.

Let's take the global commodity trade value and trade volume growth trend from the 1950s to 2013 for an example to justify the resilient scale expansion of the trading system (Fig. 19.6).

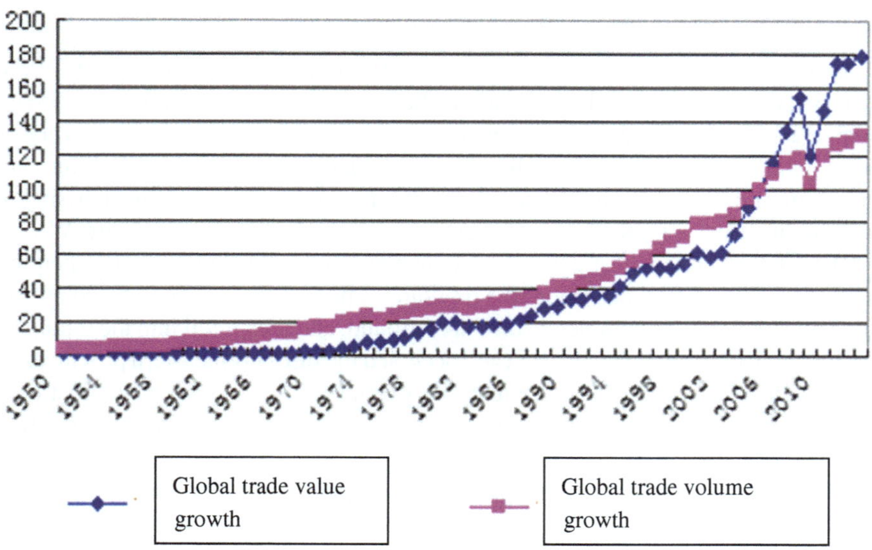

Fig. 19.6 Chart of global trade growth. *Data source* official webpage of WTO, where, both the global trade value and volume were index calculated with the Year 2005 as the benchmark of 100

International trade is only part of the trading activities in the trading system, and a large number of trading activities are completed within the trading system. Cross-border trade is just a microcosm of the expansion of trading space.

In the long run, the trading systems of all economies have undergone a continuous expansion process. Although the speed of expansion of the trading systems of various countries is not the same, the trend is basically the same. Taking the trade in China from the second half of the nineteenth century to the first half of the twentieth century for example, it can prove that the trading space has an obstinate expanding nature.

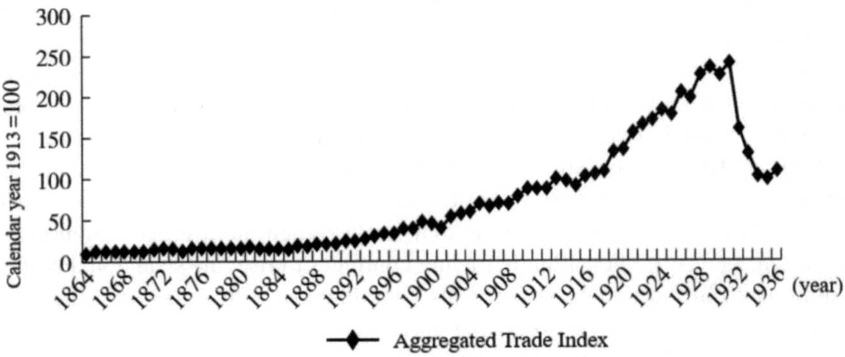

Fig. 19.7 Chart of China's trade in turmoil. *Data source* Yuqin Sun, *History of China's Foreign Trade (2nd Edition)* Tsinghua University Press, p 312–314, the trade aggregate index was calculated based on the silver price compiled by the Customs. Starting from June, 1932, the trade aggregate excludes foreign trade volume of enterprises in Northeast China

Figure 19.7 covers the trade from 1864 to 1936 during the dark period of Chinese history. After the failure of the First and Second Opium Wars, China was forced to sign a series of unequal treaties, including the Treaty of Wangxia, the Treaty of Whampoa, the Treaty of Aihun, the Treaty of Tianjin, the Treaty of Beijing, etc. The domestic situation rapidly deteriorated, and a large-scale peasant uprising—the Taiping Heavenly Kingdom Movement broke out; the Sino-Japanese War of 1894 broke out, China lost again, and signed the Treaty of Shimonoseki; then the Boxer Rebellion broke out, under the pressure of internal and external troubles, the Qing government was completely on shaky ground, and then it fell into the tumult of warlord melee before Japan invaded and occupied the three northeastern provinces of China.[2] This is a bitter period of contemporary Chinese history. Even so, international trade continues to grow, which is an outstanding showcase of the great resilience that trading space has.

The expansion of the trading space is also supported by the trading trajectory equation. The trading trajectory equation shows that as long as liquidity conditions allow, trading agent always tend to implement the maximum level of trading volume transition. The liquidity reserve of the trading agent, as part of wealth, usually maintains a certain proportional relationship with the asset scale. The expansion of the trading scale will inevitably generate a larger asset scale; conversely, the expansion

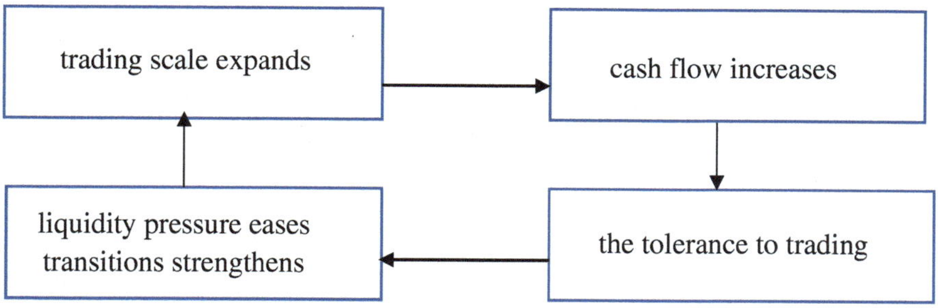

Fig. 19.8 The feedback loop of trading space

of the asset scale will inevitably increase the liquidity reserve, and a self-reinforcing mechanism is formed between trading and liquidity reserve. Reflected in the trading trajectory equation, the increase in liquidity scale improves the adapting capacity of the trading agent, reduces the sensitivity κ of the trading volume level transition and the liquidity pressure $lp(x_{t+1})$, the improvement of the trading agent's tolerance for trading volume level transition promotes the trading subject to a higher trading volume level transition, thereby driving the continuous transition of the trading volume level (Fig. 19.8).

The above is our qualitative analysis methodology to demonstrate the support of the trading trajectory equation for the expansion of the trading agent's state domain.

19.4.1.2 Proof of Trading Space Expansion

To prove the inevitability of the continuous expansion of the trading space, we only need to prove the following equivalent proposition: Given x and y are two arbitrary states on the state domain K of the trading agent a_i, and there are $|y| > |x|$ and $P_{xy} \geq p^*$; where, p^* represents the minimum action probability threshold, that is, the minimum probability requirement for the transition from state x to state y. We need to prove that there must exist a state z in the trading space Ω that satisfies $|z| > |y|$, and there is $P_{yz} \geq p^*$.

Assume that the trading agent a_i obtains the accounting matrix A_x after implementing the trading vector x at time step t, and the cash flow generated at time step $t+1$ is $l(A_x)$. If a_i transitions to the magnitude of the trading vector y, the liquidity required is $L(y)$, and the resulting liquidity gap is $\Delta L = L(y) - l(A_x)$.

It is known from the assumption that:

$$P_{xy} = \frac{E(y)}{2u_0\big(1+\kappa D_{xy}\big)(1+\text{lp}(y))} > p^* \tag{19.4.1}$$

Equation (19.4.1) implies that the liquidity pressure $lp(y)$ formed by the liquidity gap $\Delta L = L(y) - l(A_x)$ is within the tolerable range for the trading agent a_i, and can support the state x to transit to the state y, with a transition distance of $D_{xy} = |y| - |x|$.

In the trading space Ω, there exists a magnitude ring $|z| = |y| + \delta$, where $\delta > 0$ is a very small positive real number. On the magnitude ring $|z|$, any state z satisfies $|z| > |y|$. If the trading agent a_i wants to transit from state y to state z, so for a successful transition, the following liquidity and return conditions must be met:

$$L(z) - l(A_y) \leq L(y) - l(A_x) = \Delta L \tag{19.4.2}$$

$$E(z) \geq E(y) \tag{19.4.3}$$

Not all trading agents can meet conditions (19.4.2) and (19.4.3). To meet these conditions, the tradingagent must be able to ensure the rationality of the trading decision. The trading decision at time step t can bring a structurally reasonable, scale-increasing accounting matrix at time step $t + 1$, and the trading environment is also relatively friendly. We call the conditions (19.4.2) and (19.4.3) as the effective trading conditions of the trading vectors x, y, and z in terms of returns and liquidity, to distinguish between invalid trading behavior and inefficient trading agents. Obviously, under normal circumstances, effective trading conditions always exist. The standard for measuring efficiency is relative, so we can always find trading agents that meet the effective trading conditions in the trading system.

Under effective trading conditions, the liquidity pressure $lp(z)$ of the trading vector z can be realized not greater than y the liquidity pressure $lp(y)$ generated by the tradingagent a_i, that is, $lp(z) \leq lp(y)$.

$$\because \ P_{xy} = \frac{E(y)}{2u_0(1 + \kappa D_{xy})(1 + lp(y))} > p^* \tag{19.4.4}$$

According to the known conditions, we get:

$$\begin{aligned} P_{yz} &= \frac{E(z)}{2u_0(1 + \kappa D_{yz})(1 + lp(z))} \\ &\geq \frac{E(y)}{2u_0(1 + \kappa D_{xy})(1 + lp(y))} > p^* \end{aligned} \tag{19.4.5}$$

From (19.4.5) we get:

$$P_{yz} > p^* \tag{19.4.6}$$

Equation (19.4.6) shows that under effective trading conditions, driven by profit-seeking, the tradingagent will try to implement the transition of trading magnitude as much as possible. This proves that under the conditions of effective trading, the tradingagent a_i can realize the desire to continuously expand the state domain.

For micro-individuals, whether the transition of trading magnitude is successful is just a probability event, and it cannot guarantee that each trade can achieve a transition in magnitude. In some cases, there may even be a decay in magnitude.

But from the perspective of the entire trading system, since each tradingagent has the opportunity to transition in magnitude, a large number of successful transitions with small probabilities will converge into the inevitability of the expansion of the trading space, ensuring the continuous expansion of the trading state domain.

From the demonstration process of magnitude transition, it can be found that whether it is a single tradingagent or the entire trading system, its magnitude transition is a process of small steps accumulation. Through a period of accumulation, the expansion of the trading space in terms of dimensions and range can achieve significant changes.

19.4.2 Path Dependence of Trading Behavior, the Progression of Human Society's Development

From the perspective of the trading system, although the trading vector X To some extent, it presents randomness and can be regarded as a random variable. However, the behavior of trading agents strictly follows the principles of trading and has certain regularities to follow. This not only has habitual significance in behavioral terms, but is also the result of various trading constraints. The "regularity" of trading behavior leads to a certain degree of closure in the state domain of trading agents,, that is, trading behavior across the state domain falls into small probability events. This judgment not only holds for families, but also for enterprises. Families are limited by consumption habits and payment capabilities, and the state values of trading vectors usually fall within a relatively fixed area in the trading space; the trading behavior of enterprises usually revolves around the main business, due to the constraints of the scale and structure of the accounting matrix, the range of trading vector values will also be relatively stable.

The characteristic of path dependence of trading provides logical support for the closure of the state value domain. Trading behavior shows path dependence in both trading scale and trading content. Of course, path dependence is relative, and there is also the possibility of sudden changes. Technological progress is a process from quantitative change to qualitative change. In the early stage of the emergence of new technology, the impact on the market may be small. Only through the test of time, the new technology will form a strong impact on the old technology market, and the "innovative destruction" effect mentioned by Schumpeter will appear. At this time, the trading variable will transition, the old technology product market will quickly shrink, and the new product market will quickly expand.

The trading trajectory equation provides logical support for the path dependence of trading agents. Suppose a_i is any agent in the trading system T, the state domain in the trading space Ω is K, x is a state on K, that is, $x \in K$; state y is any state in the trading space Ω, very close to the magnitude of state x, the distance between the two $D_{xy} = \delta$ is a very small positive real number; the expected return of state y is not lower than the initial state x, satisfying $E(y) \geq E(x)$; because $D_{xy} = \delta << 1$, we have reason to assume that the liquidity pressure of state y is roughly the same as that of state x, that is, $lp(y) \cong lp(x)$.

Assume that state x is transferred from the state x_0 of tradingagent a_i. According to the fact that the two states have already transferred, we get from the trading trajectory Eq. (19.3.7):

$$P_{x_0x} = \frac{E(x)}{2u_0\left(1 + \kappa D_{x_0x}\right)(1 + lp(x))} > p^* \tag{19.4.7}$$

According to the trading trajectory equation, we get the calculation of transfer P_{xy}:

$$P_{xy} = \frac{E(y)}{2u_0\left(1 + \kappa D_{xy}\right)(1 + lp(y))} \tag{19.4.8}$$

$$\because D_{xy} \cong 0, \quad lp(y) \cong lp(x), \quad E(y) \geq E(x)$$

Substitute into (19.4.8) to get:

$$P_{xy} = \frac{E(y)}{2u_0(1 + lp(x))} \tag{19.4.9}$$

Transform from (19.4.9) to get:

$$P_{xy} = \frac{E(x)}{2u_0\left(1 + \kappa D_{x_0x}\right)(1 + \mathrm{lp}(x))} \frac{E(y)\left(1 + \kappa D_{x_0x}\right)}{E(x)} \tag{19.4.10}$$

$$\because \frac{E(y)}{E(x)} \geq 1,\ 1 + \kappa D_{x_0x} \geq 1$$

$$\therefore \frac{E(y)\left(1 + \kappa D_{x_0x}\right)}{E(x)} \geq 1$$

$$\therefore P_{xy} \geq p^* \tag{19.4.11}$$

Equation (19.4.11) It indicates that for any tradingagent in the trading system a_i, the probability of trading at the original trading volume level is very high, and it is also the most likely strategy to occur. This is a typical characteristic of path dependence. The path dependence of trading behavior ensures the relative stability of the trading state domain.

19.4.3 Reducibility of Trading Space, the Tendence of Society's Stratification Evolution

Symmetry breaking is the basic premise of all structure formation. The literal meaning of symmetry breaking is that the system becomes non-uniform. Within a group, if the group behavior is dominated by a self-reinforcing mechanism, its evolutionary structure will inevitably be a discrete distribution. The basic mechanism that dominates interstellar space is gravity. In Newton's law of gravity, it is easy to find a self-reinforcing mechanism. The gravitational force between two objects shortens the distance between them, the closeness of the distance increases the gravitational force between them. The greater the gravity, the faster the two approach each other. This creates a self-reinforcing mechanism between the distance between objects and the gravity between them. Under the dominance of this self-reinforcing mechanism, the universe has gradually evolved from a relatively uniform interstellar cloud to a discrete interstellar space structure. In the trajectory equation that dominates the evolution of the trading space, it also contains a self-reinforcing mechanism that causes the trading trajectory to bifurcate. Under the dominance of the self-reinforcing mechanism in the transition probability of the trading space, a reduced structure divided by many trading state domains will inevitably be formed.

We use the method of contradiction to prove the proposition of the reducibility of the trading space. Suppose the trading space Ω is irreducible, x is the state on the state domain K of any subject a_i, y is any state on the trading space Ω.

$\because \Omega$ is an irreducibly connected space.

$\therefore$ The transition probability $P_{xy} > \varepsilon$ of any state x, y, where $\varepsilon > 0$ is a very small constant.

$\because$ The financing ability of the tradingagent a_i has an upper limit.

$\therefore$ As the magnitude of the state y increases, a_i's liquidity pressure $lp(y)$ will rapidly climb at a speed exceeding the expected return $E(y)$.

Based on the above inference, we assume that the liquidity pressure $lp(y)$ satisfies the following relationship:

$$\frac{E(y)}{1 + lp(y)} \leq \pi, \quad \text{where } \pi > 0 \text{ is constant} \tag{19.4.12}$$

According to the trading trajectory Eq. (19.3.7) we get:

$$P_{xy} = \frac{E(y)}{2u_0\left(1 + \kappa D_{xy}\right)(1 + lp(y))} \geq \varepsilon \tag{19.4.13}$$

From (19.4.13) we get:

$$1+\kappa D_{xy} \le \frac{E(y)}{2u_0\varepsilon(1+lp(y))} \quad (19.4.14)$$

simplify (19.4.14) to get:

$$\kappa D_{xy} \le \frac{E(y)}{2u_0\varepsilon(1+lp(y))} - 1 \quad (19.4.15)$$

Continue to simplify to get:

$$D_{xy} \le \frac{E(y)}{2u_0\kappa\varepsilon(1+lp(y))} - \frac{1}{\kappa} \quad (19.4.16)$$

Substituting (19.4.12) into (19.4.16) and get:

$$D_{xy} \le \frac{E(y)}{2u_0\kappa\varepsilon(1+lp(y))} - \frac{1}{\kappa} \le \frac{\pi}{2u_0\kappa\varepsilon} - \frac{1}{\kappa} \quad (19.4.17)$$

$$\therefore D_{xy} \le \frac{\pi}{2\kappa u_0\varepsilon} - \frac{1}{\kappa} \quad (19.4.18)$$

In (19.4.18), it is composed of constants π, κ, ε, and the approximate value of the trading u_0. Since u_0 will increase as the magnitude of the state y increases, the value on the right side of (19.4.18) will show a trend of continuous reduction as the magnitude of the state y increases; but on the left side of (19.4.18), as the magnitude of the state y increases, the distance D_{xy} to the state x will increase accordingly. Since $x \in K$, y is any state in the trading space Ω, (19.4.18) requires that the distance D_{xy} between states x and y must be less than a certain specific value, which obviously contradicts the assumption that the trading space Ω is irreducible. This proves that the trading space is reducible.

The reducibility of the trading space Ω indicates that the evolution of the trading system inevitably leads to market and social stratification. Market stratification is evidenced as dividing the market into several levels according to the quality, price, and cost-effectiveness of goods. Trading agents at different social levels correspond to their respective markets, echoing social stratification.

The reducibility of the trading space is a probabilistic stratification, not an absolute division. This indicates that although stratification is an inevitable result of the evolution of the trading system, it does not exclude cross-level trading activities, implying that there is still the possibility of migration among different levels.

19.4.4 "Black Hole" in Trading Space, the Existence of Poverty Trap

In the evolutionary process of the trading space, the state domains of most trading agents are in a trend of continuous expansion, thus forming the microscopic basis for the expansion of the trading space. However, not every tradingagent can achieve the expansion of the state domain, and there may even be a situation where the state domain is continuously shrinking. This situation is like a black hole in interstellar space. Once it enters the capture range of the "black hole", it is difficult to escape the fate of being swallowed by it. The shrinking closed set is the "black hole" of the trading space, and both families and enterprises have the possibility of falling into the "black hole".

For enterprises, there are three types of risks that could lead to falling into the "black hole" of a shrinking closed set, namely operation, liquidity, and market risk. Operation risk takes the form as a decline in the cost-effectiveness of products, a decrease in market share, and a shrinkage of cash flow, among other things. Once an enterprise enters a state of poor management, it is very likely to enter a vicious cycle. Although there is a possibility to change the operational path, optimizing both products and technological innovation require a significant amount of capital investment, which is actually very difficult for enterprises with a continuously declining market share. In a fiercely competitive market, enterprises are like boats sailing against the current, if they do not advance, they will retreat. Once they fall behind, the distance with competitors will widen, and they will eventually be hard to escape the fate of being squeezed out of the market.

The liquidity risk of an enterprise mainly manifests as a sudden decrease in cash flow or an obstruction in asset liquidation, leading to an inability to fulfill payment obligations. Liquidity risk is usually due to problems in financial management, including the inability to obtain expected financing in time, serious mismatches in the terms of assets and liabilities, etc. Once an enterprise encounters a liquidity crisis, it must sell assets to obtain liquidity within a specific time limit. Unfortunately, under the rigid time constraints, liquidity swaps are often difficult to realize trading desires at a reasonable exchange price. Credit tools under normal circumstances are no longer accepted by the market, and creditors will also act upon the news, swarming to collect debts, resulting in a mutually reinforcing situation of a liquidity crisis and a deteriorating external financing environment, causing enterprises in a liquidity crisis to fall into a spiral of decline.

Market risk mainly manifests as a significant fluctuation in asset prices leading to damage to the integrity of the accounting matrix. Market prices change rapidly, and once the price drop exceeds the enterprise's ability to bear, the enterprise will be in a situation where its assets are not enough to cover its debts. If the situation cannot be reversed in time, the enterprise may fall into a predicament.

For families, the main cause of falling into a shrinking closed set is poverty. Poverty means low income, little wealth reserves, and fewer opportunities to participate in trading. Both in terms of scale and variety of trading, they are significantly lower than the overall social level. Families in poverty have a narrow trading space, and once they cross the threshold, the state field will show a trend of shrinking over time, as if falling into a black hole with strong gravity, firmly absorbed by poverty, and difficult to escape.

We use the trading trajectory equation to prove the existence of the "black hole" of the trading space—the shrinking closed set. To prove the existence of a shrinking closed set, we need to find conditions that satisfy the continuous shrinkage of the agent's trading volume. For this, we assume x is the initial state of the trading agent a_i, y is any state on the same magnitude as x. When the trading agent a_i falls into the shrinking closed set, it means that the transition probability P_{xy} from state x to state y will be less than the minimum action value, thus unable to maintain the original trading volume level, that is:

$$P_{xy} < p^* \tag{19.4.19}$$

Since y and x are on the same magnitude ring, that is $|y| = |x|, \quad D_{xy} = 0$. Obtained from the trading trajectory equation:

$$P_{xy} = \frac{E(y)}{2u_0(1 + lp(y))} \tag{19.4.20}$$

At time step $t + 1$, if the trading volume of the tradingagent a_i collapses, the following condition must be met:

$$\frac{E(y)}{2u_0(1 + lp(y))} < p^* \tag{19.4.21}$$

Obtained from (19.4.21):

$$lp(y) > \frac{E(y)}{2u_0 p^*} - 1 \tag{19.4.22}$$

We call (19.4.22) the "black hole" condition of the trading space. In the "black hole" condition (19.4.22), the variables on the right side of the inequality are mainly the expected return value $E(y)$ of the trading vector y, and the others are constants; the left side of the inequality is the liquidity pressure $lp(y)$. To prove the existence of a "black hole" in the trading space, we actually need to prove whether there is a possibility of reverse changes between the liquidity pressure $lp(y)$ and the expected return value $E(y)$ for any trading vector y.

In fact, when the cash flow generated by the accounting matrix of the tradingagent a_i at time step $t+1$ is less than the previous time step t, that is, when $l(A_{t+1}) < l(A_t)$ is satisfied, it means that at time step $t + 1$, the liquidity pressure $lp(y)$ formed by state y on a_i will be greater than $lp(x)$ under the condition that the external financing conditions have not changed:

$$lp(y) \geq lp(x) \tag{19.4.23}$$

Equation (19.4.23) indicates that the liquidity pressure of the tradingagent a_i increases at time step $t + 1$, which means that there will be more restrictions when choosing strategies, the number of selectable states will decrease, and the probability of occurrence of $E(y) \leq E(x)$ will increase. In this case, the "black hole" condition (19.4.22) may be satisfied. This shows that the "black hole" has the possibility of existing in the trading space.

The "black hole" condition stipulates the degree of cash flow decays, which indicates that cash flow is the key to determining whether the tradingagentfalls into the "black hole". In the short term, the scale of cash flow depends on two abilities of the trading, namely profitability and external financing ability. The stronger the profitability of the tradingagent, the stronger the repayment ability, the higher the market's acceptance of the tradingagent's debt, and the stronger the external financing ability; conversely, the stronger the external financing ability, the richer the options for the tradingagentin strategy arrangement, the greater the probability of achieving higher returns, and the stronger the profitability.

In the long term, the key to achieving abundant cash flow for trading agents lies in the efficiency of resource allocation. For enterprises, the efficiency of resource allocation is reflected in various capabilities such as product innovation, marketing, and internal organizational management; for families, the ability to allocate resources is reflected in the advantages of human capital and the ability to manage wealth. Trading agents that fall into a "black hole" inevitably have problems with low efficiency of resource allocation. The trading system maintains the efficiency of its operation by capturing inefficient agents through the "black hole" and eliminating them from the game, which is an important mechanism.

Notes

1. Paul Mantoux (1983) The Industrial Revolution in the Eighteenth Century (Trans: Yang Renpian, Chen Xiqin, Wu Xu), p 11.
2. Wang Chengren, Wu Jianjie (1985) Eighty Years of Modern China – 1840–1919, Wuhan University Press.

Part IV
Trading Economics Model

This part consists of four chapters, respectively on the transition of trading states, the economic cycle model, the economic growth model, and the trading pricing model.

Economic cycles, economic growth, and price fluctuation are important topics in mainstream economics. Trading economics, with its unique theoretical perspective and robust micro-foundation, builds a macroeconomic model of a new paradigm.

In the theoretical construct of trading economics, a trading system is the organic totality of the activities of a large number of micro-subjects under the constraints of a particular organizational structure. Notably, there is no distinction between macroeconomics and microeconomics, thus eliminating the disconnect presently between them. Successfully resolving this disconnect, which is a longstanding theoretical challenge in mainstream economics, represents one major contribution of trading economics to the modern economic theory.

Part IV
Trading Economics Model

This part consists of four chapters, respectively on the foundation of trading states, the economic cycle model, the economic growth model, and the trading pricing model.

Economic cycles, economic growth, and price fluctuations are important topics in mainstream economics (macroeconomics). Trading economics, with its more comprehensive and robust micro-foundation, builds a coherent framework for a new paradigm.

In the theoretical construct of trading economics, the trading system is the organic totality of the activities of a large number of participants, subject to the constraints of a particular organizational structure. Notably, there is no distinction between microeconomics and macroeconomics, thus eliminating the disconnect presently between them. Successfully resolving this disconnect, which is a long-standing theoretical challenge in mainstream economics, represents a key contribution of trading economics to the modern economic theory.

Chapter 20
Trade Phase Transition

The distribution of states among agents on the trading network is crucial to the operation of the trading system. Factors determining the state of an agent include both its own reasons and external causes generated by the links in the trading network. On the trading network, the synchronization of states creates economic cycles; the dispersion of states forms transitory equilibrium situations.

20.1 Concept of Trading State

The trading state can be defined from different perspectives. It can be defined from the perspective of trading intention, dividing states into high-intention states and low-intention states; it can also be defined from the perspective of decision-making confidence, dividing the states into high-confidence and low-confidence states. Here, we define the trading state from the perspective of risk preference, dividing the states of the trading agent into aggressive and conservative states. A trading agent can only choose one state at any point in time and cannot be in two different trading states simultaneously.

Trading agents are constrained by the scarcity of trading resources and must plan reverse trades based on the positive trading resources they obtain, otherwise, they cannot maintain the equilibrium of their balance sheets. When tempting enterprise opportunities appear, this principle of balancing inputs and outputs can be broken. Trading agents adopt aggressive trading strategies, increasing positive trading volume by increasing liabilities or -investing savings to maximize profits. For example, when house prices are on the rise, a strategy of increasing housing assets through debt can yield returns far above the average level. For enterprises, staying ahead of the curves can help capture the enterprise opportunities that come later. Silicon Valley genius Elon Musk saw the huge prospects of electric vehicles outside the conventional car

Z. Wang, *Trading Economics*, Contributions to Economics,
https://doi.org/10.1007/978-981-99-9875-3_20

market, tapped into the electric car market at a very low cost, and became the world's richest man within a short period of time.

Of course, everything has two sides. While aggressive trading strategies may bring high returns, they also bring risks. If judgments go wrong, or the market is hit by unexpected shocks and does not develop in the expected direction, aggressive strategies will not only fail to reap expected high returns but may also pay a heavy price. Therefore, conservative strategies are also optional choices that can compete with aggressive strategies. This strategy follows the principle of balancing inputs and outputs as much as possible, arranging reverse trades based on one's forward trades.

Now, we give the definition of aggressive and conservative states: if the trading strategy of a trading agent strictly executes its reverse trades based on the dynamic changes of the forward trades, then the set of trading strategies always stays within the scope of forward trades. We say that the trading agent is in a conservative trading state, represented by *co*.

If the trading agent executes reverse trades ahead of and beyond the scope of forward trades, we say that the trading agent is in an aggressive state, represented by *ag*.

The choice of state by the trading agent determines its marginal trading tendency. For trading agents in an aggressive state, the marginal trading tendency is higher; conversely, for trading agents in a conservative state, the marginal trading tendency is lower. On the trading network, the trading state determines the high or low trading cycle rate of the network. The higher the proportion of aggressive agents, the higher the trading cycle rate of the network; conversely, the higher the proportion of conservative agents, the lower the trading cycle rate of the network.

When the trading agent a_i is in an aggressive state, one of the important characteristics is that it has a larger set of strategies. The set of trades contains not only robust trading strategies, but also some strategies of higher risks that can bring larger returns. We denote the set of strategies of the trading agent a_i in the aggressive state as S_i; when the trading agent a_i is in a conservative state, the scale of the strategies set will shrink, and some high-risk trading strategies will be kicked out of the strategies set. The strategies remaining in the strategies set are mainly robust strategies. We denote the set of strategies of the trading agent a_i in the conservative state as S_i. Obviously, the strategies sets between the aggressive and conservative states are in an inclusion relation, that is, $s_i \subset S_i$. The difference set of the two trading strategy sets is called complementary set of the state, denoted as $\Delta S_i = S_i - s_i$.

According to the definition of trading state, $\Delta S_i \neq 0$, that is, the state complement set is a non-empty set. We know that the factors determining the size of the state complement set ΔS_i include both internal factors of the trading agent and external factors of the trading environment. Generally speaking, the more trading opportunities provided by the trading system, the larger ΔS_i will be. In terms of internal factors, the higher the potential of the trading agent, the larger ΔS_i will be. This is because higher-potential agents have greater potential to mobilize resources. On the contrary, for agents with lower trading potential, due to their limited ability to mobilize resources, the expansion of the state complement set will be more restricted.

The size of the state complement set ΔS_i plays a decisive role in the trading state. If the state complement set is small, no matter what state the trading agent chooses, it will not bring substantial changes to itself or the trading system. Since the size of the state complement set of low-potential agents is limited, agents that have a significant impact on the operation of the trading system mainly come from senior trading groups.

20.2 Phase Transition Equation of the Trading State

Assume Ω is any trading community on the trading network, a_i is the trading agent on the trading community Ω, A_i^c is the state coordination set of the trading agent a_i. In the state decision-making process of a_i, only when a_i tries to stay consistent with the majority of agents in A_i^c, it is the optimal response strategy.

The trading state is a strategy of the trading agent. Whether the choice of trading state is correct directly relates to the decision-maker's profit and risk. The key for the trading agent to determine the trading state lies in the judgment of the trading situation. If the trading situation is friendly, choosing an aggressive trading state will yield greater returns; when choosing an aggressive state, if the trading situation deteriorates, the trading agent will suffer losses. Therefore, the choice of trading state is an important part of trading decision-making, and it also follows the rules described in the trading equation.

We examine the trading state selection process of any trading agent a_i at time step t. Assume that the set of trades for a_i in the aggressive state ag is S_i, and the set of trades in the conservative state co is s_i. We use the maximum expected return of dominant strategy of the complement ΔS_i when the trading situation H is in a friendly state to represent the expected return of the aggressive state; the maximum loss that may occur when the trading situation H deteriorates represents the worst performance of the aggressive state. That is:

$$E_g(ag) = Max(\Delta S_i)$$
$$E_b(ag) = Min(\Delta S_i)$$

If the aggressive state ag suffers a loss when the situation H deteriorates, we denote it as $E_b(ag) < 0$; if the aggressive state ag can still make ends meet even when the situation H deteriorates, we denote it as $E_b(ag) \geq 0$.

Assume that at time step t, the dominant strategy on the trading set S_i has an average expected return of e_0 in the trading community Ω. We call e_0 the value threshold.

According to the above agreement, we can calculate the return risk index of the aggressive state R_g for the trading agent a_i at time step t.

$$R_g = \frac{E_g(ag) - E_b(ag)}{E_g(ag) - e_0}$$

According to the trading Eq. (14.3.27), if there are n trading agents choosing the aggressive trading state on the state synergy set A_i^c of the trading agent a_i; the prior probability of the trading situation H being friendly is p, and the prior probability of being unfriendly is q, the probability of choosing the aggressive state $\Pr(ag)$ follows the following formula:

$$\Pr(ag) = 1 - R_g \frac{q}{p} \mu^n \tag{20.2.1}$$

As for the aggressive or conservative states, when $\Pr(ag) > \frac{1}{2}$, the trading agent a_i tends to choose the aggressive state; when $\Pr(ag) < \frac{1}{2}$, the trading agent a_i tends to choose a conservative state; when $\Pr(ag) = \frac{1}{2}$ occurs, the trading agent a_i will undergo a change in trading state, that is, the original trading state will change. When the probability $\Pr(ag)$ approaches $\Pr(ag) = \frac{1}{2}$ from $\Pr(ag) > \frac{1}{2}$, the trading agent a_i will shift from an aggressive state to a conservative state; when the probability $\Pr(ag)$ approaches $\Pr(ag) = \frac{1}{2}$ from $\Pr(ag) < \frac{1}{2}$, the trading agent a_i will shift from a conservative state to an aggressive state.

From (20.2.1), we can obtain the conditions for the phase transition of the trading states:

$$1 - R_g \frac{q}{p} \mu^n = \frac{1}{2} \tag{20.2.2}$$

from (20.2.2), and we get:

$$R_g \frac{q}{p} \mu^n = \frac{1}{2} \tag{20.2.3}$$

from (20.2.3) and we get:

$$\frac{p}{q} - 2R_g \mu^n = 0 \tag{20.2.4}$$

Equation (20.2.4) depicts the equilibrium among the trading agent's prior judgment of the trading situation, the risk profile of choosing an aggressive stance, and the influence on community neighbors, revealing the basic rules of the trading agent's state transition. We call (20.2.4) the phase transition equation of the trading stance.

20.3 Discussion of the Phase Transition Equation

From the phase transition Eq. (20.2.1), it can be seen that an increase in the profit risk index R_g will reduce the probability of occurrence of an aggressive state, and decision-makers need a higher prior probability p to enter an aggressive state; conversely, as the number of aggressive agents on the state synergy set n increases, the risk filtering effect is in full play the risk factor μ^n will quickly shrink, and community residents will more easily enter an aggressive state To further explore the rules of phase transition of trading state, we put the phase transition equation of trading state (20.2.4) into the coordinate system constructed by (p, q).

Taking the prior probability p as the vertical axis and the prior probability q as the horizontal axis to form the coordinate system of the trading situation distribution, the phase transition equation of the trading state corresponds to a straight line in the coordinate system, dividing the trading state space into aggressive and conservative areas. We call this dividing line the trading stance state dividing line.

In Fig. 20.1, the square with an area of 1 represents the state space of the trading agent a_i, and state dividing line of the trading state divides the state space into two. The area above the state dividing line is the aggressive area, which we denote as a upper case S; the area below the state dividing line is the conservative area, which we denote by a Lowercase s. Obviously, the larger the aggressive area, the greater the possibility of a_i entering an aggressive state; conversely, the smaller the aggressive area, the greater the possibility of a_i entering a conservative state. The two states wax and wane.

Figure 20.1 shows that the parameter $2R_g\mu^n$ is key to determining the size relationship between the two areas. The weaker the risk filtering effect, the larger the value μ^n takes, the smaller the aggressive state S is; conversely, the stronger the risk filtering effect, the smaller the value μ^n takes, the larger the aggressive state S will be, meaning that the trading agent is more likely to enter an aggressive state. The larger the risk index of aggressive state R_g, the higher the risk of choosing an aggressive

Fig. 20.1 The distribution chart of trading states

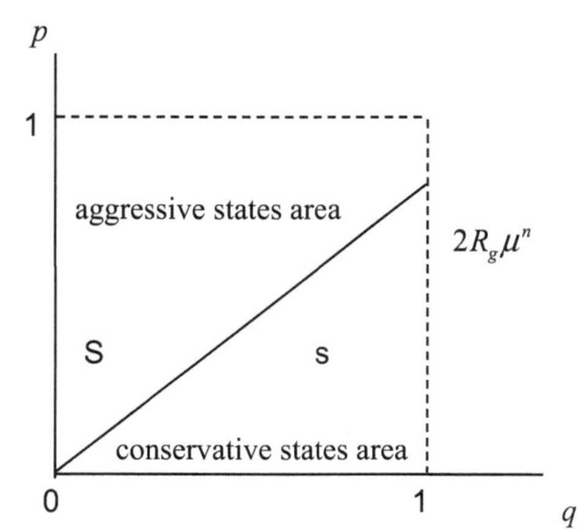

state, and the more cautious the decision-maker will be, and the stricter the conditions for choosing an aggressive state. In Fig. 20.1, the steeper the corresponding dividing line, the more compressed the aggressive state S is.

Although the state dividing line always corresponds to the agents in the trading community, the state dividing line also reflects the overall characteristics of different evolutionary periods of the trading community, including the income level of the state complement representing the aggressive state and the response intensity of the trading agent to the trading situation. By the same token, the state dividing line can also be extended to the trading system as a symbol with developmental evolutionary characteristics. The income level and the response intensity of the trading agent to the situation are also important structural features reflecting different development periods of an economy. In subsequent discussions, we often use the state dividing line at the community level or the entire trading system level.

The phase transition mechanism of the trading state results in t a cyclical oscillation pattern of trading state. As the number of agents choosing an aggressive state in the trading community increases, the risk filtering effect strengthens, $2R_g\mu^n$ begins to decline. When the number of aggressive trading agents increases to a certain number, the demand for goods increases accordingly, and the cost of implementing an aggressive state will increase; according to the supply and demand pattern of different markets and the characteristics of the production cycle, each market will have a supply critical point. When demand exceeds the supply critical point, commodity prices will rise, and the expected return of the aggressive state of the trading agent in the counter-phase $E_g(ag)$ will show a downward trend. At this time, the number of agents adopting aggressive strategies in the community will gradually decrease, and the evolutionary trend of the risk filtering factor μ^n begins to increase from small, $2R_g\mu^n$ reaches to a turning point to rally.

Correspondingly, the conservative state also has a turning point. When the conservative state continues to expand its territory, the trading situation H is on a deteriorating spiral, most trading agents adopt conservative trading strategies, with companies scaling back investment expansion, and families cutting spending. In the absence of macro-control policy intervention, the interaction of corporate conservative strategies and family conservative strategies forms a binary structure of trading feedback loops, pushing the trading situation H into a downward spiral trajectory. Driven by the contraction of the trading set of the trading agents, it will lead to a worsening trading situation, which in turn triggers a positive feedback mechanism of trading set contraction. The contraction of the trading set is not limitless. Be they families or enterprises, there is a basic trading set. The basic trading set is the trading set that maintains a normal operating level. For families, the basic trading set is the trading set that maintains the current normal living standard; for enterprises, the basic trading set is the trading set that maintains the existing scale and market share of the enterprise. Although the basic trading set may also change, there is a significant rigidity in contraction. The basic trading set is the core of the trading set, and once the trading set contracts to its core, it will stop contracting.

Enterprises are the main driving force to break conservative state. Compared to enterprises, the trading potential of families is relatively low, and the momentum that can be generated on the trading network is also quite limited. A few families are not enough to form the ability to change the state of the trading system. When most of the agents in the trading system are in a conservative state, market competition becomes extremely fierce, and enterprises enter a life-and-death period. Under such circumstances, enterprises may adopt two different strategies, one is to wait for the market environment to improve. During this period, they try to reduce uncertainty and save all possible expenses, which we can call the "hibernation strategy"; the other is an active breakout strategy. They try various innovations, including enterprise management mechanism innovation, product innovation, technology innovation, and enterprise model innovation, etc., to improve enterprise efficiency, strengthen employee incentives, and develop new product markets, thereby achieving the purpose of pushing new boundaries and emerging stronger Against the backdrop of a worsening trading situation, each enterprise will choose between the two strategies based on its own situation. Enterprises that choose the "hibernation strategy" focus on stability; enterprises that adopt the "breakout strategy" focus more on winning, much more than to get through the current predicament, and to focus on competition to come.

When most of the agents in the trading system adopt a conservative state, there are always a small part of the agents that adopt an aggressive state and try the "breakout strategy". This is the phenomenon of "mutation" invasion in the evolutionary process. When a powerful mutation—which is innovation—succeeds in its attempt, it will surely play an exemplary role. Community neighbors will follow suit and join the aggressive state. Therefore, the turning point of the conservative state will appear, and more and more agents will follow the new trading strategy, and shift to the aggressive state.

Unlike the relatively certain turning point of the aggressive state, the turning point of the conservative state has a lot of uncertainty. The turning point of the conservative state is driven by the enterprise agents that adopt the "breakout strategy" to get out of the trough, which contains two uncertainties: first, when the "breakout strategy" will succeed, and when the "successful innovation" plan can be found is highly uncertain; second, whether the successful enterprise has a significant demonstration effect on other enterprises in the community is uncertain. If the enterprise that successfully breaks out has a high-order trading momentum, the demonstration effect will be easier to spread; on the contrary, if the enterprise that successfully breaks out has a lower-order trading momentum, its demonstration effect will not be great, and its ability to lead the community out of the conservative state will be very limited.

In addition to the factors above, there is another factor that plays an indispensable role in the process of trading state phase transition, which is the value threshold e_0. Human beings are highly adaptive to environment, by actively adjusting to changes they live with. The value threshold is the minimum expected return of the trading agent, which will also spontaneously adjust with changes in the trading environment. When the trading system is in a period of prosperity, the value threshold of the trading agent e_0 will correspondingly increase. Under this mechanism, the return risk index R_g will increase, creating conditions for a phase transition in trading. After the change in the return risk index R_g mounts to a certain extent, the state dividing line of the trading system will shift, and the turning point of the trading system state is about to come. Similarly, after the trading agent experiences a period of harsh trading environment, the value threshold e_0 will gradually decrease, forming a return risk index R_g down effect, which accelerates the arrival of state turning point in the trading system.

Comparing with the different conversion mechanisms between aggressive and conservative states, we found that the evolution of the trading system is made possible in the state switching of the trading agents. When the situation of the trading system deteriorates, most agents shift to a conservative state, and part of the agents continue to push boundaries and try to innovate. The trading system enters the channel of system optimization and accelerated innovation during the period dominated by the conservative state. When the aggressive state dominates the trading system, the performance of the system optimization accumulated in the early stage can be quickly tapped, and the results of technological innovation will also be promoted and put into application faster. The trading system evolves in the process of switching between conservative and aggressive states, and each round of state alternation pushes the trading system to a new level.

According to the above analysis, the state dividing line will shift with the changes in the trading situation H. The downward movement of the state dividing line represents the expansion of the aggressive state in the state space and the contraction of the conservative state; vice versa, the upward movement of the state dividing line represents the expansion of the conservative state in the state space and the contraction of the aggressive state. The trading state dividing line swings up and down in a fan shape centered on the origin. The line at the bottom of the fan-shaped area represents the maximum expansion point of the aggressive state; the line at the top of the fan-shaped area represents the maximum expansion point of the conservative state, which are respectively called the upper and lower regression lines of the state dividing line. As shown in the Fig. 20.2.

With the upward and downward movement of the state dividing line in the fan-shaped area formed by the upper and lower regression lines, the agents' state of the trading system also follows a cyclical shift between the aggressive and conservative states. The structure of the regression line of the state dividing line fluctuation shows that in the evolutionary process of the trading system, no matter what the trading

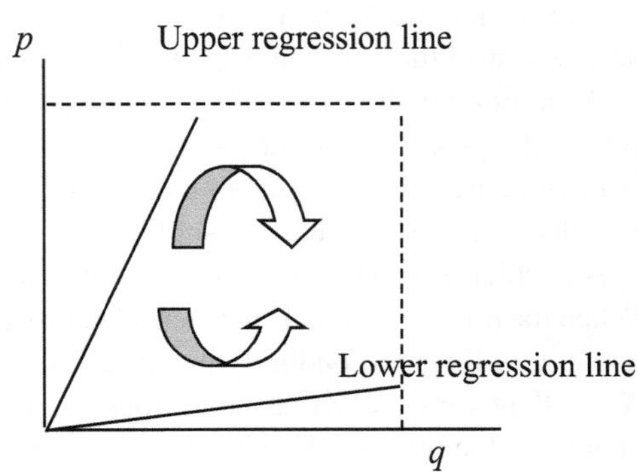

Fig. 20.2 The evolution of trading states

situation is, it is impossible for one trading state to dominate. The trading system is always in a binary state structure, with the only difference being whether dominated by the aggressive or the conservative state. The relationship between the aggressive and conservative states in the trading system is like the relationship between "yin and yang" in nature, they counteract each other to balance and coordinate.

20.4 Trading State Diffusion

We have studied the determination mechanism of a single trading state, now we study the dissemination and diffusion mechanism of the trading state on the trading network. The trading network not only provides a channel for trading agents to connect and interact with each other, but also counteract each other. The interaction between trading agents must be carried out under the framework of the trading network.

20.4.1 Trading State Diffusion Mechanism

The spread of trading sentiment on the internet can be achieved through two different mechanisms. The first mechanism manifests as the behavioral influence between neighbors within the trading community. The key to this mechanism is the dissemination and influence of trading sentiment information among neighbors. We call this mechanism the information transmission mechanism. The carrier of the information transmission mechanism is information, and the content conveyed is confidence in assessing the trading situation.

There are two key conditions for the success of information transmission: one is that the trading phase of the neighbors corresponds to the same trading situation. Only when it corresponds to the same trading situation, will their trading behaviors and state strategy contain the situation information to a_i's concern; the other is that the trading community must have an adequately high degree of aggregation. Only in this way can information be smoothly disseminated within the community, and a_i can receive behavioral information from community neighbors. Overall, the higher the degree of aggregation of the trading community, the more significant the effect of information transmission, and the more significant the effect of trading sentiment through information transmission.

The second is the trading transmission mechanism. The trading behaviors of neighbors in the lower and upper phases in the community affect the formation of the decision-maker's trading sentiment. The carrier of the trading transmission mechanism is the trading flow, and what is conveyed is the resources for the decision-maker to carry out the trade.

In the trading community, the decision-maker, as a link in the trading chain, can accurately perceive the state of the agents on the trading chain. When the lower-phase agents on the trading chain shift to an aggressive state, the decision-maker can feel the increase in trading resources and cash flow. At the same time, the trading counterpart's sensitivity to price will also show a downward trend. All these are conducive to the decision-maker entering an aggressive state; similarly, when the lower-phase agent enters a conservative state, the decision-maker will immediately feel the changes in market contraction and cash flow decline, and the market's sensitivity to price will also increase. All these will prompt the decision-maker to turn to a conservative strategy.

Compared with the influence of the lower phase, the changes in the trading sentiment of the upper-phase subjects on the trading chain have a relatively indirect impact on the decision-maker, and the mechanism is more complex. When the upper-phase agent shifts to an aggressive state, his expansionary strategy will take many forms in the market, including promotional policies and improving after-sales service, etc. As a downstream decision-maker, they will naturally benefit from it, which will undoubtedly be conducive to the decision-maker forming an aggressive strategy; another possibility is that the aggressive strategy of the upper-phase agent is manifested in expanding new enterprise areas. At this time, the aggressive state of the upper-phase subject has little to do with the existing trading chain, and the only impact is the demonstration effect. When the upper-phase agent shifts to a conservative state, the situation is relatively simple, and promotional price reduction behaviors will decrease. The decision-maker at the lower phase can directly feel the strategy change information from upstream, and this information will eventually enter the decision-maker's information set and act as the basis for adjusting the trading sentiment.

In fact, the trading transmission mechanism itself also carries information transmission. Therefore, the trading chain transmission mechanism is the overlapping of dual mechanisms, playing a more important role in the process of trading sentiment propagation and diffusion.

In the transmission process of trading states within the trading community, whether through the trading chain or the information chain, the subjects of transmission all come from the state coordination set. That is to say, the transmission of trading states is mainly restricted within the state coordination set. However, another mechanism that cannot be ignored is the permeation transmission mechanism of trading states, which occurs between different state coordination sets, through intermediate links, to achieve cross-coordination set state transmission. This permeation mechanism is realized through the extensive links of the trading network. Even between two state coordination sets that have no intersection at all, the links of the trading network will eventually realize the transmission of information flow and trading flow, which is the key to the realization of the permeation mechanism. Due to the existence of the permeation mechanism, on the trading community, any two state coordination sets are not absolutely isolated, with a large number of information flows and trading flows as permeation channels. In the transmission and diffusion process of trading states, the trading chain and information chain play the main channel role, while the permeation mechanism plays a supplementary role. Compared with the two main channels, the permeation mechanism is relatively slow in transmission speed and is a subtle and gradual process.

20.4.2 High Aggregation Community

In the high-aggregation trading community, the links between residents' trading chains and information chains present a highly interconnected structure.

In such structured communities, the residents have high coordination, and the consistency of state selection is strong. Reflected in the diffusion of trading states, the prominent feature of high-aggregation communities is that the rhythm of state adjustment is relatively lagging, but the speed of state adjustment within the community will be very rapid. Due to the high aggregation, residents share information fully, and the trading links between each other are tight. Under such circumstances, few trading agents will actively adjust their trading states, which will limit the rhythm of trading state adjustment. Assuming that the conservative state is the dominant state of the trading community Ω, few residents adopt the aggressive state, and the number of aggressive state demonstration agents in the trading community Ω will continue to hover at a low level. As can be seen from the phase transition Eq. (20.2.4), a_i as any agent on the trading community Ω, if it wants to switch from a conservative state to an aggressive state, it must meet the condition $\frac{p}{q} > 2R_g\mu^n$. Since the demonstration number n is small, so to meet the trading state conversion condition $\frac{p}{q} > 2R_g\mu^n$, it requires a_i to have greater confidence in the friendly situation H, that is, a larger prior probability value p. Obviously, this is a condition that is relatively difficult to achieve in a high-aggregation community.

In the high-aggregation community Ω, once some residents' prior probability p meets the condition $\frac{p}{q} > 2R_g\mu^n$, due to the ease of information sharing, and through information dissemination, more residents in the community Ω will meet the trading state transition condition, that is, $\frac{p}{q} > 2R_g\mu^n$, completing the transition from a conservative state to an aggressive state. As the number of aggressive state demonstrations in the trading community Ω increases, n The rapid amplification of the conversion conditions $p > \frac{q\mu^n}{R_g}$ will also reduce the requirements for prior probabilities p and the aggressive state will spread rapidly in the trading community Ω. in A vivid metaphor to describe this feature of the high-aggregation community Ω is that, the high-aggregation community Ω is like an object with a hard shell but a soft core. Breaking through the shell requires a certain intensity of strength, and once the shell is broken, there will be no impedance inside.

This feature of the high-aggregation community Ω determines that the state propagation of the trading network will not be uniform; the distribution of the trading state on the network will not be uniform, and it will inevitably present an island distribution pattern according to the size of the aggregation.

20.4.3 Low-Aggregation Community

The characteristic of the low-aggregation community is that there are relatively few trading and information connections among the residents within the community, and the external connections of the community residents are relatively more.

Due to the relatively few internal connections, there will also be a large difference in the state coordination set among the residents of the low-aggregation community. Since the residents are mainly influenced by the agents in the state coordination set, it determines that the consistency of the trading state of the community residents will also be lower, showing that each governs itself within the community, and the influence on each other in the choice of state is weak.

Another characteristic of the low-aggregation community is its high openness. Compared with internal connections, the external connections of the low-aggregation community are more extensive. This structure determines that the low-aggregation community accepts more information and influences from the outside than from the high-aggregation community. Therefore, the main characteristics of the low-aggregation community in the process of trading state propagation are exactly the opposite of the high-aggregation community: first, there is no resistance to external propagation, and new trading states can easily enter the community; second, the internal propagation speed is slow, and it is not easy to form a consistent trading state distribution within the community.

20.4.4 Closed Community

The closed community is not absolutely closed to the outside world, but a type of community with a lower degree of openness. Not only is the degree of openness of this type of community low, but the level of internal aggregation is also relatively low. Under normal circumstances, this type of community belongs to the margin of the trading network.

The residents of the closed community, due to weak trading links, are almost all in a state of dissociation. Not only is there a large difference between the state coordination sets of the residents, and the degree of consistency is low, but the scale of the state coordination set is also very small. In this case, due to the lack of input of information flow and trading flow, the closed community will stay in a conservative state for a long time, forming a state lock-in situation. The change of trading state is the result of internal interaction in the trading network. The closed community that lacks trading activities will lack the driving force for the evolution of trading states, and will inevitably be isolated from mainstream society, forming a state island on the trading network.

20.4.5 Large-Capacity Community

For communities of a larger scale, with more residents involved, the cascade effect often plays an important role in the process of trading state propagation, showing a phase change phenomenon where the propagation is slow in the early stage, but suddenly speed up after crossing the threshold.

Large-capacity community residents have a large state synergy set, and there is a significant difference between each other's synergy sets. The state decision of the trading agent requires more observations to obtain sufficient information to meet the state phase transition conditions. This leads to the threshold phenomenon of community state propagation.

Assume Ω is a large-capacity trading community, under the pattern dominated by conservative states, residents' prior judgment about the situation H appearing friendly state g is p_0, the prior probability of appearing unfriendly b state is q_0, which satisfies $p_0 < q_0$ under the current situation; if residents move from a conservative state to an aggressive state, the minimum posterior probability value needs to be p^*.

According to Bayes' theorem, the posterior probability of community Ω residents can be calculated as follows:

$$\Pr(g|n) = \frac{p}{p + q\mu^n} \tag{20.4.1}$$

The condition for the appearance of an aggressive state can be obtained:

$$p^* = \frac{p_0}{p_0 + q_0\mu^n} \tag{20.4.2}$$

From (20.4.2) we get:

$$q_0\mu^n = p_0\frac{1 - p^*}{p^*} \tag{20.4.3}$$

Let $q^* = 1 - p^*$, substitute into (20.4.3) to get:

$$\mu^n = \frac{p_0}{q_0}\frac{q^*}{p^*} \tag{20.4.4}$$

Take the logarithm on both sides of (20.4.4):

$$n \ln \mu = \ln \frac{p_0 q^*}{q_0 p^*} \tag{20.4.5}$$

From (20.4.5), it can be seen that the condition for residents of community Ω to switch from a conservative state to an aggressive state is that the number of aggressive demonstrators n^* in community Ω must reach the following level:

$$n^* = \frac{\ln \frac{p_0}{q_0} + \ln \frac{q^*}{p^*}}{\ln \mu} \tag{20.4.6}$$

$\because\ 0 < \mu < 1$

$\therefore\ \ln \mu < 0;$

$\because$ For the trading agent to enter an aggressive state, it needs to suffice $p^* \geq q^*$;
Known $p_0 \leq q_0$

$$\therefore\ \ln \frac{p_0}{q_0} < 0,\quad \ln \frac{q^*}{p^*} < 0;$$

From this, it can be seen that the minimum market norm of the aggressive state of community Ω calculated by (20.4.6) $n^* > 0$ is a meaningful positive number.

Equation (20.4.6) shows that when the number of aggressive demonstrations in community Ω reaches the level of n^*, most residents in community Ω will choose an aggressive state. This shows that there is a meaningful trading state conversion threshold n^* in the large-capacity community Ω, and it also shows the existence of the trading state phase transition threshold phenomenon.

Equation (20.4.6) shows that the smaller $\frac{p_0}{q_0}$ is, the larger the threshold of community state evolution n^* is. This shows that the general view of community residents on the situation is an important factor affecting the spread of trading states. When people's views on the situation generally tend to be pessimistic, $\frac{p_0}{q_0}$ becomes smaller, so n^* Increase; it means that the threshold of phase transition in community trading is raised. The higher the conditions for phase transition, the more difficult it is for phase transition to occur. Conversely, if people's views on the situation tend to be optimistic, it is reflected in $\frac{p_0}{q_0}$ as an increase in value, $\left|\ln\left(\frac{p_0}{q_0}\right)\right|$ will become smaller, the phase transition threshold n^* will decrease, and it will be easier for the community state to undergo phase transition.

In Fig. 20.3, the horizontal axis represents time t, n^* the position represents the time when the state evolution threshold appears, n_1^* represents a lower threshold, n_2^* represents a higher threshold; the vertical axis represents the proportion of the community that has entered the radical state through conduction.

In Fig. 20.3, the community state evolution process is divided into three areas, namely the noise area, transmission area, and penetration area. Each area corresponds to a dominant mechanism. The noise area is mainly the random fluctuation phenomenon in the group, which is an unavoidable phenomenon in any social field. Generally speaking, the noise area only occupies a very small part; the transmission area is dominated by trading and information transmission and the phase transition of the community state also occurs in the conduction area. Once it enters the threshold, the community enters the rapid phase transition process of the trading state. The conduction process is carried out within each state coordination set. When all the agents in the coordination set switch to the new state, the state transmission process ends. But at this time, not all residents of the community are covered, and some

Fig. 20.3 The infusion mechanism of trading states

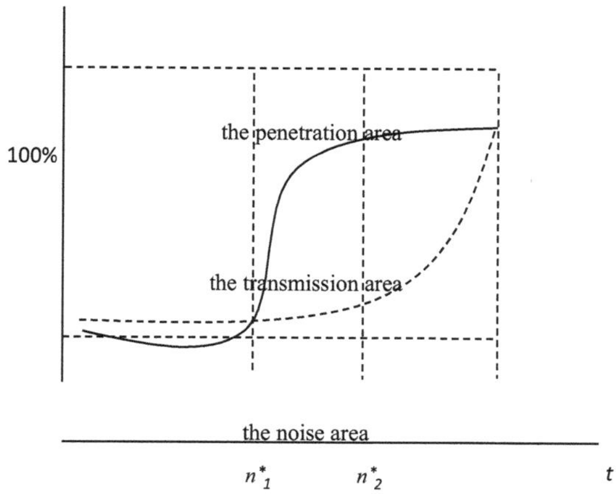

residents' coordination sets have not yet reached the threshold conditions. Through slow penetration, these residents will eventually switch to the new state.

Chapter 21
Economic Cycle Model

The economic cycle is the synchronization of the trading state on the trading network. The state of the trading agent evolves from a scattered distribution to a convergent direction, either gathering on the radical state or the conservative state; at the macro level, the two evolution trends correspond to economic prosperity and depression respectively. In this process, the state entropy of the trading system underwent two cycles.

21.1 Evolution of Economic Cycle Theory

Understanding the causes of economic fluctuations or economic cycles has always been one of the core mandates of economic theory. The theoretical research on economic cycles has become an important part of economic theory and is an indispensable content of standard economics textbooks. The formation mechanism of economic cycles and tactics have become the touchstone for testing academic schools. Where there is an economic cycle theory, there is an academic school of Economics. In the history of economic theory, scholars began to pay attention to the economic cycle fluctuations very early. Although the concept of economic cycles did not appear explicitly in early classical economics, and there was no systematic explanation of economic cycles, a lot of attention was still given to the possible causes of economic fluctuations. In 1814, Sismondi (Sismondi Jean Charles Leonard Simonde de) discussed in "*Political Economy*" and "*New Principles of Political Economy*" that the disconnection between production and consumption may lead to insufficient consumption. It is believed that the capitalist's pursuit of profit will inevitably give rise to two tendencies: on one hand, it will produce unrestrainedly; on the other hand, it will try to lower workers' wages as much as possible. The disconnection between production and consumption will inevitably lead to overproduction.

Z. Wang, *Trading Economics*, Contributions to Economics,
https://doi.org/10.1007/978-981-99-9875-3_21

In 1862, W. S. Jevons published a monograph on the theory of economic cycles, "*A Study on Periodic Commercial Fluctuations*". Jevons mainly found that the cycle of agricultural output spanned about 10 years. This cycle length coincides with the activity cycle of sunspots, hence he proposed the famous "sunspot theory". The core idea of the "sunspot theory" is that sunspot activity affects climate change while climate affects agricultural crop yields, and the supply of agricultural products ultimately affects economic operations.

Among the masters of classical economics, Marx conducted the most in-depth research on economic cycles. Marx expanded his study of economic cycles from production and trading to the field of social systems, and concluded that economic cycles are an unavoidable phenomenon in capitalist economies, and each cycle will inevitably trigger an economic crisis.[1]

The modern theory of economic cycles was initiated by John Maynard Keynes. Before the Great Depression of the 1930s, the cycle theory of neoclassical economics took a dominate position. Neoclassical economic theory acknowledges the ebbs and flows of economic systems deviating from equilibrium, and economic cycles are the result of deviations from equilibrium. Neoclassical economics also believes that the economic system has the ability to self-adjust and return to equilibrium. Unemployment cannot take place in large numbers, let alone exist for a long time. But the Great Depression in the Western world in the 1930s shattered the neoclassical theory's description of the economic system's self-adjustment. Against this backdrop, Keynes proposed a revolutionary theory, and the theory of economic cycles became the key content of this theoretical revolution. Keynes believed that insufficient effective demand was the root cause of economic depression. The interrelationships between macro variables such as investment, consumption, and income form a mutually restraining feedback loop. Without government intervention, the economy cannot spontaneously emerge from depression, but will show a spiral downward trend. The depression does not die down, but will continue to worsen.

Paul Anthony Samuelson used a model to quantify Keynes's thoughts[2]:

$$\begin{aligned} Y_t &= C_t + I_t \\ C_t &= a + bY_{t-1} \\ I_t &= K(Y_{t-1} - Y_{t-2}) \end{aligned} \tag{21.1.1}$$

where Y represents national income, C represents consumption, I represents investment; a, b, K, are three structural parameters, b represents the marginal propensity to consume; K represents the accelerator number. The three parameters satisfy the following inequalities:

$$\begin{aligned} &a > 0 \\ &0 < b < 1 \\ &K > 0 \end{aligned} \tag{21.1.2}$$

Equation set (21.1.1) describes the nested relationship among the national income Y, investment I and consumption C. The decline in national income leads to a decrease in consumption, which in turn drags down national income further, causing enterprises to reduce investment, and thus national income falls into a spiral decline. In the Keynesian cycle model (21.1.1), it includes "traps" far from equilibrium. Once the economy enters the "trap", it is difficult to break free.

There are many theories and models about economic cycles, including Austrian school cycle theory, monetarist cycle theory, rational expectation school cycle theory, new Keynesian cycle theory, real economic cycle theory, and financial cycle theory, etc. Among many schools, the real economic cycle theory representing the neoclassical economics school is currently the most influential and most widely received.

The Real Economic cycle (RBC) theory was jointly created by Kydland, Prescott, and others. In 1982, they jointly published the paper "Time to Build and Aggregate Fluctuations" in The Econometrics Journal. The two also won the 2004 Nobel Prize in Economics for this.

RBC has models of different complexity, we will analyze it using a relatively simple model[3]:

$$\begin{aligned} Y_t &= K_t^{\alpha}(A_t L_t)^{1-\alpha} \\ K_{t+1} &= (1-\delta)K_t + Y_t - C_t - G_t \end{aligned} \tag{21.1.3}$$

In (21.1.3), Y represents the output level, K represents the capital stock, L represents the labor input, δ represents the capital depreciation rate, A represents technological progress, C represents consumption, G represents government expenditure.

Essentially, the RBC model (21.1.3) is also a feedback loop model, explaining the self-reinforcing mechanism of economic fluctuations. It can be seen that both the Keynesian model (21.1.1) and the RBC model (21.1.3) simulate the dynamic characteristics of economic operation by constructing trading feedback loops. Both types of models are of economic growth, economic cycles, and economic operation.

The differences between models (21.1.1) and (21.1.3) are manifested in three aspects: first, the Keynesian model is built on the relationship of macro variables, while the RBC output equation is the Douglas production function with micro-behavioral foundations; second, the RBC model contains more variables than the Keynesian model does. RBC incorporates technological elements, labor, capital stock, capital depreciation, government expenditure, and other variables into the model. This further increases the dynamics and enhances the explanatory power of the model. Because model (21.1.3) contains more variables, including population growth, technological progress, and sudden declines in capital stock caused by natural disasters, etc., all may become reasons for economic growth or slowdown. Third, the RBC model includes a nonlinear Douglas production function, in this sense, the trading feedback loop constructed from this is more dynamic.

In the debates and challenges among different schools of thought, the theory of economic cycles has made considerable progress, and the explanation of economic cycles is becoming increasingly refined. In the fierce debates, the differences between the cycle models of different schools are gradually narrowing, showing a clear trend of convergence. From the comparison of models (21.1.1) and (21.1.3), it can be seen that the basic structure and feedback mechanism of the models are basically the same. The main differences lie in the number of variables, whether the nominal variables include monetary factors or the real economic variables exclude monetary factors, and whether expectations play an important role, as well as the strictness of the assumptions for enterprises and families.

As economics evolves over the past 300 years, the theory of economic cycles has shown a clear evolutionary path—from the early external attribution theory to today's internal attribution theory. Economists have reached some basic consensus, recognizing that the root of economic cycles is the endogenous instability of the trading system, and the endogenous instability is the result driven by the feedback loop. The debate among economists mainly focuses on whether the trading system has a self-balancing, spontaneous adjustment capacity.

21.2 The Nature of Economic Cycle

Cyclical fluctuations are a basic characteristic of natural motion. From cosmic bodies to microscopic particles; from the inorganic world to living organisms, the process of motion and evolution all show cyclical characteristics. All complex systems have fluctuations, and the essence of economic cycles is the fluctuation of the trading system. The Lotka-Volterra equation, which describes the ecological system composed of predators and prey, cannot avoid the situation of periodic famine even in a simple system as such.[4]

The core of system fluctuations is the interaction between components. From a more general level, any system with a self-reinforcing mechanism will inevitably produce a cyclical motion structure.[5] Due to the ubiquity of feedback loops, the trading system cannot avoid cyclical fluctuations.

How to view the phenomenon of economic cycles, there is a clear historical watershed in the evolution of economic thought. Before the Great Depression in the 1930s, the consensus in the economic community was that the phenomenon of economic cycles was the result of the equilibrium movement of the trading system. Even if there were non-equilibrium phenomena such as unemployment and overproduction in the short term, they were just temporary deviations from the process of the equilibrium movement of the trading system. The trading system will self-correct and will eventually spontaneously return to equilibrium. The global Great Depression that broke out in the 1930s brewed an unprecedented cognitive revolution in the economic community—the "Keynesian Revolution"—abandoning the concept that the trading system is always operating on the equilibrium trajectory, believes that the non-equilibrium state is the normal state of the trading system, while equilibrium is an occasionally achieved abnormal state. The economic cycle is the state transition of the trading system from equilibrium to non-equilibrium. However, the understanding of economic cycles has not reached a consensus in academia, and the lines between the equilibrium school and the non-equilibrium school are still clearly visible.

In the view of trading economics, the economic cycle is a phenomenon of trading state synchronization on the trading network. The trading network links a large number of trading subjects, forming a link channel for information flow and trading flow. In order to maximize profits, trading agents always switch between aggressive and conservative states. Through extensive linkages, trading agents interact on the trading network and ultimately achieve trading state synchronization.

The synchronization process can be seen as a struggle between aggressive and conservative states for trading agents on the trading network. At the beginning of the synchronization process, the trading network is divided into aggressive and conservative states, with some agents making decisions based on the characteristics of the transaction state. When a trading agent in a certain state shows a clear advantage in terms of benefits and risks, this trading state will gradually become the dominant strategy, attracting more and more trading agents, and ultimately taking over the entire trading network. In the process of achieving synchronization of the trading network, the verification of decision-making effects plays a key role. Through effect verification, different agents confirm which trading state has more advantages, thereby achieving the spread of trading states.

The speed at which the trading network achieves synchronization depends on the strength of the comparison of advantages between the two trading states. The more obvious the comparative advantage of the trading state, the faster the network synchronization is achieved. In addition, the speed at which the trading network achieves synchronization is also related to the transmission speed determined by the structure of the trading network. The denser and more compact the trading network, the faster the synchronization is achieved.

The speed at which the trading network achieves synchronization is also closely related to network capacity. On a network with only two trading agents, regardless of the trading state of the trading agent, synchronization must be maintained. Each agent's trading agents is the counter party, and the choice of trading state must be restricted by the other party's state. When the network is composed of three agents, the network needs a process to achieve synchronization. The three agents can choose different trading states, but because the number of effect verifications is relatively small that the time to achieve synchronization is also short. As the capacity of the trading network increases, it takes longer to achieve a synchronous state in reality.

Due to the influence of many factors in the process of establishing the comparative advantage of the trading state, there will be a tug-of-war phenomenon in the state competition. The larger the scale of the trading network, the more interference factors there are, the more obvious the chaotic characteristics become, and the more unstable the rhythm of state changes will be.

Under normal circumstances, the trading network will alternate between the two trading states, forming a dual-state synchronization structure. However, theoretically, the trading system may stabilize on a certain trading state for a relatively long period of time, resulting in a trading state lock-in phenomenon, which is a single-state synchronization phenomenon. When the trading system is locked in a conservative state, the economy will fall into a stagnation trap. If the trading network is stable in the excited state for a long time, it means that the economy has entered a period of rapid growth. Overall, be it a stagnation trap or sustained economic growth, both require the satisfaction of many conditions and are special phenomena in the operation of the trading system.

The formation of trading state synchronization can be divided into two stages: the first stage is the accumulation stage, which is also the establishment stage of the synchronous state. In this stage, the trading state of the nodes is divergent, and the comparative advantage of the trading state is not very obvious. The second stage is the convergence stage of the synchronous state, where the comparative strict advantage of the trading state gradually emerges, and the trading system accelerates towards the advantage state, forming a trading state synchronization pattern. Under the trading synchronization situation, the dominant state dominates the entire transaction network, while the inferior state continuously accumulates strength, waiting for the opportunity to reclaim its territory. For example, after the aggressive state has been dominant for a period of time, the number of agents that fail due to overexpansion increases, market risks gradually increase, and agents that fail in trading will join the conservative state, and some agents that are more sensitive to risk will also turn to the conservative state. As can be seen from the trading state phase transition equation, once the number of agents won by the conservative state reaches a critical level, the conservative state will seize the territory and enter the convergence stage of trading state evolution. When the conservative state replaces the aggressive state and becomes the dominant strategy on the trading network, and the aggressive state becomes the inferior strategy, the same process will restart, and so on.

In the perspective of trading economics, equilibrium and disequilibrium are no longer a theoretical dimension, and the phenomenon of economic cycles is no longer limited to the opposition of equilibrium and disequilibrium, but effectively unifies equilibrium and disequilibrium. In other words, in the logical system of trading economics, the economic cycle is the result of the rhythm of trading state transitions of a large number of agents. Trading agents interact through the trading network, and in the process of trading body selection, they are both synergistic and independent. This determines that in the operation of the economic cycle, it may always remain in equilibrium or deviate from equilibrium. Both equilibrium and disequilibrium are the results of trading agents pursuing maximum benefits, and there is no mutually exclusive relationship.

21.3 Trading Economics Cycle Model

Trading economics has chosen a more inclusive logical framework, and the economic cycle model it constructs no longer has the function of an economic growth model, and belongs to an independent economic cycle model.

21.3.1 Trading System State Entropy

Trading economics views the economic cycle as a synchronous phenomenon of the trading state of trading agents on the trading network. Under such a concept, the description of the periodic operation of the trading system is transformed into the calculation of the consistency or synchronization index of the state distribution of the trading system. For this, we introduce the concept of trading system state entropy. Entropy originated from statistical thermodynamics, and is mainly used to describe the disorder of molecular states. The second law of thermodynamics about entropy was once hailed by Einstein as an eternal law. He believes that from the dimension of time, all known laws will eventually be rewritten, and only the law of entropy increase will remain unchanged. The second law of thermodynamics is regarded by people as the basic law that dominates the universe, known as the first law of the universe. Since the trading system is a dissipative system, it no longer strictly follows the law of entropy increase. Despite this, the law of entropy increase still presents in some form. We will prove that within an economic cycle, there are two cycles of the state entropy.

Let $\{a_i\}_N$ be the capacity set of the trading system, at the time step t, any trading agent a_i chooses the probability of aggressive state as p_i, and the probability of conservative state as q_i, the two states satisfy the complementarity condition: $p_i + q_i = 1$. Under this condition, the state entropy Q of the trading system is defined as:

$$Q_t = \sum_1^N p_i \sum_1^N q_i \tag{21.3.1}$$

Since the trading state probability satisfies the inequality $0 \le p_i \le 1$ and $0 \le q_i \le 1$, the value of the trading system entropy satisfies $Q \ge 0$ condition.

According to the definition of state entropy Q (21.3.1), when all agents in the trading system enter the same trading state, if it is aggressive, then $p_i = 1, q_i = 0$; if it is conservative, then $p_i = 0, q_i = 1$, the entropy of the trading system Q reaches its minimum value, that is, $Q = 0$.

Next, let's calculate the maximum value of the entropy of the trading system state.

$$\because \quad q_i = 1 - p_i$$

$$\because \quad Q_t = \sum_1^N p_i \sum_1^N q_i = \sum_1^N p_i \sum_1^N (1 - p_i) = \sum_1^N p_i \left(N - \sum_1^N p_i \right)$$

$$\therefore \quad Q_t = N \sum_1^N p_i - \left(\sum_1^n p_i \right)^2 \tag{21.3.2}$$

Take the derivative of both sides of (21.3.2):

$$\frac{\partial Q_t}{\partial p_i} = N - 2\sum_1^N p_i \tag{21.3.3}$$

According to the condition of function extremum, when the entropy function Q reaches its maximum value, it needs to satisfy the following conditions:

$$\frac{\partial Q_t}{\partial p_j} = 0 \quad j = 1, 2, \ldots, N \tag{21.3.4}$$

According to condition (21.3.4), we get:

$$N - 2\sum_1^N p_i = 0 \tag{21.3.5}$$

From condition (21.3.5), we know that the maximum value point of the trading system entropy function must necessarily fall on the hyperplane of 2N-dimensional space $\{p_i, q_i\}$, that is:

$$\sum_1^N p_i = \frac{N}{2} \tag{21.3.6}$$

$$\sum_1^N q_i = \frac{N}{2} \tag{21.3.7}$$

On the 2N-dimensional hyperplane determined by (21.3.6) and (21.3.7), the entropy function of the trading system Q reaches its maximum value, and the maximum entropy value is:

$$Q_t = \sum_1^N p_i \sum_1^N q_i = \left(\frac{N}{2}\right)^2 \tag{21.3.8}$$

Under extremely simplified conditions, we take $N = 2$, at this time the maximum entropy value of the trading system appears on the following hyperplane:

$$p_1 + p_2 = 1 \tag{21.3.9}$$

$$q_1 + q_2 = 1 \tag{21.3.10}$$

Obviously, $p_1 = q_1 = p_2 = q_2 = \frac{1}{2}$ is on the hyperplane determined by (21.3.9) and (21.3.10). The state entropy of the trading system Q reaches its maximum value at this point. At this point, due to the maximum uncertainty of the trading state of the trading subject, the trading system is in the most disordered state.

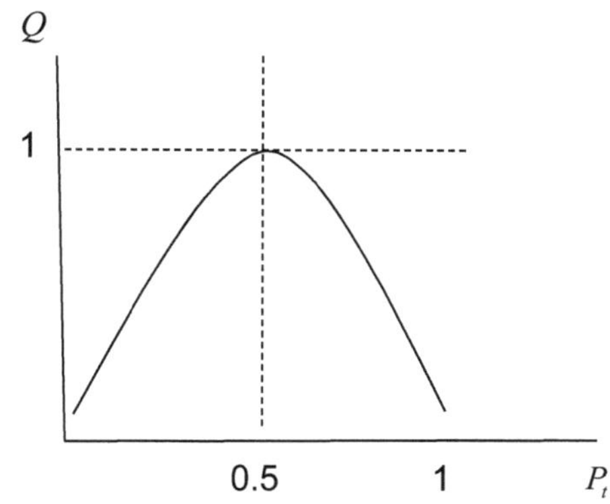

Fig. 21.1 The trajectory curve of the entropy

Observe the trajectory curve of the entropy function Q on the trading system of $N = 2$ dimensions (Fig. 21.1).

21.3.2 Trading State Synchronization Index

The state entropy Q portrays the disorder of the trading system state distribution. The trading state synchronization index is the mirror index of the disorder of the trading system state distribution The higher the trading state synchronization index, the weaker the disorder of the trading system, and the stronger the order; and vice versa. Based on the above relationship, we define the trading state synchronization index, represented by *Syn*.

$$Syn_t = \frac{\left(\frac{N}{2}\right)^2 - Q_t}{\left(\frac{N}{2}\right)^2} \tag{21.3.11}$$

In definition (21.3.11), the synchronization index *Syn* has an inverse relationship with the state entropy Q. The larger the state entropy Q, the smaller the trading state synchronization index *Syn*. When the state entropy Q reaches its maximum, that is, $Q_t = \left(\frac{N}{2}\right)^2$, the trading state synchronization index takes the value $Syn_t = 0$; on the contrary, when the state entropy $Q_t = 0$, the trading state synchronization index reaches its maximum $Syn_t = 1$.

According to the trading state synchronization index *Syn* With the mirror relationship of state entropy Q, the value range of the trading state synchronization index *Syn* is $Syn_t \in [0, 1]$. The distribution curve of the trading state synchronization index *Syn* is symmetrically inverse to the distribution curve of state entropy Q.

According to the definition of the trading state synchronization index *Syn* (21.3.11), the calculation formula can be simplified as follows:

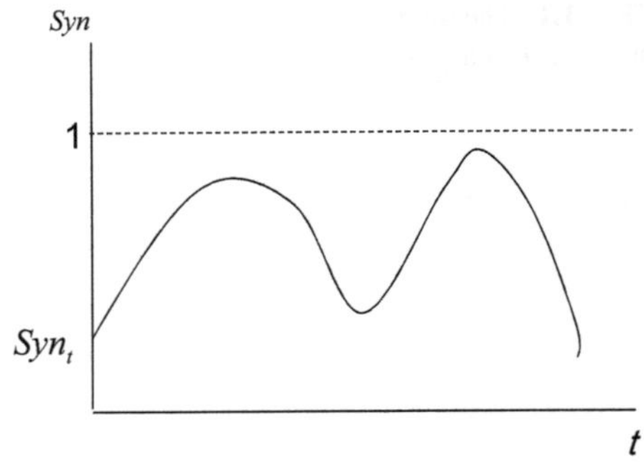

Fig. 21.2 The trajectory of synchronization index

$$Syn_t = 1 - \left(\frac{2}{N}\right)^2 Q_t \tag{21.3.12}$$

As can be seen from (21.3.12), as the capacity of the trading system N increases, the hyperplanes $\sum_1^N p_i = \frac{N}{2}$, $\sum_1^N q_i = \frac{N}{2}$, contain more possibilities of trading states. This means that it becomes more difficult for the trading system to achieve trading state synchronization, and the time required to transition from prosperity to depression in the economic cycle becomes longer.

As time t changes, the trading state synchronization index of the trading system *Syn* will form a time series $\{Syn_t\}$ in the value range [0, 1], forming a trajectory in the time coordinate system (Fig. 21.2).

The high points of the trading state synchronization trajectory correspond to two states of the trading system, which are economic prosperity and economic depression. When the economy shows a clear evolutionary direction, whether it is towards increasing prosperity or towards depression, the trading state synchronization index *Syn* shows an upward trend of the trajectory. When the economy leaves a certain clear equilibrium state and transitions to a new state, the trading state synchronization index *Syn* will show a downward trend.

21.3.3 Economic Cycle Model

Trading economics views the economic cycles as the synchronization phenomenon of the trading system. Based on this theory, we use the trading state phase transition equation to build the economic cycle model of trading economics based on the trading state synchronization index *Syn*.

The trading state phase transition Eq. (20.2.4) establishes the constraint conditions for the state selection of trading subjects, requiring the prior probabilities of the trading situation p, q, to satisfy the equation:

$$\frac{p}{q} - 2R_g\mu^n = 0 \tag{21.3.13}$$

From this, we can obtain the critical condition that the trading agent needs to satisfy when entering the aggressive state for the friendly prior probability p of the situation H.

$$\because \quad q = 1 - p \tag{21.3.14}$$

Substitute (21.3.14) into (21.3.13) to get:

$$p - 2(1-p)R_g\mu^n = 0 \tag{21.3.15}$$

Arrange (21.3.15) to get:

$$p\left(1 + 2R_g\mu^n\right) = 2R_g\mu^n \tag{21.3.16}$$

From (21.3.16), we get the critical condition for the trading agent to enter the aggressive state:

$$p = \frac{2R_g\mu^n}{1 + 2R_g\mu^n} \tag{21.3.17}$$

To avoid confusion in symbols, we will take the critical probability of the trading agent a_i p Marked as p_i^* to distinguish from the probability of the trading agent being in an aggressive state p_i.

The critical condition (21.3.17) can be restated as:

$$p^* = \frac{2R_g\mu^n}{1 + 2R_g\mu^n} \tag{21.3.18}$$

There is an inverse relationship between the probability of a trading agent successfully entering an aggressive state and the critical probability of the aggressive state. The higher the critical probability p_i^*, the less likely it is for the trading system to enter an aggressive state; conversely, the lower the critical condition p_i^*, the easier it is for the trading agent to meet the conditions for entering an aggressive state, and the greater the likelihood of entering an aggressive state. Based on this logic, we can obtain the probability p_i of any agent a_i in the trading system being in an aggressive state:

$$p_i = 1 - p_i^* \tag{21.3.19}$$

Let the return risk coefficient of a_i be R_{gi} and the risk filtering factor be μ^n, then the probability p_i of a_i successfully entering an aggressive state is:

$$p_i = 1 - \frac{2R_g\mu^{n_i}}{1 + 2R_g\mu^{n_i}} = \frac{1}{1 + 2R_g\mu^{n_i}} \tag{21.3.20}$$

According to the exclusionary relationship between aggressive and conservative states, the probability q_i of the trading agent a_i entering a conservative state has the following results:

$$q_i = \frac{2R_g\mu^{n_i}}{1 + 2R_g\mu^{n_i}} \tag{21.3.21}$$

Substitute (21.3.20) and (21.3.21) into (21.3.1) to get:

$$Q_t = \sum_1^N \frac{1}{1 + 2R_i\mu^{n_i}} \sum_1^N \frac{2R_j\mu^{n_j}}{1 + 2R_j\mu^{n_j}} \tag{21.3.22}$$

To simplify the notation, in (21.3.22), R_i represents the aggressive state return risk coefficient of the trading agent a_i; R_j represents the aggressive state return risk coefficient of the trading agent a_j; n_i represents the number of aggressive agents on the state synergy set of the trading agent a_i; n_j represents the number of aggressive agents on the state synergy set of the trading agent a_j.

Expand (21.3.22) to get:

$$\begin{aligned} Q_t &= \sum_i \sum_j \frac{2R_j\mu^{n_j}}{(1 + 2R_i\mu^{n_i})(1 + 2R_j\mu^{n_j})} \\ &= \sum_i \sum_j \frac{2R_j\mu^{n_j}}{1 + 2R_i\mu^{n_i} + 2R_j\mu^{n_j} + 4R_iR_j\mu^{n_i+n_j}} \end{aligned} \tag{21.3.23}$$

Substitute (21.3.23) into formula (21.3.12) to get:

$$Syn_t = 1 - \frac{4}{N^2} \sum_i \sum_j \frac{2R_j\mu^{n_j}}{1 + 2R_i\mu^{n_i} + 2R_j\mu^{n_j} + 4R_iR_j\mu^{n_i+n_j}} \tag{21.3.24}$$

A quantitative relationship between the trading state synchronization index and two important parameters, the return risk coefficient and the risk filtering factor, is built as per (21.3.24). Trading agents are distributed in different communities on the trading network, and the trading environment of each community is vastly different, forming a diverse trading ecosystem in the trading system. These decision parameters continue to evolve with the progress of trading activities, thereby driving the trading state synchronization index to oscillate repeatedly in the interval [0, 1].

Equation (21.3.24) not only reveals the evolution mechanism of the trading state synchronization index but also provides a calculation method for the trading state synchronization index, providing us with an effective way to understand and predict the evolution of economic cycles. We call (21.3.24) the economic cycle model of trading economics.

21.3.4 Working Mechanism of Economic Cycle Model

Each trading agent affects the rhythm of trading state synchronization in the trading network through its choice of trading state. When the risk filtering factors of all trading communities on the trading network are at a low level, the sum term in the cycle model (21.3.24) $\sum_i \sum_i \frac{2R_j\mu^{n_j}}{1+2R_i\mu^{n_i}+2R_j\mu^{n_j}+4R_iR_j\mu^{n_i+n_j}}$ immediately reaches its minimum value, thereby pushing up the trading state synchronization index of the trading system. From the perspective of dynamic evolution, when the risk filtering factor of the community $\mu^{n_j} \to 0$, there will be a result of $\sum_i \sum_j \frac{2R_j\mu^{n_j}}{1+2R_i\mu^{n_i}+2R_j\mu^{n_j}+4R_iR_j\mu^{n_i+n_j}} \to 0$, at this time the trading state synchronization index of the trading system $Syn_t \to 1$, that is, it tends to the maximum extreme value of the synchronization index *Syn*. In the state parameters of the trading system, the risk filtering factor and the return risk coefficient have a positive correlation. When $\mu^{n_j} \to 0$, it means that the trading environment is improving, and the return risk coefficient of the aggressive state R_j will correspondingly decrease.

When the return risk coefficient R_j rises above a certain critical value, the sum term of the synchronization index $\sum_i \sum_i \frac{2R_j\mu^{n_j}}{1+2R_i\mu^{n_i}+2R_j\mu^{n_j}+4R_iR_j\mu^{n_i+n_j}}$ will show a downward trend; due to the positive correlation between the return risk coefficient and the filtering factor, when the return risk coefficient R_j rises, the number of agents choosing the aggressive state in the trading community will inevitably decrease, and the risk factor μ^{n_j} will increase with the decrease in the number of demonstrative agents n. When the return risk coefficient R_j and the risk factor μ^{n_j} reach their maximum values respectively, the sum term $\sum_i \sum_j \frac{2R_j\mu^{n_j}}{1+2R_i\mu^{n_i}+2R_j\mu^{n_j}+4R_iR_j\mu^{n_i+n_j}}$ reaches its minimum value again, the trading state synchronization index *Syn* reaches its maximum value and approaches 1, that is $Syn_t \to 1$.

The above two situations appear at the two maximum points of the trading state synchronization index, corresponding to the two operating states of economic prosperity and depression. At the minimum point of the synchronization index *Syn*, it corresponds to the transition process between recession and recovery. At this time, the trading state distribution of the trading system meets the conditions $\sum_1^N p_i = \frac{N}{2}$, $\sum_1^N q_i = \frac{N}{2}$, the return risk coefficient R_j and the risk filtering factor μ^{n_j} are both in the middle value state, the situation differences of different trading communities are relatively large, and the state of trading agents presents a diverse distribution.

Because there is a certain degree of overlap between the state coordination sets of trading agents A_i^c, the same demonstrative agent may appear in the state coordination sets of multiple trading agents. This will lead to the demonstration effect $\sum_1^N n_i$. The situation is far greater than the number of demonstration agents. As can be seen from the cycle model (21.3.24), the demonstration effect plays a very important role in the evolutionary process of the trading system state, directly determining the speed of trade synchronization. Generally speaking, the higher the order of the trading agent, the greater the possibility of appearing on multiple state coordination sets, and the more obvious the spillover effect of trade state decisions. The higher

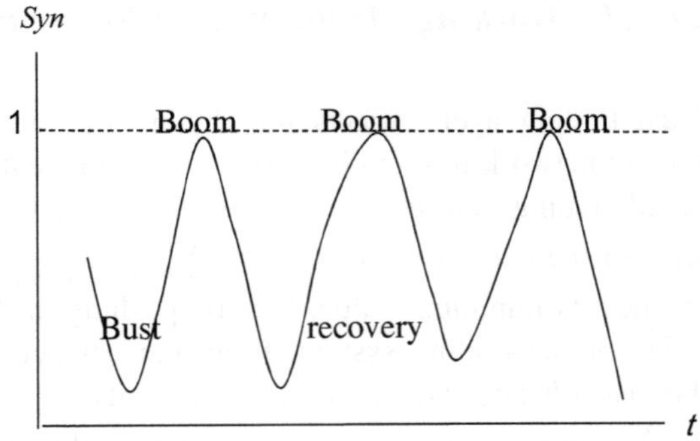

Fig. 21.3 The operation cycles of synchronization index

the order of the trade potential, the more important the role of the trading agent in the evolution of system synchronization. According to the above analysis, the trade synchronization index *Syn* fluctuates continuously under the promotion of mutual influence and interaction among trading agents, forming a recurring economic situation. The fluctuation frequency of the trade synchronization index *Syn* is higher than the fluctuation frequency of the economic cycle, and one economic cycle contains two *Syn* operation cycles (Fig. 21.3).

Bust and recovery each contain two stages: first is the deconstruction stage of the original synchronization state. Whether the trading system is in a prosperous state or a depressed state, the trading agents are in a highly synchronized state. The transition from prosperity to decline cannot be a uniform transition, but first some trading agents transition from aggressive to conservative. As the number of demonstration agents increases, the synchronization index of the trading system enters a downward channel. When the aggressive and conservative states each account for 50%, the synchronization index *Syn* reaches the lowest point, that is, $Syn_t = 0$. The trading system may stay at the lowest point of the synchronization index for a very short time, or even skip $Syn_t = 0$ point, directly transitioning from the aggressive state to the conservative state. When the trading agents gather in a conservative state, the trading system synchronization index *Syn* will enter an upward channel and eventually reach to a point completely controlled by the conservative state. It should be pointed out that the fluctuation of the trading synchronization index *Syn* does not follow a strict pattern, it may repeat in some processes; and it may also change direction before reaching the upper or lower stop point.

21.3.5 Relationship with the Main Economic Cycle Model

Fundamentally, the economic cycle is determined by the opportunities for profit and the amount of the risk in the trading system. Any factor that affects profit expectations and risk conditions may result in economic fluctuations or economic cycles, including the cyclical pattern of commercial bank credit, corporate inventory behavior, technological innovation cycles, political cycles, and agricultural cycles. In this sense, the economic cycle model of trading economics is highly compatible with other economic cycle models, and the difference lies only in entry points. The cycle model of trading economics takes the trading state as the entry point and looks for the rhythm of a large number of trading agents synchronizing. Other economic cycle models mostly take several major macroeconomic variables as entry points, revealing the transmission feedback mechanism of economic variables within the trading system through the building of relationships between different variables.

The economic cycle model of trading economics and the mainstream economic cycle model are of complimentary advantages to each other. The cycle model of trading economics is all-encompassing, and does not need to rely on too many premise assumptions, and has wide universality. The disadvantage is that it is relatively vague and difficult to perform statistical tests.

The advantage of mainstream economic cycle models lies in the clear logical relationships between economic variables, which are highly concrete, facilitating statistical testing and economic prosperity forecasting. However, the disadvantage is that the logical relationships between economic variables are all highly assumptive. Once these assumptions are not met, the usability of the model will be affected. For this reason, of the numerous economic cycle models, none can explain all economic cycle phenomena.

21.4 Effects of Monetary Policy Regulation

The basis for monetary policy to adjust economic cycles is the response in the state selection of trading agents, mainly influencing the behaviors of trading agents through three points of action, ultimately achieving the goal of adjusting economic cycles. The three points of action of monetary policy on trading agents are: first, the prior judgment value of the trading agent on the situation p. By influencing the confidence of trading agents, it changes their behaviors. This point of action is the expected point of action of monetary policy; second, the return risk coefficient R_g. Monetary policy mainly expresses policy intentions by adjusting the money supply and the price of funds, which can directly affect the value of the return risk coefficient R_g. This point of action is the trading opportunity point of action of monetary policy; third, the risk filtering factor μ^n. Monetary policy adjusts the money supply and the price of funds to create a specific trading atmosphere. Whether it is a loose monetary policy or a tight monetary policy, it will significantly change the value of the risk filtering factor in the trading environment. This point of action is the trading environment point of action of monetary policy.

Next, we will analyze the working mechanisms of the three points of action of monetary policy. In the modern trading system, all trading activities must be completed with the help of a monetary medium. Money is the most direct and widespread factor affecting trading status. We might as well assume that all trading

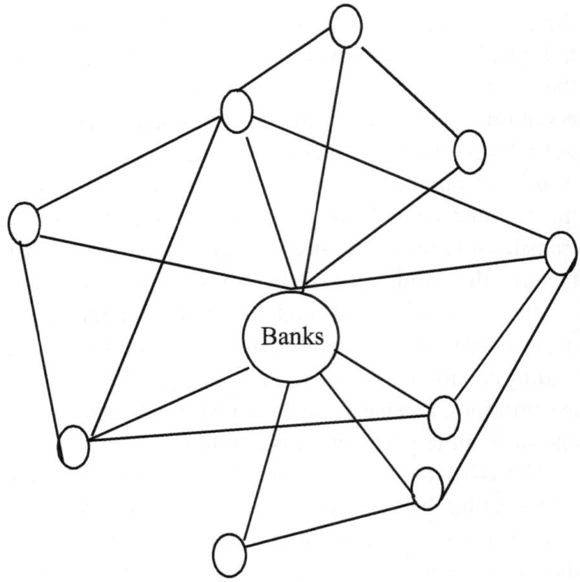

Fig. 21.4 The network diagram of modern trading system

agents in the trading system have trading links with banks, and banks are at the center of the trading network, forming the following network diagram (Fig. 21.4).

The central bank has absolute influence over commercial banks. When trading agents receive news of monetary policy from the central bank, whether it is to ease or tighten monetary policy, its impact far exceeds the influence of any other trading agent. The first is the impact on the prior probability of trading agents *p*. Of course, the prior probability of trading agents *p* does not come out of thin air, it needs to be gradually established through multiple confirmations, and there is a mechanism for mutual reinforcement between the two (Fig. 21.5).

From the announcement of the central bank's monetary policy to the adjustment of the prior probability of trading agents *p*, the public credibility of the central bank plays a crucial role. If the central bank lacks the necessary public credibility, it will be difficult to gather public expectations, and the effect of monetary policy will be discounted. In group games, whether a group can form an expectation of limit point is a key factor affecting the strategy choice of trading agents. Therefore, the central bank needs to continuously strengthen its credibility in the public to play a role in the confidence point of action of trading agents.

The credibility of a central bank is not solely the result of its own actions, but is also closely related to the compactness of the trading system. The higher the

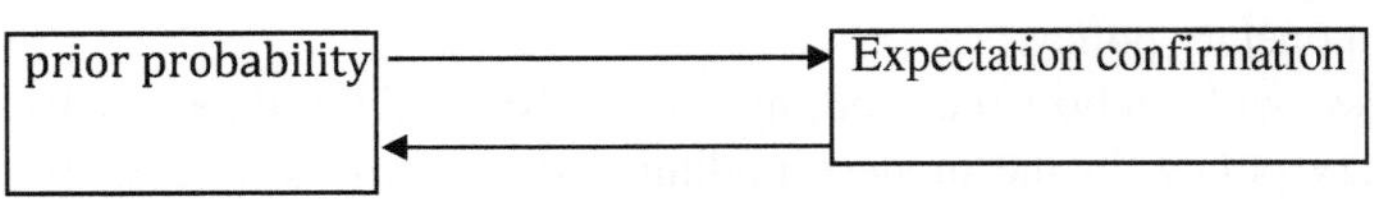

Fig. 21.5 The formulation of the prior probability

compactness of the trading system, the stronger the interconnection between trading agents, the easier it is to form limit point expectation, and the easier it is for monetary policy to take effect through these points. If the trading system is still in a stage of development with low compactness, the connections between trading agents are relatively loose, and it takes a longer time to form limit point expectation. In this case, the effects of monetary policy will not be very significant. The lag in the transmission of monetary policy lasts longer, the causal relationship between policy and effect is more ambiguous, and it is difficult for the central bank to establish sufficient credibility among the public. When monetary policy becomes more relaxed, commercial banks have abundant funds and lower funding costs. Driven by the profit motive, the loan threshold set by commercial banks will correspondingly lower down, loan interest rates will fall, the implementation cost of expansion strategies $C(\Delta S_i)$ will show a downward trend, prompting the return-risk ratio R_g to decrease. As can be seen from trading Eq. (20.2.1), the probability of trading agents choosing an aggressive stance increases. In modern trading systems, liquidity constraints are the main trading constraints. When monetary policy becomes more relaxed, commercial banks will have more abundant credit funds to increase the supply of funds. After trading agents receive liquidity support from commercial banks, their desire to trade increases. When more trading agents in the community start to tread the waters, the risk filtering factor μ^n enters a rapid decline channel. The three effect points of monetary policy are interrelated and mutually corroborative. Only when the functions of the three effect points are simultaneously in play can monetary policy achieve significant effects. However, this does not mean that the three fulcrums of monetary policy have completely equal status. In fact, the expectation effect point plays a key role in the transmission mechanism of monetary policy. Without the support of the expectation effect point, monetary policy can only work through the penetration mechanism of the trading network, and the policy effect not only has a longer lag, but also has a great randomness. This shows that the effectiveness of monetary policy must be based on public credibility. It requires not only the efforts of the central bank itself, but also the conditions provided by the trading system. Both are indispensable.

Notes

1. Song Yuhua (2007) Theory and Empirical Research of world Economic cycle, The Commercial Press, Beijing, p 7.
2. Song Yuhua (2007) Theory and Empirical Research of world Economic cycle, The Commercial Press, Beijing, p 1.
3. David Romer (1999) Advanced Macroeconomics (Trans: Su Jian), The Commercial Press, Beijing, p 198.
4. John H. Holland (2000) Hidden Order: Adaptability Creates Complexity (Trans: Zhou Xiaomu, Han Hui), Shanghai Science and Technology Education Press, Shanghai, p 15–23 (in Chinese).
5. Shen Huasong (2012) Economics after the Crisis, Southwest University of Finance and Economics Press, p 153.

Chapter 22
Economic Growth Model

Economic growth is a concomitant of the evolution of the trading system. The essence of economic growth is the result of the expansion of the scale of the trading network and the densification of its structure. Any factors that prompt the expansion of the trading network and the deepening of its connotation will trigger economic growth.

22.1 Review of Economic Growth Theory

Economic growth has always been a core issue in economic theory. The theories from Adam Smith to Alfred Marshall all contain thoughts and concepts about economic growth. In Adam Smith's *The Wealth of Nations*, division of labor and technological progress are the keys for a country to becoming wealthy, thus outlining the basic ideas of classical economics about economic growth. In Alfred Marshall's *Principles of Economics*, supply and demand determine prices, and prices guide demand and supply to achieve equilibrium, forming the underlying logic of the theory. The output of enterprises depends not only on the desire to produce but also on the production capacity; and the production capacity is determined by the stock of production factors—including land, labor, and capital. This forms the basic concept of neoclassical economics about economic growth. Today's mainstream economics still follows this logic.

The starting point of modern economic growth theory can be traced back to the 1920s, specifically in 1928 when the British genius mathematician and economist Ramsey published an article titled *A Mathematical Theory of Saving*in the *Economic Journal*.[1] In this paper, Ramsey used family intertemporal consumption and saving behavior as the starting point of analysis, linking interest rates, wage rates, population growth rates, discount rates, and corporate investment and employment behavior, and established a complete economic operation model under equilibrium conditions.

Z. Wang, *Trading Economics*, Contributions to Economics,
https://doi.org/10.1007/978-981-99-9875-3_22

The model constructed by Ramsey occupies a very important position in subsequent economic growth theory, but at that time it did not really clearly present an economic growth model, and the focus of the study was not on economic growth. In fact, before Keynes, economists believed that employment and growth were problems that market could solve on its own, and there was no need for special research. This can be also confirmed from the chapter layout of Adam Smith's "The Wealth of Nations" and Marshall's "Principles of Economics". Both classic works discussed the topic of wealth accumulation in detail, but neither had a special chapter for discussing economic growth. With the spread of the Great Depression in the 1930s, economists realized that the trading system was not perfect and that the government needed to play an active regulatory role in it.

In the history of economic theory development, the first economist to explicitly construct an economic growth model was Roy Forbes Harrod. In 1939, Harrod published a paper on "The Dynamic Theory", for the first time in history explicitly proposing the concept of economic growth. In 1948, he published "An Introduction to Dynamic Economics", systematically expounding the theory of economic growth. Harrod focused on the mechanism of capital accumulation and the relationship between capital and output. He proposed three concepts of economic growth, namely the actual growth rate, the warranted growth rate, and the natural growth rate. The actual growth rate is the growth rate achieved by the trading system, Harrod believes that actual growth is not a satisfactory growth situation; the warranted growth rate is the growth rate that ensures that the newly increased capital can be fully utilized and can ensure long-term stable equilibrium growth; the natural growth rate refers to the economic growth rate brought about by population growth and technological progress.

After Harrod, American economist Evsey David Domar published a paper titled "Expansion and Employment" in 1947, proposing an economic growth model roughly similar to Harrod's. Therefore, the Harrod growth model is also known as the Harrod-Domar growth model.

As the shadow of the Great Depression gradually dissipated, neoclassical theory returned to the center stage of mainstream economics. In terms of growth theory, neoclassical models began to emerge in the mid-to-late 1950s. In 1956, American economist Robert Solow and Australian economist Trevor Swan proposed an economic growth model in the style of neoclassical economics, known to the world as the Solow-Swan model. The typical feature of the Solow-Swan model is to use the production function as a tool, taking capital, labor, and technological progress as the three basic elements driving economic growth. In the Solow-Swan model, the production function is a first-order homogeneous concave function, reflecting the characteristic of diminishing marginal returns.

The Solow-Swan model is the first standard neoclassical growth model in history and is still frequently used today. The output function in the Solow-Swan model is $y = Ak^{\alpha}$, where y is the per capita output value, k is the per capita capital stock, and A represents technological progress. Because the Solow-Swan model requires the production function to satisfy the property of a concave function, the result is that the economic growth rate tends to 0 when the per capita capital stock increases, that is,

$\frac{dy}{dt} = A\alpha k^{\alpha-1}$, because $\alpha < 1, \lim \frac{dy}{dt} = \lim A\alpha k^{-(1-\alpha)} \to 0$. This shows that under the growth mechanism of the Solow-Swan model, the trading system cannot achieve long-term sustained economic growth solely by relying on the endogenous power of capital accumulation, and must rely on the power of technological progress. The technological progress variable A is an exogenous variable of the system, therefore, the Solow-Swan model is also classified as exogenous growth model.

Entering the 1980s, following Paul Romer and Robert Lucas, economists devoted themselves to the study of endogenous growth models. From the exogenous growth model to the endogenous model, the explanatory power of the model has been continuously enhanced, but its basic logical framework has not fundamentally changed, that is, economic growth is the process of input and output.

22.2 The Essence of Economic Growth

The approach to get to the essence of economic growth matters to not only the building of growth model, but also to the choice of the policy that spurs economic growth. In this sense, the trading economics is different from the mainstream economics.

22.2.1 The Growth from Trading Economics' Perspective

Economic growth refers to the process by which the trading system achieves a continuous increase in total value over a certain length of time.

As mainstream economics maintain, economic growth is the crystal of both family and business activities, and the aggregate value created by many trading agents. However, trading economics holds that economic growth results from the expansion of trading networks, rather than the simple superposition of non-trading agents' behaviors.

There are two ways to achieve the expansion of the trading network, namely, extension expansion and connotation deepening. The so-called extension expansion includes the increase in the capacity of the trading network and the expansion of the trading base. The result of extension expansion is to attract more trading agents to the network. Trading is the activity of trading agents, and the increase in trading agents will inevitably lead to more trading activities. The trading base is the carrier of trading, and the larger the scale of the trading base, the larger the scale of trading activities. The deepening of the connotation of the trading network is manifested as the improvement of trading efficiency, the acceleration of network circulation, and the increase in the density of the trading network. The deepening of the connotation of the trading network is the process of carrying more trading activities under the premise of a given network scale.

Based on the above understanding, we start from trading activities and analyze the trading network from two dimensions: extension and connotation. In terms of specific methods, the focus is on the cyclical nature of the trading network. Trading triggers the transfer of goods and funds between different agents, which is broadly referred to as trading circulation. Any factor that facilitates the circulation of the trading network is considered to have a positive effect on economic growth; if it goes against this, it will hinder economic growth.

In short, the expansion of the trading network is reflected in three dimensions: trading network efficiency, trading network structure, and trading network scale. The efficiency indicators of the trading network include two, namely transaction efficiency and trading circulation rate. The significance of trading efficiency for economic growth is self-evident. Under the same trading scale, the higher the trading efficiency, the more added value obtained, and the stronger the economic growth. The trading circulation rate reflects the smoothness of the trading circulation path. The smaller the resistance in the process of trading network circulation, and the more active the trading. Under the condition of constant trading efficiency, the higher the circulation rate, the faster the economic growth.

The structure of the trading network is very complex, but from the perspective of economic growth, the density of the trading network is the most important indicator. It not only shows the overall state of the network structure but also reflects the evolution intensity of the social division of labor in the trading system. Division of labor is the basis of trading. The more developed the division of labor, the more frequent the trading activities, the closer the interdependence between trading agents, the more complex the interaction mechanism between trading agents, the more significant the network effect, and the larger the trading scale.

The scale indicators of the trading network mainly include two dimensions: network capacity and trading base. The relationship between the capacity of the trading network and economic growth is relatively easy to understand. All economic activities are human activities and cannot be separated from the participation of trading agents. At a given technological level, the number of trading agents determines the maximum trading limit that the trading network can stimulate. The more trading agents, the larger the maximum trading limit of the trading system, and the greater the potential for economic growth. The trading base has a synergistic relationship with the scale of economic output. Generally speaking, the larger the scale of the trading base, the larger the total economic output. Whether it is a trading agent or a trading base, they are the basis for the operation of the trading network. The size of the network capacity and the trading base determines the scale at which the trading system carries out trading activities.

When we talk about the scale of the trading network, the total population is an important related indicator. This does not mean that a large population will definitely bring about economic development. Economic development is the result of many factors working together. Without any link, economic growth cannot be achieved. The population can only form the power of economic growth when it coexists with matching capital and a system compatible with economic growth. In the 100 years from 1800 to 1900, Germany's population did not grow on a large scale, but the economy achieved substantial growth, thus becoming the leader of the industrial revolution on the European continent after the UK. The reason is obviously not the population scale but the optimization of the trading network structure and the improvement of trading efficiency. During this period, the urbanization speed in Germany accelerated, and the number of towns increased from 4 to 50. Within a region, the change from the past scattered population to the concentrated population has caused a series of structural changes in the trading network. With the decrease in trading costs and the increase in information flow, trading efficiency is bound to improve; the gathering of the population in a region will inevitably lead to the deepening of social division of labor and the increase in the density of the trading network. In addition, urbanization has created far more trading opportunities than rural markets, stimulating the rapid growth of the number of enterprises. Taking bars and cafes as an example, under the promotion of urbanization, the number of bars and cafes in British and French towns has exploded. This phenomenon is impossible in scattered rural areas.[2]

There is a critical point effect in network capacity. A fascinating phenomenon is that only when the network capacity exceeds a certain critical value, a massive aggregation effect will occur. This is like nuclear fission, where the chain reaction only begins after the number of uranium atoms reaches a critical value. In fact, the trading system is a special action system, and capacity is the scale of this action system. Without sufficient scale support, division of labor not only fails to improve efficiency but also causes resource waste. This issue has been of concern since the time of Adam Smith. Adam Smith discussed this in *The Wealth of Nations*: "as it is the power of exchanging that give s occasion to the division of labour, so the extent of this division must always be limited by the extent of that power, or, in other words, by the extent of the market. When the market is very small, no person can have any encouragement to dedicate himself entirely to one employment, for want of the power to exchange all that surplus part of the produce of his own labour. There are some sorts of industry, even of the lowest kind, which can be carried on nowhere but in a great town. A porter, for example, can find employment and subsistence in no other place. A village is by much too narrow a sphere for him; even an ordinary market town is scarce large enough to afford him constant occupation."[3]

22.2.2 Growth Policies of Trading Economics

Based on the cognition of the nature of economic growth, trading economics is clearly differentiated from mainstream economics in terms of policy choices to promote economic growth. In the theoretical system of mainstream economics, the complex internal structure of the trading system and the interactions between the trading agents are ignored, which leads to the oversimplification of the policy logic of mainstream economics, and the policy choices are mainly focused on the behavioral induction of the trading agents, focusing on the aggregate effect and ignoring the structural problems. When there is a supply surplus, mainstream economics usually chooses policies to stimulate family consumption, advocating that the central banks lower interest rates to curb family savings, financial subsidies for consumption or reduction of specific tax rates. When there is an imbalance between supply and demand and the economy is overheating, mainstream economics advocates raising interest rates to increase the opportunity cost of consumption and discourage corporate investment expansion.

Trading economics opts for a completely different logic route, with policies focusing on both the integrity of the trading network and the stability of the cycle. When the economy is facing downward pressure, trading economics proposes first diagnosing the specific manifestations of the trading system problems, and then address the issues with the right solutions. Taking the current economic situation in China as an example, after three years of covid-19 shocks, corporate balance sheets have been severely damaged and family cash flows have shrunk. Under such circumstances, it is difficult to achieve the expected effect if the radical macroeconomic policies of increasing money supply and lowering bank credit rates is adopted. When the structure of the trading network is damaged, almost all trading agents are strongly constrained by the reduced liquidity of assets, and trading agents are forced to choose a conservative strategy and are unable to respond to an aggressive policy. It is imperative to find severely damaged trading network pivot firms as soon as possible and help them repair their balance sheets in order to stop the trading network structure from spiraling down. The bailed-out pivot firms will provide liquidity to the entire network through the penetration function of the trading network. This process of liquidity diffusion has a reliable trading background and is far more effective than the liquidity released directly by the central bank.

When there is an imbalance between supply and demand while the economy is overheating, the policy choice of trading economics is first to identify the higher-order trading loops of the trading system and choose to block the pathway of continued strengthening of the trading loops at minimal policy cost. China experienced a round of economic overheating from 2009 to 2012, with a growth rate of 9.4% in 2009, accelerating further to 10.6% in 2010, and falling back slightly to a still high 9.6% in 2011. As the economic growth rate exceeded the capacity of the trading system, prices began to rise rapidly, and the signs of economic overheating were ubiquitous. The direct cause of this round of economic overheating was that, in the face of the financial tsunami that raged in 2008, the Chinese government adopted a hedging policy in the fourth quarter of that year to increase fiscal investment and money and credit, by launching ten measures to promote economic growth, which totaled 4 trillion yuan. Stimulated by a series of loose policies, the real estate market entered into a state of rapid expansion, forming a large equivalent trading ring consisting of the real estate, the financial, building materials, home appliance, home furnishing industry with the real estate market at the core. Therefore, if speculation in the real estate market could be effectively stopped, the economic overheating would cool down. Trading economics suggests that the most effective measure to stop real estate speculation is to levy a profits tax on real estate trading. Unfortunately, this policy was not adopted at the time, instead, a dual monetary and fiscal tightening policy was adopted. Although the overheated economy was cooled down quickly, the long-tail effect of the policy cast an indelible shadow on China's economic growth prospects. Compared with mainstream economics, trading economics has two salient features in its policy choices: first, taking a holistic view is an important feature of trading economics policy. Trading economics takes upholding the integrity of the trading network and the stability of the cycle as the basic goal of its policy formulation. It focuses on the underlying correlation of the trading system, and leverages the mutual effect each trading agents imposes to multiply the best impact policies an bring. secondly, structuralizing is another prominent feature of the policy of trading economics. Trading economics pays attention to the internal structure of the trading system, and when problems arise in the trading system, it advocates that the specific structural points and links of the problems should be located first, so as to prescribe the right medication and apply the right policy precisely.

22.3 Economic Growth Model

Economic growth is supported by the trading network, achieved through internal circulation and external circulation. The value created by the trading system at time step t can be decomposed into two parts, namely the value realized by the internal circulation and the value realized by the external circulation. The so-called internal circulation refers to the trading activities generated by the internal agents of the trading system, manifested as domestic trade and its production activities; the external circulation refers to the trading activities generated by the internal agents of the trading system and the external agents of the trading system, manifested as international trade and its related production activities. Therefore, Y_t can be expressed as the sum of the two parts, namely:

$$Y_t = Y_t^1 + Y_t^2 \tag{22.3.1}$$

In (22.3.1), Y_t^1 represents the value realized by the internal circulation, Y_t^2 represents the value realized by the external circulation.

Y_t^1 can be calculated from the trading volume realized by the trading network at a given trading efficiency level, namely:

$$Y_t^1 = \mu_t \times T_t \tag{22.3.2}$$

In (22.3.2), T_t represents the trading volume realized by the trading system at time step t, μ is the trading efficiency of the trading system. According to the analysis in the previous section, the ability of the trading system to realize transactions is directly related to the capacity of the trading system, the trading base, the circulation rate of the trading network, and the density of the trading network. We can regard the trading volume T_t as a function of the above four independent variables, that is, the trading function:

$$T_t = T(N_t, M_t, \theta_t, \omega_t) \tag{22.3.3}$$

In the trading function (22.3.3), N represents the capacity of the trading system, M represents the trading base of the trading system, ω represents the density of the trading network, θ represents the circulation rate of the trading network.

As can be seen from the previous analysis, the trading volume function T has a positive correlation with the independent variables N, M, θ, and ω:

$$\frac{\partial T_t}{\partial N_t} > 0, \quad \frac{\partial T_t}{\partial M_t} > 0, \quad \frac{\partial T_t}{\partial \theta_t} > 0, \quad \frac{\partial T_t}{\partial \omega_t} > 0 \tag{22.3.4}$$

In the trading system, the trading base is composed of two parts, one part is produced within the trading system, that is, the endogenous base, denoted as M_t^1; the other part comes from trading outside the trading system, that is, the exogenous base, denoted as M_t^2. The sum of the two parts constitutes the trading base of the trading system.

$$M_t = M_t^1 + M_t^2 \tag{22.3.5}$$

For the external circulation value of the trading system Y_t^2, the statistical meaning is the net export value, which is mainly determined by two factors: firstly, the endogenous base of the trading system M_t^1 and the exogenous base M_t^2; the amount of export value depends on whether there is a sufficiently large endogenous trading base M_t^1, only when there are enough tradable goods, can the corresponding trade volume be created; the situation of imports is the same, the exogenous base M_t^2 is the basis for imports. While the trading base is not the only determinant of the external circulation value Y_t^2, it also needs to be combined with the comparison of commodity prices inside and outside the trading system, the difference in prices is reflected in the effective exchange rate R_t. The cheaper the local currency, the higher the effective exchange rate R_t, the more competitive domestic goods are, and the weaker the competitiveness of foreign goods. Therefore, the external circulation value Y_t^2 can be written in the following function form:

$$Y_t^2 = U\left(M_t^1, M_t^2, R_t\right) \tag{22.3.6}$$

U represents the external circulation function, also known as the trade function. There is the following derivative relationship with the independent variables:

$$\frac{\partial U}{\partial M_t^1} > 0, \quad \frac{\partial U}{\partial M_t^2} < 0, \quad \frac{\partial U}{\partial R_t} > 0 \tag{22.3.7}$$

According to the relationship expressed by (22.3.3) and (22.3.6), we get the output function of the trading system:

$$Y_t = \mu_t \times T(N, M_t, \theta_t, \omega_t) + U\left(M_t^1, M_t^2, R_t\right) \tag{22.3.8}$$

Let: $Y_{t+1} - Y_t = \Delta Y$

$$\because \quad \Delta Y = \frac{\Delta Y}{(t+1)-t} = \frac{\Delta Y}{\Delta t}$$
$$\frac{\Delta Y}{\Delta t} \cong \frac{dY}{dt}$$
$$\therefore \quad \Delta Y \cong \frac{dY}{dt} \tag{22.3.9}$$

According to (22.3.8) we get:

$$\frac{dY_t}{dt} = \mu_t \times \left[\frac{\partial T}{\partial N_t}\frac{dN_t}{dt} + \frac{\partial T}{\partial M_t}\frac{dM_t}{dt} + \frac{\partial T}{\partial \theta_t}\frac{d\theta_t}{dt} + \frac{\partial T}{\partial \omega_t}\frac{d\omega_t}{dt}\right] + \frac{d\mu_t}{dt} \times T_t + \frac{\partial U}{\partial M_t^1}\frac{dM_t^1}{dt} + \frac{\partial U}{\partial M_t^2}\frac{dM_t^2}{dt} + \frac{\partial U}{\partial R_t}\frac{dR_t}{dt} \tag{22.3.10}$$

Let: $Gr_t = \frac{\Delta Y}{Y_t}$
From (22.3.9) and (22.3.10) we get:

$$Gr_t = \frac{1}{Y_t} \times \left\{\mu_t\left[\frac{\partial T}{\partial N_t}\frac{dN_t}{dt} + \frac{\partial T}{\partial M_t}\frac{dM_t}{dt} + \frac{\partial T}{\partial \theta_t}\frac{d\theta_t}{dt} + \frac{\partial T}{\partial \omega_t}\frac{d\omega_t}{dt}\right] + \frac{d\mu_t}{dt} \times T_t + \frac{\partial U}{\partial M_t^1}\frac{dM_t^1}{dt} + \frac{\partial U}{\partial M_t^2}\frac{dM_t^2}{dt} + \frac{\partial U}{\partial R_t}\frac{dR_t}{dt}\right\} \tag{22.3.11}$$

In order to obtain an economic growth formula with clear meaning, we need to further organize based on (22.3.11).

$$\because \quad \frac{dN}{dt} \approx \frac{\Delta N_t}{(t+1)-t} \tag{22.3.12}$$

Multiply both sides of (22.3.12) by $\frac{1}{N_t}$ to get:

$$\frac{1}{N_t}\frac{dN_t}{dt} = \frac{\Delta N}{N_t} \tag{22.3.13}$$

Let: $r_N = \frac{\Delta N}{N_t}$
Then: $\frac{1}{N_t}\frac{dN_t}{dt} = r_N$

$$\therefore \quad \frac{dN_t}{dt} = r_N \times N_t \tag{22.3.14}$$

Similarly:

$$\frac{dM_t}{dt} = r_M \times M_t \tag{22.3.15}$$

$$\frac{d\theta_t}{dt} = r_\theta \times \theta_t \tag{22.3.16}$$

$$\frac{d\omega_t}{dt} = r_\omega \times \omega_t \tag{22.3.17}$$

$$\frac{dM_t^1}{dt} = r_{M^1} \times M_t^1 \tag{22.3.18}$$

$$\frac{dM_t^2}{dt} = r_{M^2} \times M_t^2 \tag{22.3.19}$$

$$\frac{dR_t}{dt} = r_R \times R_t \tag{22.3.20}$$

Substitute (22.3.14)–(22.3.20) into (22.3.11) to get:

$$\begin{aligned} Gr_t = \frac{1}{Y_t} \times \Bigg\{ \mu_t \left[\frac{\partial T}{\partial N_t} N_t r_N + \frac{\partial T}{\partial M_t} M_t r_M + \frac{\partial T}{\partial \theta_t} \theta_t r_\theta + \frac{\partial T}{\partial \omega_t} \omega_t r_\omega \right] + \frac{d\mu}{dt} \times T_t \\ + \frac{\partial U}{\partial M_t^1} M_t^1 r_{M^1} + \frac{\partial U}{\partial M_t^2} M_t^2 r_{M^2} + \frac{\partial U}{\partial R_t} R_t r_R \Bigg\} \end{aligned} \tag{22.3.21}$$

$\frac{\partial T}{\partial N_t} \frac{N_t}{T}$ is the elasticity of the trading function T to the system capacity N_t, denoted as $k_N = \frac{\partial T}{\partial N_t} \frac{N_t}{T}$

$$\because \quad \frac{T_t}{Y_t} \cong \frac{1}{\mu_t}$$

$$\therefore \quad \frac{\partial T}{\partial N_t} \frac{N_t}{Y_t} = \frac{\partial T}{\partial N_t} \frac{N_t}{T_t} \frac{T_t}{Y_t} = \frac{k_N}{\mu_t} \tag{22.3.22}$$

Similarly, we can calculate the elasticity relationships of several other variables:

$$\frac{\partial T}{\partial M_t} \frac{M_t}{Y_t} = \frac{k_M}{\mu_t} \tag{22.3.23}$$

$$\frac{\partial T}{\partial \theta_t} \frac{\theta_t}{Y_t} = \frac{k_\theta}{\mu_t} \tag{22.3.24}$$

$$\frac{\partial T}{\partial \omega_t} \frac{\omega_t}{Y_t} = \frac{k_\omega}{\mu_t} \tag{22.3.25}$$

$\frac{U}{Y_t}$ reflects the degree of economic dependence on the outside, we call it the degree of economic dependence on the outside, represented by λ

$$\frac{\partial U}{\partial M_t^1}\frac{M_t^1}{Y_t} = \lambda k_{M^1} \tag{22.3.26}$$

$$\frac{\partial U}{\partial M_t^2}\frac{M_t^2}{Y_t} = \lambda k_{M^2} \tag{22.3.27}$$

$$\frac{\partial U}{\partial R_t}\frac{R_t}{Y_t} = \lambda k_R \tag{22.3.28}$$

From this, we obtain the elasticity coefficients of seven aspects of the trading system k_N, k_M, k_{M^1}, k_{M^2}, $k_\theta k_\omega$, k_R. As the trading system evolves, these elasticity coefficients are also adjusting and changing.

Substitute (22.3.22)–(22.3.28) into the growth formula (22.3.21):

$$\begin{aligned} Gr_t = {} & k_N r_N + k_M r_M + k_\theta r_\theta + k_\omega r_\omega \\ & + \frac{1}{\mu_t}\frac{d\mu_t}{dt} + \lambda(k_{M^1} r_{M^1} + k_{M^2} r_{M^2} + k_R r_R) \end{aligned} \tag{22.3.29}$$

$$\because \quad \frac{1}{\mu}\frac{d\mu}{dt} \cong \frac{\Delta\mu}{\mu} = r_\mu \tag{22.3.30}$$

Substitute (22.3.30) into (22.3.29) to get:

$$\begin{aligned} Gr_t = {} & k_N r_N + k_M r_M + k_\theta r_\theta + k_\omega r_\omega \\ & + r_\mu + \lambda(k_{M^1} r_{M^1} + k_{M^2} r_{M^2} + k_R r_R) \end{aligned} \tag{22.3.31}$$

Formula (22.3.31) reflects the understanding of economic growth in trading economics, with the key takeaway that economic growth is the result of the expansion of the trading network scale and the deepening of the internal structure. To further simplify the formula, we derive the short-term and the long-term economic growth model based on this; and according to the characteristics of the economic development stage, we derive the growth model in the early stage of economic development and the growth model in the later stage of economic development.

In model (22.3.31), the net exports calculated through the trade function are nominal values that include price factors. To maintain consistency, when calculating the trading efficiency μ, nominal values need to be used, that is, $\mu = \frac{Y}{T}$ does not take comparable price into consideration. Hence, the growth rate obtained from this Gr is a nominal growth rate.

In economics, the key to defining time length is not by time itself, but by the structural parameter changes of the trading system. If the structural parameters of the system have undergone major changes, even if the time is short, short-term analysis methods cannot be used; on the contrary, during the stable period of economic development, although a long time has passed, yet the structural parameters of the system have not undergone major changes, and short-term analysis methods still apply for this case.

In the short-term view, the capacity of the trading system, the trading base, and the density of the trading network have not changed significantly, and the structural parameter values of the corresponding short-term model are as follows:

$$r_N \cong 0, \quad r_M \cong 0, \quad r_\omega \cong 0, \quad r_{M^1} \cong 0, \quad r_{M^2} \cong 0 \tag{22.3.32}$$

Unlike the five variables above, the trading turnover, effective exchange and trading efficiency are highly dynamic variables. The trading turnover rate is closely related to the expectations of the trading agents, and may also undergo major changes in a short period of time; so is the situation of the effective exchange, which is not only affected by the supply and demand relationship of different currencies, but also closely related to the inflation rate of different trading systems, these factors all have highly dynamic characteristics. Trading efficiency is also a very active variable. The expectations of the trading agents, the state of the trading, and whether there is a bubble phenomenon in the trading system, etc., will affect the value of trading efficiency. Trading efficiency has a very close relationship with the trading environment.

Substituting relation (22.3.32) into growth model (22.3.31), we can obtain the short-term growth model:

$$Gr_t = k_\theta r_\theta + r_\mu + \lambda k_R r_R \tag{22.3.33}$$

Looking at the structure of the short-term economic growth model, there are many factors that can affect economic growth, including the trading cycle rate, the elasticity coefficient of the trading system to changes in the trading cycle rate, exchange rate changes, and fluctuations in trading efficiency. Overall, the main cause of short-term economic fluctuations comes from monetary factors.

In the short term, increasing the trading cycle rate is an effective way to stimulate economic growth. There are many ways to increase the trading cycle rate, including loose monetary policy, proactive fiscal policy, improved the business environment, and infrastructure. When monetary policy is loose, the liquidity constraints of the trading agents are relaxed, financing costs are reduced, and expected returns increase, all of which can effectively increase the trading cycle rate. Fiscal policy can also effectively increase the trading cycle rate. There are many tools available for fiscal policy, which can either provide policy dividends for specific industries or opt for inclusive policies, such as tax reduction policies. Whether it is targeted fiscal policy or inclusive fiscal policy, it can ultimately increase the trading cycle rate through the transmission and diffusion of the trading network. Social security also has a significant impact on the trading cycle rate. A good social security system can reduce the worries of family residents and increase the marginal propensity to consume.

In the short term, currency depreciation is beneficial to the external economic cycle, but only if the depreciation of the exchange rate of the local currency reduces the price of the country's commodities while at the same time activating the domestic cycle and the trading efficiency; otherwise, the depreciation of the local currency will bring about inflation rather than economic prosperity.

In the long term, some short-term fluctuation indicators of the trading system, such as the trading cycle rate θ, effective exchange rate R and trading efficiency μ, will fluctuate within a certain range, showing a relatively stable long-term trend. The trading cycle rate θ is influenced by short-term factors, but deeper information comes from the structural characteristics of the trading system, including the degree of perfection of the social security system, the degree of financialization, and cultural characteristics, etc., which are all key factors affecting the long-term level of the trading cycle rate θ; the situation of the effective exchange rate is the same. In the long term, the trend line of the effective exchange rate is determined by the characteristics of the economic structure and the monetary system. The key factors affecting the long-term level of the effective exchange rate mainly include whether the trading system is dominated by external circulation or internal circulation, the competitiveness of the economy in the world, and the mechanism of money creation. Although trading efficiency is very active in the short term, it is still closely related to the structure of the trading system in the long term, including the structure of the tertiary industry and the structure of the trading network chain. These factors all have relative stability.

Based on the above analysis, in the long-term economic growth model, we take the growth rate of the trading cycle rate and the effective exchange rate and trading efficiency as 0, that is:

$$r_\theta = 0, \quad r_R = 0, \quad r_\mu \cong 0 \tag{22.3.34}$$

Substitute (22.3.34) into the growth model (22.3.31) to get the long-term growth model:

$$Gr_t = k_N r_N + k_M r_M + k_\omega r_\omega + \lambda(k_{M^1} r_{M^1} + k_{M^2} r_{M^2}) \tag{22.3.35}$$

The long-term growth model reveals the driving force for long-term economic growth, which mainly include the growth of the trading system capacity, the expansion of the trading base, the deepening of division of labor, and the improvement of international division of labor. In fact, it is very difficult to ensure that the above variables continue to improve, for it requires continuous promotion of technological innovation, improvement of the business environment, and optimization of the distribution system, otherwise there will be trade-offs to make. For example, the progression of division of labor is the main way to increase the density of the trading network and the main means to increase trading efficiency, but with the deepening of social division of labor, family functions will inevitably be weakened, which will result in a decline in family fertility rates and an aging population structure. The secondary consequences of this are an increase in social risk aversion, a decline in entrepreneurial enthusiasm, and a contraction of the trading system capacity. With the contraction of the trading system capacity, market competition weakens, trading efficiency declines, and innovation intensity decreases. As can be seen, the path of economic growth is full of various traps, and only by sidestepping from these traps can the long-term economic growth be achieved.

Economic development is the result of the evolution of the trading system, and different stages of economic development show strong stage characteristics. For example, in the early stages of economic development, induced by economic growth expectations, a large number of new trading agents emerge, which is a prominent feature of the early stages of economic development; at the same time, financial repression is another prominent feature of the early stages of economic development. Against this background, the trading turnover rate usually remains at a low level, and a high savings rate is a common phenomenon in the early stages of economic development.

In the early stages of economic development, with the rapid development of the market, the division of labor evolves at an unprecedented speed, and the density of the trading network increases significantly; correspondingly, the trading base in the early stages of economic development will also undergo a rapid expansion process, while the trading efficiency will remain at a low level, with little change, and the economy as a whole shows extensive operation characteristics.

Based on the above analysis, we can get the changes in structural parameters in the early stages of economic development:

$$r_N > 0, \quad r_M > 0, \quad r_{M^1} > 0, \quad r_\theta \cong 0, \quad r_\mu \cong 0 \tag{22.3.36}$$

From this, we can get the economic growth model in the early stages of economic development:

$$Gr_t = k_N r_N + k_M r_M + k_\omega r_\omega + \lambda(k_{M^1} r_{M^1} + k_{M^2} r_{M^2} + k_R r_R) \tag{22.3.37}$$

In the early stages of economic development, institutional obstacles are often the main factors hindering economic growth. Whether it is possible to stimulate the trading enthusiasm of trading agents through effective institutional reforms is the key to starting the wheel of economic growth. Once the willingness of trading agents to trade is mobilized, more trading agents will emerge and enter the mode of rapid expansion of the trading system. With the expansion of the trading system capacity, the process of market division of labor will spontaneously put into action, the density of the trading network will continue to increase, and the trading base will also grow.

In the early stages of economic development, trade policy plays a very important role. In order to accelerate economic growth, a one-way trade strategy of encouraging exports and restricting imports is usually adopted. Under this circumstance, the initial growth equation can have the following simplified structure:

$$Gr_t = k_N r_N + k_M r_M + k_\omega r_\omega + \lambda(k_{M^1} r_{M^1} + k_R r_R) \tag{22.3.38}$$

In the later stages of economic development, the trading system enters a mature state, and the change in the density of the trading network is relatively slow; due to the increasingly sophisticated financial system, the effective exchange rate is in a relatively stable state; in terms of the trading turnover rate, whether it is family agents or corporate agents, the trading mode is relatively mature, and the trading turnover rate is relatively stable; the trading efficiency is at a high and stable level. The main force driving economic growth comes from the expansion of the trading base driven by technological innovation. In the later stages of economic growth, there will be significant changes in the demographic structure, and the trading capacity based on the demographics will become a key constraint on economic growth. In the later stages of economic development, the basic characteristics of structural parameters are as follows:

$$r_\omega \cong 0, \quad r_\theta \cong 0, \quad r_R \cong 0, \quad r_\mu \cong 0 \tag{22.3.39}$$

The economic growth model for the later stages of economic development is obtained as follows:

$$Gr_t = k_N r_N + k_M r_M + \lambda(k_{M^1} r_{M^1} + k_{M^2} r_{M^2}) \tag{22.3.40}$$

After entering the mature stage of economic development, whether the capacity of the trading system can maintain growth should be placed in an important position among various policy objectives. The size and structure of the population are the basis for determining the capacity of the trading system. Even if the population remains unchanged or grows in size, if the age group of the population shows a rapid aging pattern, the momentum of economic growth will be greatly affected and it is very easy to fall into the trap of economic stagnation.

The above four economic growth models can be divided into two groups: short-term and long-term economic growth models in one group while early-stage s and late-stage economic development growth models in another group. The two groups of models are divided from two different dimensions, the two-term economic growth models mainly focus on the key choices on different term scales; the two development stage models focus on the prominent features presented at different stages of economic development. Whether it is the division standard or the summary of characteristics, it is empirical, and this is done merely for the convenience of application. In targeted analysis, we can summarize and set up according to the specific situation of the economy, and extract growth models that more accurately reflect the actual characteristics from the basic growth models.

22.4 Steady-State Economic Growth

In the Solow-Swan growth model of neoclassical economics, due to the condition of diminishing returns to capital added to the production function, under the dual effects of capital depreciation and labor growth, the per capita capital of the trading system eventually tends to an equilibrium point. At this equilibrium point, the growth of the trading system is completely subject to exogenous factors such as technological innovation and labor growth. In this state, the main economic variables of the trading system maintain proportional growth. Also, it is called the state steady-state growth.

The Solow-Swan model uses the most general production function, and the output value of the trading system at time step t $Y(t)$ satisfies the following relationship:

$$Y(t) = F(K, L) \tag{22.4.1}$$

The Solow-Swan model requires the above production function to satisfy the neoclassical conditions, which include three aspects: (1) the function has diminishing marginal returns to the two types of factor inputs: $\frac{\partial F}{\partial K} > 0$, $\frac{\partial^2 F}{\partial K^2} < 0; \frac{\partial F}{\partial L} > 0$, $\frac{\partial^2 F}{\partial L^2} < 0$; (2) the function satisfies the first-order homogeneity condition: $F(\lambda K, \lambda L) = \lambda F(K.L), \lambda > 0$ is any real number. The homogeneity condition in the Inada condition reflects the basic idea of monetary neutrality in neoclassical economics; (3) the function satisfies the reverse boundary condition, when the factor input tends to zero, the marginal output tends to infinity; when the factor input tends to infinity, the marginal output tends to zero. That is:

$$\frac{\lim \frac{\partial F}{\partial K}}{K \to 0} = \frac{\lim \frac{\partial F}{\partial L}}{L \to 0} = +\infty \tag{22.4.2}$$

$$\frac{\lim \frac{\partial F}{\partial K}}{K \to +\infty} = \frac{\lim \frac{\partial F}{\partial L}}{L \to +\infty} = 0 \tag{22.4.3}$$

The boundary conditions of the production function (22.4.2), (22.4.3) are called Inada conditions, first proposed by Japanese economist Kenichi Inada.

For a production function that satisfies the Inada conditions, divide both sides by the total labor force L to get:

$$\frac{Y(t)}{L} = \frac{1}{L}F(K, L) = F\left(\frac{K}{L}\right) \tag{22.4.4}$$

Let: $\frac{Y(t)}{L} = y$, $\frac{K}{L} = k$, from (22.4.4) we get:

$$y = f(k) \tag{22.4.5}$$

For a closed system in equilibrium, assume the savings rate is s, the capital depreciation rate is δ, the capital stock K rate of change K' satisfies the following equation:

$$K' = sF(K, L) - \delta K \tag{22.4.6}$$

Averaging (22.4.6) gives:

Let:

$$\frac{K'}{L} = sf(k) - \delta k \tag{22.4.7}$$

$$\because \quad k' \equiv \frac{d\left(\frac{K}{L}\right)}{dt} = \frac{K'}{L} - K\frac{L'}{L^2}$$

$$\because \quad k' + \frac{K}{L}\frac{L'}{L} = sf(k) - \delta k \tag{22.4.8}$$

Let $\frac{L'}{L} = r_1$ be the labor growth rate, obtained from (22.4.8):

$$k' + kr_l = sf(k) - \delta k \tag{22.4.9}$$

Arranged from (22.4.9):

$$k' = sf(k) - (\delta + r_l)k \tag{22.4.10}$$

This leads to the famous Solow-Swan growth model. Model (22.4.10) provides the relationship between per capita capital, labor growth, capital depreciation, and output. The model includes a steady state, where the increase in per capita capital balances with capital depreciation and labor growth, thus achieving a kind of extensive expansion growth pattern.

In the steady state contained in model (22.4.10), the rate of change of per capita capital is zero, that is: $k' = 0$. At this equilibrium point, the per capita capital amount is denoted as k^*, satisfying the following equation:

$$sf\left(k^*\right) - (\delta + r_l)k^* = 0 \tag{22.4.11}$$

$$\therefore \quad k' = sf(k) - (\delta + r_l)k = sf(k) - \frac{sf(k^*)}{k^*}k \tag{22.4.12}$$

Arranged from (22.4.12):

$$k' = sf(k) - sf\left(k^*\right)\frac{k}{k^*} \tag{22.4.13}$$

$$\therefore \quad k' = s\left[f(k) - f\left(k^*\right)\frac{k}{k^*}\right] \tag{22.4.14}$$

$\because f(k)$ is a concave function
$\therefore \frac{f(k)}{f(k^*)} > \frac{k}{k^*}$

$$\therefore \quad \text{when } k < k^*, k' = s\left[f(k) - f\left(k^*\right)\frac{k}{k^*}\right] > 0 \tag{22.4.15}$$

$$\text{when } k > k^*, k' = s\left[f(k) - f\left(k^*\right)\frac{k}{k^*}\right] < 0 \tag{22.4.16}$$

(22.4.15) and (22.4.16) show that when the trading system reaches the steady state in the Solow-Swan model, it not only presents structural stability, but per capita capital, per capita consumption, and per capita output all remain stable. Without technological progress, the only driving force for the growth of the trading system comes from the exogenous expansion of the population. At the same time, the trading system has local stability near the steady state, and when the trading system deviates from the steady state, it will spontaneously adjust back to the steady state through the adjustment of per capita capital stock. This is the meaning of steady-state growth in the Solow-Swan model. The Solow-Swan model shows that the trading system has the characteristic of spontaneously converging to the equilibrium steady state. In the absence of external uncertain factors including population and new technology inventions, the economy will no longer grow and enter a stagnant state. This is also an important reason why people call the Solow-Swan model an exogenous growth model, that is, the continuous economic growth momentum must come from outside the trading system.

In the trading growth model, is there a stable growth state? Is there a mechanism that spontaneously converges to zero growth? This depends on our understanding of steady-state growth. If strictly according to the steady-state growth conditions given by the Solow-Swan model, the trading growth model does not have a steady-state growth mechanism. However, if steady-state growth is understood as a growth pattern realized by the expansion of scale under the stable state of the trading system structure parameters, the situation of the trading growth model will change.

In the trading growth model (22.3.31), there are three variables related to the structural characteristics of the trading system, which are the trading network circulation rate, trading network density, and trading efficiency. The corresponding change rates are r_θ, r_ω, r_μ. When the trading system enters a steady-state growth state, the structural relationship of the trading system tends to be stable, and the growth rate corresponding to the structural parameters is zero, that is: $r_\theta = 0$, $r_\omega = 0$, $r_\mu = 0$, thus generating a steady-state growth model:

$$Gr_t = k_N r_N + k_M r_M + \lambda(k_{M^1} r_{M^1} + k_{M^2} r_{M^2} + k_R r_R) \tag{22.4.17}$$

The steady-state growth model of trade (22.4.17) shows that the driving force for the growth of the trading system comes from three aspects: the expansion of the trading base, the increase in trading capacity, and the changes in external demand caused by fluctuations in the actual effective exchange rate, which is consistent with the steady-state growth mechanism of the Solow-Swan model. This indicates that the trade growth model is compatible with a steady growth state.

Next, we examine the conditions for the three parameters of trade network turnover rate θ, trade network density ω and trade efficiency μ to achieve stability. Since there are no restrictions on capital depreciation hedging and diminishing returns on capital boundaries, theoretically, the three structural parameters can enter a stable state at any position. The trading system can tend to be stable at a very low level of the three parameters, whether it is trading efficiency, trading turnover rate, or trading network density, all are at a very low level; it can also achieve stability at a higher level. In the former case, due to the low efficiency level of the trading system, the number of enterprises will not increase rapidly, thus limiting the expansion speed of the trading system capacity; the trading efficiency and trading network turnover rate are low, the trading system will present a lack of vitality, market depression, and lack of expansion momentum of the trading base. In this stable state, there are a large number of idle resources in the trading system, and economic resources are seriously wasted. In this case, the trading system will be in a state of economic stagnation, corresponding to the scenario of underdeveloped economies.

When the trading system is in a high-level steady-state growth state, the situation will be another scene. The economy is operating at a high efficiency state, the trading network structure is dense, the trading cycle is smooth, and the trading system is full of vitality. In this state, the trading agents have a high willingness to trade, the economy has strong external competitiveness, and under the joint action of internal and external factors, the trading system capacity has strong expansion potential. The fully vibrant market drives enterprises to actively participate in technological innovation, and the trading base of the trading system presents a continuous expansion situation. It can be seen that the higher the steady-state level of the trading system, the greater the growth potential. Obviously, this is completely different from the picture presented by the Solow-Swan model.

The biggest difference between the steady state of the trade growth model and the Solow-Swan model is the stability of the steady state. The steady state of the Solow-Swan model has inherent stability, so the trading system will inevitably converge to the steady state; while the steady state of the trade growth model is unstable, the trading system will not spontaneously converge to the steady state. Taking the trading turnover rate as an example, when the trading turnover rate deviates from $r_\theta = 0$ equilibrium point, we discuss two situations separately. When $r_\theta < 0$, the trading network circulation volume is declining, the trading agents will respond, adjust the trading state towards the conservative direction, the trading system stops or slows down the capacity expansion, these responses will push the trading turnover rate to further decline. When $r_\theta > 0$, the trading turnover rate is on the rise, market activity will increase accordingly, stimulate the trading agents' willingness to trade, accelerate the expansion of the trading system capacity, enhance the enthusiasm for enterprise innovation, and promote the continuous expansion of the trading base; active market trading promotes the deepening of social division of labor, and the density of the trading network increases. Conversely, the trading turnover rate further increases. The situation of trading efficiency μ and network density ω is basically the same, and their changing process is dominated by the positive feedback mechanism.

22.5 Phenomenon of Accelerated Economic Growth

Any positive feedback conditions that cause two or more trading network variables to stimulate each other could potentially trigger accelerated economic growth. Generally speaking, accelerated economic growth usually occurs after major institutional changes and significant technological innovations. The most direct impact of institutional changes is the improvement of the trading environment, the reduction of trading costs, the optimization of incentive mechanisms, and the significant improvement of the trading network cycle status, which promotes economic growth from multiple aspects. During the period of economic transition, there will be major changes in the system, the dominant production and operation model, and technology, so the period of economic transition is the stage most likely to experience accelerated economic growth. Economic transition includes the transition from an agricultural economy to an industrial economy, the transition from a planned economy to a market economy, and the historical period of significant social and economic structural changes brought about by urbanization.

Major technology is a more common reason for driving accelerated economic growth. Technological innovation is an inexhaustible driving force for economic growth. Innovation can expand the dimensions of the trading system, reduce costs, increase corporate profits, and expand market demand. These are all factors that stimulate economic growth. Major breakthroughs in energy utilization technology, transportation technology, information technology, and material technology will all cause accelerated economic growth. The influence of these technologies far exceeds the scope of the department and radiates to all aspects of the economy; the impact of these technologies not only involves equipment investment, production costs, logistics management, but even involves business operation models, etc., its breadth and depth far exceed the technological innovation of a specific industry.

It is easy to understand the phenomenon of accelerated economic growth using economic growth models. The trading function contains four network variables, and these variables are increasing functions. Among the four variables, once there is a linkage between the variables and a positive feedback mechanism that stimulates each other is formed, there will be a clear and rapid network expansion, and the economy will show an accelerated growth trend. Taking the period of economic transition as an example, in the early stage of industrialization, the number of enterprises began to increase, and the number of goods in the trading system increased, and the market gradually expanded. These changes correspond to the trading system, which will cause the trading system capacity to expand, the trading network density to increase, and the trading base to expand. With the development of the economy, a series of institutional reform measures begin to be launched, the trading environment is optimized, the institutional cost of trading is significantly reduced, and the efficiency and turnover rate of trading are improved. Conversely, this change will encourage more enterprises to emerge and stimulate greater enthusiasm for technological innovation in enterprises. The trading system is once again on track for expansion in capacity, network density, and trading base, forming the second wave of rapid growth in the system.

China's reform began in the early 1980s of the last century, with large-scale institutional reforms first appearing in rural areas. During the planned economy period, the basic accounting unit of agricultural production was a production brigade composed of dozens of families. These families participated in the labor of the production brigade, but did not involve in production decisions, which were plans made from top to bottom. When the harvest season came, the production team distributed the grain produced and a small amount of people got cash from side income. After the reform began, collective land was divided into small plots and contracted to each family. Each family was responsible for production and operation on the contracted land, acting as an independent decision-maker and operator. The original communal system was broken, and after the reform, a new system of rewarding hard work was implemented, allowing those families with business acumen work hard to gain more benefits and become the first among the population to become wealthy. The massive institutional changes stimulated the enthusiasm of hundreds of millions of rural families to get rich through labor, and energized the rural markets. During this period, township governments and production brigades established a large number of township enterprises bespoke to local conditions, injecting a strong vitality into the Chinese economy.

Encouraged by the success of rural reform, industrial reform began in the late 1980s. The key point of industrial reform was to establish an incentive mechanism for workers to work actively through measures such as piecework contracting. Government departments, administrative institutions, schools, hospitals, and even the military of all levels were encouraged to establish various companies. The market began to become active for a while; under the incentive of the more work, more pay system, the production efficiency of state-owned enterprises greatly improved, and the Chinese economy, which had been plagued by shortages for a long time, began to thrive.

In the eastern coastal areas, policy incentives in terms of taxes and land were implemented, attracting a large number of foreign-funded companies to set up factories, with processing trade sprung up. The Chinese economy released huge growth potential under the intertwined forces of internal reform and opening up to the outside world.

The first twenty years of our country's reform and opening up can be described in the language of trading economics as follows: At the beginning of China's economic transformation, the trading system capacity increased exponentially as it shifted from production brigade to family units. Township enterprises joined the industrial production, increasing the number of trading agents and the number of tradable goods, and broadening the trading base. These changes accounts for China's high economic growth during the 1980s. With the advancement of reforms to urban areas, the number of trading agents in the industrial field began to increase, the number and types of goods increased rapidly, and opening up to the outside world brought Chinese products to the international market. A positive feedback loop was formed in the trading system in terms of capacity, density, trading base, and network circulation rate (Fig. 22.1).

The aforementioned feedback loop, after repeated iterations, quickly amplified the trading function of our country's trading system $T_t = T(N_t, M_t, \theta_t, \omega_t)$, driving a round of eye-catching accelerated economic growth, laying the first cornerstone for the Chinese economic miracle.

Accelerated economic growth can occur not only during the transition period, but can also at some point when industrialization is basically completed. As long as

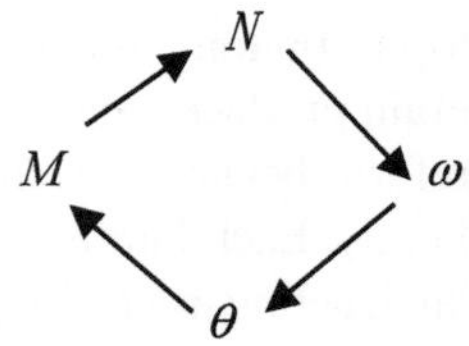

Fig. 22.1 The trading loop of China's reform and opening up at early stage

multiple structural variables in the trading system form a synergy situation, accelerated economic growth will take shape. The post-war economic miracles that have occurred in developed industrial countries in the West was a case in point (Figs. 22.2, 22.3, 22.4 and 22.5).

From the early 1950s to the early 1970s, each of these countries experienced accelerated economic growth. In these countries, there were three factors that contributed to the accelerated economic growth: First, they faced the task of large-scale economic reconstruction. Be it Germany, the United Kingdom, Italy, or France, infrastructure, production equipment, and urban buildings were severely damaged during the war. Some cities in Germany were almost in ruins at the end of the war, with Frankfurt being a typical example. Reconstruction provided a strong demand for the economy, which was the first force to jumpstart the process of accelerated economic growth. The

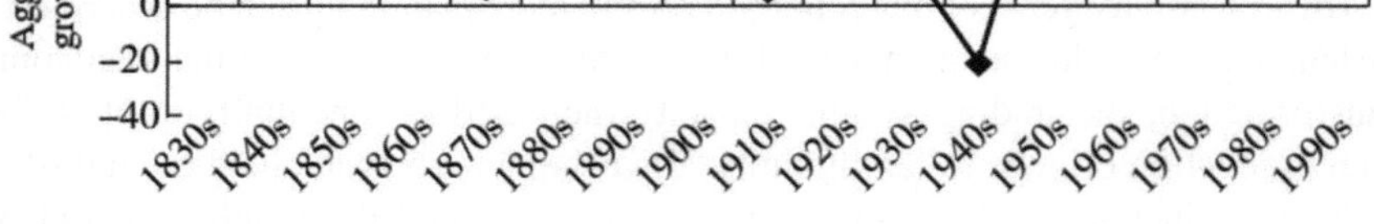

Fig. 22.2 The case of economic growth in France[4]

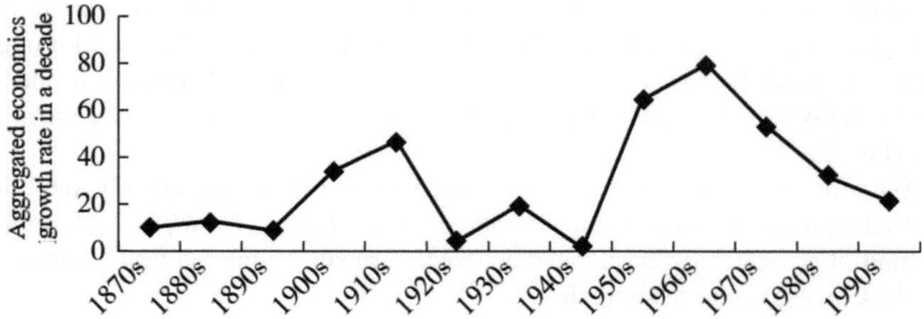

Fig. 22.3 The case of economic growth in Italy

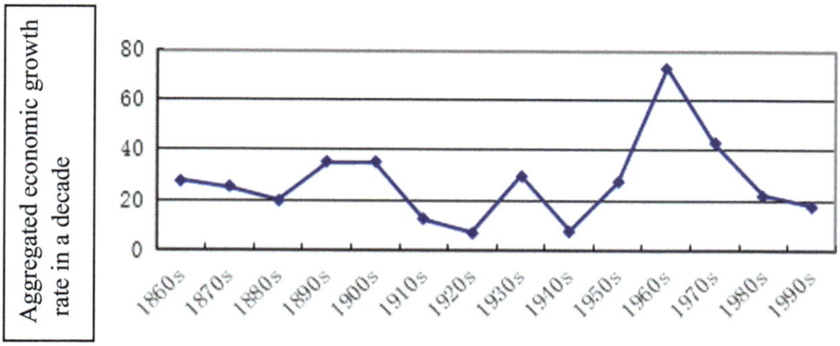

Fig. 22.4 The case of economic growth in Germany

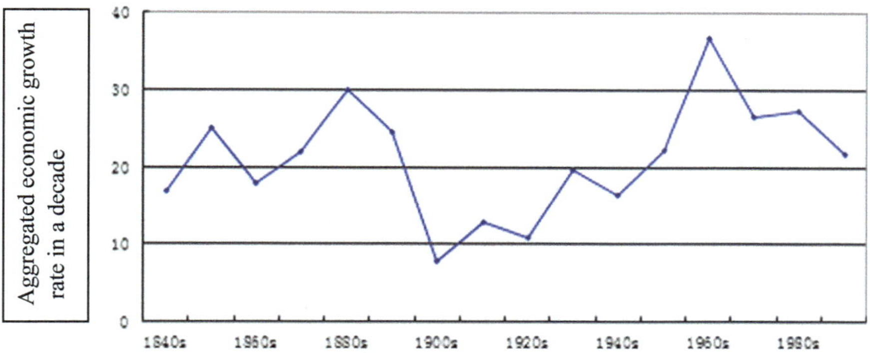

Fig. 22.5 The case of economic growth in the U.K.

second reason was that Europe, having experienced two world wars, was far behind the United States in terms of industrial production technology and they needed a large amount of investment for technological updates and transformation. The Marshall Plan played a role in helping European countries quickly improve their technological capabilities. The third factor was a significant change in the role that the government played in the operation of the economy, with the government being more proactive in market intervention and institutional construction than before. This was specifically manifested in the nationalization of important economic sectors, such as transportation, electricity, and some banking systems; a large amount of investment in social security and the expansion of public services, including pensions, family allowances, free medical care or medical subsidies, education investment, and other aspects.[5] These measures played a positive role in maintaining stable economic operation, releasing family consumption demand, and so on. This can be clearly reflected in the trend of the increasing proportion of consumer spending by governments in various countries (Tables 22.1 and 22.2).

The elimination of trade barriers played an important role in the rapid economic growth after the war. The General Agreement on Tariffs and Trade signed in Geneva

Table. 22.1 The percentage of Italian government spending in GNP[6]

1921–1930	5.6%
1931–1940	9.4%
1950–1959	12.0%
1961–1970	13.3%

Table. 22.2 The percentage of British government spending in GNP[7]

1921–1929	8.9%
1930–1939	11.4%
1950–1958	16.9%
1961–1970	18.9%

in 1947 led to the abolition of quota restrictions on international trade and the reduction of tariffs, all of which paved the way for European countries in reconstruction to expand their international markets. The establishment of the European Payments Union (EPU) had a very positive effect on promoting trade within Europe and between Europe and other countries in the world. All trade between European countries was recorded in accounts, then settled at the end of the month, with deficit countries recorded on the debit side of the central account and surplus countries on the credit side. Settlements were made in dollars or gold. The introduction of this international payment mechanism greatly facilitated trade between European countries and significantly reduced the cost of trade settlement.[8]

In the mechanisms that triggered the accelerated economic growth of Western European countries after the war, the first was initiated by post-war reconstruction. The rebuilding of infrastructure and the resetting of factory equipment led to the repair of the trade network destroyed by the war, the circulation rate of the trade network increased accordingly, and the network density began to increase. The changes in these two parameters initiated the first drive of economic growth in these countries. With the start of economic growth, the government's tax standing began to improve, social security began to be put in place, and adjustments in this aspect of the system played a role in optimizing the trading environment. The proportion of family expenditure increased accordingly, and the potential of family consumption demand was released. The circulation rate of the trade network continued to increase, constituting the second drive of economic growth. Market expansion provided motivation for companies to apply new technologies, and new products began to emerge; the facilitation of trade cooperation mechanisms further promoted increasingly active trade between European countries, and the trading system was improved in terms of commodity base and circulation rate. In the later stages of European reconstruction, the direction of international trade changed, with initial trade deficits being replaced by later trade surpluses, representing the continued expansion of the capacity of Europe's trading system as an economic whole. These changes will ultimately lead to an increase in the efficiency of the trading system.

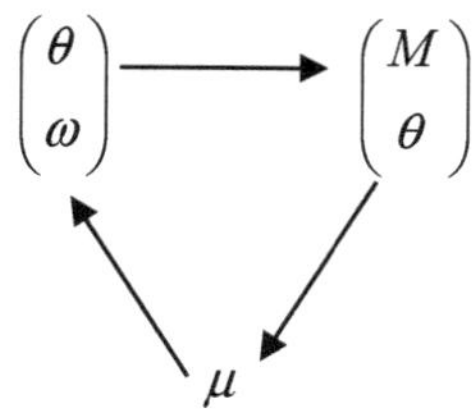

Fig. 22.6 The trading loop of the economic renaissance in Europe

The aforementioned changes further stimulated the government to carry out institutional reforms and optimizations in the established direction, the circulation rate of trade continued to rise, and eventually formed a feedback mechanism that mutually stimulated the commodity base and network density (Fig. 22.6).

Unlike European countries, the acceleration of the American economy occurred during rather than after World War II. The reason lies in that, the main battlefield of World War II was in Europe, and the United States was the provider of war munitions and materials throughout. Although the United States directly joined the Allies in declaring war on Germany and Japan after the Pearl Harbor incident, and sent troops to participate in the battles in the European and Pacific regions, the domestic economy still operated in great order. The fallout of World War II did not destroy the American economy, rather, provided it with strong growth momentum. The stimulus of the war on the American economy exceeded people's expectations, "In 1939, the gross national product of the United States, that is, the total value of products and services produced by the American people, was 91 billion dollars. But in 1945, it was as high as 215 billion dollars. Such a surge in total production is unprecedented. Unemployment used to be a thorny issue, and there were still 8 million in 1940. Now this problem has disappeared. The number of employed people has increased from 45 million to 66 million, of whom more than 5 million are women. The confidence that Americans had before the stock market crash has been restored."[9] The pull of World War II on the American economy was all-encompassing, even greatly promoting agricultural production. "By the fall of 1942, their government leaders had convinced them that they had to become the world's food suppliers. So they set about producing food again, and the harvest increased by 25% compared to the highest yield in the past. … During the Great Depression, inventors, chemists, engineers, and agronomists had already invented new fertilizers, high-yield seeds, pesticides, and new agricultural machinery. These scientific and technological changes were game changer."[10]

To meet the demands of war for armaments, the United States mobilized almost all possible resources and forces. "The assembly lines of major factories were running day and night, providing equipment for the armies of Russia, the Commonwealth, Free France, and the United States itself, preparing for the decisive battle of 1944. Even typewriter factories were making machine guns, and car factories were making bombers. In Connecticut, Igor Sikorsky completed the world's first production line for helicopters. Another factory in Stratford, Connecticut, was producing more than 6,000 "Corsair" fighters. Chrysler made 25,507 tanks for the army."[11] From the German occupation of the Low Countries and the Ardennes on May 10, 1940, to

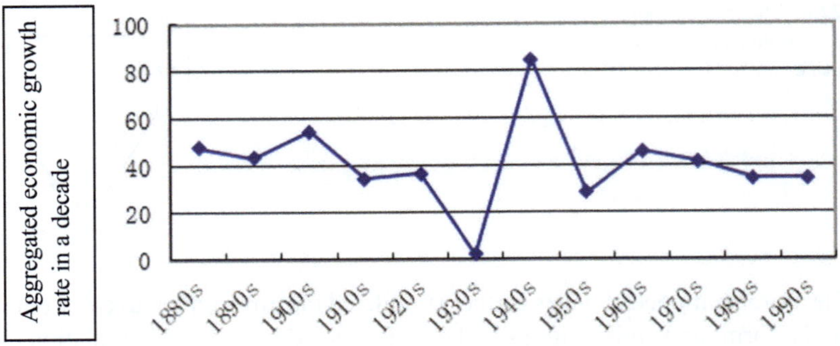

Fig. 22.7 The case of economic growth in the U.S.[12]

the end of the war in 1945, the number of all kinds of armaments produced by the United States reached an unprecedented scale (Fig. 22.7).

The external demand generated by the war on the U.S. economy is evidenced in the sudden increase in the trading cycle rate. With the war coming to an end, the external demand from Europe disappeared abruptly, and the U.S. economy was bound to suffer cycle rate contraction shock in a short time. When the external demand from Europe suddenly disappeared, the circulation volume of the U.S. economic trading network decreased accordingly. Due to the multiplier effect of economic activities, the impact of the decrease in external demand on trading volume will be several times the decrease in external demand. Under this impact, the U.S. economy inevitably generates downward pressure, resulting in a significant slowdown in growth. Due to the huge volume of the U.S. economy, the impact of the sudden disappearance of external demand, although large, cannot form a sustained downward trend.

The accelerated growth of the Japanese economy also occurred in the twenty years after World War II, in many cases similar to the situation in European countries (Fig. 22.8).

The high-speed growth of Japan's post-war economy was supported by two forces. The first was the special demand for war material supply. After the outbreak of the

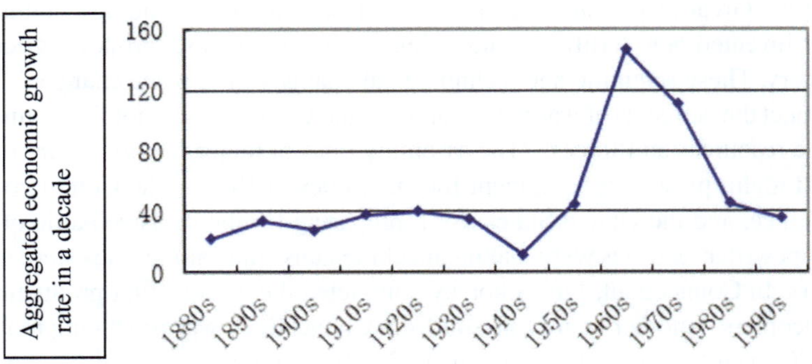

Fig. 22.8 The case of economic growth in Japan[13]

Korean War, the United States rendered Japan a rear supply station for the U.S. military on the Korean battlefield, supplying all kinds of materials including "things like hemp bags, barbed wire, gasoline barrels, steel for bridges, trucks, airplanes, car repairs, and various other demands. ... In a broad sense, special demand includes not only material demand but also the increased service demand of U.S. soldiers in Japan, which exceeds the proportion of material demand in total demand."[14] The special demand for war material supply helped the Japanese economy emerge from the post-war depression and pushed the economy into a fast lane.

While the U.S. military's special demand directly stimulated the Japanese economy, it also brought scarce dollar income to Japan. "At the end of 1949, Japan's domestic and foreign currency reserves were about 200 million dollars. Due to the impact of special demand, it increased to 4.5 times by the end of 1951, exceeding 900 million dollars in total. Japan could expand production actively through expanding equipment investment and raw material imports. In terms of equipment investment, the expansion of equipment in the steel industry was particularly notable, implementing active equipment renewal and new construction, ...".[15] These injected strong momentum into the Japanese economy.

Unlike the deep economic downturn in the United States after World War II, when the Korean War ended, the Japanese economy also faced the same cyclical downturn shock as the United States at that time, and inevitably fell into a brief recession. However, the downturn only lasted for a few months in 1954, and bottomed out and rebounded by November; the key reason was that the Japanese economy internally formed a self-reinforcing feedback loop, with urbanization being the key driving force.

The rapid urbanization process in Japan began in the 1950s and ended in the first half of the 1970s.[16] Urbanization had multiple impact on the Japanese economy. After rural labor forces moved to the city, the number of urban families increased, resulting in a corresponding surge in demand for family appliances, which drove a boom in corporate investment. With the investment to upgrade outdated equipment and expand production capacity, Japan's economy experienced the rapid growth. During this period, electrical machinery, general machinery, precision machinery, heavy chemical industry, and basic material industry enjoyed the fastest growth, faster than other industries.

Before the first oil crisis in 1973, the main support for the Japanese economy came from the expansion of domestic demand due to urbanization. With the end of the urbanization process, the growth momentum of the Japanese economy gradually shifted from internal to external, "What drove the economic growth from the second half of the 1970s to the 1980s were automobiles, electronics, and other assembly-type industries. For example, after the 1970s, Japan's automobile industry, with a pivot to the US market, rapidly expanded its exports. Especially in the US market after the oil crisis, due to the rise in gasoline prices, the demand for small cars with low fuel consumption increased, and the market share of Japanese cars expanded rapidly. In stark contrast to the stagnation of structurally depressed industries, the number of vehicles produced by Japan continued to increase steadily in the second half of the 70s after the oil crisis, and by the end of the 70s, it had reached a level

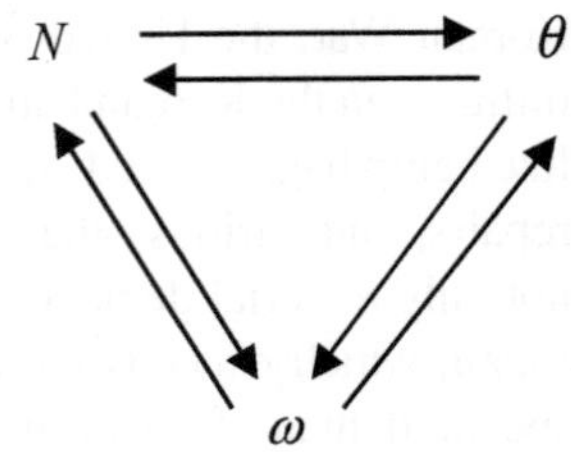

Fig. 22.9 The trading loop of economic miracle in Japan

that could compete with the largest car-producing country in the world, the United States."[17] However, during this period, the growth rate of the Japanese economy only maintained at about 3.6%, much lower than the average annual growth rate of 9.4% from 1955 to 1973.

During the period of high-speed growth of the Japanese economy, a large amount of labor moved from rural areas to cities, and corporate investment increased to expand production, forming two mutually reinforcing positive feedback loops. When there was a large gap between urban income and rural income, the process of urbanization began. As more and more farmers moved to cities, the large families in rural areas were replaced by more small families in cities, which in turn led to the expansion of family consumption demand, including the demand for housing, family appliances, cars, and other living materials. The expansion of the market led to further expansion of production by enterprises and increased equipment investment. The expansion of production created new demand for labor, attracting more labor from rural areas to cities. The flood of farmers moving to the city and the flood of corporate investment intertwined and reinforced each other, forming a feedback loop (Fig. 22.9).

The expansion of corporate investment has led to an increase in the trading cycle rate, which has accelerated the process of urbanization. The process of urbanization has in turn led to an increase in the capacity of the trading network, inducing companies to expand their investments and stimulate the trading cycle rate. After farmers move into the city, the frequency and intensity of their participation in trading are much higher than during their rural life, which has the effect of increasing the density of the trading network. The three variables mutually promote each other, forming a strong trading cycle that drives economic growth. However, the constraint boundary of the feedback loop is the surplus labor in the countryside. When the process of urbanization comes to an end, the momentum of the above-mentioned feedback loop begins to gradually decline. This is indeed the case in reality, as the growth of the Japanese economy began to noticeably slow down after the mid-1970s.

22.6 Policy Implications of Economic Growth Models

Trading economics believes that to achieve sustained economic growth, the government needs to carefully nurture and guide every link of the trading system at all times. When managing the trading system, the government should adhere to four fundamental principles, which are summarized from the dimensions of trading agents, trading environment, external relations, and trading system maintenance.

1. **Principle of Incentive Compatibility**

The growth model shows that the trading network cycle rate plays a very important role in the process of economic growth, and the role of other variables in economic growth needs to be reflected through the trading cycle rate. Whether it is system capacity, trading base, or network density, effective exchange rate, etc., this is the case. If the government wants to achieve the goal of sustained economic growth, it must pay close attention to the changes in the trading cycle rate and try to keep it running at a high level.

The trading system operates through the trading network, and the trading network is the result of spontaneous organization. Among the many factors that determine the trading network cycle rate, the profit motive of the t trading agents is the first cornerstone. If the profit motive of the trading agent is frustrated, no matter what kind of stimulus policy the government uses, it will not be able to truly stimulate economic vitality, nor can it achieve the expected economic growth target. Therefore, protecting the profit motive of the trading agent and forming an effective incentive for the profit motive of the trading agent is the first principle that the government should adhere to in managing the economy.

The object of incentive is human beings, and the goal of incentive is to arouse people's enthusiasm for trading. The incentive policy under the goal of promoting economic growth aims to stimulate the trading willingness of the trading agent. Human behavior contains multiple levels of needs, and if any need is not met, the enthusiasm for action will be suppressed, and the willingness to trade cannot be awakened. Security is a basic human need and the basis for all behavior. When people lack a sense of security, their behavior will be distorted and deformed, let alone pursuing interests. Therefore, to achieve effective incentives for trading agents, the top priority is to ensure that trading agents feel safe.

Safety includes behavioral safety, personal safety, and property safety. People's behavioral safety is based on the predictability of behavioral results. If people cannot foresee the consequences of their actions, they will be fearful and hesitant. To make people feel safe about their behaviors, there need to be simple, clear, and stable behavior rules. If the behavior rules are very strict yet very complicated, it is difficult to implement in real world, and it cannot meet people's need for security.

The rule of law is the cornerstone for people to achieve personal safety and property safety. This not only requires a complete legal system, but also needs to establish people's trust in the law. Law is a necessary means of legal system, and people's trust in law is the social foundation of the legal system.

A sense of security is only one aspect of establishing an effective incentive mechanism, social recognition is another important aspect of establishing effective incentives. Without social recognition as a foundation, the enthusiasm for profit of the trading agents will be suppressed. Building a sense of security for trading agents and creating a public opinion atmosphere of social recognition are all part of the content of effective incentives at the social level. To activate the trading intention of the trading agents, social level incentive measures alone are not enough, it is also necessary for trading activities to achieve expected returns. If the risk of trading is high and the probability of trading failure is high, even if there is a willingness to trade, it will quickly fade in the face of harsh reality. A good business environment is an important part of the effective incentive mechanism and is also a prerequisite for trading agents to achieve reasonable expected returns. In the business environment, whether the government can provide various facilitation services for enterprises is key, including business registration, tax handling, customs procedures, financial services, and worker skill training. If the government can provide good services in these areas, it will greatly reduce the institutional cost of trading and enhance the confidence of enterprises in the market. Corruption is the biggest enemy of the business environment, and cracking down on corruption is a very effective measure to create a good business environment.

Society and economy are two aspects of building an effective incentive mechanism, both of which are complementary and indispensable. In the effective incentive mechanism, the economic environment is constantly changing, with both prosperity and depression, and economic cycles are inevitable. The characteristics of the economic environment show that no matter what the trading environment is, the impact on the trading intention is short-term and temporary, the economic activities rise and fall, and the trading intention will also fluctuate. But the social environment is different, because the social environment will show stubborn trend characteristics. Once a certain value orientation is formed, it will linger for a long time, forming a long-term suppression of trading intention.

2. **Principle of Expected Stability**

The importance of expectations is self-evident. When there is a widespread phenomenon of unstable expectations in the trading system, it will greatly suppress the behavior of the trading agents, reduce the circulation rate of the trading system, and is not conducive to economic growth. This can be easily found in the trading equation. We know that the trading equation has the following form:

$$\Pr(s) = 1 - R_g \frac{q}{p} \mu^n$$

When there is widespread instability of expectations in the trading system, it means that a large number of trading agents cannot confirm the evolution trend of the trading situation. When the agents cannot confirm that the trading situation will improve, they will confirm that the trading situation will worsen, increase the prior probability q assignment, and decrease p assignment. The perception factor of the trading agent $\frac{q}{p}$ has extremely unstable characteristics. Due to the linkage of the numerator and denominator, a slight fluctuation in expectations will show a large change in the perception factor.

To provide a predictable trading environment for trading agents, the following three points need to be met: First, policy transparency. The transparency of the policy itself is very important, the public should be able to access the specific policy content while the policy statement should be clear, and will not cause misreading, misunderstanding, and should be actionable. If the policy is vague and there is a lot of room for speculation, it is easy to cause public confusion and expectation mismatch;

Secondly, it is important to maintain the consistency of policies. To stabilize expectations, policies must be consistent. If policies change overnight, especially those involving major industrial policies, it can cause confusion in expectations and result in a huge waste of resources, with mounting financial risks. Real estate is a crucial pillar industry in any country. It is absolutely unacceptable to limit purchases and loans today, and then rescue the market tomorrow with a variety of measures to prevent price drops. This approach will not effectively manage the real estate market.

The larger the scale of the industry involved in the policy, the higher the requirement for policy stability, and the longer the time that needs to be maintained. The trading system is an ecosystem dominated by self-organization. Any external disturbance will quickly spread through the extensive trading network. A large number of trading agents will react according to their own situations. This process has the characteristics of chaotic motion, with great unpredictability and uncontrollability. Therefore, to ensure precise and effective policies, extensive and thorough research must be conducted before implementing policies. Like war situation simulations, various market reactions after the implementation of policies should be simulated. The order, scope, and magnitude of market reactions should be predicted, and contingency plans should be made in advance. Only in this way can the policies achieve the expected goals and avoid the embarrassment of changing orders overnight.

Emphasizing policy stability means not pursuing immediate policy effects. In reality, we often see that soon after one policy is implemented, policy makers are bound to up the ante even before its effects are felt. As long as the effects do not meet the expected goals, the intensification will not stop. The result is that as soon as the policy effects begin to show, the problems of policies overuse become salient. Then, the policy is hastily rolled back, and counter measures are introduced. As a result, people always feel that a revolving-door policy leave them perplexed and hard to deal with.

Thirdly, policy adjustments should have a sufficient transition period. The wider the scope of the policy, the longer the transition period should be set. Policies need to be adjusted with changes in the situation, but to avoid the negative effects of unstable expectations brought about by adjustments, a transition period should be set, with a clear stipulation of the transition period. For special agents, the criteria for identification and the transition period for special arrangements should also be clearly listed.

3. **Principle of Openness**

The trading system is a dissipative complex system. Only by maintaining continuous information exchange, commodity exchange, capital flow, and human resource flow with the outside world can it foster strong vitality and continuously promote various innovative activities, including technological innovation.

Throughout human history facts have eloquently proven that openness creates competitive advantages. When the world began the process of the Industrial Revolution with the rumbling of steam engines and entered the rapidly developing eighteenth century, Australia and some indigenous inhabitants of tropical rainforests were still at the level of development of the Old Stone Age before the intrusion of modern Westerners, lagging far behind the development level of the continental world.[18] This is especially true for the Native Americans. Although the fertile American continent once nurtured the Mayan culture, it was isolated from the outside world for as long as 2500 years, and the north and south of the American continent were also isolated from each other, being in a state of disconnection from the main world. They were easily defeated by the invading Europeans, and the American continent eventually became a fertile ground for the development of European civilization.[19]

Fast forward to the contemporary era, China, a country used to stay ahead of the curve, suddenly lagged behind and gradually became a poor and weak country. The reason is that after the establishment of the Ming Dynasty in the early fourteenth century, China, which has always had an open-mindedness of a great country, suddenly began to implement a closed policy. The Ming emperor ordered the prohibition of land trade in iron, weapons, and textiles, built the Great Wall, and cut off trade with northern countries; at sea, a maritime ban was implemented. This sudden turn to a closed policy restricted China's exchanges with the outside world, forming an economic closed island. In Europe, the curtain of the Renaissance gradually opened, the train of social progress began to accelerate, and embarked on a development path completely opposite to China. "No matter what was behind China's withdrawal, but the timing of the withdrawal was terrible. For centuries, China has been a major exporter of creativity, and Western European countries have been the main importers of these ideas. Now, just as the social brain of Europe is beginning to really activate, China has chosen to give up the opportunity to exchange ideas. "[20]

Mutual stimulation are the fundamental driving forces for economic growth and social development. In a closed state, a country can be well-fed and live a peaceful life, but on the big stage of human competition, closure will inevitably lag behind and will eventually be replaced by advanced forces.

In the trading system, the trading agents in the same phase form a competitive group, and the scale of the homologous set of the same phase group determines the intensity of competition among the trading agents. No matter how large the scale of the closed system, its homologous set is always smaller than the homologous set in the open system. Therefore, the competitive pressure borne by the trading agents in the open system is always greater than the pressure borne by the agents in the closed system. The trading agents that survive under intense competitive pressure must have stronger adaptability, which is the fundamental reason why the open system always has an advantage over the closed system.

In the economic growth model, the forces driving economic growth come from both the inner cycle and the external cycle. We cannot simply look at the internal and external cycles in isolation, thinking that as long as the internal cycle is large enough, the external cycle will become insignificant. This is a misunderstanding of the operation mechanism of the trading system. No matter how large the quantitative proportion of the external cycle in the economy, it plays an irreplaceable role in stimulating the vitality of the entire trading system.

4. **Principle of Fair Development**

The evolution of the trading system is also a process of polarizing trading power. The speed of polarization is fast beyond our imagination. In just a few decades, a huge gap in trading power will form among trading agents. Under the severe polarization of trading power, the seemingly level-playing market cannot achieve true fairness. So the laissez-faire market is the oyster just for the lucky few, while the development opportunities of most trading agents are squeezed into a very small space, creating social injustice.

From the perspective of economic growth, the polarization of trading power will form two inhibitory effects: one is the circulation rate inhibitory effect. The polarization of trading power will inevitably lead to extreme wealth distribution, with a large amount of wealth concentrated in the hands of a few trading agents, inevitably forming a stagnation of the trading network, and the trading circulation rate is locked at a low level for a long time; the other is the capacity inhibitory effect. When the evolution of the trading system shows a rapid polarization trend, a few enterprises that have obtained super trading power will suppress potential competitors with their overwhelming advantages, causing a continuous deterioration of the trading environment. Just like a forest full of vitality, a few big trees occupy the limited sky, absorbing most of the sunlight, and those trees that cannot get enough sunlight will slowly wither and die. In the growth model, the capacity of the trading system is the basis for economic growth. Without a large number of small and medium-sized enterprises, the ecology of the trading system will be damaged. The two inhibitory effects produced by the polarization of trading power are undoubtedly very harmful to long-term economic growth and are also one of the key reasons for the middle-income trap.

The World Bank's *East Asia Resurgence: Views on Economic Growth* report released in 2007 pointed out that in more than half a century after the end of World War II, only 13 of the 101 middle-income economies worldwide made into the high-income development stage. Most economies have unfortunately fallen into the middle-income trap, including countries such as Brazil, Mexico, Argentina, Malaysia, Indonesia, the Philippines, and Thailand. In these countries, there are common problems such as unstable economic growth, severe polarization, serious corruption, and political instability. Polarization is the most typical characteristic. The Gini coefficient in Latin American countries is generally above 0.45, much higher than the average level of 0.35 in OECD countries while the Gini coefficient in Malaysia basically remains above 0.5. As we proved, the trading system has a natural polarization trend, and the polarization of trading power is almost an inevitable result of economic development. This is also why most middle-income countries have not been able to escape the middle-income trap. This also shows that a country's capacity to effectively avoid excessive polarization of trading power is an important prerequisite for successfully crossing the middle-income trap.

After three hundred years of development since the Industrial Revolution, humanity today, whether they are developed Western countries or many developing countries, is facing the problem of polarization of trading power. The polarization of trading power is the biggest obstacle to achieving fair development. In the trading system, a few trading agents with super trading power use the power of the market to suppress, and even kill, competitors; they use their market advantage to raise prices and force consumers to accept unfair terms, seriously eroding the efficiency of the trading system and the environment for fair competition. For the various unfair phenomena caused by the polarization of trading power, the famous American economist Joseph E. Stiglitz detailed in his "The Price of Inequality".[21]

The principle of fair development advocates for continuous system reform and optimization according to the characteristics of different stages of economic development, including market management, inclusive finance, distribution systems to social assistance in many aspects, requiring a combination of measures for continuous adjustment, effectively resolving the challenges of differentiation brought about by the evolution of the trading system.

On their path to achieving fair development, corruption is a stumbling block faced by many countries. Corruption further amplifies the unfair mechanisms that already exist in society, allowing enterprises and families with competitive advantages to obtain more opportunities through rigged operations. Corruption provides a comfortable channel for dominant groups to consolidate their advantages and avoid direct competition, completely blocking the development path of disadvantaged groups. The principle of fair development should not be simply understood as restricting competition, or even robbing the rich to help the poor. Otherwise, it will not only curb polarization, but also fundamentally nip in the bud the driving force of the evolution of the trading system and the vibrant trading ecology. Establishing a fair development environment can only be achieved through measures to fuel the development of disadvantaged groups, and cannot be achieved by suppressing dominant agents; it must be done subtly without affecting the normal trading order, and should not be done through vigorous social movements. Simply and crudely restricting competition or destroying the property rights system will not only fail to achieve the ideal result of fairness and efficiency. On the contrary, it will only stifle economic growth and lead nowhere.

Notes

1. Robert J. Barrow, Javier Sarah-e-Martin (2000) Economic growth (Trans: He Hui, Liu Mingxing), China Social Sciences Press, Beijing, p 10.
2. Edmund Phelps (2013) Great Prosperity: How Mass Innovation Brings National Prosperity (Trans: Yu Jiang), CITIC Press, Beijing, p 61–66 (in Chinese).
3. Joseph E. Stiglitz (2020) The Truth about America (Trans: Liu Binfu, Liu Yiming, Liu Jiamu), China Machine Press, Beijing.
4. Adam Smith (2009) The Wealth of Nations (Trans: Hu Changming), People's Daily Press, Beijing, p 12.
5. Angus Maddison (2009) Millennium Statistics of World Economy (Trans: Wu Xiaoying, Shi Faqi), Peking University Press, Beijing.
6. Zhou Xiaochuan (2008) Systemic Institutional Transformation - Research and Exploration in the Reform and Opening-up, China Financial Publishing House, Beijing, p 382.
7. Li Yining (2010) Industrialization and Institutional Adjustment: A Study on the Economic History of Western Europe, The Commercial Press, p 599.
8. Li Yining (2010) Industrialization and Institutional Adjustment: A Study on the Economic History of Western Europe, The Commercial Press, p 599.
9. Rondo Cameron, Larry Neal (2009) A Brief History of the World Economy from the Paleolithic Age to the end of the 20th Century (Trans: Pan Ning), 4th edn. Shanghai Translation Publishing House, Shanghai, p 386.
10. Rondo Cameron, Larry Neal (2009) A Brief History of the World Economy from the Paleolithic Age to the end of the 20th Century (Trans: Pan Ning), 4th edn. Shanghai Translation Publishing House, Shanghai, p 229.
11. Rondo Cameron, Larry Neal (2009) A Brief History of the World Economy from the Paleolithic Age to the end of the 20th Century (Trans: Pan Ning), 4th edn. Shanghai Translation Publishing House, Shanghai, p 229.
12. William Manchester (2006) Glory and Dream: American Society from 1932 to 1972 (Trans: Zhu Xie), Hainan Publishing House, Sanhuan Publishing House, Haikou, p 231.
13. Angus Maddison (2009) Millennium Statistics of World Economy (Trans: Wu Xiaoying, Shi Faqi), Peking University Press, Beijing.
14. Angus Maddison (2009) Millennium Statistics of World Economy (Trans: Wu Xiaoying, Shi Faqi), Peking University Press, Beijing.
15. Satoshi Hamano, Narihiko Izao, Munetsu Nakamura et al. (2010) The Economic History of Japan: 1600–1990 (Trans: Peng Xi, Liu Shuhan, Han Qiuyan, Tang Shuai), Nanjing University Press, Nanjing, p 234.
16. Satoshi Hamano, Narihiko Izao, Munetsu Nakamura et al. (2010) The Economic History of Japan: 1600–1990 (Trans: Peng Xi, Liu Shuhan, Han Qiuyan, Tang Shuai), Nanjing University Press, Nanjing, p 235.
17. Satoshi Hamano, Narihiko Izao, Munetsu Nakamura et al. (2010) The Economic History of Japan: 1600–1990 (Trans: Peng Xi, Liu Shuhan, Han Qiuyan, Tang Shuai), Nanjing University Press, Nanjing, p 250.
18. Satoshi Hamano, Narihiko Izao, Munetsu Nakamura et al. (2010) The Economic History of Japan: 1600–1990 (Trans: Peng Xi, Liu Shuhan, Han Qiuyan, Tang Shuai), Nanjing University Press, Nanjing, p 273.
19. Roz Murphy (2004) History of Asia, (Trans: Huang Lin), Hainan Publishing House, Sanhuan Publishing House, Haikou, p 4.
20. Stavrianos (2006) Global History: From Prehistory to the 21st Century (Trans: Wu Xiangying, Liang Chimin), Peking University Press, Beijing, p 317–331 (in Chinese).
21. Robert Wright (2014) Non-zero-sum Era: The Logic of Human Destiny, (Trans: Yu Hua), Citic Press, Beijing, p 117 (in Chinese).

Chapter 23
Trading Pricing Model

Pricing is an important component of trading decision-making. Through pricing, trading agents aim to achieve their decision-making goal of maximizing profits. The price changes in the trading system are the collective result of countless trading agents participating in pricing, competing with each other, and influencing each other. Trading pricing, which includes many random factors, is an important part of the uncertainty of the trading system.

23.1 Price Theory in Mainstream Economics

Prices occupy a very important position in the mainstream economic theory system centered on neoclassical economics, serving as a key signal guiding the trading system to achieve effective allocation of resources. Under the guidance of price signals, trading agents make trading decisions and complete the allocation of scarce resources. However, the status of price issues in the field of mainstream economic research is very subtle and does not match its logical position in the theoretical system. The price theory in mainstream economics does not discuss the mechanism of price formation, but regards price as a parameter that has been generated in a fully competitive market. The price theory of mainstream theory focuses on how trading agents accept price signals and how they react to price changes. For families, the price theory of mainstream economics uses concepts such as indifference curves, price elasticity, and substitution effects as tools to describe the behavior of family consumption activities. For enterprises, the focus of price theory is on the response to price changes, using concepts such as production functions, substitution effects, and scale effects to depict the behavioral characteristics of enterprises.[1]

The underlying logic of neoclassical economics is that perfect competition is the basic form of the market, and equilibrium is the basic state of the trading system. Under such a context, the price level of the market and the price level of the trading

Z. Wang, *Trading Economics*, Contributions to Economics,
https://doi.org/10.1007/978-981-99-9875-3_23

system are determined by a very simple logic, that is, supply and demand determine the price. For trading agents, the price is determined by the uncontrollable market; for the entire trading system, the price level is automatically set by the total supply and demand, and price changes are signals released by changes in the supply and demand pattern of the trading system. Therefore, the generation of prices and the causes of price changes have become self-evident propositions, and the price issue is thus shelved in mainstream economic theory.

In the main branches of economic theory, monetary economics also involves price issues. The well-known Fisher equation (or trading equation) is a case in point. The common form of the Fisher equation is: $MV = PY$, where M represents the money supply, V represents the velocity of money circulation, P represents the price level, and Y represents the total amount of traded goods or total economic output. The Fisher equation presents a very simple view, that is, all money is in circulation; the money supply rises in proportion to prices. This view dominated the economics community before the Keynesian revolution and is a basic view of the quantity theory of money. The quantity theory of money believes that the relationship between money and prices is very simple and intuitive, with an immediate, linear relationship; it also believes that money does not have a substantial impact on economic behaviors such as family consumption and corporate production, and has neutral characteristics, that is, the concept of monetary neutrality.[2] Economists such as David Hume, Irving Fisher, A. C. Pigou, and Knut Wicksell are the main representatives of the quantity theory of money.

The Quantity Theory of Money is not a unified school of economic theory, but a generalization of many theories from different periods under the banner of monetary neutrality. The theories of these scholars differ greatly in their expression of the quantity theory and their understanding of the function of money. Irving Fisher emphasized the direct mechanism of the change in the money stock on the trading behavior of the agent, which is also known as the Fisher mechanism; A. C. Pigou emphasized the importance of cash balances, focusing his analysis on the money market, emphasizing the impact of money supply on interest rates, and constructing the relationship between money and prices through the reaction of the trading agent's investment behavior. This monetary effect is known as the indirect transmission mechanism, corresponding to Fisher's direct transmission mechanism. Wicksell's theory uses monetary credit as the main analytical tool, focusing on the impact of interest rates on money demand. Wicksell's monetary theory had a significant impact on the Keynesian revolution and the theory of money demand.

The Great Depression ended the development of the Quantity Theory of Money, and the Keynesian revolution emerged, bringing the study of money and prices into the era of money demand theory. Keynes established a logical connection between income, consumption, interest rates, and money demand through his analysis of the motives for money demand. Keynes believed that people hold money for three motives: trading, precautionary and speculative motives. The money demand of the three different motives is affected by different factors, and the total money demand is the sum of the demands of the three motives, that is:

$$M^d = M^{tr} + M^{sp} = M(Y, r) \tag{23.1.1}$$

where, M^d represents the total demand for money, M^{tr} represents the demand for money generated by the trading motive and precautionary motive, which is positively related to income Y; M^{sp} represents the demand for money under the speculative motive, which is negatively related to the interest rate r; $M(Y, r)$ is the money demand function. The money demand function can be further expanded as follows:

$$M^d = kY + L(r) \tag{23.1.2}$$

where, $k > 0$ is the marginal propensity to consume; $L(r)$ is the liquidity preference function, which is a decreasing function of the market interest rate r.

Keynes believed that the addition of the speculative motive makes the money demand function highly unstable. Based on this judgment, Keynes advocated that in terms of stabilizing the economy, fiscal policy can play a predictable role through the relatively stable investment multiplier effect, while monetary policy cannot foresee its policy effects due to the instability of the money demand function, and the risk of policy operation is high. Friedman further expanded Keynes's money demand function, which also led to completely different policy recommendations from Keynes. Friedman's money demand function is more general, including more forms of assets, even human capital. The highlight of Friedman's money demand function is the introduction of the permanent income variable, which enhances the explanatory power of the money demand function. Friedman's demand function is as follows:

$$m^d = \frac{M_d}{P} = m^d\left(r_1, \ldots, r_n, \pi, y^p, \omega, u\right) \tag{23.1.3}$$

where, m^d is the real balance of money demand, M^d is the nominal demand for money, P is the price level, $r_1, \ldots, r_n$ represents n different types of assets, the actual rate of return is π, the immediate inflation rate is ω, and the ratio of human capital to non-human capital wealth is y^p which represents the actual permanent income.

Although Friedman's theory of money demand follows the form of Keynes's money demand function in its expression, its theoretical core mainly inherits the ideas of the quantity theory of money and is an enterprise supporter of the importance of money. Friedman denied Keynes's view, believing that the money demand function has high stability, and the stability of the money demand function and the velocity of money circulation even surpasses the stability of the consumption function. From this, Friedman asserted that monetary policy not only has predictable policy effects, but also significant policy effects.[3]

Looking back, it is not difficult to find that whether it is the price theory of mainstream economics or the money demand theory of monetary economics, the price level and inflation rate are both independent variables and belong to pre-set exogenous variables. The price generation mechanism is almost ignored in mainstream economics. Although the quantity theory of money provides a classical explanation of the price generation mechanism, the conclusion that the quantity of money determines value is too simple. Even if the direct action mechanism, indirect action mechanism, and credit action mechanism are added, it is still far from the complex reality of the price formation mechanism. In fact, money is just one of the many determinants of price. Information dissemination, pricing mechanisms, cost composition, and many other factors all play an indispensable role in the process of price formation.

The current situation of price theory is the inevitable result of the underlying logic of mainstream economic theory. The mainstream economic theory centered on neoclassical economics studies the trading system that satisfies specific attributes, that is, it satisfies the homogenization conditions of the agent, satisfies the assumption of perfect market competition, and that of market effectiveness. In such a trading system, prices are determined by both buyers and sellers, and changes in supply and demand are the only force determining prices. Based on this assumption, neoclassical economics acknowledges that prices are real information from market supply and demand changes. Since the mechanism of price formation is clear, the price generation mechanism has become a self-evident process. However, the actual trading system is far from the assumptions of mainstream economics. Not only is there a huge disparity in the trading power of the trading agents, but as the trading system evolves, the trading power presents an irreversible polarization trend; due to the information asymmetry, the trading agents cannot guarantee the effectiveness and rationality of decision-making, thereby losing the basis for the effective operation of the market. The discussion of the price production mechanism is not only necessary, but should also be an important part of economic theory.

23.2 Unilateral Pricing Mechanism

The pricing mechanism plays a very key role in the price system. The so-called pricing mechanism refers to the different roles and relative status relationships played by the trading parties in the pricing process.

There are three different types of pricing mechanisms, namely unilateral pricing mechanisms, bilateral pricing mechanisms, and multilateral pricing mechanisms. In the modern economy, the three pricing mechanisms have their own application scenarios, and they influence the operation of prices in their own different ways.

23.2.1 Unilateral Pricing Mechanism

The unilateral pricing mechanism is determined by one party of the trading, and the other party does not participate in the pricing process, can only express his/her will by accepting or withdrawing from the trading. In real world, the price is generally determined by the supply side, shopping malls and supermarkets are typical examples of unilateral pricing mechanisms.

As the economy moves past the stage of artisanal and free markets, and the scale of commodity trading rapidly expands, the pricing mechanism begins to undergo qualitative changes. The traditional pricing model of bilateral negotiation, due to its inefficiency and time-consuming nature, can no longer meet the demands of large-scale, high-frequency, and long-distance trading s. In today's globalized economy, merchants on the American continent can sell products in distant Asian countries. It is no longer possible for supply and demand parties to negotiate face-to-face as in a free market, and there is a serious asymmetry in the information structure. The equal status of the trading parties in the traditional economy no longer exists. Suppliers play a leading role in pricing, while consumers can only indirectly influence prices through the market, which is a key feature of the unilateral pricing mechanism.

23.2.2 *Price Squeeze Risk*

Although the pricing strategy of suppliers in practice is much more complex than any models discussed in economic theory, the basic principles used by trading agents behind complex pricing operations are very simple. Faced with market competition pressure, suppliers need to strike a balance between maximizing profits and market squeeze risk during the pricing process. Price squeeze risk is a key factor to pricing.

Faced with fierce market competition, trading agents are always in anxiety about losing competitive advantages. Pricing, for manufacturers, is both an important means to maximize profits and a risk that could lead to loss of competitive advantages. In order to maximize profits and minimize risks, the assessment of price squeeze risk plays a key role in the pricing decisions of suppliers. The higher the price squeeze risk, the more cautious the supplier will be. When assessing price squeeze risk, suppliers need to consider two factors: one is the possible reaction of customers to price adjustments; the other is the possible reaction of competitors. If the supplier's price exceeds that of homogeneous goods suppliers, there will be a price squeeze risk, and he may eventually be squeezed out of the market. Price squeeze risk ensures the efficiency of resource allocation in the trading system through survival of the fittest.

The size of the price squeeze risk is affected by the market structure. The price squeeze risk in a highly monopolistic market is weak, while in a fully competitive market, the price squeeze risk is more significant. Imagine the scenario of a vegetable market, if there is only one vegetable vendor in the community, the price is usually high; but if there are multiple vendors nearby, the situation will be different. The price will be cheaper, and the vendor's price premium will be much smaller than that in a monopolistic market. The reason behind this situation is the difference in price squeeze risk between two markets. For a community with only one vegetable vendor, the market forms a local monopolistic microclimate, and the price squeeze risk is limited; for a community with multiple vegetable vendors, the price squeeze risk is higher, forcing vegetable vendors to price cautiously.

The level of price squeeze risk is not only closely related to the intensity of market competition, but also to the individualization of the market. For markets with prominent individualization, the price squeeze risk will be weakened. For example, in the high-end clothing market, thanks to the brand effect, individualization works, and the price squeeze risk is relatively small. The key factor determining the market share of such goods in niche markets is often not the price, but the match between the product's individual positioning and consumer preferences. For markets with weaker individual characteristics, price plays a larger role in determining market share, and the price squeeze risk is stronger.

The process of price squeezing out risk takes time, which is based on the speed of market response. The ease of finding alternative goods is an important factor affecting the speed of price squeezing out risk. The easier it is to find alternatives, the faster the price squeezes out risk sinks in. If it is difficult to find alternative products, the speed at which the price squeeze risk sinks in is relatively slow. Generally speaking, the more distinctive the market characteristics, the more difficult it is to find alternative goods.

Price squeeze risk is also closely related to the supplier's supply adjustment ability. When a supplier raises prices, if other suppliers are unable to fill the supply gap in time, it is beyond the market's will, to react immediately as, it is impossible to quickly diffuse the price squeeze risk.

Price squeeze risk is an expectation formed by suppliers based on market supply structure, market attributes, and historical experience. We define the price squeeze risk coefficient as the expected change in sales volume that may be caused by price adjustments, represented by γ, with a value range of $[0, +\infty)$. When $\gamma = 0$, it means that price adjustments do not produce price squeeze risk; when $\gamma = +\infty$, it means that any price increase will be completely squeezed out of the market. γ the larger the value, the more obvious the price squeeze risk.

23.2.3 Optimal Pricing Strategy

Like other trading strategies, pricing strategy also follows the principle of maximum expected returns. Assume b_j is a supplier in the trading community Ω, at time step t, the product price is p_t, the realized sales volume is q_t, the fixed cost of operation is C_0, the unit variable cost of the product is c_t, and the price squeeze risk coefficient is γ_t; at time step $t+1$, the corresponding parameters are respectively denoted as $p_{t+1}, q_{t+1}, c_{t+1}$, and the changes in these parameters are respectively denoted as $\Delta p_{t+1} = p_{t+1} - p_t$, $\Delta q_{t+1} = q_{t+1} - q_t$, $\Delta c_{t+1} = c_{t+1} - c_t$.

Next, we discuss how supplier b_j will determine the price at time step $t+1$.

Use Δp_{t+1} to represent the price adjustment magnitude that b_j intends to make at time step $t+1$. When $\Delta p_{t+1} = 0$, it means to maintain the price level p_t at time step t unchanged; $\Delta p_{t+1} > 0$ means raising the price; $\Delta p_{t+1} < 0$ means lowering the price at time step $t+1$.

Assume the supplier b_j opt to adjust the price from time step t on p_t to time step $t+1$ on $p_{t+1} = p_t + \Delta p_{t+1}$. The expected return that the pricing strategy can achieve is as follows:

$$E(\Delta p_{t+1}) = \{(p_t + \Delta p_{t+1}) + (q_t + \Delta q_{t+1}) - c_{t+1}(q_t + \Delta q_{t+1}) - C_0\} \\ - \{p_t q_t - c_t q_t - C_0\} \tag{23.2.1}$$

Rearrange (23.2.1) to get:

$$E(\Delta p_{t+1}) = p_t \Delta q_{t+1} + \Delta p_{t+1} q_{t+1} + \Delta p_{t+1} q_{t+1} - c_{t+1} \Delta q_{t+1} - q_t (c_{t+1} - c_t) \tag{23.2.2}$$

From (23.2.2) we get:

$$E(\Delta p_{t+1}) = p_t q_t \left(\frac{\Delta p_{t+1}}{p_t} + \frac{\Delta q_{t+1}}{q_t} + \frac{\Delta p_{t+1}}{p_t} \frac{\Delta q_{t+1}}{q_t} - c_{t+1} \frac{1}{p_t} \frac{\Delta q_{t+1}}{q_t} - \frac{1}{p_t} \Delta c_{t+1} \right) \tag{23.2.3}$$

According to the definition of the price squeeze risk coefficient, we get:

$$\frac{\Delta q_{t+1}}{q_t} = -\gamma_{t+1} \frac{\Delta p_{t+1}}{p_t} \tag{23.2.4}$$

Substitute (23.2.4) into (23.2.3) to get:

$$E(\Delta p_{t+1}) = p_t q_t \left[-\gamma_{t+1} \frac{\Delta p_{t+1}}{p_t} + \frac{\Delta p_{t+1}}{p_t} - \gamma_{t+1} \left(\frac{\Delta p_{t+1}}{p_t} \right)^2 \right. \\ \left. + \gamma_{t+1} \frac{c_{t+1}}{p_t} \frac{\Delta p_{t+1}}{p_t} - \frac{1}{p_t} \Delta c_{t+1} \right] \tag{23.2.5}$$

Let $\pi_{t+1} = \frac{\Delta p_{t+1}}{p_t}$ and substitute into (23.2.5) to get:

$$E(\pi_{t+1}) = p_t q_t \left[-\gamma_{t+1} \pi_{t+1} + \pi_{t+1} - \gamma_{t+1} (\pi_{t+1})^2 + \gamma_{t+1} \frac{c_{t+1}}{p_t} \pi_{t+1} - \frac{\Delta c_{t+1}}{p_t} \right] \tag{23.2.6}$$

Take the derivative of both sides of (23.2.6) with respect to π and let $\frac{\partial \gamma_{t+1}}{\partial \pi_{t+1}} = \alpha_{t+1}$ Obviously, $\alpha_{t+1} \geq 0$ Substitute α_{t+1} into (23.2.6) to get:

$$\frac{dE_{t+1}}{d\pi_{t+1}} = p_t q_t \left(1 - \gamma_{t+1} - 2\gamma_{t+1} \pi_{t+1} + \gamma_{t+1} \frac{c_{t+1}}{p_t} - \alpha_{t+1} \pi_{t+1} \right. \\ \left. - \alpha_{t+1} \left(\pi_{t+1}^2 - \frac{c_{t+1}}{p_t} \pi_{t+1} \right) \right) \tag{23.2.7}$$

Assume $|\pi| \ll 1$ and $\frac{c}{p} < 1$ When $|\alpha| < K$, K is a small positive real number, consider discarding the cubic term on the right side of (23.2.7) to get the following result:

$$\frac{dE_{t+1}}{d\pi_{t+1}} = p_t q_t (1 - \gamma_{t+1} - 2\gamma_{t+1}\pi_{t+1} + \gamma_{t+1}\frac{c_{t+1}}{p_t} - \alpha_{t+1}\pi_{t+1}) \tag{23.2.8}$$

According to the principle of maximizing expected returns, the pricing strategy of supplier b_j must satisfy the maximum condition, that is, $\frac{dE}{d\pi} = 0$ and $\left.\frac{d^2E}{d\pi^2}\right|_{\pi} < 0$. Here, π^* represents the value of π at the maximum point.

According to the requirement of the extreme value condition, $\frac{dE_{t+1}}{d\pi_{t+1}} = 0$. From this we get:

$$1 - \gamma_{t+1} + \gamma_{t+1}\frac{c_{t+1}}{p_t} - \pi^*_{t+1}(2\gamma_{t+1} + \alpha_{t+1}) = 0 \tag{23.2.9}$$

The extreme solution of the pricing strategy is obtained from Eq. (23.2.9):

$$\pi^*_{t+1} = \frac{1 - \gamma_{t+1}}{2\gamma_{t+1} + \alpha_{t+1}} + \frac{\gamma_{t+1}}{2\gamma_{t+1} + \alpha_{t+1}}\frac{c_{t+1}}{p_t} \tag{23.2.10}$$

Now, we discuss the conditions for (23.2.10) as the optimal pricing strategy. From (23.2.8) we get:

$$\begin{aligned}\frac{d^2E_{t+1}}{d\pi^2_{t+1}} = p_t q_t \Big(&-\frac{d\gamma_{t+1}}{d\pi_{t+1}} - \alpha_{t+1} - \frac{d^2\gamma_{t+1}}{d\pi^2_{t+1}}\pi_{t+1} - 2\gamma_{t+1} - 2\pi_{t+1}\frac{d\gamma_{t+1}}{d\pi_{t+1}} \\ &-2\alpha_{t+1}\pi_{t+1} - \frac{d^2\gamma_{t+1}}{d\pi^2_{t+1}}\pi^2_{t+1} + \frac{d\gamma_{t+1}}{d\pi_{t+1}}\frac{c_{t+1}}{p_t} + \frac{c_{t+1}}{p_t}\alpha_{t+1} + \frac{c_{t+1}}{p_t}\pi_{t+1}\frac{d^2\gamma_{t+1}}{d\pi^2_{t+1}}\Big)\end{aligned} \tag{23.2.11}$$

Let: $\frac{d^2\gamma_{t+1}}{d\pi^2_{t+1}} = \beta_{t+1}$ Substitute into (23.2.11) and rearrange to get:

$$\begin{aligned}\frac{d^2E_{t+1}}{d\pi^2_{t+1}} &= p_t q_t (-2\alpha_{t+1} - \beta_{t+1}\pi_{t+1} - 2\gamma_{t+1} - 4\alpha_{t+1}\pi_{t+1} \\ &\quad - \beta_{t+1}\pi^2_{t+1} + 2\frac{c_{t+1}}{p_t}\alpha_{t+1} + \frac{c_{t+1}}{p_t}\beta_{t+1}\pi_{t+1} \\ &= -p_t q_t \left(2\alpha_{t+1} + 2\gamma_{t+1} - 2\alpha_{t+1}\frac{c_{t+1}}{p_t}\right) \\ &\quad - p_t q_t \pi_{t+1}\left(4\alpha_{t+1} + \beta_{t+1} + \beta_{t+1}\pi_{t+1} - \frac{c_{t+1}}{p_t}\beta_{t+1}\right)\end{aligned} \tag{23.2.12}$$

Substitute (23.2.10) into (23.2.12) to get:

$$\frac{d^2E_{t+1}}{d\pi_{t+1}^2}|_{\pi^*} = -p_tq_t\left(2\alpha_{t+1} + 2\gamma_{t+1} - 2\alpha_{t+1}\frac{c_{t+1}}{p_t}\right)$$
$$- p_tq_t\left(\frac{1-\gamma_{t+1}}{2\gamma_{t+1}+\alpha_{t+1}} + \frac{\gamma_{t+1}}{2\lambda_{t+1}+\alpha_{t+1}}\frac{c_{t+1}}{p_t}\right)$$
$$\times\left(4\alpha_{t+1} + \beta_{t+1} + \beta_{t+1}\left(\frac{1-\gamma_{t+1}}{2\gamma_{t+1}+\alpha_{t+1}} + \frac{\gamma_{t+1}}{2\gamma_{t+1}+\alpha_{t+1}}\frac{c_{t+1}}{p_t}\right) - \frac{c_{t+1}}{p_t}\beta_{t+1}\right) \quad (23.2.13)$$

Rearrange to get the following formula:

$$\frac{d^2E_{t+1}}{d\pi_{t+1}^2}|_{\pi^*} = -p_tq_t\left(2\alpha_{t+1} + 2\gamma_{t+1} - 2\alpha_{t+1}\frac{c_{t+1}}{p_t}\right)$$
$$-p_tq_t\frac{1-\gamma_{t+1}\left(1-\frac{c_{t+1}}{p_t}\right)}{2\gamma_{t+1}+\alpha_{t+1}}\left(4\alpha_{t+1} + \beta_{t+1}\left(1 + \frac{1-\gamma_{t+1}}{2\gamma_{t+1}+\alpha_{t+1}} + \frac{\gamma_{t+1}}{2\gamma_{t+1}+\alpha_{t+1}}\frac{c_{t+1}}{p_t} - \frac{c_{t+1}}{p_t}\right)\right) \quad (23.2.14)$$

From (23.2.14) we get:

$$\frac{d^2E_{t+1}}{d\pi_{t+1}^2}|_{\pi^*} = -p_tq_t\left(2\alpha_{t+1} + 2\gamma_{t+1} - 2\alpha_{t+1}\frac{c_{t+1}}{p_t}\right)$$
$$-p_tq_t\frac{1-\gamma_{t+1}\left(1-\frac{c_{t+1}}{p_t}\right)}{2\gamma_{t+1}+\alpha_{t+1}}\left(4\alpha_{t+1} + \beta_{t+1}\left(\frac{\gamma_{t+1}+\alpha_{t+1}+1}{2\gamma_{t+1}+\alpha_{t+1}} + \left(\frac{\gamma_{t+1}}{2\gamma_{t+1}+\alpha_{t+1}} - 1\right)\frac{c_{t+1}}{p_t}\right)\right) \quad (23.2.15)$$

Rearrange to get:

$$\frac{d^2E_{t+1}}{d\pi_{t+1}^2}|_{\pi^*} = -p_tq_t\left(2\alpha_{t+1} + 2\gamma_{t+1} - 2\alpha_{t+1}\frac{c_{t+1}}{p_t}\right)$$
$$-p_tq_t\frac{1-\gamma_{t+1}\left(1-\frac{c_{t+1}}{p_t}\right)}{2\gamma_{t+1}+\alpha_{t+1}}\left(4\alpha_{t+1} + \beta_{t+1}\left(\frac{\gamma_{t+1}+\alpha_{t+1}+1}{2\gamma_{t+1}+\alpha_{t+1}} - \frac{\gamma_{t+1}+\alpha_{t+1}}{2\gamma_{t+1}+\alpha_{t+1}}\frac{c_{t+1}}{p_t}\right)\right) \quad (23.2.16)$$

From the above formula we get:

$$\frac{d^2E_{t+1}}{d\pi_{t+1}^2}|_{\pi^*} = -p_tq_t\left(2\alpha_{t+1} + 2\gamma_{t+1} - 2\alpha_{t+1}\frac{c_{t+1}}{p_t}\right)$$
$$-p_tq_t\frac{1-\gamma_{t+1}\left(1-\frac{c_{t+1}}{p_t}\right)}{2\gamma_{t+1}+\alpha_{t+1}}\left(4\alpha_{t+1} + \beta_{t+1}\frac{1+(\gamma_{t+1}+\alpha_{t+1})\left(1-\frac{c_{t+1}}{p_t}\right)}{2\gamma_{t+1}+\alpha_{t+1}}\right) \quad (23.2.17)$$

For convenience, let $1 - \frac{c_{t+1}}{p_t} = k_{t+1}$ Under normal circumstances, $0 < \frac{c_{t+1}}{p_t} < 1$ Therefore, it is known that k_{t+1} satisfies $0 < k_{t+1} < 1$.

Substituting k into Eq. (23.2.17) yields:

$$\frac{d^2E_{t+1}}{d\pi_{t+1}^2}|_{\pi^*} = -p_tq_t(2\alpha_{t+1}k_{t+1} + 2\gamma_{t+1})$$
$$-p_tq_t\frac{1-\gamma_{t+1}k_{t+1}}{2\gamma_{t+1}+\alpha_{t+1}}\left(4\alpha_{t+1} + \beta_{t+1}\frac{1+(\gamma_{t+1}+\alpha_{t+1})k_{t+1}}{2\gamma_{t+1}+\alpha_{t+1}}\right) \quad (23.2.18)$$

The above equation is rearranged to:

$$\frac{d^2E_{t+1}}{d\pi_{t+1}^2}|_{\pi^*} = -p_t q_t \left\{ (2\alpha_{t+1}k_{t+1} + 2\gamma_{t+1}) + \frac{1-\gamma_{t+1}k_{t+1}}{2\gamma_{t+1}+\alpha_{t+1}} \times \left(4\alpha_{t+1} + \beta_{t+1}\frac{1+(\gamma_{t+1}+\alpha_{t+1})k_{t+1}}{2\gamma_{t+1}+\alpha_{t+1}}\right)\right\} \tag{23.2.19}$$

Given: $\alpha_t \geq 0,\ \gamma_t > 0,\ k_t > 0,$
When the relationship satisfies:

$$1 - \gamma_{t+1}k_{t+1} \geq 0 \tag{23.2.20}$$

$$4\alpha_{t+1} + \beta_{t+1}\frac{1+(\gamma_{t+1}+\alpha_{t+1})k_{t+1}}{2\gamma_{t+1}+\alpha_{t+1}} \geq 0 \tag{23.2.21}$$

Then:

$$\frac{d^2E_{t+1}}{d\pi_{t+1}^2}|_{\pi^*} < 0 \tag{23.2.22}$$

That is, the trading agent b_j will achieve the maximum expected return by adopting the pricing strategy $\pi_{t+1}{}^* = \frac{1-\gamma_{t+1}}{2\gamma_{t+1}+\alpha_{t+1}} + \frac{\gamma_{t+1}}{2\gamma_{t+1}+\alpha_{t+1}}\frac{c_{t+1}}{p_t}$.

The conditions for the optimal pricing strategy are obtained from Eqs. (23.2.20) and (23.2.21):

$$\gamma_{t+1} \leq \frac{1}{k_{t+1}} \tag{23.2.23}$$

$$\beta_{t+1} \geq -\frac{4\alpha_{t+!}(2\gamma_{t+1}+\alpha_{t+!})}{1+(\gamma_{t+!}+\alpha_{t+!})k_{t+1}} \tag{23.2.24}$$

From Eq. (23.2.24) we get:

$$\beta_{t+1} > -4\alpha_{t+1}(2\gamma_{t+1}+\alpha_{t+1}) \tag{23.2.25}$$

Substituting Eq. (23.2.23) into Eq. (23.2.25) yields:

$$\beta_{t+1} > -4\alpha_{t+1}\left(\frac{2}{k_{t+1}} + \alpha_{t+1}\right) \tag{23.2.26}$$

Since $\frac{1}{k_{t+1}} > 1$, as a prerequisite for the optimal pricing strategy, the requirements of Eqs. (23.2.23) and (23.2.26) are very relaxed, meaning they can be satisfied in a wide range of market scenarios. We therefore conclude that $\pi_{t+1}^* = \frac{1-\gamma_{t+1}}{2\gamma_{t+1}+\alpha_{t+1}} +$

$\frac{\gamma_{t+1}}{2\gamma_{t+1}+\alpha_{t+1}}\frac{c_{t+1}}{p_t}$ is the optimal pricing strategy for the trading agent b_j under a unilateral pricing mechanism.

23.2.4 Unilateral Market Pricing Equation

We have discussed the optimal pricing strategy of the pricing agent under a unilateral pricing mechanism. When the price equilibrium mechanism is disrupted, the trading agent can opt for two strategies, either to raise or to lower prices. Either way,, the optimal pricing strategy follows the following formula:

$$\pi_{t+1}^* = \frac{1-\gamma_{t+1}}{2\gamma_{t+1}+\alpha_{t+1}} + \frac{\gamma_{t+1}}{2\gamma_{t+1}+\alpha_{t+1}}\frac{c_{t+1}}{p_t}$$

In a unilateral pricing market, the pricing agents in the trading system face different situations. Trading agents have many factors such as the size of trading power, the level of technical advantages, and the distribution of sales networks, which ultimately converge to parameters such as the squeeze risk coefficient γ_t and the variable production cost c_t, forming differentiated pricing decisions of the pricing agents. The price level of the trading system is the result of the interaction of a large number of trading agents. To track and predict the value trend of the trading system, there are two ways to choose: one is to track the pricing behavior of each pricing agent through big data, estimate the pricing parameters of each pricing agent and its changes, predict the pricing strategy of each agent based on this, and finally synthesize the price trend of the trading system; the other is to treat the market as a whole, build a market macro pricing behavior model, and predict the next step of market price changes based on the pricing model. Compared with the former, the method of building a market pricing model is more feasible.

In a unilateral pricing market, all pricing agents follow the common principle of maximizing expected returns. Formally, it is manifested as satisfying a common behavioral structure equation, namely $\pi_{t+1}^* = \frac{1-\gamma_{t+1}}{2\gamma_{t+1}+\alpha_{t+1}} + \frac{\gamma_{t+1}}{2\gamma_{t+1}+\alpha_{t+1}}\frac{c_{t+1}}{p_t}$. To construct a price equation for a unilateral pricing market, we need to find the average value of market pricing behavior parameters. To this end, we only have to determine the average value of the market agent's price squeeze risk, the first derivative and variable cost averages, and average price parameters, and then construct a macro price equation containing market average parameters based on the micro pricing behavior equation.

Use uppercase Γ_t represents the mean value of the market price squeeze-out risk coefficient; use uppercase C_t represents the mean value of the market production variable cost; use uppercase P_t represents the average market price level; for simplicity, the first derivative of the price squeeze-out risk coefficient still uses α_t, π_t represents the market price change rate. The price equation of the one-sided pricing market has the following form:

$$\pi_{t+1} = \frac{1 - \Gamma_{t+1}}{2\Gamma_{t+1} + \alpha_{t+1}} + \frac{\Gamma_{t+1}}{2\Gamma_{t+1} + \alpha_{t+1}} \frac{C_{t+1}}{P_t} \tag{23.2.27}$$

In the price equation (23.2.27), three parameters, the squeeze-out risk coefficient Γ_t, the squeeze-out risk elasticity α_t and the variable cost C_t determine the pricing behavior of the one-sided pricing market. Equation (23.2.27) shows that the smaller the squeeze-out coefficient Γ_t, the greater the price increase rate π_t. When the squeeze-out coefficient Γ_t is close to 0, its elasticity α_t will also approach 0, π_t will tend to infinity, meaning that market prices will rise rapidly. Conversely, the larger the market squeeze-out coefficient Γ_t, the market price will tend to remain unchanged or downward trend.

The situation of the market average variable cost C_t is exactly the opposite of the mechanism of the squeeze-out risk coefficient Γ_t. The higher the cost C_t, the stronger the impulse to raise prices in the market. If the market average cost C_t remains at a low level, there will be no price adjustment pressure from the cost in the market.

As can be seen from (23.2.27), the larger the squeeze-out risk elasticity α_t, the more cautious the market will be in pricing, even if the price raises, it will take a small increase to avoid causing a market rebound.

The motivation for trading agents to innovate technology and develop new products is included in the pursuit of market advantage and the avoidance of squeeze-out risk. Since new products face fewer competitors, businesses with new products have an absolute advantage in market share and a small squeeze-out risk, which is also an important reason why new products are priced high. The higher the technical content and the more new technologies contained in new products, the more confident trading agents are in resisting competition, and they will have greater pricing autonomy. Suppliers can use market advantages to gain more profits.

In order to obtain higher profits, trading agents hope to minimize the constraints brought by the same phase agents in product pricing. To achieve this goal, trading agents are constantly innovating technology. Based on such motivation, the more intense the market competition, the stronger the motivation for trading agents to innovate.

Just like innovation, for greater pricing advantages, trading agents have the impulse to expand in terms of scale and scope. The larger the scale, the higher the market share, the more obvious the advantage of the trading agent in pricing. For suppliers who need to establish long-term relationships with users, market share is of greater significance. The higher the market share, the greater the expected returns, the easier it is to reduce the cost of R&D allocation, which is beneficial for the market competition of next stage. This is also the case with the automobile and aircraft manufacturing industries, where the product users and suppliers have a long-term contractual relationship, and the more customers, the better able to cover the cost of technological development.

Cost push is an important reason for suppliers being forced to raise prices. Although the risk of price squeeze is not high, this kind of price adjustment does not bring any extra benefits to suppliers, may instead lead to the risk of overall market contraction, which is not a market reaction that suppliers are happy to see. In order to avoid being forced to raise prices as much as possible, trading agents tend to expand their business scope, effectively control comprehensive costs, and reduce supply chain risks brought about by market uncertainty.

23.3 Bilateral Pricing Mechanism

The bilateral pricing mechanism is negotiated by both parties to the trading and is the traditional pricing model. Open-air markets usually adopt this pricing mechanism.

23.3.1 Bilateral Pricing Mechanism

Neoclassical economics believes that the supply–demand relationship determines commodity prices, and commodity prices in turn determine supply and demand. Price has become the core concept of neoclassical economic theory. In the process of determining prices by the supply–demand relationship, neoclassical economics believes that supply and demand are completely equivalent, that is, the impact of demand increase on prices is completely equivalent to the effect of supply reduction. In the entire neoclassical economic theory, whether it is commodity prices, capital interest rates, or labor wages, the equivalence of supply and demand is always maintained.

In the early stage of the market economy, the symmetry of supply and demand in the price formulation mechanism may be established, and the price is determined jointly by the sellers and the buyers. For example, the potato seller starts to ask for two yuan per kilogram, and the seller finds that there are many potato sellers in the market, and he thinks it is necessary to bargain the price of two yuan per kilogram. Therefore, a tentative price of 1.5 yuan per kilogram will be given; if the seller thinks this price is too low, a compromise price of 1.7 yuan per kilogram will be proposed. If the buyer can accept this price, the trading will be made, otherwise the bargaining will continue.

There are three key points in the bargaining process: one is that the buyer knows the number and scale of suppliers of similar goods in the market; the second is that the seller can roughly estimate the number of buyers and the demand by the frequency of people coming to inquire about the price; the third is that the commodity price is negotiated on an equal basis by both parties knowing each other's information. Regardless of the information held by both parties or the way of participating in the pricing process, both parties are in a symmetrical position, and neither party has an obvious advantage. We call the pricing mechanism under this mode the bilateral pricing mechanism.

The bilateral pricing mechanism is the most primitive pricing method, suitable for trading systems with small trading scales, simple trading goods, and low trading frequencies. During the long agricultural civilization era, whether it was international trade or domestic trade, it was conducted through open-air markets. The ancient

Bazzar in the Middle East was actually an open-air market. Goods transported from the Far East and Europe were traded there. The bilateral pricing mechanism has dominated in the long history of human trading system evolution and has an absolute advantage in time. It was only in modern times that new pricing mechanisms were created, and the bilateral pricing mechanism gradually gave up part of its territory, and its influence also greatly declined.

23.3.2 Bilateral Market Pricing Equation

Compared with unilateral and multilateral pricing mechanisms, an important feature of bilateral pricing mechanisms is that each party partially knows the other party's trading information. For the seller, the trading counterpart means the market, and any information conveyed by the other party is crucial; similarly, for the buyer, the counterpart is the supplier, and whether the trading can be realized depends on their acceptance of the other party. In addition, another difference between bilateral pricing and unilateral pricing is that unilateral pricing focuses on the game between the same phase agents, while bilateral pricing focuses on the game between trading counterparts.

The bilateral pricing mechanism can be summarized with the alternating offer model. Alternating offer means that one party b first gives a price, and the other party a if they agree, the trading price is successful; if they disagree, a will propose a revised price based on the price given by b if b agrees with this revised price, the trading price is completed; if they disagree, b will give another price again, if a accepts this price, then the pricing is completed; if they disagree, a will give another revised price again. The final result is only two: either reach a price accepted by both parties and complete the pricing task; or cannot reach a consensus, a and b give up their trading s with each other.

The bilateral pricing process is a process of multiple games between the two trading parties a and b Through a limited number of multiple games, the real information of the other party's psychological price is obtained. The game produces two price sequences, which are the price sequences given by a and b If these two sequences converge, the pricing task can be finally completed; if the two sequences cannot converge, the trading will be terminated.

The above-mentioned bilateral pricing game process is described in an expanded form as follows (Fig. 23.1).

Both parties in the trading have their own expected price ranges during the trading pricing process. The buyer determines a maximum acceptable price in advance, called the buyer's price ceiling, denoted as P_b. This price stipulates the maximum limit that the buyer can accept. If it exceeds this limit, the buyer will refuse the trading. The buyer hopes that the actual trading price is as low as possible, and the trading price must fall on the $(0, P_b)$ interval, which we call the buyer's expected price range.

Similarly, the seller also has a minimum acceptable price, which we call the seller's price floor, denoted as P_s. The seller's expected price range has P_s as the

Fig. 23.1 Price game tree

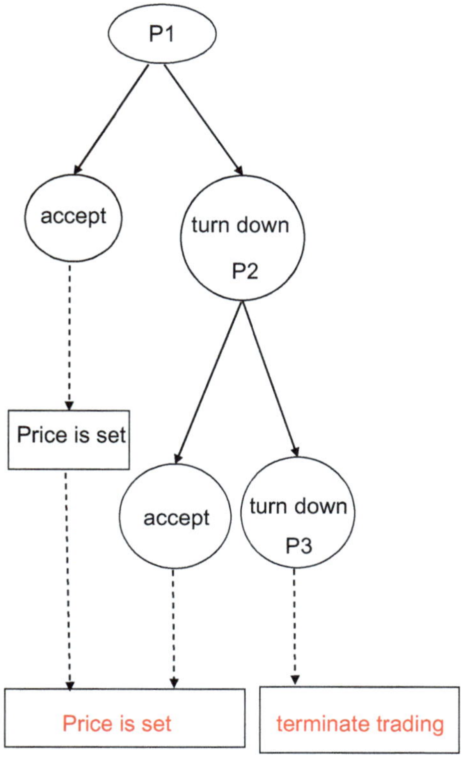

lower endpoint, and the higher the price ceiling, the better. Therefore, the seller's expected price range is $(P_s, +\infty)$.

The expected trading price range is in line with the findings of behavioral economics. Behavioral economics has found that trading utility plays a significant role in trading decisions. To achieve a trading, it is necessary to achieve a mutually acceptable equilibrium result between the two parties in a zero-sum game. If one party's trading utility becomes negative, they will withdraw from the trading, and the trading cannot be completed.[4] This is exactly the conclusion expressed by the expected price range. Here, the bottom price of the two parties corresponds to the "reference value" point in behavioral economics.

To achieve a trading between the trading agents a and b, a basic condition must be met: the expected price range of the two parties has a non-empty intersection. We call this intersection or range the trading price range:

$$[P_s,\ P_b]$$

The trading price range is constructed by the bottom price of the two parties. If this range is an empty set, the trading cannot be completed, and the trading process ends.

We know that the trading price range is usually a wide range, and where the trading price falls depends on the bargaining process of the two parties, which has a certain randomness. For the sake of calculation, we assume that the actual price is normally distributed in this range, that is, through the bargaining process of the two parties, a fair trading can be achieved.

Due to the assumption of normal distribution of the trading price range, the statistical mean of the trading price range is the midpoint of the trading price, that is, the arithmetic average of the two endpoints, and it is also the most likely trading price. Whether it is the buyer or the seller, their price bottom line will be constantly revised during the bargaining process. For example, when making the first trading, the seller always first understands the market conditions, which is a very rough price range. They will determine a preliminary price bottom line based on their eagerness to sell the goods and the comparison of their goods with similar goods. If the first buyer does not accept their offer, the seller waits for a long time, and the second buyer appears. This time, the seller will be afraid of losing the buyer again, otherwise they will have to wait longer, and the seller will appropriately lower the price limit. Similarly, if the first trading is completed quickly, the other party accepts the seller's offer, and subsequent buyers keep coming, the seller will realize that their goods are in high demand and will raise the price bottom line.

The situation is the same for buyers. Buyers first need to understand the market conditions. Based on the market conditions, buyers always hope to buy the best quality and cheapest goods on the market. If the initial price limit is very low, their offer is rejected by the first seller. In the subsequent inquiry process, it is rejected by the second one. Then, they will raise their bid limit. The speed at which the buyer adjusts their price limit is inversely proportional to the time it takes to find the next seller. After being rejected, the longer it takes to find the second seller, the faster the buyer will adjust the price. If there is only one seller, the seller is in a monopoly position, and the buyer must compromise with the seller, otherwise they cannot realize their trading intentions.

In the above analysis, we can find a very important concept—the matching time to find the trading counterparts—that is, the time the trading agent needs to wait to achieve a trading at the expected price. Take the farmers' market as an example, the vegetable seller can sensitively judge the waiting time for the next trader to appear based on the number of people who come to ask for the price and the degree of determination when they refuse the price offered by the vegetable seller and walk away. Matching time contains a lot of market supply and demand information, and is the expected value formed by traders based on various information.

If we consider both endpoints of the trading price range as time functions seeking trading counterparts at their pricing positions, according to the above analysis, we can obtain the following two equations:

$$\frac{dp_s}{dt} = \alpha(\tau_s^0 - \tau_s)$$
$$\frac{dp_b}{dt} = \beta(\tau_b - \tau_b^0) \tag{23.3.1}$$

In (23.3.1), τ represents the time to find objects at a set price, τ^0 represents the expected matching time.

Solving (23.3.1) yields:

$$
\begin{aligned}
p_s &= p_s^0 + \alpha(\tau_s^0 - \tau_s)t \\
p_b &= p_b^0 + \beta(\tau_b - \tau_b^0)t
\end{aligned}
\tag{23.3.2}
$$

In formula (23.3.2), P^0 represents the initial price floor value of the trading parties, which can generally be determined by market conditions. In the two formulas, α and β respectively represent the trading intentions of the trading parties. Obviously, the more urgent the trading, the more the trader tends to adjust their price floor.

In the same market, the matching times of the trading parties are interrelated, with one increasing as the other decreases. When the buyer's matching time becomes longer, the seller's matching time will become shorter. The linkage mechanism of trading matching time determines that the price floor functions of both parties follow the same direction of change. According to the changing rule of the price floor function, we can obtain the following price trend chart (Fig. 23.2).

On the two-dimensional plane formed by price and time, the seller's floor price line and the buyer's cap line divide the price space into three areas, namely S_1, S_2, S_3. Among them, S_1 represents the equilibrium price area. When the market is in this area, it shows a balance of supply and demand, and the price is stable; S_2 represents the seller's market, where the buyer's matching time exceeds the seller's. And the price shows a continuous upward trend in this area; S_3 represents the buyer's market, where the price shows a continuous downward trend in this area.

Now let's discuss the price floor adjustment mechanisms of the trading parties separately. First, let's discuss the seller's price floor adjustment mechanism. When the matching time exceeds the critical value, the seller tends to lower the price floor;

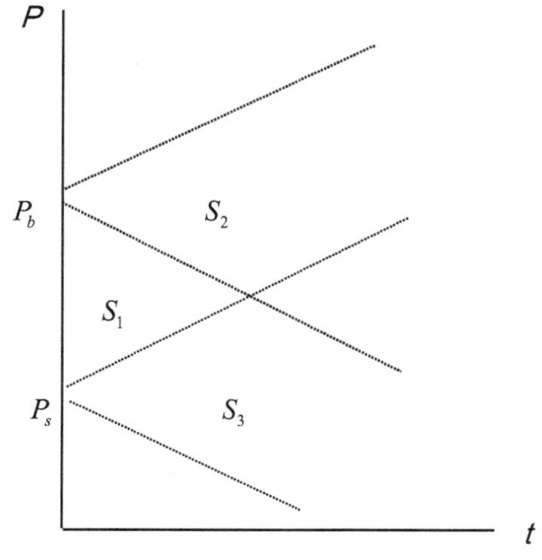

Fig. 23.2 Price game structure

on the contrary, if the matching time is shorter than the expected time, it means that the seller is in an active position, and the sales situation is in short supply. In this case, the seller tends to raise the price floor. The adjustment of the trading price floor ultimately needs to be corrected by the trading urgency coefficient. For sellers who are not in a hurry to sell, even though they wait for a long time, it does not mean that they will definitely lower the price floor. Similarly, the buyer's price floor adjusts accordingly as the trading matching time lengthens. The longer the matching time exceeds the expected time, the greater the buyer's price floor adjustment. If the matching time is much shorter than the expected time, the buyer will be in a favorable position in the trading and will lower the trading price floor to engage in more patient price bargaining with the other party.

According to the assumption of normal distribution of the trading range, the statistical price of the trading extracts the middle value of the trading price range. Any change in the price floor of either party will ultimately affect the statistical price. Theoretically, there is only one special case, that is, the two endpoints of the trading price range move an equal distance in opposite directions, and the maximum possible trading price remains unchanged. In fact, this situation will not occur in reality, because the buyers and sellers are always in opposite positions. The situation where the buyer's price cap is lowered only occurs when they are in a dominant position, which means that the seller is in a weak position. In this case, the measure the seller should take is to lower rather than raise the price floor. Because the trading parties are in a zero-sum game relationship, it determines that the two endpoints of the trading price range must move in the same direction.

The price floor function demonstrates the importance of market structure. In open markets, the reason for the existence of certain differences in vegetable prices between different districts stems from differences in market structure. If in a market of a district, there are fewer sellers and more buyers, the matching time for both parties will differ, and the bilateral pricing model indicates that this situation will inevitably lead to differences in vegetable prices between different districts.

In the price floor function, the expected matching time τ^0 has a significant impact on the price response of both parties, and the expected matching time τ^0 is closely related to the income level of the trading agent. People with higher incomes, who enter the market, do not want to spend a lot of time bargaining, often offer a higher price first, and in most cases, the seller will accept this price. Conversely, for low-income people, they are willing to spend a lot of time patiently bargaining until they reach a relatively low price. This shows that the buyer's income level is negatively correlated with the expected matching time. The higher the income, the shorter the expected matching time. This principle can explain why in a city, the prices in wealthy districts are always much higher than those in poor districts.

The price changes in the bilateral pricing market do not entirely depend on the comparison of the number of trading agents. The change in vegetable prices on rainy days is a good example. According to the comparison of the number of trading parties, on rainy days, the number of people selling vegetables will not change much, most of them will still brave the rain to buy vegetables, while the number of people buying vegetables will be much less. As long as there is a little reserve of vegetables at home, they will try not to buy vegetables, only when there are no vegetables at home, they will choose to brave the rain to buy vegetables. In the comparison of the number of trading parties, there are many fewer buyers than usual, so logically the price of vegetables should fall on rainy days, but in fact, this is not the case. This is due to the increased transportation costs on rainy days and the hard work of buying vegetables, which makes all the vegetable sellers in the market easily reach a consensus or an unspoken agreement—the price of vegetables rises. In this case, although there are fewer people buying vegetables than usual, if the buyer insists on yesterday's price, it will take a long time to match the price or it may not be possible to trade at all. In this case, if the buyer wants to buy vegetables, they must raise their maximum price. The market structure not only contains the supply and demand structure but also contains the internal structure of supply and demand—behavioral consistency. In the example of the vegetable market, the sellers reached an agreement and formed a consistent structure; while the buyers were no in position to do the same, so the trading price must be a compromise from the buyer to the seller.

Based on the price floor function of the price range, we can derive the price equation of the bilateral pricing mechanism according to the assumption of normal distribution of interval prices. In the price floor function, α and β represent the trading intentions of the seller and the buyer, respectively. Under normal circumstances, we can assume that both parties have equal trading intentions, under this setting, let:

$$\alpha = \beta = 2k \geq 0 \tag{23.3.3}$$

Under normal circumstances, the expected matching time of both parties are basically the same, we assume:

$$\tau_s^0 = \tau_b^0 \tag{23.3.4}$$

Under the above two agreements, the maximum possible price level of the bilateral pricing market is obtained from the price floor function P:

$$P = \frac{P_s + P_b}{2} = \frac{P_s^0 + P_b^0}{2} + kt(\tau_b - \tau_s) \tag{23.3.5}$$

Let $P_0 = \frac{P_s^0 + P_b^0}{2}$, substitute into (23.3.5) to get the maximum possible price at time step t:

$$P_t = P_0 + kt(\tau_b - \tau_s) \tag{23.3.6}$$

Equation (23.3.6) indicates the price change mechanism of the bilateral pricing market, where P_0 represents the market equilibrium price level, k represents the sensitivity coefficient of the bilateral pricing market. The larger value k takes, the more sensitive the market is to waiting time. Any slight deviation from equilibrium between supply and demand will be clearly reflected in the price. In such a market, prices will fluctuate around the equilibrium level P_0. When $\tau_b - \tau_s > 0$ occurs, it indicates that the buyer's waiting time is longer, the market initiative leans towards the supplier, it is a seller's market, and prices rise over time; when $\tau_b - \tau_s < 0$ occurs, the seller's waiting time becomes longer while the buyer's waiting time is shorter, with the buyer taking the initiative, and market prices enter a downward spiral.

Equation (23.3.6) presents the basic logic of neoclassical economics on how supply and demand determine prices. This is a trading scenario that neoclassical economics focuses on, and we call it the bilateral pricing equation.

23.4 Multilateral Pricing Mechanism

The multilateral pricing mechanism is a mechanism where many trading agents participate equally in price setting. This pricing mechanism often occurs at auctions, where the auctioneer determines the starting price and bidding rules, and all bidding agents participate in pricing together. Matched bidding is also a common form of multilateral pricing, and various exchanges are the main application scenarios.

23.4.1 Multilateral Pricing Mechanism

The multilateral pricing mechanism plays a very important role in the modern economy. Many financial markets use matched pricing, which is a typical multilateral pricing mechanism. The multilateral pricing mechanism is a price formation mechanism participated by many trading agents. Auctions belong to a special type of multilateral pricing. Although there are many different ways of auctions, no matter what form of auction, there is a structure corresponding to one seller and many potential buyers. As a special multilateral pricing mechanism, auctions have two significant features compared to other multilateral pricing mechanisms: one is suitable for trading s with few quantities and high value. Organizing an auction, from issuing notices, to organizing auctions, and bidding auctions, the organizational costs and time costs are much higher than general trading s, and low-value targets cannot bear these costs. Despite this, from the momentum of development, the field of trading s using the auction mechanism is increasing, from the relatively classic art collection auctions, to land auctions, to national debt auctions, to project engineering bidding, the use of auctions is increasing; the second is suitable for discontinuous trading s. One-time trading s or trading s at a certain time interval, such as auction house auctions, national debt auctions on a regular basis, etc.

In the context of the entire national economic price system, the importance of the auction, a multilateral pricing mechanism, is still one level lower compared to matching and market maker inquiries. Most financial markets use matching trading methods, including important markets such as stocks, on-exchange bonds, and bulk commodity futures. In the matching trading process, there will be a large number of participants on both sides of the trading at the same time, and each participant will have a certain impact on price formation. In this sense, matching trading is the most typical multilateral pricing.

The financial market plays a very important role in resource allocation guidance in the modern economy. Research on the multilateral pricing mechanism is very helpful for a deep understanding of the laws and characteristics of financial market price movements. Not only that, important strategic materials involving economic security and price stability, such as oil and grain, are increasingly traded through futures trading, which further enhances the importance of the multilateral pricing mechanism.

23.4.2 Pricing Behavior

Matched bidding is the most typical form of multilateral pricing, we choose matched bidding as the breakthrough point of research for multilateral pricing mechanisms. At time step t, among the simultaneously arriving trading instructions, one group is buying instructions, and one group is selling instructions. We use B to represent the set of buying instructions, and S to represent the set of selling instructions. $B_t = \{b_1, b_2, b_3, \ldots, b_m\}$, b_i represent the buying prices quoted by investors; $S_t = \{s_1, s_2, s_3, \ldots, s_m\}$, s_j represent the selling prices quoted by investors.

Matched bidding is to establish a correlation mechanism between the quote sets B_t and S_t, and determine the trading price through this mechanism. This requires a series of rules to be formulated to realize the mapping from the quote set to the trading price. The first problem to be solved is how to establish a matching order on the two quote sets. The most common rules are time priority and price priority, that is, the price that arrives first participates in the match first; for prices quoted at the same time step, the price that is most favorable to the trading counterparty participates in the match first.

At time step t, the price that gets priority matching in the selling instruction set S_t is $Min(S_t)$; the price that gets priority matching in the buying instruction set B_t is $Max(B_t)$. According to the requirements of the matched bidding rules, if $Max(B_t) < Min(S_t)$, that is, the highest buying price in the buying instruction set is lower than the lowest selling price in the selling instruction set, a trading cannot be reached between B_t and S_t. Only when B_t, S_t satisfy the following inequality:

$$Max(B_t) \geq Min(S_t) \tag{23.4.1}$$

The bidding match trading can be reached. If $Max(B_t) = Min(S_t)$, the trading directly uses the prices of both parties. If the two prices are not equal, there are multiple possible solutions, the simplest solution is to use the mid-price of the two prices:

$$P_t = \frac{Max(B_t) + Min(S_t)}{2} \tag{23.4.2}$$

Through the bidding match to get the trading price accepted by both parties (23.4.2), the match trading is completed. Since the trading instructions are randomly entered, it is impossible to guarantee that the trading instruction of $Min(S_t)$ is exactly equal to the trading instruction of $Max(B_t)$, there will always be one party's trading instructions that cannot be fully satisfied, and the unsatisfied party's trading instructions enter the matching of time step t + 1, and continue to match according to the previous round's procedure. The validity period of trading instructions is usually set as one trading day. If the trading instruction does not get the trading matching opportunity before the end of the trading day, the trading instruction will automatically expire.

Bidding matching requires strong computing power. In the setting of time steps, there are usually several intervals of a few microseconds, within which precise matching could be achieved. Since the time interval of the matching rounds is very short, the scale of the instruction sets B_t and S_t is generally small. Under the close tracking of traders, the price of market matching will show a slight and continuous change, forming a continuous price curve.

In the matching bidding process, although the trading price is set by prices quoted from two parties, one from the buyer and one from the seller, other trading instructions also play an important role and will also affect the matching price. Taking the set of buy orders as an example, the first price to be selected for matching must come from the comparison on the instruction set B_t, each price will contribute to the formation of the highest price. On the sell order set S_t, each quote also affects the lowest price.

Now, let's examine how the price generated by the matching bid changes with the expansion and contraction of the price instruction set. Suppose B_1 and B_2 are two sets of buy order prices, and they are in a containment relationship:

$$B_1 \subseteq B_2$$

Then:

$$Max(B_1) \leq Max(B_2) \tag{23.4.3}$$

Suppose S_1 and S_2 are two sets of sell order prices, and there is a relationship:

$$S_1 \subseteq S_2$$

Then:

$$Min(S_1) \geq Min(S_2) \tag{23.4.4}$$

According to the characteristics of extreme prices and the formation mechanism of matching prices, it can be inferred that when the sell order set remains unchanged, the expansion of the buy order set will cause the matching price to rise; conversely, the contraction of the buy order set will cause the price to fall. Similarly, under the premise that the buy order set remains unchanged, the expansion of the sell order set leads to a decrease in the trading price; on the contrary, the contraction of the sell order set leads to an increase in the trading price. The change in the scale of trading instructions reflects the market expectations to a certain extent. Therefore, although the bidding matching mechanism has complex pricing rules, it still follows through the basic logic of supply and demand determining prices.

Financial trading is mainly for the pursuit of investment profit. In the market, each trading agent can be a buyer and a seller at the same time, depending on which side can bring greater investment returns. Due to the nature of the matching bidding mechanism and the profit-seeking nature of trading agents, a self-reinforcing mechanism of the financial market is formed—namely the instability of rising driving rising and falling leading to falling.

As a starting point for analysis, assume that the financial market has an equal pattern between buyers and sellers at time step t:

$$B_t = \{b_1 \quad b_2 \quad \dots \quad b_m\}, \quad S_t = \{s_1 \quad s_2 \quad \dots \quad s_n\}$$

At this time, the number of trading instructions in the two instruction sets is equal, that is: $n_t = m_t$.

For some reason, the market balance pattern is broken at time step $t + 1$, and it is assumed that k investors switch to the buyer role from seller, that is:

$$n_{t+1} - m_{t+1} = k$$

From (23.4.3)–(23.4.4), it can be known that at time step $t + 1$, the trading price P_{t+1} must rise:

$$P_t \leq P_{t+1} \tag{23.4.5}$$

If the increase in trading price is large, after the upward momentum continues for a period of time, the market will form a price increase expectation. The original sellers will turn to buyers, this change further drives the price to rise, strengthens the market's price increase expectation, attracts more traders to enter the buying ranks, and drives the trading price to continue to rise sharply. Conversely, when the equilibrium situation is broken and moves in the opposite direction, more trading agents enter the selling queue, and the market price will experience the opposite price trend, with a continuous and sharp decline.

Due to the hedging relationship between the trading instructions of the buyer and seller B_t and S_t, price fluctuations in the multilateral pricing market have a strong leverage effect. Under this leverage mechanism, the market is prone to a highly unstable butterfly effect. The more components in the price system that use multilateral pricing, the more unstable the price level. Multilateral pricing is playing an increasingly important basic pricing function in the modern economy. The futures market is a typical multilateral pricing market for matchmaking trading, and the oil futures market is increasingly playing a pricing role. The leveraged trading nature of the futures market further enhances the instability of the multilateral market. Oil prices rose from $30 a barrel in 2005 to $140 a barrel in the first half of 2008. The sharp rise in oil prices did not result from major changes in supply and demand, but from a large amount of speculative funds making wave in the commodity futures market. Data shows that the proportion of investment in the oil market was as high as 81%, and futures trading that truly reflects actual demand was less than 20%.

23.4.3 Multilateral Market Pricing Equation

Multilateral pricing is sensitive and prone to market resonance. In such markets, minor factors will be magnified, possibly forming a butterfly effect. Various financial markets and commodity markets have such characteristics. In the multilateral pricing market, the state of the trading agent can be divided into three types: buying, selling, and sitting on the fences. Any increase in the state of traders will cause corresponding changes in prices. As the number of trading agents in a state increases, the price change and the corresponding states show a mutually reinforcing positive feedback relationship.

At time step t, the trader's choice of state is a probability event. We use P_b to represent the probability of the trader choosing a buying strategy. Obviously, P_b will be affected by the following three factors:

The First factor is liquidity reserves. The more abundant the funds held by investors, the better able they are to realize their trading desires. On the contrary, if the funds are insufficient, financing is difficult or the financing cost is high, the probability of entering the market to buy will decrease. Even if you opt to buy, the purchase quantity is limited. We use l to represent the amount of liquidity held by traders, which is directly proportional to P_b:

$$P_b \propto l$$

The second is actual demand. In the multilateral market, not all participants in the trading are investors, and there are a considerable number of agents with actual demands. For example, in the steel market, in addition to speculative traders, there are also some agents with production demands, including car manufacturers, equipment manufacturers, construction companies, etc. For these traders, actual demand is another important factor affecting P_b. The more and more urgent the demand, the greater the probability of purchase; vice versa. Use d to represent demand.

$$p_b \propto d$$

The above two variables are of certain objectivity. The proportion of positions, available funds, and actual demand reflect the actual situation of traders and form mandatory constraints on trading decisions.

The third is price expectation. Traders' expectations of market price trends play a very crucial role in trading decisions. For speculative trading agents, price trends are almost the only factor of concern. For these traders, they will buy when prices are expected to rise, and sell when prices are expected to fall. In frequently traded markets, traders' expectations are variable. Traders apply an empirical model to judging price trends based on experience, and form price expectations based on information evaluation. Although the models vary, due to the traders' adherence to the focal consensus of basic market cognition, the main parameters and relationships in the building of the empirical model have certain commonalities. These main variables include recent price trends; macro policies, regulations and rules, macro trends, and other factors that affect the actual supply and demand relationship of commodities; and market atmosphere, etc. Use p_e to represent price expectations, which has the following relationship with the probability of buying P_b:

$$P_b \propto p_e$$

Summarizing the relationship between the probability of buying and the above three main variables, the probability of trading agents adopting a buying strategy P_b is constructed as follows:

$$P_b = P(d,\ l,\ p_e) \tag{23.4.6}$$

And has the following relationship:

$$\frac{\partial P_b}{\partial d} > 0 \quad \frac{\partial P_b}{\partial l} > 0, \quad \frac{\partial P_b}{\partial p_e} > 0$$

In practice, the trader's current position will also have a significant impact on the probability of buying. If the trader is already in a full position and has no plans to increase the investment scale, even if the market is expected to rise in the next stage, it is difficult to continue buying. In this case, they usually maintain their existing positions and wait for prices to rise. That is to say, when traders are in a full position, even if the market is bullish, they cannot continue to buy. On the contrary, if the position is low or empty, when a bullish market appears, the probability of traders buying will be very high. There is an inverse relationship between the position ratio and the probability of buying. The higher the position ratio, the lower the probability of further buying. However, from the calculation of the position ratio, the core is still the amount of funds of the trader. The position ratio is the total value of the held trading targets as a proportion of the investor's total liquid assets. Total assets are the sum of the market value of the target and cash. With a constant position, the more funds enter the market, the lower the position ratio. Based on the above analysis, the position ratio has not been included in the buying probability function, and liquidity l has indirectly reflected the information of the position ratio.

Among the three variables that affect the probability of buying, price expectation, as a subjective judgment of traders, is of individuality and uncertainty, and is a major source of market uncertainty. In the formation of price expectations, there is an easy positive feedback trading loop between past prices p and expected prices p_e. The rise in prices affects traders' future price expectations. The longer the price rises, the easier it is to strengthen the expectation for price rises; conversely, the more traders with expectation for price rises, the higher the price will rise, thereby further consolidating the original price expectation. In the self-strengthening process of price expectations, the position volume will become the only damping factor. Theoretically, as more and more traders buy, liquidity constraints will become a damping factor. But the market is open, when the expectation of price rises is formed, a large amount of funds will flood in from outside the market, and liquidity constraints will weaken in a short time. Only after a period of time, when the influx of funds gradually decreases, will the damping effect of liquidity constraints appear.

Compared with the probability of buying, the decision-making mechanism of the probability of selling is relatively simple, mainly affected by sales demand and price expectations. Sales demand mainly comes from actual producers, who need to sell their products to the market to obtain liquidity. Use P_e Represents the probability of selling, the probability function is as follows:

$$P_s = P(s, p_e) \tag{23.4.7}$$

In Eq. (23.4.7), s represents sales demand, P_e represents price expectations.

The price in a multilateral pricing market is determined by both the buying probability and the selling probability. The buying probability and selling probability represent the proportion of market participants with different trading intentions. When the buying probability is greater than the selling probability, it indicates that the proportion of buying intentions in the market is higher than the proportion of selling intentions, and the trading price will inevitably rise; when the buying probability is less than the selling probability, it indicates that the proportion of selling intentions is higher than the buying intentions, and the trading price will inevitably fall. We express the above logic as the following mathematical relationship:

$$P = F(P_b, P_s) \tag{23.4.8}$$

And it satisfies:

$$\frac{\partial F}{\partial P_b} > 0 \quad \frac{\partial F}{\partial P_s} < 0$$

Based on the construction of the two probability functions (23.4.6) and (23.4.7), we further expand the price function (23.4.8) to obtain the following relationship:

$$P = P(s, d, l, p_e) \tag{23.4.9}$$

For a multilateral pricing market, the scale of liquidity held by market participants has a positive correlation with the money supply of the trading system. When the money supply in the trading system is abundant, the liquidity of market participants remains at a high level; on the contrary, when the money supply in the trading system shrinks, the market liquidity l will decrease. Therefore, in the multilateral market price function (23.4.9), the liquidity level l can be replaced by the money supply M of the trading system.

There are both selling demand and buying demand in the market, the ratio of the two variables affects the market price, when buying exceeds selling, the market price rises, and when selling exceeds buying, the price falls. Use σ to represent the actual supply–demand ratio of the multilateral pricing market:

$$\sigma = \frac{s}{d} \tag{23.4.10}$$

In this way, in the price function (23.4.9), the two variables of selling demand s and buying demand d can be replaced by the market structure parameter σ. Considering that the expected mean price of the market p_e is ultimately determined by supply and demand and money, the information it carries is already included in the two variables σ and M. Combining the above analysis, the price equation of the multilateral pricing market can be expressed in a more concise form:

$$P_t = P(\sigma_t, M_t) \tag{23.4.11}$$

In the price function (23.4.11), the price has the following relationship with the two variables:

$$\frac{\partial P}{\partial \alpha} < 0 \quad \frac{\partial P}{\partial M} > 0$$

23.5 Comparison of Three Pricing Mechanisms

Under the unilateral pricing mechanism, the factors that influence the pricing behavior of the agent mainly come from two aspects: one is the competition of the same phase agent; the other is the price elasticity of the market; other factors will also indirectly affect the pricing behavior of the trading agent through the above two basic elements. Generally speaking, an increase in demand or a rise in cost are reasons for the trading agent to adjust prices, but they do not play a direct role and must be transformed into two decision variables before they will ultimately affect the pricing decision of the trading agent. Take the increase in demand as an example, at time step t, the orders received by the trading agent a_i have increased, a_i may not immediately raise the price, if the price raises too much, it will face the risk of losing some customers. Only when the price squeeze risk γ_t is considered to be at a lower level, can price adjustment be made. Similarly, when a trading agent faces a situation of rising costs, before adjusting prices decision is made, it must at first understand whether there is surplus capacity in the market and whether the costs can be absorbed. Only when there is no surplus capacity in the entire industry can the rise in costs possibly prompt the trading agent to decide to raise prices. If there is a lot of surplus capacity in the industry, the competition for market share will be very intense. Even though the trading agent is under great cost pressure, due to the risk of price squeeze γ_t and the high cost, the trading agent still cannot rashly raise prices. It can be seen that due to the constraints of in-phase competition and price elasticity, under the unilateral pricing mechanism, although the supplier has the pricing power, the market price still has strong stability.

In the unilateral pricing mechanism, the number of trading s affects the final price level. Generally speaking, the more trading links, the higher the terminal price. In the unilateral pricing mechanism, adding trading links has almost no impact on the upstream, and the trading system lacks a self-restraint mechanism for the proliferation of trading links. As long as the demand is strong, it is easy to breed more trading links. The Chinese coal market and steel market have experienced increased trading links. In the mid-1990s, due to the rapid growth of fixed asset investment, construction materials such as steel were in short supply, and some speculators quickly entered the steel market. Generally speaking, the increase in trading links mostly occurs when the supply–demand relationship is tense and prices are in an upward trend. Due to the increase in trading links, demand is artificially amplified, the tension in supply and demand is further intensified, and rising prices will increase upward pressure. After the increase in trading links, the originally relatively simple market structure begins to become complicated, and trading efficiency decreases accordingly.

Compared with unilateral pricing, bilateral pricing is less stable. This is mainly because in the bilateral pricing mechanism, neither party has dominant pricing power, and the price is the result of the game price of both parties. The median price of the entire market is the product of the game of many trading agents. Therefore, no party will bear the risk of price changes. The difference in the pricing risk allocation mechanism determines that the two pricing mechanisms will inevitably show different stability characteristics.

Multilateral pricing has a lot in common with bilateral pricing, both of which have the characteristic of random fluctuations. However, due to the constraints of bilateral bargaining, the expected prices of buyers and sellers are limited by the other party at the bottom, enclosed within the trading price range, and this instability usually does not form a butterfly effect of price fluctuations. Among the three different pricing mechanisms, the multilateral pricing mechanism is the most unstable. This pricing mechanism is prone to speculative behavior, resulting in large price fluctuations.

In reality, pricing mechanisms are not immutable. When a pricing mechanism shows obvious irrationality, people will look for new pricing mechanisms. In the early days of the Industrial Revolution, workers' wages were unilaterally set by the employer, the main party in the trading. As workers had no participation in the wage-setting process, wages remained too low for a long time, leading to widespread poverty among workers. With the establishment of trade unions, unions participated in the pricing process of labor, and labor pricing changed from unilateral pricing to bilateral pricing. This change had a profound impact on the development of European society. On the one hand, workers' wage pricing became more reasonable than before, workers were able to share more corporate profits, preventing the rapid worsening of social wealth disparity, the middle class grew stronger, the tumultuous workers' movement in nineteenth-century Europe quietly subsided, and society gradually stabilized. On the other hand, because wealth distribution avoided excessive differentiation, it ensured the continuous operation of the economic cycle, providing a foundation for sustained economic growth.

The three pricing mechanisms each have their characteristics, their application scenarios, and usage conditions. When the market falls into a monopoly, the unilateral pricing mechanism will fail; although the bilateral pricing mechanism has higher stability, its pricing efficiency is low; the multilateral pricing mechanism has the characteristics of high pricing efficiency and quick and sensitive response to supply and demand, but its weakness is that it often appears excessive speculation, the market is easy to fall into chaos, and prices rise and fall dramatically.

23.6 Price Equation

The price equation is based on the decision-making mechanism of the trading agent, and also includes monetary factors and trading network structure parameters, placing the formation and changes of prices in a broader analytical framework.

23.6.1 Price Formation Mechanism in Modern Economy

The pricing system in the modern economy is a mixed system dominated by unilateral pricing and multilateral pricing. Although the bilateral pricing mechanism still has its application scenarios, it is marginalized in the modern trading system, and we no longer include it in the analytical framework when constructing the price equation.

Under the promotion of financial innovation, the role of the multilateral pricing mechanism in the economy is increasingly permeating all areas of the trading system. Although unilateral pricing still dominates commodity pricing, the influence of the futures market and financial market on the real economy is ubiquitous. Only by combining multilateral pricing and unilateral pricing can we construct a pricing model that is more in line with reality.

In the modern trading system, upstream commodities such as energy and raw materials in the industrial chain are basically priced by the futures market. The instability of the multilateral pricing mechanism enters the supply chain of the trading

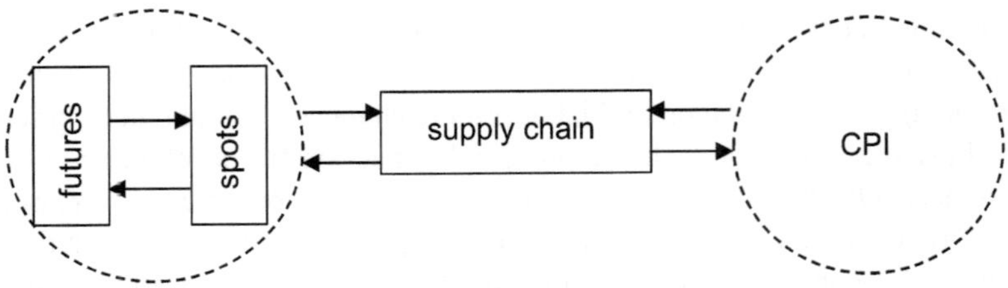

Fig. 23.3 The modern price formation mechanism

system through the futures market, through the production cost pipeline, and finally spreads its influence to the entire economy, reflected in the consumer price index.

The forward prices of bulk commodities generated through the futures market guide the spot market prices, this link is dominated by the multilateral pricing mechanism. In Fig. 23.3, the above price transmission link corresponds to the left circular part. After the pricing of bulk commodities is completed, the price information is transmitted to the CPI through the supply chain. Oil, grain, non-ferrous metals, and other bulk commodities are the basic raw materials for many industries, and oil is the benchmark that leads other energy prices, playing an important role in determining energy prices. The price of bulk commodities is an important factor in the cost of enterprise production. Changes in enterprise production costs will inevitably lead to changes in the producer price index PPI, and after the commercial circulation link, the information from the multilateral pricing market finally reaches the CPI link.

Figure 23.3 illustrates the interaction mechanism between the multilateral pricing futures market and the terminal consumer market. Driven by cost increases, the terminal consumer market price CPI will respond, and the rise in CPI will feed back demand information to the futures market of bulk commodities through the supply chain channel, forming a mutual response relationship between forward prices and demand.

23.6.2 Price Equation

In the modern pricing system, the multilateral pricing mechanism is at the upstream of the industry and belongs to the cost formation link of the trading system, while the midstream and downstream of the industry basically adopt unilateral pricing rules. Therefore, the price model of the modern trading system should be based on the unilateral pricing model, embedding the multilateral pricing mechanism into the unilateral model, and finally synthesizing the price equation.

It is known that the form of the unilateral pricing model is as follows:

$$\pi_{t+1} = \frac{1 - \Gamma_{t+1}}{2\Gamma_{t+1} + \alpha_{t+1}} + \frac{\Gamma_{t+1}}{2\Gamma_{t+1} + \alpha_{t+1}} \frac{C_{t+1}}{P_t} \tag{23.6.1}$$

The price squeeze risk coefficient Γ represents the degree of market competition. The more intense the market competition, the larger the value of the price squeeze risk coefficient Γ. From the perspective of the trading system, market competition is the way in which trading agents interact and depend on each other. The stronger the market competition, the closer the connection between trading agents, and the higher the degree of interactive response between trading agents, which will eventually be reflected in the compactness of the trading system. The more intense the market competition, the higher the compactness of the trading system ϕ; conversely, the higher the compactness of the trading system ϕ, the more intense the market competition. It can be seen that the price squeeze risk coefficient of the trading system Γ is a function of the compactness of the trading system ϕ, and has the following relationship:

$$\frac{\partial \Gamma}{\partial \phi} > 0 \tag{23.6.2}$$

In addition, the price squeeze risk coefficient of the trading system Γ is also a function of the total demand Q. The larger the total demand Q, the lower the price squeeze risk coefficient Γ; conversely, the smaller the total demand Q, the higher the price squeeze risk coefficient Γ. In the modern trading system, demand must be realized by means of currency. Under the condition of constant currency circulation speed, the total currency supply forms a corresponding relationship with the total demand. The larger the total currency supply M, the larger the total demand that can be released Q, the lower the price squeeze risk coefficient Γ; conversely, the smaller the total currency supply M, the stronger the liquidity constraint of the trading agent, the more intense the market competition, and the higher the price squeeze risk coefficient Γ. Therefore, the price squeeze risk coefficient Γ is a decreasing function of the currency supply M:

$$\frac{\partial \Gamma}{\partial M} < 0 \tag{23.6.3}$$

Squeeze-out Risk Coefficient Γ In addition to being influenced by the two variables mentioned above, external shocks also have a significant impact on the squeeze-out risk coefficient of prices. External shocks refer to disturbances from outside the trading system that are of a certain magnitude and are abnormal. The trading system faces two types of external shocks. One is demand shocks, mainly caused by panic buying when the public falls into panic or trading stagnation caused by a large number of trading agents' balance sheets being damaged by crises. The former situation is a rapid expansion of demand, and the trading system does not have enough time to adjust the supply; the latter situation is just the opposite, the balance sheets of trading agents are damaged and cannot continue to trade, the trading network presents a fragmented pattern, and the demand of the trading system encounters a sudden contraction. The other type is supply shocks. Corresponding to demand shocks, supply shocks are strong disturbances on the supply side, usually caused by major natural disasters causing supply chain paralysis, or wars causing widespread destruction of supply capacity, or severe international sanctions causing trade stagnation. These shocks will cause the supply capacity to rapidly deplete in a short period of time, causing unbearable shocks to the normal operation of the trading system. Another situation of supply shock is that a previously non-existent supply force suddenly joins, such as major resource discoveries or successful development, or a major country suddenly joining the world economic cycle, resulting in a significant increase in the scale of resource and commodity supply. These are all causes and manifestations of supply shocks.

For the convenience of expression, use p^d and p^s to represent demand shocks and supply shocks, respectively, and they both take values on $(-\infty, +\infty)$. Demand shock $p^d = +\infty$ represents a sudden infinite increase in demand; $p^d = -\infty$ represents a sudden sharp contraction in demand, and trading is almost stagnant; $p^d = 0$ represents no demand shock, and everything is normal in the trading system. Supply shock $p^s = +\infty$ represents the supply chain falling into paralysis; $p^s = -\infty$ represents a sudden large increase in supply; $p^s = 0$ represents normal supply, and there is no supply shock in the trading system.

Usually, external shocks are in a dormant or invisible state, that is, p^d and p^s hover around 0, almost having no impact on the operation of the trading system. Once external shocks occur, whether they are demand shocks or supply shocks, they will cause great damage to the trading system, and even cause the trading system to completely collapse.

The squeeze-out risk coefficient of prices is the supplier's expectation and assessment of the size of the market squeeze-out risk. In external shocks, the positive demand shock $p^d > 0$ causes the squeeze-out risk coefficient of prices Γ to drop rapidly; the larger the value of the demand shock p^d, the greater the drop in the squeeze-out risk coefficient of prices Γ, quickly returning to zero from a larger value; on the contrary, the negative demand shock $p^d < 0$. The smaller, the price squeezes out the risk coefficient Γ. It may show a jump-like increase, this relationship can be expressed as follows:

$$\frac{\partial \Gamma}{\partial p^d} < 0 \tag{23.6.4}$$

Supply shocks will also squeeze out the risk of price Γ have a significant impact. The stronger the positive supply shock $p^s > 0$. The weaker the squeeze out risk coefficient Γ. Conversely, the smaller the negative supply shock $p^s < 0$ The stronger the squeeze out risk coefficient Γ. The relationship between supply shock and risk squeeze out coefficient is as follows:

$$\frac{\partial \Gamma}{\partial p^s} < 0 \tag{23.6.5}$$

Combining the above analysis, the price squeeze out risk coefficient of the trading system Γ is a function of the compactness of the trading system ϕ, Money supply

M and external shocks p^d, p^s and other four variables. These variables reflect the structure of the trading network, the state of the trading system, and the environment of the trading system. The price squeeze out risk function gives Γ the response to changes in three variables. Considering the lag in monetary transmission, we introduce the lag amount τ, then the price squeeze out risk function of the trading system is as follows:

$$\Gamma_{t+1} = \Gamma(p_{t+1}^d, p_{t+1}^s, \phi_{t+1}, M_{t-\tau}) \tag{23.6.6}$$

Now, let's discuss the variable production cost variable of the trading system C_t. Considering that the main determinants of variable costs are concentrated in the upstream of the industry and are closely related to commodity prices, the cost variable of the trading system C_t is mainly determined by the multilateral pricing mechanism. The higher the commodity prices, the higher the variable costs of the trading system C_t. On the contrary, the cheaper the commodity prices, the lower the variable costs of the trading system C_t. In the multilateral pricing market, the money supply M Is a key variable determining the price. The price function is $P = P(\sigma, M)$, And there is $\frac{\partial P}{\partial \sigma} < 0$ $\frac{\partial P}{\partial M} > 0$. Based on this analysis, the cost variable of the trading system C_t. There is a positive correlation between the price function of the multilateral pricing market:

$$C_t = kP(\sigma_t, M_t) \tag{23.6.7}$$

According to the usual expression habits, we still use C_t represents the cost function, that is:

$$C(\sigma_t, M_t) = P(\sigma_t, M_t) \tag{23.6.8}$$

The variable cost function can be expressed as:

$$C_t = kC(\sigma_t, M_t) \tag{23.6.9}$$

$k > 0$ is a constant, reflecting the structural characteristics of the trading system from the multilateral pricing market to the consumer terminal, we call it the supply chain parameter. Considering the variety of commodities, we regard the cost function C_t As the average price of all commodities; the market supply–demand ratio σ As the average supply–demand structure of different commodity markets. In the cost function C_t In, the money supply M Without including the time lag factor τ, the money supply M in the price squeeze function Γ corresponds to the value of the time lag variable τ.

Substituting (23.6.6) and (23.6.9) into (23.6.1), we get the following price equation:

$$\pi_{t+1} = \frac{1 - \Gamma(p_{t+1}^d, p_{t+1}^s, \phi_{t+!}, M_{t-\tau})}{2\Gamma(p_{t+1}^d, p_{t+1}^s, \phi_{t+1}, M_{t-\tau}) + \alpha_{t+1}} + \frac{\Gamma(p_{t+1}^d, p_{t+1}^s, \phi_{t+1}, M_{t-\tau})}{2\Gamma(p_{t+1}^d, p_{t+1}^s, \phi_{t+1}, M_{t-\tau}) + \alpha_{t+1}} \frac{kC(\sigma_{t+!}, M_{t+1})}{P_t} \tag{23.6.10}$$

Replace the time subscript $t + 1$ in (23.6.10) with the commonly used time subscript t to get a more concise form of the price equation:

$$\pi_t = \frac{1 - \Gamma(p_t^d, p_t^s, \phi_t, M_t)}{2\Gamma(p_t^d, p_t^s, \phi_t, M_{t-\tau}) + \alpha_t} + \frac{\Gamma(p_t^d, p_t^s, \phi_t, M_{t-\tau})}{2\Gamma(p_t^d, p_t^s, \phi_t, M_{t-\tau}) + \alpha_t} \frac{kC(\sigma_t, M_t)}{P_{t-1}} \tag{23.6.11}$$

The price equation (23.6.11) is constructed based on the pricing model under the unilateral pricing mechanism of micro-agents. In its construction process, it takes into account the characteristics of the mixed pricing mechanism of the modern trading system, has both the behavioral basis of micro-agents and the macro characteristics of the trading system, and reveals the basic laws of price movement in the modern trading system.

The price equation (23.6.11) shows a very interesting result. The two terms on the right side of the equation correspond to the two main channels of inflation: one is the mechanism dominated by the squeeze risk function, representing the price change mechanism driven by demand; the other is the mechanism dominated by the cost function, representing the price change mechanism driven by cost.

Another interesting phenomenon is that the price equation includes two different mechanisms of money. The money supply in the price squeeze risk function has a time lag; while the money supply in the cost price function does not have a time lag; the response relationship of the price change rate of the trading system π_t to the change of money supply depends on the size of the roles played by the price squeeze risk channel and the cost-driving channel in price increases. If cost-driving becomes the main force of price increases, the time lag of the money effect will be smaller.

The price equation (23.6.11) shows that the effect of money on prices is closely related to the compactness of the trading system. The higher the compactness of the trading system ϕ, the higher the price squeeze risk faced by the trading agents, the more restrained the response to loose monetary policy will be, and there will not be a situation where a slight increase in money supply will lead to a rise in inflation. We know that the compactness of the trading system ϕ has distinct stage characteristics. The more developed the trading system, the higher the value of compactness ϕ, the more obvious the inhibitory effect on price squeeze risk. Even if there is an oversupply of money, it usually does not immediately lead to inflation, but settles within the trading system, lowering the velocity of money circulation, and showing a slowing trend of money circulation velocity accompanying the evolution of the trading system. The relationship between money and prices is in a dynamic evolution process; at different stages of the trading system's evolution, the relationship between money and prices also presents different forms, and there is no universally applicable, unchanging relationship between money and prices for all trading systems.

23.7 Application of the Price Equation

Compared with the mainstream theory's price model, the price equation (23.6.11) incorporates more structured variables of the trading system, enhancing its explanatory power for price phenomena. Here, we choose two representative price issues and attempt to explain them using the price equation (23.6.11) to demonstrate the explanatory power of the trading pricing model.

23.7.1 Inflation Threshold Phenomenon

The non-linear characteristics of the trading system are manifested in many aspects, and the non-linear characteristics of price operation are an important manifestation. In the process of price movement, there is a definite inflation threshold; before and after the threshold, the characteristics of price movement are completely different, showing typical characteristics similar to phase transition.

The force driving the acceleration of inflation comes from the positive feedback loop behind it. The price feedback loop is composed of the money supply M, price squeeze risk coefficient Γ and inflation rate π_t. Once these three variables form a mutually stimulating positive feedback relationship, the trading loop that drives the acceleration of inflation is activated, and prices enter an accelerated upward channel.

In the feedback loop described in Fig. 23.4, once money becomes a force to push up prices, the rise in prices will reduce the price squeeze risk coefficient Γ, increasing the possibility of trading agents adjusting prices upwards, and the rise in prices will further increase the demand for money. The entire feedback process, starting from increasing money, eventually returns to the starting point of increasing money, forming a closed feedback loop.

In the price equation (23.6.11), the price squeeze risk coefficient Γ is the key variable determining the price trend of the trading system. Due to the self-reinforcing

Fig. 23.4 The trading loop of runaway inflation

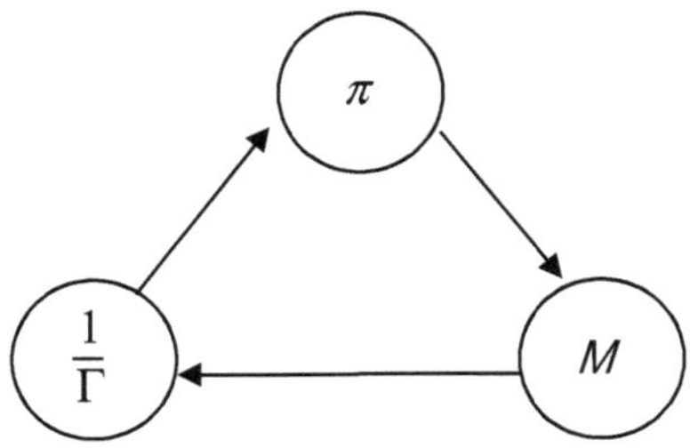

characteristics of the feedback loop, once the trading loop is activated, the price squeeze risk coefficient Γ will accelerate to decrease. Companies that have removed the squeeze risk constraint will undoubtedly become bolder in their pricing strategy choices; in the price equation (23.6.11), there is also another channel to push up prices—the cost-driven channel. When the money supply M continues to increase, the cost function C_t will be manifested. Under the dual effects of the decrease in squeeze risk and the cost-driving effect, prices enter an accelerated upward channel. The so-called inflation threshold is the starting value of the price trading loop. The inflation threshold, like a watershed, separates moderate inflation from accelerated inflation. The task of monetary policy is to control inflation within the threshold to avoid inflation getting out of control.

The inflation threshold of the trading system is determined by the structure of the trading system. As the trading system evolves, the inflation threshold will also shift. In order to effectively control inflation, monetary authorities need to ascertain the exact position of the inflation threshold and keep inflation levels below this threshold. For the healthy operation of the trading system, moderate inflation is not to be feared, what is to be feared is uncontrolled inflation. Unfortunately, inflation is easily out of control. Once the threshold is crossed, it will enter an acceleration channel. Economist Brown found the phenomenon of inflation acceleration when studying the inflation of OECD countries from 1951 to 1979. In 29 years, there were 76 instances of inflation acceleration in OECD countries, of which 29 occurred only within a certain year; 28 lasted for 2 years; 14 lasted for 3 years; 4 lasted for 4 years, and 1 lasted for 5 years (slow and steady acceleration of inflation in Canada from 1962 to 66). He also found that the most common length of the inflation acceleration phase is 2 to 3 years. The acceleration phase of inflation accounts for almost 50% of the time length in the cycle of inflation.[5]

23.7.2 Stagflation Phenomenon

In mainstream economic theory, prices are determined by supply and demand. When supply exceeds demand, prices fall; when demand exceeds supply, prices rise. According to this logic, there can only be two possible combinations in reality, namely price increase, economic growth; or price decrease, economic stagnation or slowdown. This is also the logic expressed by the Phillips curve. In mainstream economic theory, it is impossible for prices and growth to have a third combination—price increase, economic stagnation, unemployment rate increase—the so-called stagflation phenomenon. Unfortunately, this situation has occurred. When the United States fell into stagflation twice in the 1970s, the economic theory community also fell into a state of confusion. To this day, the problem of stagflation is still a chasm in front of neoclassical economics and Keynesian macroeconomic theory.

After the end of World War II, Western capitalist countries gradually entered a golden development period, with rapid economic expansion, low unemployment rates, and well-controlled inflation. The three major policy goals of macroeconomics have reached an unprecedented ideal state (Table 23.1).

However, after entering the 1970s, the situation began to reverse. On the one hand, economic growth slowed down, with growth rates hovering around 2%, and the unemployment rate continued to rise, reaching a level of 10%; on the other hand, the inflation rate remained high, reaching more than 10%.

The emergence of stagflation has dealt a serious blow to the thriving Keynesian theory. People began to doubt the Keynesian theory, believing that in some sense, "Keynesianism has proven to be wrong."[7] The widespread occurrence of stagflation in developed economies indicates that there are serious flaws in Keynesian demand management policies. At least it can be said that the establishment of Keynesian theory is conditional, and it can only be correct under the condition that the economy has not reached its potential output level. The Keynesian school tries to save Keynesian theory through the concept of asymmetry in wage and price movements. It is believed that the asymmetry of prices, economic growth, and unemployment rates led to the emergence of stagflation, which is merely a lagging response to macro-control effects. The Keynesian school's explanation for stagflation is as follows: when the economy is operating in a state of high growth, high inflation, and low unemployment, the authorities implement contractionary control policies to control inflation, and total demand responds first. The economic growth rate begins to decline, and inflation lags due to inertia. Due to wage stickiness, it will not be quickly reduced, and the asymmetry of the three main macro variables in response to contractionary macro control has caused the three to be out of sync. The Keynesian school believes that after a period of lag, the pace of the three variables will be synchronized again. These situations did indeed occur after entering the 1980s.[8] However, this explanation has not been widely accepted in the economic community, and economists have proposed various explanations, including policy failure explanation, OPEC oil supply shock explanation, and Great Depression shadow explanation, etc.[9]

In fact, stagflation, like deflation, is just a temporary phenomenon in price phenomena, a kind of abnormal state. It is precisely the abnormal price phenomena

Table 23.1 The macroeconomic states of major developed economies[6]

Country	Annual productivity growth rate on average		Annual inflation rate on average		Annual unemployment rate on average	
	1963–1973	1974–1979	1963–1973	1974–1979	1950–1973	1974–1983
Canada	2.4	0.1	4.6	9.2	4.8	7.2
France	4.6	2.7	4.7	10.7	2.0	4.5
Italy	5.4	1.4	4.0	16.1	5.2	6.6
Japan	8.7	3.3	6.2	10.2	1.2	1.9
Britain	3.0	0.8	5.3	15.7	3.0	5.3
The U.S.	1.9	-0.1	3.6	8.6	4.5	6.7
Germany	4.6	2.9	3.6	4.7	0.8	3.2

that have become a challenge to existing theories. In traditional price theory, the price formation mechanism is overly simplified, and the price phenomenon is only attributed to the comparison of supply and demand relationships, which limits the price theory's explanation of the stagflation phenomenon produced by the combination of nearly two contradictory elements.

According to the characteristics of stagflation, the cause of demand-pull inflation should be excluded first in the causes of stagflation, so we can only look for it from the cost-push aspect. High and unyielding costs put all companies under tremendous profit pressure, and the common situation reduces the risk of price squeeze for companies Γ. In this case, even though market demand has not significantly increased, or even may be shrinking, due to the weakened constraints of the risk of cost transfer squeeze, companies will still raise prices unanimously.

In an interconnected trading system, the supply end where the cost is located cannot change in isolation from the demand end, resulting in cost-push inflation. This is exactly where the mainstream price theory faces the logical dilemma of stagflation. In fact, the openness of the trading system determines that the system state cannot be fully explained by endogenous factors, and a large number of exogenous disturbance factors inevitably affect the operation of the trading system. The price equation reflects the open characteristics of the trading system, and the external disturbance factors are represented by the external shock variables p_s and p_d, incorporated into its own logical system, which provides the possibility for explaining the phenomenon of stagflation.

In the price equation (23.6.11), cost-push can either come from upstream price fluctuations or from external disturbance shocks. The peculiarity of stagflation is that the cause of the cost increase does not come from within the trading system, but from outside the system. Supply shocks $p_s \gg 0$ suddenly awaken from a dormant state, and cause a significant shock to the trading system. The two instances of stagflation that occurred in the United States in the 1970s were caused by the Middle East oil crisis. Oil prices rapidly rose from 2–3 dollars per barrel in the early 70s to 40 dollars per barrel, an increase of more than ten times. The huge supply shock was undoubtedly indigestible for the US economy, which heavily relies on fossil energy.

Although cost-push inflation induced by supply shocks is the basic cause of stagflation, not all cost-push inflations will eventually evolve into stagflation. Only when the cause of the cost increase comes from outside the trading system and has sufficient shock power, can it possibly trigger stagflation. Even so, whether it can ultimately trigger stagflation depends on the state of the trading system. If the economy is in a vigorous state, even if there is an exogenous cost shock, the economy has a strong absorption capacity. As the economic cycle passes through each link, due to the sufficient cash flow of the trading agents, companies can absorb some of the cost pressure by sacrificing some profits. Each trading link will become a pressure reducer to absorb cost pressure, and after passing through multiple links, the cost pressure will eventually be absorbed by the trading system. While companies absorb some of the cost pressure, the upstream companies do not feel the shrinkage of the trading volume due to the support of the expanding cash flow. Thus, to a certain extent, exogenous cost-push will not cause a comprehensive shock to the entire price system, the overall price level of the economy still maintains a relatively stable trend, and the economy is still growing.

If the economy is in a stagnant state, the cash flow of the trading agents is shrinking. In this case, the rise in costs will inevitably lead to a shrinkage in the trading volume of upstream companies. At the same time, the shrinking cash flow weakens the company's ability to absorb cost pressure, and companies have to transfer the cost pressure downstream, eventually leading to comprehensive inflation. In the 1970s in the United States, after a long period of Keynesian stimulus policies, problems such as bloated government departments, rigid state-owned enterprises, inefficient government investment, and rising fiscal deficits emerged; coupled with the rapid rise of the European and Japanese economies, the United States' advantageous position in the international market was greatly challenged. The proportion of exports to world exports fell from about 30% in 1947 to 15.5% in 1970; as a former world trade powerhouse, it ran a trade deficit for the first time in 1971, the decline in the competitiveness of the US economy created conditions for the subsequent stagflation.

Stagflation is an abnormal state of the economy and is inevitably short-lived. The two instances of stagflation that occurred in the United States in the 1970s, one occurred from 1973 to 1975; the other occurred from 1979 to 1980. The former lasted three years, and the latter lasted two years. After each stagflation, the economy will eventually get out of the mire of stagflation after a period of self-adjustment. Taking the supply shock brought by the oil crisis as an example, the rise in oil prices is an exogenous cost-push. As the harm of stagflation to the US economy deepens, the economic recession eventually crosses borders, leading to a global economic recession or decline. Globally, oil prices have become endogenous variables. Once the external shock is internalized, the main variables affecting prices in the trading system will spontaneously return to normal relations.

When the trading system experiences stagflation, monetary policy falls into a difficult and embarrassing situation. If the goal of monetary policy is to promote economic growth and expand employment, the already high inflation will become even more rampant under the stimulus of loose monetary policy. If the main policy goal is to curb inflation, the existing high unemployment rate will also become more severe under the pressure of tight monetary policy. In fact, once stagflation appears, monetary policy will be squeezed into a very narrow space. Fortunately, stagflation usually does not become a lingering cloud and has a transient characteristic.

Notes

1. Sonia Jaffe, Robert Minton, Kathy B. Marrigan, et al. (2021) Chicago Price Theory (Trans: Li Yihang, Dai Yuwen, Li Yang, Zhou Qiong), Oriental Press, Beijing.
2. Jagdish Handa (2005) Monetary Economics (Trans: Peng Zhiwen, Zhang Wei, Sun Yunjie, et al.), China Renmin University Press, Beijing, p 31.
3. Jagdish Handa (2005) Monetary Economics (Trans: Peng Zhiwen, Zhang Wei, Sun Yunjie, et al.), China Renmin University Press, Beijing, p 49.
4. Dong Zhiyong (2005) Behavioral Economics, Peking University Press, Beijing.

5. A. Brown (1996) Contemporary Inflation in the West, (Trans: Liu Xiaochuan et al.), Oriental Press, Beijing.
6. John Etwell, Murray Milgate, Peter Newman (1996) The New Palgrave Dictionary of Economics (Volume 4), (Compiled by: Chen Daisun), Economic Science Press, Beijing, p 507.
7. John Etwell, Murray Milgate, Peter Newman (1996) The New Palgrave Dictionary of Economics (Volume 4), (Compiled by: Chen Daisun), Economic Science Press, Beijing, p 508.
8. John Etwell, Murray Milgate, Peter Newman (1996) The New Palgrave Dictionary of Economics (Volume 4), (Compiled by: Chen Daisun), Economic Science Press, Beijing, p 508.
9. Brian Snowden, Howard R. Wen (2012) Encyclopedia of Macroeconomics (Trans: An Jia), Jiangsu People's Publishing House, Nanjing, p 654.

Part V
Nature and Evolutionary Endpoint of Trading System

This part contains three chapters, covering the equilibrium, efficiency decay, and imperfection of trading system. This part offers a full review of the basic characteristics of the trading system and shows the key features of its evolution. Based on discussions of the laws governing this evolution, trading economics answers the ultimate question the human society is facing.

By clarifying what equilibrium means, we find that general equilibrium is one of the innumerable possible states of the trading system, which makes it difficult to achieve in normal circumstances. The more common state is an approximation of the general equilibrium, or α-equilibrium.

Possessing the characteristics of a living being, a trading system follows the same evolutionary laws that apply to all forms of life. It is destined to go through the whole cycle of birth, growth, functional decline, and disintegration and reconstruction. Uncertainty runs throughout the process and may halt the progress at any stage. At the same time, we will show that in the later stages of the evolution, polarization will inevitably take hold and lead to falling resource allocation efficiency; this is also the only definite endpoint in the evolution of a trading system.

Chapter 24
Trading System Equilibrium

Equilibrium is a signature concept of neoclassical economics and an important sign of economic theory evolution from classical to neoclassical. When the concept "equilibrium" was enshrined in economic theory, great strides were made in the understanding of economic principles, thus laying a solid foundation for the belief of the "invisible hands".

This chapter, through the improvement of the concept of equilibrium, introduces a more realistic α—equilibrium concept and extreme point residence concept, proving the weak stability of the trading system.

24.1 Concept of Equilibrium

In standard economics textbooks, it is almost impossible to find a strict definition of the concept of equilibrium only with a brief description. In the eyes of economists, the concept of equilibrium should be self-evident. In t Mechanics, the concept of equilibrium is widely applied in everyday life. Therefore, "economic equilibrium" is considered to be akin to the "static state" in the mechanical system.[1] "In economics, when an economic quantity reaches a relatively static state under the interaction of other economic forces, the economic quantity is said to be in equilibrium. Therefore, the market price of a certain commodity is the result of the interaction of supply and demand in the market. When the forces of supply and demand reach a balance, the price or price mechanism is in a relatively stable state, at this time, the determined market price is called the equilibrium price, and the quantity where supply equals demand is called the equilibrium quantity."[2] Paul Samuelson, the famous American economist also had a similar statement in his classic textbook *Economics and he said that*: "The market equilibrium comes at that price and quantity where the forces of supply and demand are in balance. At the equilibrium price, the amount that buyers want to buy is just equal to the amount that sellers want to sell. The reason we call

Z. Wang, *Trading Economics*, Contributions to Economics,
https://doi.org/10.1007/978-981-99-9875-3_24

this an equilibrium is that, when the forces of supply and demand are in balance, there is no reason for price to rise or fall, as long as other things remain unchanged."[3]

Compared with the evolutionary process of the utility concept, the equilibrium concept is much simpler. Since 1769, when James Stuart, the British economist first introduced the concept of equilibrium into the field of economics, economists' understanding of the concept of equilibrium has basically not changed much, and overall it still maintains the tone of using the "balance" concept in Newtonian mechanics as a template.

In terms of methodology, the concept of equilibrium can be divided into partial equilibrium and general equilibrium. The partial equilibrium method is mainly represented by Alfred Marshall, while the general equilibrium method is mainly represented by Leon Walras. The partial equilibrium method focuses on a specific market or trading activity, assuming that other conditions remain unchanged; the general equilibrium places all trading activities in an interactive and mutually influential trading system to solve the equilibrium result of an item or a market. The partial equilibrium method simplifies the solving process, making it easy for practical use, which is the main reason why the partial equilibrium method is more familiar and widely used. However, the partial equilibrium method has shortcomings in the accuracy of the results, and the results obtained using the partial equilibrium method can only be regarded as an approximation of the real situation. Although the general equilibrium method is more rigorous in theory, it often falls short when dealing with specific problems due to the massive calculations involved. Both partial equilibrium and general equilibrium have their strengths and complement each other in practical applications, enriching the analytical tools of economics.

The partial equilibrium method is an important contribution by Marshall to economics. Based on this, Marshall further refined the concept of equilibrium in the time dimension, proposing the concepts of temporary equilibrium, short-term equilibrium, and long-term equilibrium. According to Marshall's definition, temporary equilibrium is the equilibrium state achieved by the market under the condition of strictly limiting the total supply in a very short time. The temporary equilibrium price depends entirely on the total demand; short-term equilibrium is a slight relaxation of the conditions for temporary equilibrium, and the supplier can make a limited response to the market according to changes in market conditions; long-term equilibrium is the complete release of supply constraints, and both supply and demand are in a state of free choice.

The introduction of the concept of equilibrium is of great significance for studying complex trading systems. Equilibrium is both a special state of the trading system and a key node in the evolution of the trading system. In terms of the definition of equilibrium, neoclassical economics basically stays on the description of equilibrium results, and basically does not touch on the micro-mechanism for achieving equilibrium, which leads to a disconnect between real scenarios and conceptual descriptions.

Taking general equilibrium as an example, the trading system is divided into product markets and factor markets. In the product market, there are K products, and the consumer's demand for products x_i depends on the price of the product p_i, and is affected by the prices of other products p_{-i}. The trading system's demand function for each product can be expressed in the following form:

$$x_i = x_i(p_i, p_{-i}), \quad (i = 1, 2, \ldots, K) \tag{24.1.1}$$

The supplier's willingness to supply the product y_i also depends on the product's price:

$$y_i = y_i(p_i, p_{-i}), \quad (i = 1, 2, \ldots, K) \tag{24.1.2}$$

The condition for the trading system to achieve equilibrium is:

$$x_i = y_i, \quad (i = 1, 2, \ldots, K) \tag{24.1.3}$$

From this, we get the K equations for the price p_i:

$$x_i(p_i, p_{-i}) - y_i(p_i, p_{-i}) = 0, \quad (i = 1, 2, \ldots, K) \tag{24.1.4}$$

Under specific conditions, the equation group (24.1.4) can obtain a unique equilibrium price.

In the factor market, a set of equilibrium conditions can also be found. Assuming that there are R types of factor goods in the factor market, the enterprise, as the demand side of the production factor, the demand for each factor X_j depends on the product price and factor price. The demand function is as follows:

$$X_j = X_j\left(P_j, P_{-j}, p_1, p_2, \ldots, p_K\right), \quad (j = 1, 2, \ldots, R) \tag{24.1.5}$$

Families, as the supply side of the factor, the willingness to supply the factor Y_j depends on the factor price and product price, and the supply function is as follows:

$$Y_j = Y_j\left(P_j, P_{-j}, p_1, p_2, \ldots, p_K\right), \quad (j = 1, 2, \ldots, R) \tag{24.1.6}$$

For the factor market to achieve equilibrium, the following conditions need to be met:

$$X_j = Y_j, \quad (j = 1, 2, \ldots, R) \tag{24.1.7}$$

For a closed trading system, in the absence of monetary participation, the trading system cycle must satisfy the budget constraint condition of equal income and expenditure:

$$\sum_{i=1}^{K} x_i p_i = \sum_{j=1}^{R} Y_j P_j \tag{24.1.8}$$

The system of Eqs. (24.1.4), (24.1.7) and (24.1.8) expresses the simplified Walrasian general equilibrium idea. Walras's original expression is very complex.[4]

Market clearing is at the core of the Walrasian equilibrium definition. The equilibrium Eqs. (24.1.4), (24.1.7) and (24.1.8) are also derived from the equality condition of market clearing. Such a definition method is logically clear and characteristic. However, due to the lack of a micro-mechanism for achieving equilibrium, such an equilibrium definition cannot provide us with much information about the process of achieving equilibrium. Walras also realized this and tried to compensate by introducing the method of the Walrasian auctioneer, but it could not fundamentally solve the problem because the Walrasian auctioneer does not exist in reality. How the market allows buyers and sellers to quickly reach a trading intention and achieve market clearing is still an unresolved issue in the theoretical framework of neoclassical economics.

The intention of introducing the concept of equilibrium is to find a special state of the trading system. In this state, all agents of the trading system have the intention to maintain the status quo. Let's go back to the real trading process, if each trading agents of the trading system has achieved the maximum expected return under the given constraints, rational decision-makers will not actively change the trading strategy. This means that for the trading system to achieve equilibrium, all trades must achieve Nash equilibrium. From this, we find the connection between the macro state of the trading system equilibrium and the micro state of the trading agent, providing us with a way to restate the concept of equilibrium: Equilibrium is a special state of the trading system. In this state, all agents in the trading system achieve effective matching with an optimal strategy. Under the condition that the trading situation does not change, no trading agent is willing to change the trading strategy.

We can prove that the restated concept of equilibrium is completely equivalent to the mainstream theory of equilibrium. There are two key elements in the original concept of equilibrium, namely the stability of the trading state and market clearing. The stability of the trading system state is reflected in price stability and trading scale stability; market clearing is reflected in the satisfaction of the trading intentions of both supply and demand in the market. First, when the trading system meets the restated equilibrium conditions, since all trading agents have achieved the maximum return under the constraint conditions, any change means a decrease in return, and the trading agent will maintain the current trading strategy, including trading prices and quantities. On the macro level, the market statistical price will remain stable, and the trading scale will remain unchanged. Secondly, when the trading system meets the restated equilibrium requirements, it means that all trading agents' trading intentions are satisfied, and each market must be in a clearing state. Therefore, we conclude: when the trading system meets the restated equilibrium requirements, it must meet the conditions of the mainstream theory of equilibrium.

When the requirements of the mainstream theory equilibrium concept are met, prices and trading volumes are in a stable state. If there are some trading agents in the trading system whose trading strategies have not been able to achieve effective matching, they will inevitably adjust their trading strategies, which may cause changes in the price and volume of the trading system. Obviously, this contradicts the stable state of the trading system, so when the trading system is in equilibrium, all games in the trading system must be in a Nash equilibrium state, that is, each trading agent has achieved the optimal strategy; secondly, when the trading system enters equilibrium, all markets clear, meaning that the trading intentions of all trading agents in the trading system have been met within the specified time. The above argument shows that when the trading system meets the equilibrium requirements of mainstream theory, it must meet the redefined equilibrium conditions.

In the redefined concept of equilibrium, the so-called effective matching refers to the ability of trading agents to find trading objects in the trading system and achieve trading that satisfy their intentions, and the trading results meet expectations. Due to the limitations of information costs and constraints, trading agents can only make decisions based on insufficient information in many cases, and they cannot always find trading agents that meet their own constraints; even if they find trading counterparties, they cannot guarantee that the final trading results fully meet expectations. In reality, it is very difficult for the trading system to reach an effective matching state where all trading desires are met. This requires us to slightly relax the equilibrium conditions and introduce a new concept of equilibrium, α-equilibrium.

24.2 α-Equilibrium

When we return to the real world from theory, we will find that it is a very lucky thing for trading agents to achieve effective matching. It needs to meet many conditions, including reasonable expectations, suitable trading partners, and accurate judgment of the trading situation. In fact, the trading agents that can achieve effective matching only account for a part of the trading system, and we call this ratio the effective matching degree of the trading system, represented by P_t. The specific definition is as follows:

Let $\{a_i\}_N$ be the set of trading agents in the trading system. At time step t, the trading matching status of trading agent a_i is represented by p_i. $p_i = 0$ indicates that a_i has not found a trading partner to realize its trading desire; $0 < p_i < 1$ indicates that a_i has found a trading partner and realized its trading intention, but has not realized its expected trading return. If $v(s)$ represents the actual return realized by trading agent a_i, $e(s)$ represents the expected return, a_i's trading matching degree p_i is given by the following formula:

$$p_i = \frac{v(s)}{e(s)} \tag{24.2.1}$$

In (24.2.1), when $v(s) < 0$, let $p_i = 0$; when $v(s) > e(s)$, let $p_i = 1$. At time step t, if trading agent a_i has no trading intention, as there is no gap between desire and reality, let $p_i = 1$.

According to the above assignment rules, the effective matching degree of the trading system P_t is given by the following formula:

$$P_t = \frac{\sum_i p_i}{N} \tag{24.2.2}$$

According to definition (24.2.2), if the trading system is in equilibrium, it needs to satisfy the effective matching condition, that is, the effective matching degree of the trading system $P_t = 1$. Similarly, if the effective matching degree of the trading system $P_t = 1$, it indicates that the trading system is in equilibrium at time step t. It can be seen that, $P_t = 1$ is a necessary and sufficient condition for the trading system to achieve equilibrium.

According to definition (24.2.2), at each time step t, we can calculate the effective matching degree of the trading system P_t, thus forming an effective matching degree sequence that changes with time $\{P_t\}_t$. This sequence reflects the basic characteristics of the evolution of the trading system.

As trading agents with limited rationality, constrained by limited cognitive abilities and incomplete information, it is difficult to perfectly realize the realm of trading expectations. The more complex the trading strategy, the lower the probability of perfectly realizing expected returns. The ability of trading agents to realize expected returns is closely related to the level of trading potential. Specifically, the higher the order of trading potential, the stronger the ability to realize expected returns; the lower the order of trading potential, the weaker the ability to realize trading expectations. In the trading system, the trading potential of trading agents cannot all be distributed at high orders, the proportion of agents with high-order trading potential is extremely low, and most trading agents' trading potential is at low orders. Therefore, it can be asserted that the effective matching degree $P_t = 1$ is not the normal state of the trading system operation, and the more common situation is the sub-equilibrium state of the trading system's effective matching degree $P_t < 1$, we call this state α—equilibrium state.

The α—equilibrium state is a state where the trading system is close to equilibrium. At this time, the effective matching degree of the trading system satisfies the $\alpha \leq P_t < 1$ condition. When the trading system enters the α—equilibrium state, although there are still trading agents in the trading system that account for $1 - \alpha$ of the total that have not achieved effective matching, because the proportion is relatively small, it is not enough to have a significant impact on the market pattern, and the trading system still maintains a stable price and market clearing pattern. Since the evolution of the trading system presents phased characteristics, the critical parameter α of each trading system will have different values at different times. α as a structural parameter of the trading system, has a close internal relationship with other structural parameters of the trading system. For example, the higher the natural unemployment rate, the smaller the value of the trading system's α; on the contrary, the lower the natural unemployment rate, the higher the value of α.

When the effective matching degree of the trading system $P_t < \alpha$ at time t, due to the high proportion of trading agents that have not realized their trading intentions in the entire system, these agents will adjust their trading strategies at time $t + 1$. This proactive force seeking change will impact the operation of the trading system, triggering a response from trading agents that have already achieved effective matching, leading to changes in the entire trading system. After some trading agents proactively adjust and the remaining agents respond, the trading system will return to the α-equilibrium state.

It should be noted that when the trading system spontaneously adjusts and returns to equilibrium, it is usually not the same equilibrium point, and both prices and trading volumes will change. The trading system evolves through such deviations and returns. We call the time length for which the trading system takes to spontaneously adjust and return to equilibrium, the equilibrium cycle of the trading system, represented by T_α. The equilibrium cycle T_α is an important parameter reflecting the structural characteristics of the trading system. Due to the structural differences between trading systems at different evolutionary stages and between different trading systems, these differences will be reflected in the length of the equilibrium cycle T_α. Generally speaking, the higher the evolutionary level of the trading system, the better the overall quality of the trading agents, and the more evenly distributed the information within the trading system, the shorter the equilibrium cycle T_α, reflecting the stronger resilience of the trading system.

The equilibrium cycle of the trading system T_α is an unstable variable. The length of the return cycle depends on the degree to which the trading system deviates from equilibrium. The greater the degree of deviation of the effective matching degree P_t from $1-\alpha$, the longer time required for the equilibrium cycle T_α. When the effective matching degree of the trading system P_t is below a certain threshold, the trading system's ability to spontaneously restore equilibrium will be damaged, forming a peculiar phenomenon—pole residence. At this time, the equilibrium cycle will tend to infinity, that is, $T_\alpha = +\infty$.

24.3 Pole Residence

Each and every stable system has the ability to self-regulate and return to the equilibrium point, but this spontaneous equilibrium ability is limited. Once it exceeds the limit, the system will lose its self-adjustment ability and stay out of equilibrium for a long time. We call the critical point where the system loses its adjustment ability the system's limit point, and the state of staying far from equilibrium is called the pole residence state. The trading system also has a limit value that the system can withstand, represented by β. When the system's effective matching degree is $P_t < \beta$, the trading system will lose its spontaneous adjustment ability. Without the assistance of exogenous forces, the trading system cannot automatically return to equilibrium in a short time.

The micro-mechanism of the trading system falling into a state of extreme residence originates from the liquidity paradox, that is, under certain conditions, the logical dilemma that trading activity and liquidity are prerequisites for each other. Under the conditions of currency trading, trading activity is based on liquidity, and the cash flow that generates liquidity comes from trading. The pincer relationship between trading and liquidity is the key to the emergence of the liquidity paradox.

This has exactly the same nature as the mother–child paradox of "chicken-and -egg story". Taking one form of trading activity—consumption behavior—as an example, consumption needs to be based on income. When income decreases, consumption demand decreases accordingly; the result of decreased consumption will lead to a reduction in the scale of corporate production, and the decrease in corporate production scale will further reduce consumers' income, forming a logical cycle. John Maynard Keynes discovered this logical pincer relationship that is mutually causal in the trading system, and thus proposed the theory of demand management.

Due to the extreme residence state caused by the liquidity paradox, it only occurs under certain conditions. Specifically, when the effective matching degree of the trading system is $P_t < \beta$, due to the excessively low trading matching degree causing a large number of trades to be unrealizable, as liquidity is exhausted, a large number of trading agents will face the situation of balance sheet damage, forcing the trading agents to exit the trading system, leading to the fragmentation of the trading network; the trading system cycle is "locked" by liquidity, presenting a dead "super stability". Without the intervention of external forces, the trading system cannot escape from the residence state.

The "stable" phenomenon caused by extreme residence is very similar to the stable state of equilibrium, but the two are essentially different. The equilibrium state is the result of trading agents maximizing their profits, and all kinds of resources are fully utilized. However, extreme residence is the helpless result of trading agents, the space that trading agents can choose is extremely compressed, and a large amount of resources in the trading system are idle and wasted. It can be seen that extreme residence is a pseudo-equilibrium state, and the super "stability" and equilibrium stability presented are at the two ends of the distribution range of the trading system operation state.

The common cause of the trading system falling into a residence state is various sudden crisis events, including financial-, economic, currency, supply chain, major public health crises, etc. These events will have a major impact on the normal operation of the trading system, causing the trading matching degree to drop significantly. The global COVID-19 outbreak at the end of 2019 is a typical major public health safety crisis, which caused a wide range of economic activities to stop, a large number of companies went bankrupt due to cash flow exhaustion, and many families faced financial difficulties. In this situation, if the government does not have effective aid and support measures, the economy will inevitably fall into a stagnant state of extreme residence.

It should be noted that extreme residence and market dysfunction are two different concepts. Market dysfunction refers to the situation where the trading agent is subject to specific restrictions causing the market to be unable to effectively allocate resources. Extreme residence, on the other hand, refers to a more extreme situation where the trading system falls into a basic paralysis state, and the ability of the trading system to allocate resources is severely damaged.

24.4 Equilibrium Point Displacement

Theoretically speaking, the equilibrium of the trading system corresponds to the stable state of the trading system, but it does not mean that the trading system enters a relatively static state. The equilibrium state of the trading system contains self-negating power. Each trading will cause the accounting matrix of the trading agent to mutate, which means that the trading agent a_i. The accounting matrix at time step t + 1 A_{t+1} will inevitably change compared to the accounting matrix A_t at the previous time step t. The accounting matrix is the basis for trading agents to construct their trading strategy sets, and changes in the accounting matrix will inevitably lead to changes in the strategy sets of trading agents. In this case, the equilibrium strategy at time step t is bound to change compared to the equilibrium strategy at time step t + 1, resulting in different equilibrium points, thus forming a spontaneous movement of the equilibrium point of the trading system, rather than a result of external disturbances.

The equilibrium point of the trading system can be described in the coordinate system formed by price and trading volume. Based on the trading base, we can calculate the price index of the trading system. The resulting price index is similar to the GDP deflator index; the trading volume indicator is more intuitive, and the total of all trades can be used to obtain the trading volume of the trading system at time step t. P is used to measure the price index of the trading system; Q represents the total trading volume index of the trading system at time step t. Each equilibrium state of the trading system corresponds to a point on the P–Q coordinate system (Fig. 24.1).

As time step t progresses, the equilibrium state of the trading system continues to move, drawing a trajectory line in the P–Q state space, which we call the equilibrium trajectory line of the trading system (Fig. 24.2).

Since the equilibrium trajectory line describes the trajectory line generated by the trading system evolving under equilibrium conditions, it represents the result of the trading system maximizing the use of all types of resources under established constraints and institutional rules, and is the optimal evolution path.

Fig. 24.1 The diagram of equilibrium coordinate of trading system

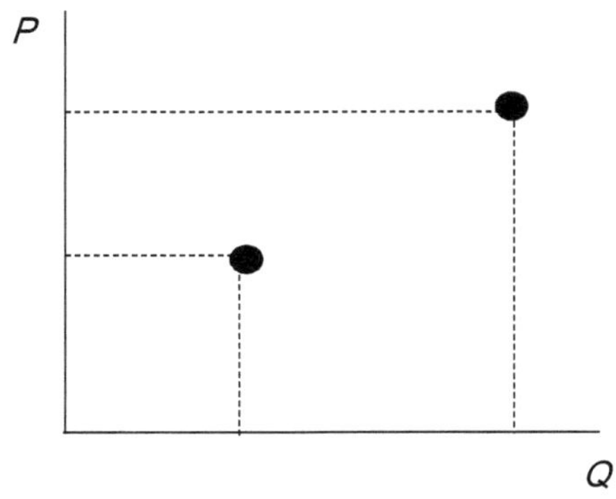

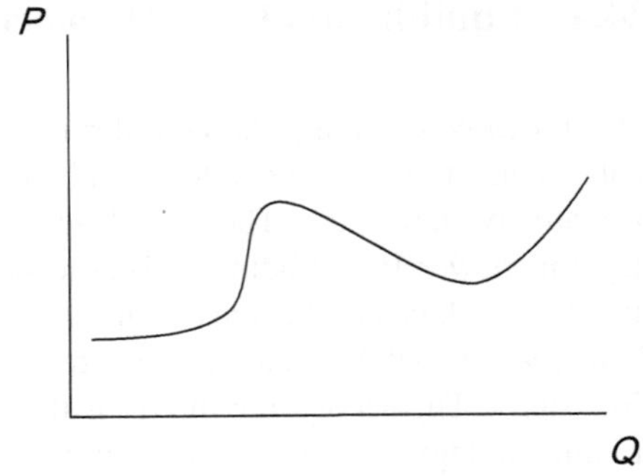

Fig. 24.2 Equilibrium trajectory line of the trading system

It should be noted that the equilibrium trajectory line of the trading system cannot always maintain an upward trend. The operation of the trading system has various possibilities, including the possibility of expansion and contraction. The key is the overall trend of changes in the balance sheets of trading agents.

Since the equilibrium point of the trading system is the result of the synthesis of the optimal strategies of a large number of trading agents, the existence and uniqueness of the equilibrium point of the trading system at any time step t depends on the existence and uniqueness of each game equilibrium in the trading system. Game theory research proves that any game has a Nash equilibrium; if a pure strategy Nash equilibrium cannot be found, there must be a mixed strategy Nash equilibrium. However, when it comes to uniqueness, it is not the case, as some games may have several Nash equilibrium results. From this, it can be inferred that at time step t, there are multiple possible equilibrium points in the trading system, leading to a certain degree of uncertainty in the trading system, which means that we cannot accurately predict the operation of the trading system at time step t + 1. In fact, we must face two realities: one is that all trading agents have trading constraints and must make choices within these constraints; the second is that due to the constraints of incomplete information and the uncertainty of the trading situation, all trading agents have decision path dependence. Under the constraints of these two factors, the optimal trading strategy of each trading agent is almost unique, and even if a few trading agents have multiple dominant trading strategies, the equilibrium result finally synthesized in the trading system is almost unique due to the mutual offset within the trading system. The reason why we use the judgment of "almost unique" is because whether it is restrictive conditions or decision path dependence, their precondition for influencing the decision-making behavior of trading agents is that the trading situation remains stable; but there is a logical nesting relationship between the trading situation and the decision-making of trading agents, which makes it impossible for us to directly conclude the uniqueness of the trading system equilibrium.

Due to the existence of the positive feedback mechanism in the trading system, even without the influence of external disturbances, the trading system in equilibrium can automatically deviate from equilibrium, which is the key difference between the trading system and the physical system. The root of this difference comes from the initiative of the trading agent and the decision-making mechanism under incomplete information. Taking the real estate market as an example, real estate bubbles can evolve in the equilibrium state of the trading system. The severe bubble phenomenon experienced by the Chinese real estate market from 2007 to 2017 is a typical case. Before 2007, the Chinese real estate market was in a stable development state. Although house prices rose after 2005, the increase was relatively moderate. Entering 2007, after two years of rising house prices, people's expectations of house prices began to take shape. In fact, the changes in the real estate market are not only from the psychological expectation level of the trading agent. In 2007, China's economy had been growing rapidly for 7 years, with an average growth rate of 9.3%. Economic growth has accelerated urbanization, leading to a rapid increase in demand for urban housing. Under these circumstances, house prices across the country began to rise rapidly. The huge trading ring formed between housing demand, money supply, house price expectations, and land prices has driven China's economy away from equilibrium and into overheating. The economic growth rate that year reached a high level of 13%, and the consumer price index CPI reached a high of 4.8%, while the CPI index in 2006 was only 1.3%, a difference of 3.6 times.

It's fair to say that not all deviations from the equilibrium trajectory are bad. Short-term, small-scale deviations are not only the norm of economic operation, but they may also help to accelerate economic growth. The market that causes the trading system to deviate from equilibrium may become a source of economic growth and be in a position of economic growth. Looking back at the growth history of China's economy from 2000 to 2010, especially in 2006, the economy was clearly running on a deviating equilibrium trajectory, but overall the economy was running smoothly, inflation was moderate, and the international balance of payments maintained a twin surplus. The current account surplus was 249.9 billion US dollars while the capital account surplus was 1 billion US dollars. The fiscal balance was basically balanced, with fiscal revenue of 3.93 trillion yuan; fiscal expenditure was 4.02 trillion yuan, and the fiscal deficit rate that year was only 1.6%, far below the fiscal deficit warning line of 3%. From all aspects, China's economy achieved very impressive results in 2006, with a growth rate of 11.6%, which was 2.63% higher than the average growth rate of 8.97% from 2000 to 2005. The situation in 2007 changed, the trading system deviated from the equilibrium trajectory to a greater extent, and of course the growth rate was higher. The GDP growth rate that year reached an astonishing 13%, which obviously exceeded the range that the trading system could bear. The speed of price increases began to accelerate, the tendency of asset bubbles became obvious, and the proportion of real estate loans in new loans that year increased rapidly, squeezing the real economy. It can be seen that a large deviation from the equilibrium state of the trading system is not conducive to the long-term healthy development of the economy. The optimal development path of the economy should be a small fluctuation around the equilibrium trajectory of the trading system, as shown in Fig. 24.3.

In Fig. 24.3, the solid line represents the real operating trajectory of the trading system, and the dashed line represents the equilibrium trajectory.

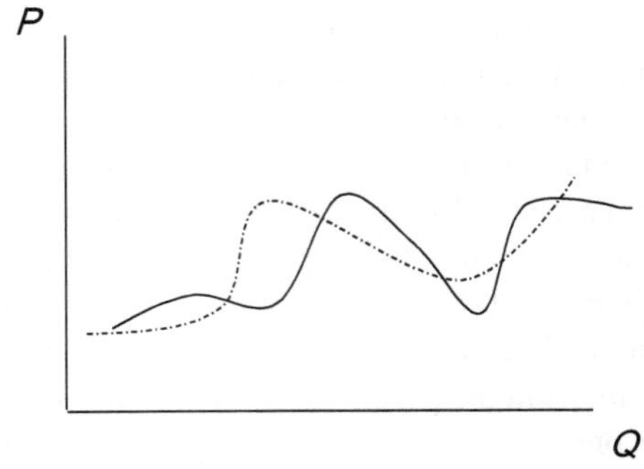

Fig. 24.3 The optimal development path of the economy. The operating trajectory line and the equilibrium trajectory line of trading system

Based on the factors that lead to a decrease in effective matching, the imbalance of the trading system can be divided into two basic types: supply-side imbalance and demand-side imbalance. Within each type, depending on the direction of variable imbalance, it can be further divided into expansionary and contractionary categories. With this classification, there are four types of scenarios where the trading system deviates from equilibrium, namely supply expansionary deviation, supply contractionary deviation; demand expansionary deviation, and demand contractionary deviation.

These four types of imbalances present different manifestations in the operation of the trading system. Supply expansionary imbalance, at the macro level, manifests as a decrease in prices. Under this stimulus, demand remains strong, and economic growth remains robust. The economic situation experienced by economies represented by the United States for a considerable period after China joined the WTO in 2001 is the imbalance of this type. The trading system in this type of imbalance is easy to restore balance, and it will hardly have a negative impact on economic growth.

The situation of supply contractionary imbalance is just the opposite. Due to sudden fluctuations in the supply chain, regardless of where it occurs, it will quickly spread to the entire trading system, resulting in price increases, demand contraction, and the economy falling into stagnation. The Russo-Ukrainian conflict in 2022 led to a sudden reduction in the supply of oil, natural gas, and food, and major economies such as Europe and the United States encountered high inflation unseen in 40 years. The highest inflation rate in EU countries exceeded 10%, and the highest inflation rate in the United States approached 9%; while African countries suffered a food crisis, and saw its economic growth rate slow down.

The main manifestation of demand expansionary imbalance is inflation. Under the stimulus of demand expansion, the economy will show a trend of accelerating growth, and there may even be an overheating economy. In addition to inflation, demand expansionary imbalance may also lead to the accumulation of financial risks. The 2008 US subprime mortgage financial crisis was caused by demand expansionary imbalance induced by low interest rates.

The main manifestation of demand contractionary imbalance is deflation, economic growth stagnation, or economic depression. This kind of situation usually occurs after a major crisis, and the Great Depression of the US economy in the 1930s is a typical case in point.

For ease of summarization, we might as well place the above conclusions in a matrix for observation (Table 24.1).

From the above typology matrix, it can be seen that whether it is supply-side imbalance or demand-side imbalance, it will be reflected in prices. Both types of imbalances will lead to price increases and decreases. The fundamental difference between the two types of imbalances lies in the relationship between prices and economic growth. Supply-side imbalance shows the inverse relationship between price changes and the speed of economic growth. When prices rise, the speed of economic growth decreases; when prices fall, the speed of economic growth remains the same or slightly accelerates. For demand-side imbalance, price increases and economic growth show a positive relationship, that is, when prices rise, the speed of economic growth accelerates; when prices fall, the speed of economic growth decreases.

In order to observe the economic laws of the two types of imbalances more thoroughly, we will place them in the coordinate space. The vertical axis represents the supply side, and the horizontal axis represents the demand side.

In Fig. 24.4, the first quadrant of the coordinate system formed by the supply axis *S* and demand axis *D* represents an expansionary trend; the third quadrant represents a contractionary trend. In the first quadrant, the area above the 45-degree demarcation

Table 24.1 The classification of economic imbalance

	Supply-side imbalance		Demand-side imbalance	
	Supply expansionary	Supply contractionary	Demand expansionary	Demand contractionary
Manifestation	Falling prices, steady demand, and growth remains unchanged	Rising prices, falling demand and slower economic growth	Rising prices, increased supply, and faster economic growth	Falling prices, decreased supply, and slower or stagnating economic growth
Mechanism	With no increase in demand, an increase in supply inevitably leads to a fall in prices. The demand side, in the face of changing budgetary constraints, will slightly increase consumption. This is reflected in economic growth, which remains unchanged or accelerates slightly. This is often the case in food markets	While the active factor causing the economic imbalance is a reduction in supply, when prices rise, consumers will inevitably act accordingly to spend less. Therefore, the actual trading volume is bound to be reduced	With inevitable lag in supply adjustment and demand expansion, when prices rise, the supply side acts accordingly, which leads to an increase in the volume of real transactions and a faster rate of economic growth	When demand falls, prices decrease, and the supply side then reacts by scaling back supply. The contraction of both supply and demand will inevitably lead to a slowdown in economic growth, or even a recession

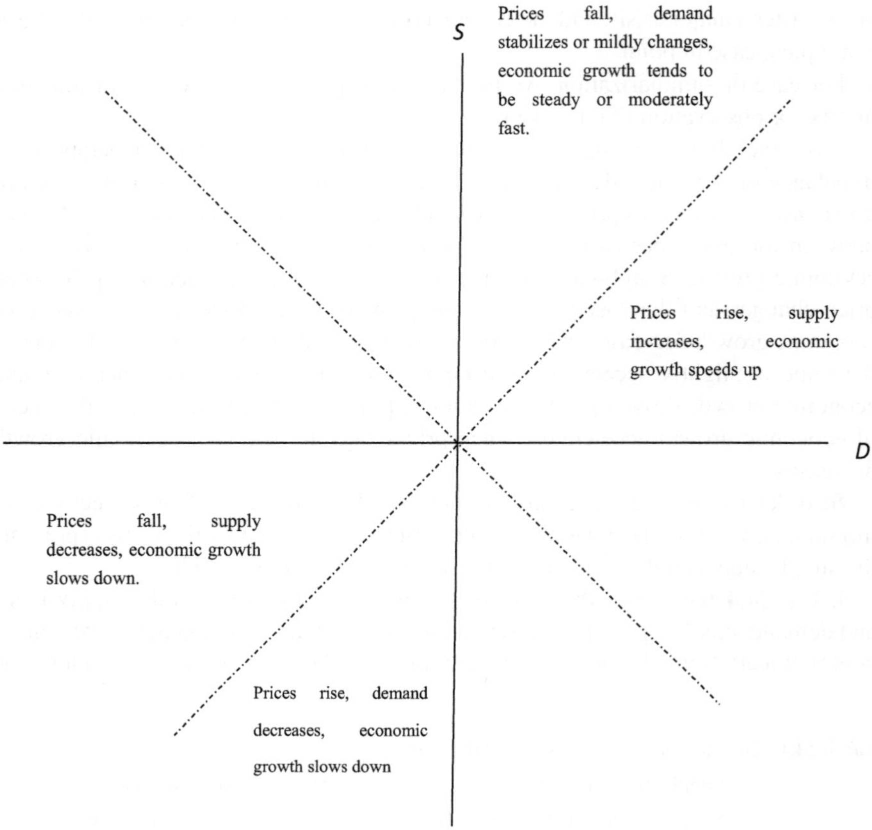

Fig. 24.4 The diagram of macroeconomic illustrations

line represents supply expansion, and the area below the line represents demand expansion. In the third quadrant, the area above the demarcation line represents demand contraction; the area below the line represents supply contraction. The entire supply–demand coordinate space is divided into four regions by the demarcation lines of quadrants one and three, and quadrants two and four. Observing the situations in these four regions, we can easily find that, on the upper side of the demarcation line of quadrants one and three, whether in the first or third quadrant, there is a phenomenon of falling prices; below the demarcation line, there is a uniform phenomenon of rising prices. On the upper side of the demarcation line of quadrants two and four, mainly distributed in the first quadrant, both situations show the characteristic of accelerating economic growth; below the demarcation line, that is, the two situations in the third quadrant, both show a trend of slowing economic growth. Based on this rule, we call the demarcation line of quadrants one and three the price line; the demarcation line of quadrants two and four the growth line. Based on the above, we can summarize the following rules: When the trading system enters the area above the price line, prices show a downward trend; when it enters the area below the price line, prices show an upward trend. When the trading system enters the area above the growth line, the economic growth rate shows an accelerating trend; when it enters the area below the growth line, the economic growth rate shows a downward trend.

24.5 Weak Stability of the Trading System

In the evolution process of the trading system, the effective matching degree P_t shows a random walk state, in which the parameters α and β play a very crucial role. When $P_t > \alpha$, the trading system enters the α-equilibrium state, and the main indicators of the trading system, including price indicators, trading volume indicators, and market structure indicators, show a relatively stable trend. The α-equilibrium state has self-maintaining characteristics and can maintain the stability of the trading system without large external shocks. When P_t crosses the α boundary and enters the $\beta < P_t < \alpha$ interval, it begins to oscillate. In this state, a considerable number of traders have not realized their trading intentions or expectations, they will not be willing to maintain the status quo, and will constantly try to find their optimal trading strategy. This process will inevitably cause some indicators of the trading system to change significantly until the trading system returns to the α-equilibrium state.

When the effective matching degree P_t falls beyond the limit boundary β of the trading system, it will enter another state, namely the extreme point residence state. In the extreme point residence state, the main indicators of the trading system show a continuous deterioration trend, and the process may be very slow, so that it is very close to the stable state of the trading system in appearance. Only after a long period of stagnation or under the action of exogenous forces, the trading system will leave the extreme point residence state.

According to the above analysis, the random walk process of the effective matching degree P_t of the trading system can be shown graphically as follows (Fig. 24.5).

Fig. 24.5 The random walk process of effective matching in trading system

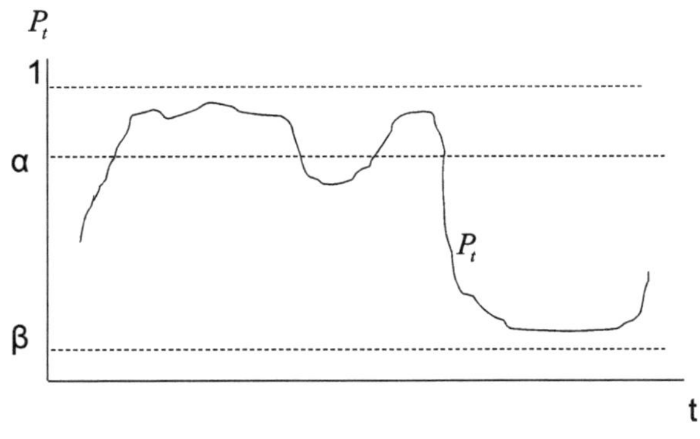

In the evolutionary process of the trading system, the equilibrium period T_α as an important parameter reflecting the evolution characteristics, has a clear response to α and β.

In Fig. 24.6, the solid line represents the trend of changes in the equilibrium period T_α, when $P_t \in [\beta, \alpha)$, the equilibrium period T_α Having limited values means that within a finite time, the trading system, after spontaneous adjustment, returns to the equilibrium state. The equilibrium period T_α on $[\beta, \alpha)$ shows a downward trend, indicating that the greater the deviation of the trading system from the equilibrium state, the longer the time required to return to the equilibrium state. When $P_t \in [0, \beta)$, it means that the trading system has entered the residence interval, and the equilibrium period P_t will quickly extend, even to infinity, showing the characteristic of the extreme residence state being "locked". Since the equilibrium period P_t represents the time for the trading system to return to the α-equilibrium state, when $P_t \geq \alpha$, it means that the trading system is already in the equilibrium state, hence the result of $T_\alpha = 0$.

The limit point β of the trading system is an important parameter of the system, reflecting the limit ability of the trading system to maintain stability, and its size depends on the robustness of the trading system. The robustness of the trading system is a reflection of the overall health of the balance sheet of the trading agents, including whether the asset-liability ratio is in a reasonable range, the liquidity of the balance sheet, and the situation of cash flow and profitability indicators. Theoretically speaking, the stronger the robustness of the trading system, the stronger the ability of the trading system to withstand shocks, and the greater the degree of effective matching P_t oscillation it can withstand, which is reflected in a smaller value of β.

Various rescue mechanisms and internal risk-sharing mechanisms in the trading system can also affect the position of the system's extreme points to a certain extent. For trading systems with well-established crisis relief mechanisms and efficient risk

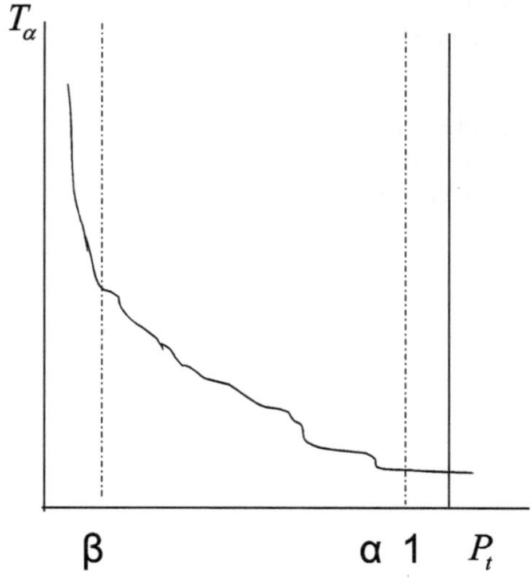

Fig. 24.6 The distribution curve of equilibrium period of T_α

diversification mechanisms, the ability of trading agents to withstand risks will be stronger. These mechanisms can effectively resolve and absorb some of the destructive effects of external shocks on the balance sheets of trading agents, thereby enhancing the resilience of the trading system.

From the perspective of evolution, as the risk management capabilities of trading agents strengthen, the means of risk diversification and risk avoidance provided by the financial market are becoming increasingly rich, and with the improvement of macro-prudential management and regulatory mechanisms, the resilience of the trading system is continuously strengthening, and the position of the system's extreme points will continue to decline. This has been confirmed by the achievements of modern society's development.

Comparing developed economies with developing economies, there are clear differences in the resilience of the trading system. Generally speaking, the more developed the economy, the stronger the resilience of the trading system, and the lower the position of the system's extreme points. The trading systems of developing economies, whether in terms of the management skills of trading agents for balance sheets and the health of balance sheets, or in terms of macro-prudential management and macroeconomic adjustment capabilities, are still in an imperfect state. The trading system is relatively fragile, the position of the system's extreme points is relatively high, and it is more likely to fall into a crisis under the impact of external shocks or sudden events.

Combining the above analysis, we can draw a conclusion about the stability of the trading system: The trading system is a weakly stable system. Under the condition of effective matching degree $P_t \geq \beta$, the trading system is stable and has the ability to absorb external disturbances. When the system deviates from the equilibrium state, it can return to the equilibrium state after spontaneous adjustment. However, when the external shock is too strong, the effective matching degree $P_t < \beta$ at times, the trading system will lose its ability to self-adjust, falling into a "locked" state of extreme residence, far from the equilibrium point. This is the connotation of the weak stability of the trading system.

Notes

1. Douglas Gale (2008) The Strategic Basis of General Equilibrium: Dynamic Matching and Bargaining Game (Trans: Wesson, trans), Gezhi Publishing House, Shanghai People's Publishing House, Shanghai, p 37.
2. Wu Yifeng, Liu Fengliang, Wu Hanhong (1999) Western Economics, China Renmin University Press, Beijing, p 30.
3. Paul A. Samuelson, William D. Nordhaus (2014) Economics (Trans: Xiao Chen), Posts & Telecom Press, Beijing, p 46.
4. He Zhengbin (2009) 300 Years of Economics, 2nd edn. Hunan Science and Technology Press, Changsha, p 190–191 (in Chinese).

Chapter 25
Efficiency Decay of Trading System

Resource allocation is the basic function of the trading system, and the efficiency of resource allocation in the trading system is a key indicator to measure the evolution of the trading system, and it is also a key factor in forming the core competitiveness of a country. We would like to prove that, with the evolution of the trading system, after the efficiency of resource allocation in the trading system has undergone a continuous rise, it will reverse the direction of evolution, showing a trend of efficiency decay, and plunge into the second half of the complete evolutionary cycle. This is an inevitable law that the evolution of the trading system cannot resist.

25.1 Optimal Conditions for Trading System Efficiency

The equilibrium state of the trading system is a state where all trading agents can realize their trading intentions. Due to the limitations of the trading agents' cognitive abilities and information, even when the trading system is in a state of equilibrium, there may still be room for increasing profits. If the equilibrium state is to reach Pareto optimality, the trading system should not have situations where trading intentions are restricted, decision-making errors exist, and resources are idle or potential is underutilized. This requires the trading system to meet three conditions: complete competition, complete information, and complete rationality. Complete competition means that every trading agent in the trading system can make decisions and trading according to their own wishes, and will not be restricted by the government or suppressed by competitors or other trading agents. At the same time, there are no unequal constraints. Complete information means that there is no information asymmetry. Trading decisions are based on information, and only underpinned by sufficient and complete information, will there be no trading failure. Complete rationality means that trading agents have strong enough abilities to use and process information

Z. Wang, *Trading Economics*, Contributions to Economics,
https://doi.org/10.1007/978-981-99-9875-3_25

based on complete information, and will not misjudge the trading situation or make decision-making errors.

The above three conditions all contain the determiner "complete", corresponding to complete in English. Therefore, we can generally call it the 3-C condition for the equilibrium state to meet Pareto optimality. The 3-C conditions of trading specify the decision-making status, information conditions, and decision-making ability of trading agents, ensuring that the trading system operates at the most efficient state.

Under the 3-C conditions of trading, the trading system in equilibrium meets Pareto optimality. First, the market is in a completely clearing state, and each trading agent is in a state of maximizing profits (or utility). Since it is the result of voluntary trading by trading agents, the trading system cannot increase the profits of another trading agent without reducing or retaining the profits of other trading agents, and therefore no agent wants to change the status quo.

Pareto also proposed three conditions to achieve optimality, namely trading conditions, production conditions, and combined conditions of exchange and production. Their essence is that all participants in the trading system can achieve their maximum utility and profit. Consumers achieve equal marginal utility for all consumer goods, producers achieve equal marginal conversion rates for all inputs, and between consumers and producers, the marginal substitution rate of consumers equals the marginal conversion rate of producers. If the three conditions are met at the same time, it means that the trading system has achieved optimal resource allocation.

The 3-C condition, compared to Pareto's three marginal conditions, is also centered on maximizing the benefits of the trading agents. The conditions set are to ensure that the trading agents can fully utilize their potential and endowments. Only when every trading agent in the trading system can fully utilize its own potential and fully use its own endowments to maximize benefits, can we say that the trading system has reached the optimal overall efficiency. This is the core idea of Pareto optimality. The difference between the 3-C condition and Pareto's marginal conditions lies in the discourse system. The 3-C condition uses game theory language, which is more intuitive and easy to understand and verify; Pareto's marginal conditions use the marginalist discourse system, which has a heavy mathematical analysis tone, but is more abstract and difficult to operate in practical tests.

Welfare economics proposes six conditions different from Pareto's marginal conditions: (1) complete and symmetrical assumption of economic information. (2) assumption of a perfectly competitive market. (3) assumption of constant or decreasing returns to scale. (4) assumption of no external effects and public goods. (5) assumption that trading costs can be ignored. (6) assumption of complete rationality of economic parties. These six conditions are at different logical levels. For example, the assumption of constant or decreasing returns to scale is to avoid market monopoly and destroy the condition of a perfectly competitive market. Therefore, it is at the upper level of condition 2, and is a further strengthened condition. From the final result, it is already included in condition 2 and can be eliminated.

The precondition of no externality and public goods is set to meet the requirements of Pareto optimality, that is, it is impossible to increase anyone's welfare without reducing the welfare of others. Due to the sharing characteristics of public products, a person's increase in welfare from the use of public products does not presuppose a reduction in the welfare of others. Take the public road as an example, one person's passage usually does not affect another person's passage. But in fact, the use of public products also incurs costs, for instance, people will not wander on the street all day just because they don't have to pay for walking on the street. In the discourse system of trading economics, when making decisions, the trading agents will fully weigh the costs and benefits of different strategies and consider the overall trading. In addition to liquidity constraints and regulatory constraints, trading agents must also face the scarcity of time, after all, everyone's life span is limited. Therefore, this condition can also be omitted.

Condition 5 is set to achieve the result of instantaneous adjustment of the trading system, to ensure that the trading system is always in a state of equilibrium, and has no direct relationship with Pareto optimality itself. According to the requirements of condition 5, there is no possibility of achieving Pareto optimality in reality. This is obviously inconsistent with the facts. Even if trading costs exist, or even if trading costs are high, the optimal resource allocation result can be achieved through the mutual game of trading agents, which is determined by the Nash equilibrium.

As can be seen, the 3-C condition is a simplified statement of the six conditions of welfare economics. Even so, it is still very difficult to meet the 3-C conditions. In general, the trading system cannot meet the requirements of Pareto optimality. The first is that the condition of complete competition cannot be met. In reality, trading agents have different trading powers, and the gap in trading power will continue to expand with the evolution of the trading system, which determines that it is impossible for trading agents to compete on an equal footing. In addition, government regulation and control of economic activities is inevitable, which will undoubtedly form rigid constraints on the trading behaviors of trading agents. For example, the government's restrictions on residents' purchase of houses, regulatory requirements for banks' fund investment by regulatory agencies, etc., will have a significant impact on the operation of the trading system.

Secondly, the condition of complete information cannot be satisfied. Information asymmetry is a fundamental characteristic of human society, which is not only due to the constraints of information costs, but more importantly, it is determined by human cognitive characteristics. The trading agent is both the information demand agent and the information supply agent. The profit-seeking motive determines that people intentionally control the supply of information to achieve their own beneficial purposes. This creates the paradox of the information role of the trading agent: For information demanders, they hope to obtain as comprehensive and truthful information as possible; For suppliers, they hope to effectively control information to maximize their own interests. The trading agent pursuing maximum profit can never eliminate this information paradox, and the world can never eliminate information asymmetry.

Thirdly, the condition of complete rationality cannot be satisfied. Whether in processing information or controlling emotions, human abilities are limited. Faced with the rapidly changing trading situation and the explosion of information flow, trading agents with limited rationality cannot guarantee the absolute correctness of decisions. In fact, in terms of information processing ability, people vary vastly, which determines that the real trading system cannot meet the condition of complete rationality.

The above analysis shows that under normal circumstances, the trading system in equilibrium cannot meet the Pareto optimal standard, at most it can only be an approximation or approximation of Pareto optimality. The distance from Pareto optimality depends on the gap between reality and the 3-C conditions. The larger the real gap, the further the trading system is from Pareto optimality. For trading systems that have not reached equilibrium, the gap from Pareto optimality will be even greater. If we use η_t to represent the degree to which the trading system can achieve Pareto optimal efficiency at time step t, use k to represent the degree of the trading system meeting the 3-C conditions on the whole, and use P_t to represent the effective matching degree of the trading system at time step t, then the following relationship exists:

$$\eta_t = kP_t \tag{25.1.1}$$

In Eq. (25.1.1), k is a structural parameter of the trading system, reflecting the rules and institutional efficiency of the trading system. We call it the structural efficiency factor of the trading system. The larger the value of k, the higher the efficiency of the trading system. When $k = 1$, it means that the trading system is in a completely rational state and can achieve the efficiency standard of Pareto optimality. As a structural parameter of the trading system, the value of k is relatively stable over a long period of time and can be treated as a constant. k takes values in the open interval from 0 to 1, that is, $0 < k < 1$.

When the trading system is in equilibrium, the effective matching degree $P_t = 1$, at this time, the efficiency ratio realized by the trading system η_t is:

$$\eta_t = k \tag{25.1.2}$$

Equation (25.1.2) shows that the institutional arrangement of the trading system is the key factor determining the efficiency of the trading system. This is a very important conclusion, indicating that institutional arrangements play a crucial role in economic development. Excessive trading costs and lack of incentive institutional arrangements will become the main obstacles to the release of trading system efficiency. This explains why there is a huge development gap among different countries. In today's world where economy increasingly moving towards global competition, efficiency is the basis of national competitiveness. Losing efficiency advantages will lose the opportunity for economic development.

The factors affecting the value of the efficiency factor k in the trading system come from three aspects. First is the system, which includes market management, income distribution, tax, ownership, and property inheritance systems, etc. These systems directly affect the rationality of income distribution and wealth possession, the effectiveness of incentive mechanisms, and so on. Second is the quality of the trading agents. The efficiency of the trading system in allocating resources stems from the decision-making ability of all trading agents, therefore, the educational quality of the trading agents is the basis of the efficiency of the trading system. Generally speaking, the higher the level of education of the citizens, the stronger their cognitive abilities, and the better they can fully utilize their resource endowments to maximize their returns, the higher the efficiency of the trading system in allocating resources. The third is the business environment. A good business environment is a prerequisite for trading agents to form stable expectations. In a turbulent and fraudulent business environment, both trading costs and trading risks will be high, and the trading system cannot achieve efficient resource allocation.

Looking at the economic development of countries around the world, they generally follow a basic rule: economically developed countries perform better in the above three aspects, whether it is the incentive compatibility of institutional design, the educational quality of citizens, or market order, they all perform excellently; while economically backward countries are the opposite, with inefficient institutional arrangements, poor incentive compatibility, and high institutional trading costs. In terms of education, there is generally a low level of education, high illiteracy rates, and a large amount of human resources are untapped and wasted. In terms of market order and trading environment, due to low judicial efficiency, various infringements are not punished, crime costs are low, and trading risks are high.

In reality, it is difficult for the trading system to achieve 100% trading matching degree, and it can usually only achieve an α-equilibrium state, that is, the effective matching degree P_t enters the interval $\alpha \leq P_t < 1$ which is greater than α. In this case, the efficiency ratio that the trading system in equilibrium can achieve is at the following level:

$$\eta_t \approx k\alpha \tag{25.1.3}$$

Under normal circumstances, the actual resource allocation efficiency of the trading system is far from reaching the Pareto optimal level. If there are serious institutional obstacles, the trading system will operate inefficiently, and there are many examples in the real world. This is the case in some underdeveloped countries in Africa, such as Malawi, Burundi, Central Africa, Niger, and other countries.

It should be noted that the above conclusion about the relationship between the equilibrium state of the trading system and Pareto optimality does not dismiss the basic law of welfare economics, that is, the trading system in equilibrium under the condition of complete competition can achieve the Pareto optimal efficiency of resource allocation. However, we will later prove that the spontaneous evolution of the trading system results in the polarization of trading potentials, including the polarization of wealth possession and income distribution, as well as the polarization of market competitiveness. Social stratification and market monopoly will be inevitable results, inevitably deviating from the Pareto optimal track. This shows that the trading system is a system that cannot be self-guarded. In the evolutionary process of the trading system, it presents distinct stage characteristics. At different evolutionary development stages, the problems restricting the efficiency of resource allocation in the trading system have their own characteristics. Generally speaking, the later the evolutionary process of the trading system, the greater needs for government intervention and reform and improvement of institutional arrangements, the greater needs there are to impose external constraints on the trading system, but this is contrary to the 3-C conditions for the trading system to achieve Pareto optimality, which is an important manifestation of the inherent contradiction of the trading system.

25.2 Social Welfare Function of Trading Economics

Arrow's impossibility theorem once plunged the social welfare function into a logical dilemma. It states that there are no such procedures whatsoever—none, anyway, that satisfy certain apparently quite reasonable assumptions concerning the autonomy of the people and the rationality of their preferences. In other words, it is impossible to establish a welfare function that meets the standards of all independent decision-making agents.[1] We must abandon the view of seeing social groups as rational decision-making agents and give up the establishment of social welfare functions in terms of choice. Arrow's impossibility theorem shows that social groups, as a whole composed of many members, inherently have irrational characteristics, which is the inevitable result of interpersonal differences in value standards.

Against such a cognitive background, we need to see the social welfare function as the output result of the trading system. By comparing various possible results, we can assess the resource allocation efficiency of the trading system. Even so, we still cannot sidestep the issue of value orientation. For this reason, it is always difficult for people to reach a consensus on the form of the social welfare function. Different values have significant differences in the choice of the balance point between fairness and efficiency. It should be seen that the contradiction between efficiency and fairness only exists in a small time dimension. Once this issue is viewed on a large-scale time axis, the seemingly sharp contradiction between fairness and efficiency will immediately disappear.

In the long run, a highly polarized society is unsustainable. Not only is there a risk of system collapse, but from the perspective of efficiency, the trading potential of a large number of trading agents is suppressed, and the most valuable resource of the trading system—the potential of trading agents—is untapped and wasted. Once we regard the agent as part of the trading resources, fairness and efficiency will be unified and will become two indispensable aspects of maintaining the efficient operation of the trading system.

Trading potential refers to the state where all endowments of the trading agent are fully utilized under given technical conditions and economic development levels. In this state, the trading agent can implement trading on the largest possible trading strategy set.

The social welfare function of trading economics aims at sustainable development, builds a welfare function with the full development of the trading agent's potential as the standard, and uses the trading strategy set as a tool.

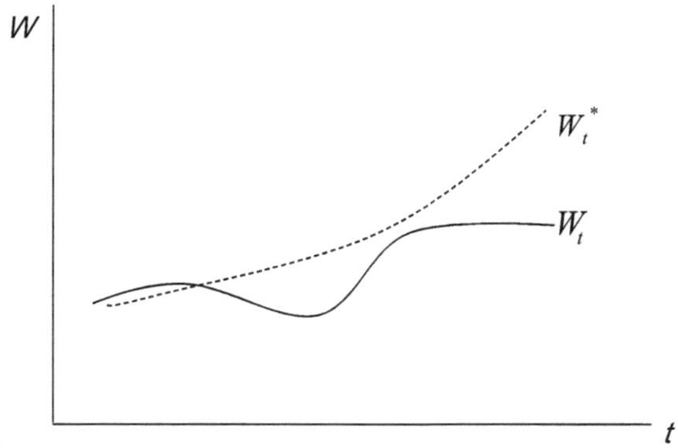

Fig. 25.1 The operating state of the trading system

Suppose $\{a_i\}$ is the capacity set of the trading system, S_{it} is the trading strategy set of any trading agent a_i at time step t, $E(S_{it})$ is the maximum expected return value realized on the trading strategy set S_{it}, W_t is the social welfare value realized by the trading system at time step t, its value is defined as follows:

$$W_t = \sum_{i=1}^{N} E(S_{it}) \quad (25.2.1)$$

If the trading system operates at the optimal state, that is, fully utilizing the potential of all resources including trading agents, the realized social welfare is the social welfare boundary, denoted as W^*. In the optimal state of trading system, the trading agent needs to fully develop its own potential, and the trading activity is carried out on the largest possible trading strategy set S_{it}^*. In Reality, this level can hardly be reached, that is, $S_{it} \subset S_{it}^*$, at this time $W_t \ll W_t^*$. The relationship between the two is shown in Fig. 25.1.

The larger $W_t^* - W_t$ is, the greater waste of resources in the trading system, and the lower efficiency of resource allocation. The reasons for the inefficiency of the trading system are multifaceted, which could be due to outdated systems or the result of high polarization.

Compared with other social welfare functions, the welfare function of trading economics has a clear value unit. This shows a basic value concept, that is, social welfare is built on the basis of value creation.

25.3 Potential Optimal State of Trading System

Pareto optimality can be described in many different ways, which often as: in an economic state, no if there are no economic changes can make one individual better off without making at least one other individual worse off., which indicates that under the given production technology and preference structure, resource allocation has reached to the optimal state.[2]

The Pareto optimality expressed in the language of trade economics is as follows: in a trading system, if each trading agent fully utilizes the trading resources under the given constraints and achieves the maximum benefit under the constraints, the trading system is said to be in the Pareto optimal state of resource allocation.

Without a doubt, given reality, the efficiency of resource allocation in the trading system cannot be better than the standard of Pareto optimality. However, if we consider the possibility of unreasonable systems in reality and the resulting unreasonable distribution status, there is still room for improvement in Pareto optimality.

To test the efficiency of the trading system in resource allocation, we cannot presuppose the rationality or validity of the existing situation, instead, we should see whether the operation of the trading system can fully mobilize all resources and fully tap the potential of all resources, including the human resource potential of the trading agent. In this principle, the criterion for the effectiveness of resource allocation should be: whether each trading agent in the trading system has maximized the trading potential. Based on the above views, the concept of potential optimality in the trading system is described as follows:

Under the given technical level, when and only when all trading agents can realize the trading potential, we call the trading system in the potential optimal state of resource allocation.

Compared with Pareto optimality, the standard of potential optimality has been further improved. Not only economic resource endowments are included within the standard range, but also human resource endowments are included, with both efficiency and fairness under the expanded concepts of efficiency. When the trading system achieves the potential optimal state, it will also achieve the result of maximizing social welfare, a perfect unity of achieving potential optimality and maximizing social welfare in trade economics. We can prove the correctness of this conclusion.

Assuming that the trading system meets the potential optimal standard, at this time, any agent of the trading system a_i all execute the trading on the largest possible strategy set. If the trading welfare function W_t has not reached the level of the welfare boundary W_t^*, that is:

$$W_t < W_t^*$$

$$\because \quad E(S_{it}) \geq 0, \quad E\left(S_{it}^*\right) \geq 0$$

$\therefore$ in the welfare function W_t, at least one item has not reached the welfare boundary. Assume a_k is this trading agent, that is:

$$E(S_{kt}) > E\left(S_{kt}^*\right)$$

$\because$ The trading system is in a potentially optimal state.
$\therefore a_k$ It is on its maximum strategy set

$$\therefore\ E(S_{kt}) = E\left(S_{kt}^*\right)$$

Obviously, it contradicts with the inequality $E(S_{kt}) > E\left(S_{kt}^*\right)$.
This proves that the trading system operates on the social welfare boundary.

25.4 Efficiency Decay of Trading System

The three states of the trading system operation, namely equilibrium state, Pareto optimal state, and potentially optimal state, represent three levels of resource allocation efficiency of the trading system, with the potentially optimal state at the highest level.

Equilibrium is a sign of resource allocation efficiency. When the trading system enters an equilibrium state, all trading agents have realized their trading intentions under the expectation of maximizing profits. It should be said that under given constraints, including liquidity constraints, information constraints, regulatory constraints, etc., through trading, all trading agents have realized their desire for optimal resource allocation. As we already know, due to external disturbances and internal trading cascades, the trading system does not always operate along the equilibrium trajectory, but often deviates from it. Therefore, achieving equilibrium is an important sign of effective resource allocation by the trading system. The transition from non-equilibrium to equilibrium is the first level transition in the efficiency of resource allocation in the trading system.

Due to the limitations of bounded rationality, limited information, and imperfect market competition, even a trading system in equilibrium cannot reach the efficiency standard of Pareto optimality. The transition from the resource allocation efficiency achieved in equilibrium to Pareto resource allocation efficiency is the second level efficiency transition of the trading system.

Due to institutional constraints, government regulatory interventions, and polarization, the potential of trading agents and the full use of trading resources are restricted, forming the third level transition in the efficiency of resource allocation in the trading system, that is, the transition from Pareto optimal to potentially optimal.

If the trajectory line is used to represent the dynamic evolution trend of the resource allocation efficiency of the trading system, three efficiency curves will appear: upper, middle, and lower.

In Fig. 25.2, W_t^* represents the social welfare function of potential optimality; W_t' represents the social welfare function of Pareto optimality; W_t represents the social welfare function under the equilibrium state of the trading system. As can be seen, the three trajectory lines operate at three efficiency levels.

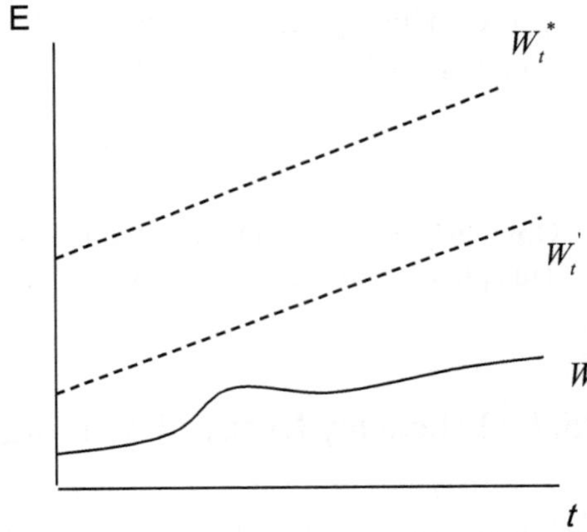

Fig. 25.2 The efficiency hierarchy of the trading system

From the perspective of the evolution of the trading system, $W_t^* - W_t$ the gap is showing an increasingly large development trend, indicating that the trading system has an efficiency decay trend. From the perspective of dynamic evolution, the main cause of this result is the polarization of trading potentials, including the polarization of wealth distribution in the family sector and the polarization of market control rights in the enterprise sector.

According to the definition of the social welfare function, $W_t^* - W_t$ the value is calculated by the following formula:

$$W_t^* - W_t = \sum_{i=1}^{N} \left[E\left(S_i^*\right) - E(S_i)\right] = \sum_{i=1}^{N} E\left(S_i^* - S_i\right) \tag{25.4.1}$$

In (25.4.1), $E\left(S_i^*\right) - E(S_i) \geq 0$. If there is a continuously increasing term on the right side of the equation, it will lead to a situation where the gap between the resource allocation efficiency of the trading system and the potential optimal $W_t^* - W_t$ continues to expand.

Under the market economy system, the gap between the strategy set implemented by the trading agents and the maximum possible strategy set is mainly constrained by competitors. In the evolutionary process of the trading system, the higher the degree of trading polarization, the more obvious the pressure from strong competitors on the weak agents, and the smaller the trading strategy set. Based on this logic, we can get the following relationship:

$$E\left(S_i^* - S_i\right) = k\left(\psi_i^* - \psi_i\right) \tag{25.4.2}$$

where, ψ_i^* represents the maximum trading potential among the potential competitors of the trading agent a_i; ψ_i is the trading potential of a_i; $k > 0$ is the structural parameter of the trading system. From this we get:

$$W_t^* - W_t = \sum_{i=1}^{N} k\left(\psi_i^* - \psi_i\right) \tag{25.4.3}$$

According to the trading potential theorem, the difference in trading potential between any two agents in the trading system satisfies the following relationship:

$$\psi_i^* - \psi_i = \psi_i^{*0} e^{(\pi_i^* - 1)t} - \psi_i^0 e^{(\pi_i - 1)t} \tag{25.4.4}$$

where, ψ_i^{*0} is the initial value of ψ_i^*, ψ_i^0 is the initial value of ψ_i, π is the feedback factor of the trading agent. As the largest potential competitor of the trading agent a_i, the feedback factor satisfies the basic condition of $\pi_i^* - 1 > 0$.

Without loss of generality, we assume $\psi_i^{*0} \geq \psi_i^0$.

From this we get:

$$\psi_i^* - \psi_i \geq \psi_i^0 e^{(\pi_i^* - 1)t} - \psi_i^0 e^{(\pi_i - 1)t} \tag{25.4.5}$$

$$\therefore \quad \psi_i^* - \psi_i \geq \psi_i^0 \left(e^{(\pi_i^* - 1)t} - e^{(\pi_i - 1)t}\right) = \psi_i^0 e^{(\pi_i^* - 1)t}\left(1 - e^{(\pi_i - \pi_i^*)t}\right) \tag{25.4.6}$$

As an ordinary trading agent, the feedback factor of a_i satisfies the following relationship:

$$\pi_i - \pi_i^* < 0 \tag{25.4.7}$$

$e^{(\pi_i^* - 1)t} \to +\infty,\ e^{(\pi_i - \pi_i^*)t} \to 0,\ t \to +\infty$

$$\therefore \quad \psi_i^* - \psi_i \to +\infty, \quad t \to +\infty \tag{25.4.8}$$

According to the power law distribution characteristics of trading potential, the number of agents with high-order trading potential will rapidly decrease as the value of trading potential increases. This means that, in the above equation, the situation of $\pi_i - 1 \leq 0$ occupies the majority, and as time t increases, the situation of $\pi_i - 1 \leq 0$ will continue to increase. In this case, the efficiency difference of the trading system $W_t^* - W_t$ continues to expand over time, that is:

$$W_t^* - W_t = \sum k\left(\psi_i^{*0} - \psi_i^0\right)e^{gt} \to +\infty, \quad t \to +\infty \tag{25.4.9}$$

Equation (25.4.9) shows that, with the evolution of the trading system, under the trend of continuous increase in the degree of trading potential polarization, the efficiency of the trading system in allocating resources will show a continuous decline, and the gap with the potential optimal efficiency will become larger and larger.

25.5 Institutional Suppression

From a more macro perspective, the causes of the decline in the efficiency of resource allocation in the trading system results from two completely different mechanisms: one is the result we have proven, that is, the process of trading potential polarization induced by the evolution of the trading system, which is an endogenous cause; the other is institutional suppression, which can also lead to a decline in the efficiency of the trading system. For the trading system, the institution has a certain degree of exogeneity. We call the decline in the efficiency of the trading system caused by institutional suppression an exogenous cause.

Institutional repression is a special phenomenon where the government excessively intervenes in the market, compressing the trading space of the entire society. When institutional repression occurs, the trading set will fall into a situation of continuous shrinkage, and the decision-making space of the trading agents will be squeezed.

In the evolution process of the trading system, endogenous efficiency decay usually appears at the high-order evolution stage, which is the main challenge faced by developed economies; while exogenous efficiency decay usually appears in the low-order process of the trading system evolution, which is the main problem faced by developing countries, and is also the main reason for these countries' economic backwardness and poverty. In this regard, Peru in the twentieth century provides us with a very persuasive case. "In Peru, a self-made entrepreneur has to take 13 years to overcome various legal and administrative hurdles to establish a food retail market, freeing street vendors from street vending; 21 years to get permit to build a legal, property-owned house on wasteland; 26 months to get permit to open a new bus route; and roughly a year (with 6 h of commuting every day), to get a legal permit to use a sewing machine for commercial purposes… Our legal system is not aimed at establishing fair and reasonable laws and regulations to protect the interests of the Peruvian people, and to make detailed allocations of power and responsibility, to protect everyone's property rights as much as possible, and to encourage citizens to engage in business activities. It does not provide enterprises with the motivation to create wealth. Rather, it is obsessed with directly interfering with business operations, ultimately leading to all parties competing for possible benefits as always… In such a country, the uncertainty of the future makes every Peruvian live in fear, confusion, and bewilderment. They know that since the administrative organs can issue about 110 rules and decisions every day, they can change the rules of the game at any time without prior consultation or discussion."[3]

Facing institutional repression, trading agents are always seeking possible ways to increase profits under the drive of profit-seeking motives. When the trading space within the system is compressed, people will look for trading opportunities outside the system. The more severe the institutional repression, the more prosperous the shadow trading. In the last 40-plus years of the twentieth century, Peru experienced a rapid urbanization process. A large number of residents who flooded into the city from the countryside, including associated activities in housing, production, commerce, transportation, etc., were mostly outside the law and became shadow trading outside the system. Among them, 48% of Peru's economically active population, 61.2% of working hours, and 40% of the economic value of GDP are all outside the system, belonging to the category of gray trading. In its capital, Lima, 42.6% of the total housing area does not have government-licensed property rights; 91,455 street vendors are in a completely autonomous state, not subject to government control; 93% of urban public transportation is unlicensed.[4]

The prevalence of shadow trading indicates a serious lack of effectiveness of the system, which is a typical feature of institutional repression. Shadow trading can neither get effective protection from the government, nor lack effective supervision from the government, and are completely in a self-organizing state of self-survival. The large scale of shadow trading not only seriously erodes the legal basis for the healthy operation of the trading system, but also injects a huge uncertainty into the trading system, exposing each trading agent to huge uncertain risks.

Systemic repression inevitably leads to corruption. In order to engage in legal trading within the narrow confines of the system, trading agents will inevitably try all possible means. Within an imperfect system, bribery is often the most effective means of passage. The more severe the systemic repression, the more obvious the shielding effect of the system on competition, the stronger the desire of trading agents to break through the system barriers and enter the system space, and the more widespread the phenomenon of corruption. Ubiquitous corruption not only distorts the inherent logic of resource allocation in the trading system, but also causes serious damage to social justice, greatly dampening the trading agents' willingness to trade, and accelerating the decay of the trading system's efficiency.

Under systemic repression, people will always try to break through systemic constraints in order to meet their survival needs; the government, in order to strengthen its own control, will continuously intensify control and increase the severity of punishment. In the game between control and evasion, systemic repression will continuously self-strengthen, possibly reaching a level that completely suffocates society.

The two mechanisms leading to efficiency decay differ greatly in their effects. Endogenous efficiency decay is the result of the polarization of trading power. Trading agents with strong competitiveness and high efficiency gradually gain market dominance after winning in competition, suppressing weaker trading agents. The greater the disparity in trading power between trading agents, the more obvious the suppression effect of higher-order trading agents on lower-order ones. Based on this mechanism, the endogenous efficiency decay process within the trading system is inevitably gradual and local, and the process is indirect. In this process, the potential of trading agents with strong competitiveness and high organizational efficiency is maximized. Therefore, a trading system in efficiency decay can still release powerful innovative capabilities and maintain high economic vitality.

Exogenous efficiency decay is the result of systemic repression. Under systemic repression, all trading agents in the trading system will inevitably be suppressed. In this process, government agencies do not need a process of power accumulation, and their intervention in the market directly restricts the free decisions of trading agents and compresses the trading space of the whole society. Therefore, the exogenous efficiency decay of the trading system is direct and global, and the decay process will be much faster than endogenous decay.

25.6 Income Trap

In 2006, the World Bank first proposed the concept of the "middle-income trap" in its "East Asia Economic Development Report," which immediately attracted widespread attention from governments and economists around the world. The report pointed out that many developing countries lose the effectiveness of their original development strategies and economic policies after their per capita income reaches \$3000 to \$10,000. With the change in the structure of domestic economic elements, the international competitive advantages they once had no longer exist. At the same time, problems accumulated during the early stages of economic development, including polarization and social corruption, have become major obstacles to further economic growth. In East Asia, the Philippines and Malaysia are typical representatives of the "middle-income trap". Taking the Philippines as an example, as early as 1980, the per capita GDP had reached \$671; after nearly thirty years of development, the per capita GDP in 2006 was still hovering around \$1,100. After excluding inflation factors, the per capita GDP of the Philippines has hardly changed. Although the situation in Malaysia is slightly better, with the per capita GDP rising from \$1812 in 1980 to \$8209 in 2008, it has always been hovering outside the threshold of high-income countries, unable to make the leap from a middle-income country to a high-income country. Similar situations are more common in Latin America, with Argentina, Brazil, and Mexico all being typical representatives of the "middle-income trap".

In the evolution process of the trading system, "traps" are everywhere, not only the "middle-income trap", but also the "low-income trap" and the "high-income trap", covering almost the entire process of the evolution of the trading system. Whether it is the "low-income trap", the "middle-income trap" or the "high-income trap", they are all characterized by a decline in economic vitality and stagnant growth. Their differences mainly focus on different stages of the evolution of the trading system and their causes. As the name suggests, the "low-income trap" occurs in the early stage of the evolution of the trading system, during the development period with lower per capita income, mainly appearing in the group of low-income countries; the "middle-income trap" occurs in the middle stage of the evolution of the trading system, mainly appearing in the group of moderately developed countries; while the "high-income trap" occurs in the later stage of the evolution of the trading system, mainly appearing in the group of developed countries.

Polarization is a main cause of the "middle-income trap". According to the estimation of the evolution equation of the trading system (19.2.9), the differentiation structure parameters α, β of the trading systems of major Latin American countries, are 5 times that of the US trading system, which means that for the same economic growth rate, the differentiation cost that the Latin American countries' trading system needs to cover is 5 times higher than that of the US. From this, it can be inferred that the decay rate of the trading system efficiency of Latin American countries represented by Brazil, Mexico, and Argentina is 5 times faster than that of the US. This can explain why, starting from almost the same starting point, after 300 years of development, the gap in comprehensive national power between Latin American countries and the US has become so huge; it can also explain why Latin American countries have become the hardest hit areas of the "middle-income trap".

If we say that polarization is the key to the "middle-income trap", institutional repression is the fundamental cause of the "low-income trap". Among low-income countries, common characteristics include abundant labor resources, poor educational quality, backward infrastructure, and high uncertainty risks; in the global industrial chain division, they mainly provide cheap raw materials and agricultural products. On the surface, these phenomena should be regarded as reasons for locking the economy in a stagnant and backward state. However, a deeper analysis reveals that institutional repression is the key factor hindering the economic development of low-income countries. Economic backwardness means that the domestic market is in an undeveloped state, and there could be many investment opportunities. It is precisely because of severe institutional repression that the trading system strategy set is severely squeezed, and the potential of the trading agent cannot be effectively released. Bribery has almost become the only way to obtain legal trading. In such countries, the vested interest class will form an interest alliance to prevent institutional reform and plunge the economy into a long-term stagnation.

Entering the ranks of high-income countries means that they have successfully broken through the barrier of institutional repression and achieved a successful breakout from the "low-income trap"; it means overcoming the "economic development paradox" and successfully crossing the "middle-income trap". However, this does not mean that the road to economic development is smooth from now on. It is also very difficult to escape the fate of the "high-income trap"; countries that can luckily escape the curse of the "high-income trap" are still rare. We know that developed economies have completed the transition from traditional society to modern society, have a relatively complete legal system and social governance system; they have established a wide-ranging, high-level social security system. This is also the key reason why developed economies can successfully prevent the decay of the trading system efficiency. However, it is precisely because of the developed social division of labor and the complete, high-quality social security system that families realize the externalization of functions at a higher level. Children no longer bear the responsibility of maintaining family continuity and supporting their parents in old age. Raising children has become a manifestation of parents' social responsibility and love. On the other hand, raising children requires parents to spend a lot of precious time. In modern society where time is life and time is money, choosing to raise children means paying a very high time cost. The more developed the economy, the more perfect the social division of labor, the more distorted the cost–benefit relationship of raising children, and the weaker people's willingness to have children. With the intensification of the phenomenon of fewer children, population aging is almost an unavoidable fate on the road of human social development. When an aging society comes, people's entrepreneurial enthusiasm will decrease, the number of business agents will also decrease, and the trading system will inevitably face the situation of capacity shrinkage.

From the economic growth model (23.3.40), we know that for developed economies, the capacity of the trading system is an important variable driving economic growth. When the population is aging, developed economies will fall into a state of slow economic growth, or even stagnation. Therefore, we say that population aging is the basic cause of the "high-income trap". Avoiding excessive population aging and preventing the shrinkage of the trading system capacity are key steps for developed economies to overcome the curse of the "high-income trap".

Notes

1. Kenneth J. Arrow (2020) Social Choice and Individual Value (Trans: Ding Jianfeng), 3rd edn. Gezhi Publishing House, Shanghai Sanlian Publishing House, Shanghai People's Publishing House, Shanghai, p 68.
2. Tan Jun, Sun Yueping (2006) Applied Welfare Economics, 2nd edn. Economic Management Press, Beijing, p 18.
3. Hernando de Soto (2007) Another Path—an economist's sage advice to jurists, legislators, and governments (Trans: Yu Haisheng), Huaxia Publishing House, Beijing, p 228–229.
4. Hernando de Soto (2007) Another Path—an economist's sage advice to jurists, legislators, and governments (Trans: Yu Haisheng), Huaxia Publishing House, Beijing, p 13–14.

Chapter 26
The Imperfection of the Trading System

The trading system, like all evolving systems, contains a mechanism of self-negation. We have proven that the polarization of trading power is an inevitable product of the evolution of the trading system; when polarization exceeds a certain threshold, the efficiency of resource allocation in the trading system will rapidly decay. We will also prove that we cannot build a perfect institutional system that balances fairness and efficiency in the trading system. This means that we cannot effectively prevent the metamorphosis of the trading system, nor can we guarantee the perfect evolution of the trading system.

26.1 Distribution of Institutional Lineages

The trading system must operate under the norms of regulation. Institutional construction and optimization are important aspects of the evolution of the trading system. The higher the evolutionary stage of the trading system, the more complex the structure of the trading system, and the higher dependence on institutional rules. Fairness and efficiency are the two main dimensions of the institution, which also constitute the two coordinates for measuring the characteristics of the institutional system.

26.1.1 Concept of Institution

Institutions refer to the rules established on the trading system to constrain and regulate trading behaviors. Institutions include rules determined by various laws and regulations, as well as parameters determined by various policies. Maintaining the operation of the trading system requires a large number of various institutional rules. With the evolution of the trading system, the institution composed of various

Z. Wang, *Trading Economics*, Contributions to Economics,
https://doi.org/10.1007/978-981-99-9875-3_26

rules is always changing. Some institutional rules are abolished, some new rules are brought into the institutional system, and some institutional rules are revised. These are the specific forms of the evolution of the trading system's institutions. Since the institutional system is built on a large number of rule combinations, there bound to be great differences in the institutional systems of any two trading systems.

S represents the set of institutional alternatives at time step t. The size and structure of S will change with people's cognition and social environment, and it is a function of time t. Therefore, we denote the set of institutional alternatives as S_t. s_i represents any optional institution on the optional set S_t, representing an institutional system composed of many rules.

26.1.2 Distribution of Institutional Lineages

Institutions include efficiency and fairness dimensions. Each institution will form a projection on these two dimensions, and the projection coordinates are the strength of the institution in efficiency and fairness. We use p to represent the efficiency coordinate; use q to represent the fairness coordinate. When the institutional system s_i takes the value $p = 0$, it means that the institutional system s_i is absolutely inefficient; when $p = 1$, it means that the institutional system s_i is absolutely efficient; similarly, when $q = 0$, it means that the institutional system s_i is absolutely unfair; when $q = 1$, it means that the institutional system s_i is absolutely fair.

The efficiency characteristic of the institutional system is reflected in whether it can effectively stimulate the potential of the trading agents; the fairness characteristic of the institutional system is reflected in the strength of support for disadvantaged groups and the effectiveness of maintaining a fair competitive order.

We can locate the coordinates of the institution in three steps. First, we need to analyze the characteristics of the rules in the institutional system on the trading agents, and classify the rules accordingly. Rules that incentivize trading activities and encourage competition are classified into the efficiency group. Rules that maintain a fair competitive order and are conducive to reducing polarization are classified into the fairness group. In reality, the impact of laws and policies on trading agents is often multifaceted. For example, China's *Anti-Unfair Competition Law* enacted in 1993 and revised in 2019, and the United States' *Sherman Act* enacted in 1890, the *Clayton Act* enacted in 1914, and the *Robinson-Patman Act* enacted in 1936, all of which maintain a fair trading order while also promoting trading prosperity. For such regulations that have dual functions, they can appear in both the fairness group and the efficiency group.

The second step is to assign values to each rule according to the strength of its effect on the trading agents. For rules that appear in both the efficiency group and the fairness group, it is necessary to give a specific assessment based on the role of the rule in efficiency and fairness.

The third step, after assigning values to each rule, we can calculate the total values of the efficiency group and the fairness group. On this basis, the total values of the two groups are added to get the total value of the trading system. The proportion of the efficiency group's value in the total value of the system is used as the efficiency coordinate value; the proportion of the fairness group's value in the total value of the system is used as the fairness coordinate value of the system. The specific calculation steps are as follows.

Assume $s \in S_t$ is any institutional system on the alternative set S_t of the trading system T at time step t, $s = \{ru_k\}_N$ contains N rules, $\{ru_i\}_{N_1}$ is the efficiency subset; $\{ru_j\}_{N_2}$ is the fairness subset. According to the grouping criteria, the two rule subsets satisfy $N_1 + N_2 \geq N$.

The rule assignment is based on the principle that the greater the effect on the trading agents, the greater the assignment. Assume the assignment of the efficiency group rule ru_i is p_i; the assignment of the fairness group rule ru_j is q_j. From this, we can get the two coordinate values of the institutional system s on the institutional coordinate system:

$$p = \frac{\sum_1^{N_1} p_i}{\sum_1^{N_1} p_i + \sum_1^{N_2} q_j} \tag{26.1.1}$$

$$q = \frac{\sum_1^{N_2} q_j}{\sum_1^{N_1} p_i + \sum_1^{N_2} q_j} \tag{26.1.2}$$

From (26.1.1) and (26.1.2), it can be seen that the coordinate values (p, q) of any institutional system $s \in S_t$ on the alternative set S_t all satisfy the following id agent relationship:

$$p + q = 1 \tag{26.1.3}$$

All systems on the alternative set S are distributed on the line connecting (1,0) and (0,1). We call this line the trading system T of the institutional lineage distribution line.

Looking at the distribution of institutional lineages, there are infinite possibilities for institutions. Different positions of institutions on the lineage distribution line imply different tendencies in the two dimensions of efficiency and fairness. The trading system is always in dynamic evolution, and the challenges and problems it faces will change as the system evolves. Institutions will also adjust according to the evolution of the trading system. When the main challenge comes from efficiency, the institution should adjust in a direction that promotes efficiency; when the main challenge comes from fairness, the institution needs to lean towards reducing polarization and increasing fairness.

26.2 The Impossibility Theorem of Perfect Institutions

The so-called perfect institution refers to a system under which the trading system can maintain resource allocation efficiency while preventing the polarization of trading potentials from exacerbating, and meet the requirements of both efficiency and fairness at the same time. We use s^* to represent the perfect institution.

26.2.1 Statement of the Impossibility Theorem of Perfect Institutions

The Impossibility Theorem of Perfect Institutions can be stated in two different ways.

Statement Form 1

At any time step t of the institutional alternative set S, $s_i \in S_t$ is any optional institution, then s_i must have some deficiencies and cannot meet the conditions of a perfect institution.

Statement Form 2

At any time step t of the institutional alternative set S_t, there is no perfect institution s^*, that is, $s^* \notin S_t$.

26.2.2 Proof of the Impossibility Theorem of Perfect Institutions

We can use four different methods to prove the Impossibility Theorem of Perfect Institutions, in order to understand the fact that perfect institutions do NOT exist from multiple perspectives.

First Proof of the Impossibility Theorem of Perfect Institutions

Let $s^* \in S_t$ be a perfect institution. According to the definition of a perfect institution, a trading system operating under the institution s^* is both efficient and fair.

Let a_i be any trading agent in the trading system T, which can be an enterprise or a family. Assume that the basic motivation of a_i is to obtain as much benefit as possible (including monetary income and material products or service products) with the least payment (including monetary payment, physical and mental effort, etc.). The behavior of the trading agent must be carried out under clear instructions. There are only two scenarios that instructs the trading agent a_i to act: either instructions come from within the trading agent, that is, they are decided by the trading agent itself; or they come from outside the trading agent, that is, it takes third-party instructions. We call the behavior pattern of autonomous decision-making the first behavior pattern.

The set of trading strategies under this behavior pattern is autonomously constructed by the trading agent based on the information set, and includes many strategies with different rates of return and constraint conditions. We call the behavior pattern of accepting third-party instructions the second behavior pattern, and its action strategy set is not autonomously constructed by the trading agent based on the information set, but comes from third-party instructions. Under the second behavior pattern, the strategy set of the trading agent only contains a single strategy, that is, the third-party instruction.

The trading system adopting the first behavior pattern belongs to the ordinary system discussed in trading economics; while the trading system adopting the second behavior pattern has significant differences from the ordinary trading system, but it can still be unified under the concept of the trading system, and we regard it as a special case of the trading system.

Next, we will discuss the two driving models separately.

Under the first behavior pattern, a_i makes decisions according to the rules defined by the perfect system s^*. According to the behavioral motivation of the trading agent, a_i seeks the best trading opportunities in the trading system T to achieve the behavioral motivation of maximizing returns. In order to obtain as much profit as possible, a_i will make the greatest effort.

In the trading system T, information is disseminated among members through interpersonal communication and various media channels. If a_i's decision is successful and achieves the expected return, it will attract more same-phase trading entities a_j to imitate a_i's trading strategy, and form a certain sense of competition with a_i. Under the condition of scarce resources, the more the same-phase entities join the ranks, the more intense the competition will be.

Autonomous decision-making and mutual competition are the basic characteristics of the market system, which shows that s^* has the attributes of a market economic system. As known from the principle of trading polarization, Polarization is an inevitable trend under the market economic system. Once there is a huge disparity in the distribution of trading potentials, the trading environment featuring fair competition will be damaged to some extent. Obviously, this contradicts the premise that s^* is a perfect system.

If the perfect system s^* includes rules to suppress polarization and protect fair competition, the trend of polarization in the trading system will undoubtedly be controlled. Assume that this rule is ru^* (there may be a set of such rules). In order to achieve the effect of effectively suppressing polarization, the rule ru^* must implement transfer payments from the dominant trading agent a_i to the weak trading agent a_j. Assume the transfer amount is Δw, Δw must be with a_i and a_j income gap is proportional, otherwise, it is impossible to achieve the goal of suppressing polarization. Under this mechanism, the trading agent a_i tends to reduce potential output in order to bridge the income gap with a_j. Otherwise, the additional potential payment will be transferred to a_j, obviously, this is a disadvantageous outcome for a_i. Under the rule ru^*, the disadvantaged trading agent a_j tends to widen the income gap with a_i, so as to get more transfer income. Under this motivation, the trading agent a_j lose the appetite to trade, leaving their potential untapped.

As can be seen, due to the implementation of the rule ru^*, while suppressing polarization, it will also lead to the idling of some potential of the dominant and disadvantaged trading entities. The higher the transfer intensity Δw, the more serious the idling or waste of the trading agent's potential. This outcome contradicts the characteristics of the s^* perfect system.

In the second behavior pattern, a_i economic behavior comes from third-party instructions. In this case, a_i earnings will be determined by the instructing party. Since a_i economic activities must be carried out according to third-party instructions, even if they are dissatisfied with the earnings, a_i cannot change the earnings status quo through autonomous choices. In this case, a_i can only adjust the relationship between potential input and output by reducing the output, so as to achieve cost-effectiveness. Regardless of the behavior pattern, the motivation of the trading agent will not change. In the case where the earnings are determined by the instructing party, a_i will inevitably choose the strategy of least potential input possible.

In the trading system, the potential of the trading agent is an important yet scarce resource. Therefore, in the second behavior pattern, s^* there is a state of resource waste or idling, which is a characteristic of inefficient systems. Obviously, it contradicts the assumption that s^* belongs to a perfect system.

In the second behavior pattern, if the third party applies the method of supervising the behaviors of members to reduce delinquency, it needs to pay the supervision cost, represented by *Sc*. Obviously, the size of the supervision cost *Sc* is proportional to the supervision effect and the number of supervised entities. Suppose the trading system *T* capacity is *N*, in the second behavior pattern, it means that the number of third-party supervision entities is *N*; assuming *Le* To reduce the total economic loss caused by potential payments for all trading entities, then $\frac{1}{Le}$ can be used as a measure of the supervision quality. The larger value the potential loss *Le* takes, the smaller the reciprocal $\frac{1}{Le}$ value will be; conversely, the smaller value the potential loss *Le* takes, the larger the reciprocal $\frac{1}{Le}$ value will be.

Based on the proportional relationship between supervision cost *Sc* and the effect of supervision and the number of supervised entities, we can get the following equation:

$$Sc = \alpha \frac{N}{Le} \tag{26.2.1}$$

where, $\alpha > 0$ is a balance constant. From (26.2.1) we get:

$$Sc \times Le = \alpha N \tag{26.2.2}$$

Equation (26.2.2) shows that there is a zero-sum relationship between supervision cost and potential loss of the trading system. Since the capacity of the trading system has relative stability, Eq. (26.2.2) shows that the product of supervision cost and potential loss of the trading system is a stable constant, we call αN the efficiency constant of the trading system *T*. The value of the efficiency constant αN represents the intensity of system efficiency loss when implementing the second behavior pattern in a trading system with a capacity of N. Equation (26.2.2) shows that the efficiency loss of the trading system cannot be eliminated by strengthening supervision. The larger the capacity N of the trading system, the more severe the efficiency loss under the second behavior pattern. This contradicts the assumption that s^* is a perfect system.

The above argument shows that regardless of the behavior pattern, the assumption of a perfect system will lead to contradictory results. This proves that the perfect system s^* does not exist, that is $s^* \notin S_t$.

Second proof of the impossibility theorem of a perfect system

In fact, we can have a more direct and simpler proof method. According to the definition of a perfect system s^*, the coordinates of a perfect system s^* on the system coordinate system should satisfy both: $p = 1, q = 1$.

As can be seen from Fig. 26.1, the coordinate (1,1) corresponds to the point $E(1,1)$, and the point $E(1,1)$ is not on the system spectrum distribution line $p + q = 1$. Therefore, $s^* \notin S_t$. Even if we lower the requirements of a perfect system and bring its conditions to the level of $p > 0.5$、 $q > 0.5$, the rule combination that meets such conditions is still not on the system spectrum distribution line $p + q = 1$. This proves that a perfect system does not exist, that is $s^* \notin S_t$.

Proof of the Third Theorem of the Impossibility of a Perfect System

We view the arrangement of systems as a process of social choice, and use Arrow's impossibility theorem to prove the impossibility of a perfect system.

Arrow's impossibility theorem is an important theorem proven by Kenneth Joseph Arrow, the American economist and 1972 Nobel laureate in economics, in the 1950s. Currently, Arrow's impossibility theorem has become an important theoretical foundation of welfare economics, having a significant impact on the research direction of the entire field of social sciences. Arrow's impossibility theorem consists of a definition, four axioms, and a conclusion. Arrow's impossibility theorem is based on the concept of a social welfare function, which Arrow defines as: a social welfare function is a social preference order on a finite set of social states $\{x, y, z \dots\}$, and

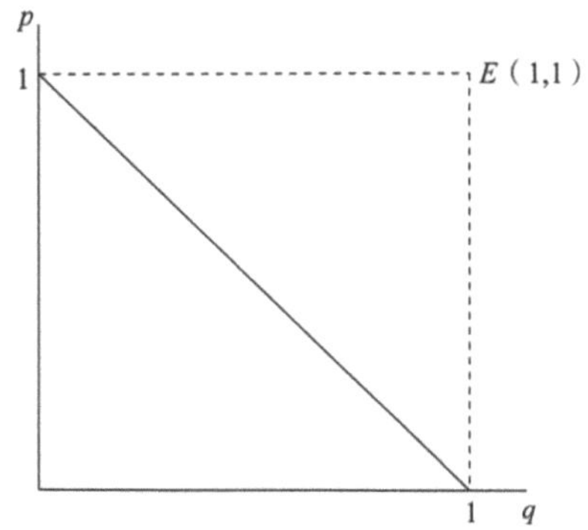

Fig. 26.1 The assessment coordinates of institutions

the social preference order is a general function generated based on the preference order of each member of society for social states.

In order to prove the conclusion that a social welfare function generated based on the preference order of social members cannot exist, Arrow proposed the following four axioms as basic premises:[1]

U (Unrestricted Domain Axiom): For any logically consistent individual preference, there exists a social preference order;

I (Independence of Irrelevant Alternatives Axiom): For any group $\{x, y\}$ of social preference orders, it only depends on the individual sequence for *x* and *y*;

P (Pareto Principle Axiom): If all individual preferences have social state *x* superior to social state *y*, then the entire society's preferred state *x* is superior to state *y*, expressed as *xPy*;

D (Non-Dictatorship Axiom): There is no social member a_i, so that when a_i has *xPy*, regardless of other members' preferences, there is a social preference that satisfies *xPy*.

Axiom U is for the conditions that the social welfare function needs to meet, that is, the social welfare function must cover the preference information of all members and respond to the preference choices of each member.

Axiom I is for the convention of social member preference choices, requiring that when social members make preference choices for social states *x*, *y*, they will not be affected by information unrelated to social states *x*, *y*. Specifically, they will free from the influence of other social states *z* of. Although behavioral economics has proven through a large number of behavioral experiments that it is impossible to completely exclude the interference of factors outside the alternatives in the process of decision-making, the main factors that determine people's choices are still the characteristics of the alternatives themselves. In this case, the Independence Axiom I still has a high degree of rationality.

P (Pareto Principle Axiom) is the result of applying the basic principle of Pareto optimality to social choices. This axiom stipulates the value of the social welfare function at the extreme point. When all members of society prefer state *x* over *y*, the social welfare function should satisfy the value of *xPy*. This axiom requires that the social welfare function can reflect the demands of all members of society, ensuring that the results obtained by the social welfare function do not come at the expense of any member's interests.

D (Non-Dictatorship Axiom) has a very special position among the four axioms. As a premise for discussing social choices, non-dictatorship is self-evident, otherwise social choice would become a pseudo-proposition. The reason for including it in the axiom system is mainly for the logical rigor of the proof.

One conclusion of Arrow's impossibility theorem is: it is impossible to exist (or construct) a social welfare function that satisfies the four axioms.

Arrow proposed the impossibility theorem mainly with the electoral system in Western countries as the research object. In fact, although the process of system choice or system building can also be seen as this kind of social choice behavior, although the system usually does not require all adult citizens to participate in the election like a presidential election, the process of formulating regulations and policies usually needs to be completed by voting. Whether it is parliamentary voting or monetary committee voting, it can be seen as social choice under specific rules. In Arrow's argument, social choice allows for various all possibilities, it can be the majority voting principle, or the majority rule, or even the representative principle. All principles that conform to human rational logic can theoretically become rules that are followed by public opinion to realize social choices. Obviously, whether it is the formulation of laws or policy decisions, they all meet the standards of social choice.

For the trading system T, assume that the system alternative set at time step t is S_t, $s \in S_t$ is any institutional arrangement on the alternative set, and the system s includes a set of rules $\{ru_i\}_N$. For any rule that constitutes the system s, there will be different preferences among the trading entities in the trading system. According to the Unrestricted Domain Axiom U, each trading agent has its own preference rules, and thus forms the preference ranking of all systems in the system alternative set S_t.

On this understanding basis, we define the concept of optimal system. The so-called optimal system is the alternative system that ranks first in the social preference order on the system alternative set, represented by s'. The optimal system s' can be seen as Arrow's social welfare function.

We will prove that the perfect system must be the optimal system. According to the definition, the perfect system is a set of rules that are both efficient and fair in the trading system. If the system s^* is a perfect system, it means that all trading entities in the system s^* Everyone can be motivated and give their potential into full play; at the same time, due to the fairness of s^*, there are no unreasonable constraints or suppressions on the trading activities of any trading agent in the trading system. Obviously, trading entities governed by the principle of maximizing expected returns will inevitably place the perfect system s^* at the top of their preference ranking. According to the Pareto rule axiom P, we can infer that s^* must be at the top of social preferences, meeting the requirements of the optimal system s'.

According to Arrow's impossibility theorem, it is impossible for a social welfare function that satisfies the four axioms (U, I, P, D) to exist on the alternative set of the trading system S_t, so it is also impossible for the optimal system s' to exist. If the perfect system s^* exists in the alternative set S_t, it must be the optimal system on S_t, meaning that the optimal system s' does exists. This conclusion contradicts Arrow's impossibility theorem.

The fourth theorem of the impossibility of a perfect system proves.

Let a_i and a_j be any two trading entities in the trading system, and $E(a_i)$, $E(a_j)$ the efficiency levels of a_i and a_j respectively. Assume that at time step t, the efficiency levels of a_i and a_j have the following relationship:

$$E(a_i) > E(a_j)$$

Assume s^* is the perfect system on the alternative set; at time step t, the trading entities a_i and a_j under the continuous effect of the perfect system s^*, the profit is ultimately reflected in their own accounting matrix, that is:

$$s^*(a_i) = A_i, \quad s^*(a_j) = A_j$$

To further prove the impossibility theorem of a perfect system, we introduce the following three lemmas:

Lemma 1 The accounting matrices A_i and A_j of trading entities a_i and a_j, are the results of continuous trading iteration under a specific system.

Lemma 1 is self-evident. As a tool to describe the economic achievements of trading entities, the accounting matrix must have the ability to accurately reflect the results of the behavior of trading entities. The scale of net assets, asset structure, and liquidity of assets reflected by the accounting matrix all result from the trading iteration of trading entities.

Lemma 2 The larger the accounting matrix, the more trading opportunities for the trading agent.

Trading behavior is a choice under constraints. The stronger the ability of the trading agent to overcome constraints, the larger the space for strategic choice. The accounting matrix of the trading agent is the result of past trading iterations, the larger the accounting matrix, the stronger the ability of the trading agent to overcome trading constraints. At the same time, the accounting matrix is the starting point of the trading, the larger the accounting matrix, it means that the trading agent has more resources, and the more trading strategies can be chosen. The strategy set represents the trading opportunities that the trading agent has, the larger the trading strategy set, the more trading opportunities trading agent has.

Lemma 3 The higher the efficiency of the trading agent, the faster the aggregated returns from trading iterations.

The efficiency of the trading agent represents the ratio of input to output of the trading agent. The higher the trading efficiency, it means that the trading agent gets more output value with the same input; the growth rate of net assets after the iteration of the accounting matrix is also faster.

$$\because \; E(a_i) > E(a_j)$$

From Lemma 1 and Lemma 2, we can conclude:

$$|A_i| > |A_j|$$

Let $S^*(\Delta A) = |A_i| - |A_j|$.

From Lemma 2, we know that with the continuation of time step t, $S^*(\Delta A)$ will continue to increase. For any positive real number K, there exists a time step t that can satisfy the inequality:

$$s^*(\Delta A) \geq K \tag{26.2.3}$$

Since s^* is a perfect system, no matter how big the efficiency difference between trading agents a_i and a_j, under the constraint of the perfect system s^*, the difference reflected in the accounting matrix of the trading agents should be limited within a certain range, that is, there exists a positive real number K, for all time steps t must satisfy the inequality:

$$s^*(\Delta A) < K \tag{26.2.4}$$

Obviously, (26.2.3) and (26.2.4) contradict each other, indicating that the perfect system s^* does not exist.

26.3 Implications of the Impossibility Theorem of Perfect Systems

The impossibility theorem of perfect systems dismisses not only the existence of perfect systems, but also the feasibility of comparing the merits and demerits between different systems directly. If a direct comparison is made between different systems, without asking about the evolution stage and state of the trading system, and ignoring the main challenges emerged in the operation of the trading system, and simply comparing the merits and demerits of different system choices on the set of alternative systems, it means that we can establish a kind of social preference order on the set of alternative systems S_t. Obviously, this contradicts Arrow's impossibility theorem.

The choice of system must be based on an evaluation of the merits and demerits of different alternative systems, otherwise any choice will lack a reliable basis. These seemingly conflicting facts indicate that when choosing a system, we cannot simply choose based on preferences for system efficiency scales and fairness scales. We must also introduce information about the characteristics of the trading system itself to construct a system selection space with more dimensions and richer selection constraint information. To do this, we must delve into all levels of the trading system, and conduct detailed research on many aspects such as the stage characteristics of the evolution of the trading system, the structural distribution of trading agents, and the main challenges present in the operation of the trading system. We cannot simply choose the best option on the set of system alternatives, but rather look for the system that best addresses the main challenges faced by the trading system; look for the system that best fits the evolutionary stage of the trading system.

From the perspective of the evolution of the trading system, the adaptability and effectiveness of any system are stage-specific. Once out of the effective range of the system, a system that used to have a high percentage of match will be ineffective and hinder the evolution of the trading system Therefore, system arrangements must change with time, through continuously reforming, adjusting, and optimizing system arrangements.

From the distribution of system lineages, there is a trade-off between fairness and efficiency. Improving the efficiency incentive of the system will inevitably come at the cost of heightened polarization; conversely, increasing social fairness will inevitably come at the cost of reducing the efficiency of the trading system. In a world where gains are exchanged for costs, there is no perfect choice. Choices must be made based on one's own needs and the main challenges faced.

Generally, in the early stages of the evolution of the trading system, the problem of polarization is not prominent, and system arrangements should adhere to the principle of efficiency first. System design should lean towards efficiency *p*, maintaining the system to operate in relation to satisfying $p > q$. When the trading system enters the later stages of evolution, the trading system is already at a high level of efficiency and has a clear advantage in international competition. Under these conditions, system design should be adjusted accordingly, giving more space to fairness, so as to maintain the system in a basic equilibrium between efficiency and fairness, which satisfies $p \approx q$ basic relationship. A system structure that is basically balanced between efficiency and fairness is a state that can be maintained in the long term.

Note

1. Eric Maskin, Amartya Sen et al. (2016) The Paradox of Choice: Arrow's Impossibility Theorem and the Truth of Social Choice (Trans: Huang Yong), CITIC Publishing Group, Beijing, p 22.

MIX
Papier aus verantwortungsvollen Quellen
Paper from responsible sources
FSC® C105338

If you have any concerns about our products,
you can contact us on
ProductSafety@springernature.com

In case Publisher is established outside the EU,
the EU authorized representative is:
Springer Nature Customer Service Center GmbH
Europaplatz 3, 69115 Heidelberg, Germany

Printed by Libri Plureos GmbH
in Hamburg, Germany